CRITICAL SURVEY
OF
LONG FICTION

CRITICAL SURVEY
OF
LONG FICTION

English Language Series

Authors
Pro-Stua

6

Edited by
FRANK N. MAGILL

Academic Director
WALTON BEACHAM

SALEM PRESS
Englewood Cliffs, N.J.

LIBRARY OF CONGRESS CATALOG CARD NUMBER: 83-61341
Complete Set: ISBN 0-89356-359-5
Volume 6:   ISBN 0-89356-365-X

PRINTED IN THE UNITED STATES OF AMERICA

LIST OF AUTHORS IN VOLUME 6

CRITICAL SURVEY
OF
LONG FICTION

FREDERIC PROKOSCH

Born: Madison, Wisconsin; May 17, 1908

Principal long fiction

The Asiatics, 1935; *The Seven Who Fled*, 1937; *Night of the Poor*, 1939; *The Skies of Europe*, 1941; *The Conspirators*, 1943; *Age of Thunder*, 1945; *The Idols of the Cave*, 1946; *Storm and Echo*, 1948; *Nine Days to Mukalla*, 1953; *A Tale for Midnight*, 1955; *A Ballad of Love*, 1960; *The Seven Sisters*, 1962; *The Dark Dancer*, 1964; *The Wreck of the "Cassandra,"* 1966; *The Missolonghi Manuscript*, 1968; *America, My Wilderness*, 1972.

Other literary forms

Frederic Prokosch has published five books of poetry. Some of his poems enjoyed a transitory popularity and appeared in anthologies, notably those of Oscar Williams. In addition, he has translated the love sonnets of Louise Labé, some of the poetry of Friedrich Hölderlin, and the *Medea* of Euripides.

Many of the poems in his first collection, *The Assassins* (1936), celebrate places and journeys and aspire to create an exotic mood. The collection also contains one of his most anthologized poems, "The Dolls," where Prokosch writes at his musical best of the sweet, crescent-eyed shapes, which, reaching into the poet's "secret night," become the "furies" of his sleep. Dylan Thomas later parodied this poem, giving to his own poem the title, "The Molls."

Prokosch's second volume of poems, *The Carnival* (1938), depends less on the dazzling imagery of geography and more on the ordinary things of life and was an attempt, according to the author, to convey the darkness of the prewar decade, as in "Fable," where the "rippled snow is tracked with blood,/ And my love lies cold in the burning wood." The volume contains a long, autobiographical "Ode" that describes the phases of Prokosch's first thirty years of life and his various discoveries (of fairy tales, his body, the past, Asia). His "Nocturne," beginning "Close my darling both your eyes,/ Let your arm lie still at last," shares similarities with W. H. Auden's well-known poem, "Lay your sleeping head, my love,/ Human on my faithless arm."

The poems contained in *Death at Sea* (1940) concern the plight of the individual in a chaotic world. In "The Festival," for example, a pair of lovers who are apparently homosexual note the "coming tempest" and follow "Silent the paths of longing and regret/ Which all our learning taught us to despise"; the poem is set against a backdrop of earrings trembling in the dark and fairies huddling by a bridge.

Reviewers were not kind to Prokosch the poet, and time itself has been still less kind. Although he assembled an anthology of *Chosen Poems* in 1944, it was not until 1983 that he published his next volume of verse, *The Sea*, a collection of sonnets that once again reflects Prokosch's fascination with geography.

Finally, in 1983, Prokosch published his memoirs, *Voices*, a series of vignettes in which many of the literary giants of the twentieth century appear in a decidedly unheroic light.

Achievements

Prokosch is said to have created the novel of geography, a distillate of the reflective travelogue. More than half of his sixteen novels fall into this category, and even those that do not are dominated in some way by the theme of geography and involve cosmopolitan, travel-loving characters. With the publication of his first novel, *The Asiatics*, in 1935, a book highlighted by Asian scenes and attitudes when other American novelists were writing realistic novels set in their own country, Prokosch achieved instant fame and maintained a high reputation for approximately the next ten years. William Butler Yeats was deeply struck by Prokosch's poetic gifts, and André Gide, Thomas Mann, and Albert Camus all praised his works during his stellar decade. Even his later works were praised by Somerset Maugham, Thornton Wilder, and Marianne Moore. *The Asiatics*, which was translated into seventeen foreign languages and was even more popular in Europe than in the United States, has been in print for nearly fifty years. *The Seven Who Fled* won the Harper Novel Prize, awarded by a panel of judges consisting of Thornton Wilder, Sinclair Lewis, and Louis Bromfield. In 1940, Warner Brothers made *The Conspirators* into a motion picture starring Hedy Lamarr and Paul Henreid.

Radcliffe Squires has observed that Prokosch's recurring theme—the death-defying search-for-truth in travel—began to seem irrelevant to a postwar generation looking for stability in suburbia. Subsequently, his novels were not so much condemned by the critics as they were ignored. Nevertheless, no complete discussion of twentieth century literature can afford to gloss over the fictional subgenre pioneered by the wunderkind Prokosch, the novel of geography.

Biography

Frederic Prokosch was born in Madison, Wisconsin, on May 17, 1908, the middle child of three children born to Eduard and Mathilde Dapprich Prokosch. His father, who had left Austria to escape a duel, was professor of Germanic philology at the University of Wisconsin, and his mother was an accomplished pianist. In 1913, Eduard Prokosch assumed a position at the University of Texas at Austin, which he lost six years later as a result of the anti-German hysteria that followed World War I.

Prokosch was sent in 1914 to spend a year in Europe, visiting his grandfather in Austria and attending private schools there and in Munich. His Austrian-

Slavic-Germanic ancestry and his early acquaintance with European culture encouraged Prokosch's cosmopolitan spirit and love for geography. As a child, he developed an interest in fairy tales, and this he credits for his fascination as a novelist with picaresque and allegorical characters who strive inexorably for fulfillment.

In 1920, the family moved to Bryn Mawr, where Prokosch attended high school and then, in 1922, Haverford College. In college, he became an athlete, particularly in tennis and squash, which, indeed, he did not abandon for years to come; he won the national squash championship of France in 1939 and that of Sweden in 1944. Always an avid lepidopterist, in later years he became as dextrous wielding his butterfly net as he had been with a racket.

After receiving his first master's degree from Haverford in 1928, Prokosch proceeded to earn a second one from King's College, Cambridge in 1930. Two years later, he earned his doctorate at Yale. While a doctoral student, Prokosch taught English (from 1931 to 1933), continuing as a research fellow in 1934. The following year, *The Asiatics* appeared, and he returned to England, later visiting Africa and Asia. In 1936 and 1937, he was teaching at New York University, but when in 1937 he received both a Guggenheim Fellowship and the Harper Novel Prize of $7,500, he abandoned teaching altogether. He was then at the apogee of his renown as a writer, and he could write from Prague in 1937 that one of his main interests was "trying to avoid the vulgarizations of money and publicity." Ironically, the vagaries of the reading public would facilitate this goal considerably in coming years.

After the fall of France, Prokosch spent two years in Lisbon, which served as the setting for *The Conspirators*. When the United States entered the war, Prokosch returned home to enter government service in the Office of War Information and then spent two years (1943 to 1944) as an attache in the American Legation in Stockholm. After the war, he went to Rome (1947 to 1953), where, on a Fulbright Scholarship (1951 to 1952), he researched in the Vatican Library the material for his first attempt at a historical novel, *A Tale for Midnight*, about the Renaissance Cenci family.

The 1960's found Prokosch living in Paris, and he finally settled in Grasse in the South of France, where he lives today. In his memoirs, he characterizes himself as a loner ("lonely by nature, lonely by habit, lonely by instinct, lonely by desire") who has experienced occasional bouts of gregariousness.

Analysis

The creator of the novel of geography, Frederic Prokosch is obviously a lover of travel and even of maps themselves. In *America, My Wilderness*, he defines the place-name as a "talisman that guides us through the terror of anonymity," and his novelist's fascination with place-names is, at its best, lyrical and evocative, at its worst, pedantic and tedious. It follows that such a lover of the places of this world would be a proponent of internationalism, and in most of his novels written after 1940, Prokosch urged his American readers to abandon their isolationism and to nurture links and bonds with the other peoples of the world.

All of Prokosch's fiction is an attempt in some way to probe the spiritual malaise characteristic of this century. In his novels of the 1930's, there is an abiding, non-Western fatalism. A sense of impending doom for the world saturates *The Asiatics* as the natives philosophize to the young American traveler about the resignation implicit in the Asian personality. This doom is counterbalanced by the lyrical nature of the writing and by the luxuriance of detail, however, and the beguiling, unutterable beauty of life strains to prevail even in these prewar novels. When the fear and foreboding of the 1930's was eventually replaced by worldwide optimism after the war, the tenor of Prokosch's novels changed in tune with the times. In *Storm and Echo*, the emphasis is on Africa as a new continent rather than on Asia as a dying one, and the hint of a positive note in the destiny of man is unmistakable.

In the picaresque narrative of *The Asiatics*, the nameless young American hero crosses the entire Asian continent from Lebanon to China. The character of the hero is elusive and vague, and many of the secondary characters with whom he forms friendships—friendships that are sometimes intense but always temporary—seem to take on more life than he. The hero is jailed in Turkey, suffers a plane crash in Iran, but always keeps his mind open and unbiased in order to soak up all the aphorisms proffered him both by the Asians and by the Western travelers whom he encounters. There is a chillingly prophetic mood to the novel; Asis is old and tired and waiting for death. When the hero enters a snowy-domed dagoba in Kandy and begins to converse with an old monk, it is of the coming of the twenty-fifth Buddha and of the accompanying dissolution of the world into Nirvana that they speak. The novel never ceases to analyze and emphasize the decadence and resignation of the enigma that is Asia.

In *The Seven Who Fled*, Prokosch weaves an allegory around a group of seven travelers, each representing a country in Europe (England, France, Spain, Germany, Austria, Belgium, and Russia), set adrift in the hostile vastness of Chinese Turkestan. After their caravan reaches Aqsu from Kashgar, the two German-speaking geologists are put into prison by local authorities; two others are kept as hostages; and the Frenchman de la Scaze falls prey to a fever. Only the Englishman Layeville and de la Scaze's beautiful Spanish wife are free to proceed; the former joins a caravan to Tibet, and the latter continues eastward on a caravan in the company of Dr. Liu, a wealthy Chinese merchant. Much of the first half of the book details the disintegration and eventual death of Layeville in the icy summits of Tibet. In his relationship with the barbaric and tantalizing Tansang, his Turgot guide whose powerful face combines the strengths of "a young man, a woman and a child," Layeville feels the possibility of a renewal of his spirit, but he loses his last chance when Tansang dies.

Like Layeville and Tansang, the hostages back in Aqsu, the Russian Serafimov (an inarticulate bear of a man) and the Belgian thief Goupilliere, form an uneasy pair. When Serafimov is rejected by the Russian prostitute Madame Tastin while his companion Goupilliere is accepted, Serafimov consummates his hatred for the Belgian by murdering him. The two geologists, the German Wildenbruch (who worships heroism and ambition) and the blond, angelic Austrian Von Wald, escape from prison together and travel to Shanghai, where the tubercular Wildenbruch departs for home and Von Wald decides to remain. The last pair, the most mismatched of all, are Paul and Olivia de la Scaze. Olivia, who abandons her husband in Aqsu, comes under the complete control of Dr. Liu and ends up joining a house of prostitution in Shanghai. Paul recovers from his fever, eventually catches cholera from a dancing girl, and dies.

Although the seven characters do not correspond exactly to the seven cardinal sins of medieval theology, each sin is very much in evidence. Certainly sloth is implied in the flight of the seven from the responsibilities of their European lives to the distractions of adventure abroad. Lust is evident in Layeville's reminiscences of homosexuality, in Olivia's eventual choice of occupation, and in Serafimov's obsession with Madame Tastin. Wildenbruch feels envy for the innocence of Von Wald, and only Von Wald seems relatively immune to the ravages of the deadly sins.

Nine Days to Mukalla is the story of four plane-crash survivors who make their way from an island in the Indian Ocean to Mukalla in Arabia, where they will be able to get a boat for Aden and return to civilization. The novel employs the rich, evocative style that characterizes Prokosch's best work and allegorizes the contrasting sensibilities of the four victims lost in a mysterious Arabia, which, in its capacity to distill good and evil, "reveals the human skeleton." The group is composed of two Englishwomen, Miss Todd and Sylvia Howard, and two Americans, an archaeologist, Dr. Moss, and David Gilbert, who is the only survivor by the end of the novel. David, described by Miss Todd as not quite a typical American, seems symbolic of a new, postwar, cosmopolitan America. Miss Todd, although she dies early in the narrative, possesses such great vitality that her spirit persists throughout the novel. It is the gift of her jewelry to David that enables him to reach Mukalla successfully. Dr. Moss is Miss Todd's foil, and just as the party's Bedouin guide thinks of Miss Todd as their good spirit, Moss is viewed by him as their bad spirit. He steals some of Miss Todd's jewels, abandons the party in his own interest, and is finally murdered in the desert. The primness of Sylvia Howard, the sketchiest of the four characters, is broken down in the Arabian desert, and before she dies of exhaustion when she actually reaches Mukalla, she asks David to make love to her.

The Seven Sisters is Prokosch's first novel in which an American setting

(Bishop's Neck, Maryland) is handled as powerfully as the foreign settings are in his earlier works. Each of the seven Nightingale sisters has a story, and the story of each sheds light on the character of Peter, an orphan who lives with the family. Peter is another of Prokosch's searching artists, but this time, untypically for Prokosch, his search ends in a kind of maturity. Five of the seven sisters, after frantic struggles, gradually achieve a kind of maturity as well.

The death of one of the sisters, young Elizabeth, who succumbs to a snake bite while still innocent, signals the real start of the action of the novel, suggesting a world divested of its innocence. The oldest sister, the repressed Augusta, marries a neighboring aristocrat, recognizes that the marriage is a mistake, and returns to her parents' home. Daphne leaves home dressed as a boy, falls in with a Lesbian, meets a runaway New Yorker named Pancho, loses him to another man and to death, rejects the Lesbian, and returns home. The elfin and visionary Grace never leaves home, but follows the advice of a ouija board, becomes pregnant, and goes to a cave, where she dies in the act of childbirth.

Consuelo, Barbara, and Freya, in the company of Peter and their mother, go to Europe. Consuelo links up with a Hungarian refugee. Blonde, beautiful Barbara marries a wealthy, aging Italian prince, falls in love with his handsome nephew, and ends up, after losing both, praying for forgiveness for her vanity and pride. Freya gives up her career as a painter and goes to Brazil as a social worker, where she perishes in the jungle. It is the character of Peter that acts as the cohesive force in the novel; it is with him that the novel begins and ends.

The Skies of Europe is Prokosch's first realistic novel and covers the events that led up to World War II. Philip, a young American journalist, loves Saskia, a failed artist who does not love him. The novel abounds in characters who are unsuccessful artists and neglected poets; one such unnamed character seems intended to represent Hitler. *The Skies of Europe* has affinities with a later novel, *A Ballad of Love*, Prokosch's most nearly autobiographical novel, his "portrait of the artist as a young man." It is, moreover, a portrait of a *defeated* artist. The hero, Henry, is a poet who grows up in Austria, Texas, and Wisconsin and becomes involved in a disastrous love affair similar to those in *The Skies of Europe* and *The Idols of the Cave*.

Three of Prokosch's novels are set against the backdrop of World War II. *The Conspirators*, which takes place in a wartime Lisbon filled with refugees and reeking of espionage, relates the detection and murder of a Nazi agent. Its atmosphere of historical change is haunting, and the degree of conventional suspense is rare in Prokosch's work. *Age of Thunder*, dedicated to the memory of Antoine de Saint-Exupéry, is not as realistic or as successful as *The Conspirators* and suffers from a preponderance of sketchily drawn characters, whereas the latter concentrates on a select few. As in all of Prokosch's novels, many of the scenes are brilliant, and they faithfully evoke the hypnotic atmosphere of war, but the dreamlike mission of the hero, Jean-Nicholas, through the Haute-Savoie seems to lack significance in the overall picture of the war. *The Idols of the Cave* makes use of the wartime atmosphere of New York as *The Conspirators* did with Lisbon. The city's brooding and sinister air is such that it almost overpowers the reader, and the unsuccessful love-story plot is little more than a duplication of that of *The Skies of Europe*.

Night of the Poor, the title of which was taken from a painting by Diego Rivera, is perhaps the author's weakest novel and amounts to little more than a conventional travelogue. It is the first of Prokosch's novels that has an American setting, and American place-names are savored and enumerated to such an extent that they tax the reader's patience. The plot chronicles the travels of Tom on his way to Texas after the death of an uncle in Wisconsin, and the gamut of depravity and inhumanity that he encounters on the way. Thirty-three years later, Prokosch would rework the same idea in *America, My Wilderness*, dressing it up with generous amounts of surrealism and modernistic bizarrerie. After the murder of his uncle in the Middle West, a half-black outcast named Pancho Krauss wanders from the Atlantic to the Pacific, savoring the "slow transition of one landscape into another."

Storm and Echo follows the pattern of Prokosch's first two novels, and the landscape of Africa is even more brilliantly painted than that of Asia in his earlier novels. There is a Conradian power in this tale of an American's search for a mysterious friend who has gone off to Mount Nagala. Central Africa is typically fraught with dangers of all kinds, but the friend is found (albeit as a corpse impaled upon a rock), and the protagonist emerges victorious over his own death wish.

Prokosch's historical novels include *A Tale for Midnight*, *The Dark Dancer*, and *The Missolonghi Manuscript*. The first, characterized by its author as "dedicated to storytelling per se and above all," seems to be just that, chronicling the murder of Count Francesco Cenci in 1599 by his wife and children and stressing the effect of the crime on the main conspirator, his daughter Beatrice. Its portrayal of sixteenth century Rome as plague-ridden, flood-ridden, and sin-ridden is graphic and effective. *The Dark Dancer* is laid in seventeenth century India at the zenith of the Mogul Golden Age, when Emperor Shah Jahan built the Taj Mahal for his wife Arjumand. The Emperor, however, is dispossessed of his empire by his sons, even as he himself had murdered to secure it, and gets to see the monumental building only when, as a prisoner, he is too weary even to admire it. *The Missolonghi Manuscript*, which purports to be the long-lost memoirs of Lord Byron unearthed by an American professor, is the strongest of Prokosch's postwar novels. Praiseworthy for its sensitive probing of Byron's personality and for its historical accuracy, the book is perhaps flawed by its overemphasis on the homosexual side of Byron's undeniably bisexual life-style.

The Wreck of the "Cassandra" is similar to *Nine Days to Mukalla*, but lacks the latter's allegorical sweep. Here, nine survivors of a shipwreck somewhere between Hong Kong and Australia reach a large island and settle down idyllically for a short time before the spirit of the island distills their personalities into various shades of good and evil. The presence of hostile natives adds to the tensions in the group; they confront one another violently; and some of their number are lost before their inevitable rescue.

Major publications other than long fiction

POETRY: *The Assassins*, 1936; *The Carnival: Poems*, 1938; *Death at Sea: Poems*, 1940; *Chosen Poems*, 1944; *The Sea*, 1983.

NONFICTION: *Some Poems of Friedrich Hölderlin*, 1943 (translation); *Love Sonnets of Louise Labé*, 1947 (translation); *Medea* in *Greek Plays in Modern Translation*, 1947 (translation, Dudley Fitts, editor); *Voices*, 1983.

Bibliography

Austen, Roger. *Playing the Game: The Homosexual Novel in America*, 1977.
Kunitz, S. J., and H. Haycroft. *Twentieth Century Authors*, 1942.
Peter, Max. *Frederic Prokosch, ein Romantiker des 20. Jahrhundrets*, 1969.
Squires, Radcliffe. *Frederic Prokosch*, 1964.

Jack Shreve

JAMES PURDY

Born: Fremont, Ohio; July 14, 1923

Principal long fiction

Malcolm, 1959; *The Nephew*, 1960; *Cabot Wright Begins*, 1964; *Eustace Chisholm and the Works*, 1968; *Jeremy's Version*, 1970; *I Am Elijah Thrush*, 1972; *The House of the Solitary Maggot*, 1974; *In a Shallow Grave*, 1976; *Narrow Rooms*, 1977; *Mourners Below*, 1981.

Other literary forms

In addition to his novels, James Purdy has written in a variety of genres, including poetry, the short story, and drama. The most important of these other works are *63: Dream Palace* (1956); *Color of Darkness: 11 Stories and a Novella* (1957); *Children Is All* (1962), ten stories and two plays; and a volume of poetry, *The Running Sun* (1971).

Achievements

Purdy is an experimental novelist and does not cater to a mass audience. His themes, topics, and stylistics indicate that he is writing for an audience that delights in literary craftsmanship and epistemological complexities. Along with Thomas Pynchon, John Barth, John Hawkes, Walker Percy, and Kurt Vonnegut, Purdy is now acknowledged to be one of the best of the generation of post-Joycean experimental authors. Although his writing is unique, Purdy does share certain characteristics with these writers: he experiments with a wide variety of styles; he treats bizarre and serious themes in a comic and unusual manner; he never presents the reader with definite answers, achieving ambiguity through the use of subtexts; and he indicts much of modern American culture. Altogether, Purdy's novels are quite complex, and, because of the nonrational motivations of many of his characters, they are, at times, quite baffling. Nevertheless, he is a writer who must be examined if the texture and themes of the postmodern novel are to be appreciated.

Biography

Because he is reluctant to discuss his life, little is known about James Purdy. He lives in Brooklyn and teaches at New York University. He has studied at the University of Chicago and at universities in Mexico and Spain. His interest in languages—in particular, Spanish, French, and classical Greek—is apparent in his novels.

Analysis

Since James Purdy is so hesitant to make public the details of his private life, it is impossible to correlate any of his works with his personal experiences. His works are hermetically sealed from his life, and must be examined as entities in themselves. Purdy's themes, style, and ideas change, develop, and expand from novel to novel, so it is not possible to delineate any one particular aspect of his work that is found consistently throughout. There are certain preoccupations, however, that are found, in varying degrees, in most of his works, and certain characteristics that are typical of postmodern fiction.

The characters in Purdy's novels are bizarre, grotesque, and governed by abnormal impulses and desires. Purdy uses his characters for purposes of symbolic manipulation, rather than for the purpose of character development in the traditional sense. Many of his characters are physically and/or mentally mutilated: they are tattooed, wounded, stabbed, raped, and, in one case, crucified. One of the major characteristics of all of his novels is his use of "unreal" characters whose thinking processes are "nonrealistic."

A primary concern of Purdy is the relationship of children to their parents; most of his novels include a domineering phallic woman, the search for a father, and the interrelationships within a family matrix. Many of his characters are orphans, illegitimate children, or children who have been abandoned by their parents. Along with these motifs, Purdy is preoccupied with the idea of being "grown-up" or mature. Within the quest for a father-figure, the idea of becoming mature is interwoven into the text, and within this framework Purdy usually parodies the search for identity and its resultant ambivalence.

The interplay of sex, love, and violence occurs frequently throughout his writing. Virtually no love between man and woman appears in Purdy's novels—the male/female relationships are either those of a prostitute and a man, or a man who rapes women. Purdy does include a number of homosexual affairs between men in his works, but these usually end in obsession and violence. In addition, many of the novels involve incest. Also interwoven in the stories are themes of tyranny, freedom, dominance, and obsessive love. Frequently, the female characters are aggressive and domineering, and often the male characters are passive and dominated. Many of the characters are attempting to find their "freedom." The nature of obsessive love is grotesquely related to many of the homosexual affairs found in the novels, and related to obsessive love are forms of hero-worship. Finally, in some manner or another, Purdy's novels all involve a writer within the narrative. In some books, this figure takes on more importance than in others; this device, typical of self-conscious "metafiction," serves to emphasize the autonomous reality of the fictive world.

Many of the themes, motifs, and preoccupations of his subsequent novels are found in Purdy's first novel, *Malcolm*. The orphan motif that occurs so frequently in Purdy's works plays a vital part in *Malcolm*. Malcolm (no last name given), the reader is told, belongs nowhere and to nobody. His father has disappeared, and Malcolm's search for him forms the central psychological structure of the book. The fifteen-year-old Malcolm is sitting on a park bench outside of the hotel where he is staying when Mr. Cox, an astrologer, takes an interest in him. He gives Malcolm a series of addresses in order to interest him in "things," and the ensuing visits to the people who live at the respective addresses form the core of the action in the novel. Malcolm becomes a parody of the picaro, for instead of acting he is acted upon. His main concern is to find his father, but his actions are governed by the tyrannical Mr. Cox and his circle of friends.

Within Mr. Cox's circle are Madame Girard and Girard Girard, an eccentric billionaire. At one point in the novel, Malcolm is offered a chance to be Girard Girard's son, but Malcolm tells him he has only one father and Girard Girard cannot take his place. Later, after Malcolm marries Melba, a famous black singer, he believes that he sees his father at a restaurant. Malcolm follows this man into the restroom. The man, however, disclaims that he is Malcolm's father and throws Malcolm down, causing Malcolm to hit his head. After this incident, Malcolm, who has deteriorated physically since his marriage, becomes too weak to get out of bed and eventually dies.

Thus, in this first novel, Purdy reveals many of his recurring preoccupations. In addition to the orphan's search for the father (paralleling the search for identity), Purdy also explores the topic of tyranny and the theme of the fatality of a loveless marriage. A concern with the maturation process is also found in *Malcolm*. Gus, one of Melba's ex-husbands, is chosen to help Malcolm mature before his marriage. Gus's solution to "maturing" Malcolm is to have Malcolm tattooed and to have him visit a prostitute.

In *Malcolm*, the characters are constantly questioning the substantiality of their existence; they are two-dimensional, almost comic-book figures. Malcolm is given addresses, not names, and consequently, places and events take primacy over the development of the personality. Malcolm himself has no last name, and when he dies there is no corpse in his coffin. All that is left of Malcolm are three hundred pages of manuscript that he had written, which Madame Girard attempts to organize.

In *The Nephew*, Purdy turns to the small town of Rainbow Center for his setting and tells a story which superficially resembles a slice of small-town life. Yet, underneath the seemingly placid exterior of Rainbow Center, as beneath the surface of the novel, much is happening. The text is surcharged with meanings, and the experience of reading this novel is similar to that of watching a movie with the sound track slightly off.

The plot is simple and straightforward. Alma Mason and her brother Boyd receive news that their nephew, Cliff, is missing in action during the Korean War. Cliff, another of Purdy's orphans, had lived with the Masons. In order to alleviate some of the grief of his death, Alma decides to write a memorial honoring Cliff. The novel focuses on Alma's attempts to gather material for the writing of Cliff's memorial. During this process, she discovers many facets of Cliff's existence of which she had been unaware—particularly that Cliff had hated the town and that he had had a homosexual affair with Vernon—which lead her to some revelations about herself and her relationship to Boyd and others in the community.

One of Purdy's concerns that can be noted throughout the novel is the inadequacy of judging people by their actions and by what they say. Communication is always inadequate and misinterpreted. Alma never does finish her memorial to Cliff, another indication that one can never fully understand another person. By the end of the story, though, Alma does become much more tolerant in her attitude toward what she considers the foibles of others.

Like *The Nephew*, *Cabot Wright Begins* concerns the attempt to write about another person—in this case, a businessman-rapist named Cabot Wright. Instead of one narrative voice, as in *The Nephew*, many emerge in *Cabot Wright Begins*, and this blending and confusion of narrative voices further demonstrates the impossibility of learning the true story about another person.

Purdy's third novel is an extremely pessimistic indictment and extended meditation upon modern American culture. In *Cabot Wright Begins*, people are controlled by media-think, big business, and popular culture, and by all the superficial aspects of modern existence. Feelings, emotions, and actions are all superficial, and even the rape scenes involving Cabot Wright are narrated in a dispassionate manner—much like secondhand violence seen on television or in the cinema. People exist on the screen of the text, and their ability to function in normal human terms is questioned.

Cabot Wright, another orphan, is twenty-six years old during the time of the novel. He is a stockbroker turned rapist. Bernie Gladhart, a used-car salesman, has been cajoled by his wife into writing the great American novel and has decided that a life history of Cabot Wright would be the perfect subject matter. In fact, the tentative title of Bernie's novel is "Indelible Smudge," which indicates Purdy's judgment about American culture at this time. Princeton Keith, the owner of a large publishing house, however, has commissioned Zoe Bickle to write the story in terms of popular fiction. Through a skylight, Zoe literally falls upon Cabot Wright himself, and Cabot offers to help her ghostwrite his biography. In the process of turning his life into popular fiction, however, he becomes alienated from himself. To him, the story does not portray his real self.

Cabot Wright seems to symbolize the attempt of modern man to assert his identity through violence. Only through the act of rape can Cabot penetrate the surface of another, but even then he becomes increasingly alienated and less alive. For Cabot, there are no answers.

In *Eustace Chisholm and the Works*, Purdy presents his concept of the sacrificial, violent, and grotesque aspects of love. In many horrific scenes he shows the results of obsessional love. The story revolves around the homosexual love Daniel Hawes has for seventeen-year-old Amos Ratcliff. Amos, an illegitimate son, has been rejected by his father and has had incestuous relationships with his cousin (later revealed to be his mother). Daniel attempts to repress his feelings for Amos, but they finally become so overwhelming that he reenlists in the army to escape. Instead of escaping, however, he permits his homosexual love for Amos to be brought to the surface and projected upon his commanding officer, Captain Stadger. During the affair between these two, Captain Stadger becomes increasingly more sadistic until finally he kills Daniel by disemboweling him, and then commits suicide. This incident is the first in a series of homosexual blood-sacrifices found in Purdy's novels.

Once again, as in all the previous works, there is an author involved in an attempt to write the story. In this case, Eustace Chisholm is the writer who is attempting to incorporate the story of Amos and Daniel within the context of a larger epic poem that he is writing.

Purdy's next novel, *Jeremy's Version*, was written as Part I of a series called *Sleepers in the Moon-Crowned Valleys*. Although Purdy had dealt with orphans, the search for a father-figure, and interrelationships among families in his previous works, this was his first novel in which the family matrix formed the basis for the entire work.

Again, there is a writer—in this case, Jeremy Cready—narrating the story being told to him by Uncle Matt. The basic story (that actually occurred more than fifty years before) involves the battle of wills between two strong women, Elvira Summerlad and Winifred Fergus, a divorce case, and the interrelationships of the three sons with one another and with their mother and father. Elvira Summerlad and Wilders Fergus were married, much against the wishes of his sister, Winifred, who thought the marriage was doomed. In a sense, Winifred was right, because Wilders abandoned Elvira and their sons. Winifred, however, goes to Wilders and tells him that since his sons are almost grown, he is needed at home. When he arrives, Elvira starts divorce proceedings against him.

The basic conflict is between Elvira and Winifred for custody of the children. Wilders is indifferent to the whole affair. One of Purdy's major themes—that of the son confronting the father—occurs during the divorce proceedings, when the homosexual oldest son, Rick, confronts Wilders. Rick demands that Wilders tell him the reason for his existence since his father has never been around before to teach him—he has only had his mother, who, he claims, has emasculated him. After Elvira wins the divorce case, her second son, Jethro, attempts to shoot her, but Matt saves her and is wounded. A similar shooting scene, between mother and son, occurs again in *The House of the Solitary Maggot*.

I Am Elijah Thrush is a dreamlike, ornate, and highly stylized book, populated with strange characters and filled with unusual events. More than any of Purdy's other novels, this book exists in the realm of allegory and symbols.

Among the major characters are a famous mime, Elijah Thrush; his great-grandson, a mute, called the Bird of Heaven; Millicent De Frayne, a tyrannical old dowager who retains her youth by drinking the seminal fluid of young men; and Albert Peggs, the black memoirist who tells the story and who, himself, has a bizarre "habit." In addition, the novel incorporates many elements of mythology in a comic manner, suggesting the debasement of culture in modern America.

As in many of Purdy's previous novels, the plot in *I Am Elijah Thrush* involves a person (in this case, Albert Peggs) being hired by someone to write the story. Millicent De Frayne hires Albert to recount the story of Elijah Thrush. Once again, this story involves a clash of wills between two strong people—Millicent and Elijah. For more than fifty years, she has been trying to gain control of Elijah and marry him. Eventually, she succeeds by manipulating Albert, the Bird of Heaven, and Elijah onto her boat, where she finally marries him. Late in the novel, Albert's "habit" is discovered: he sustains the life of a golden eagle by permitting the eagle to feed upon him. At the wedding feast of Millicent and Elijah, the eagle is served as the entrée. After this incident, Albert "becomes" Elijah Thrush.

One of Purdy's major themes is that of confirming, or finding, an identity. In his novels, there is a plethora of name-changes, mistaken identities, disguises, masquerades, and other such motifs. The dreamlike structure of the narrative suggests that Albert Peggs is attempting to discover his identity by telling this story.

The House of the Solitary Maggot is Part II of the series called *Sleepers in Moon-Crowned Valleys*. The story is reconstructed—this time on a tape-recorder—by one of the characters, and, as in Part I of the series, *Jeremy's Version*, the family matrix is the psychological focus in the novel. The story involves Mr. Skegg, the magnate (the "solitary maggot"); Lady Bythewaite; and their three illegitimate sons: Clarence, who is legally "acknowledged" by the father; Owen, who is "acknowledged" by the mother; and Aiken, who is not "acknowledged" by either parent until later in the book.

The novel takes place in a dying community called Prince's Crossing. Owen, the youngest son, hero-worships his brother Clarence, who goes to New York to become a famous silent-film star. After Clarence leaves, Owen turns to the other older brother, Aiken, whom he also worships. The two become inseparable. Aiken, who himself has no acknowledged father or mother, serves as a father-figure to Owen, "maturing" him by giving him his first shave and taking him to visit a prostitute. After visiting the whore, Owen loses his sight. Aiken, who has finally been acknowledged by Lady Bythewaite as her long-lost son, buys the Acres, the showplace of the community. When Clarence returns and refuses to accept Aiken as his brother, Aiken, whose pride is hurt, burns down the house and marries the prostitute. This marriage is a failure, and Aiken decides to leave.

Although Aiken has been estranged from Owen; he loves him obsessively. When Aiken goes to say good-bye to Owen and their mother, Owen shoots him. Lady Bythewaite, one of Purdy's typical strong-willed, castrating, women, then shoots Owen. In another of Purdy's characteristically grotesque scenes, Owen's eyeballs fall out and Aiken swallows them. While Aiken remains unconscious in the hospital, Clarence returns and wants to be acknowledged as Aiken's brother. When the unconscious Aiken cannot comply, Clarence slits his own throat. Eventually, Aiken comes to live with his mother. Mr. Skegg acknowledges him as his son and takes care of him in his illness. The story concludes with the death of Aiken, who, in a dreamlike sequence, tries to ride off on a horse with the dead Owen.

The protagonist of Purdy's next novel, *In a Shallow Grave*, is Garnet Montrose, a war hero who has been so badly wounded that he is turned almost inside-out and is the color of mulberry juice. Garnet seeks "applicants" to take messages from him to the Widow Rance, whom he wishes to court, but the applicants are so appalled by Garnet's appearance that they cannot accept the job. Finally, Quintus, a black adolescent, shows up by accident at Garnet's house and accepts the position. Quintus' responsibilities are to read to Garnet and to rub his feet. Later, one Daventry shows up. Even though he is not an applicant, he takes the position of messenger to the Widow Rance. Within this narrative structure, Purdy pursues many of his recurring themes.

One of the primary scenes involves a communion among Garnet, Quintus, and Daventry. Garnet is about to have his property taken away, but Daventry says that he will save Garnet's land and property if Garnet will commune with him. Daventry takes his knife, slits open his chest, and the three of them drink his blood. Later, they discover that Garnet's property has been saved by the Veteran's Administration, who heard of his plight and paid the mortgage. The wounding and shedding of blood, along with the religious connotations of the scene, seem to indicate that language is inadequate for portraying emotions, and that the only way to "love" another person is to shed blood for him.

Again, homosexual love appears in the novel, for Daventry and Garnet fall in love. They consummate their love in the dance hall where Garnet goes to dance by himself and relive the moments in the past when he was "normal." With Garnet's permission, Daventry marries the Widow Rance, but on his wedding night, he is swept up by a strong wind, smashed against a tree, and is killed.

Narrow Rooms is a story about the love-hate relationship between Roy Sturtevant (the renderer) and Sidney De Lakes. Roy Sturtevant had been in love with Sidney since the eighth grade, until Sidney slapped him publicly and humiliated him; from that time, Roy has been planning his revenge. The story opens after Sidney has returned from prison, where he has served time for killing Brian McFee. He finds a job as keeper of Gareth Vaisey, who has been injured in a fall from a horse. Sidney and Gareth fall in love and have an affair, but Roy Sturtevant still exercises a strange power over them. In the central scene in the novel, after Roy and Sidney have had a sexual encounter, Roy commands Sidney to crucify him on the barn door and then bring the body of Brian McFee to view the crucifixion. Roy, still alive, is taken down from the barn door and carried into the house. Sidney and Roy then pledge their love for each other, and Gareth, jealous, shoots them both. Subsequently, Gareth also dies. Though the subject matter of *Narrow Rooms* is largely sensational, the novel continues Purdy's exploration of the destructive nature of obsessive love.

In his most recent novel, *Mourners Below*, Purdy returns to the theme of hero-worship. Seventeen-year-old Duane Bledsoe is mourning the death of his two half-brothers, Justin and Douglas, who have been killed in the war. Eugene Bledsoe, the father, with whom Duane lives, is aloof and psychologically distant. The central episode in the novel occurs when Duane goes to a fancy-dress ball at the mansion of Estelle Dumont (who had been Justin's lover), and Estelle seduces him. After the ball, another of Purdy's rape scenes occurs when Duane is homosexually assaulted by two men along the roadside. During the brief affair between Duane and Estelle, Estelle conceives a child, also named Justin. At the end of the story, Duane is given the child to rear, and Eugene states that it is Duane's destiny to rear a son.

Although this novel incorporates many of Purdy's familiar conceptions, it appears to be much more optimistic about the human condition than his previous novels. For example, Eugene and Duane do become reconciled in many ways, and there are many indications that Duane will make a good parent for the child. Furthermore, many of the grotesque and sadistic aspects of love are absent in this book. The men and the women in the story are not the tyrannical types found in previous works; they exhibit much more normal motivation. *Mourners Below* seems to indicate a new phase in Purdy's development, for in this novel he emphasizes the hopeful qualities of love and human existence.

Major publications other than long fiction

SHORT FICTION: *Don't Call Me by My Right Name and Other Stories*, 1956; *63: Dream Palace*, 1956; *Color of Darkness: 11 Stories and a Novella*, 1957; *Children Is All*, 1962.

PLAYS: *Mr. Cough Syrup and the Phantom Sex*, 1960; *Wedding Finger*, 1974.

POETRY: *The Running Sun*, 1971; *Sunshine Is an Only Child*, 1973.

Bibliography

Adams, Stephen D. *James Purdy*, 1976.

Pomeranz, Regina. "The Hell of Not Loving: Purdy's Modern Tragedy," in *Renascence*. XV (Winter, 1963), pp. 149-153.

Weales, Gerald. "No Face and No Exit: The Fiction of James Purdy and J. P. Donleavy," in *Contemporary American Novelist.* CLXXXIII (Spring, 1964), pp. 143-154.

Earl Paulus Murphy

BARBARA PYM
Mary Crampton

Born: Oswestry, England; June 2, 1913
Died: Oxford, England; January 11, 1980

Principal long fiction
Some Tame Gazelle, 1950; *Excellent Women*, 1952; *Jane and Prudence*, 1953; *Less Than Angels*, 1955; *A Glass of Blessings*, 1958; *No Fond Return of Love*, 1961; *Quartet in Autumn*, 1977; *The Sweet Dove Died*, 1978; *A Few Green Leaves*, 1980; *An Unsuitable Attachment*, 1982.

Other literary forms
Barbara Pym is known only for her novels.

Achievements
Pym was a writer of distinctive qualities who, having suffered discouragement and neglect for fifteen years, was rediscovered toward the end of her life, to take her rightful place as a novelist of considerable originality and force. Often compared favorably with Jane Austen's novels, Pym's are essentially those of a private, solitary individual, employing precise social observation, understatement, and gentle irony in an oblique approach to such universal themes as the underlying loneliness and frustrations of life, culture as a force for corruption, love thwarted or satisfied, and the power of the ordinary to sustain and protect the men and women who shelter themselves under it. Also like Austen, she has no illusions about herself and very few about other people: "I like to think that what I write gives pleasure and makes my readers smile, even laugh. But my novels are by no means only comedies as I try to reflect life as I see it."

The story of Pym's early achievements, her long enforced silence, and her remarkable rediscovery perhaps says more about the publishing world than about either her books or her readers. Between 1949 and 1961, while working as an editorial assistant at the International African Institute, Pym wrote a novel every two years. As each manuscript was finished, she sent it off to Jonathan Cape. Her first six novels established her style, were well-received by reviewers, and enjoyed a following among library borrowers. *Excellent Women*, her most popular novel, sold a little more than six thousand copies.

Then, in 1963, Pym put her seventh novel, *An Unsuitable Attachment*, in the mail. A short time later, it was returned: times, she was told, had changed. The "swinging sixties" had no place for her gently ironic comedies about unconventional middle-class people leading outwardly uneventful lives. "Novels like *An Unsuitable Attachment*, despite their qualities, are getting increasingly difficult to sell," wrote another publisher, while a third regretted that the novel was unsuitable for their list.

Being a woman of determination and a certain modest confidence in herself, Pym went to work on an eighth novel, *The Sweet Dove Died*, and she sent it off to Cape; it too came back. She adopted a pseudonym—"Tom Crampton"—because "it had a swinging air to it," but twenty publishers turned down the novel. Humiliated and frustrated, she began to feel not only that her new books were no good, but also that nothing she had ever written had been good. *No Fond Return of Love* was serialized by the British Broadcasting Corporation (BBC) and Portway Reprints reissued five others; her books retained their popularity among library borrowers; and Robert Smith published an appreciation of her work in the October, 1971, issue of *Ariel*—but despite these signs of the continuing appeal of her work, Pym could not find a publisher, and by the mid-1970's, her name appeared to have been forgotten.

A renaissance in Pym's fortunes came with startling suddenness in 1977, when, to celebrate three-quarters of a century of existence, *The Times Literary Supplement* invited a number of well-known writers to name the most over- and underrated novelists of the century. Both Philip Larkin and Lord David Cecil—for years staunch admirers of hers—selected Pym as having been too long neglected, the only living writer to be so distinguished in the poll. Larkin praised her "unique eye and ear for the small poignancies and comedies of everyday life." Cecil called her early books "the finest example of high comedy to have appeared in England" in this century.

The publicity surrounding the article, not surprisingly, had positive effects on Pym's reputation. MacMillan published her new novel, *Quartet in Autumn*, near the end of 1977; later it was shortlisted for the Booker Prize. Cape began to reissue her earlier books; Penguin and Granada planned a series of paperbacks; she was widely interviewed; and she appeared on "Desert Island Discs" as well as in a television film called "Tea with Miss Pym." *The Sweet Dove Died* was published in 1978, followed by her last novel, the posthumously published *A Few Green Leaves* (1980). The manuscript of *An Unsuitable Attachment* was found among her papers after her death and published in 1982 with an introduction written by Philip Larkin. A book is being prepared from her diaries and short stories.

Pym's novels are distinguished by an unobtrusive but perfectly controlled style, a concern with ordinary people and ordinary events, and a constant aim to be readable, to entertain in a world that is uniquely her own. They are also distinguished by a low-key but nevertheless cutting treatment of assumptions of masculine superiority and other sexist notions—all this well in advance of the women's movement, and without the rhetoric which mars so much feminist fiction. Although hers is a closed world—what Robert Smith called "an enchanted world of small felicities and small mishaps"—it is also real and varied in theme and setting, with its own laws of human conduct and values, its peculiar humor and pathos. Middle-aged or elderly ladies, middle-aged or elderly gentlemen, civil servants, clergymen, anthropologists and other academics—these are the people about whom Pym develops her stories.

The world in which Pym's characters live, whether urban or provincial, is also a quiet world—evoked in such detail as to make the reader feel that the action could not possibly take place anywhere else. Taken together, her novels constitute that rare achievement: an independent fictional world, rooted in quotidian reality yet very much the creation of Barbara Pym. Central characters from one novel appear in passing or are briefly mentioned in another; delightful minor characters turn up in unexpected places. This pleasure of cross-references is characteristic of Pym's art, in which formal dexterity and a marvelous sense of humor harmonize with a modest but unembarrassed moral vision. "I prefer to write about the kind of things I have experienced," Pym said, "and to put into my novels the kind of details that amuse me in the hope that others will share in this."

Biography

Barbara Pym (the pen name of Mary Crampton) was born on June 2, 1913, in Oswestry, Shropshire, a small English town on the border of Wales. Like many of her characters, she led a quiet but enjoyable life among middle-class people with an Anglican background. Her father, Frederick Crampton, was a solicitor and sang in the choir; her mother, Irena (Thomas), was of half Welsh descent and played the organ. Pym was given a good education (Huyton College, a boarding school near Liverpool; and St. Hilda's College, Oxford, from which she received a B.A., 1934, in English language and literature); saw some wartime service (Postal and Telegraph Censorship in Bristol, 1939, and the Women's Royal Naval Service in England and Italy, 1943-1946); and lived in various sections of London: Pimlico, Barnes, and Kilburn. She wrote down everything she saw in a series of little notebooks, and later "bottled it all up and reduced it, like making chutney."

In 1948, Pym began working at the International African Institute, first as a research assistant and later as an assistant editor of the journal *Africa*. She was given the job of preparing the research for publication, and regretted that more of the anthropologists did not turn their talents to the writing of fiction. In their work, she found many of the qualities that make a novelist: "accurate observation, detachment, even sympathy." Needed was a little more imagination, as well as "the leavening of irony and humour." Several of her novels draw on her years at the Institute to study the behavior patterns and rituals of a group of anthropologists. In *Less Than Angels*, for example, she portrays an anthropologist and his female co-workers, gently mocking the high seriousness with which they pursue their research among primitive African tribes and the shameless jargon in which they converse. No doubt the narrator is speaking for Pym herself when she concludes: "And how much more comfortable it sometimes was to observe [life] from a distance, to look down from an upper window, as it were, as the anthropologists did."

Although her first novel did not appear until 1950, Pym began writing when she was a schoolgirl, and even completed a novel when she was sixteen. After leaving Oxford, she started to write seriously and finished two more novels, but did not succeed in getting them published. By then, however, her literary tastes were well-set. Above all, she was addicted to novels. Anthony Trollope and Jane Austen were her favorite novelists, and she knew their works intimately; but she read all the fiction she could, and listed among her favorites Ivy Compton-Burnett, Anthony Powell, and Iris Murdoch. She was less tolerant of contemporary novels, and viewed popular and sentimental fiction with the critical eye of the satirist. Nowhere in her own fiction does the reader find the sentimental excesses and sensational unrealities of current popular fiction.

In 1971, Pym had a serious operation, and in 1974, she retired to live with her sister near Oxford. She died on January 11, 1980, at the age of sixty-six.

Analysis

"In all of her writing," Philip Larkin has written of Barbara Pym, "I find a continual perceptive attention to detail which is a joy, and a steady background of rueful yet courageous acceptance of things." In this statement, Larkin points to perhaps the single most important technique—and theme—in Pym's work. *Excellent Women*, *A Glass of Blessings*, and *Quartet in Autumn* develop their effects, as indeed do all of Pym's ten novels, by exploiting the comedy of contemporary manners. Like her anthropologists, whom she quietly mocks for their esoteric detachment, Pym scrupulously notes and records the frustrations, unfulfilled desires, boredom, and loneliness of "ordinary people, people who have no claim to fame whatsoever." The usual pattern for the heroine is either retrenchment into her own world or, as a result of interaction with others, self-realization. By representing intensively the small world most individuals inhabit, it is Pym's method to suggest the world as a whole as well.

Usually Pym appoints a heroine to comment on the intimate details of social behavior. In *Excellent Women*, the assignment falls to Mildred Lathbury, who, as an observer of life, expects "very little—nothing, almost." Typical of Pym's "excellent women," Mildred is preoccupied with order, stability, and routine, but her special interest centers on the lives and crises of those around her—including her new neighbors, Rockingham and Helena Napier; the vicar, Julian Malory; and the anthropologist, Everard Bone. Faced with Mildred's honesty, diffidence, and unpretentiousness, the crises are resolved happily.

In Pym's fifth novel, *A Glass of Blessings*, the heroine is Wilmet Forsyth, a young and leisured woman bored with her excessively sober civil-servant husband. Her near-romances with a priest, her best friend's husband, and Piers Longridge (in whose friend Keith she discovers a rival) are only some of the pairings in this intricate drama of romantic errors. When the possibility of a love affair fails to materialize, Wilmet finds a different kind of consolation in religion.

Finally, Pym's anti-heroic view of life is particularly obvious in her most somber work, *Quartet in Autumn*, the first of her novels to be published after fifteen years of silence. Whereas her earlier work was a small protest against everyday life, *Quartet in Autumn* offered a formal protest against the conditions both of life itself and of certain sad civilities. The comedy is cold and the outlook is austere in this story of four people in late middle age who suffer from the same problem: loneliness. In its manipulation of the narrative among Edwin, Norman, Letty, and Marcia, the novel also represents Pym's greatest technical achievement.

Excellent Women, described by one critic as the most "felicitous" of all of Pym's novels, explores the complications of being a spinster (and a religious one, at that) in the England of the 1950's. The setting is a run-down part of London near Victoria Station, but the very high Anglican Church of St. Mary's also provides the background for some of the events described. In the quiet comfort of this world, where everything is within walking distance and a new face is an occasion for speculation, the pleasantness and security of everyday life dominate. Only small crises—such as an argument between Winifred and Alegra over how to decorate the church altar—form the counterpoint to comfort. As the narrator says, "life was like that for most of us—the small unpleasantnesses rather than the great tragedies; the little useless longings rather than the great renunciations and dramatic love affairs of history or fiction."

Mildred Lathbury, the narrator, is representative of one of Pym's favorite character-types: the "excellent woman." She lives very much as she did growing up in a country rectory, working part-time for the aid of impoverished gentlewomen and devoting herself to the work of the parish. As one who tends to get involved in other people's lives, she knows herself, she says, "capable of dealing with most of the stock situations or even the great moments of life—birth, marriage, death, the successful jumble sale, the garden fête spoilt by bad weather."

In all of Pym's novels, says Philip Larkin, "a small incident serves to set off a chain of modest happenings among interrelated groups of characters." In this instance, it is the entry into Mildred's life of Rockingham Napier. A flag lieutenant to an admiral, Rockingham has just returned from Italy, where he served his country by being charming to dull Wren officers. His wife Helena, an anthropologist, does not welcome his return. Scornful of his easy charm and lack of serious purpose, she has become infatuated with another anthropologist, Everard Bone, her co-worker in Africa. As Helena pursues, however, Everard flees.

The reader depends upon Mildred for ironic commentary. Helena leaves her husband, who then departs for a cottage in the country. Excellent woman that she is, Mildred is invited by Rockingham to send him the Napier furniture; by Helena to get it back; by both to effect their reconciliation; and by Everard to read proof and make the index for his forthcoming book. Because the vicar, Julian Malory, needs to be protected from designing women and Everard needs her help with the book, it seems to Mildred that she may look forward to a "full life." Then she remembers Rockingham's smile and reads from Christina Rossetti: "Better by far you should forget and smile,/ Than that you should remember and be sad." "It was easy enough to read those lines and be glad at his smiling," she acknowledges, "but harder to tell myself there would never be any question of anything else." Still, Everard's affection is genuine, if undemonstrative—and not unmixed with a pragmatic desire to find a suitable typist, indexer, and all-around "helpmate"—and the reader is happy to learn, in a subsequent novel, that Mildred and Everard do indeed go on to wed.

Again set in the 1950's, town and country are contrasted in *A Glass of Blessings*, which Larkin regards as the "subtlest" of Pym's books. The novel opens in St. Luke's Church on the feast of its patron, the "beloved physician," as St. Paul called him. Celebrating the feast and her thirty-third birthday, Wilmet Forsyth, the narrator and heroine, is the well-to-do but aimless wife (subject to "useless little longings") of a typical Pym husband—hopelessly imperceptive, though well-intentioned and reliable. Like Jane Austen's Emma, whom Pym has in mind throughout the novel, Wilmet is unused and spoiled. A beautiful woman, always exquisitely dressed, Wilmet is childless, idle, and snobbish. She is also utterly unknown to herself, unable to imagine another life, and afraid to risk herself, even on the London buses, certain that any disturbance will be disillusioning. Bored, without training for a career, despising routine, she plans "to take more part in the life of St. Luke's, to try to befriend Piers Longridge and perhaps even go to his classes."

Piers Longridge is a sour, moody homosexual, a fact Wilmet never quite seems to grasp until well into the novel. He has taken a seemingly useless degree and now teaches Portuguese in adult education classes. Believing that she might relieve his unhappiness, she forces herself on him, hoping for the grand passion of her life, another fact that she never really admits. Finally, in a scene of high comedy and bitter pain, exasperated by Wilmet's attentions and her naïveté, Piers confronts her with his secret lover, Keith, a male model, and accuses Wilmet of being incapable of affection. It is the first time anyone has told her anything near the truth, and in response, she says to Mary Beamish, "sometimes you discover that you aren't as nice as you thought you were—that you're in fact rather a horrid person, and that's humiliating somehow."

When she witnesses the courtship and marriage of Mary Beamish, an orphan and ex-Anglican nun, and Father Marius Lovejoy Ransome, Wilmet begins to perceive the possibilities of being useful in the parish and even of passion. After she finds out that Rodney has had an innocent flirtation with his secretary, Wilmet sees him differently, thinking, "I had always regarded Rodney as the kind of man who would never look at another woman. The fact that he could—and indeed had done so—ought to teach me something about myself, even if I was not quite sure what it was." The truth of it is that Wilmet has failed to recognize her society, including the parish of St. Luke's, for what it is—an erotic conclave of beauty and variety, both dangerous and enlivening. It is like George Herbert's "glass of blessings," full of the "world's riches"—"beautie . . . wisdome, honour, pleasure."

In her first six novels, Pym treats her characters with warm compassion and gentle irony. With *Quartet in Autumn*, however, her tone becomes harsher, more bitter, as she examines with bleak detachment the lonely rejection of the retired. Letty Crowe, another of Pym's excellent women, is sixty-five and faces retirement from the unspecified office job she has shared for many years with her colleagues, Marcia, Norman, and Edwin. For Letty, life in a rooming house is "a little sterile, perhaps even deprived." Retirement gives her a feeling of nothingness, as if she had never existed. During sleepless nights, her life unrolls before her, like that of a drowning man: forty years wasted looking for love. Images of dead leaves drifting to the pavement in autumn and being swept away recur throughout the novel. Indeed, Letty tries not to dwell on the image of herself lying among the autumnal leaves "to prepare for death when life became too much to be endured."

Her former colleagues are of no help to Letty. Norman is a scrawny, sardonic bachelor. Edwin is a widower preoccupied with "the soothing rhythms of the church's year." Marcia is gravely ill and at least slightly mad—collecting tins of food she never opens and milk bottles which she hoards in a shed. The only pleasures she knows are visits to the clinic for check-ups and bus trips to look at the mansion of her adored surgeon. Incapable of thought, she is far more pathetic than Letty.

Unlike her colleagues, Letty does try to act bravely, reading books on sociology, participating in church activities, still caring for her hair and her dress. "She told herself, dutifully assuming the suggested attitude toward retirement, that life was still full of possibilities." At the close of the novel, she is, like Mildred and Wilmet, where she was at the beginning. Yet, at the slightest change in the routine of her eventless days, she courageously assures herself, "at least it made one realize that life still held infinite possibilities for change."

In *Excellent Women*, *A Glass of Blessings*, and *Quartet in Autumn*, Pym relies neither on violence nor on the bizarre. Nothing outwardly momentous happens, but the frustrations of a half dozen or more characters emerge clearly and poignantly. Some critics have felt that the narrowness of her life inevitably imposed limitations on her work. Beneath the calm surface of her novels, however, the events of the day do make an imprint—to a degree appropriate to the lives of ordinary middle-class people. Each novel is a miniature work of art, distinguished by an air of assurance, an easy but firm control of the material, and the economy of means to achieve it.

Bibliography

Clapp, Susannah. "Genteel Reminders," in *The Times Literary Supplement.* July 7, 1978, p. 757.

Clemons, Walter. "The Pleasures of Miss Pym," in *Newsweek*. April 16, 1979, pp. 90-91.

Fitzgerald, Penelope. "A Secret Richness," in *London Review of Books.* November 20-December 4, 1980, p. 19.

King, Francis. "Fairly Excellent Women," in *The Spectator*. CCXLV (July 19, 1980), pp. 21-22.

Larkin, Philip. "The World of Barbara Pym," in *The Times Literary Supplement.* March 11, 1977, p. 260.

Smith, Robert. "How Pleasant to Know Miss Pym," in *Ariel*. II (October, 1971), pp. 63-68.

Dale Salwak

THOMAS PYNCHON

Born: Glen Cove, New York; May 8, 1937

Principal long fiction
V., 1963; *The Crying of Lot 49*, 1966; *Gravity's Rainbow*, 1973.

Other literary forms
In addition to his novels, Thomas Pynchon has published a handful of short stories. These include "The Small Rain" (1959), "Mortality and Mercy in Vienna" (1959), "Low-Lands" (1960), "Entropy" (1960), and "The Secret Integration" (1964). Two other magazine publications, "The World (This One), the Flesh (Mrs. Oedipa Maas), and the Testament of Pierce Inverarity" (1965) and "The Shrink Flips" (1966), are extracts from *The Crying of Lot 49*. "Under the Rose" (1961) is a version of Chapter 3 of *V.* Pynchon has also published an article, "A Journey into the Mind of Watts" (1966) in *The New York Times Magazine*.

Achievements
Among those contemporary novelists who enjoy both a popular and an academic following, Pynchon stands out as a virtual cult figure. His novels and stories stand up to the most rigorous critical analysis; they prove, like all great works of art, to be the product of a gifted sensibility and careful craftsmanship. At the same time, Dr. Samuel Johnson's "common reader" cheerfully wades through much abstruse matter because this author never fails to entertain—with bizarre plots, incandescent language, anarchic humor, and memorable characters.

With only three major works of fiction to his credit, Pynchon has an enormous, diverse, and fanatically loyal following. Already there are ten books and four collections of essays on his work, not to mention a triquarterly journal (*Pynchon Notes*, published at Wesleyan University) and special issues of òther scholarly journals. Much of the fascination he holds for readers derives from his reclusive habits. He refuses to be interviewed, photographed, or otherwise made into a darling of the media. His residence, which probably changes frequently, is not a matter of public record.

Pynchon has been honored with a number of literary awards. He received the William Faulkner Foundation Award for *V.*, the 1967 Rosenthal Foundation Award of the National Institute of Arts and Letters for *The Crying of Lot 49*, and the National Book Award for *Gravity's Rainbow* in 1974. Though the judging committee unanimously voted to award the Pulitzer prize for fiction to Pynchon for *Gravity's Rainbow*, the committee was overruled by an advisory board which found the novel immoral and "turgid." The Howells Medal, awarded once every five years, was offered to Pynchon in 1975, but he declined it.

Though Pynchon has published only three novels, he remains, in the eyes of most followers of the current fiction scene, in the front rank. More than one distinguished critic has declared him America's finest novelist, and few would deny him a place among the best novelists now writing in the United States.

Biography

Because of Thomas Pynchon's passion for privacy, little is known about his life. His father was an industrial surveyor, and the family lived in Glen Cove, East Norwich, and Oyster Bay—all on Long Island in New York. His father, a Republican, eventually served as town supervisor of Oyster Bay. Pynchon was sixteen when he was graduated from Oyster Bay High School in 1953. He was class salutatorian and winner of an award for the senior attaining the highest average in English. With a scholarship at Cornell University, he first majored in engineering physics but, though he was doing well academically, abandoned that curriculum after the first year. A year later, he decided to do a hitch in the Navy before completing his baccalaureate degree. He attended boot camp at Bainbridge, Maryland, and did advanced training as an electrician at Norfolk, Virginia. The two years in the Navy, partly spent in the Mediterranean, provided Pynchon with a number of comic situations and characters, which he has exploited in "Low-Lands," *V.*, and *Gravity's Rainbow*. Pynchon finished at Cornell as an English major and was graduated in 1959. While at Cornell, Pynchon took a class taught by Vladimir Nabokov; Nabokov's wife, Vera, who did her husband's grading, remembers Pynchon for his distinctive handwriting.

Pynchon lived briefly in Greenwich Village and in uptown Manhattan before taking a job with the Boeing Company and moving to Seattle. With Boeing for two and a half years (until September, 1962), he worked in the Minuteman Logistics Support Program and wrote for an intramural publication called "The Minuteman Field Service News." After leaving Boeing, he lived in California and Mexico and completed *V.*, which was published in 1963 and hailed as a major first novel.

Rumors of Pynchon's whereabout circulate often, some indicating that he has been seen in California, Mexico, and Oregon; in the late 1970's, he made a trip to England that mysteriously got noted in the national newsmagazines. Otherwise, there are only apocryphal stories of Pynchon which accompany the novels that have followed *V.* Would-be biographers have been frustrated, and some have simply written articles about their search for Pynchon, a search as beguiling and as ultimately inconclusive as the quests that figure in each of Pynchon's novels.

Analysis

The quest would seem to be the one indispensable element in the fictions of Thomas Pynchon, for each of his novels proves to be a modern-dress version of the search for some grail to revive the wasteland. Pynchon's characters seek knowledge that will make sense of their unanchored lives and their fragmented times; Pynchon hints that questing has a value irrespective of the authenticity of that for which one quests. The quest lends purpose to life, enabling one to function, to see life as worthwhile. At the same time, however, Pynchon invites his more privileged reader to recognize that the ordering principle thus projected is factitious. What is real are the gathering dissolution, the passing of human beings, civilizations, and all attempts to discover or create order and system.

Even so, as Pynchon's career has developed, one notes what may be a tendency to define some grail of his own, an inclination to search for a way out of the cul-de-sac of a metaphysics perhaps unduly in thrall to the principle of entropy (broadly defined as the gradual deterioration of the universe caused by irreversible thermodynamic equalization). Pynchon's critics disagree sharply on this point. Some maintain that the intimation of counter-entropic orders in *The Crying of Lot 49* and *Gravity's Rainbow* is merely a hook by which to catch the unwary reader, a means of seducing him into system-making as delusive as that of any of Pynchon's characters. Other critics, unwilling to believe that Pynchon's frequently noted affinity with modern science has been frozen at a point attained some time in the 1950's, suspect that Pynchon means to hint at transcendental alternatives implicit in the vast mysteries of contemporary astronomy and particle physics.

Whether Pynchon is on a grail quest of his own (with all the propensity for mysticism that seems indispensable to such a quester), he continues to create intricate labyrinths in which readers experience the paranoia that also figures as a prominent theme in his work. Paranoia is the conviction that mighty conspiracies exist, that all things are connected "in spheres joyful or threatening about the central pulse of [one]self." Pynchon's protagonists come to believe in this infinite reticulation of conspiracy because it is preferable to the possibility that "nothing is connected to anything." Pynchon's readers, by the same token, encounter fictive structures that formally imitate the paranoid premise: all is connected in great, seamless webs of interdependent detail.

The dialectic between order and disorder is the dialectic between art and life, and it is with reference to this neglected commonplace that one should analyze Pynchon's artifice. Art is traditionally man's imitation—sometimes pious, sometimes impious—of the divine prerogative of creation, the establishment of order where all before was without form and void. Pynchon gives evidence, since the almost nihilistic *V.*, of a fascination with the religious belief that there are "orders behind the visible," orders analogous to those found beneath the surface in works of art ostensibly reflecting life in all its chaotic aspects. *Gravity's Rainbow*, for example, strikes one at first as a complete mishmash, a welter of all-too-lifelike confusion, but one subsequently discovers it to be as finely crafted as James Joyces' *Ulysses* (1922) or *Finnegans Wake* (1939). Perhaps Pynchon is ready, like William Blake, William Butler Yeats, and D. H. Lawrence, to counter the smugness and complacency of a scientific age with a calculated antirationalism. Though he was rumored in the mid-1970's to be working on another comic novel, a parody of Japanese monster movies (one heard, too, of a novel for which he was doing research on the Mason-Dixon line), perhaps what the world will actually receive from him next time will be something unabashedly visionary.

These remarks adumbrate the last major topos in Pynchon's work—science and art. More than any other great writer, Pynchon knows and makes artistic use of science. He has, if nothing else, dispatched legions of humanists in search of information about modern physics, chemistry, and engineering—disciplines to which they had previously been indifferent. As noted above, however, science serves vision, not the other way around. Pynchon has done more than any other writer—scientific or literary—to reverse the widening "dissociation of sensibility" that T. S. Eliot noted as part of the intellectual landscape since the seventeenth century. In Pynchon, and in his readers to a remarkable extent, C. P. Snow's "two cultures" become one again.

In his first novel, *V.*, Pynchon brilliantly interweaves two narratives, one in the present (mid-1950's), the other in the period 1880 to 1943. The historical narrative, presented obliquely, concerns an extraordinary woman who appears originally as Victoria Wren and subsequently under *noms de guerre* in which the letter *V* of the alphabet figures prominently: Veronica Manganese, Vera Meroving. This is V., who turns up whenever there is bloodshed in the course of the twentieth century. In 1898, for example, she appears at the periphery of the Fashoda crisis in Egypt, and the following year she gravitates to Florence, where the spies of several nations are jockeying for position, engaging in what Pynchon calls "premilitary" activity. In 1913, she is in Paris, involved in a bloody theater riot which, like the crises in Egypt and Florence earlier, proves an earnest of World War I—a kind of fulfillment for V. in her early phase. When World War I ends with Western civilization intact, though permanently altered, V. begins to be involved with those elements that will figure in the more satisfying carnage of the century's real climacteric, World War II. In 1922, she is in German South-West Africa, where the massacre of the native Hereros reenacts the even greater massacre of two decades earlier and anticipates the really accomplished genocide in Europe between 1933 and 1945. On and off after 1918, she is on Malta, consorting with a group sympathetic to Mussolini and his Fascists. V. dies in an air raid on Malta in 1943—just as the tide turns against the Fascist cause with which she has become increasingly identified.

V.'s affinity with Fascism complements a decadent religiousity, and she comes to personify the drift to extinction of Western culture and of life itself. She gradually loses parts of her body and becomes more and more the sum of inanimate parts: false eye, false hair, false foot, false navel. She is a brilliant metaphor for entropy and the decline of civilization, and her baleful influence is projected in the novel's present in the decadence of the contemporary characters, most of whom are part of a group called the Whole Sick Crew. The Crew is exemplified by its newest member, the winsome schlemiel Benny Profane. Profane is incapable of love and emotional involvement; he is also perennially at war with inanimate objects. His dread of the inanimate suggests that he intuits the cultural situation as the century wanes. Though he is no thinker, he realizes that he and his fellows are Eliot's hollow men, on the way to their whimpering end. His inability to love is presented in comic terms—though fat, he is doted on by various desirable women, including the Maltese Paola Maijstral and the beautiful Rachel Owlglass. The failure is that of his entire circle, for though there is much sex among the Whole Sick Crew, there is no commitment, no love, no hope. The one baby generated by all the sexual freedom is aborted.

The Whole Sick Crew is what Western civilization has become as a result of entropic processes that are utterly random and mindless. The meaning-lessness of entropy is something difficult for the human mind to accept, however, and in Herbert Stencil, a marginal member of the Crew, Pynchon presents what becomes his standard character, a person who must discover conspiracy to deal with the fragmentation of life and culture. It is Stencil who does the mythmaking, the elevating of Victoria Wren from mere perverted adventuress to something awesome and as multifaceted as Robert Graves's White Goddess. Nor is Stencil alone, for the undeniable desire for connect-edness is quintessentially human. It is also shared by the sophisticated reader, who flings himself into the literary puzzle and becomes himself a Stencil, a quester for meaning in the convoluted plot of *V.* and in the identity of the mysterious personage who gives the novel its name. Pynchon's genius man-ifests itself in his ability to keep his readers suspended between his two mutually exclusive alternatives: that the clues to V.'s identity are the key to meaning and that V. is nothing more than a paranoid fantasy, the product of a mind that cannot deal with very much reality.

The fascination with which readers have responded to *V.* indicates that Pynchon is himself a brilliant mythmaker. Even after one has "solved" the mystery of V. and arrived at an enlightenment that Stencil explicitly rejects as a threat to his emotional and mental stability, one still finds the myth trenchant, moving, even terrifying. The decline of the West is a theme that one has encountered before, but never has one encountered it so cogently as in this woman who loves death and the inanimate. The real conspiracy, then, is an artistic one; the connectedness is that of the novel, the cabal between author and reader.

Pynchon's second novel, *The Crying of Lot 49*, seems slight between *V.* and *Gravity's Rainbow*, but some readers believe it to be his most perfect work of art. It is the story of Oedipa Maas, who is named "executor, or she supposed executrix" of the estate of an ex-lover, the millionaire Pierce Inverarity. In carrying out her duties, she stumbles upon evidence of a conspiracy to circumvent the United States Postal Service. She discovers Tristero, a *sub rosa* postal system at war for centuries with all officially sanctioned postal services, first in the old world, then in the new. Tristero subsumes an extraordinary number of revolutionary or simply alienated groups. In its new-world phase, it seems to bring together all those within the American system who are disenfranchised, disaffected, or disinherited—all those defrauded of the American dream.

Oedipa, like Herbert Stencil, finds that the harder she looks, the more connections to Tristero she discovers, until the connections start revealing themselves in such number and variety that she begins to doubt her sanity. Oedipa's mental condition, in fact, becomes the book's central conundrum. She first confronts the question in a flashback early in the story. She recalls visiting a Mexico City art gallery with Pierce Inverarity and seeing a disturbing painting by Remedios Varo. In the painting, a group of girls are imprisoned at the top of a circular tower and made to embroider *"el Manto Terrestre"*— the earth mantle. The tapestry they create, extruded through the tower's windows, contains "all the other buildings and creatures, all the waves, ships and forests of the earth," for "the tapestry was the world." Oedipa recognizes in the painting a representation of the fact that she—like any other human being—is imprisoned mentally and perceptually in the tower of her individual consciousness. External reality, in other words, may be nothing more than what one weaves or embroiders in one's cranial tower. Oedipa weeps at human isolation. Later, tracking down the clues to Tristero (which seems coextensive with Inverarity's estate and enterprises), she cannot free herself from the suspicion that the proliferating connections she is discovering all have their throbbing ganglion in her own mind. She realizes that she is becoming a classic paranoid.

Though Pynchon does not resolve the question of Oedipa's sanity, he hints that becoming sensitized to the problems of twentieth-century American culture (and to the horrors of the spiritual void contingent on certain twentieth century habits of mind) involves a necessary sacrifice of sanity or at least serenity. At the end, Oedipa is faced with a harrowing choice: either she is insane, or Tristero—with its stupendous reticulation—really exists. When Oedipa attempts to rephrase the dilemma, she finds that the paranoia is somehow inescapable:

> There was either some Tristero beyond the appearance of the legacy America, or there
> was just America and if there was just America then it seemed the only way she could

continue, and manage to be at all relevant to it, was as an alien, unfurrowed, assumed full circle into some paranoia.

Pynchon implies that Tristero, whatever its status as literal reality, is in effect a necessary fiction, a metaphor for the idea of an alterntive to a closed system.

Oedipa's experiences are almost certainly an imaginative version of Pynchon's own. At the time of the novel, 1964, Oedipa is twenty-eight years old—the same age as Pynchon was in that year. Like Pynchon, she has attended Cornell and then gravitated to the West Coast. Like Pynchon, too, she comes to view herself as an "alien," unable to fit into the furrow of American success, prosperity, and complacency. Thus, one can read the novel as Pynchon's account of why he has gone underground. He has made common cause with America's disadvantaged; in all of his fiction, not to mention his article "A Journey into the Mind of Watts," one notes an obvious sympathy with minorities and something like loathing for the mechanisms of corporate greed responsible for the spoilage of the American landscape, both literal and psychic. *The Crying of Lot 49*, then, is a fictional hybrid of the spiritual autobiography—in the same tradition as St. Augustine's *Confessions* (397-401) and William Wordsworth's *The Prelude* (1850).

These speculations—the need for an alternative to a closed system, the hints of spiritual autobiography—are supported by Edward Mendelson's brilliant essay "The Sacred, the Profane, and *The Crying of Lot 49*" (the single most satisfying reading of the novel, this essay has been reprinted in Mendelson's *Pynchon: A Collection of Critical Essays*). Mendelson points out the novel's high density of language with religious connotations; he argues that what Oedipa really searches for—and behind her twentieth century man—is a new species of revelation, a way out of the agnostic, positivistic cul-de-sac of contemporary rationalism. He also provides an explanation of the novel's odd title. "Lot 49" is a group of stamps—Tristero forgeries—to be sold as part of the settlement of Pierce Inverarity's estate. The novel ends as lot 49 is about to be "cried" or auctioned. Oedipa, present at the auction, expects to confront some representative of the mysterious Tristero, who will attempt to acquire the evidence of the secret organization's existence. Mendelson suggests that the number "49" refers obliquely to the forty-nine-day period between Easter and the descent of the Holy Spirit at Pentecost; the revelation that awaits Oedipa at the crying of lot 49 is symbolically the revelation awaited by modern man, whose existence so tragically lacks a numinous dimension. Thus, Pynchon ends his novel on a note of expectation, a yearning for some restoration of mystery, some answer to what the narrator calls "the exitlessness, the absence of surprise to life" in the modern age.

All of Pynchon's books are filled with bizarre characters and incidents, but *Gravity's Rainbow* is especially dense and demanding. The hero is Tyrone Slothrop, an American army lieutenant attached to an allied intelligence unit in World War II. Slothrop's superiors become aware that the map of his sexual conquests (or his sexual fantasies; this is kept ambiguous) coincides with the distribution of German V-2 rockets falling on London. Significantly, the erection *precedes* the arrival of the rocket. This fact, which calls into question the usual mechanism of cause and effect (it complements the fact that the rocket, traveling faster than the speed of sound, is heard falling *after* it has exploded) is of central importance to the novel, for Pynchon means to pit two scientific models against each other. The older model, which few laymen question, posits a mechanistic universe that operates according to the laws of cause and effect.

The character associated with this world view is the sinister Dr. Pointsman, a diehard Pavlovian threatened by the new model, which posits a universe in which physical phenomena can be plotted and predicted only in terms of uncertainty and probability (Pynchon is on sound theoretical ground here; he is presenting the physics of Werner Heisenberg and Max Planck). The character who embraces the more up-to-date world view is the sympathetic Roger Mexico, a statistician. Between these two, poor Slothrop—a kind of Everyman—tries to stay alive and if possible free. Pointsman and his minions concoct an experiment with Slothrop; they will provide him with the best information they have on the German rocket and then observe him closely for further revelations. Slothrop, aware that he is being used, goes AWOL to embark on a private quest to discover the truth of his personal destiny— and perhaps the destiny of his age as well.

Pynchon picks his historical moment carefully, for World War II was the moment when technological man came of age. Technology offers man complete control of his environment and his destiny; it offers him something very like transcendence—or it offers him annihilation. Pynchon's novel is a meditation on the choice, which is seen nowhere more clearly than in the new rocket technology. Will man use the rocket transcendentally, to go to the stars, or will he use it to destroy himself? The answer has been taking shape since the German rocket scientists were sent east and west after World War II, and Pynchon concludes his great narrative with the split second before the ultimate cataclysm: the apocalyptic rocket plunges toward the "theatre" in which the film *Gravity's Rainbow* has unreeled before the reader. Critical opinion is split on the degree of bleakness in this ending. Figuratively, says Pynchon, the world is separated from its end only by "the last delta-t," the last infinitesimal unit of time and space between the rocket and its target. The delta-t, however, is a relative unit of measure. Modern man's folly has indeed set in motion the process of his own destruction, but the process might still be arrested by a reordering of priorities, human and technological.

As for Slothrop, he simply fades away. Pynchon says he becomes "scattered," and the world reveals a characteristic aspect of Pynchon's genius. Just as Joyce forced religious and liturgical language to serve his aesthetic ends,

Pynchon forces technological language to serve humanistic and spiritual ends. "Scattering," a trope from particle physics, refers to the dispersal of a beam of radiation, but it also evokes *sparagmos*, the ritual dismemberment and dispersal of the divine scapegoat. Slothrop has been associated all along with Orpheus, whose dismemberment became the basis of one of the many fertility cults in the Mediterranean and Near East. In a sense, Slothrop dies for the sins of modern man, and his scattering coincides with the founding of the Counterforce, a group of enlightened, anarchic men and women devoted to reversing the technology of violence and death. The Counterforce, which has affinities with various countercultural movements waxing at the moment of this novel's composition, is not particularly powerful or effective, but it offers hope for a planet hurtling toward destruction.

One wonders, though, what Pynchon makes of the 1970's and the 1980's, in which the counterculture seems in abeyance and the forces of reaction or at least complacency are resurgent. Perhaps it is this frightening and disheartening development that is behind Pynchon's long silence. Has he abandoned a book or books that came to seem unattuned to the post-1960's *Zeitgeist*? Will he present his readers now with something bleak indeed? Perhaps Pynchon has been impressed by the promotion of "moral art" by his contemporary, the late John Gardner. Perhaps he agrees that the artist has a responsibility to provide what Gardner calls "models of virtue" and to create fictions that offer hope to an embattled humanistic ideal. Perhaps he is finding such a task rather hard just now.

Bibliography

Cowart, David. *Thomas Pynchon: The Art of Allusion*, 1980.
Fowler, Douglas. *A Reader's Guide to "Gravity's Rainbow,"* 1979.
Levine, George, and David Leverenz, eds. *Mindful Pleasures: Essays on Thomas Pynchon*, 1976.
Mackey, Douglas A. *The Rainbow Quest of Thomas Pynchon*, 1980.
Mendelson, Edward, ed. *Pynchon: A Collection of Critical Essays*, 1978.
Pearce, Richard, ed. *Critical Essays on Thomas Pynchon*, 1981.
Plater, William M. *The Grim Phoenix: Reconstructing Thomas Pynchon*, 1978.
Schaub, Thomas H. *Pynchon: The Voice of Ambiguity*, 1981.
Siegel, Mark Richard. *Pynchon: Creative Paranoia in "Gravity's Rainbow,"* 1978.
Slade, Joseph W. *Thomas Pynchon*, 1974.
Stark, John O. *Pynchon's Fictions: Thomas Pynchon and the Literature of Information*, 1980.

David Cowart

MRS. ANN RADCLIFFE

Born: London, England; July 9, 1764
Died: London, England; February 7, 1823

Principal long fiction

The Castles of Athlin and Dunbayne, 1789; *A Sicilian Romance*, 1790; *The Romance of the Forest*, 1791; *The Mysteries of Udolpho*, 1794; *The Italian: Or, The Confessional of the Black Penitents*, 1797; *Gaston de Blondeville*, 1826.

Other literary forms

In addition to her novels, Ann Radcliffe published *A Journey Made in the Summer of 1794 Through Holland and the Western Frontiers of Germany* (1795). It recounts a continental journey made with her husband and includes copious observations of other tours to the English Lake District. The work became immediately popular, prompting a second edition that same year retitled *The Journeys of Mrs. Radcliffe*. Following a common practice of romance-writers, Radcliffe interspersed the lengthy prose passages of her novels with her own verses or with those from famous poets. An anonymous compiler took the liberty of collecting and publishing her verses in an unauthorized edition entitled *The Poems of Ann Radcliffe* (1816). This slim volume was reissued in 1834 and 1845. Radcliffe's interest in versifying was increasingly evident when her husband, in arranging for the posthumous publication of *Gaston de Blondeville*, included with it a long metrical romance, *St. Alban's Abbey* (1826). Radcliffe also wrote an essay, "On the Supernatural in Poetry," which was published in *The New Monthly Magazine* (1826). The record of her literary achievement remains available today as all of her novels and the poems are in print.

Achievements

Mrs. Radcliffe's fame as a novelist today in no way compares to the popularity she enjoyed in the 1790's. With the publication of her third novel, *The Romance of the Forest*, this relatively unknown woman established herself as the best-selling writer of the period, receiving rave reviews from the critics and increasing demand for her works from circulating libraries.

Radcliffe's five Gothic romances, published between 1789 and 1797, owed a portion of their motivation to Horace Walpole's *The Castle of Otranto* (1765) and two earlier Gothic writers, Sophia Lee and Clara Reeve. The Gothic tale reached its full development with Radcliffe's ability to manipulate the emotions of love and fear in such a manner as to provoke terror in both her characters and readers alike. Though managing an effective use of the little understood complexities of the imagination, she offered her readers stereotyped plots, characters, and settings. Her disguises of foreign characters and lands were as thin as the supernatural illusions which often seemed anticlimactic in their emotional appeal. These weaknesses did not deter Radcliffe's public, who remained fascinated by her distinctive brand of romanticism, which combined the gloomy darkening vale of the more somber poets of the graveyard school, the extremes of imaginative sensibility (as in Henry Mackenzie's *The Man of Feeling*, 1771), and the medieval extravagance of the Ossianic poems of James Macpherson, as well as the pseudoarchaic fabrications of Thomas Chatterton's Rowley poems (1777).

Radcliffe nurtured this cult of melancholy, primitivism, sentimentalism, exoticism, and medievalism in her novels, becoming the epitome of the Gothic genre to her contemporaries. *The Mysteries of Udolpho*, her best-known work, was satirized by Jane Austen in *Northanger Abbey* (1818) as representative of the entire mode. Her later importance was seen in a number of major Romantic writers who read her romances in their childhood. Percy Bysshe Shelley's *Zastrozzi* (1810), an extravagant romance, was a youthful answer to the genre. Lord Byron's *Manfred* (1817) appears as a Gothic villain committing spiritual murder in a landscape of "sublime solitudes." Matthew G. Lewis and Mary Wollstonecraft Shelley clearly benefited from Radcliffe's strengths as a novelist of suspense, mystery, and the picturesque. In America, Washington Irving's, Edgar Allan Poe's, and Nathaniel Hawthorne's tales of terror, along with Charles Brockden Brown's *Edgar Huntley* (1799), were suggested by Radcliffe's work.

As the most popular and perhaps most important novelist between the eighteenth century masters and Austen and Sir Walter Scott, Radcliffe continues to claim the attention of academicians. Psychological, feminist, folklorist, and the more traditional thematic studies have proved the strengths of her art. In 1980, Devendra P. Varma (*The Gothic Flame*, 1957) began serving as advisory editor for the Arno Press collection, *Gothic Studies and Dissertations*, which has published at least thirty-four texts dealing with Radcliffe's literary output; of those, fifteen discuss Radcliffe's novels at length. It is clear that there is at present a remarkable revival of interest in the Gothic and in Radcliffe's work.

Biography

Mrs. Ann Radcliffe, *née* Ward, was born on July 9, 1764, in Holborn, a borough of central London, the only child of William Ward and Ann Oates Ward. Her father was a successful haberdasher who provided the family with a comfortable life, allowing Radcliffe access to a well-stocked library and the time to read the works of every important English author, as well as numerous popular romances.

This quiet, sheltered existence was enlivened by the visits of her wealthy and learned uncle, Thomas Bentley, who was the partner of Josiah Wedgwood, the potter. Bentley's London home was a center for the literati; there, among others, the pretty but shy girl met Mrs. Hester L. Thrale Piozzi, the friend and biographer of Samuel Johnson; Mrs. Elizabeth Montagu, "Queen of the Blue-Stocking Club"; and "Athenian" Stuart.

In 1772, Radcliffe joined her parents at Bath, where her father had opened a shop for the firm of Wedgwood and Bentley. She remained sequestered in this resort until her marriage to the young Oxford graduate, William Radcliffe, in 1788. William Radcliffe had first decided to become a law student at one of the Inns of Court but abandoned this for a career in journalism. The couple moved to London soon thereafter, where William subsequently became proprietor and editor of the *English Chronicle*. The marriage was happy but childless, and the couple's circle of friends were primarily literary, which added encouragement to William Radcliffe's argument that his wife should begin to write.

With her husband away on editorial business, Radcliffe spent the evenings writing without interruption. Her first book, *The Castles of Athlin and Dunbayne*, was unremarkable, but her next two novels established her reputation as a master of suspense and the supernatural. *A Sicilian Romance* and *The Romance of the Forest* attracted the public's voracious appetite for romances. Both works were translated into French and Italian and numerous editions were published, as well as a dramatization of *The Romance of the Forest*, performed in 1794. Radcliffe's success culminated in the appearance of *The Mysteries of Udolpho*; her decision to rely less on external action and more on psychological conflict produced ecstatic reviews. The excitement created by the book threatened the relative solitude of the Radcliffes, but the publisher's unusually high offer of five hundred pounds freed them to travel extensively on the Continent.

In the summer of 1794, the Radcliffes journeyed through Holland and along the Rhine to the Swiss frontier. On returning to England, they proceeded north to the Lake District. While traveling, Radcliffe took complete notes concerning the picturesque landscape and included detailed political and economic accounts of the Low Countries and the Rhineland. These latter observations were probably contributed by her husband, though both Radcliffes found the devastation of the Napoleonic Wars appalling. In 1795, there appeared *A Journey Made in the Summer of 1794 Through Holland and the Western Frontiers of Germany*.

Radcliffe's interest in the human misery of these regions and the legends and superstitions of the great fortresses and Catholic churches of the Rhineland suggested her next work, *The Italian: Or, The Confessional of the Black Penitents*. As a romance of the Inquisition, it explored character motivation in great detail, while action became a method of dramatizing personalities and not a simple vehicle for movement from one adventure to another. *The Italian*, though not as popular as *The Mysteries of Udolpho*, was translated immediately into French and even badly dramatized at the Haymarket on August 15, 1797.

At the age of thirty-three, Radcliffe was at the height of her popularity; though she had never decided on writing as a potential source of income, her means by this time had become quite ample. With the deaths of her parents between 1798 and 1799, she found herself independently wealthy. Whether it was because of her secure financial condition or her displeasure with the cheap imitations of her novels, Radcliffe withdrew from the public domain and refrained from publishing any more works in her lifetime. Innumerable reports surfaced that she was suffering from a terminal illness, that the terrors of which she had written in her novels had driven her mad, or that she had mysteriously died. These reports were without substance; in fact, she wrote another novel, a metrical romance, and an extensive diary.

After her death, Radcliffe's husband found among her papers a novel, *Gaston de Blondeville*, which he arranged to have published. Written after Radcliffe's visit to the ruins of Kenilworth Castle in 1802, it came near to comparing with the historical romances of Scott but lost itself in a preoccupation with historical precision, leaving action and character to suffer from a lack of emphasis. The narrative poem, *St. Alban's Abbey*, appeared posthumously with this last novel; though Radcliffe had been offered an early opportunity for publication, she broke off negotiations with the publisher.

Content with retirement and relative obscurity, she wrote in her last years only diary entries concerning the places she and her husband had visited on their long journeys through the English countryside. From 1813 to 1816, she lived near Windsor and probably at this time began suffering from bouts of spasmodic asthma. From all reports, she enjoyed the company of friends, maintained a ready wit and a sly humor, but insisted on delicacy and decorum in all things. Shortly before her final illness, she returned to London; she died there on February 7, 1823, in her sixtieth year. The "Udolpho woman" or "the Shakespeare of Romance Writers," as one contemporary reviewer called her, has achieved a secure place in the history of English literature.

Analysis

The novels of Ann Radcliffe serve as a transition between the major English novelists of the eighteenth century and the first accomplished novelists of the nineteenth century. In the years between 1789 and 1797, her five novels established a style which profoundly affected English fiction for the next twenty-five years and had a considerable impact in translation as well. From the negligible first novel, *The Castles of Athlin and Dunbayne*, to the sophisticated romances, *The Mysteries of Udolpho* and *The Italian*, Mrs. Radcliffe demonstrated an ability to enrich the motives, methods, and machineries of each succeeding work. Manipulating the conventions of the Gothic while introducing new thematic concerns and experiments with narrative techniques, Radcliffe became a master of her craft.

Improved control over the complex atmosphere of the Gothic romance proved an early factor in her success. Radcliffe went beyond the traditional Gothic devices of lurking ghosts and malevolent noblemen torturing innocent girls to an interest in natural description. This delight with nature's sublime scenery gave tone and color to her settings while emphasizing the heightened emotions and imagination that were produced in reaction to the landscape. A skillful use of numerous atmospherical factors such as sunsets, storms, winds, thunderclaps, and moonlight, intensified the romantic tendencies of her time.

A scene typifying the Radcliffe concept of landscape portraiture has a ruined castle in silhouette, arranged on a stern but majestic plain at nightfall. This view does not depend on precision of outline for effect but instead on an ominous vagueness, creating in the reader a queer mixture of pleasure and fear. Her delight in the architecture of massive proportions and in the picturesque derived in part from her reading of the nature poets and her study of the paintings of Claude Lorrain, Nicolas Poussin, and Salvator Rosa. She reflected a mid-eighteenth century English passion in cultivating an acute sensibility for discovering beauty where before it had not been perceived. While she made landscape in fiction a convention, it was her combining of beauty in horror and the horrible in the beautiful that reflected the romantic shift away from order and reason toward emotion and imagination.

Radcliffe's novels rely not only on strategies of terror, but also on the psychology of feelings. The novels of sensibility of the past generation offered her alternatives to the Gothic trappings made familiar in Horace Walpole's *The Castle of Otranto*; those Gothic aspects now became linked to various emotional elements in a total effect. By drawing on the poetry of Thomas Gray and Edward Young or the fiction of Oliver Goldsmith and Henry Mackenzie, Radcliffe created a minority of characters with complex natures who not only exhibited melancholy and doubt, love and joy, but also hate and evil intentions. She was one of the first English novelists to subject her characters to psychological analysis.

Of particular psychological interest are Radcliffe's villains. Cruel, calculating, domineering, relentless, and selfish, they are more compelling than her virtuous characters. Since their passions are alien to the ordinary man, she dramatically explores the mysteries of their sinister attitudes. Radcliffe's villains resemble those created by the Elizabethan dramatists, and their descendants can be found in the works of the great Romantics, Byron and Shelley.

At her best, Radcliffe manifested strengths not seen in her first two novels nor in her last. Her first novel, *The Castles of Athlin and Dunbayne*, exhibits the most obvious borrowings, from sources as well known as *The Castle of Otranto* to numerous other Gothic-historical and sentimental novels. Though immature, the work offers her characteristic sense of atmosphere with the marvelous dangers and mysteries of feudal Scotland depicted to full advantage. Its weaknesses become evident all too soon, however, as stock characters populate strained, often confused incidents while mouthing rather obvious parables about morality. Didacticism seems the motivating principle of the work; as David Durant observes in *Ann Radcliffe's Novels* (1980), "The characters are so controlled by didactic interests as to be faceless and without personality." The rigid obligations of *The Castles of Athlin and Dunbayne* to the morality of sentimental novels, the uniformity of a neoclassical prose style, and the repetitious, predictable action of the romance plot, trap Radcliffe into a mechanical performance.

Mrs. Radcliffe's second novel, *A Sicilian Romance*, has a new strategy, an emphasis on action and adventure while subordinating moral concerns. This approach, however, was not effective because of the obvious imbalance between the two methods, and characterization suffered before a mass of incident. The interest in fear was expanded throughout the tale as a long-suffering wife, imprisoned in the remote sections of a huge castle by a villainous nobleman (who has an attachment to a beautiful paramour), struggles helplessly until rescued, after much suspense, by her gentle daughter and the young girl's lover. The characters' shallowness is hidden by a chase sequence of overwhelming speed which prevents one from noticing their deficiencies. To dramatize the movement of plot, Radcliffe introduced numerous settings, offering the reader a complete vision of the romantic landscape.

Though *A Sicilian Romance* lacks the sureness of technique of the later novels and remains a lesser product, it did establish Radcliffe's ingenuity and perseverance. It was followed by the three novels on which her reputation rests: *The Romance of the Forest*, *The Mysteries of Udolpho*, and *The Italian*. Radcliffe's last novel, the posthumous *Gaston de Blondeville*, which was probably never meant for publication, exhibits the worst faults of the two earliest romances. Lifeless characters abound in a narrative overloaded with tedious historical facts and devoid of any action. In reconstructing history, Radcliffe was influenced by Sir Walter Scott but clearly was out of her element in attempting to make history conform to her own preconseptions. The primary innovation was the introduction of a real ghost to the love story. This specter, the apparition of a murdered knight demanding justice, stalks the grounds of Kenilworth Castle at the time of the reign of Henry III. Radcliffe detracts from this imposing supernatural figure when she resorts to explanations of incidents better left mysterious.

With the publication of her third novel, *The Romance of the Forest*, Mrs. Radcliffe moved from apprenticeship to mastery. Her technique had advanced in at least two important elements: the chase with its multitude of settings is scaled down to an exacting series of dramas set among a few extended scenes, and characterization of the heroine is improved with the reduction of external action. Though suspense is extended rather illegitimately in order to produce a glorious final surprise, the novel is a genuine exploration of the realm of the unconscious. This remarkable advance into modern psychology gave life to the standard situations of Radcliffe's stories, allowing the reader to create his own private horrors.

Radcliffe's new emphasis on internal action makes her protagonist, Adeline, more credible than the stock romantic heroines whom she in many ways resembles. Adeline suffers from a nervous illness after mysteriously being thrust upon the LaMotte family, who themselves have only recently escaped, under curious circumstances, from Paris. Soon the group discovers a Gothic ruin, which contains the requisite underground room, rotten tapestries, blood stains, and a general aura of mystery.

Instead of the familiar chase scenes, a series of unified set-pieces portray the exploration of the ruin, the seduction of the heroine, and the execution of the hero. The entire plot depends upon the actions of a vicious but dominating sadist, the Marquis Phillipe de Montalt, and his conspiratorial agent, Pierre de LaMotte, against the unprotected Adeline. Because of the uncertainty of her birth, the sexual implications of this situation involve the risk of incest. Among contemporary readers, *The Romance of the Forest* became an immediate success, owing to its well-constructed narrative, the charm of its description of romantic landscape, and a consummate handling of the principle of suspense.

Mrs. Radcliffe's next novel, *The Mysteries of Udolpho*, remains her best-known work. The sublimity of her landscapes and the control which she demonstrates in this novel mark an important change from her earlier novels; Radcliffe's handling of action and character also reached new levels of subtlety and success, moving the novel a step beyond the rather strict conventions of the sentimental mode to one of psychological inquiry.

The period of the novel is the end of the sixteenth century. The principal scenes are laid in the gloomy enclave of the Castle of Udolpho, in the Italian Apennines, but many glances are directed toward the south of France—Gascony, Provence, and Languedoc—and the brightness of Venice is contrasted with the dark horrors of the Apennines. Emily St. Aubert, the beautiful daughter of a Gascon family, is the heroine; she is intelligent and extraordinarily accomplished in the fine arts. Though revealing all the tender sensibilities of the characters associated with a hundred sentimental tales, Emily emerges as a credible figure who seems aware of the connections between the scenery around her and the characters who inhabit it. As a painter, she sees and thinks of life as a series of pictures. As David Durant explains in *Ann Radcliffe's Novels* (1980), "She does not merely feel fright, but conjures up imaginary scenes which elicit it . . . scenery inhabits the inner life of the heroine, as well as locating her actions." A further element of Emily's characterization that adds to her credibility is her internalizing of the suspense produced by the action in the narrative. Her heightened sensibility reacts to fear and terror in an all-inclusive way; this acuteness of sensibility makes her an easy prey for the villain, Signor Montoni. This sinister figure marries Emily's aunt for her money, and then conveys Emily and her unhappy aunt to the "vast and dreary" confines of the castle.

This impossible castle becomes a superbly appointed stage for the playing of the melodrama. As the melodrama has hopes of communicating a real sense of mystery, its action and characters remain subordinate to the environment which pervades the entire texture of the work. Description of landscape is a major part of the book's concept, and Radcliffe pays homage to Salvator Rosa and Claude Lorrain in emphasizing pictorial detail. The somber exterior of the castle prepares the reader for the ineffable horrors that lie within the walls and adumbrates the importance of landscape and massive architecture in the novel.

There are certain shortcomings in Radcliffe's method: landscape description strangles action; the visual aspects of the novel have been internalized; and the device of the chase over great stretches of land has been subordinated by mental recapitulation of past scenes—action becomes tableaux. This internal action is slow-moving, tortuously so in a novel of 300,000 words. Critics have also objected to Radcliffe's penchant for a rational explanation of every apparent supernatural phenomenon she has introduced; others, however, point out that Radcliffe's readers enjoyed terror only if they were never forced into surrendering themselves.

The Mysteries of Udolpho brought new energy to the picturesque, the sentimental, and the Gothic novel. Radcliffe alternated effectively between the picturesque vagueness of the landscape and the castle's hall of terrors. Her deft handling of sexual feeling, shown as antagonism between Montoni and Emily, is characteristic of her refusal to acknowledge sex overtly except as a frightening nameless power. The artificial terror, heightened sensibility, and the pervading air of mystery produced a powerful effect on her readers, yet many felt cheated by her failure to satisfy fully the intense imaginative visions awakened by the book. These readers would have to wait for *The Italian*, probably Radcliffe's finest work and the high-water mark of Gothic fiction.

The unity, control, and concentration of *The Italian* display a superb talent. Mrs. Radcliffe's narrative technique is more sophisticated than at any previous time, particularly in the subtle revelation of the unreliability of feelings based on first impressions rather than on rational judgment. The dramatic pacing remains rigorous throughout and relatively free from digressions. The story's impulse depends upon the Marchesa di Vivaldi's refusal to allow her young son, Vincentio, to marry the heroine, Ellena di Rosalba, whose origins are in doubt. The Marchesa relies on the sinister machinations of her monk-confessor, Schedoni, who decides to murder Ellena. Radcliffe's antipathy to

Roman Catholicism is evident in her account of the horrors of the Carmelite abbey and its order, including the labyrinthine vaults and gloomy corridors. A strange blend of fascination and disgust is evoked here and in the scenes of the trial in the halls of the Inquisition, the ruins of the Paluzzi, and in the prison of the Inquisition. Clearly, the Gothic aspects of *The Italian* function as representations of a disordered and morally evil past.

The vividness continues through to the climax of the story, when Schedoni, dagger in hand, prepares to murder Ellena but hesitates when he recognizes the portrait miniature she wears. Believing the girl is his lost daughter, he tries to make amends for his crimes. Though the solution involves more complex developments, the excitement of the confrontation between these two figures remains exceptional. Ellena has been a paragon of virtue, displaying piety, sensibility, benevolence, constancy, and a love of nature. To this catalog, Radcliffe adds intelligence, courage, and ingenuity. As an idealized character, Ellena represents the strengths necessary to prevail in the romantic conflict against external malign forces.

Schedoni, the devil/priest, is a figure of strong and dangerous sexual desire, associated, as is often the case in Radcliffe's work, with incest. Radcliffe counters the passivity and weakness of Ellena's virtues with this masculine version of desire—the lust of unregulated ambition. She describes him thus: "There was something terrible in his air, something almost superhuman. . . . His physiognomy . . . bore traces of many passions . . . his eyes were so piercing that they seemed to penetrate at a single glance into the hearts of men, and to read their most secret thoughts." His pride, greed, and loneliness combine to form a demonic figure vaguely suggesting John Milton's Satan.

Eino Railo, in *The Haunted Castle* (1964), believes *The Italian* and the central character, Father Schedoni, were created under the revivified romantic impulse supplied by the tragic monastic figure in Matthew G. Lewis' *The Monk* (1796). According to Railo, the difference between Ambrosio and Schedoni is that the latter "is no longer a young and inexperienced saint preserved from temptations, but a person long hardened in the ways of crime and vice, alarmingly gifted and strenuous, hypocritical, unfeeling and merciless." Radcliffe was inspired by "Monk Lewis" to write a more impressive book than earlier conceived; her bias against sexual and sadistic impulses and toward heightened romantic effect win out in *The Italian*. While Ambrosio's passions remain tangled and confused by his need for immediate satisfaction and his lack of any lasting goal, Schedoni has well-defined goals for power, wealth, and status. His Machiavellian inclinations blend with pride, melancholy, mystery, and dignity, making him Radcliffe's most fully realized character. Her protest against *The Monk* created a story of tragic quality that goes beyond the conventional Gothic paraphernalia and toward the psychological novel.

Mrs. Radcliffe remains the undisputed mistress of the Gothic novel and a central figure in the Gothic revival, beginning in the late 1950's, which has seen the resurrection of hordes of forgotten Gothic novelists and their tales. The generous volume of Radcliffe criticism in recent decades has redefined her place in literary history, acknowledging the prodigious sweep of her influence. On first reading her works, one must remember to search behind the genteel exterior of the artistry to discover the special recesses of terror, subconscious conflict, and the psychology of feelings which played a major role in the evolution of dark romanticism.

Major publications other than long fiction
NONFICTION: *A Journey Made in the Summer of 1794 Through Holland and the Western Frontiers of Germany*, 1795.
POETRY: *The Poems of Ann Radcliffe*, 1816; *St. Alban's Abbey*, 1826.

Bibliography
Birkhead, Edith. *The Tale of Terror: A Study of the Gothic Romance*, 1921.
Durant, David S. *Ann Radcliffe's Novels: Experiments in Setting*, 1980.
Frank, Frederick S. "A Bibliography of Writings about Ann Radcliffe," in *Extrapolation*. XVII (1975), pp. 54-62.
Murray, E. B. *Ann Radcliffe*, 1972.
Smith, Nelson C. *The Art of the Gothic: Ann Radcliffe's Major Novels*, 1980.
Summers, Montague. *The Gothic Quest: A History of the Gothic Novel*, 1938.
Tompkins, J. M. S. *Ann Radcliffe and Her Influence on Later Writers*, 1980.
Varma, Devendra P. *The Gothic Flame*, 1957.
Wieten, A. S. S. *Mrs. Radcliffe: Her Relation to Romanticism*, 1926.

Paul J. deGategno

RAJA RAO

Born: Hassan, India; November 5, 1908

Principal long fiction

Kanthapura, 1938; *The Serpent and the Rope*, 1963; *The Cat and Shakespeare: A Tale of India*, 1965; *Comrade Kirillov*, 1976.

Other literary forms

Raja Rao's first efforts as a writer were in Kannada, his mother tongue. Between 1931 and 1933, he published three essays and a poem in Kannada in a journal called *Jaya Karnataka*. Around that time, he began to publish his earliest stories in English. These and others were collected and published as *The Cow of the Barricades and Other Stories* in 1947. A later collection, *The Policeman and the Rose* (1978), includes seven stories published in the earlier volume and three new ones written chiefly during the 1960's. In addition to novels and short stories, Rao has published essays, travelogues, and biographical sketches in various journals and popular magazines; these have not been collected as yet. Rao has also edited three books: the first two, anthologies of essays on India, are *Changing India* (1939) and *Whither India* (1948), coedited with Iqbal Singh; the third is *Soviet Russia: Some Random Sketches and Impressions* (1949) by Jawaharlal Nehru.

Achievements

Rao, with Mulk Raj Anand and R. K. Narayan, is generally regarded as one of the most important modern Indian English novelists. The reasons for his preeminence are both historical and artistic. Rao is important historically because his first novel, *Kanthapura*, was published during the decade of the 1930's, when Indian English fiction first began to gain recognition. Although the Indian English novel is considered to begin with Toru Dutt's incomplete romance, *Bianca: Or, The Young Spanish Maiden* (1878), it was in the 1930's that Indian English fiction began to demonstrate maturity and accomplishment with the publication of Anand's *Untouchable* (1935), Narayan's *Swami and Friends* (1935), and Rao's *Kanthapura*.

Artistically, Rao is important because of his unique formal and thematic accomplishments. Although his four novels seem meager in comparison to Anand's or Narayan's more prolific output, Rao's achievement is considerable. Formally and stylistically, he is the most adventurous of the three. As M. K. Naik has elaborated in his monograph *Raja Rao* (1972), Rao has consistently tried to adapt the Western form of the novel to suit his Indian subject matter. He uses traditional Indian genres such as Purana, *sthalakatha*, and the Indian beast fable to structure his works. Thus, formally, his novels are based on Indian models. Furthermore, they are written in an English that is uniquely Indian in style, tone, mood, and rhythm. This Indianness of style is achieved by relying heavily on translation, quotation, and the use of Indian proverbs, idioms, and colloquial patterns. Rao adroitly manipulates vocabulary and syntax to enhance the Indian flavoring of his English. The result is a style which, although distinctly Indian, is evocative and perfectly intelligible to Western readers as well.

Thematically, too, Rao is somewhat different from the other two major Indian English novelists, Anand and Narayan. Rao is a metaphysical novelist whose concerns are primarily religious and philosophical. *Kanthapura*, for example, shows a strong Gandhian influence as it documents the progress of a nonviolent agitation against the British in a remote South Indian village. *The Serpent and the Rope* and its sequel *The Cat and Shakespeare* are expositions of the ancient Indian philosophical outlook, Vedanta. *Comrade Kirillov* is an evaluation of the efficacy of Communism. Thus, in Rao's works there is an ongoing discussion of major philosophical systems, chiefly of India but also of the West.

Both stylistically and thematically, then, Rao succeeds in capturing the spirit of India in his works. His formal and stylistic innovations have expanded the expressive range of English and have influenced other writers who share Rao's predicament: the task of writing about a culture in a language that is not native to it. Although Rao's oeuvre is small, his reputation appears to be secure.

Rao was awarded the Sahitya Akademi Prize for 1964 by the Academy of Indian Literature. In 1969, he received the Padma Bhushan from the Indian government. He has been invited to lecture by several institutions in India, France, and the United States.

Biography

Raja Rao was born into a respected Brahmin family in Hassan, South India, the eldest son in a family of two brothers and seven sisters. His father taught Kannada at Nizam's College in the neighboring Hyderabad state. The earliest influence on young Rao was his grandfather, with whom he stayed both in Hassan and in Harihalli, while his father was in Hyderabad. Rao seems to have imbued a spiritual orientation from his grandfather; his preoccupation has stayed with Rao throughout his life and is evident in all his work.

Rao joined his father in Hyderabad, going there to attend high school. He was then sent to Aligarh Muslim University in North India. These Aligarh days proved to be crucial in shaping Rao's intellectual growth. Under the influence of Eric Dickinson, a minor poet and a visiting professor from Oxford, Rao's literary sensibility was awakened. He met other interesting students such as Ahmed Ali, who became a famous novelist, and Chetan Anand, who became an influential film producer. Rao also began learning

French at Aligarh, which contributed to his decision to go to France a few years later. After matriculating in 1927, he returned to Hyderabad to enroll as a student for the B.A. at Nizam's College. Two years later, he was graduated, having majored in English and History.

In 1929, two other important events occurred in Rao's life: first, he won the Asiatic Scholarship of the Government of Hyderabad for study abroad. This marked the beginning of a new phase in his life; he left India for the first time to study at the University of Montpellier in France. Second, in that same year, Rao married Camille Mouly, who taught French at Montpellier. Camille was undoubtedly the most important influence on Rao's life during the next ten years. She not only encouraged him to write, but supported him financially for several years. In 1931, his early Kannada writing began to appear in the journal *Jaya Karnataka*. For the next two years, Rao researched the influence of India on Irish literature at the Sorbonne. His short stories were published in journals such as *Asia* (New York) and *Cahiers du Sud* (Paris). In 1933, Rao abandoned research to devote himself completely to writing.

Although he never settled permanently in India, Rao's awareness of Indian culture grew during his stay abroad. He became a compulsive visitor, returning to India again and again for spiritual and cultural nourishment; indeed, in a sense, Rao never completely left India. In 1933, he visited Pandit Taranth's ashram in his quest for self-realization. In 1938, his small masterpiece, *Kanthapura*, although written earlier, was published from London. One year later, Rao's marriage disintegrated; he found himself back in India, his spiritual search renewed. In the next few years, Rao visited a number of ashrams and religious teachers, notably Ramana Maharshi of Tiruvannamalai, Narayana Maharaj of Kedgaon, and Mahatma Gandhi at Sevagram. Around this time, Rao also became active in several social and political causes. He edited, with Singh, *Changing India* (1939), an anthology of modern Indian thought from Ram Mohan Roy to Nehru. He participated in the underground "Quit India" movement of 1942, boldly associating with a group of radical Socialists. In 1943-1944, he coedited with Ali a journal from Bombay called *Tomorrow*. He was the prime mover in the formation of a cultural organization, Sri Vidya Samiti, devoted to reviving the values of ancient Indian civilization; this organization failed shortly after inception. In Bombay, he was also associated with Chetana, a cultural society for the propagation of Indian culture and values. Finally, in 1943, Rao's quest appears to have been fulfilled when he met his spiritual preceptor in Atmananda Guru of Trivandrum. Rao even thought of settling down there, but returned to France following the death of his guru.

In 1960, twenty-two years after *Kanthapura*, Rao's masterpiece *The Serpent and the Rope* was published. Its sequel, *The Cat and Shakespeare*, came relatively soon, in 1965. About ten years later, *Comrade Kirillov* was published in English, although it had appeared in a French translation, *Le Comrade Kirillov* (1965) much earlier. From 1965 until his recent retirement, Rao was Professor of Philosophy at the University of Texas at Austin. In that same year, 1965, he married Katherine Jones, an American stage actress. They have one son, Christopher Rama. Teaching one semester a year, Rao has divided his time among the United States, France, and India.

Analysis

An understanding of Raja Rao's art is enhanced by contextualizing his novels. Although Rao admits to several Western influences, his work is best understood as a part of the Indian tradition. Rao regards literature as *Sadhana* or spiritual discipline; for him, writing is a consequence of his metaphysical life. His novels, hence, essentially represent a quest for the Absolute. From *Kanthapura* to *Comrade Kirillov*, Rao's protagonists grapple with the same concerns: What is Truth? How is one to find it? Their methods vary, as do their results, but they share the same preoccupation. The novels, thus, become chronicles of this archetypal search. Formally, too, all four novels share certain features. Plot is deemphasized; the narrative is generally subjective—even idiosyncratic—and episodic. The progression of the narrative is not linear, but circular; in the *puranic* manner of storytelling which Rao adapts to the form of the Western novel, there are digressions, stories within stories, songs, philosophical disquisitions, debates, and essays. Characters, too, are frequently symbolic figures; often, the motivations for their actions might seem puzzling or insufficient. Finally, because the narration is subjective, the language of the narrator, too, tends to be unique, reflecting the narrator's peculiarities—his or her social, regional, and philosophical makeup.

Rao's first novel, *Kanthapura*, is the story of how a small, sleepy, South Indian village is caught in the whirlpool of the Indian freedom struggle and comes to be completely destroyed. In the Foreword, Rao himself indicates that the novel is a kind of *sthala-purana* or legendary history, which every village in India seems to have. These local *sthala-puranas* are modeled on the ancient Indian Puranas—those compendia of story, fable, myth, religion, philosophy, and politics—among which are the Upa Puranas, which describe holy places and the legends associated with them. Hence, several features of *Kanthapura* are in keeping with the tradition of *sthala-puranas*. The detailed description of the village at the opening of the novel is written in the manner of a *sthala-purana*, wherein the divine origin or association of a place is established. The village is presided over by Goddess Kenchamma, the *Grama-deveta* (village-deity) and the novel provides a legend explaining her presence there, recalling several similar legends found in the Puranas. Like the "place-Gods" of the Puranas, Kenchamma operates within her jurisdiction, where she is responsible for rains, harvests, and the well-being of the villagers. She cannot extend her protection to other villages or to outsiders. Thus, the village-deity symbolizes local concerns such as famine, cholera, cattle-diseases, and poor harvests, which may have little to do with the world outside the village. Like Kenchamma, the river Himavathy, too, has a special significance in the novel and recalls passages describing famous rivers in the Puranas, such as the description of the river Narmada in *Matsyapurana* and *Agnipurana*.

Similarly, *Kanthapura* shares certain narrative techniques with the Puranas. The story is told rapidly, all in one breath, it would seem, and the style reflects the oral heritage also evident in the Puranas. Like the Puranas, which are digressive and episodic, *Kanthapura* contains digressions such as Pariah Siddiah's exposition on serpent lore. The Puranas contain detailed, poetic descriptions of nature; similarly, *Kanthapura* has several descriptive passages which are so evocative and unified as to be prose-poems in themselves. Examples are the coming of Kartik (autumn), daybreak over the Ghats, and the advent of the rains. Finally, the narration of *Kanthapura* has a simplicity and lack of self-consciousness reminiscent of the Puranas and quite different from the narrative sophistication of contemporary Western novelists such as Virginia Woolf or James Joyce.

Kanthapura is also imbued with a religious spirit akin to that of the Puranas. The epigraph of the novel, taken from the *Bhaghavad Gītā* (c. fifth to second century B.C.), is the famous explanation of the Hindu notion of incarnation: "Whensoever there is misery and ignorance, I come." The doctrine of incarnation is central to the Puranas, too, most of which are descriptive accounts of the avatars of Vishnu. The avatar in *Kanthapura* is Gandhi, whose shadow looms over the whole book, although he is himself not a character. Incarnation, however, is not restricted to one Great Soul, Gandhi, but extends into Kanthapura itself, where Moorthy, who leads the revolt, is the local manifestation of Gandhi, and by implication, of Truth.

Although the form of *Kanthapura* is closely modeled on that of the *sthalapurana*, its style is uniquely experimental. Rao's effort is to capture the flavor and nuance of South Indian rural dialogue in English. He succeeds in this by a variety of stylistic devices. The story is told by Achakka, an old Brahmin widow, a garrulous, gossipy, storyteller. The sentences are long, frequently running into paragraphs. Such long sentences consist of several short sentences joined by conjunctions (usually "and") and commas; the effect is of breathless, rapid talking. The sentence structure is manipulated for syntactic and rhythmic effect, as in the first sentence of the novel: "Our village—I don't think you have ever heard about it—Kanthapura is its name, and it is in the province of Kara." Repetition is another favorite device used to enhance the colloquial flavor of the narrative. In addition to these techniques, translation from Kannada is repeatedly used. Nicknames such as "Waterfall Venkamma," "Nose-scratching Nanjamma," "Cornerhouse Moorthy" are translated; more important, Kannada idioms and expressions are rendered into English: "You are a traitor to your salt-givers," "The Don't-touch-the-Government Campaign," "Nobody will believe such a crow and sparrow story," and so on. The total effect is the transmutation into English of the total ethos of another culture. *Kanthapura* with its *Kannadized* English anticipates the lofty *Sanskritized* style of *The Serpent and the Rope*, which, stylistically, is Rao's highest achievement.

Kanthapura is really a novel about a village rather than about a single individual; nevertheless, Moorthy, the Brahmin protagonist of the villagers' struggle against the government, is a prototypal Rao hero. Moorthy is the leader of a political uprising, but for him, as for Gandhi, whom he follows, politics provide a way of life, indistinguishable from a spiritual quest. In fact, for Moorthy, Action is the way to the Absolute. In Gandhi, he finds what is Right Action. Thus, for him, becoming a Gandhi man is a deep spiritual experience which is appropriately characterized by the narrator as a "conversion." At the culmination of this "conversion" is Sankacharaya's ecstatic chant "Sivoham, Sivoham. I am Siva. I am Siva. Siva am I," meaning that Moorthy experiences blissful union with the Absolute. Indeed, the chant, which epitomizes the ancient Indian philosophical school of Advaita or unqualified nondualism, is found in all Rao's novels as a symbol of the spiritual goal of his protagonists. Moorthy, the man of action, thus practices *Karma Yoga* (the Path of Action), one of the ways of reaching the Absolute as enunciated in the *Bhaghavad Gītā*. In the novels after *Kanthapura*, Rao's protagonists, like Moorthy, continue to seek the Absolute, although their methods change.

Published twenty-two years after *Kanthapura*, *The Serpent and the Rope* is Rao's most ambitious work. If the former is modeled on an Upa Purana (minor Purana), the latter is a kind of Maha Purana (major Purana) or epic: geographically, historically, philosophically, and formally, its sweep is truly epical. The novel includes a variety of settings, ranging from Paris to Ramaswamy's ancestral home in a South Indian village, from European locales such as Aix, Montpalais, Pau, Montpellier, Provence, Cambridge, and London to Indian locales such as Hyderabad, Delhi, Lucknow, Bombay, Bangalore, and Beneras. Rao delves into almost the whole of Indian history, from the invasion of the Aryans to the advent of British rule; European history, chiefly the Albigensian heresy; Chinese history—all of these come under discussion as the protagonist, Rama, a historian by training, expounds his theories in conversations with the leading characters. Philosophically, too, the novel's sweep is formidable: Rao discusses Hinduism, Buddhism, Catholicism, Islam, Taoism, Marxism, Darwinism, and Nazism. Hence, it is not surprising to find *The Serpent and the Rope* extremely diverse in form as well. Rao quotes from an array of languages, including Sanskrit, Hindi, French, Italian, Latin, and Provençal; only the Sanskrit quotations are translated. There are long interludes and stories, such as Grandmother Lakshamma's story of a princess who became a pumpkin and Ishwara Bhatta's "Story of Rama." In addition, the novel contains songs, myths, legends, and philosophical discussions in the manner of the Puranas. The main narrative, the gradual disintegration of Rama's marriage with his French wife, Madeleine, is thus only a single strand holding a voluminous and diverse book together.

The Serpent and the Rope is an extremely challenging work thematically as well; Savithri's words in the novel sum it up well: it is "a sacred text, a cryptogram, with different meanings at different hierarchies of awareness." It may be approached on at least two different levels, the literal and the symbolic, although the two usually operate simultaneously. On the literal level of plot, the novel may appear puzzling and unsatisfying. The crux is: Why does the marriage of Rama and Madeleine disintegrate? Critics have attempted various answers, ranging from incompatibility between the Indian Rama and the French Madeleine, to Rama's infidelity. Although such answers are plausible, they do not satisfy completely because these reasons are not perceived by the characters themselves. Rama and Madeleine are both aware of the growing rift between them, but they do not attempt to bridge it on a practical level. Instead, both watch the dissolution of the union with an almost fatalistic helplessness. Similarly, it is hard to understand why Rama seeks fulfillment in other women while averring his love for Madeleine at the same time, or why he never tells her of his affairs in spite of his claim that he keeps no secrets from her. Rama, the narrator, does not answer such questions; he only chronicles the breakdown of the relationship, almost impersonally, as if there were little *he* could do to save it. He also does not feel himself responsible for having affairs with other women, one of which involves a ritual second marriage, while being married to Madeleine at the same time. What is lacking, then, is an adequate motivation for the actions of the characters, something that most readers are conditioned to expect from the novel. Perhaps a better approach, however, instead of asking of the novel something that it did not intend to give, is to consider what it does clearly provide; indeed, questions which appear unresolved on the literal level are resolved more satisfactorily on the symbolic level.

Rama, the Brahmin hero, is a seeker of Truth both by birth and by vocation (a Brahmin is one who seeks Brahma, or the Absolute). As an Indian scholar in France, Rama is seeking Truth in the form of the missing link in the puzzle of India's influence on the West. According to Rama, this missing link is the Albigensian heresy: he thinks that the Cathers were driven to heresy by the influence of Buddhism, which had left India. Rama's quest for Truth is also manifested in his search for the ideal Woman because in the Hindu tradition, the union of man and wife is symbolic of the union of man and God. The marriage of Siva and Parvathi is one such paradigmatic union in which Siva, the Absolute, the abstract, the ascetic, is wedded to Parvthi, the human, the concrete, the possessor of the Earth. Another such union is that between the mythical Savithri and her husband Satyavan ("Satya" means "Truth"); Savithri, through her devotion, restores her dead husband to life.

In keeping with these paradigms, Rama—the thinker, the meditator, the seeker of Truth—can only find fulfillment in a Parvathi or a Savithri who can bring him back to Earth by her devotion. Madeleine, however, who has given up her Catholicism for Buddhism, becomes an ascetic, renouncing the Earth, denying her body through abstinence and penance. Significantly, her union with Rama is barren: both their children are stillborn. Madeleine also regards Truth as something outside herself, something that has to be striven for, in order to be realized. Her dualism is the philosophical opposite of Rama's nondualism; Rama believes, following the Advaita Vedanta, that the self is a part of Truth, as the wave is a part of the sea, and that all separateness is illusion, like the illusion in which a rope is mistaken for a serpent. Rama's true mate is an Indian undergraduate at Cambridge named, interestingly, Savithri. Savithri, despite her modishness—she dances to jazz music, smokes, wears Western clothes, and so on—is essentially an Indian. Unlike Madeleine, Savithri does not seek Truth, but instinctively and unselfconsciously *is* Truth. Her union with Rama is thus a natural and fulfilling one. Savithri, however, like Rama's sister Saroja, opts for an arranged marriage in the traditional Indian manner with someone else; hence, her relationship with Rama is never consummated. At the end of the book, Rama, divorced from Madeleine, sees a vision of his guru in Travancore and plans to leave France for India.

Rama's path to Truth, unlike Moorthy's *Karma Yoga*, is *Jnana Yoga* (the Path of Knowledge), also enunciated in the *Bhaghavad Gītā*. Rama is not a man of action but an intellectual. Although he has accumulated knowledge, he still does not apprehend Truth clearly; like the deluded seeker in the fable, he mistakes the rope for the serpent, failing to see himself already united with Truth as Savithri is. Traditionally, a guru is necessary for the *Jnana Yogi* because only a guru can cure his delusion by *showing* him that what appears to be a serpent is really a rope. Thus, in the end, Rama resolves to seek his guru to be cured of his delusion.

The Cat and Shakespeare, described by Rao as "a metaphysical comedy," clearly shows a strong formal *Upanishadic* influence. The spiritual experiences of its narrator, Ramakrishna Pai, are reminiscent of the illuminative passages in the *Chandogya Upanishad*, which describe the experience of the Infinite. The dialogues in the novel are also *Upanishadic* in their question-and-answer patterns; the best example is the conversation between Govindan Nair and Lakshmi in the brothel. Nair's metaphysical speculations, such as "Is there seeing first or the object first?," seem to be modeled on philosophical queries in the Upanishads. The cat links the novel to the Indian beast fable, and Nair's comic roguery shows similarities to the rogue fable in the *Pancha Tantra*. The major Western debt is to William Shakespeare, who is acknowledged in the title. Shakespeare is a symbol for the universal; according to

Rao, Shakespeare's vision transcends duality and arrives at a unified view of the universe. There are numerous allusions to *Hamlet* (1600-1601) in the novel, culminating in the "rat-trap episode" in which a cat is trapped in a large rat-trap; this prompts Nair to deliver a parody of *Hamlet* which begins: "A kitten sans cat, that is the question."

The Cat and Shakespeare is Rao's sequel to *The Serpent and the Rope* in that it shows what happens after a seeker's veil of illusion has been removed by the guru. Its theme may be summed up in Hamlet's words to Horatio toward the end of the play: "There's a divinity that shapes our ends,/ Rough-hew them how we will." A similar view of grace is embodied in the novel in what Nair, the man who is united to Truth, calls "the way of the Cat." The "way of the Cat," simply, is the notion that just as the kitten is carried by the scruff of its neck by the mother cat, man is completely at the mercy of the divine; consequently, the only way to live is to surrender oneself totally to divine grace, as the helpless kitten surrenders itself to the mother cat. Nair lives this philosophy and is responsible for teaching it to his ignorant neighbor, the narrator Pai. Pai is like the innocent hunter in the story who unknowingly heaped leaves on Siva and was rewarded with a vision.

Between Pai's house and Nair's is a wall over which Nair leaps everytime he visits Pai. The wall is an important symbol because it represents the division between illusion and Truth. Nair crosses it easily, but Pai has never gone across. Toward the end of the novel, following Nair's cat, Pai accidentally crosses the wall. Like the lucky hunter, he, too, is vouchsafed a divine vision: for the first time, Pai sees the whole universe as a unity. The novel ends with Pai's spiritual as well as material fulfillment, having partially realized his lifelong ambition of owning a three-story house. *The Cat and Shakespeare*, although not as ambitious as *The Serpent and the Rope*, is as successful on its own terms. The novel is an elaborate puzzle which the author challenges the reader to solve; a solution is not only possible at all levels, but is completely satisfying as well. The way to the Absolute here is not *Karma Yoga* or *Jnana Yoga* of the two previous novels, but *Bhakti Yoga*, or the path of devotion. The seeker recognizes himself as completely dependent on divine grace for his salvation and surrenders himself to the Benevolent Mother like a trusting kitten.

Comrade Kirillov, published in English in 1976, is generally recognized as Rao's least ambitious novel; it is clearly a minor work compared to its three illustrious predecessors. Formally, it is an extended *Vyakti-Chitra*, or character sketch, a popular genre in Indian regional literature. The main story, narrated by one "R.," is a mere ninety-three pages in large type, to which are appended twenty-seven pages of the diary of Kirillov's wife, Irene, and a concluding seven pages by the narrator; the effect is of a slight, sketchy novella. Kirillov, alias Padmanabha Iyer, leaves India for California to propagate Theosophy but, after a period of disillusionment, becomes a Communist. From California, he moves to London, where, marrying a Czech immigrant, Irene, he settles down to the life of an expatriate intellectual. Like Rao's other protagonists, Kirillov starts as a seeker of Truth, but after becoming a Communist, he is increasingly revealed by the narrator to be caught in a system which curtails his access to Truth. Thus, Kirillov continuously rationalizes the major events in the world to suit his perspective. Nevertheless, following a visit to India several years after he has left, he realizes that his Communism is only a thin upper layer in an essentially Indian psyche. Irene also recognizes in her diary that he is almost biologically an Indian Brahmin, and only intellectually a Marxist. By the end of the book, Kirillov is shown to be a man of contradictions: attacking and worshiping Gandhi simultaneously, deeply loving traditional India but campaigning for a Communist revolution, reciting Sanskrit *shlokas* but professing Communism.

The narrator is Kirillov's intellectual opposite, an adherent of Advaita Vedanta. There are numerous interesting discussions on Communism in the book, which has great value as a social document, capturing the life of an Indian expatriate intellectual between 1920 and 1950. Also of interest is Kirillov's relationship with Irene, which recalls Rama's relationship with Madeleine. Numerous similarities aside, this relationship is more successful: this marriage lasts, and the couple have a child, Kamal. Soon after Kirillov's return from India, however, Irene dies in childbirth, followed by her newly born daugher. Kirillov leaves for Moscow and is last heard of in Peking. The novel ends with the narrator taking Kamal, now in India, to Kanyakumari. Despite its humor, pathos, and realism, *Comrade Kirillov* falls short of Rao's three previous novels.

It is interesting to note that *Comrade Kirillov*, first published in a French translation in 1965, was written earlier. Thematically, it represents the stage of negation before the spiritual fulfillment of *The Cat and Shakespeare*. Kirillov, as a Communist and atheist, has negated the *Karma Yoga* of *Kanthapura* and the *Jnana Yoga* of *The Serpent and the Rope* by denying the existence of the Absolute; thus, his quest results in failure. The *Bhakti Yoga* of *The Cat and Shakespeare*, especially in the character of Nair, is the culmination of the various stages of spiritual realization in the earlier novels. Nair is the first character in Rao's novels who does not merely seek Truth, but who has found it, who actually practices it. The question is what direction will Rao take next. He has told the present writer that his work in progress, *The Chessmaster and His Moves*, about eight hundred pages long, is an extended dialogue between a Brahmin and a rabbi, among other things. Its publication will be a literary event worth awaiting.

Major publications other than long fiction

SHORT FICTION: *The Cow of the Barricades and Other Stories*, 1947; *The*

Policeman and the Rose, 1978.

Bibliography
Naik, M. K. *Raja Rao*, 1972.
Narasimhaiah, C. D. *Raja Rao: A Critical Study of His Work*, 1972.
Sharma, K. K., ed. *Perspectives on Raja Rao*, 1980.

Makarand Paranjape

MARY RENAULT

Born: London, England; September 4, 1905

Principal long fiction

Purposes of Love, 1939 (published in the United States as *Promise of Love*, 1940); *Kind Are Her Answers*, 1940; *The Friendly Young Ladies*, 1944 (published in the United States as *The Middle Mist*, 1945); *Return to Night*, 1947; *North Face*, 1948; *The Charioteer*, 1953; *The Last of the Wine*, 1956; *The King Must Die*, 1958; *The Bull from the Sea*, 1962; *The Mask of Apollo*, 1966; *Fire from Heaven*, 1969; *The Persian Boy*, 1972; *The Praise Singer*, 1978; *Funeral Games*, 1981.

Other literary forms

All but two of Mary Renault's published works have been novels. *The Lion in the Gateway: Heroic Battles of the Greeks and Persians at Marathon, Salamis, and Thermopylae* (1964) is a children's history of ancient Greek battles. *The Nature of Alexander* (1975) is a heavily documented biography placing the charismatic leader in the context of his time and customs, a book that also defines the two abiding preoccupations of Alexander's life and Renault's art. "Outward striving for honour," the Greek *to philotimo*, balances *arete*, the profound inward thirst for achievement knowingly made beautiful. Together, as Alexander himself wrote, they win immortality: "It is a lovely thing to live with courage,/ and die leaving an everlasting fame."

Achievements

Critics praised Renault's first five novels, written and set around World War II, for their realism, psychological depth, and literary technique. In 1946, one year prior to its publications, *Return to Night* won the MGM Award, $150,000, then the world's largest literary prize. Although this novel was never made into a motion picture, the award brought Renault American acclaim, augmented later by the success of her Greek novels, but her work has never gained the academic attention it deserves. She received the National Association of Independent Schools Award in 1963, and the Silver Pen Award in 1971, and she is a Fellow of the Royal Society of Literature.

Biography

Mary Renault (the pen name of Mary Challans), a physician's daughter, was born on September 4, 1905, in London. At eight, she decided to become a writer, and she read English at St. Hugh's College, Oxford, from 1924 to 1927, where she preferred to study the Middle Ages, the setting of an attempted historical novel she destroyed after several rejections. She had once thought of teaching, but after graduation she entered nurses' training at Radcliffe Infirmary, Oxford, where she received her nursing degree in 1936. She dates her literary career from 1939, though she continued as a neurosurgical nurse at Radcliffe Infirmary throughout the war, writing in her off-duty hours. Her first novels were widely popular, but "She claims that if her early novels were destroyed irrevocably, she would feel absolutely no loss" (Bernard F. Dick, *The Hellenism of Mary Renault*, 1972).

Renault's postwar travels in the eastern Mediterranean provided the impetus for a new literary phase marked by her emigration to South Africa in 1948. Since then, her exhaustive self-taught knowledge of ancient Greek history and philosophy has made her a mesmerizing novelist able to re-create a lost world. In the estimation of Bernard F. Dick, Renault is "the only bona fide Hellenist in twentieth century fiction."

Analysis

Mary Renault's novels celebrate and eulogize man's potential but transitory glory, a combination difficult for a world that has relinquished its acquaintance with the classics. Peter Wolfe regards Renault's first five novels as her literary apprenticeship, "1930's novels" marked by then-fashionable themes of political engagement and sexual liberation. Bernard F. Dick, her only other major commentator, believes her early fiction was influenced by the restrictive, pain-filled atmosphere of a World War II surgical hospital. Both are partly correct; Renault's early work deals with the individual's freedom from contemporary power structures and stifling social conventions.

Such topical concerns, however appealing to modern readers, are nevertheless peripheral to the core of Renault's art, the Platonism which she followed to the mythic depths of her later novels. When she began to write, Renault was already familiar with the Theory of Ideas developed in Plato's dialogues, wherein everything perceptible by human senses is imitative of changeless perfect Ideas beyond time and space. Each Idea corresponds to a class of earthly objects, all of which must inevitably change, leaving the Ideas the only objects of true knowledge in the universe. A transitory earthly object, however, may remind men of the Idea it represents. Plato theorized that before entering the body, the soul had encountered the infinite Ideas, and that once embodied, the soul might vaguely remember them. Renault often convincingly incorporates Plato's anamnesis, the doctrine that "learning is recollection," in her fiction. Plato also believed that human recognition of such natural truths as the mathematically perfect circle could lead men stepwise to the contemplation of Absolute Truth, which he equated with Absolute Goodness and Absolute Beauty. He taught that the immortal human soul may be reborn through metempsychosis, transmigration, another concept found throughout Renault's work.

Renault's novels are also informed by Plato's theory of love as defined by

Socrates in *The Symposium*: love is the desire for immortality through possession of or union with the Beautiful. Love manifests itself on its lowest levels by human sexuality, proceeds upward through intellectual achievement, and culminates in a mystical union of the soul with the Idea of Beauty. That Renault's heroes aspire to such union is their glory; that being mortal they must fail is the fate she eulogizes.

Plato, like most classical Greeks, allowed heterosexual love only the lowest rung on his ladder of love, as the necessary element for reproduction. Only the homosexual relationship was considered capable of inspiring the lifelong friendships which offered each partner the ideal of *arete*. All of Renault's novels illustrate some aspect of Platonic love; in the first, *Promise of Love*, she shows Vivian, a nurse, and Mic, who loves her because she resembles her brother Jan, achieving self-knowledge not through sexual passion but by affection, the ultimate stage of Platonic love, which at the close of the novel "recalls the true lover of [Plato's dialogue] the *Phaedrus* who is willing to sleep like a servant at the side of his beloved."

Renault's other early novels also have strong Platonic elements. *Kind Are Her Answers* foreshadows her interest in theater as mimetic form, Plato's first literary love, which she realized more fully in *The Mask of Apollo*. Her third novel, *The Middle Mist* concludes with references to Plato's *Lysis*, his dialogue on friendship which claims that erotic satisfaction destroys *philia*, the more permanent nonphysical union promised by Platonic love, a theme to which Renault returned more successfully in *The Last of the Wine*. Renault attempted unconvincingly in *Return to Night* and *North Face* to state the *amor vincit omnia* tradition of "women's fiction" in mythological metaphors, and found that she had to develop a new fictional mode capable of expressing her archetypal themes with Platonic concepts.

Not published in the United States until 1959 because of its forthright treatment of homosexuality, *The Charioteer* (1953) is the only Renault novel to incorporate a systematic development of Platonic philosophy as the vehicle for commentary on contemporary life. In the *Phaedrus*, Plato depicted reason as a charioteer who must balance the thrust of the white horse of honor against the unruly black horse of passion. The image unifies Renault's tale of Laurie Odell, wounded at Dunkirk, who must come to terms with his homosexuality. After his friendship with the sexually naïve conscientious objector Andrew Raines dissolves, Laurie finds a lifelong partner in Ralph Lanyon, who brought him back wounded after they had fought at Dunkirk. Laurie attains an equilibrium between the two conflicting halves of his nature in a Platonic denial of sexual excess. As Renault comments in the epilogue, a Greek device she favors, "Now their [the horses'] heads droop side by side till their long manes mingle; and when the charioteer falls silent they are reconciled for a night in sleep."

In the ideal Platonic pattern, the older man assumes a compassionate responsibility for the honor of the younger, altogether transcending physical attraction and cemented by shared courage in battle. Renault is hindered in *The Charioteer* from an entirely convincing presentation of such friendship by the intolerance with which homosexual relationships are usually viewed in modern society and the often pathetic insecurity it forces upon them. Despite these handicaps, Renault sympathetically portrays Laurie as "a modern Hephaestus, or maimed artist," as Wolfe notes, a character who wins admiration through striving to heal his injured life and nature and make of them something lasting and beautiful.

From roots far deeper than Plato's philosophy, Renault developed the vital impulse of her eight Greek novels, her major literary achievement. Central is the duality of Apollo and Dionysus, names the Greeks gave to the forces of the mind and of the heart, gods whose realms the mythologist Walter Otto described in *Dionysus, Myth and Cult* (1965) as "sharply opposed" yet "in reality joined together by an eternal bond." In Greek myth, Zeus's archer son Apollo, wielder of the two-sided weapon of Truth, endowed men with the heavenly light called Art, by which he admonished mankind to self-knowledge and moderation through his oracle at Delphi. Paradoxically, Apollo shared his temple and the festival year at Delphi with his mysterious brother Dionysus, god of overwhelming ecstasy, born of mortal woman and all-powerful Zeus, torn apart each year to rise again, offering both wine's solace and its madness to mankind. Thought and emotion were the two faces of the Greek coin of life—in Otto's words, "the eternal contrast between a restless, whirling life and a still, far-seeing spirit."

Each of Renault's Greek novels focuses on a crucial nexus of physical and spiritual existence in Greek history. The age of legendary heroes such as Theseus of Athens, subject of *The King Must Die* and *The Bull from the Sea*, was followed by the Trojan War, 1200 B.C., the stuff of classical epic and tragedy and the harbinger of Greece's Dark Age, when only Athens stood against the Dorian invasion. By the sixth century B.C., the setting of *The Praise Singer*, Athens, under the benevolent tyrant Pisistratus, had become the model polis of the Greek peninsula, building a democracy that repelled imperial Persia and fostered the world's greatest tragedies in their Dionysian festivals. *The Last of the Wine* treats Athens' fall to Sparta in the Peloponnesian Wars, 404 B.C., torn by internal strife and bled by foreign expansion. The restored Athenian democracy of a half-century later is the milieu of *The Mask of Apollo*. Shortly after Plato's death, his pupil Aristotle taught a prince in Macedon who dreams of Homeric deeds in *Fire from Heaven*, accomplishes them in *The Persian Boy*, and leaves an empire to be shattered by lesser men in *Funeral Games*—Alexander the Great.

The Last of the Wine, like most of Renault's Greek fiction, is ostensibly a memoir, a form favored by classical authors. Its fictional narrator, a young and "beautiful" Athenian knight named Alexias, endures the agonizing aftermath of Athens' ill-fated Sicilian venture under Alkibiades, the magnetic but flawed former student of Sokrates. With Lysis, the historical figure on whom Plato modeled his dialogue on ideal friendship, Alexias begins the idealistic attachment they learned together from Sokrates, but physical passion, handled with sensitivity by Renault, overcomes them, and they ruefully must compromise their ideal. Sacrificing his honor for Lysis during the famine caused by the Spartan siege of Athens, Alexias models for sculptors, at least one lascivious, to feed his wounded friend, and in the battle to restore Athenian democracy, Lysis falls gloriously with Alexias' name upon his lips.

The novel's title, an allusion to the Greek custom in which the wine remaining in a cup is tossed to form the initial of a lover's name, metaphorically represents Athens' abandonment of the ideals of its Golden Age. Renault poignantly shows Lysis, a gentleman athlete in pursuit of *philotimo*, the hero's struggle for outward glory to emulate his ideal, beaten sadistically in the Isthmian Games by a monstrous professional wrestler, just as Athenian democracy is becoming warped by politicians such as the vicious Kritias and the cold-blooded Anytos, who will help condemn Sokrates. Alkibiades' personal disaster, abandoning Athens for its Spartan enemies, is an exemplary case of a leader who cannot resist abusing his charismatic gifts.

The Greek ideal of democracy learned at Sokrates' side and based on individual *arete*, inward pursuit of honor, still allows Lysis a moral victory often overlooked in this splendidly elegiac novel of the death of an era. "Men are not born equal in themselves," Lysis tells Alexias over wine one evening in Samos; "A man who thinks himself as good as everyone else will be at no pains to grow better." Lysis fights and dies for "A City where I can find my equals and respect my betters . . . and where no one can tell me to swallow a lie because it is expedient." At the end of the novel, as he listens to the distorted minds of bureaucrats, Alexias remembers the lamps of Samos, the wine-cup on a table of polished wood, and Lysis' voice: "Must we forsake the love of excellence, then, till every citizen feels it alike?"

Renault analyzes the ideal of kingship in *The King Must Die* and *The Bull from the Sea*. In the earlier novel, she traces Theseus' early life from Troezen and Eleusis, where with the bard Orpheus he establishes the Sacred Mysteries, to the labyrinthine palace of Crete, where he destroys the brutal son of King Minos, who oppresses Athens. In the second, she pursues Theseus' progressive rule in Athens through his abandonment of Ariadne to Dionysus' bloody cult and his capture of the Amazon Hippolyta to the great tragedy of his life, his fatal curse on their son Hippolytus. Stylistically more evocative of Homer's mighty simplicity than the Attic cadences of *The Last of the Wine*, Renault's Theseus novels treat kingship as a manifestation of the divine inner voice that chooses the moment of willing consent when the monarch sacrifices himself for his people.

Both novels discuss a past so dim that its events have become the raw material of myth. Theseus' birth meshes the earthly with the supernatural, since it results from the divinely inspired compassion of the Athenian King Aigios for the stricken land of Troezen; the reader is left, as is customary in Renault's fiction, to decide where history ends and metaphysics begins. Until his son's death, Theseus practices the lesson learned from his grandfather's ritual sacrifice of the King Horse, one of the shocking joys hidden in pain that opens much of Renault's fiction: "The consenting . . . the readiness is all. It washes heart and mind . . . and leaves them open to the god."

By closing himself to the speaking god, however, obeying not his reason but his emotional reaction to his wife Phaedra's false accusations of Hippolytus, Theseus is lost. Only two bright moments remain to him, an anamnetic dream of Marathon where he fights beside the Athenians defending their City, his name their stirring war cry; and a glimpse before he dies of the boy Achilles, "as springy and as brisk as noonday, his arm round a dark-haired friend." Prescient, Theseus watches tragedy in the making: "The god who sent him that blazing pride should not have added love to be burned upon it," but—consoled that his own reputation has become Achilles' "touchstone for a man"—Theseus for the last time consents to the god of the sea.

By the mid-fourth century B.C., late in Plato's life, sophisticated Athenians had accepted the gods as metaphysical forces within the human personality. In *The Mask of Apollo*, Renault poses the primal duality of Apollo and Dionysus in Greek culture, the calm, farseeing force of reason and art balanced against the irresistible force of ecstasy. An old mask of Apollo, reputedly from the workshop of the Parthenon's architect Phidias, accompanies Renault's narrator Nikeratos through his successful acting career, the fascinating backdrop to the political career of Dion of Syracuse, Plato's noble friend, who might have become the ideal philosopher-king Plato postulated in *The Republic*.

Though Dion is a model soldier and a principled statesman, circumstances force him to abandon his philosophical ideals to save Syracuse from devastation. Renault parallels his fall with Nikeratos' performance in Euripides' *The Bacchae* (405 B.C.), the enigmatic masterpiece named for the followers of Dionysus. As he meditates before Apollo's mask, Nikeratos hears his own voice: "With *The Bacchae* he [Euripides] digs down far below, to some deep rift in the soul where our griefs begin. Take that play anywhere, even to men unborn who worship other gods or none, and it will teach them to know themselves."

Plato's tragedy, acted out by Dion, was the "deep rift" that made men unable to follow him with united minds and hearts: "No one would fight for Dion, when he gave, as his own soul saw it, his very life for justice." By serving Apollo and Dionysus equally, however, Nikeratos the artist earns his gifts, one a Platonic dream of acting in a strange revenge drama, speaking lines beside an open grave to a clean skull in his hand. Through his love for his protégé Thettalos, whom he frees for achievements he knows will be greater than his own, Nikeratos plays Achilles in Aeschylus' *The Myrmidons* in a performance viewed by Alexander, a boy for whom men will fight and die, "whether he is right or wrong," a prince who "will wander through the world . . . never knowing . . . that while he was still a child the thing he seeks slipped from the world, worn out and spent." Had he encountered Plato's Ideals, which he instinctively sought, Renault proposes as the curtain falls on *The Mask of Apollo*, the Alexander of history might have made the philosopher-king Plato's Dion never could have been; but Nikeratos observes that "No one will ever make a tragedy—and that is well, for one could not bear it—whose grief is that the principals never met."

Renault's Alexander grows from boy to king in *Fire from Heaven*, in which she abandons the memoir form for more objective narration, as though no single point of view could encompass Alexander's youthful ideals, fired by the blazing Homeric *philotimo* in Achilles' honor he learned at the epic-conscious Macedonian court. Modern archaeology supports Renault's conviction that Alexander deliberately patterned his actions, even his father Philips' funerary rites, upon the *Iliad* (c. 800 B.C.), which he read as though returning home, recognizing his mutual love with Hephaistion the tragic bond of Achilles and Patroclus, the basis of the Western world's first, perhaps greatest, poem.

Arete, which cloaks the heavenly Idea of excellence in earthly beauty, came to Alexander less from Aristotle than through his instinctive attraction to Sokrates through Plato's works, which he read as a boy in Macedon. After defeating Thebes's Sacred Band at Cheironeia, where Philip's Macedonians secured the domination of all of Greece, Alexander stands "with surmise and regret" at Plato's tomb in Athens, listening to his disciple Xenokrates: "What he [Plato] had to teach could only be learned as fire is kindled, by the touch of the flame itself."

The novel in which Renault most precariously treats the question of homosexuality, *The Persian Boy*, is narrated by Bagoas, the handsome eunuch once King Darius' favorite and now the lover of Alexander. Renault's choice of Bagoas' point of view reflects her belief that Alexander was not corrupted by Persian luxury and imperial power, as many historians from classical times to the present have asserted, but that he sought to assimilate Eastern ways as a means of uniting his realm in spirit as well as military fact. Just as Alexander's "passionate capacity for affection" could allow him to accept affection wherever it was sincerely offered from the heart and yet remain wholly true to Bagoas' "victor now, forever," Hephaistion, who Renault feels is the most underrated man in history, Alexander felt "Macedon was my father's country. This is mine"—meaning the empire he had won for himself.

Renault believes that Alexander's eventual tragedy was that he was humanly unable to achieve equilibrium between his followers' personal devotion to him and their pragmatic selfish desires. Through Alexander's complex relationship with his dangerous mother Olympias, herself a devotee of Dionysus, Renault exemplifies the peril of neglecting the god of ecstasy basic to *The Bacchae*, in which Olympias herself had acted during Alexander's youth as a shocking challenge to Philip's authority. Toward the end of his own life, Dionysus' cruelty touches even Alexander. Renault shows his purported deterioration as less his own fault than his men's when he must hold them by force as well as by love, even violating Macedon's dearest law, killing before their Assembly had condemned a man to death. The powerful god leads Alexander to excess; Bagoas sees that "His hunger grew by feeding." The Roman historian Arrian, following the memoir of Alexander's only faithful general Ptolemy, commented, "If there had been no other competition, he would have competed against himself."

Bagoas better than any also sees that "Great anguish lies in wait for those who long too greatly." Alexander loses Hephaistion and with him nearly abandons his own senses, emerging only after his friend's funeral, in which he watches Thettalos, without Nikeratos for the first time, perform *The Myrmidons* one last time; "'Perhaps,' Bagoas thought, 'the last of the madness had been seared out of him by so much burning.'"

At the close of *The Persian Boy*, Renault notes in her Afterword, "When his [Alexander's] faults (those his own times did not account as virtues) have been considered . . . no other human being has attracted in his lifetime, from so many men, so fervent a devotion. Their reasons are worth examining." In her two novels of Alexander's life, Renault not only has examined the reasons, but also has brilliantly probed to the heart of one of the greatest human mysteries: how one man can ask, as did Homer's Achilles, "now as things are, when the ministers of death stand by us/ In their thousands, which no man born to die can escape or even evade,/ Let us go."—and how other men, with all their hearts, can answer.

Such "true songs are still in the minds of men," according to the aged bard Simonides, narrator of *The Praise Singer*, recalling the "lyric years" when tragedy was being born of song and Athens was becoming the center of the earth. "We die twice when men forget," the ghosts of heroes seemed to tell him as a boy, and he has spent his life in "The bright and perilous gift of making others shine." In this novel, where Renault's heroic epitaph for *to philotimo* and her noble elegy for man's hope of *arete* have given place to a gentler, less exalted nostalgia, she recognizes that "praising excellence, one serves the god within it." Renault also notes in her Afterword that "the blanket generalization 'absolute power corrupts absolutely' is a historical absurdity," and she demonstrates that the respected rule of Pisistratus, nominally a "tyrant," formed the solid foundation on which Pericles erected Athenian democracy, even presaging through a discredited seer "a lightning flash from Macedon."

In Alexander's time, Renault has remarked, "the issue was not whether, but how one made [war]." At his death, brought about at least in part by his self-destructive grief for Hephaistion, Alexander's generals embarked on a cannibalistic power struggle—only Ptolemy, his half-brother, emerging with any of the dignity Alexander had worn so easily in conquering his empire. Renault's *Funeral Games* is "the ancestral pattern of Macedonian tribal and familial struggles for his throne; except that Alexander had given them a world stage on which to do it."

The most violent of Renault's Greek novels, *Funeral Games* contains a darkness that is alleviated only by flashes of Alexander reflected through the decency of the few who knew him best—Ptolemy; Bagoas; Queen Sisygambis, who looked upon Alexander, not Darius, as her son. In them, something of Alexander's flame lingers a little while, a heavenly light extinguished at last in the wreckage of his empire of human depravity which Alexander could not prevent nor Renault fail to record.

In her eight novels of ancient Greece, Renault far surpasses conventional historical fiction. She achieves a mythic dimension in her balance of Apollonian and Dionysian psychological forces and philosophical precision in her treatment of Platonic doctrines. Her style is adapted to the Greek literature of each period she delineates, Attic elegance for *The Last of the Wine* and *The Mask of Apollo*, Hellenic involution counterpoised against Alexander's Homeric simplicity of speech. Renault links all eight novels with a chain of works of art, a finely crafted touch the classical Greeks would have applauded: the great tragedies, *The Myrmidons* and *The Bacchae*, Polykleitos' sculpture of Hermes modeled on Alexias, and the bronze of the liberator Harmodios in Pisistratos' day all serve as shaping factors in the portrait of her ultimate hero, Alexander. Mastering time, space, and modern ignorance of the classical world, Renault captures the "sadness at the back of life" Virginia Woolf so aptly cited as the essence of Greek literature, the inevitable grieving awareness of man at the impassable gulf between his aspirations and his achievement. In the face of the eternal questions of existence, Renault's novels offer a direction in which to turn when, in Woolf's words, "we are sick of the vagueness, of the confusion, of the Christianity and its consolations, of our own age."

Major publications other than long fiction
NONFICTION: *The Nature of Alexander*, 1975.
CHILDREN'S LITERATURE: *The Lion in the Gateway: Heroic Battles of the Greeks and Persians at Marathon, Salamis, and Thermopylae*, 1964.

Bibliography
Burns, Landon C., Jr. "Men Are Only Men: The Novels of Mary Renault," in *Critique*. VI (1964), pp. 102-121.

Dick, Bernard F. *The Hellenism of Mary Renault*, 1972.
Otto, Walter. *Dionysus, Myth and Cult*, 1965.
Wolfe, Peter. *Mary Renault*, 1969.

Mitzi M. Brunsdale

JEAN RHYS

Born: Roseau, Dominica Island, West Indies; August 24, 1894
Died: Devonshire, England; May 14, 1979

Principal long fiction

Postures, 1928 (published in the United States as *Quartet*, 1929); *After Leaving Mr. Mackenzie*, 1931; *Voyage in the Dark*, 1934; *Good Morning, Midnight*, 1939; *Wide Sargasso Sea*, 1966.

Other literary forms

Though Jean Rhys is now primarily remembered for her novels, her first published book was a collection of short stories, *The Left Bank and Other Stories* (1927). As Ford Madox Ford pointed out in the Preface to the collection, Rhys's heroines are geographically, psychologically, and emotionally of "the Left Bank," not only of Paris—though Rhys captured the Paris of the 1920's as well as anyone—but also of all of the cities of the world. They are underdogs, alone, betrayed, on the edge of poverty; they are women in a man's world.

Besides *The Left Bank*, Rhys published two other collections of stories: *Tigers Are Better-Looking* (1968) and *Sleep It Off, Lady* (1976). At her death, she left an essentially completed first section of an autobiography with Diana Athill, who had edited *Wide Sargasso Sea* and *Sleep It Off, Lady*. Athill published this section and a less completed second section as *Smile, Please: An Unfinished Autobiography* in 1979.

Achievements

When *Wide Sargasso Sea*, her last novel, was published, Jean Rhys was described in *The New York Times* as the greatest living novelist. Such praise is overstated, but Rhys's fiction, long overlooked by academic critics, is undergoing a revival spurred by feminist studies. Rhys played a noteworthy role in the French Left Bank literary scene in the 1920's, and between 1927 and 1939, she published four substantial novels and a number of jewellike short stories. Although she owes her current reputation in large measure to the rising interest in female writers and feminist themes, her work belongs more properly with the masters of literary impressionism: Joseph Conrad, Ford Madox Ford, Marcel Proust, and James Joyce. She began to publish her writing under the encouragement of her intimate friend, Ford Madox Ford, and continued to write in spite of falling out of favor with his circle. As prizes and honors came to her in her old age after the publication of *Wide Sargasso Sea*, it must have given her grim satisfaction to realize that she had attained entirely by her own efforts a position as a writer at least equal to that of her erstwhile friends.

Biography

Jean Rhys was born Ella Gwen Rhys Williams in the West Indies on the island of Dominica in 1894, the daughter of a Welsh father and a part-Creole mother. English society classified her as "colored." Her child associates were often Creole and she was surrounded by ideas peculiar to their culture, such as voodoo and witchcraft. At the same time, she attended a convent school and seriously considered the life of a nun. The colonial mentality was strong in Dominca, and the "proper" role for a well-bred young woman was sharply defined: passive, obedient, submissive.

In 1910, Rhys left Dominica and went to live in Cambridge, England, with her aunt, Clarice Rhys Williams. After a short term in a local school, she enrolled in the Royal Academy of Dramatic Art in London. Her father died soon after she arrived in England, and she found herself short of money. The transition from the West Indies to England must have been extremely painful for the sixteen-year-old girl: the climate harsh, the people cold, the social and economic situation threatening. Those who knew her as a young woman testified that she was strikingly beautiful. After a term at the Royal Academy of Dramatic Art, she toured as a minor actress or chorus girl with provincial theater troupes and did modeling. A young woman alone under these circumstances would have seen at firsthand how male dominance and financial control in British society combined to exploit the female. Many of her stories and novels reflect scenes from her career on the stage, and most of them hinge on the theme of male exploitation of women through financial domination.

Near the end of World War I, Rhys married Jean Lenglet (alias Edouard de Neve), an adventurer who had served in the French Foreign Legion and who was probably employed by the French secret service during the war. The newlywed couple lived in Paris, constantly moving from one cheap hotel to another, although de Neve secured temporarily a position with the international mission administering Vienna. A son was born to them in 1919, but lived only three weeks. A daughter born in 1922 lived, but required special medical care. Rhys tried to earn a living in Paris by modeling and writing. Pearl Adam, the wife of a correspondent for *The Times* of Paris, took an interest in some of her sketches and introduced her to Ford Madox Ford, then editor of *The Transatlantic Review*. Through him, she entered into the expatriate community of the early 1920's, meeting James Joyce, Ernest Hemingway, and other prominent writers. Shortly after Rhys met Ford in the autumn of 1924, her husband was sent to prison for illegal dealing in antiques. Ford was living at the time with the artist Stella Bowen. Rhys, penniless, moved in with them and soon formed an intimate relationship with Ford. A casual episode in Ford's generally messy life was something much more serious for the young woman; Rhys treats this affair in her first novel, *Quartet*. De Neve never forgave her for her involvement with Ford. After her divorce from de Neve, Rhys became closely involved with a literary agent, Leslie

Tilden Smith. They were eventually married and lived together until his death in 1945. Subsequently, she married his cousin, Max Hamer, who later served time in prison for mismanagement of his firm's funds. Throughout the 1940's and 1950's, Rhys suffered greatly from poverty, poor health, and family problems. Her books were all out of print.

She was not, however, entirely forgotten. The actress Selma Vaz Diaz adapted a dramatic monologue from *Good Morning, Midnight* for stage use in 1949. Eight years later, the BBC's third program presented Selma Vaz Diaz's monologue, which received excellent notices. The publication of *Wide Sargasso Sea* in 1966 and the rapid growth of feminist studies led to a Rhys revival, and the reprinting of all her works followed.

Analysis

Jean Rhys's first novel, *Quartet*, reflects closely her misadventures with Ford Madox Ford. The heroine, Marya Zelli, whose husband is in prison, moves in with the rich and respectable Hugh and Lois Heidler. Hugh becomes Marya's lover, while Lois punishes her with petty cruelties. The central figure is a woman alone, penniless,.exploited, and an outsider. In her next novel, *After Leaving Mr. Mackenzie*, the central figure, Julia Martin, breaks off with her rich lover, Mr. Mackenzie, and finds herself financially desperate. *Voyage in the Dark* tells the story of Anna Morgan, who arrives from the West Indies as an innocent young girl in England, has her first affair as a chorus girl, and descends through a series of shorter and shorter affairs to working for a masseuse. In *Good Morning, Midnight*, the alcoholic Sasha Jensen, penniless in Paris, remembers episodes from her past which have brought her to this sorry pass. All four of these novels show a female character subject to financial, sexual, and social domination by men and "respectable" society. In all cases, the heroine is passive, but "sentimental." The reader is interested in her feelings, rather than in her ideas and accomplishments. She is alienated economically from any opportunity to do meaningful and justly rewarding work. She is an alien socially, either from a foreign and despised colonial culture or from a marginally respectable social background. She is literally an alien or foreigner in Paris and London, which are cities of dreadful night for her. What the characters fear most is the final crushing alienation from their true identities, the reduction to some model or type imagined by a foreign man. They all face the choice of becoming someone's gamine, *garçonne*, or femme fatale, or of starving to death, and they all struggle against this loss of personal identity. After a silence of more than twenty years, Rhys returned to these same concerns in her masterpiece, *Wide Sargasso Sea*. While the four early novels are to a large degree autobiographical, *Wide Sargasso Sea* has a more literary origin, although it, too, reflects details from the author's personal life.

Wide Sargasso Sea requires a familiarity with Charlotte Brontë's *Jane Eyre*

(1847). In Charlotte Brontë's novel, Jane is prevented from marrying Rochester by the presence of his madwoman in the attic, an insane West Indian wife who finally perishes in the fire which she sets, burning Rochester's house and blinding him, but clearing the way for Jane to wed him. The madwoman in *Jane Eyre* is depicted entirely from the exterior. It is natural that the mad West Indian wife, when seen only through the eyes of her English rival and of Rochester, appears completely hideous and depraved. Indeed, when Jane first sees the madwoman in Chapter XVI of the novel, she cannot tell whether it is a beast or a human being groveling on all fours. Like a hyena with bloated features, the madwoman attacks Rochester in this episode.

Wide Sargasso Sea is a sympathetic account of the life of Rochester's mad wife, ranging from her childhood in the West Indies, her Creole and Catholic background, and her courtship and married years with the deceitful Rochester, to her final descent into madness and captivity in England. Clearly, the predicament of the West Indian wife resembles that of Rhys herself in many ways. In order to present the alien wife's case, she has written a "countertext," an extension of Brontë's novel filling in the "missing" testimony, the issues over which Brontë glosses.

Wide Sargasso Sea consists of two parts. Part I is narrated by the girl growing up in Jamaica who is destined to become Rochester's wife. The Emancipation Act has just been passed (the year of that Imperial Edict was 1833) and the blacks on the island are passing through a period of so-called apprenticeship which should lead to their complete freedom in 1837. This is a period of racial tension and anxiety for the privileged colonial community. Fear of black violence runs high, and no one knows exactly what will happen to the landholders once the blacks are emancipated. The girlish narrator lives in the interface between the privileged white colonists and the blacks. Although a child of landowners, she is impoverished, clinging to European notions of respectability, and in constant fear. She lives on the crumbling estate of her widowed mother. Her closest associate is Christophine, a Martinique obeah woman, or voodoo witch. When her mother marries Mr. Mason, the family's lot improves temporarily, until the blacks revolt, burning their country home, Coulibri, and killing her half-witted brother. She then attends a repressive Catholic school in town, and her kindly colored "cousin" Sandi protects her from more hostile blacks.

Part II is narrated by the young Rochester on his honeymoon with his bride to her country home. Wherever appropriate, Rhys follows the details of Brontë's story. Rochester reveals that his marriage was merely a financial arrangement. After an uneasy period of passion, Rochester's feelings for his bride begin to cool. He receives a letter of denunciation accusing her of misbehavior with Sandi and revealing that madness runs in the family. To counter Rochester's growing hostility, the young bride goes to her former companion, the obeah woman Christophine, for a love potion. The nature of the potion is that it can work for one night only. Nevertheless, she administers it to her husband. His love now dead, she is torn from her native land, transported to a cruel and loveless England, and maddeningly confined. Finally, she takes candle in hand to fire Rochester's house in suicidal destruction.

In Brontë's novel, the character of the mad wife is strangely blank, a vacant slot in the story. Her presence is essential, and she must be fearfully hateful, so that Jane Eyre has no qualms about taking her place in Rochester's arms, but the novel tells the reader almost nothing else about her. Rhys fills in this blank, fleshing out the character, making her live on a par with Jane herself. After all, Brontë tells the reader a great deal about Jane's painful childhood and education; why should Rhys not supply the equivalent information about her dark rival?

It is not unprecedented for a writer to develop a fiction from another writer's work. For example, T. H. White's *Mistress Masham's Repose* (1946) imagines that some of Jonathan Swift's Lilliputians were transported to England, escaped captivity, and established a thriving colony in an abandoned English garden, where they are discovered by an English schoolgirl. Her intrusion into their world is a paradigm of British colonial paternalism, finally overcome by the intelligence and good feeling of the girl. This charming story depends on Swift's fiction, but the relationship of White's work to Swift's is completely different from the relationship of Rhys's work to Brontë's. Rhys's fiction permanently alters one's understanding of *Jane Eyre*. Approaching Brontë's work after Rhys's, one is compelled to ask such questions as, "Why is Jane so uncritical of Rochester?" and, "How is Jane herself like the madwoman in the attic?" Rhys's fiction reaches into the past and alters Brontë's novel.

Rhys's approach in *Wide Sargasso Sea* was also influenced by Ford Madox Ford and, through Ford, Joseph Conrad. In the autumn of 1924, when Rhys first met Ford, he was writing *Joseph Conrad: A Memoir*. Some thirty years earlier, when Joseph Conrad was just beginning his career as a writer, his agent had introduced him to Ford in hopes that they could work in collaboration, since Conrad wrote English (a language he had adopted only as an adult) with great labor. Ford and Conrad produced *The Inheritors* (1901) and *Romance* (1903) as coauthors. During their years of association, Ford had some hand in the production of several works usually considered Conrad's sole effort, although it has never been clear to what degree Ford participated in the creation of the fiction of Conrad's middle period. About 1909, after Ford's disreputable ways had become increasingly offensive to Conrad's wife, the two men parted ways. Immediately after Conrad's death in 1924, however, Ford rushed into print his memoir of the famous author. His memoir of Conrad is fictionalized and hardly to be trusted as an account of their association in the 1890's, but it sheds a great deal of light on what Ford thought about writing fiction in 1924, when he was beginning his powerful Tietjens tetralogy and working for the first time with Rhys. Ford claimed that he and Conrad invented literary impressionism in English. Impressionist fiction characteristically employs limited and unreliable narration, follows a flow of associated ideas leaping freely in time and space, aims to render the impression of a scene vividly so as to make the reader see it as if it were before his eyes, and artfully selects and juxtaposes seemingly unrelated scenes and episodes so that the reader must construct the connections and relationships that make the story intelligible. These are the stylistic features of Rhys's fiction, as well as of Ford's *The Good Soldier* (1915), Conrad's *Heart of Darkness* (1899), Henry James's *The Turn of the Screw* (1898), and Joyce's *Ulysses* (1922).

An "affair"—the mainspring of the plot in an impressionist novel—is some shocking or puzzling event which has already occurred when the story begins. The reader knows what has happened, but he does not understand fully why and how it happened. The story proceeds in concentric rings of growing complication as the reader finds something he thought clear-cut becoming more and more intricate. In Conrad's *Lord Jim*, the affair is the scandalous abandonment of the pilgrim ship by the English sailor. In *The Good Soldier*, it is the breakup of the central foursome, whose full infidelity and betrayal are revealed only gradually. Brontë's *Jane Eyre* provided Rhys with an impressionist "affair" in the scene in which the mad West Indian wife burns Rochester's house, blinding him and killing herself. Like Conrad's Marlow, the storyteller who sits on the veranda mulling over Jim's curious behavior, or *The Good Soldier*'s narrator Dowell musing about the strange behavior of Edward Ashburnham, Rhys takes up the affair of Rochester and reworks it into ever richer complications, making the initial judgments in *Jane Eyre* seem childishly oversimplified. "How can Jane simply register relief that the madwoman is burned out of her way? There must be more to the affair than that," the secondary fiction suggests.

One of the most important features of literary impressionism is the highly constructive activity which it demands of the reader. In a pointillist painting, small dots of primary colors are set side by side. At a certain distance from the canvas, these merge on the retina of the eye of the viewer into colors and shapes which are not, in fact, drawn on the canvas at all. The painting is constructed in the eyes of each viewer with greater luminosity than it would have were it drawn explicitly. In order to create such a shimmering haze in fiction, Ford advises the use of a limited point of view which gives the reader dislocated fragments of remembered experience. The reader must struggle constantly to fit these fragments into a coherent pattern. The tools for creating such a verbal collage are limited, "unreliable" narration, psychological timeshifts, and juxtaposition. Ford observes that two apparently unrelated events can be set side by side so that the reader will perceive their connection with far greater impact than if the author had stated such a connection openly. Ford advises the impressionist author to create a verbal collage by unexpected selection and juxtaposition, and *Wide Sargasso Sea* makes such juxtapositions on several levels. On the largest scale, *Wide Sargasso Sea* is juxtaposed with *Jane Eyre*, so that the two novels read together mean much more than when they are read independently. This increase of significance is what Ford called the "unearned increment" in impressionist art. Within *Wide Sargasso Sea*, Part I (narrated by the West Indian bride) and Part II (narrated by Rochester) likewise mean more in juxtaposition than when considered separately. Throughout the text, the flow of consciousness of the storytellers cunningly shifts in time to juxtapose details which mean more together than they would in isolation.

Because *Wide Sargasso Sea* demands a highly constructive reader, it is, like *The Good Soldier* or *Heart of Darkness*, an open fiction. When the reader completes *Jane Eyre*, the mystery of Rochester's house has been revealed and purged, the madwoman in the attic has been burned out, and Jane will live, the reader imagines, happily ever after. *Jane Eyre* taken in isolation is a closed fiction. Reading *Wide Sargasso Sea* in juxtaposition to *Jane Eyre*, however, opens the latter and poses questions which are more difficult to resolve: Is Jane likely to be the next woman in the attic? Why is a cripple a gratifying mate for Jane? At what price is her felicity purchased?

The *Doppelgänger*, twin, or shadow-character runs throughout Rhys's fiction. All of her characters seem to be split personalities. There is a public role, that of the approved "good girl," which each is expected to play, and there is the repressed, rebellious "bad girl" lurking inside. If the bad girl can be hidden, the character is rewarded with money, love, and social position. Yet the bad girl will sometimes put in an appearance, when the character drinks too much or gets excited or angry. When the dark girl appears, punishment follows, swift and sure. This is the case with Marya Zelli in *Quartet*, Julia Martin in *After Leaving Mr. Mackenzie*, Anna Morgan in *Voyage in the Dark*, and Sasha Jensen in *Good Morning, Midnight*. It is also the case in Brontë's *Jane Eyre*. The education of Jane Eyre consists of repressing those dark, selfish impulses that Victorian society maintained "good little girls" should never feel. Jane succeeds in stamping out her "bad" self through a stiff British education, discipline, and self-control. She kills her repressed identity, conforms to society's expectations, and gets her reward—a crippled husband and a burned-out house. Rhys revives the dark twin, shut up in the attic, the naughty, wild, dark, selfish, bestial female. She suggests that the struggle between repressed politeness and unrepressed self-interest is an ongoing process in which total repression means the death of a woman's personal identity.

Major publications other than long fiction

SHORT FICTION: *The Left Bank and Other Stories*, (1927); *Tigers Are Better-Looking*, 1968; *Sleep It Off, Lady*, 1976.

NONFICTION: *Smile, Please: An Unfinished Autobiography*, 1979.

Bibliography

Baldanza, Frank. "Jean Rhys on Insult and Injury," in *Studies in the Literary Imagination*. XI, no. 2 (Fall, 1978), pp. 55-65.

Bender, Todd K. "Jean Rhys and the Genius of Impressionism," in *Studies in the Literary Imagination*. XI, no. 2 (Fall, 1978), pp. 43-53.

Staley, Thomas F. *Jean Rhys: A Critical Study*, 1979.

Todd K. Bender

DOROTHY RICHARDSON

Born: Berkshire, England; May 17, 1873
Died: Beckenham, England; June 17, 1957

Principal long fiction
Pilgrimage 1938, 1967 (includes *Pointed Roofs*, 1915; *Backwater*, 1916; *Honeycomb*, 1917; *The Tunnel*, 1919; *Interim*, 1919; *Deadlock*, 1921; *Revolving Lights*, 1923; *The Trap*, 1925; *Oberland*, 1927; *Dawn's Left Hand*, 1931; *Clear Horizon*, 1935; *Dimple Hill*, 1938; *March Moonlight*, 1967).

Other literary forms
Dorothy Richardson's literary reputation rests on the single long novel, *Pilgrimage*. She referred to the parts published under separate titles as "chapters," and they were the primary focus of her energy throughout her creative life. The first appeared in 1915; the last—unfinished and unrevised—was printed ten years after her death. Before 1915, she wrote some essays and reviews for obscure periodicals edited by friends and also two books growing out of her interest in the Quakers. She contributed descriptive sketches on Sussex life to the *Saturday Review* between 1908 and 1914. During the years writing *Pilgrimage*, Richardson did an enormous amount of miscellaneous writing to earn money—columns and essays in the *Dental Record* (1912-1922), film criticism, translations, articles on various subjects for periodicals including *Vanity Fair*, *Adelphi*, *Little Review*, and *Fortnightly Review*. She also wrote a few short stories, chiefly during the 1940's. None of this material has been collected. A detailed bibliography is included in *Dorothy Richardson: A Biography* by Gloria G. Fromm (1977).

Achievements
The term "stream of consciousness," adapted from psychology, was first applied to literature in a 1918 review of Richardson's *Pointed Roofs*, *Backwater*, and *Honeycomb*. In the twentieth century, novels moved from outward experience to inner reality. The experiments that marked the change were made almost simultaneously by three writers unaware of one another's work: the first two volumes of Marcel Proust's *Remembrance of Things Past* appeared in 1913; James Joyce's *Portrait of the Artist as a Young Man* began serial publication in 1914; the manuscript of *Pointed Roofs* was finished in 1913.

Richardson was the first novelist in England to restrict the point of view entirely to the protagonist's consciousness, to take for content the experience of life at the moment of perception, and to record the development of a single character's mind and emotions without imposing any plot or structural pattern. Her place in literature (as opposed to literary history) has been less certain; some critics feel that her work is interesting only because it dates the emergence of a new technique. The absence of story and explanation make heavy demands on the reader. Since the protagonist's own limited understanding controls every word of the narrative, readers must also do the work of evaluating the experience in order to create meaning.

Richardson wrote what Virginia Woolf called "the psychological sentence of the feminine gender"; a sentence that expanded its limits and tampered with punctuation to convey the multiple nuances of a single moment. She deliberately rejected the description of events, which she thought was typical of male literature, in order to convey the subjective understanding that she believed was the reality of experience. The autobiographical basis of *Pilgrimage* was not known until 1963. Richardson, like her protagonist and like other women of her period, broke with the conventions of the past, sought to create her own being through self-awareness, and struggled to invent a form that would communicate a woman's expanding conscious life.

Biography

Dorothy Miller Richardson, born on May 17, 1873, was the third of four daughters. Her father, Charles Richardson, worked in the prosperous grocery business that his father had established, but he wanted to be a gentleman. He abandoned Nonconformity for the Church of England and, in 1874, sold the family business to live on investments. During Dorothy's childhood, periods of upper-middle-class luxury (a large house, servants, gardens, membership in a tennis club) alternated with moves arising from temporarily reduced circumstances.

Charles Richardson had hoped for a son, and he took Dorothy with him to lectures in Oxford and meetings of scientific associations. She was sent at age eleven to a private day school for the daughters of gentlemen. It was late enough in the century for the curriculum to emphasize academic subjects; her studies included logic and psychology. In 1890, realizing that her family's financial condition had become seriously straitened, Dorothy looked to the example of Charlotte Brontë and *Villette* (1853) and applied for a post as pupil-teacher in a German school. Six months in Hanover were followed by two years teaching in a North London private school and a brief spell as governess for a wealthy suburban family.

By the end of 1893, Charles Richardson was declared bankrupt; in 1895, two of Dorothy's sisters married. Her mother, Mary Richardson, was troubled by an unusually severe bout of the depression that had gripped her for several years. Dorothy took her mother to stay in lodgings near the sea and found that she required almost constant companionship and supervision. On November 30, 1895, while her daughter was out for a short walk in the fresh air, Mary Richardson committed suicide.

At the age of twenty-two, responsible for her own support and severely shaken by the past two years' events, Richardson moved to an attic room in a London lodging house and took a job as secretary and assistant to three Harley Street dentists. For young women at that time, such a step was unusual, by taking it Richardson evaded the restraint, protection, and religious supervision that made teaching an acceptable profession for young women of good family. The nineteenth century was drawing to a close and London was alive with new ideas. Richardson explored the city, made friends with women who worked in business offices, and lived on eggs and toast so that she could afford concert tickets.

Soon after moving to London, she was invited for a Saturday in the country by an old school friend, Amy Catherine Robbins, who had married her science instructor at London University—a man named H. G. Wells. He had just published *The Time Machine* (1895). Richardson was fascinated by Wells and by the people and ideas she encountered at his house but angered by his way of telling her what to do. She was aware that she stood outside the class system and between the Victorian and modern worlds. She was drawn both to picnics with cousins at Cambridge and to Anarchist and Fabian meetings. She sampled various churches (including Unitarian and Quaker) but refrained from committing herself to any group or cause.

In 1902, Richardson began contributing occasional articles and reviews to *Crank* and other magazines edited by a vegetarian friend. She refused a proposal from a respectable physician and broke her engagement to a Russian Jew, Benjamin Grad. Her friendship with Wells passed at some point into physical intimacy, but she continued to struggle against being overwhelmed by his ideas and personality. In 1906, finding herself pregnant, she brought the affair to an end; she looked forward to rearing the child on her own and was distressed when she suffered a miscarriage.

Exhausted physically and mentally, Richardson left her dental job and went to Sussex to recover and think. In 1908, she began writing sketches for the *Saturday Review*. Then, as her fortieth year approached, she began deliberately searching for the form that would allow her to create what she called "a feminine equivalent of the current masculine realism."

Pointed Roofs was at first rejected by publishers; when it was published in 1915 it puzzled readers, distressed some reviewers, and failed to make money. Richardson persisted, however, on the course she had set, even while living an unsettled life in YWCA hostels and borrowed rooms and earning a minimal income by proofreading and by writing a monthly column for the *Dental Record*. In 1917, she married the artist Alan Odle, who was fifteen years younger than she and had been rejected for military service by a doctor who told him he had six months to live.

Richardson's books attracted some critical recognition in the years after World War I, but they never earned money; she was usually in debt to her publishers. She supported herself and Odle (who lived until 1948) and also coped with all the practical details of their life—housekeeping, paying taxes, writing checks, doing his business with publishers and exhibitors. The couple moved frequently, spending the off-season (when lodgings were less expensive) in Cornwall and going to rooms in London for the summer. During the early 1930's, Richardson took on the burden of five full-length translations from French and German. Returning to *Pilgrimage* and the state of mind in which it was begun became increasingly difficult for Richardson; the later volumes were weakened by extraliterary distractions and also by the psychological difficulty for the author in concluding the work that was based on her own life. The final segment, *March Moonlight*, was found unfinished among her papers after she died on June 17, 1957, at the age of eighty-four.

Analysis

Pilgrimage is a quest; the protagonist, Miriam Henderson, seeks her self and, rejecting the old guideposts, makes her own path through life. The book remains a problem for many readers, although since 1915 most of Dorothy Richardson's technical devices have become familiar: unannounced transitions from third-person narration to the first person for interior monologue, shifts between present and past as experience evokes memory, disconnected phrases and images and fragmentary impressions representing the continuous nonverbal operations of the mind. Looking back on the period when she was trying to find a way to embody Miriam Henderson's experience, Richardson described her breakthrough as the realization that no one was "*there* to *describe* her." Impressed by Henry James's control of viewpoint, she went one step further. The narrator and the protagonist merge; the narrator knows, perceives, and expresses only what comes to Miriam's consciousness. Furthermore, the narrator does not speak to any imagined reader and therefore does not provide helpful explanations. The scenes and people are presented as they impinge on Miriam's awareness—thus the most familiar circumstances are likely to be undescribed and the most important people identified only by name, without the phrases that would place them or reveal their relationship to Miriam. Many readers are discouraged by the attempt to follow the book and make meaning of it; some are tempted to use Richardson's biography as a pony to find out what "really" happened and others prefer to read isolated sections without regard to sequence, responding to the feeling and imagery as if it were poetry. Because there is no narrative guidance, meaning is continually modified by the reader's own consciousness and by the extent of identification.

The first three titles show Miriam Henderson in the last stages of her girlhood and form the prelude to her London life. *Pointed Roofs* covers her experience in Hanover; in *Backwater*, she is resident teacher in a North London school and still drawn to the possibility of romance with a young man from her suburban circle; in *Honeycomb*, she briefly holds a post as governess before her sisters' weddings and her mother's death complete the disintegration of her girlhood family. *The Tunnel* begins Miriam's years in London and introduces situations and characters that reappear in the next several volumes: the dental job, the room at Mrs. Bailey's lodging house, the new women Mag and Jan and the dependent woman Eleanor Dear, a visit to her school friend Alma who has married the writer Hypo Wilson. In *Interim*, Miriam perceives the difficulty of communicating her current thoughts and experiences to her sister and other old friends. *Deadlock* treats her acquaintance—growing into an engagement—with Michael Shatov. In *Revolving Lights*, she has decided not to marry Shatov and becomes increasingly involved with Hypo Wilson. *The Trap* shows her sharing a cramped flat with a spinster social worker and growing despondent about the isolation which, she realizes, she imposes on herself to avoid emotional entanglements. *Oberland* is a lyrical interlude about a holiday in Switzerland. In *Dawn's Left Hand*, Miriam has an affair with Hypo Wilson and an intense friendship with a young woman (Amabel) who becomes a radical suffragist. *Clear Horizon* concludes much of the practical and emotional business that has occupied Miriam for several years; she disentangles herself from Wilson, Shatov, and Amabel and prepares to leave London. In *Dimple Hill*, she lives on a farm owned by a Quaker family, absorbs their calm, and works at writing. *March Moonlight* rather hastily takes Miriam up to the point of meeting the artist who would become her husband and to the beginning of her work on a novel.

This summary of events is the barest framework. Life, for Miriam Henderson, exists not in events but in the responses that create her sense of awareness. The books are made up of relatively independent sections, each treating a single segment of experience or reflection. Because of the depth with which single moments are recorded, the overall narrative line is fragmentary. Despite *Pilgrimage's* length, it embodies isolated spots of time. Frequently, neither narration nor the memories evoked by subsequent experience indicate what events may have taken place in the gaps between. Furthermore, the book concentrates on those moments important to Miriam's interior experience, and it leaves out the times when she acts without self-awareness—which may include significant actions that take place when Miriam is so engrossed by events that she does not engage in thought or reflection.

Richardson disliked the phrase "stream of consciousness" because it implies constant movement and change. She preferred the image of a pool—new impressions are added, and sometimes create ripples that spread over the previously accumulated consciousness. Thus, Miriam's interior monologue becomes steadily more complex as she grows older. Her consciousness widens and deepens; fragmentary phrases show her making connections with her earlier experiences and perceptions; her understanding of past events alters with later awareness. The earlier volumes have more sensory impression and direct emotion; later, as Miriam grows more self-aware, she has greater verbal skill and is more likely to analyze her responses. Because of her more sophisticated self-awareness, however, she also grows adept, in the later volumes, at suppressing impressions or fragments of self-knowledge that she does not want to admit to consciousness.

In many ways, Miriam is not likable—readers are sometimes put off by the need to share her mind for two thousand pages. In the early books, she is a self-preoccupied, narrow-minded adolescent, oppressively conscious of people's appearance and social class, annoyingly absorbed in wondering what they think about her, defensively judgmental. The wild swings in mood and the ebb and flow of her energies during the day appear to have little cause and to be unworthy of the attention she gives them. Most people, however, would appear unpleasantly selfish if their minds were open for inspection. Miriam creates her self by deliberate consciousness. The danger is that she tends to withdraw from experience in order to contemplate feeling.

The events of *Pilgrimage* span the decades at the turn of the century but, because of the interior focus, there is relatively little physical detail or explicit social history to create an objective picture of the era. Women's developing self-awareness, however, must be seen as one of the period's significant events. Miriam reflects the mental life of her times in her range of responses to religion, the books she reads, and the people, ideas, and movements she encounters.

A good deal of life's texture and even its choices take place at levels that are not verbalized. Richardson's first publisher described her work as "female imagism." Miriam responds particularly and constantly to the quality of light. Readers are also aware of her reaction to places, objects, and physical surroundings; ultimately, it is through mastering the emotional content of this response that she is able to discover what she needs to have in her life.

Another continuing thread is created by Miriam's thoughts about men, about men and women together, and about the roles of women in society. Her basic animosity toward men gives shape to a series of statements on their personal, emotional, social, and intellectual peculiarities that falls just short of a formal feminist analysis. Each possible romance, each rejected or forestalled proposal amounts to a choice of a way of life. The matter is, however, complicated by Miriam's sexual reticence. Even though she can talk about free love, she is not conscious—or perhaps will not permit herself to become conscious—of overt sexual urges or of physical attraction to men or to women. She struggles not to let her feeling for certain women lead her to be absorbed by their lives or roles. In *Backwater*, Miss Perne's religion is dangerously comfortable; Eleanor Dear's passive feminine helplessness forces Miriam to become her protector; Amabel's possessiveness is as stifling as Hypo Wilson's. At the end—in *March Moonlight*—there is a hint of emotional involvement with the unidentified "Jane." Struggling to know herself, Miriam is constantly faced with the problem of knowing other women.

Pointed Roofs comes close to being a structural whole—it begins with

Miriam Henderson's journey to Hanover and ends with her return home six months later. She is on her first trip away from home, looking at new scenes, anxious about her ability to do her job and earn her wages, having her first taste of independence. Since Miriam is seventeen—and, as a Victorian daughter, a relatively innocent and sheltered seventeen—the reader often understands more than Miriam does and can interpret the incidents that develop her sense of who she is and where she fits in the world. Some of Miriam's reactions are cast in the form of mental letters home or imaginary conversations with her sisters, which provide a structured way to verbalize mental processes. Miriam pays attention to the sights and sounds and smells of Hanover because they are new, giving readers a sense of the physical setting absent in many of the later books.

Miriam's moods are typically adolescent. An incident or object can set off a homesick reverie or a bout of self-recrimination; the sound of music or the sight of rain on paving stones can create an inexpressible transport of joy. She is alternately rebellious and anxious for approval; she is glad to learn that her French roommate is Protestant (because she could not bear living with a Catholic), proud of the skill in logic that allows her to criticize the premises of a sermon, moved by the sound of hymns in German. She worries about her plainness, her intellectual deficiencies, her inability to get close to people. Observing class and cultural differences lets her begin to understand that she has unthinkingly absorbed many of her tastes and ideas; she starts to grow more deliberate. This portrait of Miriam at seventeen—which forms the essential background for the rest of *Pilgrimage*—is also interesting for its own sake.

Because the narrative is limited to Miriam's consciousness, the reader is able to supply interpretation. In one key scene, the middle-aged Pastor Lahmann, chaplain to the school, quotes a verse describing his ambition for "A little land, well-tilled,/ A little wife, well-willed" and then asks Miriam to take off her glasses so that he can see how nearsighted her eyes really are. Miriam, who is both furious at being "regarded as one of a world of little tame things to be summoned by little man to be well-willed wives" and warmed by the personal attention that makes her forget, for a moment, that she is a governess, is oblivious to the sexual implications of Pastor Lahmann's behavior, and cannot understand why the headmistress is angry when she walks in upon the scene. Although Miriam's consciousness will develop in subsequent volumes, her combination of receptivity to male attention, anger at male assumptions, and blindness to sexual nuance will remain.

Deadlock contains a greater proportion of direct internal monologue than the earlier books. Miriam has grown more articulate; she interprets her emotional states and examines the premises underlying her conflicts. During her first years in London, she had cherished the city for the independence it gave her. By such acts as smoking, eating alone in restaurants, and dressing without regard to fashion, she deliberately rejected Victorian womanhood. In *Honeycomb*, she refused a marriage that would have satisfied her craving for luxuries because she could not accept a subordinate role. In *Deadlock*, Miriam is faced by the loneliness that seems inextricably linked to independence. Her work has become drudgery because she no longer has the sense of a social relationship with her employer. A Christmas visit to her married sister reveals the distance that has grown betwen them; Miriam had not even realized that Harriet's marriage was unhappy.

Deadlock is shaped by the course of Miriam's relationship with Michael Shatov. The romance forces her conflicts to the surface. Shatov is a young Jew recently arrived from Russia; a lodger at Mrs. Bailey's arranges for Miriam to tutor him in English. As she shows Shatov London, tired scenes recapture their original freshness. Miriam is excited by her ability to formulate ideas when she argues about philosophy or works on a translation. Yet, although Miriam is buoyed by the joy of sharing her thoughts with another person, Shatov's continual presence comes between her and the life that was her own. Her love has a maternal quality: though Shatov is only three years younger than Miriam, he is a foreigner and also, Miriam finds, rather impractical; she feels protective. She is also sexually reticent: because she has despised traditional femininity she does not know how to behave as the object of a courtship. The romance ends when Miriam deliberately engages Shatov in an argument that reveals his views of woman's limited nature. (The final scene restates the problem more concretely when Miriam visits an Englishwoman married to a Jewish man.) Beneath these specific difficulties lies the friction between Miriam's individualism and Shatov's tendency to see problems in the abstract—she talks about herself, he dwells on the future of the race. For Richardson, the conflict reflects the irreconcilable difference between masculine objectivity (or materialism) and feminine subjectivity. The images of darkness accumulate as Miriam realizes the extent of her deadlock; unable to be a woman in the sense that men see women, she seems to have no path out of loneliness and alienation.

Dawn's Left Hand is a prelude to the deliberate detachment and observation that would turn Miriam into a writer. *Oberland* (the preceding book) vibrates with the sensory detail of a two-week holiday in Switzerland that makes London complications seem far·away; returning, Miriam sees people objectively even when she is with them. The transitions between third-person narrative and internal monologue are less noticeable; Miriam and the narrator have virtually merged. The visual content of scenes reveals their meaning. Miriam looks at pictorial relationships and examines gesture and tone for the nonverbal communications that, to women, are often more meaningful than words. (During the years that she worked on *Dawn's Left Hand*, Richardson wrote regularly about films—which were still silent—for the magazine *Close Up*.)

Images of light carry emotional and symbolic content throughout *Pilgrimage*. When Miriam visits Densley's medical office early in *Dawn's Left Hand*, the drawn shades are keeping out the light; she refuses his proposal— one last offer of conventional marriage—with a momentary wistfulness that is immediately replaced by a great sense of relief. She is increasingly aware of herself as an actor in the scenes of her life. Self-observation allows physical compositions to reveal power relationships: when Hypo Wilson comes into Miriam's room she notices that he stands over her like a doctor, and when he embarks on a program of seduction to the music of Richard Wagner, she disputes his control by rearranging the chairs. On another occasion, in a hotel room, Miriam looks in the mirror to observe herself and Wilson. Her own position blocks the light and thus the scene is chilled even before she begins to see him as a pathetic naked male.

During the final stages of the Wilson affair, Miriam is increasingly preoc- cupied by a beautiful young woman—soon to be a radical suffragist—who pursues her ardently and pays homage to her as a woman in ways that bring home to Miriam the impossibility of real communion with men. Yet the deep commitment demanded by Amabel is frightening; her intense adoration forces Miriam into a role that threatens her independence more crucially than Hypo Wilson's overt attempts at domination. The advantage of being with people who interact only on superficial levels, Miriam realizes, is that she can retain her freedom.

Although Richardson struggled to bring the events in *March Moonlight* up to 1912, the year that she began writing *Pilgrimage*, her form and subject virtually required the book to remain unconcluded. The narrative techniques of *March Moonlight* grow more deliberate; when Miriam begins to write, she thinks and sees differently and is aware of selecting and arranging details. Thus, the book's ending is only a middle: Miriam's sense of self would inev- itably change as she reexamined and re-created her experiences in order to write novels. Once traditional formulas are rejected and *being* itself becomes the subject, there can be no ending; there is no epiphany, no coming of age, no final truth but rather a continuous process of self-making through self- awareness.

Major publications other than long fiction

NONFICTION: *The Quakers Past and Present*, 1914; *Gleanings from the Works of George Fox*, 1914; *John Austen and the Inseparables*, 1930.

Bibliography

Blake, Caesar R. *Dorothy Richardson*, 1960.
Edel, Leon. *The Modern Psychological Novel, 1900-1950*, 1955.
Fromm, Gloria G. *Dorothy Richardson: A Biography*, 1977.
Gregory, Horace. *Dorothy Richardson: An Adventure in Self-Discovery*, 1967.

Rosenberg, John. *Dorothy Richardson: The Genius They Forgot*, 1973.
Showalter, Elaine. *A Literature of Their Own: British Women Novelists from Brontë to Lessing*, 1977.
Staley, Thomas F. *Dorothy Richardson*, 1976.

Sally Mitchell

SAMUEL RICHARDSON

Born: Derbyshire, England; July 31 (?), 1689
Died: London, England; July 4, 1761

Principal long fiction

Pamela: Or, Virtue Rewarded, 1740-1741; *Clarissa: Or, The History of a Young Lady*, 1747-1748; *Sir Charles Grandison*, 1753-1754.

Other literary forms

In addition to the three novels on which his fame and reputation rest, Samuel Richardson's best-known work is a collection of fictitious letters which constitutes a kind of eighteenth century book of etiquette, social behavior, manners, and mores: *Letters Written to and for Particular Friends, on the Most Important Occasions* (1741), customarily referred to as *Familiar Letters*. It had been preceded, in 1733, by a handbook of instruction concerning the relationship between apprentices and master printers, which grew out of a letter Richardson had written to a nephew in 1731, *The Apprentice's Vade Mecum: Or, Young Man's Pocket Companion* (1734). Throughout his life, Richardson, like so many of his contemporaries, was a prolific letter-writer; notable selections of his correspondence include six volumes edited by his contemporary and early biographer, Anna L. Barbauld, the first of which was published in 1804; and his correspondence with Johannes Stinstra, the Dutch translator of his novels to whom Richardson had sent a considerably important amount of autobiographical material. A good recent representative collection is *Selected Letters of Samuel Richardson* (1964, John Carroll, editor). Of only minor interest is Richardson's *A Collection of the Moral and Instructive Sentiments, Maxims, Cautions, and Reflexions, Contained in the Histories of Pamela, Clarissa, and Sir Charles Grandison*, published anonymously in 1755, a series of excerpts emphasizing his conviction that "instruction was a more important obligation to the novelist than entertainment."

Achievements

Perhaps Richardson's most important contribution to the development of the novel was his concern for the nonexceptional problems of daily conduct, the relationships between men and women, and the specific class-and-caste distinctions of mid-eighteenth century England. He sought and found his material from life as he had observed and reflected upon it from childhood and youth as a member of the working class in a highly socially conscious society to his position as an increasingly successful and prosperous printer and publisher. He contemplated this material with passionate interest and recorded it with a kind of genius for verisimilitude that sets him apart from most of his predecessors. What one critic has called Richardson's "almost rabid concern for the details" of daily life and his continuing "enrichment and complication" of customary human relationship, account in large measure for his enormous contemporary popularity: In *Pamela*, for example, the relationships beteween Pamela and Squire B. are so persistently grounded in the minutiae of ordinary life as to create a sense of reality seldom achieved in prose fiction prior to Richardson; at the same time, the outcome of the emotional and physical tugs-of-war between the two main characters and the happy outcome of all the intrigue, sensationalism, and hugger-mugger have about them the quality of conventional romantic love.

Richardson learned to *know* his characters, so intimately, so thoroughly, as to triumph over his prolixity, repetetiveness, moralizing, and sentimentality. Equally important was his development of the epistolary novel. Other writers had used letters as a storytelling device, but few if any of Richardson's predecessors had approximated his skill in recording the external events and incidents of a narrative along with the intimate and instant revelation of a character's thought and emotions in the process of their taking place, a method so flowing, so fluid, so flexible, as almost to anticipate the modern technique of stream of consciousness. Richardson's works, along with those of his three great contemporaries—Henry Fielding, Tobias Smollett, and Laurence Sterne—prepared the way for the great achievements of the nineteenth century English novel.

Biography

The exact date of Samuel Richardson's birth is uncertain, but he was born in Derbyshire, probably on July 31, 1689. His father was a joiner and, according to Richardson, a "good draughtsman" who "understood architecture" and whose ancestors had included several generations of small farmers in Surrey; of his mother, the second wife of Richardson *père*, little is known. The family returned to London, where Richardson may have attended the Merchant Taylor's School in 1701 and 1702, at which time his formal education ended. In 1706, he was apprenticed to the Stationers' Company, and in 1715, he became a "freeman" of the Company. He married his former employer's daughter, Martha Wilde, in November 23, 1721, set up his own business as a printer, was admitted to the Stationers' Company in 1722, and soon became what his major biographers—T. C. Duncan Eaves and Ben D. Kimpel—term a "prosperous and respected" tradesman. Six children, none of whom survived infancy or early childhood, preceded their mother's death in January, 1731. Two years later (February 3, 1733), Richardson remarried, this time to Elizabeth Leake, also the daughter of a printer; four of their six children survived.

Richardson's career as an editor continued to prosper—among other distinctions, he was eventually awarded the lucrative contract to print the journals of the House of Commons—and by the mid-1730's, he had moved into a large house in Salisbury Court, where the family would live for the next two decades and where he would write the three novels on which his reputation rests.

For some time, two of Richardson's "particular friends," both of them London booksellers, had been urging him to compile a "little book . . . of familiar letters on the useful concerns of common life." An almost compulsive letter-writer since early childhood—before he was eleven he had written to an elderly widow, reprimanding her for her "uncharitable conduct"—Richardson began the undertaking, one letter of which was an actual account he had heard some years before, the story of a virtuous servant who eventually married her master. The recollection of the incident stimulated his imagination, and so, at the age of fifty, he temporarily abandoned the letters-project. In two months, writing as much as three thousand words a day, he completed the novel that, on November 6, 1749, without the author's name on the title page, was to explode upon the English scene:

> *Pamela: Or, Virtue Rewarded. In a Series of Familiar Letters from a beautiful Young Damsel, to her Parents. Now first published in order to cultivate the Principles of Virtue and Religion in the Minds of the Youth of both Sexes. A Narrative which has its Foundation in Truth and Nature; and at the same time that it agreeably entertains, by a Variety of Curious and affecting Incidents, is entirely divested of all those Images, which, in too many Pieces calculated for Amusement only, tend to inflame the Minds they should instruct.*

Pamela as an instant success, going through five editions in less than a year (in the interim, Richardson completed *Familiar Letters*, which was published January 23, 1741) and inspiring numerous burlesques, imitations, and parodies, including *An Apology for the Life of Mrs. Shamela Andrews* (1741, probably the work of Henry Fielding and the only parody of interest today) and serving as the impetus for Fielding's *The History of the Adventures of Joseph Andrews* (1742). *Pamela* was also dramatized in several forms and translated into German, French, and Dutch; its success, for the worse rather than the better, led Richardson to write a sequel, centering around his heroine's life after her marriage.

Meanwhile, Richardson continued to combine the roles of successful and prosperous businessman and author. Exactly when he began the novel which was to be his masterpiece is uncertain—one of his biographers thinks he was considering it as early as 1741—but he had the concept of *Clarissa* "well in mind" before 1744, began the actual writing in the spring or summer of that year, and by November was ready to send parts of the manuscript to his old friend Aaron Hill. Unlike *Pamela*, *Clarissa* did not have its origins in "real life"; Clarissa and Miss Howe, Richardson insisted, were "entirely creatures of his fantasy." The novel, almost a million words in length, was three years in the writing, including two "thorough" revisions, and published in seven volumes between December 1, 1747, and December 7, 1748; a subsequent eight-volume edition, "with Letters & passages restored from the original manuscript," was published between 1749 and 1751.

Though *Clarissa* was somewhat less controversial than *Pamela*, its reception was tumultuous; among other things, the author was accused of indecency because of the dramatic fire scene, and Richardson took the charges seriously enough to write an eleven-page pamphlet defending it. Sarah Fielding wrote what has been called an "ambitious defense" of the novel, and her brother Henry, whose masterpiece *The History of Tom Jones* was published soon after the last volumes of *Clarissa* in 1749, lavishly praised Richardson's work, although Richardson's dislike of what he considered Fielding's improprieties, along with the opening sections of *Joseph Andrews* and Fielding's possible authorship of *Shamela*, made any friendship between the two impossible (indeed, their relationship—or, more accurately, the lack of it—reflects little credit on Richardson).

One of Richardson's closest friends, Lady Bradshaigh, had written him soon after publication of the fourth volume of *Clarissa*, entreating him not to let his heroine die, and subsequently urged him to write a "novel about a Good Man." How much this influenced Richardson, if at all, is purely conjectural, but early in 1750, he had begun what was to be his last novel. Despite his stated intention not to publish this "new work," the first six volumes of *Sir Charles Grandison* were published late in 1753 (November 13 and December 11), and the concluding volume on March 14, 1754. As had been the case with *Pamela* and *Clarissa*, Dutch, German, and French translations soon followed.

In his Preface to *Sir Charles Grandison*, Richardson, in his guise as the "editor" of the manuscript, announced that after this third novel he would write no more. He had, however, been in the process of compiling a series of selections from his novels which was published in March, 1755, as *A Collection of the Moral and Instructive Sentiments, Maxims, Cautions, and Reflexions, Contained in the Histories of Pamela, Clarissa, and Sir Charles Grandison*. He continued to be active as a printer and to make minor revisions in his novels, particularly *Pamela*, but his "dislike to the pen" continued. During his last years, he devoted more and more time to his correspondence—since the early 1740's, he had kept copies of all or most of his letters—apparently with the idea of eventual publication. On June 28, 1761, he suffered a stroke that resulted in his death a few days later on July 4, 1761.

Analysis

"Why, Sir, if you were to read Richardson for the story, your impatience would be so much fretted that you would hang yourself. But you must read him for the sentiment, and consider the story as only giving occasion to the sentiment." Samuel Johnson's comment is only partly relevant. As James E. Evans states in his Introduction to Samuel Richardson's series of excerpts, the revival of Richardson's reputation in recent decades grows out of the assertion that he "remains a great writer in spite of his morality" and must be read "'for the story' (psychological realism and conscious artistry), because we no longer read 'for the sentiment.'"

Richardson himself stated quite clearly, in his Prefaces to *Pamela* and *Clarissa*, and in his letters, that his purpose as an author was to depict "real life" and "in a manner probable, natural, and lively." At the same time, however, he wanted his books to be thought of as instruments of manners and morals intended to "teach great virtues." Fiction, he insisted, should be "useful & instructive"; it should edify readers of all ages, but particularly should be relevant and appealing to youth. Richardson observed with passionate interest and recorded with a genius for infinite detail the relationships between men and women; the concerns of daily life; and the particular class and caste distinctions of mid-eighteenth century England. This intense interest in the *usual* sets him apart from such predecessors as Daniel Defoe or the seventeenth century writers of prose romances. In all of his novels, and particularly, perhaps, in *Pamela*, the relationship between his main characters has about it the quality of traditional romantic love; at the same time, the novels are so realistically grounded in the accumulation of a mass of day-to-day realistic details as to create a remarkable sense of authenticity. Characteristic of this creation of the illusion of real life is the account, possibly apocryphal, of *Pamela*'s being read aloud by the local blacksmith to a small group of the village's inhabitants on the village green; finally, when Pamela's triumph by her marriage to Squire B. was assured, the villagers indulged in a spree of thanksgiving and merrymaking; it was *their* Pamela who had conquered.

Richardson, then, was both a conscious, self-avowed realist, and also an equally conscious, self-avowed teacher and moralist. This dualism permeates all three of his novels and is perhaps most apparent—and transparent—in *Pamela*. It is, indeed, Richardson's hallmark, and is the source both of his strength and weakness as a novelist.

Reduced to its simplest terms, the "story" or "plot" of the first volume of *Pamela* is too well known to warrant more than the briefest summary. The heroine, a young servant girl, is pursued by her master, Squire B., but maintains her virginity in spite of his repeated and ingenious efforts, until the would-be seducer, driven to desperation, marries her. Thus is Pamela's virtue rewarded. The continuation of the novel in Volume Two, a decided letdown, is virtually plotless, highly repetitive, and highlighted only by Squire B.'s excursion into infidelity. Volumes Three and Four, written partly because of Richardson's indignation with the various parodies of the first volume of *Pamela*, have even less to recommend them. Labeled as "virtually unreadable" by one modern commentator, even Richardson's most understanding critic-biographers, T. C. Duncan Eaves and Ben D. Kimpel, have dismissed them as "Richardson at his worst, pompous, proper, proud of himself, and above all dull."

Despite his frequent excursions into bathos and sentimentality, when he is not indulging in sermonizings on ethics and morality, the Richardson of the first volume of *Pamela* writes vigorously, effectively, and with keen insight and intimate understanding of his characters. *Pamela* contains many powerful scenes that linger long in the reader's memory: the intended rape scene, the sequence in which Pamela considers suicide, even parts of the marriage scene (preceded by some prodigious feats of letter-writing to her parents on the day prior to the wedding, from six o'clock in the morning, half an hour past eight o'clock, near three o'clock [ten pages], eight o'clock at night, until eleven o'clock the same night and following the marriage) are the work of a powerful writer with a keen sense for the dramatic.

In the final analysis, however, the novel succeeds or fails because of its characters, particularly and inevitably that of Pamela herself. From the opening letter in which she informs her parents that her mistress has died and Squire B., her mistress' son, has appeared on the scene, to the long sequence of her journal entries, until her final victory when her would-be seducer, worn out and defeated in all his attempts to have her without marriage, capitulates and makes the "thrice-happy" Pamela his wife, she dominates the novel.

In effect, and seemingly quite beyond Richardson's conscious intent, Pamela is two quite different characters. On the one hand, she is the attractive and convincing young girl who informs her parents that her recently deceased mistress had left her three pairs of shoes that fit her perfectly, adding that "my lady had a very little foot"; or having been transferred to Squire B.'s Lincolnshire estate, laments that she lacks "the courage to stay, neither can I think to go." On the other hand, she is at times a rather unconvincing puppet who thinks and talks in pious platitudes and values her "honesty" as a very valuable commodity, a character—in Joseph Wood Krutch's words—"so devoid of any delicacy of feeling as to be inevitably indecent."

Squire B. is less interesting than Pamela, and his efforts to seduce Pamela tend to become either boring or amusing. Her father, the Old Gaffer, who would disown his daughter "were she not honest," similarly frequently verges upon caricature, although one distinguished historian of the English novel finds him extremely convincing; and Lady Davers, Squire B.'s arrogant sister, tends to be more unbelievable than convincing, as do Pamela's captors, the odious Mrs. Jewkes and the equally repulsive Colbrand.

In spite of its shortcomings, *Pamela* cannot be dismissed, as one critic has commented, as "only a record of a peculiarly loathsome aspect of bourgeois morality." *Pamela* has great moments, scenes, and characters that pass the ultimate test of a work of fiction, that of *memorableness*: scenes that remain in the reader's consciousness long after many of the events have become blurred or dimmed. It is equally important historically: among other things, its popularity helped prepare the way for better novelists and better novels, including what Arnold Bennett was to call the "greatest realistic novel in the world," Richardson's *Clarissa*.

Unlike *Pamela*, *Clarissa* did not have its origins in "real life"; his characters, Richardson insisted, were "entirely creatures of his fantasy." He commenced the novel in the spring or summer of 1744; it was three years in the making, two of which were primarily devoted to revision (it has been said that when his old friend Aaron Hill misread *Clarissa*, Richardson devoted a year to revising the text for publication). Almost a million words in length—the longest novel in English—the plot of *Clarissa* is relatively simple. Clarissa Harlowe, daughter of well-to-do, middle-class parents with social aspirations, is urged by her family to marry a man, Solmes, whom she finds repulsive. At the same time, her sister Arabella is being courted by an aristocrat, Robert Lovelace. Lovelace, attracted and fascinated by Clarissa, abandons his luke-warm courtship of Arabella and, after wounding the girl's aroused brother in a duel, turns his attention to Clarissa, in spite of her family's objections. Clarissa lets herself be persuaded; she goes off with Lovelace, who imprisons her in a brothel, where he eventually drugs and rapes her; she finally escapes, refuses the contrite Lovelace's offers of marriage, and eventually dies. Lovelace, repentant and haunted by his evil act, is killed in a duel by Clarissa's cousin, Colonel Morden.

Counterpointing and contrasting with these two major characters are Anna Howe, Clarissa's closest friend and confidante, and John Belford, Lovelace's closest friend. Around these four are a number of contrasting minor characters, each of whom contributes to the minutely recorded series of events and climaxes, events which in their barest forms verge upon melodrama, and at times even farce. Even so, the novel in its totality is greater than the sum of its parts: it has about it the ultimate power of Greek tragedy, and Clarissa herself, like the major characters of Greek drama, rises above the occasionally melodramatic or improbable sequences to attain a stature not seen in English prose fiction before, and seldom surpassed since.

Much of the power and the drama of *Clarissa* grows out of the author's effective use of contrast—between Clarissa and Anna Howe; between Lovelace and Belford; and between the country life of the upper middle class and the dark, rank side of urban England. This and the richness and variety of incident redeem the sometimes improbable events and lapses into didacticism and give the novel a sense of reality larger than life itself.

In the final analysis, the great strength of the novel is the creation of its two main characters. Clarissa, with her pride and self-reliance, "so secure in her virtue," whose feelings of shame and self-hatred are such that she begs Lovelace "to send her to Bedlam or a private madhouse" (no less a master than Henry Fielding praised Clarissa's letter after the rape as "beyond any-thing I had ever read"), could have degenerated into bathos or caricature but instead attains a level of intensity and reality unique in the novel prior to 1740.

Though Clarissa dominates the novel, Richardson is almost as successful with Lovelace, despite the fact that in the early portions of the novel he seems for the most part like Squire B., just another Restoration rake. His transformation, following his violation of Clarissa, grows and deepens: "One day," I fancy," he reflects, "I shall hate myself on recollecting what I am about at this instant. But I must stay till then. We must all of us have something to repent of." Repent he does, after his terse letter announcing the consummation of the rape: "And now, Belford, I can go no further. The affair is over. Clarissa lives."

Belford, like the reader, is horror-stricken. By the rape, Lovelace has acted not as a man, but an animal, and his expiation is, in its own way, much more terrible than Clarissa's, who at times somewhat complacently contemplates her own innocence and eventual heavenly reward. Lovelace remains a haunted man ("sick of myself! sick of my remembrance of my vile act!") until his death in a duel with Colonel Morden, a death which is really a kind of suicide. The final scene of the novel, and Lovelace's last words, "Let this Expiate!," are among the most memorable of the entire novel, and Richardson's portrayal of a character soiled and tarnished, an eternally damaged soul, is unforgettable.

As early as February, 1741, an anonymous correspondent had asked Richardson to write the "history of a Man, whose Life would be the path that we should follow." By the end of the decade, with *Pamela* and *Clarissa* behind him, and influenced by old friends, including Lady Bradshaigh, Richardson began thinking seriously about such a novel. Despite increasing ill health and the continuing demands of his business, he was soon immersed in the project, a novel designed to "present" the character of a "Good Man," and to show the influence such a character exerted "on society in general and his intimates in particular." Although he had at one time decided not to publish the novel during his lifetime, the first volumes of *Sir Charles Grandison* came out in 1753. Even before the seventh and last volume was in print the following year, some critics were stating their dissatisfaction with Sir Charles's "Unbelievable Perfection," a criticism Richardson repudiated in a concluding note to the last volume: "The Editor (that is, Richardson himself) thinks human nature has often, of late, been shown in a light too degrading; and he hopes from this series of letters it will be seen that characters may be good without being unnatural."

Subsequent critical opinion of the novel has varied widely, a few critics considering it Richardson's masterpiece, while many regard it as his least successful novel. *Sir Charles Grandison* differs dramatically from its predecessors in its concern with the English upper class and aristocracy, a world which Richardson freely acknowledged he had never known or understood: "How shall a man obscurely situated . . . pretend to describe and enter into characters in upper life?" In setting, too, the novel was a new departure, ranging as it does from England to Italy and including a large number of Italians, highlighted by Clementina, certainly the most memorable character in the novel. The conflict in Clementina's heart and soul, her subsequent refusal to marry Sir Charles because he is a Protestant, and her ensuing madness are as effective as anything Richardson ever wrote, and far more convincing than Sir Charles's rescue of Harriett Byron following her abduction by Sir Hargrove Pollexfen and their eventual marriage. Harriett, though not as interesting a character as either Pamela or Clarissa, shares with them one basic habit: she is an indefatigable letter-writer, perhaps the most prolific in the history of English prose fiction, at times sleeping only two hours a night and, when not admiring Grandison from afar, writing letters to him (not uncharacteristic of her style is her appeal to the clergyman who is supposed to marry her to Sir Hargrove: "Worthy man . . . save a poor creature. I would not hurt a worm! I love everybody! Save me from violence!").

Sir Charles himself is similarly less interesting than either Squire B. or Lovelace, and it is difficult today for even the most sympathetic reader to find a great deal to admire in the man who is against masquerades, dresses neatly but not gaudily, is time and time again described as a "prince of the Almighty's creation," an "angel of a man," and "one of the finest dancers in England." Most of the other characters, including the Italians (with the notable exception of Clementina), are similarly either unconvincing or uninteresting, except for two small masterpieces of characterization: Aunt Nell, Grandison's maiden aunt; and Lord G., Charlotte Grandison's husband, a gentle and quiet man, in love with his temperamental wife, often hurt and bewildered by her sharp tongue and brusque actions.

Horace Walpole is said to have written off *Sir Charles Grandison* as a "romance as it would be spiritualized by a Methodist preacher"; and Lord Chesterfield also dismissed it, adding that whenever Richardson "goes, *ultra crepidem*, into high life, he grossly escapes the modes." On the other hand, Jane Austen specifically "singled . . . [it] out for special praise," and Richardson's major biographers believe that in *Sir Charles Grandison*, his "surface realism and his analysis of social situations are at their height."

Whatever his weaknesses, Richardson was one of the seminal influences in the development of the novel. His impact upon his contemporaries and their immediate successors was profound, not only in England but on the Continent as well, and eventually on the beginnings of the novel in the United States. He popularized the novel of manners as a major genre for several decades, and his use of the epistolary method added another dimension to the art of narrative. Though his novels have frequently suffered in comparison with those of his major contemporary, Henry Fielding, in recent years a renewed interest and appraisal of Richardson and his work have placed him securely in the ranks of the major English novelists, great in spite of his frequent sentimentality and verbosity.

Major publications other than long fiction

NONFICTION: *The Apprentice's Vade Mecum: Or, Young Man's Pocket Companion*, 1734; *Letters Written to and for Particular Friends, on the Most Important Occasions*, 1741; *A Collection of the Moral and Instructive Sentiments, Maxims, Cautions, and Reflexions, Contained in the Histories of Pamela, Clarissa, and Sir Charles Grandison*, 1755; *The Correspondence of Samuel Richardson*, 1804 (Anna Barbauld, editor).

Bibliography

Baker, Ernest A. "From Richardson to Sterne," in *The History of the English Novel*, 1929-1938, 10 volumes.

Brophy, Elizabeth. *Samuel Richardson: The Triumph of Craft*, 1974.

Carroll, John, ed. *Samuel Richardson: A Collection of Critical Essays*, 1969.

_____ . *Selected Letters of Samuel Richardson*, 1964.

Dobson, Austin. *Samuel Richardson*, 1902.

Doody, Margaret Anne. *A Natural Passion: A Study of the Novels of Samuel Richardson*, 1974.

Downs, Brian W. *Richardson*, 1928.

Eaves, T. C. Duncan, and Ben D. Kimpel. *Samuel Richardson: A Biography*, 1971.

Golden, Morris. *Richardson's Characters*, 1963.

Kinkead-Weakes, Mark. *Samuel Richardson: Dramatic Novelist*, 1973.

McKillop, Ian D. *Samuel Richardson, Printer and Novelist*, 1936.

Slattery, William C., ed. *The Richardson-Stinstra Correspondence and Stinstra's Prefaces to Clarissa*, 1969.

Thomson, Clara L. *Samuel Richardson: A Biographical and Critical Study*, 1900.

Warner, William Beatty. *Reading Clarissa: The Struggle of Interpretation*, 1979.

Watt, Ian. *The Rise of the Novel: Studies in Defoe, Richardson, and Fielding*, 1957.

Wolff, Cynthia Griffin. *Samuel Richardson and the Eighteenth-Century Puritan Character*, 1972.

William Peden

MORDECAI RICHLER

Born: Montreal, Canada; January 27, 1931

Principal long fiction

The Acrobats, 1954; *Son of a Smaller Hero*, 1955; *A Choice of Enemies*, 1957; *The Apprenticeship of Duddy Kravitz*, 1959; *The Incomparable Atuk*, 1963 (also known as *Stick Your Neck Out*); *Cocksure: A Novel*, 1968; *St. Urbain's Horseman*, 1971; *Joshua Then and Now*, 1980.

Other literary forms

As a professional writer, spurning academic life for wider creative possibilities, Mordecai Richler has produced short stories, essays, articles, film scripts, television plays, and children's literature. Much of his work first appeared in prestigious magazines such as *The Atlantic*, *The New Yorker*, the *New Statesman*, and *Encounter*. Some of his individual stories, which often end up as chapters in his novels, have been collected in *The Street: Stories* (1969). A children's book, *Jacob Two-Two Meets the Hooded Fang* (1975), and a novel, *The Apprenticeship of Duddy Kravitz*, have been made into motion pictures, the latter winning the Golden Bear Award at the Berlin Film Festival in 1974. Richler's screenplay for this film was also nominated for an Academy Award and won a Screenwriter's Guild of America Award.

Achievements

Forsaking Canada for the more exciting atmosphere of Paris, Richler struggled with his work and lived in poor circumstances, publishing very few stories. Here, however, he met some significant figures of the new literary set who reacted favorably to his work; among them were Allen Ginsberg, Herbert Gold, and Terry Southern. After returning to Canada for a short while, Richler finished his first novel, *The Acrobats*. As is so often the case with Canadian writers, Richler preferred to publish outside his own country, where he felt more appreciated. His first effort was accepted by André Deutsch in London. In recent years, with his reputation secure, he has decided to publish with the Canadian house, McClelland and Stewart.

In order to make a living exclusively as a writer, Richler left Canada again. Still using his Canadian experience as the substance of his work, Richler was very productive in England, publishing stories and novels that met with much acclaim. Even his film scripts for *No Love for Johnnie* (1961), *Young and Willing* (1964), and *Life at the Top* (1965), which Richler considers inferior work for an often superficial medium, were positively reviewed. Richler twice has won Canada's foremost literary prize, the Governor General's Award, for *Cocksure* and *St. Urbain's Horseman*. Although he has achieved a certain notoriety for his searing portraits of Canadian life, he has finally gained acceptance as one of Canada's most distinguished novelists.

Biography

Mordecai Richler was born in Montreal, Canada, in 1931, in the heart of the Jewish ghetto. His father was a junk dealer and his mother was a housewife who has recently written a book about her life. Her father was a rabbi whose influence ensured an orthodox household. By turning away from orthodoxy at a young age, however, Richler ran into trouble at home, which perhaps accounts for some of his perceptive but acerbic reflections on family life. To further compound his problems as a youth, his parents were divorced when he was thirteen. As a response to the breakdown at home, Richler joined a Zionist labor group called Habonim and dreamed of settling in Palestine. Only later did he go to Israel as a journalist.

In his adolescent years, Richler attended Baron Byng High School, a predominantly Jewish school even though it was part of the Protestant school system. In his stories and novels it is transformed into Fletcher's Field High, and Richler peoples it with characters known to him as a schoolboy. After high school, Richler attended Sir George Williams University in Montreal (now Concordia University), since his grades were not good enough for McGill University. Although he returned to Sir George as writer-in-residence, the academic life did not appeal to him. He once remarked that "academe, like girls, whiskey, and literature, promised better than it paid." Rejecting a life of scholarship, Richler decided on the uncertain life of a free-lance writer in Europe, where he could develop his own style and not merely put a stamp of approval on someone else's.

After living in Paris for two years, where he published his first story in a magazine called *Points* and got his first taste of expatriate life, Richler returned to Montreal. There he joined the Canadian Broadcasting Company for a short time, earning enough money to complete his first novel, *The Acrobats*. The novel aroused more attention in England than in Canada, which perhaps convinced him that the richer literary heritage there would fuel his talents. For the best part of twenty years, then, Richler lived in England, producing many novels, short stories, and film scripts.

Although Richler needed this geographical and cultural change to gain an ironic and critical distance in his work, he used his Canadian experience as the basis of his fiction; he has said that the first twenty years of a writer's life determine the character of his writing and inform his imaginative vision. Even after many years in England, Richler never felt sufficiently integrated into English society to capture the essence of that particular culture. Feeling himself an outsider in England and cut off from the social context of Canada, Richler returned to Montreal in 1972, where he continues to live with his wife and five children.

Analysis

In an article, "Why I Write," Mordecai Richler repeats the honest answer given by George Orwell to the same question: sheer egotism, aesthetic enthusiasm, political purposes, and historical impulse. These reasons, modified by Richler's unique perception, are clues to the form and content of his work.

Richler's egotistical desire to be talked about has, no doubt, been fulfilled, as he is the victim of attacks from both Jews and Protestants for what they consider to be unjust satirical portraits of their respective communities. He has even said that to be a Jew and a Canadian is to emerge from the ghetto twice, as a sense of self-consciousness and envy pervading both societies. His satire, however, even when confined by the geography of Montreal, is more universal than some critics have assumed, and this element has enhanced his status as a significant writer. Although Richler has never wanted to acquire the role of writer as personality (he avoids the talk-show circuit as much as possible and loathes being cast as the kind of figure Norman Mailer has become), his fierce attacks on provincialism, pretension, community arrogance, envy, and class economic superiority have marked him as a highly visible, eccentric, and often vicious outsider.

While there is a great deal of harshness in Richler's writing, it is not merely personal vindictiveness, but a narrative strategy of accurate observation informed by imagination; it is a grotesque comic style designed to emphasize the absurdity of the human condition and to mock those whose misdirected values merely cause suffering. In *The Acrobats*, Richler dissects a generation of hollow men who infest the corrupt world of Spain's festival time, in which a loss of belief is symbolized by *fallas*, empty wood and papier-mâché dolls. It is a nightmare world of confusion and fantasy which culminates in the death of antihero André Bennett. Without capturing the flavor and intensity of Hemingway's lost generation, Richler, in a limited way, sets the themes for his later novels by attacking all attitudes which he thinks are essentially destructive.

Richler has admitted to a certain sense of guilt prompted by the discrepancy between his life at home facing a blank page and the memory of his father going to work in his junkyard in subzero weather. Perhaps this recognition of the severity of ordinary life has given him the focus of his work, the precisely observed but critically and ironically rendered life of the common man fighting circumstances greater than himself.

Richler's intelligence, however, does not allow him to glorify uncritically his protagonists. The tension between what is and what ought to be is always present; the result is a controlled realism balanced by a satirical distance which allows fantasy, nightmare, and a morally grounded sense of the ridiculous. As George Woodcock has observed, Richler was influenced by the realism of André Malraux, Albert Camus, and Louis-Ferdinand Céline, but Richler himself has praised Evelyn Waugh as the greatest novelist of his time, and there is in his work much of the energy, sensibility, and bawdiness of American writers such as Philip Roth.

When Richler speaks of a political purpose, he follows Orwell's idea that a novelist should push the world in a certain direction, that in fact any serious novelist is therefore a moralist. Although many of his stories end tragically, there is still a sense that his characters exist not as victims of a cruel, impersonal fate, but as victims of their own and others' actions. The choices they make are important ones and often lead to disaster when they are not based on a consistent moral viewpoint. Norman Price in *A Choice of Enemies* recognizes that choices are significant, but no longer has the courage to make the difficult ones that confront his modern generation. He ends up complacently accepting values from his friends. In *The Apprenticeship of Duddy Kravitz*, Richler succeeds in making Duddy a partially sympathetic character, often a victim of powerful people even more ruthless than he is, but Duddy, blinded by ambition, is the indirect cause of his friend Virgil's paralysis from a motor accident. In his enthusiasm for the direct, specific attack, however, Richler's moral position often seems diffuse or simply confusing. His last two novels, *St. Urbain's Horseman* and *Joshua Then and Now*, manifest a more coherent intention which makes the satire even more meaningful.

Much of the force of Richler's work comes from his observation and memory of life in the Montreal ghetto of his youth. Even novels such as *Cocksure* and *The Acrobats* are distilled through the experience of the expatriate Canadian trying to make sense of a less provincial foreign world. Richler has said that he feels rooted in Montreal's St. Urbain Street, and because that was his time and place, he has elected to get it right. To this end, Richler often writes about the same characters from Fletcher's Field High School as they experience life at different stages of intellectual and emotional growth. A peripheral character such as Jake Hersh, for example, in *The Apprenticeship of Duddy Kravitz* and *The Street*, will become the focus of *St. Urbain's Horseman*.

There is so much comic energy in *The Apprenticeship of Duddy Kravitz* that the reader can easily underestimate the social and moral implications of the work. Richler has stated that to a certain extent the reader should sympathize with Duddy, who must rise above the poverty of the St. Urbain ghetto to challenge and defeat powerful manipulators such as Jerry Dingleman, the Boy Wonder. The ambiguity of Duddy's character creates a problem of moral focus, however, in that some of his victories are at the expense of truly kindhearted people, such as Virgil Roseboro and Yvette.

There are certainly many reasons for Duddy's aggressive, almost amoral behavior. His mother died when Duddy was very young, leaving him without the female stability he needed at the time. His father, Max the Hack, who drives a Montreal cab and pimps on the side, lets Duddy fend for himself, as most of his affection and attention went to the older son, Lenny. Duddy remembers that his father wrote many letters to Lenny when he worked at a resort, but Max refuses to write to Duddy. Max also encourages Lenny to go to medical school and is proud of his achievements; he makes it obvious that he expects little from Duddy and does not perceive the extent of Duddy's ambition nor his loyalty to his family. Duddy is also often humiliated by the affluent university students with whom he works as a waiter at the Hotel Lac des Sables. Irwin Shubert, for instance, considers Duddy a social inferior and, using a rigged roulette wheel, cheats him out of three hundred dollars.

Although eliciting sympathy by explaining Duddy's situation, Richler undercuts a completely sympathetic attitude toward Duddy by detailing the results of his actions. His exploitation of the other students of Fletcher's Field High School leads even his friend Jake Hersh to believe that he makes everything dirty. Duddy's schemes to make money are clever enough; he works out a system to steal hockey sticks from the Montreal Canadians, but he does not realize that the blame rests on the stick boy, who is trying to earn money through honest, hard work. More seriously, Duddy, through a cruel practical joke, is responsible for the death of Mrs. Macpherson, the wife of one of his teachers. Later, as he tries to make his dream of owning land come true, Duddy rejects his lover Yvette, causes the paralysis of his friend, Virgil, from whom he also steals money, and alienates his grandfather, Simcha, who cares for him more than anyone else.

Duddy's relationship with Simcha provides both the moral tone and the narrative drive of the novel. Simcha, a man trusted but not loved by the elders of the St. Urbain ghetto for his quiet, patient integrity, is loved by his favorite, Duddy. Like many others of his generation, Simcha feels the weight of the immigrant's fear of failure and instills Duddy with the idea that a man without land is a nobody. For Simcha, this cliché is a more complex concept associated with the traditional struggles of the Jews and presupposes a sense of responsibility. Duddy misinterprets the implications of his grandfather's advice and perceives it as being a practical imperative to be gained at any cost, involving himself in many schemes—from importing illegal pinball machines to filming bar mitzvahs with a bizarre, alcoholic documentary director—in order to purchase land for commercial development.

For a short time, Duddy's plans misfire; he goes bankrupt and is unable to pay for the land he wants so badly. Upon hearing that the Boy Wonder, the ghetto "miracle" who has escaped his environment by drug peddling and other corrupt means, covets the same land, Duddy forges checks in Virgil's name to get enough money to make the purchase. In a closing scene, Duddy brings his family to see his property. By coincidence, the Boy Wonder arrives, and Duddy drives him away with verbal abuse. His father is more impressed with this act of defiance than with Duddy's achievement, and later, among his circle of friends, Max begins to create a legend about Duddy in much the same way as he created the legend of the Boy Wonder. Although his victory has been effected by deceit and victimization, Duddy's behavior seems vindicated; he smiles in triumph, unaware that he continues only under the spell of a shared illusion. The reader is left elated to a certain extent at the defeat of the Boy Wonder, yet sobered by the figure of Simcha, crying in the car, after having been informed by Yvette of Duddy's method of acquiring the land.

Unlike Duddy Kravitz, whose life is defined by the wealth he acquires, Jake Hersh of *St. Urbain's Horseman* is defined by the exploits of his cousin, Joey, the "Horseman" of the title. In his quest for certainty and identity in a world of confusion and moral ambiguity, Jake chooses a dubious model of behavior which eventually becomes an obsession. Much of the comedy and much of the human drama in the book come from the discrepancy between Jake's illusions of the Horseman and the reality of his own life.

Richler experiments with a cinematic style of flashbacks and flash-forwards, not only to create a sense of suspense, but also to show the role memory plays in developing a character. It is obvious that Jake is involved in some sort of sex scandal which threatens his married and professional life. As the trial progresses, the narrative is punctuated by the events in Jake's life which have led him to this degradation. In his youth, he wanted to escape the St. Urbain ghetto and the provincial nature of Canada itself. Typically, however, he leaves Canada to escape boredom only to find it everywhere.

Although Jake's loving relationship with his wife offers the promise of real stability, Jake seems to believe that only his cousin Joey leads a meaningful life, fighting injustice wherever he can find it. Specifically, he thinks Joey is the lone avenger riding after Joseph Mengele, the feared *Doktor* of the Nazi extermination camps. At first, Joey is simply the black sheep of the Hersh family, leaving home at a young age and returning periodically to disrupt the mundane lives of his relatives. Jake, who is eleven years younger than Joey, perceives him to be a hero and dismisses the accusations that he is just a criminal taking advantage of others for his own gain. Uncle Abe even tells Jake that the famed Horseman is more likely to blackmail Mengele than kill him.

By adulthood, Jake's fantasies and nightmares about his cousin assume mythic proportions, and he incorporates this mythology into his daily concerns, measuring himself against the Horseman he has created. Jake's consequent search for Joey in Israel and Germany uncovers the grim reality of Joey's fraud, drug smuggling, and disastrous love affairs, but Jake only rationalizes his negative impression; he places the Horseman's quest for "justice" beyond the sphere of ordinary moral culpability or human responsibility.

Jake reasons that he is a product of his generation, conceived in the Depression. He and others like him lived through the Spanish Civil War, World War II, the Holocaust, Hiroshima, the Israeli War of Independence, McCarthyism, the Korean War, and finally the Vietnam War. They were always the wrong age to be involved; they were merely observers, moral bystanders who could protest and give advice, but who were fundamentally impotent. Jake wants answers to his plight, but feels even more alienated from the important issues of his time because he is a case history of the Jewish intellectual born into the Canadian working class. He finds his generation and its concerns trivial and peripheral, easily susceptible, in his thinking, to the guilt induced by the "injustice collectors"—the prison-camp survivors and the starvelings of Africa.

These issues, these betrayals of age, are contrasted with the more personal betrayals of life: Jake's father rejects his marriage to a non-Jew; Luke Scott decides to choose a British director instead of Jake, his best friend, for his first major script; Jenny dismisses Jake as a lover because he is too young; and Harry Stein implicates Jake in the rape of a young au pair girl. Jake is no more capable of understanding these events than the historical events of more significant import.

After the trial, in which Jake is found guilty of indecent assault and fined, he receives word that the Horseman has been killed in a plane crash while smuggling cigarettes. He retreats to his attic and finds a gun hidden in the Horseman's saddle. It fires only blanks, its efficacy as illusory as the Horseman's exploits. Upon discovering this, Jake seems to have returned to reality, but later in his nightmare, he dreams that he is the Horseman extracting gold fillings from Mengele's teeth with pliers. He wakes up and changes the Horseman's journal to read "presumed dead." The irony is that Jake will probably continue to search for certitude and will live a tolerable life based on illusion; he does not realize that the love of his wife is the stable point which will exist despite the illusion.

There are many similarities between *St. Urbain's Horseman* and *Joshua Then and Now*: the time-schemes are not linear but shift backward and forward in a search for meaning which takes precedence over simple historical considerations; the characters are again graduates of Fletcher's Field High School who gain obvious material success, but who are not immune to even the minor ravages of time; the major issues of the world are always present, but private and personal issues dominate; and Joshua Shapiro, like Jake Hersh, tries to make sense of his own life in terms of facing the past. The important difference between the two novels is that Richler's attitude toward life in *Joshua Then and Now* is much more humane, and love is seen as the moral imperative that makes all other attitudes seem trivial.

Joshua Then and Now begins close to the present with Joshua in a cottage retreat suffering from multiple fractures incurred in a car accident. Because of hints of a sex scandal, he is guarded from the press by his father Reuben and father-in-law, Senator Stephen Hornby. Joshua reads many letters from his fans and colleagues who have scorned him for what they think is his atrocious behavior, but he is able to put this criticism into perspective. He believes this public display of disapproval is what he deserves for the roguish behavior of his youth. Reflecting on his life, he now is able to see clearly what was of real importance.

Joshua's background seems almost surreal; certainly it is more colorful than the lives of his friends in St. Urbain. Joshua's aspiration to be a sportswriter derived from his father, Reuben, who was a Canadian boxing champion. After his retirement from the ring, Reuben became an enforcer for a gangster named Colucci. As a youngster, Joshua had to suffer both his father's long absences and the resentment of the neighborhood over Reuben's involvement with Colucci. Joshua's mother, Esther, is an eccentric who bewilders him even more than his father. At Joshua's bar mitzvah, Esther has too much to drink and decides to let the young boys see her perform as an exotic dancer. She shocks them with the explicitness of her movements and even lets them fondle her. Later in life, she gets involved in pornographic movies and in running a massage parlor. It seems that Joshua's independent and sometimes improbable behavior is the logical result of his upbringing.

In trying to prolong his adolescence, Joshua becomes as ridiculous as his parents, and although his exploits seem harmless, they do have consequences; Joshua's fake letters about the novelist Iris Murdoch's homosexual activities, written to make money at the expense of the University of Texas, end up being made public, to Joshua's disgrace. The pranks that he plays to gain revenge on his enemies—taking labels off Pinsky's valuable wine bottles, defacing Jonathan Coles's original painting, and planting illegal currency at Eli Seligson's house—conclude with Joshua's injuring himself in a high-speed car chase. For Joshua, at least, these episodes are a learning experience; they are stages on his way to maturity.

Joshua has many friends from his youth who still get together as the "Mackenzie King Memorial Society," the name being an ironic comment on a prime minister whom they consider a fraud. As successful as they are, however, in their middle age they are susceptible to law suits, tax-evasion inquiries, bypass operations, hair transplants, and cancer. The struggle for material wealth and its attainment now seem inadequate as values. More important is Joshua's involvment with the WASP, country-club circle. After marrying Pauline, Joshua is introduced to Jane and Jack Trimble and Pauline's brother Kevin. Joshua marries above his social class, but he takes a resentful and superior attitude to his wife's friends and relatives. He does as much as he can to sabotage a group that he believes has all the advantages. Through the years, however, he sees the disintegration of the Trimble marriage, the dashed hopes of the senator, and the death of Pauline's dependent brother, which precipitates her madness, and realizes that, even with their pretensions, they were only trying to survive.

The echoes of the past are most vividly sounded when Joshua returns to Ibiza, Spain, to confront Mueller, a German, who had disgraced him more than twenty-five years before. To gain revenge on Mueller, Joshua leaves his wife at a crucial time in her life, when she needs his comfort to fight off impending madness. In Spain, he notices remarkable changes: the friends he had are gone; many of his former haunts have been destroyed; the road to Almeria, the route of the retreating Republican army, is now dotted with hotels, condominiums, and commercial signs; and more significantly, Mueller is dead, a victim of cancer. To cleanse himself of the past, however, Joshua pays a price. His wife is institutionalized; then, after a prolonged stay at the hospital she disappears.

The novel ends with a loving reconciliation which suggests a change in Richler's perspective. Still on crutches as a result of his accident, Joshua recuperates at Hornby's cottage, accompanied by his children, the senator, and Reuben. In the final scene, Pauline returns, and Reuben sees Joshua in the vegetable garden without his cane, being supported by Pauline.

Richler has been praised widely for the richness of his comic vision and for his keenly observed, unsentimental portrait of the inhabitants of the Montreal ghetto. Through an imaginative extension of this vision, Richler has developed into a novelist of importance: his message has transcended the limited boundaries of St. Urbain Street to assume universal significance.

Major publications other than long fiction
SHORT FICTION: *The Street: Stories*, 1969; *Notes on an Endangered Species and Others*, 1974.
NONFICTION: *Hunting Tigers Under Glass: Essays and Reports*, 1968; *Canadian Writing Today*, 1970 (edited); *Shovelling Trouble*, 1972; *The Great Comic Book Heroes and Other Essays*, 1978.
CHILDREN'S LITERATURE: *Jacob Two-Two Meets the Hooded Fang*, 1975.

Bibliography
Dooley, David. *Moral Vision in the Canadian Novel*, 1979.
Sneps, G. David. *Mordecai Richler*, 1970.
Woodcock, George. *Mordecai Richler*, 1970.

James C. MacDonald

CONRAD RICHTER

Born: Pine Grove, Pennsylvania; October 13, 1890
Died: Pine Grove, Pennsylvania; October 30, 1968

Principal long fiction

The Sea of Grass, 1937; *The Trees*, 1940; *Tacey Cromwell*, 1942; *The Free Man*, 1943; *The Fields*, 1946; *Always Young and Fair*, 1947; *The Town*, 1950; *The Light in the Forest*, 1953; *The Lady*, 1957; *The Waters of Kronos*, 1960; *A Simple Honorable Man*, 1962; *The Grandfathers*, 1964; *The Awakening Land*, 1966 (includes *The Trees*, *The Fields*, *The Town*); *A Country of Strangers*, 1966; *The Aristocrat*, 1968.

Other literary forms

Conrad Richter wrote fourteen novels, all of which were published by Knopf, but in addition to the longer fiction which Richter produced between 1937 and 1968, he also wrote short stories and a variety of nonfiction. He was nearly as prolific a short-story writer as he was a novelist, his earliest published story appearing in 1913. His first volume of collected short stories includes twelve stories under the title *Brothers of No Kin and Other Stories* (1924); nine more stories were collected in a volume entitled *Early Americana and Other Stories* (1936). Richter wrote short fiction throughout his career, producing more than thirty-one stories, most of which appeared in the *Saturday Evening Post*. Many of Richter's stories still remain uncollected, but a number were gathered in a collection entitled *The Rawhide Knot and Other Stories* (1978). Richter's nonfiction includes three book-length essays on his eclectic personal philosophy: *Human Vibrations* (1926); *Principles in Bio-Physics* (1927); and *The Mountain on the Desert* (1955). Six of Richter's novels have been adapted for motion pictures and television, and Richter himself worked periodically as a writer for Metro-Goldwyn-Mayer in Hollywood between 1937 and 1950, but found that writing for motion pictures was not his forte. His continuing popularity as a writer is reflected by the fact that at present, nearly sixteen years after his death, ten of Richter's books are still in print, yet to date, his notebooks, correspondence, and other papers that would make for scholarly appreciation and analysis of his craft as a writer remain to be published.

Achievements

Richter did not achieve widespread recognition during his long career as a writer despite the fact that he won the Pulitzer Prize for Fiction in 1951 for *The Town* and the National Book Award for Fiction in 1960 for *The Waters of Kronos*, beating out Harper Lee's *To Kill a Mockingbird* and John Updike's *Rabbit Run* among the competition. A reclusive man who spent much of his life in rural Pennsylvania and in the isolated mountains of New Mexico, Richter was not a colorful figure whose life drew attention to his work. Because much of his work appeared in serial form for popular and pulp magazines, he has been too hastily dismissed by academic critics. At his best, Richter is a historical novelist of the first rank. He re-creates the past, not as a historian would, but rather, by reproducing the actualities of frontier experience which are conveyed by fidelity to details and local expression. When Richter's purposes as an artist are more fully understood, it seems certain that critical assessments of his work will acknowledge the judgment of the general reader, with whom Richter continues to be popular.

Biography

Conrad Michael Richter was born in Pine Grove, Pennsylvania, on October 13, 1890. The eldest of three sons of a Lutheran minister, he grew up in several small rural Pennsylvania towns where his father had congregations. He came from mixed German, French, and Scotch-Irish blood. One of his forebears served with George Washington's Continental Army and another fought as a Hessian mercenary for the British. His grandfather, uncle, and great-uncles were preachers. Richter was brought up in bucolic surroundings, and he passed a happy boyhood in a score of central and northern Pennsylvania villages. In 1906, he was graduated from Tremont High School and during the next three years took a number of odd jobs—clerking, driving teams, pitching hay, and working as a bank teller. His first permanent job was as a reporter for the Johnstown, Pennsylvania, *Journal*, which he began at nineteen. His first published story, entitled "How Tuck Went Home," was written in 1913 while he was living in Cleveland, Ohio. In 1914, a second story, "Brothers of No Kin," was awarded a twenty-five-dollar prize for being one of the best stories of the year. In 1915, Richter was married to Harvena Maria Achenbach. Taking his bride West to find his fortune in a silver mine venture at Coeur d'Alene, Idaho, he made a short sojourn as a speculator in the mine fields. After returning East, where a daughter was born in 1917, Richter started writing children's literature and published a periodical for juveniles called *Junior Magazine Book*. Meanwhile, his short stories had been appearing in magazines such as *Ladie's Home Journal* and *Saturday Review*.

Richter's early work as a newspaper reporter and editor influenced his literary style. His sparse method of expression was a product of his journalistic training, and the typical length of his novels is about two hundred pages. In lieu of formal education, Richter, like many self-taught people, became a voracious reader. In an interview, he said, "All my life I have been a reader and one of my joys as a boy and young man was a good book in which I could lose myself." His reading was eclectic, ranging from the adventure writer W. H. Hudson to scientific authors such as Michael Faraday and G. W. Crele, whose theories of chemistry and physics influence Richter's later philosophical works. Ralph Waldo Emerson, Henry David Thoreau, and John Burroughs also helped shape his idealistic views on nature. The most important influence on his own writing came, however, from Willa Cather, whose pioneer characters and Western backgrounds provided the model for much of Richter's fiction.

In his early short fiction, Richter used the formulas of the popular literature of the period, which still abided by the conventions of the genteel tradition. The typical tale revolved around stock plots such as a case of mistaken identity, a rich youth's rehabilitation through hardships shared with the common people, a city girl coming to terms with country life, and so on. As might be expected, these stories used cardboard characters and were tailored to readers' moral and social assumptions. Richter's first stories were self-admitted "potboilers" from which he only expected to get a bit of money for his family. During the period between 1917 and 1928, when Richter was engaged in hackwriting and publishing for a living, he started to develop his ideas on "psychoenergics," as he called his theory of human personality. This theoretical interest led to three works, *Human Vibration, Principles in Bio-Physics*, and a privately printed monograph called "Life Energy." These essays contained the germ of another book-length essay that he published twenty-eight years later as *The Mountain on the Desert*, his fullest attempt to articulate his personal philosophy.

In 1928, Richter's wife's illnesses caused a move to the Southwest, an event that would have a major effect on his career as a writer and mark a turning point in his life. What had started as a misfortune would turn out otherwise. Stimulated by the culture and climate of New Mexico, Richter published a second volume of stories *Early Americana and Other Stories* and his first novel, *The Sea of Grass*.

The writer's material was enlarged. He had always taken the ingredients of his fiction from family memories and observations; when he moved to New Mexico, as he later wrote in his unpublished *A Few Personal Notes*, "The backlog of my material still came from first sources, fine old-time men and women, chiefly from New Mexico and Arizona, Texas and Indiana territory, who lived through many of the early days. . . ."

In 1940, Richter published *The Trees*, the first volume of a trilogy that would be completed with *The Fields* in 1946 and *The Town* in 1950. After the publication of his Southwestern novel *Tacey Cromwell* in 1942, Richter received his first literary award, the gold medal for literature given by the Society of Libraries of New York University. In 1944, an honorary Litt.D. degree was conferred upon him by Susquehanna University in recognition of a native son's attainments. During the decade of the 1940's, Richter also received the Ohio Library Medal Award for Literature.

In 1950, Richter returned to his native heath, Pine Grove, Pennsylvania, where he would remain for the rest of his life except for return trips to the

Southwest, and winters in Florida. In 1951, Richter won the Pulitzer Prize for Fiction for *The Town*. Although he wrote one more novel about the West, *The Lady*, most of Richter's remaining career was given over to the subjects with which he had started as a writer—the people and land of his birthplace. He completed his best-selling novel *The Light in the Forest* after his return home; like his later novel, *A Country of Strangers*, it was inspired by the beauty of the Eastern landscape and by the deeper sense of history one feels in the East. At the close of the 1950's, Richter was awarded his second honorary doctorate, this time by the university of his adopted state, New Mexico. In the early 1960's he completed two volumes of his projected Pennsylvania trilogy—*The Waters of Kronos* and *A Simple Honorable Man*. Richter won the National Book Award for the former; he was at work on the third volume of the trilogy when he died in 1968 at the age of seventy-eight. Since his death, two works have appeared: a novel, *The Aristocrat* and a book of stories, *The Rawhide Knot and Other Stories*.

Analysis

Conrad Richter's qualities as a writer are partly described by the title of one of his late novels, *A Simple Honorable Man*. Although the book is about his father, the same terms might be used to characterize Richter's fiction, which is simple, concise, and concerned with basic virtues. Thus, it is something of a paradox that Richter's novels and stories are underpinned by a rather complex theory of human life and history, and that these philosophical, quasi-scientific ideas provide a conceptual framework over which the characters, plots, and settings of his fiction are stretched like a covering fabric. Another major tendency of Richter's fiction is that it is intensely autobiographical, deriving from family traditions and experience. In his youth, Richter heard stories of frontier experiences from relatives who had been pioneers themselves. It was his fascination with the way things had been and his conviction that he could inspire his readers to cope with modern problems by showing how ordinary people in the past had overcome the adversities of their frontier that prompted him to become a historical novelist.

Equally important to Richter's development as a novelist, however, were the quasi-scientific philosophical principles which he developed long before his first novel was published. Thus, Richter is unlike most writers in that his fiction does not represent the developing and unfolding of a philosophy, but rather the extension of a belief system that was essentially static after being established. This being the case, it is important to grasp some of the rudiments of Richter's philosophy before discussing his longer fiction, for his themes as a novelist grow out of his philosophical notions.

It must be pointed out that despite their would-be scientific titles and vocabulary (*Human Vibration* and *Principles in Bio-Physics*), Richter's book-length essays lack the rigor of scientific methodology. At first glance, his theory of life seems to be based upon an odd merging of materialism and idealism. His first premise is that man functions in response to bodily cellular vibrations or "vibes" which are regulated by the reserves of psychical or physical energy. If energy abounds, man is in harmony with life. The ultimate expression of human harmony is compassion for one's fellow man. Other signs are charity, fortitude, and the confidence to prevail against hardship, a sense of unity with nature, a tendency toward betterment in history, and a quest for freedom. On the other hand, if energy sources are low, there is a lack of harmony in life. Conflict with nature, with other men, and with oneself all signify a deficiency of energy; other such manifestations are restless wandering, fruitless searching for intangibles, and historic change for the worse. Thus, as Richter explains it, human life and history are governed by mechanical laws.

Richter's second premise is based on quasi-scientific ideas. He holds that man responds in mind and body with "cellular energy" to outside stimuli. Activity causes the cells in one's body to overflow, revitalizing the weak cells. The process is like that of an electrical circuit in which there is a constant reenergizing while the operation continues. Therefore, constant use insures a steady power source, whereas disuse can cause the source to decline and lose power. In human terms, mental and physical exertion stimulates the release of energy and speeds up "energy transfer" through the cell structure.

Like many American autodidacts, Richter combined Yankee know-how and practicality with the visions of the crank philosopher. His "bio-physics" serves as a point of departure for accurate historical fiction about the actualities of pioneer life. By Richter's own admission, much of what he produced before he moved to New Mexico in 1928 was hack-writing for the pulp magazines, but there, led to new literary subjects, he launched his career as a serious author with a series of stories and novels; inspired by the grand surroundings of his Western residence and informed by extensive research and the philosophical themes which would run through his subsequent fiction, he produced his first novel.

The Sea of Grass was well-received on publication and is still highly regarded by readers and critics. The similarities between Richter's story of a strong-willed Southwestern pioneer woman and Willa Cather's *A Lost Lady* (1923) were quickly noted. The central idea of *The Sea of Grass* was sounded in a short story entitled "Smoke over the Prairie," published two years earlier in *Saturday Evening Post*. The novel is set in New Mexico during the last decades of the nineteenth century. It revolves around a feud between cattle ranchers, led by Colonel James Brewton, who use the open grasslands for grazing and growing numbers of farmers, called "nesters" by the cattlemen, who are supported by Brice Chamberlain, a federal judge. A subplot concerns a love triangle between Brewton, his wife Lutie, and Chamberlain, which ends with the tragic death of the son of Brewton and Lutie, whose paternity is uncertain,

Critical Survey of Long Fiction

since it is implied that Chamberlain might well have been the boy's father.

The major theme is the decline of the grasslands, a historic change for the worse. The story is narrated as a reminiscence by Hal Brewton, a nephew of Colonel Brewton. He tells the story of an era that has already passed and thus conveys an aura of nostalgia which Richter himself apparently felt for these bygone days. In fact, Hal Brewton is actually a persona for the author and reflects his attitudes toward events. For this reason, Hal remains a one-dimensional character, yet his role as narrator serves to create an objective view of the material. Hal is involved in the events he describes but not so closely as to have his judgment obscured. He is a boy when the story starts and is the town doctor when the story ends twenty-five years later. The first part of the book is devoted to Lutie, a lively and lovely belle from St. Louis, who comes to Salt Fork, New Mexico, to marry the cattle baron Jim Brewton. The "Colonel," as he is called, has a battle going on with the nesters because he believes that the dry lands are doomed to be blown away if they are plowed. The marriage results in three children, but Lutie grows tired of her life as a rancher's wife and simply walks out, staying away for fifteen years. She had left thinking that her lover Brice Chamberlain would come with her, but he remains to support the cause of the farmers.

The title of the book implies that it is a story about the land, and it is indeed, for the basic conflict of the novel arises from how the land will be used. Yet *The Sea of Grass* also introduces the typical Richter hero and heroine in Colonel and Lutie Brewton. The Colonel embodies the best combination of idealism and pragmatism, but he is not complex. He reflects the virtues Richter admires—integrity and courage; he exercises his control over his world with sure authority. Lutie, on the other hand, is the first in a line of female characters in Richter's fiction who are not in harmony with their existence, and who achieve maturity only through hardship and suffering. When she returns to the Southwest, she has finally learned that she needs the sense of fulfillment that comes from the exertion required to survive on the sea of grass. *The Sea of Grass* is ultimately a novel in which the triumph belongs to the earth, for it is the land itself that finally, through a drought, defeats the persistent nesters and subdues Lutie's willful romanticism when her son is destroyed by the violence of the Southwest. Although *The Sea of Grass* is a lasting achievement, it has some of Richter's characteristic flaws as well. There is a thinness to the writing that gives the impression of a screenplay or an extended short story rather than a fully realized novel, a charge leveled with even more justification against Richter's next novel, *Tacey Cromwell*.

Tacey Cromwell was generally not as well-received as *The Sea of Grass*, perhaps because the heroine is a prostitute and the hero a gambler. Recalling his Idaho experience, Richter sets the plot of *Tacey Cromwell* in a mining town called Bisbee; his treatment of this setting reflects extensive research concerning life in early Western mining towns. He shows the ethnic diversity of the miners and the pretensions of the leading townsmen, who have risen from humble origins to positions of wealth and power. The plot of the novel is built around the conflict between the rough-and-ready immigrants and the new rich ruling class in town. The narrator is again a small boy, Wickers Covington, who is both an observer and a partial participant in the action, about which he reminisces as he tells the story after the fact.

The book begins with the runaway boy Wickers escaping from an uncle in Kansas who has mistreated him. Changing his name to Nugget Oldaker, he heads to Socarro, New Mexico, where his half brother Gaye Oldaker is living. He finds his kinsman in a house of tolerance called the White Palace, which is ironically named, for it is a place of prostitution. His brother's mistress is a prostitute named Tacey Cromwell. Fearing that an upbringing in a bordello would prejudice the lad's morals, the couple moves away to give Nugget a decent home. They relocate in a mining town in Arizona, where they settle down and start the climb to success. Tacey and Gaye never marry, but they remain something of a team. She shows incredible altruism toward her former lover, even after he leaves her and takes the richest woman in town as his wife. Tacey's conversion to respectability is hastened by the adoption of two children of a neighbor killed in a mine accident. The good woman of the town, however, take umbrage at the children being reared by even a reformed prostitute, and they bring legal action against Tacey, which results in her losing the children.

Undaunted by disappointment in love, community treachery, and sickness, Tacey starts a business as a dressmaker. At first she is boycotted by the priggish ladies, but one of her creations is worn at an annual ball by a lady who did not know or care about Tacey's reputation. The dress is a sensation, and her future as a dressmaker and designer is made overnight. Meanwhile, Gaye has been appointed territorial treasurer, a position he sought after being encouraged by Tacey. His wife, the haughty and puritanical Rudith Watrons, is drenched in a rainstorm that leads to a long illness and finally to her death. Nugget, who has grown up and become a mining engineer, returns to Bisbee, and one of the foster children taken from Tacey is restored to her. Thus, the novel ends with things returned to their original condition, but with the new harmony that hardship always hands to those who accept it in Richter's fictional worlds.

The novel also illustrates the conception of "westering," the process of evolution in which a region goes from frontier to community. Such a process, in Richter's conception, involves more than historical change. On the physiological and psychological levels, *Tacey Cromwell* depicts Richter's theory of altruism. Tacey's selfless assumption of guilt, both hers and her gambler-lover's, so that Gaye and his children might prosper, is close to the formula plot of the prostitute with a heart of gold used by Bret Harte in his Western fiction. Richter, however, has Tacey's sacrifice pay off, and she finally rises to respectability and eventual reunion with her lover and loved ones.

The Lady, Richter's ninth novel and his third with a Southwestern setting, was published fifteen years later in 1957. *The Lady* was better received by the critics and evidences Richter's increased competence as a writer. It is a stronger novel because the central character, Dona Ellen Sessions, is more fully developed than Tacey Cromwell. The plot is partly based on an actual case, an unsolved New Mexico mystery of the frontier period, that involved the disappearance and probable murder of a judge and his young son. The conflict in this book centers around the struggle between Spanish-American sheepherders and Anglo-American cattle ranchers. The story is told by a narrator named Jud, who tells of events which happened sixty years before, when he was a boy of ten. He, like the juvenile narrators of *The Sea of Grass* and *Tacey Cromwell*, is both a participant and a witness. Jud is taken in by his cousin, the Territorial Judge Albert Sessions, after his own father has abandoned him. The judge's wife is the charming and arrogant "Dona Lady Ellen," as she is styled because of her noble Spanish and English bloodlines. She is the mistress of a giant sheep spread, inherited from her parents. In addition to breeding and wealth, she has acquired skills as a horseback rider and markswoman. The villain of the piece is her brother-in-law, a mercenary and unethical lawyer, Snell Beasley. The violent feud that is the focus of the book is begun when Beasley drives a cattle herd through her ranch; there is shooting that results in the death of some of the cattlemen.

The chain of events that leads to the disappearance of Judge Sessions and his young son Wily is set in motion. Thinking Dona Ellen is now vulnerable, Snell Beasley sets out to destroy her completely. She is forced to sell her once great ranch, and it seems that her humiliation is complete, yet in the final scene of the novel, poetic justice is served. In a buggy race between Dona Ellen and Snell, there is an accident and her adversary is killed; thus, the heroine gets her revenge in a somewhat melodramatic ending. Her victory underscores Richter's central themes of endurance in the process of "westering" and the mystic bond between people and landscape. It is fitting that Richter's last book about his adopted Southwest should be concluded with a glorification of the land which had inspired him to write the type of fiction that would be his forte—historical romances.

While working on his Southwestern novels, Richter began in the early 1940's his trilogy about the Pennsylvania-Ohio frontier, which was conceived from the first as a whole. The first novel of the trilogy, *The Trees*, is set in the late eighteenth and early nineteenth centuries; the novel unfolds the story of a typical pioneer family, the Tuckett clan, whose frequent migrations through the great sea of woods that covers the Ohio Valley and the Alleghany mountains is the basis of the plot. In this novel, Richter vividly depicts the darkness of the forest floor as well as the moral darkness in the heart of man. The protagonist of *The Trees* is a "woods woman" named Sayward Tuckett, a larger-than-life figure who is the focal character of the entire trilogy. She is married to Portius Wheeler, who, for reasons never explained, has abandoned his native New England, where he was educated as a lawyer, and has become a loutish and drunken backwoodsman. Although nearly all traces of culture and civilization have been erased from him by the time he is married to Sayward, she nevertheless prevents him from further decline, and he honors her by making a reformation.

In addition, *The Trees* tells how Sayward as a girl had wandered with her nomadic family, breaking away from that way of life to marry Portius and settle down. Richter intended that Saywards' experiences should reflect the whole pioneer experience of movement, settlement, and domestication. Using the span of one woman's life, the process of historical change in the Ohio Valley from hunters to farmers to town dwellers is reflected. Thus, like Richter's Southwestern novels, *The Trees* traces social evolution; it also resembles his Southwestern novels in being episodic, in having a strong heroine, and in its themes of hardship and endurance, ending in ultimate triumph. It differs most from the earlier books in that there is no boy-narrator; Richter's point of view is omniscient in the trilogy, and he uses more dialect in the dialogue. Further, in an effort to make his depiction of pioneer life more convincing, he uses folktales and superstitions in order to reflect the primitive way of life on the frontier.

The final two volumes of the trilogy *The Fields* and *The Town*, continue the portrait of Sayward and depict the conquering of the land through the process of civilization. *The Fields* tells of Sayward's ten children and her husband's affair with the local schoolmarm, who bears him an illegitimate daughter. Sayward is devasted by Portius' unfaithfulness, yet she recovers from this crushing experience when she hitches a pair of oxen to a plow and begins to till the fields. She sees in the great brutes' tolerance and strength and in the permanence of the earth a prescription for her own survival.

The Town, though not any more successful artistically than the first two parts of the trilogy, was awarded the Pulitzer Prize in 1951, more for the entire series than for its concluding volume. *The Town*, which is set in pre-Civil War Ohio, deals mostly with the romance between Sayward's youngest son, Chancey, and her husband's illegitimate daughter, Rosa Tench. The love between the half brother and sister is marked by tragedy; she dies in a fatal balloon accident. The rest of the book completes Sayward's story. The conflict that fills out the plot is between mother and son: Sayward tries to make a pioneering man out of Chancey, but he refuses to accept her value-system and goes off to edit a liberal newspaper in Cincinnati. The newspaper, which is supported by an unknown patron, publishes Chancey's socialist views, which are an affront to his mother. Just before her death, he learns that she was the secret benefactor who had supported his newspaper career over the years.

Chancey has to reexamine his philosophy in the light of this revelation. He concludes that his mother's doctrine of hard work and self-reliance is a better one than his own. Thus, Sayward dies at eighty having won her last victory, rescuing her baby son from the heresy of socialism; the puritan faith in work of the older generation remains superior to modern liberal social theory.

Thus, in his trilogy, Richter brings full circle the "westering" process in which wilderness gives way to farms and farms become towns—historic change for the better; that is the essence of the American experience. Yet as civilization conquers the wilderness, something is lost as well as gained. The frontier's hardships had tested men and honed their character. Modern Americans lack hardiness, vigor, and self-reliance, those qualities of mind and spirit which their ancestor's had in abundance, as the heroine of his Ohio trilogy so amply shows.

Richter produced some half-dozen minor novels on various historical subjects and themes, but the major achievements of his later career are *The Waters of Kronos* and its sequel, *A Simple Honorable Man*, the first two volumes of a projected trilogy which he did not live to complete. The former is regarded as one of Richter's highest artistic successes and won wide critical acclaim, earning the National Book Award for 1960. The book is one of Richter's most autobiographical. His main character, a man named John Donner, resembles Richter himself; the character's parents are very much like his family as well. *The Waters of Kronos* is an almost mystical story in which John Donner, an ill and aged man, returns from the West to his Pennsylvania hometown, which is covered by a man-made lake, to visit the graves of his ancestors. At the cemetery, he meets an old man, who takes Donner down a steep hill where, to his incredulous eyes, he finds his town just as it looked sixty years ago. The remainder of the plot is a reexamination of the scenes of his childhood and a reunion with friends and relatives. The journey into the past enables him to learn that what he has always feared is not true—that the gap between his faith and that of his father is not as wide as he once thought. He discovers that he is his father's spiritual son. His final realization from his return to the past is that they have both worshiped the same god in different ways. Having come to terms with his father's god in his novel, Richter's next book shows how he gains further understanding of his parents as a person.

A Simple Honorable Man describes the life of John Donner's father, Harry, who at age forty gives up a career in business for a lifetime of service to the Lutheran Church. Like *The Waters of Kronos*, this book is clearly autobiographical, but it is more than a nostalgic family history, for in this novel as in the previous one, Richter tries to come to grips with a number of philosophical problems. The novel emphasizes that the most important things in life are not social status, or power of office, or money, but altruistic service to others. Harry Donner's greatest satisfaction is not in putting money in the bank but in helping those who are in need.

The third volume of the trilogy, on which Richter was at work when he died, was intended to show, as the first two books had done, his reconciliation with his actual father, his final reconciliation with his spiritual father. The two volumes that he did complete are a fitting capstone to Richter's career as a writer. His personal struggles, reflected through those of the Donners, show him to be a man of spiritual and intellectual integrity. The order and lucidity of the narrative reveal his artistry; the restrained realism that characterizes his fiction mutes the sentimentality inherent in such materials, and even though dealing with personal subject of a moral nature, he never lapses into overt didacticism.

Except for *The Sea of Grass*, Richter's reputation will rest most firmly on the books written in the last stages of his career, especially *The Waters of Kronos*; nevertheless, he will probably continue to attract readers who admire exciting, concise, sometimes lyrical stories and novels about the early history of this country and the common people who experienced it.

Major publications other than long fiction

SHORT FICTION: *Brothers of No Kin and Other Stories*, 1924; *Early Americana and Other Stories*, 1936; *The Rawhide Knot and Other Stories*, 1978.

NONFICTION: *Human Vibrations*, 1926; *Principles in Bio-Physics*, 1927; *The Mountain on the Desert*, 1955; *A Philosophical Journey*, 1955.

Bibliography
Barnes, Robert J. *Conrad Richter*, 1968.
Clifford, Duane E. *Conrad Richter's Ohio Trilogy*, 1971.
Gaston, Edwin W. *Conrad Richter*, 1965.
Lahood, Marvin J. *Conrad Richter's America*, 1975.

Hallman B. Bryant

ELIZABETH MADOX ROBERTS

Born: Perryville, Kentucky; October 30, 1886
Died: Orlando, Florida; March 13, 1941

Principal long fiction

The Time of Man, 1926; *My Heart and My Flesh*, 1927; *Jingling in the Wind*, 1928; *The Great Meadow*, 1930; *A Buried Treasure*, 1931; *He Sent Forth a Raven*, 1935; *Black Is My Truelove's Hair*, 1938.

Other literary forms

Before Elizabeth Madox Roberts was a novelist, she wrote poetry, including children's verse—facts which explain much about her work as a novelist— and she continued to produce some poetry throughout her career. Her first collection of verse, privately printed in 1915, was *In the Great Steep's Garden*, a pamphlet consisting of a few short poems accompanying photographs. A second collection of poetry, *Under the Tree*, appeared in 1922, published by Huebsch, Inc., which soon became The Viking Press, publisher of Roberts' subsequent work. A revised edition of *Under the Tree* appeared in 1930, and a third collection of Roberts' poetry, *Song in the Meadow*, came out in 1940.

In addition, Roberts wrote short stories, which, like her poetry, found a ready market in leading magazines of the day. Her short fiction was collected in *The Haunted Mirror* (1932) and *Not by Strange Gods* (1941).

Achievements

Roberts' reputation as a writer furnishes an interesting case study in literary fashions and critical evaluation. Few novelists have begun their careers to such popular and critical acclaim as Roberts achieved with *the Time of Man* in 1926, acclaim that was renewed and confirmed by *The Great Meadow* four years later. With the 1935 publication of *He Sent Forth a Raven*, however, Roberts' literary reputation went into a precipitous decline. By her death in 1941, it had struck bottom. Since then, there have been intermittent attempts, including several book-length studies, to resurrect her reputation, frequently with highly inflated praise. Claims that she is among the half dozen or so great American novelists of the twentieth century do her as much disservice as does the vague "regionalist" label which her special pleaders decry.

Perhaps as a result of her early success and her relative isolation in Kentucky, Roberts seems likewise to have overestimated her powers: with talents along the lines of a May Sarton, Roberts was apparently encouraged to think of herself as another William Faulkner, with a little Herman Melville and Thomas Mann thrown in for good measure. Her style, so often termed "poetic," achieves some fine effects indeed, but at immense cost to the narrative flow of her novels. Her style is allied to her narrative focus, almost invariably the novel's female protagonist, whose perceptions and sentiments are spun out at length while the reader waits for something to happen. Little does happen, except that the heroines take long walks. The effect is somewhat reminiscent of an agrarian Virginia Woolf. Perhaps the reader is treated to such a subjective focus because Roberts' protagonists, however different, are to some extent alter egos of their author, whose own comments blend imperceptibly into their observations. The results of all this are slow-moving and sometimes flimsy plots, dimly realized characters (except usually for the protagonist), loss of authorial perspective, and tedium. As if these results were not unhappy enough, Roberts also had trouble dealing with ideas and with the overall plans for her novels.

Despite all these limitations and failings, Roberts is due for, and deserving of, a revival. Most readers will find her lighter novels, *A Buried Treasure* and *Black Is My Truelove's Hair*, still entertaining, and *The Great Meadow* possesses some epic qualities. All of Roberts' novels involve significant themes, and all deal incidentally with significant social issues, such as economic conditions, racism, and sexism. In particular, both feminists and antifeminists will find much of interest in Roberts' depiction of her female protagonists, in her treatment of male-female relationships, and in Roberts' own biography.

Biography

Elizabeth Madox Roberts' life was marked by a few salient facts. Descended from early settlers of Kentucky, she was the second of eight children born to Mary Elizabeth Brent and Simpson Roberts, Confederate veteran, teacher, grocer, and occasional surveyor/engineer. Roberts lived most of her life in Springfield, a small county-seat town on the southwestern edge of the Kentucky Bluegrass. She attended high school in Covington, Kentucky (1896-1900), and college at the University of Chicago (1917-1921; Ph.D. with Honors, English, 1921; David Blair McLaughlin Prize for prose, Fiske Poetry Prize, president of Poetry Club, Phi Beta Kappa), beginning college at the age of thirty-one because limited finances and ill health delayed her. She suffered from poor health much of her life. From 1910 to 1916, she made various stays with a brother and a sister in Colorado, in part to recuperate from what was possibly tuberculosis. At the height of her literary career, she experienced sever headaches and a skin rash, both possibly nervous in origin. During her last years, when she wintered in Florida for her health, she suffered severely from Hodgkin's disease (cancer of the lymphatic system), the eventual cause of her death.

Because of her ill health and perhaps her own disposition, Roberts led a quiet personal life, at times almost reclusive. She never married, though she always enjoyed a circle of friends, including friends from her Chicago years whom she later wrote and sometimes visited. In a sense, she never left the family circle, building her own house onto her parents' Springfield home when she came into money from her writing. She also enjoyed contacts and visits with her brothers and sisters. At heart, she was a solitary, introspective individual who guarded her privacy, growing a hedge around her backyard garden. Besides reading and writing, her favorite activities included listening to music, gardening, sunbathing, and taking long walks into secluded areas of the countryside (from which she returned to make voluminous notes).

These conditions of Roberts' life exercised strong influences, both positive and negative, on her writing career. Her family's proud pioneer heritage not only stimulated her imagination, but it also encouraged her to paint an overly idyllic picture of Kentucky's past and present. The sleepy farming region around Springfield was also a rich source of material—indeed, her prime source—but at the same time it effectively isolated her from literary circles which might have served to encourage, temper, and appreciate her efforts. These functions were served briefly by her stay at the University of Chicago. Her heady experience of Chicago, where literary circles flourished both inside and outside the university, filled her with ideas and propelled her into sustained literary production, but perhaps this hothouse experience also encouraged her to overreach herself as a writer.

The effects of Roberts' cirucmscribed personal life can also be detected in her fiction, particularly in her efforts to depict character and to describe male-female relationships, possibly also in her habitual narrative focus. To a great extent, Roberts' fiction provides an ironic counterpoint to her personal life. In most of her novels, the main narrative interest is her heroines' search for identity, worked out through the rituals of courting and mating: her heroines suffer their shipwrecks but eventually find safe harbor in marriage. The men in their lives are either grandfatherly, brutish, bucolic, or childishly vengeful; the heroines get advice from the grandfatherly ones, are hurt by the brutish ones, and marry either the bucolic or childishly vengeful ones. Fathers are frequently possessive, obstructing their daughters from marriage; one can only wonder about Roberts' relationship with her father, who refused her money for college and then had her underfoot for the rest of his life. To Roberts' credit, it must be said that in her novels, men, however unpromising, are absolutely vital to the scheme of things.

On the other hand, too, if Roberts' personal life had been less circumscribed, she might not have taken up writing at all. Writing became her means of achieving identity—and against stronger odds than any of her heroines had to face. However sickly and easily demoralized Roberts might seem, she had a vein of iron in her character that also came out in her heroines and in her themes. Even Roberts' ill health furnished her with potent material. Her heroines frequently develop by means of long illnesses and convalescences, from which they emerge born again, like a butterfly from its pupa. It was perhaps toward such a rebirth that Roberts was aiming in her writing.

Analysis

Although commentators on Elizabeth Madox Roberts like to describe her main theme in such terms as "the ordering of chaos" or "the triumph of spirit over matter," one need not be so high-minded and vague. A hardheaded Kentucky version of her major theme would be more specific: ownership of the land. This theme reflects an old, revered attitude in Kentucky, where in some parts even today one can be shot for trespassing. The theme also reflects an old, revered American (even Anglo-Saxon) attitude, a pioneer urge to settle and possess, if necessary by violence—an urge that today achieves its debased avatar in the mass media and advertising. In its gentler, more settled aspects, however, Roberts' theme embodies a Jeffersonian, agrarian vision of American democracy, the American dream of independence through ownership of the land. The theme eventually embodies a more universal vision, a vision of harmony with the land, a realization, serenely accepted, that those who possess the land are also possessed by it. Unhappily, whether expressed by Roberts or by other American writers whose characters want to own chicken farms or raise rabbits, the theme is a poignant reminder that many Americans have in actuality been vagabonds, whether the pioneer variety or today's rootless variety. In this sense, then, the theme embodies an idyllic but unrealized American dream; it was apparently Roberts' conviction, however, that this dream came very close to being realized in Kentucky.

In developing her theme, Roberts reveals the influence of her favorite philosopher, George Berkeley, the eighteenth century bishop who denied the existence of matter, holding that "things" exist only as "ideas" or "spirits" in the minds of God and man. Such a philosophy would seem, at first, to preclude any relationship with the land; on the contrary, it points to a divine immanence, to the spiritual nature of all "things," including the land. The philosophy also implies the worth of "subjective" truth, justifying Roberts' narrative focus on the lengthy observations of her protagonists. As a result of this focus, her novels are full of loving descriptions of the land, the flora and fauna, the weather. Held constantly before the reader, the land forms an immense backdrop or tableau against which human action is played out, a background so overwhelming at times that the characters seem to emerge out of it and then sink back into it.

Because of their closeness to the land, many of Roberts' characters exhibit a sameness: Mostly simple farmers, their lives governed by the imperatives of the seasons, crops, animals, they identify with the soil in their talk and in their impulses. Rather inarticulate, they have a blood-knowledge of the earth that requires little discussion. The continuity of their lives with the land is also reflected in their impulses to create life, to mate and procreate. To Roberts, these characters represent an ideal, a settled state, though to her readers they might seem too bucolic to be interesting.

The state of health represented by such characters is what Roberts' protagonists aspire to and her maladjusted characters lack. Like the bucolic characters, Roberts' protagonists seek to mate and procreate. The protagonists do not achieve their aims easily, though, having to reenact the archtypal struggle of their pioneer ancestors before they reach a settled state. When misfortune frustrates their desires, they get back in touch with the earth through the simple therapies of raising chickens, growing a garden, sunbathing, or taking rides in the country. Some end up marrying farmers. Such is the ultimate salvation of Theodosia, the highbred protagonist of *My Heart and My Flesh*, whose alienation from the land is an index of her initial maladjustment. Other unhappy characters in Roberts' novels are similarly out of touch with the land, such as Stoner Drake in *He Sent Forth a Raven* and the evil Langtry in *Black Is My Truelove's Hair*.

These patterns of behavior exhibited by her characters are the prime means through which Roberts' develops her theme, with examples of each pattern generally to be found in each of her novels. To some extent, however, each novel emphasizes a particular aspect of her theme, with *He Sent Forth a Raven* being Roberts' most ambitious effort to pull all her characteristic motifs together in a single work.

Although *The Great Meadow* was Roberts' fourth novel, it was apparently the first conceived. This is appropriate, since thematically *The Great Meadow* comes first among her novels. Set around the time of the American Revolution, it celebrates the early settlement of Kentucky, that other Eden, that paradise, that promised land. The epic qualities of this novel have led some commentators to compare it to Homer's *Odyssey* (c. 800 B.C.), though it could more appropriately be compared to Vergil's *Aeneid* (c. 29-19 B.C.). Like Latium, Kentucky has to be wrested from the "aborigines." The novel even has its epic heroine with a noble name, Diony, and noble progenitors, sturdy Pennsylvania Methodists and Quakers on her mother's side and Virginia Tidewater gentry on her father's. Diony is, in truth, the founder of "a new race," though before she marries and sets out for Kentucky, she has to get her father's permission (in typical fashion for Roberts' possessive fathers, he at first denies her).

After a slow start in Albermarle County, Virginia, the novel follows Diony, her husband, and a small party of settlers as they trek across the rugged Appalachians to Harrod's Fort, where they proceed to fight off the Indians and establish farms. The growth of their settlement corresponds to Diony's growth as a person, largely a development of awareness. A convinced Berkeleian who frequently quotes from the philosopher's works, she receives a real challenge to her beliefs when she is banged in the head with a tomahawk, but the tomahawk incident and the scalping of her mother-in-law are only smaller parts of the overall challenge represented by the alien wilderness. In the beginning, Diony had imagined God as a benevolent deity creating "a world out of chaos," but since everything which exists is a thought of God's,

He must also have created the wilderness, where wolves howl and savages prowl. Unlike Daniel Boone—or for that matter the Indians—Diony cannot feel at home in the wilderness; instead, she must remake the wilderness into her vision of home, a vision of a settled, orderly, agrarian society where the land is "owned."

Although Diony clings stubbornly to her vision of order, the wilderness does make her more tolerant of disorder. Even before she leaves for Kentucky, she has a "wilderness marriage . . . without law" (performed by a Methodist minister). Later, her experiences of hardship and deprivation at Harrod's Fort lead her to observe that "men wanted law to live by" but that women and babies "followed a hidden law"—that is, a law based on concrete, immediate human needs. This frontier tradition of making do the best one can, without too much scrupling about moral and legal niceties, serves Diony well at the end of the novel. Her husband, Berk Jarvis, goes off into the wilderness to seek revenge against the Indian, Blackfox, who has his mother's scalp. When Berk does not return in a year or so, he is presumed dead, and Diony marries Evan Muir, who had helped provide for her after Berk left. Then, three years after he left, Berk shows up. Faced with two husbands and a child by each, Diony exercises the frontier woman's option: she sends Evan away, takes Berk back, and then goes to bed for a good, sound sleep.

The same spirit of make-do morality also characterizes the settlers' relations with the Indians. Diony's mother, Polly, influenced by Quaker thought, not only opposes the slaveholding favored by the Tidewater gentry, but also opposes taking land from the Indians. At the dinner table where the men are enthusiastically discussing "the promise land" of Kentucky, Polly angrily announces that Kentucky "belongs to the Indians" and that white trespassers there will get "skulped." Quiet reigns while the men contemplate images of "battle, fire . . . rapine, plunder." These thoughts, however, dampen their enthusiasm only momentarily. Striking the table for emphasis, they argue that Kentucky, "a good country," belongs to those strong enough to take and hold it—that is, "the Long Knives." Later, the last term is revised to "civilized man." Apparently, the latter argument is the one Roberts favors, since the rest of her novel eulogizes the settlers' taking of Kentucky. For example, as Diony's party breaks through Cumberland Gap, Roberts describes them as marching forward, "without bigotry and without psalm-singing," to take "a new world for themselves . . . by the power of their courage, their order, and their endurance." Thus is a time-honored Kentucky tradition established.

If *The Great Meadow* celebrates the vision of this other Eden, *A Buried Treasure* and *Black Is My Truelove's Hair* celebrate the realization of the vision. Like all of Roberts' novels except *The Great Meadow*, they are set in early twentieth century Kentucky, roughly contemporaneous with the period of their composition. Both novels were expanded from shorter pieces and show the effects of padding and lengthening, but at the same time they are

Roberts' most entertaining novels and exhibit, in its purest form, her theme of living on the land. Generally light and pleasant works, they depict a pastoral scene where the land is the source of happiness and renewal.

A Buried Treasure differs from other novels in its comic tone and in its older protagonist, Philadelphia Blair. Philly's farmer husband, Andy, finds a pot of old gold and silver coins under a stump on their land, and the rest of the novel concerns their efforts to announce their find and at the same time protect it from thieves. The flimsy plot is complicated somewhat by Philly's machinations to slip away her cousin's daughter, Imogene (whose possessive father, Sam Cundy, will not let her wed), and marry her to Giles Wilson. In addition, a subplot, introducing experimentation with point of view and synchronous time, treats seventeen-year-old Ben Shepherd's search for his ancestors' graves. To a great extent, the whole novel is an extended pun on the meanings of "buried treasure." Ben Shepherd finds the graves of his ancestors, who naturally go all the way back to the pioneer settlers of Kentucky. Imogene marries her beau, a jolly young farmer who wears horseshoes. Philly becomes more aware of her deep love for Andy, particularly when he loans the widow Hester Trigg (who gives him cherry pie) his two pearls he got from the treasure pot and normally wears in a small sack tied around his lower abdomen. Both Philly and Andy become more aware of their love for the land, from whence the treasure pot came, put there perhaps by some ancestor. Despite an evil old hen that eats her own eggs, and the threat of two itinerant housepainters who are thieves, the novel ends happily in a communal ring dance out in the pasture under the moonlit sky of the summer solstice.

Compared to *A Buried Treasure*, *Black Is My Truelove's Hair* is somewhat less satisfactory. Its title drawn from an Appalachian ballad containing the line "I love the ground whereon he stands," *Black Is My Truelove's Hair* concerns a young woman, Dena Janes, who "loved too much" and whose first lover, the black-hearted Langtry, is untrue. A truck driver who brags that he has no home, Langtry takes Dena on the road, refuses to marry her, treats her brutally, and threatens to kill her if she ever loves another man. After six days, Dena flees home, walking most of the way. Beginning at this point (the affair with Langtry is told through brief flashbacks), the novel treats Dena's gradual rehabilitation in the rural community and her eventual engagement to marry the miller's son, Cam Elliot. Although received at first with leering remarks and invitations, Dena is not given the Hester Prynne treatment. Even on her way home from the Langtry affair, the distraught Dena maintains she has "a right to a life that makes good sense." Apparently the people of the community agree.

Dena restores herself with the help of time, a sympathetic sister, routine chores of gardening and tending animals, sunbathing, and the advice of the local oracle, the apple-grower Journeyman, who observes that Dena is like one of his overburdened apple trees, "destroyed by its own abundance." As

Dena recovers, the passage of time is marked by great to-dos over a strayed gander and a lost thimble; these comic commotions are supposed to be highly symbolic, but to the reader they may seem merely silly. The reader is also likely to find the ending anticlimactic. The fearsome Langtry shows up, gun in hand, but when he chases Dena into Journeyman's moonlit orchard and views her abundance, he shoots to miss. The story is resolved when Journeyman appears, destroys the gun, and buries it in the earth, leaving Dena free to go her own way.

While *The Great Meadow* and the pastoral novels emphasize the positive aspects of Roberts' theme, *The Time of Man* and her other novels emphasize negative aspects. Dealing with poor tenant farmers who move from place to place, *The Time of Man* shows the plight of people who live on the land but do not own it. They have, in effect, been reduced to beasts of burden. Laboring mainly for others, they receive only enough from their labors to insure their continuing usefulness, their subsistence. Their inability to escape from this cycle probably means that their children will continue it.

Although Roberts' subject raises weighty social issues, suggesting a novel along the lines of John Steinbeck's *The Grapes of Wrath* (1939), *The Time of Man* is not a novel of social protest. Instead, with Roberts' narrative focus on the mind of her protagonist, *The Time of Man* is more a *Bildungrsroman*, tracing the development of Ellen Chesser from a girl of fourteen to a woman in her mid-thirties.

The reader follows Ellen as she bounds about the woods and fields, joins a group of other teenagers, gets a boyfriend, loses her boyfriend, withdraws into her hurt, meets another man, marries him, has four children, is estranged from her husband when he is unfaithful, has a fifth child die, and is reconciled with her husband. In short, whatever her social status, Ellen's experience of life over a generation is typical of most people's; in this sense, then, her experience is representative of "the time of man"—experiences of beauty and love, disappointment and tragedy, all within the context of passing time. Her ability to hold her experiences within this context is the key to her appreciation of beauty and love and her endurance of disappointment and tragedy. This ability derives from her closeness to the land, her sense of the seasons and participation in the rhythms of the earth: her jaunts through the woods, her work in the fields and garden, her courtship and marriage, her children.

Ellen illustrates what the Indians knew—that one can live in harmony with the land without owning it. To this extent, the several moves she makes from farm to farm, first with her parents and then with her husband, are almost irrelevant. Still, Ellen is aware of the inequities and injustices of the landowner/tenant system, a carryover from slave plantations, with some landowners continuing to act as if they own their tenants. She is incensed when her husband, while she and the children starve, identifies with, even takes pride in, the richness and show of their arrogant landlord. Both she and her husband carry around a vision of having their own farm someday, in "some better country." Perhaps they are headed toward this vision when, at the end of the novel, after her husband has been wrongly accused of barnburning and run out of the country, they are on the road again.

Roberts' first novel, *The Time of Man* is judged by some critics to be her best. Her exposition of her heroine's mind and development is a consummate job, and the novel does include some recognition of social problems in "the great meadow" of Kentucky; many readers, however, will feel that Roberts dwells too long on Ellen's early years, so that the first part of the novel drags.

Roberts' other novels could all be called "novels of maladjustment," since they all show, in one manner or another, people who are out of touch with the land. Of these, *Jingling in the Wind*, which includes Roberts' only depiction of an urban setting, presents the most extreme case. There is much that Roberts finds artificial, even bizarre, in the city, such as neon advertisements that usurp the stars. In short, *Jingling in the Wind*, sometimes described as a satiric fantasy, is an outright attack on many trends of modern civilization. The loose plot concerns a couple of rainmakers, Jeremy and Tulip, who give up their unnatural profession in order to marry and have children. Usually considered Roberts' worst novel, *Jingling in the Wind* is interesting for its contribution to her grand theme.

Another novel of maladjustment is *My Heart and My Flesh*, centering around Theodosia Bell, a neurasthenic product of the wealthy landowning class. In this Faulknerian work exhibiting the results of Southern decadence, the protagonist gradually loses everything which has insulated her from contact with the land—her wealth, her boyfriends, her home, her grandfather and sottish father, even her feelings of racial superiority (she discovers she is a half-sister to three mulattoes in town, including one idiot). As a child, Theodosia is so out of place in the countryside that a pack of hounds attack her. As an adult, when disillusionment, poverty, and sickness have brought her down to earth, she moves in with the pack, even eats their food. Later she finds health and happiness by teaching in a country school, living in her pupils' homes and marrying a farmer. Thus, the pattern of rebirth through contact with the land is perfectly illustrated by Theodosia.

Conversely, a negative example is provided by Stoner Drake, the mono-maniacal old man in *He Sent Forth a Raven*. The title's biblical reference to Noah, who trusted in God, provides a lucid contrast to Drake's blasphemous behavior. When his second wife dies, Drake vows never to set foot on God's green earth again. His anger hardening into inflexible principle, he keeps his word, never venturing from the house and managing his farm from a rooftop observatory, summoning workers and family members with blasts on a hunting horn or conch shell. The blasts symbolize not only his pathetic defiance of God but also his alienation from other people and the land. To Drake, of course, they symbolize command, and in his house he is an absolute dictator.

His rancorous behavior is self-punishing, but it also takes a toll on the people around him. For example, he prevents his daughter, Martha, from entertaining suitors. When one finally ventures a polite visit as a guest, Drake confronts him and Martha with loud, vile charges of fornication. The young man leaves, and Martha, thunderstruck, falls into fever and delirium, temporarily losing her hearing; when after some weeks it returns, the first things she hears are "the loud horn and the screaming of the swine." She thereafter reconciles herself to being a spinster and to banking the fires at night (so the house will not catch fire and her father burn up with it).

Standing in contrast to Drake is his granddaughter Jocelle, the novel's heroine, who takes a lesson from her aunt's fate. Growing up in the house with Drake and Martha, Jocelle manages to live a relatively normal life because she is free to roam the fields, sometimes even beyond the range of the horn. Like all of Roberts' female protagonists, Jocelle does suffer her traumas, but she is strong enough to bounce back. For example, when she is raped by Walter, Drake's nephew, Drake renews his ridiculous vow, but Jocelle eventually recovers from her shock. At the end of the novel, she is happily married and a mother, her husband the manager of the farm, while Drake sits before the fireplace and hardens into brittle senility, unable to remember the reason for his vow.

Major publications other than long fiction
SHORT FICTION: *The Haunted Mirror*, 1932; *Not by Strange Gods*, 1941.
POETRY: *In the Great Steep's Garden*, 1915; *Under the Tree*, 1922, 1930; *Song in the Meadow*, 1940.

Bibliography
Campbell, Harry Modean, and Ruel E. Foster. *Elizabeth Madox Roberts: American Novelist*, 1956.
McDowell, Frederick P. W. *Elizabeth Madox Roberts*, 1963.
Rovit, Earl H. *Herald to Chaos: The Novels of Elizabeth Madox Roberts*, 1960.
Wagenkenecht, Edward. *Cavalcade of the American Novel*, 1952.

Harold Branam

SINCLAIR ROSS

Born: Shellbrook, Canada; January 22, 1908

Principal long fiction
As for Me and My House, 1941; *The Well*, 1958; *Whir of Gold*, 1970; *Sawbones Memorial*, 1974.

Other literary forms
The Lamp at Noon and Other Stories (1968) is a volume of ten short stories available in a New Canadian Library (McClelland and Stewart) paperback edition. Most of Sinclair Ross's eighteen uncollected short stories may be found in *Queen's Quarterly*, a Canadian scholarly journal. In addition to their intrinsic merit, the short stories are important as proving grounds for many of the plots, themes, and characters of Ross's novels.

Achievements
The fact that *As for Me and My House*, Ross's first novel and the one on which his reputation rested for many years, was published in the United States and not in his native land is indicative of his early struggle for recognition in Canada. Previously, he had published several short stories that gained little attention, perhaps because of their rather somber view of the human condition as reflected in the lives of the characters: Canadian prairie dwellers during the Depression. A few copies of *As for Me and My House* sold in Canada, but the reading public there was not interested in the Canadian West, a region apart from the rest of the world, and the merits of the novel went largely unappreciated until publication of the New Canadian Library paperback edition in 1957. Today, *As for Me and My House* holds a secure place among the classics of Canadian fiction. Like Mark Twain's *The Adventures of Huckleberry Finn* (1884) and F. Scott Fitzgerald's *The Great Gatsby* (1925), it is a parable by which a country can measure its imaginative life. In its complex rendering of humans struggling with inner conflict and the psychological effects of landscape and the elements, and in its richly resonant language, it surpasses the best of Frederick Philip Grove, the leading prairie realist before Ross, and it maps a fictional terrain that is still being explored by Margaret Laurence, Rudy Wiebe, Robert Kroetsch, and others. Though his next two novels, *The Well* and *Whir of Gold*, fail to match the achievement of *As for Me and My House*, a renewing fourth novel, *Sawbones Memorial*, is of high quality.

In his best fiction, a sentence or two of Ross's lean, spare, honest prose can illuminate the life of an entire community. In his best fiction, too, Ross has the ability to identify with his characters and with their time and place.

Margaret Laurence has said that "he got his time and place in the prairies exactly right." Ross could not have asked for a more satisfying tribute.

Biography

A very private man, Sinclair Ross is reticent about his personal life and prefers to let his art speak for him. A few articles, interviews, and recollections of friends, however, make it possible to piece together at least the outward facts of his life.

Born January 22, 1908, in northern Saskatchewan, James Sinclair Ross was the third child of Peter and Catherine Ross, who met and married in Prince Albert, Saskatchewan, in 1897. Peter had been born on an Ontario farm to Scottish parents, and Catherine had been born in Scotland. When he was three, Ross's parents separated, his mother taking custody of him and his father taking the two older children. After the separation, Mrs. Ross found employment as a housekeeper on several farms. Ross assisted with farm chores and learned the vagaries of horses and men, as well as the daunting effects of landscape and climate on the prairie dwellers. He has strong memories of his isolation in those years.

After he was graduated from high school in 1924, Ross went to work for the Royal Bank of Canada, his sole employer until his retirement in 1968. In 1933, the bank rewarded Ross's stints in several small Saskatchewan towns by sending him to Winnipeg, Manitoba, where he remained until 1946, except for World War II military service, and finally to Montreal. Upon retirement, he lived in Greece for three years and then moved to Spain in 1971. Culture and climate (he suffers from arthritis) influenced Ross's decision to live by the Mediterranean Sea. Competent in Spanish and French, somewhat less so in Greek, Ross reads the original versions of the literatures of these languages. Living abroad, he believes, has given him a stronger sense of his Canadian identity. Although the pattern of Ross's life is one of gradual withdrawal eastward from the pioneer prairies toward older, more cosmopolitan cultures, his true subject and setting remain the Canadian prairies, specifically rural Saskatchewan and its people.

Few of Ross's colleagues at the bank knew him as a writer, though he has always been a "compulsive scribbler," he says, despite having had "so little success." Isolated from any real literary community, some of Ross's determination to write, mostly at night after long days at the bank, must be credited to his mother, the strongest influence in his life and a model for some of the women in his fiction. Ever conscious of her moral and intellectual refinement (her father had studied theology at the University of Edinburgh, taught at Oberlin College in Ohio, and eventually been ordained a Unitarian minister), Catherine encouraged her young son to take piano lessons, experiment with oil painting, and read widely. In particular, Ross remembers reading Sir Walter Scott, Charles Dickens, and Thomas Hardy, whose *The Return of the*

Native (1878) may well have influenced him he says, though he has never been aware of any literary influences. For many years he had to support his mother as well as himself in the succession of small towns and cities to which she followed him, making it impossible to resign from the bank to devote his full energy to writing.

Ross's most productive period was the 1930's. Many of his best short stories were published then; one of them, "No Other Way," won third prize in a competition for unpublished writers. In 1941, *As for Me and My House* appeared. Ross had already destroyed the manuscripts of two earlier, unsatisfactory novels, and would later destroy another, a possibly autobiographical story of a Canadian soldier from Manitobawritten during World War II.

Discouraged by the reception of *As for Me and My House*, Ross did not publish his second novel, *The Well*, until 1958, but it was greeted with even less enthusiasm than his first. *The Well* was influenced by his negative reaction to Montreal, where for twenty-two years the ascetic Ross lived largely within himself, avoiding the "literary swim," as he calls it. Much of his third novel, *Whir of Gold*, was also written in Montreal, then completed after retirement. Written in Europe, his fourth novel, *Sawbones Memorial*, is a forgiving reminiscence of the prairies as Ross knew them in the 1930's and 1940's. Bearing an obvious kinship to its predecessors, it is nevertheless a more mellow novel, striking a better balance between humorous detachment and bitterness, rejection and grudging nostalgia. If his new awareness of his Canadian identity ensures continued psychic access to the time and place that is the strongest foundation of his art, Canadian literature and Ross's readers both stand to benefit.

Analysis

Despite his relatively small output and rather limited fictional world, Sinclair Ross succeeds in universalizing the human concerns of his novels. Drought, poverty, and the hardship and anxiety they cause, are universal concerns, but life on the Canadian prairies in the 1930's and 1940's becomes in Ross's works a paradigm of the human condition everywhere. Moreover, at its most intense there is a characteristic mood in Ross's fiction, a synthesis of human isolation, claustrophobia, and threatening nature, that serves as his trademark, making his writing as distinctive and recognizable as that of his contemporaries Ernest Hemingway and William Faulkner.

"Most writers," Ross has said, "have only one or two themes that they constantly develop in their work." Actually, Ross has three: communication, or more often the failure of communication, in human relationships; the struggle to find an authentic self and live a fulfilled existence; and man's struggle against the land and the elements. In Ross's novels, man-woman relationships, in particular, are vitiated by a failure to communicate, or even a failure to attempt communication. In *As for Me and My House*, the Bentleys are isolated from each other by their emotional and psychological shortcomings. In *The Well*, a generation gap of attitudes and values separates the old farmer, Larson, and his young wife, Sylvia. In *Whir of Gold*, Sonny McAlpine's emotional immaturity and prairie Calvinist attitudes destroy his chances of happiness with the good-hearted prostitute, Madelaine. Among the prairie homesteaders, poverty, climate, physical toil, pessimism about the future, and a repressive Puritan morality are hardly conducive to romance.

Writing about women in Canadian and American prairie fiction, the novelist Robert Kroetsch asks, "How do you establish any sort of *close* relationship in a landscape—in a physical situation—whose primary characteristic is distance?" Thwarted in their attempts at closeness, Ross's women become domineering and manipulative (Mrs. Bentley), sexually aggressive (Sylvia), or maternal and possessive (Madelaine). Love becomes a power struggle. The women's superior social and intellectual backgrounds, or their emotional needs, cause them to treat their men as sons rather than lovers. As for the men in Ross's novels, Oedipal overtones—their failure in heterosexual love, their need for mothering women, the lack of adequate father figures in their youth, for example—are present in the principal male characters, and may conceal a latent homosexuality which Ross does not overtly confront until *Sawbones Memorial*. Indeed, Ross's men seem to have better rapport with animals than with other people, and the best-written passages in his later novels are those involving animals, especially horses. Horses serve as companions or as daring symbols of sexuality, independence, and the imaginative life.

For the artist, a recurrent figure in Ross's world of outsiders and misfits, the failure of communication is especially acute. The aspirations of the artist find little nourishment in prairie society, or—by implication—in Canada and North America as a whole. The failure of Ross's struggling painters and musicians to communicate their vision is symptomatic of the larger failure of the national imagination. In *As for Me and My House*, Philip Bentley's paintings are as stillborn as his first child. In *Whir of Gold*, Sonny McAlpine's musical ambition is blunted by prairie attitudes that burden him even in distant Montreal. In this respect, Sonny, like Philip, is a typical Canadian literary protagonist, incapable of great art or memorable literary heroism on account of the domination of a persistent puritanism. The failed artist as modern literary hero is a familiar type, best exemplified perhaps by James Joyce's Stephen Dedalus, but when the Canadian protagonist discovers he is in disagreement with the dictates of the system, whether religious, social, or other, his peculiar Calvinist-Puritan conditioning causes him to blame himself, internalizing the tension and engaging in painful and destructive soul-searching in an attempt to discover his deficiencies.

Philip Bentley's self-absorption, his unfinished pictures of headless figures and the false fronts of the town are a measure of the frustration of his search for meaning and significance in life. In this respect, Philip and the other artist-protagonists in Ross's fiction represent man's search in modern North America for an authentic existence, either by coming to terms with a repressive social, cultural, and natural environment (the Canadian way), or by overthrowing it entirely (formerly the America way). Ross's characters are locked into themselves and unable to find a means of escape. This in turn leads to a withholding of emotion and strained relationships devoid of real communication. The trap preventing self-realization in Canada has been called by Northrop Fry the "garrison mentality," the tendency of frontier societies to barricade themselves psychologically and culturally against the alien wilderness behind the ordered "civilized" propriety of a transported Eastern culture, rather than adapt to the new environment. The superficial Christianity that Bentley practices, for example, is inadequate to reconcile man with nature on the prairie; there are hints in *As for Me and My House* that a natural, pastoral paganism would be more helpful. Frozen in its own negations and reinforced in the Depression by an overwhelming sense of failure, Christianity engenders guilt and self-destructive behavior (in the turning to crime of the protagonists of *Whir of Gold* and *The Well*, for example), rather than encouraging self-realizing ambition, individualism, and instinct.

Indeed, by the time Ross came to write *The Well* and *Whir of Gold*, he felt that the real wilderness was in the human chaos of the modern city. The true prairie, as opposed to the garrison, was regenerative; it was the way to redemption and self-realization. Completely alienated from society, the criminal is the ultimate outsider, but in *The Well*, Chris Rowe, the small-time Montreal thug hiding out on a prairie farm, does find regeneration in nature, the courage to face punishment for his crimes, and probably an authentic existence within the community of prairie dwellers. Whereas in *The Well* a life in nature regenerates a young criminal, in *Whir of Gold*, his experience in the city almost destroys Sonny McAlpine. The keys to survival are his nostalgic recollections of his prairie upbringing, especially those involving his horse, which serve as an anchor of self and identity amid the disorientation and venality of Montreal.

Ross's third major theme, man's struggle with the land and the elements, probably derives from experience and observation as well as from his reading of the literary naturalists, especially Thomas Hardy. Moods are known to be affected by climate and geography, but on the prairies of Ross's novels, as on Hardy's moors, characters and their relationships seem to be deterministically influenced by wind, heat, drought, dust, rain, snow, and ice. The psychological and emotional toll these elements exact lead characters to regard nature as part of an indifferent, even hostile universe. Ross was also, however, the first of the Canadian prairie realists to go beyond this naturalistic treatment of the landscape; his characters are not only psychologically conditioned by the prairie, but they also project their own subjectivity onto the external environment. In effect, they interact with it, so that not only is character determined by external environment, but environment also becomes an extension of the mind. Its challenge can test and strengthen the endurance of those who survive, uniting them in the common struggle against it, it can be a regenerative sanctuary for an urban fugitive such as Chris Rowe.

The defeated ones find little in religion to sustain the human spirit, at least the version of it proferred by prairie Christianity. One of Philip Bentley's redeeming qualities is precisely that he cannot believe in deliverance through a faith reduced to hollow forms and meaningless rituals that hypocritically ignore the Christian virtues of charity and compassion. In a deeper sense, however, Ross is a religious writer in that the underlying concern of his fiction is man's struggle "with the implacable blunderings of Nature" in an indifferent universe. In the face of this daunting situation, Ross holds up rationalists and humanists, such as Mrs. Bentley and Paul Kirby in *As for Me and My House* and Doc Hunter in *Sawbones Memorial*, who stake their faith on human courage, reason, and idealism, "all the things that really are humanity," in Mrs. Bentley's words. Others, such as Sonny McAlpine and old Larson, find solace in the illusory world of the past, a youthful world of happiness and material and spiritual well-being, unthreatened by darker realities. If Ross's characters are escapist-dreamers, though, their dreams must sometimes be blown away, like the false fronts of main street in a wind storm, to reveal the reality in which a new, authentic self can be forged.

As a youth in Saskatchewan, Ross was encouraged by a United Church minister to enter the ministry rather than banking. Already skeptical about organized religion, although he taught Sunday school and played the organ in church, Ross "was not tempted in the least. But I began to think, 'Suppose I did, or someone else did who did not really believe in it, and felt trapped in the ministry.' That was the origin of *As for Me and My House*." Ross has revealed also that he once knew a minister whose plight resembled Philip Bentley's. Mrs. Bentley appears to have been based, at least in part, on Ross's mother, to judge by his recollections of her.

Like Ross's next two novels, *As for Me and My House* is the story of an inner quest for the authentic self. It thus belongs to a literary genre that includes works as diverse as John Bunyan's *The Pilgrim's Progress* (1678), Johann Wilhelm von Goethe's *Wilhelm Meister's Apprenticeship* (1795-1796), Henry David Thoreau's *Walden* (1854), and Walt Whitman's *Leaves of Grass* (1855). It is also kindred to a large number of Canadian works in which the search for personal and national identity is a dominant theme. Ross's ironic vision is nowhere better illustrated than in the fact that Bentley's search for an authentic self compels him to reject the church's way, which is to follow the teachings of Jesus Christ. Finally, he tears down the facade of his old self, but the new, authentic self must be forged in the secular, humanist crucible of art rather than in the empty chalice of the church. Sandra Djwa's perception of the "latter-day Puritanism of the psychological search for self," in a world where "Christianity has become a meaningless form without spirit, where people must learn to reject the false gods without before it it is possible to find the true God within and an authentic sense of direction," suggests the continuing contemporaneity of the book, if one thinks of the self-realization movements of the 1960's and 1970's.

As for Me and My House is a taut, intense, and bitter record of repressed, static lives in rural Saskatchewan in the 1930's. It deals with the Bentleys' year in Horizon, the fourth small-town prairie residence in twelve years for the thirty-five-year-old minister and his wife. Told in journal form by Mrs. Bentley, the book is an indictment of puritanical moral attitudes and cultural sterility. It is also bleakly pessimistic about the possibility of communication in human relationships, especially marriage. Outsiders by virtue of their position in the community and their parishioners' awareness that to them Horizon is merely a way station in a stultifying series of prairie pastorates, the Bentleys are estranged from the townsfolk as well as from each other. With no real vocation as a minister of the gospel, Bentley wants to believe he has some talent as a painter, but his daubing shows little evidence of this, mainly because his creativity is frozen by self-lacerating guilt arising from his clerical charade.

Embittered by his failure as a minister and twelve years of entrapment in drought and depression-ridden prairie towns, Philip seeks consolation through an adopted son whose natural father had abandoned him, but—in keeping with the melancholy pattern of discontinuity between the generations in Ross—societal pressure (the boy's Catholicism is unacceptable, as is his parental background) forces the Bentleys to give up their son. Philip lacks a natural father as well as a son. Having sired Philip illegitimately, his father died before he was born; Philip's own child was stillborn. Despite, or on account of, the scorn to which his illegitimacy subjected him, Philip followed his father's path, first into the ministry and then into art. He saw the church's offer of an education in return for a commitment to the ministry as a means of escaping humiliation, but planned to leave it quickly for a painting career. He is prevented from doing so by an inanition of the soul that arises from marital responsibilities, economic conditions, and guilt over abandoning his flock. Adultery seems briefly to offer a way out for Philip, but Mrs. Bentley soon learns of it, and the other woman dies giving birth to Philip's child. In what can be interpreted as a hopeful conclusion, though, the Bentleys adopt this child, and with the money Mrs. Bentley has saved, they leave Horizon for a city life as owners of a used bookstore. Their hope is that the bookstore will allow Philip time to pursue his painting without the crippling emotional and psychological burdens of the past.

The essence of Ross's achievement in *As for Me and My House* lies in the rich complexity of character and theme realized through brilliant manipulation of point of view and language. For almost three decades after the book's publication, it was assumed that Mrs. Bentley's reporting was accurate and that her point of view was reliable. Certainly, if the reader accepts the point of view of her journal, then the town and her husband both fail her. She is the long-suffering, supportive wife; the superior woman languishing in a cultural and domestic wasteland. As late as 1957, in his Introduction to the New Canadian Library edition of the book, Roy Daniells called her "pure gold and wholly credible." If the reader accepts Ross's implicit invitation to read between the lines, however, Mrs. Bentley's self-indulgent meanness, her lonely pride, and her manipulation of Philip to satisfy her own ego are the reasons for her defeat and, to some extent, her husband's. The many inconsistencies and outright contradictions in her journal suggest that her single perspective is actually a source of considerable ambiguity in the book and of ambivalence on the reader's part. Several questions are raised: How accurate are her perceptions and assessments of her husband and the townspeople? How accurate are her perceptions of her own behavior and attitudes? Is the fact that the reader never learns her first name a clue to how *non*-revealing her journal is? In 1969, William H. New argued that the reader's ambivalence toward Mrs. Bentley arises not so much from uncertainty about her credibility as from Ross's ironically pitting the reader's viewpoint against hers in such a way that the reader comes to appreciate the depth and complexity of the narrator's situation, and Ross's control of his material. Through ironic use of symbols such as lamps, moths, Philip's study door, railroad tracks, and the false fronts of Horizon's main street, and through imagery involving gardens, horses, heat, dust, rain, snow and the prairie itself, Ross reveals Mrs. Bentley's journal to be an exercise in self-deception and evasiveness. In the final analysis, this book about communication and its failure informs the reader of the impossibility of taking sides, despite the human inclination to do so.

When *The Well* was published in 1958, Ross had been living in Montreal for twelve years. The new urban environment awakened an interest in the motivations of the criminal mind, while remoteness from the prairie prompted a realization of its regenerative potential. In *As for Me and My House*, Philip Bentley leaves the prairie to seek an authentic self in the city; in *The Well*, Chris Rowe flees the city and achieves authentic selfhood through his moral regeneration on the prairie. Apart from this about-face, the two novels bear a close kinship. Once more the setting is rural Saskatchewan; once more the characters fail to communicate and are claustrophobically trapped by the past as well as the present; once more they are psychologically conditioned by the prairie environment, while projecting their own subjectivity onto it; and once more there is discontinuity between the generations.

The Well is a story of three barren misfits whose lives converge in the little prairie community of Campkin in the 1940's. The central character, Chris Rowe, is a fatherless twenty-year-old criminal from Montreal whose petty larcenies have culminated in the shooting of an intended robbery victim whose fate the novel leaves in doubt. Handsome, tough, and arrogant, Chris never-theless has a potentially sensitive, gentle, nature which has been brutalized by his urban upbringing. Fleeing on westbound trains to escape arrest, Chris accepts an offer of farm work in Campkin, his intention being to maintain a low profile for a while before resuming his westward flight. He soon finds himself enmeshed, however, in a conflict for domination over him between Larson, his employer, and Larson's wife, Sylvia.

Like Chris, Larson is pursued by the past. Ten years before, Larson's first wife had died; his son, also named Chris, died soon after. Grief has warped Larson's mind several degrees beyond eccentricity, despite outward symbols of material success such as his Cadillac and new young wife. Pathetically trying to relive the past, Larson makes a virtual shrine of the old homestead he began with his first wife. Its chief icon is the well they dug together, a symbol of their shared achievement and happy union. Larson also keeps a horse with the same name as his dead son's horse, and he even imagines that Chris Rowe is the dead son returned. He treats Chris as a surrogate son, assuming he will take over the farm eventually and reestablish continuity with the Edenic past. To the extent that Larson's aversion to the present stems from his longing for the pretechnological past when farming offered pride of individual accomplishment and close identity with the soil, Ross is sounding a theme found in other prairie realists such as Grove and Laurence: the human costs of increasing technology on the prairie farms. As usual, Ross's focus is on the dynamics of one or two human relationships, but *The Well* can be read as a work of social criticism that probes, as Robert Chambers, in his *Sinclair Ross and Ernest Ruckler* (1975), states, "some neglected side effects of that new prairie trinity: mechanization, mobility, and money."

Larson's wife, the voluptuous, ambitious Sylvia, had married Larson five years earlier to escape the poverty and drudgery of life as a waitress in Campkin. Partly because of a thirty-year age difference, there is neither love nor communication between them; in fact, Sylvia's plan is to kill Larson and abscond with his money. If Mrs. Bentley's designs for Philip are manipulative, those of Sylvia for Chris are evil and predatory. Her fantasy is that the adulterous relationship that quickly develops between them will make it easier to coerce Chris into helping her murder Larson, stuff his body down the well, persuade the townspeople that he suddenly left on a train, as he often talked of doing. After a judicious interval, the two would marry and retire to Cali-fornia. In a lurid climax, Sylvia shoots her husband after wresting the gun from Chris, whose loyalty to his new surrogate father prevents him from doing so. Sylvia is eventually forced out of the house, never to be seen again. Larson expires, but not before he has written a note indicting Sylvia, exculpating Chris, and leaving the farm to him as well. Chris still faces uncertain punish-ment for the Montreal shooting but the important thing is that he now has the courage to do so. His refusal to be further tempted into crime by Sylvia, coupled with his loyalty to Larson, is redemptive. Once free of the entramelling past, his best instincts released by the regenerative powers of nature and the rhythms of farm life, Chris will have a chance to achieve authentic selfhood, an end to alienation, and even community with the prairie dwellers.

If *As for Me and My House* is Ross's best novel, *The Well* is in many ways his weakest. Ross has admitted his failure to "get inside" the criminal mind to make Chris Rowe a sympathetic character. The ending is wildly melodramatic, as Ross has also acknowledged. "I would like to do it again and give it a different ending," he has said. "I see now how it should be done." The book suffers also from a thinness of texture, a lack of intensity and power, attributable to Ross's decision to substitute the flat, banal language of barely literate characters for the richly metaphorical prose of *As for Me and My House*, and to the general lack of complexity of character, theme, and point of view. In view of these flaws, the book's cool reception seems justified.

In two important ways, *Whir of Gold*, Ross's third novel, is a reverse image of *The Well*. The latter is a Rousseauistic study of a victim of urban corruption in Montreal whose innate goodness is brought out by the morally regenerative life in nature; the former is a Hobbesian study of the nasty and brutish life of a prairie youth in the same city. Again, a man and a woman compete for domination of the young hero, but whereas in *The Well* the man is basically decent, despite his misfortunes in life, and the woman grotesquely evil, in *Whir of Gold* the reverse is true. In other ways, *Whir of Gold* resembles *The Well* quite closely. Like Chris Rowe, Sonny McAlpine is arrogant, alienated, and female-dominated. Like Chris, Sonny is drawn into crime. In common with both of the earlier novels, *Whir of Gold* is concerned with entrapment, the failure of communication, and the baneful influence of the past. Its conclusion is more pessimistic than those of Ross's previous novels. Indeed, Sonny McAlpine's struggle and eventual defeat as a musician may represent Ross's pessimistic answer to the question of whether Philip Bentley's move to the city will really enable him to develop an authentic self. In the thirty years between *As for Me and My House* and *Whir of Gold*, Ross seems to have concluded that neither the rural nor urban environment in Canada is capable of nourishing the artistic imagination.

The plot is simple and familiar, sometimes to the point of cliché. Determined to prove his superior musical talent and plagued by guilt over his sensible choice of a career in popular rather than classical music in the Saskatchewan farm community where he was reared, the young, innocent Sonny takes his clarinet to Montreal, but competition and commercialism in the wicked city combine to thwart his ambitions. Out of money and hope, he is comtemplating retreat to the West when he meets Madelaine, a good-hearted nightclub floozie as lonely as he. Mad, as she is called, is from Nova Scotia, a place as remote in spirit from Montreal as is Saskatchewan. Comrades in alienation, the two decide to live together in Sonny's skid-row rooming house immediately after a first-night sexual encounter. More spontaneous and generous than other female characters in Ross's works, Mad nevertheless had comparable plans for her man. Once he is sexually involved with her, her idea is to return with him to Nova Scotia, where they will manage a restaurant, and live a simple, healthy life far from the psychological rat race and moral wasteland of Montreal. In effect, she tries to trap Sonny into domesticity, as Sylvia tried to trap Chris Rowe through her plot to kill Larson.

As Mad sees it, the chief obstacle to this scheme is Sonny's neighbor, Charlie, the only other character of consequence in the small, claustrophobic world of the novel. A small-time, street-mean crook, Charlie exploits Sonny's weaknesses (primarily, a self-destructive urge arising from the guilt he feels about wasting his musical talent) to involve him, against the vehement opposition of Mad, in robbing a jewelry store. In the robbery, Sonny is shot and is himself robbed of his share of the loot by Charlie. The relationship between Sonny and Mad is likewise doomed, as are most male-female relationships in Ross's novels. The protagonist's emotional immaturity causes him unconsciously to seek an Oedipal relationship, which Mad's need to mother conveniently satisfies. Because of his insecurity, however, Sonny is unwilling to risk commitment, treating Mad's mothering as a smothering possessiveness, and her praise of his sexual prowess as proof of his limited talent. Ross implies that Sonny's past background, specifically his repressive prairie puritanism, is largely responsible for both his lack of feeling for Mad and his guilt over his shabby treatment of her.

Sonny, it appears, was Mad's "whir of gold," a fleeting vision of happiness, beauty, and self-fulfillment. The book's title and central symbol derives from an incident in Sonny's childhood. Out of curiosity and cruelty, he once pursued and killed a flicker bird in an attempt to capture it. The bird's wings "flashed like a whir of gold, a gust of feathered light," before it died. Years later, his pursuit of a musical career leads to the deathly alienation of the criminal world, and his aborted relationship with Mad to the bleak realization, once she leaves, that he has rejected probably the best chance for happiness he will ever have. The whir of gold is a fragile thing, impossible to capture. To attempt to do so is to destroy it, and also to destroy oneself through its false promise of permanence.

Ross's deep pessimism about human relationships in *Whir of Gold* is presaged in much of his earlier fiction, where Puritan constraints conflict with the human instinct for beauty, imagination, freedom, and daring. Sonny has an innate predilection for these, but his farm upbringing and moral background have indoctrinated him with practicality, restraint, discipine, and caution, values dictated also by a prudent regard for the often hostile natural elements of the prairie. Not that beauty, imagination, freedom, and daring flourish in Montreal, but Sonny's failure there is partly a deterministic result of his projection of prairie attitudes onto the city, just as earlier Ross characters projected their fears onto the external prairie environment. Unfortunately, *Whir of Gold* is not a powerfully realized novel. It does not make a profound or relevant statement about psychological repression and cultural alienation. In deferring to trends in popular fiction—inarticulate characters, limited lives, disjointed language, sordid settings—Ross denies it depth of meaning. Referring to the novel's "desperate brand of naturalism," Robert Chambers points out that "Ross's pages are covered with mundane and trivial things, as though the endless plates of bacon and eggs and all those nice hot cups of coffee will somehow cohere to underpin a work of art." The use of Sonny's first-person point of view weakens the novel further. Sonny is a vapid Candide, a vacuous Ulysses, and the other characters mere literary extensions of his personality. Ross professes an interest in the motivations of the criminal mind (though he admits he probably lacks sufficient insight), but Sonny is incapable of understanding Charlie's character or his own drift toward crime. Similarly, the forays into metaphorical language, so successful in *As for Me and My House*, seem artificially literary because they are inappropriate to Sonny's character. Again, *As for Me and My House* is rich in symbols, but the present novel has only two of any significance: the whir of gold and Sonny's horse, Isobel. Finally, the structure of the book is poorly balanced, with the central Sonny-Mad relationship starved for development in the second half because of Ross's increasing preoccupation with the robbery.

Apart from its successful interweaving of several perspectives in time, *Whir of Gold* did not advance Ross's reputation as a novelist any more than did *The Well*. In fact, it confirmed the uneasy doubts of some that Ross was a one-book author who had reached his peak in his first novel. Perhaps he was essentially a short-story writer, albeit a good one, lacking the technical resources or sustaining vision required of the novelist.

Sawbones Memorial reassured the doubters by proving convincingly that Ross was more than a one-book novelist, though its success is attributable in part to a form which utilizes the economy and precision of the short story. It succeeds also because in it Ross returns to the time and place he knows best, the Canadian prairies during the 1930's. Like *As for Me and My House*, it has a central intelligence who is perceptive and ironically detached. Unlike the two-or-three-person relationships he minutely dissects in earlier novels, Ross creates a large, diverse cast of thirty characters in *Sawbones Memorial*; and while the townspeople seem no less petty and narrow-minded than before, those on the side of life, a generous and enlightened few, dominate the action in his fourth novel. If, as Ronald Sutherland insists, a new Canadian literary hero has replaced the old, Doc Hunter must be counted a member of the new breed. Certainly his self-reliance, independence, and acceptance of life are preferable to Philip Bentley's intense struggle with his demons of guilt and self-doubt. Perhaps, as one reviewer stated, Ross himself "has stopped fighting life and come to terms with it." Perhaps the fact that the book was written in retirement in Europe, at several removes in time and space from Ross's Saskatchewan of the 1930's, explains the mellow, often humorous tone. In any case, the book is more hopeful than any of its predecessors, despite its return to some of Ross's familiar, depressing themes.

Sawbones Memorial is actually a collection of reminiscent vignettes depicting life in Upward, the small town that Doc Hunter has ministered to through forty-five years of pioneering, drought, and depression. The *raison d'être* of the vignettes is a ceremony held in April, 1948, to mark the doctor's retirement and the opening of the new Hunter Memorial Hospital. Accordingly, both reminiscing and looking to the future are in order. Though the action is limited to a few hours of the present, by the end of the novel Ross has roamed back and forth through four generations and several decades to lay bare the attitudes and preoccupations, the tensions and antagonisms, and the hypocrisies and prejudices of Upward's citizens.

Representing the full diversity of the community, the characters include farmers, storekeepers, teachers, ministers, and housewives, people old and young, living and dead, absent and present. They do not develop psychologically so much as they show the effects of time. Through the episodes in which they appear and reappear, they comment on the action, on Doc Hunter, and on one another. Occasionally, the same incident is retold by different characters, the contrasting viewpoints giving rise to comic or tragic irony. Little by little, the reader comes to know the characters. Doc Hunter's is the unifying point of view for those of the thirty characters whose stories constitute the book; conversely, the reader comes to know him through his shamanlike role in the lives of the other characters. The central character and intelligence, Doc is also the focus of attention at the gathering, as he has been the focus of the town's hopes and fears for over four decades. His own suffering, it is implied, broadens and deepens the efficacy of his mission as a doctor. It seems he was married too long to a frigid wife, and thus shares with other Ross protagonists an unfulfilled emotional life, though his experience has neither embittered him nor lessened his philosophical tolerance of human imperfection, of which there is God's plenty in Upward.

As with many fictional studies of small towns, from Winesburg, Ohio, to Peyton Place and beyond, Upward's appearance of respectability, especially its straitlaced attitudes concerning sexual morality, conceals a closetful of skeletons: rape, abortion, incest, murder, euthanasia, to name only a few. As the town's sole physician for almost half a century, Doc Hunter knows the contents of the closet better than anyone, a fact that gives pause to those who would prefer to forget their past in order to gossip more self-righteously. The more admirable characters, on the other hand, are often outsiders, defined as anyone who deviates from Upward's conventional standards of moral and social behavior. More so than Ross's earlier outsider-protagonist, these are very human characters whose struggles and triumphs the readers can share.

Sawbones Memorial is also more ambitious in form and conception than Ross's earlier novels. The large number of characters, the experimentation with multiple points of view, the reliance on dialogue, monologue, speeches, and flashbacks to convey information, reveal personality, and establish mood (much as in drama and film), are all new. The dialogue is especially remarkable in that each character is individuated through diction, idiom, intonation, or rhythm. (Ross has said that the idea of using nothing but the speech of his characters to construct a novel came to him as he overheard fragments of reminiscences at the opening of the Royal Bank's new head office in Montreal.) It is true that the book turns against two familiar themes, the failure of communication and the stultification of the spirit in the small prairie towns of Ross's time. The roots of man's alienation, whether personal or social, are still to be found in his agonized confusion over sexuality, but Ross deals with a larger range of human experience than before, including such timeless concerns as the nature of human evil and the evil of human nature, birth and death, youth and age, courage and cowardice, cruelty and compassion. For one day in time, at least, in the spring of 1948, these are reconciled as Doc Hunter speaks of retirement and the continuity symbolized by the new doctor's arrival. It is all beginning again, "just as it was all beginning that day" when he first arrived.

Major publication other than long fiction
SHORT FICTION: *The Lamp at Noon and Other Stories*, 1968.

Bibliography
Chambers, Robert. in *Sinclair Ross and Ernest Buckler*, 1975.
Latham, David. "Sinclair Ross," in *The Annotated Bibliography of Canada's Major Authors*. III (1981), pp. 365-393.
McCourt, Edward. "Sinclair Ross," in *The Canadian West in Fiction*. 1949, pp. 94-99.
McMullen, Lorraine. *Sinclair Ross*, 1979.
New, W. H. "Sinclair Ross' Ambivalent World," in *Canadian Literature*. XL (Spring, 1969), pp. 26-32.
Ricou, Laurence. "The Prairie Internalized: The Fiction of Sinclair Ross," in *Vertical Man/Horizontal World: Man and Landscape in Canadian Prairie Fiction*. 1973, pp. 82-94.

John H. Ferres

PHILIP ROTH

Born: Newark, New Jersey; March 19, 1933

Principal long fiction

Letting Go, 1962; *When She Was Good*, 1967; *Portnoy's Complaint*, 1969; *Our Gang*, 1971; *The Breast*, 1972; *The Great American Novel*, 1973; *My Life as a Man*, 1974; *The Professor of Desire*, 1977; *The Ghost Writer*, 1979; *Zuckerman Unbound*, 1981.

Other literary forms

More than a dozen of Philip Roth's published short stories remain uncollected. "The Conversion of the Jews," "Defender of the Faith," "Epstein," "You Can't Tell a Man by the Song He Sings," and "Eli the Fanatic" appeared, along with the title novella, in *Goodbye, Columbus* (1959). An unproduced screenplay, "The Great American Pastime," was anthologized in 1968. Two of Roth's works, "Goodbye, Columbus" and *Portnoy's Complaint*, were adapted to film by others. Roth is also an essayist and reviewer, and *Reading Myself and Others* (1975) collects some of his interviews and literary and cultural criticism. Since 1975, he has edited the "Writers from the Other Europe" series for Penguin Books.

Achievements

Though each denies any but a casual acquaintance with the others or sufficient affinities to constitute a genuine school, Roth, Saul Bellow, and Bernard Malamud are widely considered to constitute a triumvirate of major contemporary American Jewish novelists. Of Roth's fictions with invented characters, only *When She Was Good* does not focus on a character who is recognizably Jewish. He specializes in the depiction of second- and third-generation Jews struggling to come to terms with the attractions and repulsions of American society. Roth's work has helped to foster, and has benefitted from, the development of ethnic awareness and pride during the 1960's. His considerable critical and commercial success has encouraged others to treat explicitly Jewish themes, though he himself has been castigated from pulpits and by such influential critics as Irving Howe and Norman Podhoretz for the unflattering mirror he holds up to contemporary Jewish culture and for the paucity of his grounding in a genuinely Judaic tradition.

Especially since the momentous *succès de scandale* of *Portnoy's Complaint*, Roth has been defensive about his presumed role as Jewish spokesman. He sees as his artistic challenge the fractious variety of American actuality. His 1961 essay "Writing American Fiction" bemoans the imagination's inability to rival the grotesque reality of contemporary American life. Roth is fascinated by the cultural myths of the United States and outraged by its politics, and his fictional strategies for conveying his sense of the American scene include precise social observation, fantasy, and farce. As a self-consciously Jewish writer, he is drawn to the theme of cultural assimilation and to the tensions between traditional ethical restraints and the libidinous temptations of contemporary materialism.

Roth has become a celebrity even for those who do not read his books, and his works have increasingly concerned themselves with the burdens of fame. Sensitive to charges of vulgarity and to attempts at biographical reductionism, Roth has turned to metafiction, reflexive structures in which earnest, troubled writers examine the demands of art and its relationship to their own disordered lives. Such characters as David Kepesh, Otto Spielvogel, Peter Tarnopol, and Nathan Zuckerman return in later novels for further analysis by a master of comic invention and vernacular voice who is not content with the roles of entertainer or autobiographer.

Biography

Philip Milton Roth was born in Newark, New Jersey, on March 19, 1933, to Herman and Bess Finkel Roth. He grew up in a lower-middle-class Jewish section of the city and was graduated from Weequahic High School in 1950. After one year at Newark College of Rutgers University, Roth transferred to Bucknell University, where he edited the literary magazine and received a B.A. in English, magna cum laude, in 1954. After receiving an M.A. in English from the University of Chicago in 1955, he enlisted in the United States Army, but, as a result of a back injury sustained in basic training, received a medical discharge. He returned to Chicago, where he spent a year as a Ph.D. candidate and an instructor in English.

"The Contest for Aaron Gold," first published in *Epoch*, was selected for inclusion in *The Best Short Stories of 1956*, the first of several appearances by Roth in that anthology and in *The O. Henry Prize Stories*. *Goodbye, Columbus*, published in 1959, won a Houghton Mifflin Literary Fellowship and the National Book Award. In the same year, Roth married Margaret Martinson Williams, who was to die in an automobile accident in Central Park in 1968. The two were legally separated in 1963 and divorced in 1966.

Roth has received several prestigious grants, including ones from the Guggenheim and Ford Foundations. Currently an adjunct faculty member at the University of Pennsylvania, he has also taught at the Iowa Writers Workshop, Princeton University, and the State University of New York at Stony Brook. He maintains residences in both London and upstate New York.

Since the publication of his second novel, *When She Was Good*, in 1967, Roth's books, which have always encountered widespread critical attention and commercial success, have been appearing almost annually. When, in 1969, *Portnoy's Complaint* became the best-selling and most controversial novel of the year and the film *Goodbye, Columbus* became a box-office hit, Roth found himself wealthy and an uncomfortable celebrity. Despite numerous apparent parallels between his fictions and his life, as there are between his fictive authors and their own creations, Roth has remained reticent about his private life. As a member of the National Institute of Arts and Letters and of the International Association of Poets, Playwrights, Editors, Essayists, and Novelists, he has spoken out on political issues with particular relevance to the position of the artist in society. A visit to Czechoslovakia in 1972, led to his taking on the general editorship for Penguin Books of a continuing series of translations of twentieth century Eastern European writers.

Analysis

"Sheer Playfulness and Deadly Seriousness are my closest friends," Philip Roth declared in a 1974 interview, and his novels may be grouped naturally according to which of Roth's two friends is dominant. *Portnoy's Complaint*, *Our Gang*, *The Breast*, and *The Great American Novel* are his most rambunctious works, while *Letting Go* and *When She Was Good* most soberly address the complexities of contemporary social experience. It is perhaps when both comrades are equally supportive, in *My Life as a Man*, *The Professor of Desire*, *The Ghost Writer*, and *Zuckerman Unbound*, that Roth produces his most completely satisfying books. He is at once a spirited, comic inventor and an incisive chronicler of life in America in the second half of the twentieth century, especially among Jews, academics, and writers.

Roth has absorbed such influences as Henry James, Jonathan Swift, Nikolai Gogol, Franz Kafka, and Anton Chekhov in developing a voice that is emphatically his own and that articulates the panic of a self beset by powerful forces intent on domesticating it. In his earliest works, the locus of oppression is the family, and a young protagonist demonstrates his insurgency by declaring the sovereignty of outlawed appetites. He is the hapless stage for the combat of id and superego. Roth sings of civilization and its discontents—earnest young men beleagured by mothers and other lovers. As a family romancer, he provides both implicit and explicit psychoanalysis. Libby Herz seeks help from a Dr. Lumin and David Kepesh from Dr. Klinger, while Alexander Portnoy and Peter Tarnopol, characters from separate Roth novels, receive not entirely successful treatment from the same psychiatrist, Dr. Otto Spielvogel.

As Roth's career has developed, his protagonists have become no less obsessive, but their anxieties no longer stem only from smothering love or the coercions of ethnicity. Roth's drama has increasingly been a confrontation between the reality of contemporary America and a desperate imagination convinced of its own inadequacy. Just as, after the publication of *Portnoy's Complaint*, Roth found himself transformed from an obscure literary craftsman into a notorious public figure, a profligate Jewish heresiarch, so his characters began to wrestle with the disparity between their obdurate lives and the verbal mockery they make of them. The strategies which they and their author deploy in an effort to unbind themselves and to capture the rest of the world range from burlesque to servile transcription. All are haunted, however, by the realization that the aspiration is as presumptuous and as ludicrous as Neil Klugman's *parvenu* lust for Brenda Patimkin in "Goodbye, Columbus" or Nathan Zuckerman's for Sharon Shatsky in *My Life as a Man.* The alluring external world remains as irreducibly Gentile as Maureen Johnson and Lydia Ketterer, but Roth's later works struggle toward serenity through a realization and acceptance of life as a man.

In Roth's first novel, *Letting Go,* one can see the extent to which he has always been conscious of working in the tradition of great fiction. The preoccupation with his life as a writer and with his literary antecedents which informs Roth's latest novels is also evident in *Letting Go.* Henry James serves as the tutelary genius to this long, ambitious novel of fine consciences, and the shifting relationships among Gabe Wallach, Paul and Libby Herz, and Martha Reganhart, and between these figures and others, recall the quadrilles performed among characters in James's novels. Like James, Roth also alternates his posts of consciousness throughout the novel among his dramatis personae.

During the seven years covered by the novel, the reader follows Gabe, son of an affluent New York Jewish dentist, through graduate school at the University of Iowa and a faculty position in English at the University of Chicago. Though Gabe's father is feckless, his mother is resolutely manipulative, and the book begins with her deathbed letter regretting a lifetime of fierce control of herself and those around her. Gabe is determined not to commit the same transgressions; only at the end of the novel does he realize that he, too, has been incapable of letting go of others.

Gabe becomes involved with Marge Howells, a graduate student from Kenosha, Wisconsin, who is in awe of his Jewishness, but he abruptly and callously terminates the relationship when it threatens to exact any commitment on his part. The pattern is repeated in his destructive flirtations with Libby Herz and in his affair with Martha Reganhart. He is hesitant about marriage to Martha and averse to assuming responsibility for her two young children. She sends them to live with her former husband, where her son Markie dies accidentally. Though Martha is overwrought with guilt, Gabe refuses to acknowledge any role in Markie's death. After the collapse of his relationship with Martha, Gabe attempts to arrange for Paul and Libby to adopt a baby. He is motivated much more by a sense of self-importance than by altruism, and when the adoption proceedings become delayed by severe problems, Gabe suffers a nervous breakdown and flees to Europe.

Unlike Gabe, Paul has always been financially insecure and is not a notable academic success. Whereas Gabe evades commitment, Paul embraces it, marrying Libby out of a sense of obligation after having taken her virginity. The marriage alienates Paul from his parents, who cannot accept a Gentile daughter-in-law. Problems caused by the couple's poverty are exacerbated when Libby becomes pregnant. After she has an abortion, her normally frail health deteriorates, and so does her relationship with Paul, complicated by Gabe's role in their lives. Although tempted to abandon Libby, Paul resolves to strengthen his commitment through their adoption of a child.

Letting Go is a detailed study in individual freedom and moral choice. Its characters represent a spectrum from evasion to engagement and from coercion to a respect for the sovereignty of others. Drawing on Roth's own background at the University of Chicago, it is a solid first novel that announced a commitment to examining the blighted lives on the American social landscape.

It was five years before Roth published his next novel, *When She Was Good,* and the result was a relentlessly naturalistic account of the pattern of compulsions in five generations of a Protestant family in a small, upper-midwestern town. Like *Letting Go, When She Was Good* makes careful use of point of view. Beginning from an omniscient perspective, it gradually shifts into the represented discourse of Willard, Lucy, and Roy before returning, at the end, to detached omniscience. It is a somber, relentless demonstration of psychological determinism.

The most obvious antecedent of the pronoun in the title is Lucy Nelson, whose life has been shaped by two traumatic scenes in which she discovers her alcoholic father, Whitey, abusing her mother, Myra. In the first, she summons the police and has Whitey arrested. In the second, although she no longer lives with her parents, she comes to the rescue of her mother and locks Whitey out of the house and out of their lives. Lucy resents her irresolute father, who proves incapable of remaining in a responsible job and of establishing his own household apart from that of his in-laws. The dominant male presence in Lucy's upbringing is her grandfather, Willard Carroll, whom she, like Myra, continues to call "Daddy Will." Lucy also resents her pampered mother for the excessive indulgence she sees her extending to her charming but improvident husband.

Self-righteous and eager to escape her family, Lucy is very receptive to the attentions of Roy Bassart, a young veteran whom she meets through Ellen Sowerby, a friend from a more estimable background than her own. Though concerned about her honor and eager to establish a respectable social position for herself, Lucy is seduced by Roy in the back seat of his car on a lover's lane known as Passion Paradise. Her subsequent pregnancy puts an end to her dreams of attending college and rising above her parents' station. Marriage to Roy convinces Lucy that he, like Whitey, is another irresponsible male content with his own failures and unwilling to assert the kind of authority appropriate to the head of a family. She increasingly badgers him about his weaknesses until he abandons her and their son Eddie. Roy eventually returns, but word that Whitey is about to come back to town feeds Lucy's paranoia and triggers hysterical confrontations with him and members of both their families. Lucy runs off in the middle of the night and is found three days later, frozen to death, alone on Passion Paradise.

It is ironic that Lucy, who is doomed to reenact the same termagant role with a shiftless father and husband, spends her brief life in a town north of Chicago named Liberty Center. Roth devotes considerable attention to the social structure, rituals, and human topography of life in such a provincial setting. His only novel with a non-Jewish protagonist, *When She Was Good* also lacks the boisterous humor that was to leaven his subsequent books.

It is perhaps hyperbolic (and hence appropriate to the manner of the book itself) to maintain that *Portnoy's Complaint* radically altered (rather than reflected a radical alteration in) the tone of American culture. It certainly marked a dramatic departure from the style of Roth's previous two books, and it precipitously made him a wealthy celebrity, the center of strident controversy. Ribald, flamboyant, deliberately outrageous, *Portnoy's Complaint* is cast in the form of the extended self-examination Alexander Portnoy conducts in the office of his psychoanalyst, Dr. Otto Spielvogel. Portnoy is an energetic young Assistant Commissioner for Human Opportunity of the City of New York and a coddled Jewish son reared with a very strict sense of what is proper. Despite, and because of, his careful upbringing and his august position as municipal do-gooder, Alex yearns for his own downfall, for abandonment to the outlaw forces of the id.

His confessions are indeed unrestrained, and *Portnoy's Complaint* has become for the general public synonymous with licentiousness; as a result of an activity rarely before portrayed by a mainstream author, it has acquired a reputation as an epic of masturbation. Yet there is more to Roth's third novel than that—indeed, there are fellatio, cunnilingus, anal penetration, group sex, and other varieties of sensual experience shocking to the middle-class reader of 1969. Roth also incurred the wrath of numerous Jewish leaders, who regarded the book as an extended ethnic slur.

Though only the monologist himself is given more than spectral reality in this book-length *kvetch*, Alex is obsessed with his protective, domineering mother, Sophie. By contrast, his father, Jack Portnoy, is portrayed as suffering from a case of terminal constipation and is another of Roth's ineffectual male authority figures. A succession of sexual interests, stunning Gentile women Alex embraces in an attempt to defy the exemplary discipline Sophie inculcates in him, flit through the pages. None has much identity beyond the nicknames—such as The Pilgrim, The Pumpkin, and The Monkey—which Portnoy assigns them, and none is successful in freeing him from the syndrome of Portnoy's complaint: "A disorder in which strongly-felt ethical and altruistic impulses are perpetually warring with extreme sexual longings, often of a perverse nature." When Alex journeys to Israel and attempts to establish relationships with women who are, like his mother, Jewish, he finds himself impotent.

Portnoy's Complaint introduced a burlesque element that was to be central to Roth's next three books as well. In addition, it drastically altered Roth's relationship to his public, a relationship which itself was subsequently to become a theme in his writing.

Roth's next novel, *Our Gang*, was an exercise in moral outrage, a Juvenalian satire directed at the regnant Nixon Administration. Its immediate occasion was Roth's perception of an incongruity between Richard Nixon's opposition to abortion and his support for those responsible for the massacre of the Vietnamese village of My Lai. A savage caricature of the policies and mannerisms of the thirty-seventh President of the United States, *Our Gang* proceeds as a series of interviews, press conferences, cabinet meetings, and political speeches in which the voice of the actual Chief Executive was finely mimicked. The central character is called Trick E. Dixon, and the book's other broad onomastic assaults on powerful public figures include an attorney general named John Malicious, a secretary of defense named Melvin Lard, and a former president named Lyin B. Johnson.

In a smarmy, self-righteous parody of logic, Dixon declares his support not only for the rights of the unborn to be protected against abortion, but also, in what he, facing reelection, believes a clever campaign ploy, for the extension of suffrage to fetuses. The strategy seems to backfire when the Boy Scouts of America, thinking that Dixon is thereby encouraging sexual intercourse, march on the White House to protest. In order to divert attention from the domestic disorder, Dixon directs an invasion of Denmark, where former baseball star Curt Flood is living. Flood had unsuccessfully challenged the right of his team to trade him without his consent, and Dixon regards his refusal to play under these conditions an act of treason and Denmark's willingness to let him stay there an international provocation. Shortly thereafter, Dixon is assassinated by being stuffed into a plastic bag and abandoned to suffocate from his own thermal air. The coda of *Our Gang* finds Dixon electioneering against Satan for leadership in Hell.

In *Our Gang*, Roth's patron saint is not James but rather Swift. His most timely fiction but for that very reason perhaps his least enduring, the book does effectively dramatize Roth's continuing frustration with the egregious mismatch between contemporary American reality and the powers of the imagination. Just as "Writing American Fiction" had bemoaned fiction's infirmity in the face of events that were each day more fantastic, *Our Gang* was itself being outdone by the further extravagances of a man it presumed to ridicule. As a work of impassioned polemical intent, it inadvertently demonstrated the impotence of verbal constructions when Richard Nixon was overwhelmingly reelected in 1972.

Equally a product of Roth's antic phase, *The Breast* was, in addition, written under the sign of Kafka. Reminiscent of the misfortunes that befall Gregor Samsa, this spare book is narrated by a man who has not only read "Metamorphosis" but who also lectures on it as a professor of comparative literature. David Alan Kepesh, a successful thirty-eight-year-old academic and man of reason, suddenly finds himself transformed into a six-foot-long female breast. While Kepesh provides some sketchy information on his earlier life, including a disastrous former marriage, most of *The Breast* concentrates on the consequences of the extraordinary physical change he involuntarily undergoes. Kepesh's relationships—to his psychoanalyst, Dr. Klinger, to the woman with whom he has been involved for three years, Claire Ovington, and to the dean of his college, Arthur Schonbrunn—are drastically altered. Most distressing to the victim, though, is his inability to begin to understand why this might have happened to him.

Kepesh is another of Roth's conscientiously reared neurotic Jewish men, and he simply cannot accept this overt intrusion of the irrational into his life. The particular form he assumes, that of a huge mammary gland, not only obviously affects his sexuality but also forces him to ponder the grotesque mysteries of sex. Kepesh as helpless breast is another vivid occasion for Roth to suggest the absurdity of the external world, its incongruity with our conceptions of it. While many critics have attempted to dismiss *The Breast* as slight and an embarrassing joke, it clearly shares themes and characters with other Roth books. A monstrous fantasy narrated in precise, realistic detail to intensify the horror, *The Breast* inverts the method to be employed by *The Great American Novel*, which takes publicly verifiable realities and bizarrely magnifies them into the dimensions of a tall tale.

"Oh, to be a center fielder, a center fielder—and nothing more!" was probably the purest of Alexander Portnoy's ejaculations. When, in *Our Gang*, Roth wanted to confront pervasive American attitudes, he seized on the case of baseball player Curt Flood. Like such other Jewish novelists as Mark Harris, Bernard Malamud, and Jay Neugeboren, the sons and grandsons of immigrants, Roth finds in baseball a means of coming to terms with the quintessential American experience. That is precisely his audacious ambition in *The Great American Novel*, whose dual focus is the folklore of the great American pastime and the myth of the supreme national masterpiece.

The Great American Novel takes the form of the memoirs of one Word Smith, the resident of an old age home named Valhalla. "Call me Smitty" is his opening fusillade, in a bid to rival Herman Melville's achievement. Smitty recounts the story of the Ruppert Mundys, a baseball franchise in a defunct organization called the Patriot League. Because of its strategic value for dispatching troops overseas during World War II, the Ruppert Mundys are obliged to abandon their stadium and wander about, playing forever on the road. Smitty's exhuberant narrative is a mock epic lampooning the amalgam of sports, commerce, religion, and politics shaping American life.

The Ruppert Mundys, players with misshapen physiognomies and grotesque names such as Hothead Ptah, Jolly Cholly Tuminikar, and Frenchie Astarte, are monumentally inept. Equally incredible is the Tri-City Greenbacks pitcher Gil Gilgamesh, who is utterly invincible. Smitty's vernacular, vulgar voice rambles through episodes in the history of the Patriot League, such as Gilgamesh's seventy-seven consecutive strikes, that are absolutely and comically implausible.

Roth makes sly allusions to Jewish themes in the eternal wanderings of the homeless Ruppert Mundys and in Abraham Ellis, avaricious owner of the Tri-City Greenbacks. Ellis' seven-year-old son Izzy is a mathematical genius who splits the atom in his spare time. When he decides to manage his father's team, Izzy devises strategies and chemical substances that assure victory, but his players balk. They would prefer to lose games rather than betray the spirit of baseball to Jewish wiles.

A large book written as broad farce, *The Great American Novel* is Roth's canny attempt to twit the traditional chimera of one consummate work that will capture the entire range of American experience and that will displace all other novels. It is certainly not that work, but its humor is knowing and effective. The metafictional nature of this narrative which explicitly examines its own pretensions and characteristics links *The Great American Novel* to later works in which Great American literary creation becomes more insistently Roth's theme.

While not entirely abandoning the preposterous zaniness of Roth's four previous books, *My Life as a Man* introduces a structural and tonal complexity not found in the earlier works. It represents the attempt by Peter Tarnopol, a Jewish writer in his middle thirties to exorcise the ghost of Maureen Johnson Mezik Tarnopol, the frenetic Gentile to whom he was married for seven years in a ruinous bond that threatened to deprive both of their precarious holds on sanity. Again, an intractable reality goads both Roth and a troubled character into an awareness of the inadequacy of their conceptual inventions.

My Life as a Man begins with two short stories by Peter Tarnopol which refashion elements of the author's own life in much the same way as the entire novel does Roth's. "Salad Days" is a comical third-person account of the adolescent experiences of Nathan Zuckerman—"the puppyish, protected, upbringing above his father's shoe store in Camden," his rebellion against that background, his glory as undergraduate intellectual at Bass College, his affair with Sharon Shatsky, a sexually compliant Jewish princess, and his first experience of insecurity in the alien world of the Army. "Courting Disaster (or Serious in the Fifties)" is Zuckerman's more somber, even lurid, first-person account of his marriage to Lydia Jorgenson Ketterer, a divorcée five years his senior and the mother of a ten-year-old daughter. After Lydia's suicide, Nathan, whose career as a writer and teacher at the University of

Chicago has been disintegrating, is left with the child. These two short stories represent the two poles of Roth's writing, the comic and the solemn; they move toward an ideal synthesis in Peter Tarnopol's confessional "My True Story," which constitutes the bulk of the novel.

Tarnopol terms the two Zuckerman stories "useful fictions," and, though Dr. Otto Spielvogel and Peter's enraged wife both make use of them for their own purposes, the usefulness of fiction in subduing an intractable reality remains problematic. The manner in which Peter has been duped into marriage, when Maureen buys a urine sample from a poor black woman to substitute for her own in a pregnancy test, leaves the earnest author utterly incredulous. So, too, does the manner in which he is finally freed of his marital scourge, through a fatal automobile accident in Central Park. Tarnopol's narrative echoes Zuckerman's, as it does those of other conscientious Jewish Roth men disastrously lured by the bizarre and the outlaw. *My Life as a Man* alludes to other Roth books, notably *Letting Go* and *Portnoy's Complaint*, as well as to stages of Roth's own career and his marriage to a woman who also died in an accident in Central Park. In tone and organization, it is a sophisticated reworking of themes common to Roth's fictions, as well as an affecting meditation on the capacities of fiction.

For his next book, Roth returned to the figure of David Alan Kepesh in order to write a kind of reverse sequel to *The Breast*; *The Professor of Desire* examines in detail Kepesh's life during the years preceding his bizarre metamorphosis. The story presented as a series of notes Kepesh is writing for an introductory autobiographical lecture he will deliver to "Desire 341," a comparative literature seminar he will conduct in the fall following the final summer scene of the novel. Details of his life include childhood at a Catskill hotel run by his doting parents, graduation from Syracuse University, a Fulbright year in London where he and two Swedish women form a catastrophic *ménage à trois*, and a tempestuous marriage to the beautiful but chaotic Helen Baird.

Kepesh is a professor of desire not merely in the texts by Leo Tolstoy, Thomas Mann, and Gustave Flaubert he chooses to teach. He is a seasoned veteran of unfulfilled, and unfulfillable, longings. From bitter personal experience and from insights drawn from the literature he studies, he is well qualified to lecture on Roth's universe, in which sexual combat is inevitable and the moral self and the libidinous one are irreconcilable. When, after the collapse of his marriage, Kepesh meets Claire Ovington, an orderly and unusually loving woman, he appears at last to be moving toward an equilibrium that has eluded him before. Yet even then, he feels some vague intimations of dissatisfaction, as if perfection itself were a flaw. In the final, nocturnal scene of the novel, Kepesh's father and a friend sleep tranquilly in the idyllic Catskill house he and Claire rent for the summer. Kepesh's sleep is haunted by strange foreboding, as if his arduously achieved contentment were soon to be torn from his breast.

Kepesh's doctoral dissertation was, appropriately, on romantic disillusionment in Chekhov's short stories, and the tone of melancholy serenity at the conclusion of *The Professor of Desire* suggests the Russian master. Kafka, however, has not yet been discarded. Kepesh travels with Claire to Bruges in order to deliver a lecture on "Hunger Art" in Kafka. On the way, he visits Kafka's grave in Prague and has an unsettling dream of meeting a woman who claims to be "Kafka's Whore." Clearly, *The Professor of Desire*, more even than Roth's earlier books, is saturated with literary allusions and haunted by the issue of fiction's ability to harmonize the forces that sunder his characters. It struggles to achieve, in its closing pages, that mellowness that is the central concern of Roth's next novel.

Roth next returned to another earlier fictional creation, one invented by his own fictive author Peter Tarnopol. *The Ghost Writer* is Nathan Zuckerman's retrospective account of the December, 1956, day he visited E. I. Lonoff and his wife Hope at their Berkshire home. At the time, Nathan was only twenty-three years old and just beginning his career as a fiction writer. Having distressed his father by publishing a short story entitled "Higher Education," Zuckerman is eager to adopt Lonoff, a reticent Jewish literary master, as his artistic father. Though dead in 1961, Lonoff is in some ways suggestive of Bernard Malamud, in other ways of Isaac Bashevis Singer, just as a writer they discuss named Felix Abravanel is suggestive of Saul Bellow. Lonoff teaches at a small New England women's college and leads a secluded life zealously devoted to his craft. With their "celebrated blend of sympathy and pitilessness," his exquisite stories express "visions of terminal restraint."

Lonoff befriends the younger writer and persuades him to spend the night with them. Zuckerman eagerly consents but cannot sleep. He is disturbed by signs of strain with Hope, who as an attractive Yankee socialite had married the exotic young Lonoff and who, now white-haired, is feeling neglected. He is also intrigued by a mysterious young beauty, a visitor who calls herself Amy Bellette. During the night, Zuckerman overhears a compromising conversation between Amy and the older man. He also convinces himself that Anne Frank has survived the Holocaust and that she is living pseudonymously in America as Amy Bellette. The next morning at breakfast, Hope becomes distraught over her husband's obvious preference for the other woman. She runs off into the snow while Lonoff declares to the apprentice writer: "I'll be curious to see how we all come out someday."

The Ghost Writer, then, is very much about the processes of creation, indeed about its own genesis. It provides the opportunity not only for Nathan Zuckerman to recall an episode twenty years old, but also for Roth, who in 1956 was also beginning a literary career after Newark, Chicago, and the Army, to take the measure of his own career. Zuckerman, Tarnopol, and Roth all incensed Jewish community leaders with early works thought to malign their own people. Zuckerman spends part of his sleepless night drafting a letter to his father justifying his work. Like Roth himself, Nathan has to contend with figures such as Judge Leopold Wapter of Newark, who, after reading "Higher Education," queries: "Can you honestly say that there is anything in your short story that would not warm the heart of a Julius Streicher or a Joseph Goebbels?" During the same night, in what are perhaps evocations of *Letting Go* and *Portnoy's Complaint*, respectively, Zuckerman also reads a copy of James's "The Middle Years," and masturbates.

The Ghost Writer lacks the shrillness and pyrotechnics of Roth's earlier work. It gently blends the fantasy of Anne Frank's survival with a mellow account of how one man spent part of a winter vacation long ago. Roth is again concerned with the nature of the Jewish community and with a writer's responsibility to it. No more than in *The Professor of Desire* does this novel's dominant key of retrospective tranquillity entirely displace anxiety; but it at least teases with the possibility of earned wisdom.

Roth returned yet again to Peter Tarnopol's alter ego Nathan Zuckerman in an attempt, through such distancing, to come to terms with later developments in his own career. In *Zuckerman Unbound*, an older, successful Nathan's talents have been released to a huge audience, but the author himself is captive of his public image. He has recently published a sexually explicit novel entitled *Carnovsky* which, like *Portnoy's Complaint*, has earned its author a fortune and the contempt of those who saw it "depicting Jews in a peep-show atmosphere of total perversion, for depicting Jews in acts of adultery, exhibitionism, masturbation, sodomy, fetishism, and whoremongery." Zuckerman now finds himself incapable of riding a New York City bus without attracting a crowd of curious gawkers. Among those who try attaching themselves to him is Alvin Pepler, a fellow Newark Jew who insists on telling his tale of woe, of his own promising career ruined by a quiz-show scandal. Nathan also receives anonymous telephone threats to kidnap his mother unless he accedes to a fifty-thousand-dollar extortion demand.

Emily Dickinson had little in common with the authors of *Portnoy's Complaint* and *Carnovsky*, but her observation that "Success is counted sweetest/ By those who ne'er succeed" might have served as an apt epigraph to *Zuckerman Unbound*, a novel about the exorbitant wages exacted by literary success. Instead, Roth provides as epigraph a statement E. I. Lonoff made to his wife at the time of Zuckerman's visit to their rural home in *The Ghost Writer*: "Let Nathan see what it is to be lifted from obscurity. Let him not come hammering at our door to tell us what he wasn't warned." His agent, André Schevitz, now warns him that he should travel with an armed chauffeur and that it has become unseemly for him to be seen in anything but custom-tailored clothing. Nathan is prey to the lurid imaginations of gossip columnists, who are delighted to seize on his affair with the glamorous screen actress Caesara O'Shea. Like *How to Save Your Life* (1978), which Erica Jong published after the scandalous success of *Fear of Flying* (1973) suddenly transformed her into a celebrity and led millions of strangers to identify an earnest author with her bawdy narrator, *Zuckerman Unbound* is an attempt by Roth, still a casualty of the prodigious success of *Portnoy's Complaint*, to examine the interaction between fiction and life.

Nathan's third marriage, to a WASP social activist named Laura, has ended, and his relations with his family are strained by his new notoriety. He flies to Florida to be at his father's deathbed and arrives in time to receive the old man's final statement: "Bastard." In the final scene of the novel, Nathan has an armed chauffeur drive him to his old neighborhood in Newark. There, on the blighted urban streets where none of his people live any more, he ponders who he is and what he has lost by gaining the world. Thus, Nathan returns to the Jewish background that has nurtured his illustrious career—as Roth has throughout his fictions—only to find himself a lonely stranger in a rented limousine.

Major publications other than long fiction
SHORT FICTION: *Goodbye, Columbus*, 1959.
NONFICTION: *Reading Myself and Others*, 1975.

Bibliography
Jones, Judith Paterson, and Guinevera A. Nance. *Philip Roth*, 1981.
McDaniel, John N. *The Fiction of Philip Roth*, 1974.
Meeter, Glenn. *Philip Roth and Bernard Malamud: A Critical Essay*, 1968.
Pinsker, Sanford. *The Comedy That "Hoits": An Essay on the Fiction of Philip Roth*, 1975.
Rodgers, Bernard F., Jr. *Philip Roth*, 1978.

Steven G. Kellman

SUSANNA ROWSON

Born: Portsmouth, England; 1762
Died: Boston, Massachusetts; March 2, 1824

Principal long fiction

Victoria, 1786; *The Inquisitor: Or, Invisible Rambler*, 1788; *Mary: Or, The Test of Honour*, 1789; *Charlotte: A Tale of Truth*, 1791 (published in the United States as *Charlotte Temple*, 1797); *Mentoria: Or, The Young Lady's Friend*, 1791; *Rebecca: Or, The Fille de Chambre*, 1792; *Trials of the Human Heart*, 1795; *Reuben and Rachel: Or, Tales of Old Times*, 1798; *Sarah: Or, The Exemplary Wife*, 1813; *Charlotte's Daughter: Or, The Three Orphans*, 1828.

Other literary forms

Susanna Rowson was a prolific, well-rounded writer. Besides her ten works of long fiction, she produced three volumes of poetry: *Poems on Various Subjects* (1788), *A Trip to Parnassus* (1788), and *Miscellaneous Poems* (1804). Between 1794 and 1797, she wrote about seven dramatic works, most of which were probably performed but not published; the most popular of these was *Slaves in Algiers: Or, A Struggle for Freedom* (1794). She also composed the lyrics for numerous songs and contributed to the production of at least two periodicals: the *Boston Weekly Magazine*, for which she wrote articles on a wide range of subjects and apparently also served as editor between 1802 and 1805; and the *New England Galaxy*, which was founded in 1817 and for which Rowson wrote chiefly religious and devotional prose pieces. Finally, she wrote and had published six pedagogical works: *An Abridgement of Universal Geography* (1805); *A Spelling Dictionary* (1807); *A Present for Young Ladies* (1811); *Youth's First Step in Geography* (1818); *Exercises in History* (1822); and *Biblical Dialogues* (1822).

Achievements

Opinions of Rowson's achievements as a novelist have fluctuated widely since the nineteenth century. Earlier critics were high in their praises of the moral tendency of her work and her storytelling skills, while more recent estimates have tended to disparage both and to find her writing limited and ordinary.

Among the handful of Americans who wrote novels in the late eighteenth century, Rowson was both the most prolific and most coherent. As Dorothy Weil has shown, a well-developed system of aims and values emerges from all of Rowson's writings and gives her work notable unity and breadth. In particular, as Weil has demonstrated, Rowson's belief in the equality of the sexes and her concern with feminist issues and positive goals for women deserve wider recognition than they have received. In other respects, Rowson's novels are typical of the novelist's theory and practice in newly independent America and are interesting and revealing as a window on the nature of fiction in the late eighteenth century.

Biography

Susanna Haswell Rowson's remarkably full, active life began in Portsmouth, England, where she was born in 1762. Her mother died shortly after, and Rowson's first visit to America occurred when her father settled and married in Massachusetts and, in 1767, brought his daughter to join him, his new wife, and his three stepsons. Some of Rowson's experiences during this visit, including a shipwreck, appear later in _Rebecca_. By 1778, she was back in England, her father's apparently doubtful loyalty having led the fledgling American government first to confiscate his property and intern his family and him and then return them to England.

Rowson's initiative and independence soon showed themselves. By the time she was in her twenties, she had secured a position as governess in the family of the Duchess of Devonshire, beginning a life of service through teaching and writing; she also helped her father gain a pension, and she began publishing her fiction and poetry.

Rowson was twenty-four when her first novel, _Victoria_, appeared in London in 1786. The work's subtitle, a sign of her aims and interests as a novelist, declared that _Victoria_ was "calculated to improve the morals of the female sex, by impressing them with a just sense of the merits of filial piety." Later in 1786, she married William Rowson, and though he was apparently an ineffectual person, they shared an interest in music and theater and remained married for thirty-eight years.

Between Rowson's marriage and her emigration to America in 1793, she wrote prolifically, publishing five novels and two books of verse. In 1792, following the failure of her husband's hardware business, the couple, along with Rowson's sister-in-law Charlotte, decided to join a theater company and tour the British Isles. The decision was fateful, because in 1793 they were seen by Thomas Wignell, an American who was recruiting players for the theater he was about to open in Philadelphia. Wignell took them to America in 1793, and thus began Rowson's American period, during which she blossomed both as a performer and as an educator amd moralist who attempted to serve others through many activities, including novel writing.

Rowson published her four-volume novel, _Trials of the Human Heart_, in 1795, and continued acting and writing in the theater until 1797. Then, once again, she turned her life and her career of service in a new direction. She opened a Young Ladies' Academy in Boston in 1797. Starting with only one pupil, she had one hundred and a waiting list within a year. She continued to instruct young women in her school until 1822, but she also continued to do so through her writing. She published the novels *Reuben and Rachel* and *Sarah* as well as another book of poetry, various songs and odes, and a theatrical piece. Her major works, however, were the six pedagogical books she wrote and published between 1805 and 1822 for use in her school.

All of this got done even as Rowson found time and energy for rearing several adopted children and for supporting church and charity, which included holding the presidency of Boston's Fatherless and Widow's Society. When she died on March 2, 1824, Rowson left in manuscript her final work, *Charlotte's Daughter*, the sequel to *Charlotte*; it was published posthumously in 1828.

Analysis

Benjamin Franklin certainly had neither women nor novelists foremost in his mind when he published his "Information for Those Who Would Remove to America" in 1782. Yet Susanna Rowson, who would remove to America a little more than a decade later, was exactly the sort of migrant Franklin would have wanted. America, he said, required useful members of society rather than persons "doing nothing of value, but living idly on the labour of others." Citizens of the new nation "do not inquire concerning a stranger, *what is he?* but *what can he do?* If he has any useful art, he is welcome; and if he exercises it and behaves well, he will be respected by all that know him."

Rowson understood the kind of labor Franklin meant, and the years she spent in America as writer and educator show that she cared about becoming a useful, respected member of society. Doing this as a novelist was no easy task, for while fiction might be popular among young readers, the "common verdict with respect to novels," as Noah Webster expressed it in 1788, was that "some of them are useful, many of them pernicious, and most of them trifling."

Rowson responded by producing novels that consistently stress Franklin's service ideal, especially for the young women she saw herself addressing. "We are not sent into the world to pass through it in indolence," says one of Rowson's wise widows to the heroine of *Trials of the Human Heart*. "Life which is not serviceable to our fellow creatures is not acceptable to our Creator."

Such was the ideal that Rowson held up to the women for whom she wrote and that she herself sought to embody by writing novels that would be an honor to herself and a benefit to society. For many modern readers and writers of fiction, there may well be something objectionable about regarding novel writing as akin to useful arts of the kind Franklin mentions with approval in his prospectus—farming, carpentry, tanning, weaving, shoemaking, and the like—but Rowson and a few other scrupulous early American novelists were in effect trying to do just that: produce fiction that would be of direct, lasting benefit to its readers by helping them live happy, fulfilled lives.

Rowson's novels typically exhibit a clear moral purpose and an unmistakable connection between virtue and happiness. The strong didactic element which modern readers may find distasteful in Rowson and her contemporaries was in fact the essential finishing touch for many early American novelists. Of what use, these writers might have said, was an uncultivated field or undeveloped talent? Almost from the outset, Rowson stressed that the moral purpose of her fiction and the well-being of her readers were more important to her than financial or critical success.

Rowson realized, of course, that there were too many novels which were either trifling or pernicious, as Webster said, and did their readers no good. Her awareness was sharp enough that in *The Inquisitor* she offers a detailed summary of what she considered a typical "Modern Novel." To Rowson, the problem with such novels was that they were more likely to harm than improve the reader, mislead rather than enlighten. They tended to encourage vice and error by showing that they lead to happiness rather than suffering, thus making them attractive instead of repugnant to the unwary reader. Novels such as these, and writers such as Jean Jacques Rousseau and Johann Wilhelm von Goethe, were said to misuse the power of fiction by ennobling errant behavior such as suicide or adultery and charming the reader into accepting and even living by untruths made too attractive.

For Rowson and her contemporaries, fiction was never to make error noble and vice fascinating, deluding the reader and ultimately causing her unhappiness; it should have exactly the opposite psychological effect. Rowson would have agreed with what Columbia College student Daniel Tompkins, in 1794, called fiction's "true design and intent." Novels, he wrote in his journal, "are representations of men and things qualified to excite to the love of virtue and the detestation of vice." Such novels used the power of narrative and the feelings and imaginations of readers to move the reader away from vicious behavior and toward that which was virtuous and rewarding. As Rowson describes this process in her Preface to *Trials of the Human Heart*, she hopes to "awaken in the bosoms of . . . youthful readers a thorough detestation of vice, and a spirited emulation to embrace and follow the precepts of Piety, Truth, and Virtue."

At the heart of Rowson's novels, then, is her concern with what she likes to call the "true felicity" of her readers and her belief that virtue leads to happiness as surely as vice and error do not. In changing the reader for the better, the novels seek to be both moral and affective. They work through the feelings and imagination and end in well-rooted, satisfying behavior. A closer look at three representative novels of Rowson's will show how she tried to achieve these results.

As Dorothy Weil observes in her recent study of Rowson, *In Defense of Women* (1976), *Charlotte* (entitled *Charlotte Temple* in the American edition of 1797) is one of the wonders of American literature, primarily because of

its immediate and long-lasting popularity. It was widely read upon its publication in America in 1797—about twenty-five thousand copies sold shortly
after it appeared—and by the middle of the nineteenth century it had become
the most frequently published popular novel in America. By 1905, it had
gone through as many as two hundred editions, and in 1932, in his bibliographical study of Rowson, R. W. G. Vail claimed that more people had read
Charlotte than any other work of fiction printed in America. Fueled by the
novel's popularity, legends about the real-life identities of its main characters
have flourished. In New York City's Trinity Churchyard, the grave of Charlotte Stanley, supposedly the model for the novel's heroine, now bears a slab
with the inscription "Charlotte Temple."

The novel is also a revealing example of one kind of narrative by which
Rowson tried to affect her readers as useful fiction was supposed to do. She
does this by relating and having her readers imaginatively participate in one
of the eighteenth century's favorite plots: the story of the causes and consequences of youthful error and delusion in which the heroine herself, and
thus the reader, learns by bitter experience to love virtue and hate vice.
Rowson also presents the heroine's learning process in a moral context of
clearly stated values, thereby insuring that the nature of virtue and vice is
well defined throughout.

The main events of the novel are easily summarized. Charlotte Temple is
a fifteen-year-old student at a boarding school in Chichester, England; the
year is 1774. One day, she meets Lieutenant Montraville, who, finding Charlotte attractive and eventually deciding that he loves her, persuades her to
see him and then to accompany him to America. Although she doubts herself
the moment she decides to go, Charlotte nevertheless leaves her friends and
her parents behind and, in the company of her lover, his deceitful friend
Belcour, and her evil teacher Madmoiselle La Rue, sails to America. Once
there, Montraville falls in love with another woman even as Belcour deceives
him into believing that Charlotte has been unfaithful; Montraville abandons
her, though she is now pregnant with his child. Virtually alone and friendless,
Charlotte has her baby and dies just after her distracted father has finally
located her. Montraville kills Belcour in a duel and lives out his days married
to the woman he loves but still sad and remorseful over his part in Charlotte's
ruin. La Rue later dies in misery brought on by her life of dissipation.

This is the grisly narrative that Rowson attempts to make useful and instructive to the "young and thoughtless of the fair sex." She does this first by
anchoring the events of the story in a context of contrasting values. In a novel
designed to make virtue lovely and vice and error detestable, the reader
should be very certain just what virtue and its opposites are. Among the
important good people offered as attractive examples of the life of virtue are
Charlotte's parents and Mrs. Beauchamp, her only real friend in America.
These characters are distinguished by that active service to others that Rowson

valued so highly. Each possesses a feeling heart and a generous hand, and each knows the exquisite satisfaction of comforting less fortunate fellow creatures. Moreover, these characters have given up fast-paced city life in favor of the simple, contented rural existence that befits men and women of feeling.

In contrast to such characters are the novel's bad people, especially La Rue and Belcour, who represent the false pleasures and values of selfishness. These clear contrasts between virtue and vice are established early in the novel and are regularly reinforced by a narrator who both relates and freely comments on the story. "Oh, my dear girls, for to such only am I writing," she says at one point in a typical utterance, "listen not to the voice of love unless sanctioned by parental approbation . . . pray for fortitude to resist the impulse of inclination when it runs counter to the precepts of religion and virtue."

The secret of fiction's power to further the happiness of readers lay not in static commentary and contrast, however, as much as in *process*—the learning process which the feeling reader would go through by participating imaginatively in the experience of the novel's heroine, Charlotte Temple. She is a poor deluded child who must learn by adversity that virtue leads to happiness, vice to misery. The novel is thus a psychological history of the causes and effects of error and vice, with Charlotte starting the novel as "an innocent artless girl" and ending "a poor forsaken wanderer" suffering "extreme agitation of mind" and "total deprivation of reason" as a result of her mistakes.

Rowson tries to show that Charlotte's basic problem is her inability to resist an impulse when it runs counter to the precepts of religion and virtue. Despite the fact that she was reared by exemplary parents, Charlotte falls, and she does so, Rowson shows, because she allows herself to come under the influence of bad people who disable her power to resist dangerous, delusive inclinations in herself—just what was said to happen to weak, unwary readers of pernicious novels. Charlotte thus ends as "the hapless victim of imprudence and evil counsellors," the "poor girl by thoughtless passion led astray."

Like bad novels, the evil counsellors who overwhelm Charlotte's discretion and good sense are capable of using appearances—particularly the power of language and dress—to disable and deceive. A sorceress possessed of the "art of Circe," La Rue convinces Charlotte to meet, and later to continue seeing Montraville against her own better judgment. Thus does Charlotte "forsake the paths of virtue, for those of vice and folly." Eloping to America with Montraville, becoming pregnant and then left abandoned "to die with want and misery in a strange land," the very opposite of a useful and respectable member of society, Charlotte is "held up as an object of terror, to prevent us from falling into guilty errors." The reader, Rowson would hope, sees and feels that deviation from virtue is "an object of detestation," and vice and error themselves as detestable as their opposites, embodied in happy characters, are desirable. The ideal reader is the "reader of sensibility" who will "acutely feel the woes of Charlotte" and therefore behave so as to avoid them.

Implicit in *Charlotte* is a pattern for a second type of useful novel which Rowson employed in *Mentoria*. As noted, the third-person narrator of *Charlotte* both relates and comments on the tale, making sure her readers understand its moral import and learn from it. In *Mentoria*, the nameless, wholly reliable preceptress of *Charlotte* becomes the story's main character. Her name is Helena Askham, and, in a series of letters to Lady Winworth's three daughters for whom she earlier was governess, Helena dispenses stories and lessons based on her own experience, which are designed to instruct young women on subjects of concern to them.

Like Charlotte, Helena combines humble origins with a good education. Unlike Charlotte, she is strong enough to resist impulses which run counter to the precepts of religion and virtue. She is able to do so because, sensitive and feeling though she is, she is also "endowed with discernment and sense far superior to the generality of young women of her age."

She shows her mettle early on when, placed in a situation very much like Charlotte's with Montraville, she is courted by Lady Winworth's son. Unlike Charlotte, who allowed the rhetoric and appearance of La Rue and Montraville to disable her judgment and excite errant, delusive hopes, Helena displays the control of feeling and pleasing inclination that is the mark of Rowson's strong women, and that enables her to stifle her rising passion for her suitor and reject him. Later, he does in fact marry someone closer to him in rank and fortune, and so does Helena, until her husband's death leaves her free to become governess and then mentor to the three Winworth children.

As this wise widow, a woman who, like the narrator of *Charlotte*, combines sensibility with strong good sense, Helena becomes the central character of *Mentoria*. The several stories she relates, therefore, are meant to do what the single story of Charlotte did: use the power of narrative as a memorable, striking means of instruction for young women, a way of making "a lasting impression on the minds of fair readers" and thereby of advancing their happiness.

For example, the life of Helena's friend Louisa Railton is offered as "a model by which every young woman who wishes to promote her own felicity, will regulate her conduct." The beauty of the virtue of filial piety is illustrated by Louisa's choosing, after her mother's death, "a low roofed mansion, scanty meals, and attendance on a sick peevish father, to the lofty apartments, plenteous table, and variety of amusements she might have enjoyed with Lady Mary," her rich relative. She thereby gains, however, "a contented happy mind, [and] serenity dwelt in her heart and cheerfulness beamed in her eyes. . . . She lived beloved by all and died universally regretted." Made desirable and attractive, and distinguished as in *Charlotte* from its selfish opposite, the virtue of filial devotion should impress the reader and prompt her to imitation. As Helena writes her pupils, "Be wise, my dear children, follow Louisa's example, so shall your lives be happy and your last moments peace." Helena continues to deal similarly with such topics as friendship, reputation, love, pleasure, and marriage, using the force of the striking instance to impress readers with the felicity of the virtuous life and the miseries of vice and error.

In *Trials of the Human Heart*, Rowson demonstrates a third type of "useful fiction." Her aim is to achieve the same effect as before—"to awaken in the bosoms of my youthful readers," as she says in the novel's Preface, "a thorough detestation of vice, and a spirited emulation, to embrace and follow the precepts of Piety, Truth and Virtue." Like *Charlotte*, *Trials of the Human Heart* is a story of adolescent initiation, but rather than involving the reader in the misfortunes of a heroine such as Charlotte whose imprudence is her undoing, Rowson offers the character of Meriel Howard, who is the undeserving victim of the cruelty or caprice of others and as a result suffers through what one character calls "some of the heaviest trials to which the human heart is incident"—four volumes' worth, in fact, related through letters exchanged among the characters.

Like other Rowson heroines, Meriel is artless and innocent at the start— having indeed spent much of her childhood in a convent—and she possesses a generous heart as well. As she writes her convent friend Celia, "I am weak as an infant, whenever a scene of distress or happiness meets my eye; I have a tear of sympathy for the one, and a smile of gratulation for the other." Thus endowed, Meriel leaves the convent and enters a world that ends up causing her far more distress than happiness.

The first incidents of the novel, when Meriel is about sixteen, are typical of the pattern of disappointed expectation that repeats itself in Meriel's life and occasions her learning and uttering many lessons about life. On her way home to Bristol, she thinks about the coming reunion with her parents, whom she has not seen for most of her childhood. "I pictured them to myself, as very amiable old people—and, in fancy, felt their embraces and kissed off the tears of joy I saw falling from their eyes." What she finds instead is a "suffering saint" of a mother, her settled melancholy the result of living with a husband who is cruel and unfeeling and a son notable for "frigid coldness." Meriel soon discovers that her father—who much later in the novel turns out *not* to be her father—is a freethinker and a hypocritical villain, concealing under the "mask of integrity and honour every vice which can disgrace human nature." Indeed, it was because of her father's vitiated morals that Meriel was originally placed in a convent. She now finds him ardently pursuing an adulterous affair; after she succeeds in breaking that up, she herself becomes the object of his amorous attention, an event one character describes as "too dreadful, too shocking to human nature, to wear even the face of probability."

Soon after, Meriel reflects that she no doubt has many more trials yet to endure, and she is absolutely right. In one episode after another, she—like her counterpart Rebecca, the heroine of the novel of the same name—attracts the compromising notice rather than the solicitude of married men and the venom rather than the pity of other women. As Meriel remarks later, looking back over her life, "how hard is my fate. Possessed as I am of a heart moulded to compassion, glowing with universal affection toward my fellow creatures, I am constantly thrown among people, whose every feeling is absorbed in self."

For Meriel as for the reader of this and virtually every other Rowson novel, the purpose of the heroine's experiences is to teach about truth and error— what Meriel calls the "useful lessons taught me in the school of adversity." Born to be the sport of fortune, Meriel learns that "this is a sad—very sad world to live in.—For if we love anything we are sure to lose it." The truly important lesson, however, follows on this. Having so painfully discovered the error of her innocent belief that "every heart glowed with humanity, friendship and sincerity toward each other," Meriel periodically entertains the opposite error. "What a world this is," she writes to her enviably placid convent friend. "Were it not impious, I could wish I had never entered it."

Despair is indeed impious, and the heroine, like the reader, learns that such feelings run counter to the precepts of religion and virtue. Unlike Charlotte, however, Meriel is capable of pulling back from harmful vice and error. The proper response to misfortune is, first, to bear up under it; one's duty, as Meriel says, is "to submit without repining, to the will of Him, who never lays on his creatures the rod of affliction but for some wise purpose." Second, one must serve, not retreat: "We are not sent into the world to pass through it in indolence," Meriel is told. "Remember, that life which is not in some measure serviceable to our fellow creatures, is not acceptable to our Creator." As Meriel and the reader learn, the suicidal response in any form is never appropriate. At the end of the novel, Meriel anticipates a happy marriage and hopes both to deserve and preserve her good fortune "by exerting the abilities with which I am amply endowed to chear the desponding heart, sooth the afflicted spirits and soften the bed of pain."

Like other Rowson heroines, Meriel has found the secret of happiness. For her readers, Rowson wanted nothing less. Living happily in the real world of human folly and disappointment is the ideal which her many novels and her own varied life embody. To have found so many ways to demonstrate that ideal is surely a tribute to her strength and her inventiveness.

Major publications other than long fiction

PLAYS: *Slaves in Algiers: Or, A Struggle for Freedom*, 1794; *The Volunteers*, 1795; *The Female Patriot*, 1795; *Americans in England*, 1796 (revised as *The Columbian Daughter*).

POETRY: *Poems on Various Subjects*, 1788; *A Trip to Parnassus*, 1788; *Miscellaneous Poems*, 1804.

NONFICTION: *An Abridgement of Universal Geography*, 1805; *A Spelling*

Dictionary, 1807; *A Present for Young Ladies*, 1811; *Youth's First Step in Geography*, 1818; *Exercises in History*, 1822; *Biblical Dialogues*, 1822.

Bibliography

Brown, Herbert Ross. *The Sentimental Novel in America, 1789-1860*, 1972.
Martin, Terence. *The Instructed Vision: Scottish Common Sense Philosophy and the Origins of American Fiction*, 1961.
Nason, Elias. *A Memoir of Mrs. Susanna Rowson*, 1870.
Petter, Henri. *The Early American Novel*, 1971.
Vail, R. W. G. "Susanna Haswell Rowson, The Author of *Charlotte Temple*: A Bibliographical Study," in *Proceedings of the American Antiquarian Society*. XLII (April 20, 1932), pp. 47-160.
Weil, Dorothy. *In Defense of Women: Susanna Rowson (1762-1824)*, 1976.

Michael Lowenstein

J. D. SALINGER

Born: New York, New York; January 1, 1919

Principal long fiction
The Catcher in the Rye, 1951.

Other literary forms
Little, Brown and Company has published three collections of J. D. Salinger's short fiction: *Nine Stories* (1953), *Franny and Zooey* (1961), and *Raise High the Roof Beams, Carpenters and Seymour: An Introduction* (1963). An unauthorized paperback collection of his stories in two volumes, apparently published by an unidentified source in Berkeley, California, *The Complete Uncollected Short Stories of J. D. Salinger*, was issued in 1974. It provoked Salinger's first public statement in some years, denouncing the collection, which was suppressed by the copyright holders. There has been one film adaptation of his work, produced by Samuel Goldwyn and adapted by Julius J. and Phillip G. Epstein from Salinger's "Uncle Wiggily in Connecticut," renamed *My Foolish Heart* (1950) and starring Susan Hayward and Dana Andrews. Salinger was so upset by the screen version that he has since banned all further adaptations of his work into any other medium.

Achievements
In the post-World War II years, Salinger has been unanimously acclaimed by both the literate American youth and the critical establishment. His only novel has sold steadily since its publication, and not only does it still generate high sales, but it also generates intense discussion as to its appropriateness for classroom use. Although his productivity has been slow, his popularity both in terms of sales and critical articles and books written about him has continued unabated since the early 1950's.

The Catcher in the Rye has been cited as one of the most read and influential postwar novels and has entered the culture as a statement of youth's view of the complex world. The novel has been translated into German, Italian, Japanese, Norwegian, Swedish, French, Dutch, Danish, Hebrew, Czechoslovakian, Yugoslavian, and Russian, and has been highly successful. In Russia, possession of a copy of *The Catcher in the Rye* is something of a status symbol for young intellectuals. Although there have been problems in translating the particularly American idiom into foreign languages, the story somehow touches a nerve that cuts across cultural and global lines. The novel has also been favorably compared to Mark Twain's *The Adventures of Huckleberry Finn* (1884) in terms of its portrayal of the "phoniness" of society, the coming of age of a young man, and its use of colloquial language.

Salinger's reputation, paradoxically, has been aided by his refusal to give interviews or to be seen in public. Under his cloak of secrecy, critics and magazine writers have pursued him relentlessly, trying to discover his thoughts, concerns, and approaches to literature and writing. Partly as a result of their speculation, more has been written about Salinger than any other postwar author. Since 1953, all of his short fiction has appeared exclusively in *The New Yorker*. He is said to be working currently on a novel about the fascinating Glass family, whose members have appeared in most of his work since the publication of *The Catcher in the Rye*.

Biography

Jerome David Salinger was born in New York, New York, on January 1, 1919, the second child and only son of Sol and Miriam (Jillich) Salinger. Since the details on Salinger and his parents' life is clouded, one can only assume that this date is correct. Salinger's father was born in Cleveland, Ohio, and has been noted as being the son of a rabbi, but he drifted far enough away from orthodox Judaism to become a successful importer of hams and to marry a gentile, the Scotch-Irish Marie Jillich, who changed her name soon after to Miriam to fit in better with her husband's family.

Salinger attended schools on Manhattan's upper West side, doing satisfactory work in all subjects except arithmetic. He probably spent most of his summers in New England camps like most sons of upper-middle-class New York families; he was voted the "most popular actor" in the summer of 1930 at Camp Wigwam in Harrison, Maine. When he reached high school age, he was placed in Manhattan's famed McBurney School, a private institution, where, although interested in dramatics, he flunked out after one year. In September of 1934, his father enrolled him at Valley Forge Military Academy in Pennsylvania.

During his two years at Valley Forge, Salinger did satisfactory, but undistinguished, work. He belonged to the Glee Club, the Aviation Club, the French Club, the Non-Commissioned Officers' Club, and the Mask and Spur, a dramatic organization. He also served as literary editor of the academic yearbook, *Crossed Sabres*, his senior year. He is credited with writing a three-stanza poetic tribute to the academy that has since been set to music and is sung by the cadets at their last formation before graduation. Although not yet the recluse that he would later become, Salinger began to write short stories at that time, usually working by flashlight under his blankets after "lights out." Astonishingly, he also appeared interested in a career in the motion-picture business, either as a producer or a supplier of story material. He was graduated in June of 1936.

It is unclear what Salinger did after graduation, but he enrolled at least for the summer session of 1937 at Washington Square College in New York. Salinger, in one of his rare interviews, has mentioned that he spent some time in Vienna, Austria, and Poland learning German and the details of the ham importing business; it is not clear if his father accompanied him or not, but his trip probably occurred before Adolf Hitler's *Anschluss*, possibly in the fall of 1937.

On his return, Salinger enrolled at Ursinus College, a co-educational institution sponsored by the Evangelical and Reformed Church at Collegeville, Pennsylvania, not far from Valley Forge. Although he remained only one semester, he wrote a humorous and critical column, "The Skipped Diploma," for the *Ursinus Weekly*. He returned to New York and enrolled in Whit Burnett's famous course in short-story writing at Columbia University. It has been noted that Burnett was not at first impressed with the quiet boy who made no comments in class and seemed more interested in playwriting. Yet Salinger's first story, "The Young Folks," was impressive enough to be published in the March, 1940, issue of *Story*, edited by Burnett.

After publishing in a magazine famous for discovering new talent, Salinger spent another year writing without success until, at age twenty-two, he broke into the well-paying mass circulation magazines with a "short, short story" in *Colliers* and a "satire" in *Esquire*; he even had a story accepted by *The New Yorker*, which delayed publication of "Slight Rebellion off Madison," until after the war. This story proved to be one of the forerunners to *The Catcher in the Rye*.

During 1941, he worked as an entertainer on the Swedish liner *M. S. Kungsholm*. Upon his return to the United States, he wrote to the military adjunct at Valley Forge, Colonel Milton G. Baker, to see if there was some way that he could be inducted into the service, even though he had been classified as 1-B because of a slight cardiac condition. After Selective Service standards were lowered in 1942, Salinger was inducted and attended the Officers, First Sergeants, and Instructors School of the Signal Corps. He also reportedly corrected papers in a ground school for aviation cadets. He applied for Officers' Candidate School but was transferred to the Air Service Command in Dayton, Ohio, and wrote publicity releases. Finally, at the end of 1943, he was transferred to the Counter-Intelligence Corps. He also conducted a long correspondence with Eugene O'Neill's daughter Oona (later the last Mrs. Charles Chaplin).

He continued to write whenever he found the opportunity, publishing again in *Colliers*, *Story*, and at last in the well-paying and highly celebrated *Saturday Evening Post*. One of the *Saturday Evening Post* stories marks the first mention of the character Holden Caulfield. Salinger also sent Whit Burnett two hundred dollars from his earnings from the "slicks" to be used to encourage young writers and be applied to future writing contests for college undergraduates, such as the one won by Norman Mailer in 1941.

After training in Tiverton, Devonshire, he joined the American Fourth Division and landed on Utah Beach five hours after the initial assault wave on D-Day. He served with the Division through five European campaigns as a special agent responsible for security of the Twelfth Infantry Regiment. There is an unsupported story that Salinger had an audience with author and war correspondent Ernest Hemingway, who shot off the head of a chicken to either impress Salinger or to demonstrate the effectiveness of a German Luger. This incident has been used to explain why Salinger has written about Hemingway in a bad light in his stories and has Holden Caulfield in *The Catcher in the Rye* detest Hemingway's *A Farewell to Arms* (1929). There are also undocumented reports that during the war Salinger married a French woman who was a doctor, possibly a psychiatrist. He has never admitted the marriage, and no divorce records exist to substantiate the story that he was granted a divorce in Florida after the war.

After the war, Salinger decided to make a living by selling stories to the so-called "slicks," publishing again in the *Saturday Evening Post* and *Collier's*, which issued "I'm Crazy" in its Christmas issue. "I'm Crazy" featured the long-delayed debut of Holden Caulfield, who had been mentioned as missing in action in several of Salinger's wartime stories. *Mademoiselle, Good Housekeeping*, and *Cosmopolitan* also published Salinger's work. *Cosmopolitan* featured a short novelette, "The Inverted Forest," an involved, obscure allegory of an artist, his possible muses, and his fate. During part of this period, Salinger lived with his parents but also kept a Greenwich Village apartment to entertain various young women. He also, supposedly, began to develop an interest in Zen Buddhism that is illustrated in his stories following publication of *The Catcher in the Rye*, especially the Glass family saga, but there is no suggestion that he actually converted to Buddhism.

After the disastrous film version of "Uncle Wiggily in Connecticut" and stories in *Harper's* and *World Review*, he settled down with a contract to produce stories exclusively for *The New Yorker* and has published exclusively for that magazine since. At that time, Salinger was also his most public: he lived in Tarrytown, New York, and even visited a short-story class at Sarah Lawrence College. Although he seemed to enjoy the conversation and interaction, he never repeated it. It was during that period that he decided to avoid all public appearances and concentrate his efforts on writing.

The Catcher in the Rye finally made its appearance on July 16, 1951, although years earlier Salinger submitted, had accepted, and then withdrew a much shorter version. It was not the immediate hit that time suggests, but it did gain Salinger enormous critical praise and respect. The novel was successful enough to cause Salinger to have his picture removed from the dust jacket of the third edition and all subsequent editions; annoyed by the letters, autograph seekers, and interviewers that sought him, he apparently sailed to Europe to keep his composure and avoid publicity.

In 1952, Salinger moved to Cornish, New Hampshire, where he has lived since. He often visited nearby Dartmouth College, where he met his future wife, Claire Douglas, at a cocktail party in Manchester, New Hampshire. He fraternized with high school students in the area, attending high school basketball games and entertaining them at their parties. In November, 1953, he granted Shirley Blaney an interview for the high school page of the Claremont, New Hampshire, *Daily Eagle*. He reputedly became upset when the interview was printed prominently on the editorial page. At that point, he ceased entertaining the students and built a fence around his home that still stands.

In 1955, he returned to print in *The New Yorker* with the publication of "Franny," the first of the Glass Family series that occupied all of his forthcoming stories. He supposedly dedicated it to his new bride, whom he married in Barnard, Vermont, on February 17, 1955. On December 10 of that year, the Salingers became the parents of their first child, Margaret Ann; on February 13, 1960, his only son, Matthew, was born. Since then, Salinger has concentrated his efforts on rearing his family and documenting the Glass family. Little has been heard or read from Salinger since the 1965 publication of "Hapworth 16, 1924" in *The New Yorker*. He was divorced from his wife in November, 1967.

Analysis

J. D. Salinger's characters are always extremely sensitive young people who are trapped between two dimensions of the world: love or "squalor." The central problem in most of his fiction is not finding a bridge between these two worlds but bringing some sort of indiscriminate love into the world of squalor: to find a haven where love can triumph and flourish. Some characters, such as the young, mixed-up Holden Caulfield, adopt indiscriminate love to aid them in their journey through the world of squalor, while others, such as Seymour Glass, achieve a sort of perfect love, or satoris, and are destroyed, in Seymour's case by a bullet through his head. Each of these characters is metropolitan in outlook and situation and is introverted: their battles are private wars of spirit, not outward conflicts with society. The character's minds struggle to make sense of the dichotomy between love and squalor, often reaching a quiet peace and transcending their situation through a small act.

Frederick L. Gwynn and Joseph L. Blotner, in *The Fiction of J. D. Salinger* (1958), offer an analysis of Salinger that claims he is the first writer in Western fiction to present transcendental mysticism in a satiric mode, or simply to present religious ideas satirically. Although much has been made of Salinger's Zen Buddhism, the stories do not seem to be about applying Buddhist principles to modern life, nor do they present a clear and coherent statement of what these principles entail or signify. Holden Caulfield does not react as a Buddhist would, nor does he seek consolation from Buddhism. The Glass Family may mention Buddhism, but because of their acquaintance with all religions and their high intelligence and hyperkinetic thirst for knowledge, Salinger suggests they they have picked and chosen aspects from various religions and created a composite of them all. If anything, Salinger's characters seem to move toward a "perfect" Christian ideology—indiscriminate love.

The normality of the characters in Salinger's stories is a primary attraction for readers. Holden Caulfield is no better or no worse than any young high school boy; he is merely a bit more articulate and honest in his appraisals, more open with his feelings. Even though the Glasses are brilliant, they are not cerebral or distanced from the reader because of their brilliance; and all the characters live in the same world and environment as the readers do. Their moments of pain and delight are the same as the readers', but Salinger's characters articulate these moments more naturally and completely.

Another element that draws readers into Salinger's world is his use of satire. The satire not only touches upon the characters descriptions and reactions to the world, but also touches on the characters themselves. Holden Caulfield's confrontation with Maurice, the brawny elevator operator/pimp, shows not only the ridiculousness of the antagonist but also Holden's stupidity for attempting to reason with him. Even if he does not realize it, Holden does many of the things that he tells readers he hates. He is critical enough, however, to realize that these things are wrong.

All of Salinger's work has also a strong focus on the family; it is held as an ideal, a refuge, and a raft of love amid a sea of squalor. Although the family does not provide the haven that Salinger suggests it might be, it is through coming home that the characters flourish, not by running away. Holden Caulfield, in *The Catcher in the Rye*, never realistically considers running away, for he realizes that the flight cannot help him. At the critical moment his family may not be ready to grant him the salvation that he needs, but it is his only security. If the world is a place of squalor, perhaps it is only through perfect love within the family unit that an individual can find some kind of salvation. It is important to notice that the family unit is never satirized in Salinger's fiction. Perhaps, as Warren French has noted, Salinger will become more public once his own family has grown and left him, but for now, the family is of ultimate importance in both Salinger's life and his art.

The basic story of *The Catcher in the Rye* follows the adventures of sixteen-year-old Holden Caulfield, during a forty-eight-hour period after he has been expelled from Pencey, the latest in a long line of expulsions for Holden. After a few confrontations with various fellow students at Pencey, he goes to New York City, his hometown, to rest before confronting his parents with the news. During the trip he tries to renew some old acquaintances, has an adventure or two, and tries to come to grips with the headaches that he has been having lately. Eventually, after two meetings with his younger sister, Phoebe, he returns home. At the book's opening, he is somewhere in California recovering from an illness (it is not clear if it is physical or mental) and has reconciled himself to his lot by returning to the bosom of his family. The entire story is told through the first person narration of Holden who uses adolescent phrasings and profanity as he tries to reconstruct his "crazy" period of the previous year.

Holden Caulfield is a normal sixteen-year-old, no better and no worse than his peers, except that he is slightly introverted, a little sensitive, and willing to express his feelings openly. His story can be seen as a typical growing process. As he approaches and is ready to cross the threshold into adulthood, he begins to get nervous and worried. His body has grown, but his emotional state has not. He is gawky, clumsy, and not totally in control of his body. He seeks to find some consolation, some help during this difficult time but finds no one. The school cannot help him, his peers seem oblivious to his plight, his parents are too concerned with other problems (his mother's nerves and his father's business activities as a corporate lawyer). His girl friend, Sally Hayes, is no help, and his favorite teacher merely lectures him drunkenly. The only people with whom he can communicate are the two young boys at the museum, the girl with the skates at the park, and his younger sister Phoebe: all of whom are children, who cannot help him in his growing pains but remind him of a simpler time, one to which he wishes he could return. Eventually, he does cross the threshold (his fainting in the museum) and realizes that his worries were unfounded. He has survived. At the end of the book, Holden seems ready to reintegrate himself into society and accept the responsibilities of adulthood.

Through Holden's picaresque journeys through New York City, he grows spiritually. He slowly begins to recognize the "phoniness" around him and the squalor that constantly presses down on him. Although he castigates himself for doing some of the phony things, lying especially, Holden does realize that what he is doing is incorrect: this understanding sets him above his fellows; he knows what he is doing. Holden never hurts anyone in any significant way; his lies are small and harmless. Conversely, the phony world also spins lies, but they are dangerous since they harm people. For example, Holden mentions that Pencey advertises that it molds youth, but it does not. He is angry with motion-pictures because they offer false ideals and hopes. Yet, his lies help a mother think better of her son. Like Huck Finn, he lies to get along, but not to hurt, and also like Huck, he tries to do good.

By the end of the book, Holden has accepted a new position—an undiscriminating love for all mankind. He even expresses that he misses all the people who did wrong to him. Although not a Christ-figure, Holden does acquire a Christlike position—perfect love of all mankind, good and evil. He is not mature enough to know what to do with this love, but he is mature enough to accept it. In this world, realizing what is squalor and what is good, and loving it all is the first step in achieving identity and humanity: compassion is what Holden learns.

Recalling all the suffering and pain that he has witnessed, Holden develops a profound sense of the human condition and accepts Christ's ultimate commandment. In the passage regarding Holden's argument with his Quaker friend, Holden argues that Judas is not in hell because Jesus would have had the compassion and love not to condemn Judas to hell. Also, Jesus did not have time to analyze who would be perfect for his Disciples; thus, they were not perfect and would have condemned Judas if they had had the chance. In this discussion, Holden points out his own dilemma, not having time to analyze his decisions, and his belief in the perfect love that he embraces at the end of the book. Although not a would-be saint, Holden does become a fuller human being through his experiences.

The title symbol of the novel comes from Holden's misreading of a line from a song. His wish, as expressed to his sister, is that he wishes to be a catcher in the rye, standing beneath a cliff waiting to catch any child that falls over the cliff: he wants to spare children the pain of growing up and facing the world of squalor. He also wishes to provide some useful, sincere activity in the world. The catcher-in-the-rye job is a dream, a hope, and a job that Holden realizes is impractical in the world as it is. Only by facing the world and loving it indiscriminately can anyone hope to live fully within it and have any hope of changing it.

In the novel, Holden is also constantly preoccupied with death. He worries about the ducks freezing in the winter, the Egyptian mummies, and his dead brother Allie. He cries to Allie not to let him disappear. This symbolizes Holden's wish not to disappear into society as another cog in the great machine, and his wish not to lose what little of himself he feels that he has. To Holden, the change from childhood to adulthood is a kind of death, a death he fears because of his conviction that he will become other than he is. This fear proves groundless by the end of the book. His name also provides a clue: Holden—hold on. His quest is to hold on to his adolescent self and to save other children from the pain of growth. His quest fails, but his compassion and the growth of his humanity provide him with better alternatives.

In terms of sex, Holden is often puritanical. His trouble lies in the fact that he begins to feel sorry for the girls he dates, and he has too much compassion for them to defile their supposed virtue. This problem ties in with his compassion: he tries to see people as they are and not as types. He looks quickly and may make rash judgments, but once he talks to or acquaints himself with someone, he sees them as individuals. His mentioning of the boring boy he knew in school who could whistle better than anyone is the perfect example: Holden cannot help but confront people as individuals. Again, this shows his growing compassion and indiscriminate love. He sympathizes with the girl's position, which is a very mature quality for a teenager, and with anyone's position once he gets to know them.

The Catcher in the Rye also reflects the art of a maturing author. Although there is no indication that Holden will become a novelist, there are clues scattered throughout the novel that he has an artistic sensibility. His sensitivity, his compassion, his powers of observation, and his references to himself as an exhibitionist are several such clues.

Later, Salinger more fully develops the contrast between squalor and love in the world and reintroduces various elements of his Caulfield family saga in his grand design of charting the story of the Glass family. The compassion, the satire, the heights of perfect love, the love of the family unit, and the use of brilliant conversational language that characterized Salinger's great novel, *The Catcher in the Rye*, will continue to set his fiction apart.

Major publications other than long fiction
SHORT FICTION: *Nine Stories*, 1953; *Franny and Zooey*, 1961; *Raise High the Roof Beam, Carpenters, and Seymour: An Introduction*, 1963.

Bibliography
Belcher, William F., and James W. Lee, eds. *J. D. Salinger and the Critics*, 1962.
French, Warren. *J. D. Salinger*, 1963.
Grunwald, Henry Anatole, ed. *Salinger: A Critical and Personal Portrait*, 1962.
Gwynn, Frederick L., and Joseph L. Blotner. *The Fiction of J. D. Salinger*, 1958.
Simonson, Harold P., and Philip E. Hager, eds. *Salinger's "Catcher in the Rye" Clamor vs. Criticism*, 1963.

Domenic Bruni

WILLIAM SAROYAN

Born: Fresno, California; August 31, 1908
Died: Fresno, California; May 18, 1981

Principal long fiction

The Human Comedy, 1943; *The Adventures of Wesley Jackson*, 1946; *The Twin Adventures: The Adventures of William Saroyan*, 1950; *Rock Wagram*, 1951; *Tracy's Tiger*, 1951; *The Laughing Matter*, 1953 (reprinted as *The Secret Story*, 1954); *Mama I Love You*, 1956; *Papa You're Crazy*, 1957; *Boys and Girls Together*, 1963; *One Day in the Afternoon of the World*, 1964.

Other literary forms

Despite his many novels, William Saroyan is more famous for his work in the short story, the drama, and autobiography. Each of these areas received emphasis at different stages in his career. In the 1930's, he made a spectacular literary debut with an avalanche of brilliant, exuberant, and unorthodox short stories. Major early collections were: *The Daring Young Man on the Flying Trapeze and Other Stories* (1934), *Inhale and Exhale* (1936), *Three Times Three* (1936), and *Love, Here Is My Hat and Other Short Romances* (1938). *My Name Is Aram* (1940), a group of stories detailing the experiences of Aram Garoghlanian growing up in a small California town, marks the culmination of his short-story artistry.

Most of Saroyan's plays and his productions on Broadway were concentrated in the years between 1939 and 1942. *My Heart's in the Highlands* was produced by the Group Theatre in April, 1939. His second major production, *The Time of Your Life* (1940), was awarded both the Pulitzer Prize and the New York Drama Critics' Circle Award and is still considered Saroyan's best play. *Hello Out There* (1942), a one-act play, is also regarded as a fine drama.

In 1951, Saroyan and Ross Bagdasarian published a very popular song, "Come On-a My House." Saroyan also wrote several television plays, including an adaptation of *The Time of Your Life*. Starting with *The Bicycle Rider in Beverly Hills* (1952), Saroyan composed extensive memoirs, including *Here Comes, There Goes, You Know Who* (1961), *Not Dying* (1963), *Days of Life and Death and Escape to the Moon* (1970), *Places Where I've Done Time* (1972), *Sons Come and Go, Mothers Hang in Forever* (1976), *Chance Meetings* (1978), and *Obituaries* (1979).

Achievements

A thorough evaluation of Saroyan's achievement as a writer has yet to be made. By the age of twenty, he had already decided his role in life was to be that of a professional writer, and throughout his remaining fifty years he dedicated himself to that vocation, publishing voluminously in all literary forms, with the exception of poetry. The sheer bulk of his work and his admission that much of it was done merely to earn money have worked against him. Further, his frequent arguments with his critics and his increasingly difficult personality left him with few strong critical advocates. Currently, his literary reputation is quite low.

Saroyan's lasting literary achievement is in the area of the short story, where he expanded the genre by linking narrative form to the essay and infusing his work with a highly individual vision of poetic intensity. Many of his stories feature a character modeled on Saroyan, a writer-persona who, though often obsessed with his own ideas and feelings, is vitally alive to the world of his immediate experience. Several of the most successful stories concern childhood experiences in an ethnic, small-town environment modeled on Saroyan's Fresno. Saroyan impressed his early readers with his rediscovery of the wondrous in the texture of ordinary American life. *The Saroyan Special: Selected Stories* (1948) is a collection of his best stories. *My Name Is Aram* delineates with some beautiful character portraits Saroyan's sense of the poetic interplay of values in the ethnic community.

Saroyan's plays oppose the vitality of personality and individual dreams to the force of social institutions and the threats of war. In their sense of improvised movement, his plays were a deliberate challenge to the strictly plotted productions of the commercial theater.

Starting in the mid-1940's, Saroyan turned his attention to longer fiction, writing over the next two decades a series of novels concerned with marriage and divorce. Apparently inspired by his own experiences, the books become increasingly skeptical about romantic love and reflect Saroyan's growing cynicism about the man-woman relationship while retaining his fondness for the charm of childhood.

Saroyan's longer fiction grows gradually out of those short stories concerned with growing up in a small town. *My Name Is Aram*, a story collection moving toward novelistic unity, leads directly to *The Human Comedy*, where Saroyan finally succeeds in making a novel out of his childhood material. While *The Adventures of Wesley Jackson* must be regarded as a failed attempt to write in the picaresque mode, *Rock Wagram* is a surprisingly mature handling of the thematic scope provided by the novel form. Whereas *The Adventures of Wesley Jackson* presents marriage as an idyllic goal for the solitary man, *Rock Wagram* focuses on the crushing effect of the title character's failed marriage. Several shorter book-length works—*Tracy's Tiger, Mama I Love You*, and *Papa You're Crazy*—seem more tied to Saroyan's earlier material in their confinement to the perspectives of childhood and youth and, for the most part, are limited in theme and story situations. Saroyan's other novels—*The Laughing Matter, Boys and Girls Together*, and *One Day in the Afternoon of the World*—are deliberate forays into social areas where relationships are often intense and events are somber in their finality. Like *Rock Wagram*, each of these books centers on a male's struggle with marriage, death, and divorce. The last novel, *One Day in the Afternoon of the World*, features a character who at last seems to have acquired the wisdom to deal with such personal crises. Though his longer fictions are professionally wrought, Saroyan's achievements in the novel form are limited.

The mood of the later novels is picked up and carried to greater extremes in Saroyan's memoirs, a series whose loose formats encourage the author to reveal, often in free associations, his deep anxiety about his relationship to his society. Saroyan's memoirs, generally his weakest works, become increasingly preoccupied with death, the significance of his literary achievements, and with his struggle to ward off a bitterness that he occasionally admits but wants to deny.

Biography

So much of William Saroyan's work—especially his fiction—is drawn from the circumstances of his life that it has a biographical dimension. He was born in 1908, in Fresno, California, the city where he died on May 18, 1981. The child of Armenian immigrants, he faced his first hardship when, at his father's death in 1911, he was placed for four years in the Fred Finch orphanage in Oakland. During these years, his mother worked in San Francisco as a maid, finally gathering the money to move back to a house in Fresno with her four children. Here Saroyan lived from age seven to seventeen, learning Armenian, acquiring an irreverence for the town's chief social institutions, the church and the school, and working as a newspaper boy and as a telegraph messenger to help support the family. At fifteen, he left school permanently to work at his Uncle Aram's vineyards. In 1926, he left Fresno, first to go to Los Angeles, then, after a brief time in the National Guard, to move to San Francisco, where he tried a number of jobs, eventually becoming at nineteen, the manager of a Postal Telegraph branch office. In 1928, determined to make his fortune as a writer, he made his first trip to New York. He returned to San Francisco the following year, somewhat discouraged by his lack of success. In the early 1930's, however, he began to write story after story, culminating with his decision in January, 1934, to write one story a day for the whole month. That year, *Story* published "The Daring Young Man on the Flying Trapeze," and suddenly Saroyan stories were appearing in many of the top periodicals. His first book of stories was published that year, and the following year he had enough money to make an ethnic return, a trip to Soviet Armenia.

Except for a few months in 1936 spent working on motion pictures at the Paramount lot, Saroyan spent the majority of the 1930's in San Francisco. By 1939, he had shifted his activities to drama, writing and producing plays on Broadway. After *The Time of Your Life* won both the New York Drama Critics' Circle Award for the best play of 1939 to 1940 and the Pulitzer Prize, Saroyan made headlines by rejecting the Pulitzer on the grounds that he was opposed to prizes in the arts and to patronage. More controversy followed when he wrote *The Human Comedy* as a screenplay for M-G-M, then argued about directing the film and tried to buy his work back for twenty thousand dollars, more than he was paid for it. At that time he was also, in a letter to *The New York Times*, publicly denouncing the Broadway theater.

Even though he had pacificist sympathies, Saroyan was inducted into the United States Army in October, 1942, serving until 1945. His most traumatic experience in the 1940's, however, was his marriage to Carol Marcus, which lasted from 1943 to 1949, and which was resumed briefly from 1951 to 1953, before a final divorce. The couple had two children, Aram and Lucy.

In the 1950's, Saroyan began to write more long fiction, much of it dealing with marital difficulties. In addition, in 1951, he was the coauthor of a hit song, "Come On-a My House," and in the late 1950's, he began writing television plays. From 1952 to 1959, he lived in a Malibu beach house, an environment which encouraged him to work very steadily. During this time, he lived a less public existence and, feeling monetary pressure because of his gambling and his huge income tax debt, he increasingly developed a reputation as a difficult personality.

In 1960, after some travel about the world, he settled in a modest apartment at 74 Rue Taitbout, Paris. The following year he was briefly a writer-in-residence at Purdue University. By 1962, he arranged to buy two adjacent houses in Fresno and thereafter alternated living between Fresno and Paris. He spent most of the last fifteen years of his life working on various volumes of memoirs. Five days before his death he called the Associated Press to give this statement: "Everybody has got to die, but I have always believed an exception would be made in my case. Now what?" After much success (much money earned by writing, much money lost by gambling), much international travel, much controversy, much fame, and much obscurity, William Saroyan died of cancer in his hometown, Fresno, in 1981.

Analysis

William Saroyan's work habits were a major determinant (for better or worse) of his unique literary effects. He regarded writing as work, something that required disciplined effort, but also as an activity whose chief characteristic was the free play of the mind. As he explained his practice, Saroyan would often give himself assignments, a story or a chapter a day (or so many hours of writing), but would seldom work from a detailed organizational plan. Uncomfortable with mulling over possible styles, attitudes, narrative directions, he would often prefer to plunge into writing, fueled by coffee and cigarettes, hoping that whatever got down on paper would inspire the story to "take off on its own." Whatever relationships would be worked out would be those of deep structure, drawn from his inner being rather than from rhetoric.

At times he would begin with a "theory" or abstract idea. (For example, the theory stated at the end of "War" is that hatred and ugliness exist in the heart of man.) The act of writing itself was to clarify and refine the idea for the writer. In "Myself upon the Earth," the writer's own situation, his dead father, and his attitudes toward the world begin to weave into the free connections that substitute for a conventional plot. Thematically, the apparently undisciplined becomes the true discipline as the dedication expressed in an attitude toward life—toward humanity—is transformed through the narration into a dedication to art.

There are obvious difficulties with this method of composition. "The Man with His Heart in the Highlands" begins in the course of its improvisation to split in two; when Saroyan puts it into the form of a full-length play, the theme of the importance of acceptance in forming the new American community is finally seen as a basic articulation in the material. Saroyan also acknowledged revision as an important stage in the writing process, but much of his work suffers from a lack of objectivity, the ability to see his own work clearly and revise it accordingly.

While the act of writing was for Saroyan both a kind of thinking and a performance, the materials of his art were usually the materials of his life. Much in the manner of Thomas Wolfe (an early influence), Saroyan's fiction was often drawn directly from his experience. A letter to Calouste Gulbenkian (in *Letters from 74 Rue Taitbout*, 1969) shows how Saroyan drew in detail on his external experience and his frame of mind for most of the content of "The Assyrian." Writing, he came to believe, was connected with "noticing" life and with the sense that life itself was theatrical. Although Saroyan acknowledged that the process of writing had to discover form in its materials and that the writer had to be transformed into a character framed by his art, the sense of witnessed scene and character in his best work lends a necessary solidity to his creative exuberance.

The favorite writer-personas in Saroyan's early fiction were poet-philosophers in the manner of Walt Whitman; American wiseguys (the young grown suddenly smarter about the ways of the world than their elders); or combinations of the two. His later long fiction featured the writer as a veteran of life, sometimes bitter but with his own philosophic resignation, a mode of stoic humility about what he might be able to accomplish. Saroyan's typical themes—the advocacy of love and a condemnation of war and violence—are less important than the way in which he plays the narrator (usually a writer) against the narrator's circumstances. In the most deep-seated manifestation of this paradigm—the ethnic boy responding to his American environment—Saroyan associates the ethnic self in the ethnic community with naturalness, lack of self-consciousness, true being, and dignity of person. The American environment, while it promises opportunity with its training and its competitive games, also has institutions which seem to specialize in modes of restriction, punishment, and prejudice.

The ethnic responds to his environment with a complex involvement and detachment. On the one hand, he is willing, even eager, to be assimilated; on the other hand, however, he is always aware of a kind of existence that has no adequately defined relationship to the American world of conventional social fact. The ethnic's psychological relationship to the world recalls Whitman's democratic paradox of man being intensely individual and at the same time like everyone else. In Saroyan's fiction, there is at times an emphasis on the individual's alienation—as when the protagonist in "The Daring Young Man on the Flying Trapeze" feels "somehow he had ventured upon the wrong earth" and the central character in "1,2,3,4,5,6,7,8" feels the room he is living in is not a part of him and wants a home, "a place in which to return to himself." Invariably, however, the ethnic family and its small-town environment expand quite naturally for Saroyan into a version of the democratic family of man.

This sense of communal home, however, is not easily preserved—as Saroyan's novels with their marital catastrophes and lonely protagonists repeatedly demonstrate. From the beginning, the fate of Saroyan's ethnic was complicated by the fact that his deepest allegiance was to a national community that no longer existed. In an early story, "Seventy Thousand Assyrians," the Assyrian states, "I was born in the old country, but I want to get over it . . . everything is washed up over there." Though Saroyan could be sympathetic to such practicality, he tried to achieve, often with a deliberate naïveté, a poetic point of view that would embrace both existence in the old community of family values (which was a basic part of his being) and existence in the practical new world (which offered the only opportunity for becoming).

From the perspective of Saroyan's writer-persona, the world outside is continually new, funny, sometimes strange, often wonderful, a place of innocent relationships and suspended judgments. A recurring situation in his work has someone who is apprehended for theft trying to explain that he is not guilty because his value system is different from that of his accusers. On the one hand, Saroyan believes in an attitude of joyful acceptance: here he sees man "on the threshold of an order of himself which must find human reality a very simple unavoidable majesty and joy, with all its complications and failures." On the other hand, he imagines, like Whitman, a more somber mystic vision based on "the joyous sameness of life and death." In this mysterious crucible, life is fate, perhaps only glimpsed fully when "drawing to the edge of full death every person is restored to innocence—to have lived was not his fault." Saroyan's basic impulse is to preserve, recapture, and restore the innocence that the world has lost that state of being which sees experience only as a fantastic fate which serves ultimately to redeem the primal self.

Like Sherwood Anderson's *Winesburg, Ohio* (1919) and William Faulkner's

The Unvanquished (1938), *My Name Is Aram* is a book that falls midway between short-story collection and novel. The stories are separate and distinct, but they all concern the small-town experiences of the same boy, Aram, with his Armenian relatives. There is little sense of sequence but rather an accumulated manifestation of the potential wisdom in this world. Saroyan emphasizes the preservation of innocence, the warding off of the absolute element in the values of the adult culture. Aram and his friends turn social rituals into human games, and in the course of their experiences demonstrate that the many social failures in these stories have really two constituents, the innocent immediacy of the experience (its essential value) and the cultural "truths" and judgments applied to it. Through vital participation in their world, Aram and his friends begin to negotiate its preconceived ideas.

The setting, the characters, and the young man's perspective which predominate in *The Human Comedy* all have their sources in Saroyan short stories. The background is World War II, and the California small town has accordingly become "the home front." In the book's basic drama, the innocence in this environment—its vulnerable children, young people, and women and its emotional closeness—must come to terms with death and its finalities.

Within the context of the small-town milieu, the novel focuses primarily on the Macauley family and most often on Homer Macauley, a fourteen-year-old telegraph messenger boy. As Homer delivers telegrams announcing the deaths of soldiers, he finds himself getting caught up psychologically in the shock of the family reactions. On his first such delivery, to Rosa Sandoval, the woman responds with an eerie, calm hysteria in which she confuses Homer with her dead son and begins to think of both as little boys. Feeling at first both compassion and an urge to flee, Homer gradually arrives at an awareness of the meaning of death. With the help of his mother (whose husband has recently died), he fights through feelings of loneliness and isolation toward the idea that death and change afford perspectives for redeeming the values of innocence, love, and life itself.

The ideal of the community dominates the book. The novel implies in its moments of crisis and healing—Homer becoming briefly transformed into the son of another woman; Tobey taking the place of the dead Marcus in the Macauley family—that mankind is a single family. Though the fact of death and the awareness of death are constant threats to the individual, the book, as the allusions to Homer's *Odyssey* (c. 800 B.C.) imply, is about to return home, the coming back from the ugly realities of the outside world to the love and security which the family of man can provide.

The book seems intent on assuring its readers that despite economic tribulations, the discontent of restless desire, the anxiety connected with competition, and the confining tendency of its institutions, the community is an active, positive force. A working out in the rhythms of experience of the differences between people—age, sex, degrees of formality—invariably shows positive contrasts. The many relationships Homer has with older people are all thematically active ingredients for dramatizing the closeness of the community. *The Human Comedy* insists—perhaps too facilely at times—on the capacity of the American community to regulate the experience of life and the encounter with death.

The Adventures of Wesley Jackson may be Saroyan's worst novel. It is marred by two closely related problems, an uncertain grasp of form and a confusion about its issues. Saroyan's indiscriminate use of his own military experience takes the novel hopelessly out of control. Evidently attempting to give himself ample latitude with the novel form, Saroyan chose to employ the picaresque form, referring in his comments on the novel to Mark Twain's *The Adventures of Huckleberry Finn* (1884). Unfortunately, Wesley is much too introverted to be an effective picaro of any kind. He is intended to be a nonconformist, but, except for a few anti-Army establishment opinions, his personal idealism and prosaic earnestness only serve to make him seem as remote from the realities of Army life as from the realities of war. Lacking a feeling for the actual operations of the Army, the book meanders haphazardly from the bureaucratic to the personal, from one location to another, from family concerns to writing ambitions, succeeding finally in giving the impression of an Army journal rather than a picaresque novel.

At times the book develops an antiwar theme; at times the theme seems to be the pettiness of the Army bureaucracy. No one theme, however, is developed consistently. Wesley's self-absorbed narration does provide some shaping by turning the officers into bad fathers (cruel figures of authority), the women into sympathetic (though vague) images, and his fellow soldiers into boys, sometimes naughty but basically innocent. In sporadic, almost desultory, fashion the first part of the book features Wesley's search for his father, the essentially good man who has been displaced and ignored by organized society. The last part of the book becomes concerned with Wesley's search for a son (actually a search for a woman to bear him a son). Were Wesley's narration less limited, less egotistical, these thematic threads might have made firmer connections.

The split structure of *Rock Wagram*—approximately half the novel taking place in September, 1942, and half in February, 1950—emphasizes the drive of Rock Wagram (pronounced Vah-GRAM) to be married to Ann Ford and his resultant puzzled desperation when that marriage fails. The chronological gap, by omitting the marriage and Rock's military experience, accents the negative quality of this part of his life. Yet by leaving out the specific difficulties that are so much a part of his later depression, the novel makes Rock's psychology a problematic frame for understanding events instead of using the events of the past to put his psychology in an understandable perspective. At times, the failure of the marriage seems explained by Ann's frivolous, lying character. At other times, the failure seems to grow out of Rock's ethnic assumption that man must become involved in a family existence.

Rock Wagram explores the tensions between man as individual and man as social animal. In his motion-picture career, Rock has become successful as an individual star, but his acquaintance with Ann Ford kindles his memories of certain values from his Armenian background, particularly the notion that a man is not complete until he had founded his own family, been husband to his wife, father to his children. Unhappily for him, Ann turns out to be like so many other characters whose departures from their true natures disturb him; her lies signify to him that she is refusing to be herself, hoping for something better. Earlier Rock has met a series of males rebelling against their heritage: Paul Key, the Hollywood producer who hates being a Jew; Sam Schwartz, Paul's nephew, who devotes himself to becoming the image of success; and Craig Adams, the completely assimilated Armenian. Although these men are denying both their heritage and their own individuality, they are better adapted to the world of casual social relationships than he, and the book raises doubts about the possibilities of a deeply authentic existence.

Rock chooses to see his life—and the life of man—as involving continual adjustment to a Shavian life force, a power which, once he begins to perceive it through his Armenian ethnic environment, becomes his ultimate guide to true being. To get in tune with this force, he tries to be uninhibited in his social relationships, to go with the flow of events, to pay attention to his circumstances and to the people he is with, and to be, as he puts it, "a good witness" to his own experience and to his world.

Part of Rock's effort to live in terms of true being is a half-conscious cultivation of strategies toward death. His reaction to the death of his brother Haig is rage; at the death of his friend Paul Key, he affects a Hemingwayesque stocisim; and to his mother's death, he responds by plunging deeply and intensely into his subjective nature. In spite of all attempts to come to terms with the reality of death, he seems at last depressed, left with a sense of being part not only of a dying culture, but also of a dying world. As he goes back to acting at the end of the narrative, his feeling for his art is one of obligation rather than enthusiasm for an individualized expression of himself. Yet, as the humor in his last statement indicates, he is finally not without hope in probing his lonely situation for its satisfactions.

The laughter of *The Laughing Matter* is that of black comedy. From the time Swan Nazarenus announces to her husband that she is pregnant with another man's child, *The Laughing Matter* moves powerfully but erratically toward what seems an almost self-indulgently gruesome ending. The story line is captive to the emotional tensions and explosions of Evan Nazarenus as he attempts to sort out a future direction for himself, Swan, and their two children, Red and Eva. As he resorts successively to drink, violence, a return to family harmony, an abortion, and more violence, the problem-pregnancy tends to be obscured by his confusing attempts at solution. Since his personality is never clarified in the characterization, and since he often gives the impression of running aimlessly about the countryside, Evan becomes progressively less sympathetic in his shifting relationship to people and events.

The accompaniment to the mad rhapsody of his behavior is more carefully controlled. The children are innocent victims, becoming increasingly aware that something is wrong and even acting out some of the tensions themselves. The Walzes, a neighbor couple, have their own fights, and Evan's brother, Dade, who has, after years of domestic turbulence, lost his family entirely, conveniently defines one possible outcome.

Complicating the question of what to do is the issue of who is to blame. In one scene between Evan and Dade, the two brothers—who often speak in an old-country tongue—review their ethnic fate as heads of families, Evan wondering what they as males have done wrong. Evan debates whether he ought to be more feminine, more kindly, or strive to retain his masculine pride in the face of what may be an essential challenge to his person. His solution, the abortion, is less an act of harsh morality (as he later views it) than the result of a desire to begin again, to regain a kind of innocence by reversing events.

The ironies and the deaths pile up so rapidly at the conclusion that they achieve only a blurred effect. The fact that so much violence results from simple ignorance begins to make the characters comic rather than tragic, and this may have been the prompting behind Saroyan's title. When Evan accuses the wrong man as the adulterer (pushing the poor lonely man toward suicide), and when he shoots and kills his brother Dade under the mistaken notion that they have been responsible for Swan's death from abortion, Evan seems more the incompetent than the grief-stricken victim. His own death in an auto accident may have been meant to suggest that the whole chain of events was merely a series of accidents, but this must be weighed against the remarks of the doctor who explains to Dade that Swan committed suicide and that she had evidently had a strong death wish for several years. For all its masculine madness, this book begins and ends by pointing an accusing finger at the woman.

Boys and Girls Together is a realistic study of a husband-wife relationship that moves with an understated satire toward black humor. The husband, Dick, is a writer who finds that his current domestic relationship has made it impossible for him to work, thus heaping financial strain upon his already turbulent marriage to Daisy. In the course of their sporadic fighting, the couple discovers greater and greater depths of incompatibility. Dick comes to the conclusion that she is ignorant, trivial, and selfish; Daisy accuses him of being egotistical and immature. Were it not for the two children (Johnny, five, and Rosey, two and a half), the writer, who is a family man, would undoubtedly leave.

As this account of a few days in their lives demonstrates, what keeps the marriage together is their socializing with other couples. The slight story line follows the meeting of Dick and Daisy with two other couples for a few days of fun in San Francisco. Though only casual friends, all the couples have common characteristics: In each instance, the husband has achieved prominence in the arts; in each case, the husband is many years older than the wife; and in each instance, the difference in age seems part of the strain on the marriage. Before all six can get together, the oldest husband, Leander, dies of a heart attack, an episode witnessed by Oscar Bard (the actor) and his wife, and by Leander's wife Lucretia. Dick and Daisy arrive soon after the attack and seem generally ineffective in preventing the scene from sliding from seriousness to farce. Dick eventually begins to act as satiric observer, commenting on Oscar's egotistical discomfort and on Lucretia's performance as grieving widow. The scene has its climax in Oscar's long speech on the difficulties of their kind of marriage. While he begins by pointing out realistically that the women they have married are not for them, he finally comes to the conclusion that it is sexual attraction that gives the necessary life to all partners in such marriages and which makes them continue to put up with each other. Dick does not disagree. Soon the survivors are planning a trip to Reno as another distraction from the harsh realities around them. Earlier, Dick had resented it when his wife teased him about being a fool for sex. In the last part of the novel, his understated satiric vision outlines them all as characters in a sexual farce.

If all of William Saroyan's writing can be regarded as his attempt to understand and define his position in the world, his long fiction must be seen as his deliberate recognition of the crueler circumstances in that world—death, the failure of love, divorce, the recalcitrant details of life itself. His own marital troubles undoubtedly inspired the novels of the 1950's and 1960's with their fragmented families, and while the intently masculine perspective in these books reveals a serious but virtually unexamined reverence for love and marriage, it also demonstrates the author's own very personal irritation with wives. In nearly all of his novels, the formal problem tends to be the male protagonist's varied reactions to his situation. In *Rock Wagram* and *The Laughing Matter*, Saroyan is successful in focusing these reactions by means of intense emotional pressures, but his confusion about final blame for the marital breakdown makes a fictional closure difficult. With *Papa You're Crazy* and *Mama I Love You*, he moves to the detachment of the child's point of view but is still uncertain about the extent to which the world's facts ought to—and must—impinge on the individual family member. (To what degree, for example, does the particular existence of the parent doom or mold the life of the child?) In *Boys and Girls Together* and *One Day in the Afternoon of the World*, Saroyan gets mixed results from mining the attitudes of his male protagonists for a perspective that would be both a consistent and legitimate interpretation of their marital situations. In Saroyan's long fiction, as well as in his other writing, both his strengths and his weaknesses derive from his insistent emotional presence.

Major publications other than long fiction

SHORT FICTION: *The Daring Young Man on the Flying Trapeze and Other Stories*, 1934; *Inhale and Exhale*, 1936; *Three Times Three*, 1936; *A Gay and Melancholy Flux: Short Stories*, 1937; *Little Children*, 1937; *Love, Here Is My Hat and Other Short Romances*, 1938; *The Trouble with Tigers*, 1938; *3 Fragments and a Story*, 1939; *Peace, It's Wonderful*, 1939; *My Name Is Aram*, 1940; *Saroyan's Fables*, 1941; *The Insurance Salesman and Other Stories*, 1941; *48 Saroyan Stories*, 1942; *31 Selected Stories*, 1943; *Some Day I'll Be a Millionaire: 34 More Great Stories*, 1943; *Razzle Dazzle*, 1942; *Dear Baby*, 1944; *The Saroyan Special: Selected Stories*, 1948; *The Fiscal Hoboes*, 1949; *The Assyrian and Other Stories*, 1950; *The Whole Voyald and Other Stories*, 1956; *William Saroyan Reader*, 1958; *Love*, 1959; *After Thirty Years: The Daring Young Man on the Flying Trapeze*, 1964; *Best Stories of William Saroyan*, 1964; *The Tooth and My Father*, 1974.

PLAYS: *The Hungerers*, 1939; *Three Plays: My Heart's in the Highlands, The Time of Your Life, Love's Old Sweet Song*, 1940; *A Special Announcement*, 1940; *Subway Circus*, 1940; *The Ping Pong Game*, 1940; *Three Plays: The Beautiful People, Sweeney in the Trees, Across the Board on Tomorrow Morning*, 1941; *The People with Light Coming Out of Them*, 1941; *Razzle Dazzle*, 1942; *Get Away Old Man*, 1944; *Jim Dandy: Fat Man in a Famine*, 1947; *Don't Go Away Mad and Two Other Plays*, 1949; *The Slaughter of the Innocents*, 1952; *The Cave Dwellers*, 1958; *Once Around the Block*, 1959; *Settled Out of Court*, 1962 (adaptation with Henry Cecil); *The Dogs: Or, The Paris Comedy and Two Other Plays*, 1969.

NONFICTION: *The Time of Your Life*, 1939; *Harlem as Seen by Hirschfield*, 1941; *Hilltop Russians in San Francisco*, 1941; *Why Abstract?*, 1945 (with Henry Miller and Hilaire Hiler); *The Bicycle Rider in Beverly Hills*, 1952; *Here Comes, There Goes, You Know Who*, 1961; *A Note on Hilaire Hiler*, 1962; *Not Dying*, 1963; *Short Drive, Sweet Chariot*, 1966; *Look at Us: Let's See: Here We Are*, 1967; *I Used to Believe I Had Forever: Now I'm Not So Sure*, 1968; *Letters from 74 Rue Taitbout*, 1969; *Days of Life and Death and Escape to the Moon*, 1970; *Places Where I've Done Time*, 1972; *Sons Come and Go, Mothers Hang in Forever*, 1976; *Chance Meetings*, 1978; *Obituaries*, 1979.

CHILDREN'S LITERATURE: *Me*, 1963; *Horsey Gorsey and the Frog*, 1968.

Bibliography

Burgum, Edwin B. "Lonesome Man on the Flying Trapeze," in *The Novel and the World's Dilemma*, 1963.

Carpenter, Frederick I. "The Time of William Saroyan's Life," in *American*

Literature and the Dream, 1955.
Floan, Howard R. *William Saroyan*, 1966.
Gray, James. *On Second Thought*, 1946.
Kherdian, David. *A Bibliography of William Saroyan, 1934-1963*, 1965.

Walter Shear

MAY SARTON

Born: Wondelgem, Belgium; May 3, 1912

Principal long fiction

The Single Hound, 1938; *The Bridge of Years*, 1946; *Shadow of a Man*, 1950; *A Shower of Summer Days*, 1952; *Faithful Are the Wounds*, 1955; *The Birth of a Grandfather*, 1957; *The Small Room*, 1961; *Joanna and Ulysses*, 1963; *Mrs. Stevens Hears the Mermaids Singing*, 1965; *Miss Pickthorne and Mr. Hare: A Fable*, 1966; *The Poet and the Donkey*, 1969; *Kinds of Love*, 1970; *As We Are Now*, 1973; *Crucial Conversations*, 1975; *A Reckoning*, 1978; *Anger*, 1982.

Other literary forms

A poet as well as a novelist, May Sarton has published a considerable number of volumes of verse. Her *Collected Poems, 1930-1973* appeared in 1974. She has also written a fable, *Miss Pickthorne and Mr. Hare*; an animal fantasy story, *The Fur Person: The Story of a Cat* (1957); several volumes of autobiography: *I Knew a Phoenix: Sketches for an Autobiography* (1959), *Plant Dreaming Deep* (1968), and *A World of Light: Portraits and Celebrations* (1976); and several journals of her life in Nelson, New Hampshire, and York, Maine: *Journal of a Solitude*, (1973, enlarged edition, 1979); *The House by the Sea: A Journal* (1977), and *Recovering: A Journal* (1980). She has written essays on various topics such as gardening, houses, and travel for popular magazines such as *Vogue*.

Achievements

It was after World War II, with the novel *The Bridge of Years* and the poems collected in *The Lion and the Rose* (1948), that Sarton's reputation began to grow. Her novels have met with a mixed response from critics and reviewers, sometimes condemned for awkward or imprecise style, an odd charge against a practicing poet. Even Carolyn Heilbrun, Sarton's defender, admits that confusing shifts of viewpoint occur in her fiction. On the other hand, Sarton's honesty in presenting human problems, seeing them from varied perspectives, has generally been acknowledged. In some ways, novels such as *Mrs. Stevens Hears the Mermaids Singing* and *Crucial Conversations* are dramatized debates about art, feminine culture, interpersonal relationships, tradition, and memory. Sarton has also been accused of sentimentality and preciousness, and she has tried to shift her style to a more direct, less self-conscious one since the early 1970's, perhaps answering critics of *Mrs. Stevens Hears the Mermaids Singing*, who saw it as too arch, too knowing. She has tended to take current issues or fashions such as the Vietnam War, death-and-dying, feminine consciousness, and Jungian psychology as material for her novels. Autobiographical material frequently enters into her fiction, particular persons being reinvoked in various works and especially types such as authoritarian women, supportive women, and rebellious young people.

Sarton has complained of the lack of serious critical scrutiny of her work and has expressed disappointment as well at her failure to achieve a large popular success. She has been stereotyped as a woman's writer, presumably creating slick plot situations, overdramatic dialogue, and conventional characters in romantic duos or trios. Some of these charges are true; she herself, noting the difficulty of supporting herself by her work even as late as the 1970's although she is a prolific and well-established writer, has spoken of the difficulties of being a single woman writer not sustained by a family or a religious community. Nevertheless, she continues to affirm the possibility of self-renewal, commenting: "I believe that eventually my work will be seen as a whole, all the poems and all the novels, as the expression of a vision of life which, though unfashionable all the way, has validity." The recent surge of interest in her work, particularly among feminist scholars, would seem to confirm Sarton's hopes.

Biography

May Sarton was born Elèanore Marie Sarton in Wondelgem, Belgium, on May 3, 1912. Her mother, Mabel Elwes Sarton, an English designer who worked at Maison Dangette, Brussels, was a determined craftsperson and an uncompromising seeker of high standards. Her father, George Sarton, pampered by his Belgian upper-middle class family after losing his mother early, was an active socialist who did mathematical studies at the University of Brussels before settling into his life's work as a major historian of science; he founded the leading journal in the field, *Isis*, in 1912. He was a methodical scholar who even after his day's scholarly labors would make notes in the evening concerning recent research by other scholars. May's mother compromised her talents for her husband's career, but Mrs. Sarton's gift of "refashioning things magically" inspired her daughter's own verbal artistry.

One close friend of her mother was Céline Dangotte Limbosch or "Mamie," whose home near Brussels Sarton has recalled as the one place in the world which would not change and whose traits appear in the heroine of *The Bridge of Years*. Her husband, Raumond Limbosch, a poet who never published his poems, also figures in that novel as a philosopher.

Sarton's earliest years were spent in Belgium, but with the coming of World War I, the family fled to England. In 1915, the Sartons went to America, staying briefly in New York before settling in Washington, where the Carnegie Institute gave support to Mr. Sarton's projected history of science. May's mother founded Belgart, specializing in handmade fashion apparel. May's father's somewhat informal appointment at Harvard University led the family to Cambridge, Massachusetts, in 1918. There, young May attended Shady Hill School, a Spartan institution run by an educational innovator, Mrs. Ernest Hocking, wife of a well-known philosopher, who combined the study of philosophy with poetry. Miss Edgett, an imaginative math teacher, inspired Sarton to be a poet, but Sarton also received encouragement from a family friend in Cambridge, Edith Forbes Kennedy. Edith was the inspiration for a character, Willa MacPherson, in *Mrs. Stevens Hears the Mermaids Singing*, whose friendship and encouragement push young Hilary Stevens along on her poetic career. School plays also awakened Sarton's interest in drama.

In 1919, the family briefly returned to settle their affairs in Belgium. For a short time, Sarton attended the Institute Belge de Culture Française, which she later attended for a year at age twelve. The institute was presided over by Marie Closset, who published poetry as "Jean Dominique," and two other women. Literature was taught from great works, and memorization was required. Sarton spent that year with the Limbosches while her parents were in Beirut so that her father could learn Arabic for his research. The literary atmosphere and general culture which she encountered there influenced Sarton greatly.

A 1926 graduate of Cambridge Latin High School, Sarton recalls attending Boston Repertory Theater, reading poems with friends, and feeling revolutionary about Henrik Ibsen during these years. Her parents had settled into Channing Place, Cambridge, which was the center of Sarton's life until her parents' deaths. Sarton spent two years wanting to be an actress, doing summer stock in Gloucester before joining Eva LeGallienne's Civic Repertory Theater in 1929. She spent three years with the theater company; from 1931 to 1932, Sarton was in Paris working as director of the company's apprentices. While in Paris, she became friends with Aurélian-Marie Lugné-Poë, a founder of Theatre de L'Oeuvre, a theater which brought many new plays to France. Lugné-Poë appears as a director in *The Bridge of Years*. Although he thought Sarton had more talent as a writer, he was willing to help her improve her acting skills. Their unsuccessful romantic relationship parallels that which occurs in *A Shower of Summer Days*, whose heroine goes to a country home in Ireland to overcome a love affair.

When LeGallienne ran out of money, Sarton, together with Eleanor Flexner and Kappo Phelan, kept the Apprentices Theater going, settling in Dublin, New Hampshire, and appearing elsewhere on tour. That venture failed after two years, a considerable shock for Sarton which turned her in the direction of writing fiction. In the following year, she wrote several short stories, none of which sold. In June, 1936, she went to Cornwall, England, first staying with Charles Singer, the historian of science, and then moving to London. She met Elizabeth Bowen, who was to become a friend over the next several decades and was the subject of passionate feelings; Juliette and Julian Huxley, at whose apartment over the London Zoo she spent a month; and Virginia

Woolf. She also met James Stephens, the Irish poet, and became a particular friend of S. S. Koteliansky, editor and mentor of various writers, including Katharine Mansfield. From 1936 to 1940, Sarton visited Belgium each spring, and for decades she could not decide whether she was European or American. She began writing poetry at the age of twenty-six. Wanting funds and having no settled career, she returned to the United States in 1939 to read her poetry at various colleges. Despite feeling "the inward disturbance of exile," she felt the love and friendship of many different people.

During the years of World War II, she worked for the Office of War Information in the film department. In 1943, she set up poetry readings at the New York Public Library to provide cultural experience for wartime workers. She returned to England in 1944 to visit her friend Elizabeth Bowen, who also visited Sarton whenever she was in the United States. With *The Bridge of Years*, Sarton's novel-writing began again in earnest. Novels and other fiction and volumes of poetry have appeared at close intervals since. Her early poetry won her the Gold Rose for Poetry and the Edward Bland Memorial Prize (1945).

Sarton supported herself by teaching, serving as Briggs-Copeland instructor in composition at Harvard from 1950 to 1952, poet-in-residence at Bryn Mawr from 1953 to 1954, and lecturing on poetry at Harvard, the University of Iowa, the University of Chicago, Colorado College for Women, and Wellesley and Beloit colleges. In 1953, she met Louise Bogan, whose calm and order she valued considerably, though Bogan, poetry editor of *The New Yorker*, did little to forward Sarton's career. Other novels appearing in the early 1950's earned Sarton a Guggenheim Fellowship from 1954 to 1955. Her reputation had grown with *A Shower of Summer Days*, though the critical reception, as with later novels, was mixed.

The Birth of a Grandfather came at a turning point in Sarton's life: her mother had died in 1950 after a long illness and her father died quite suddenly in 1956. The family home in Cambridge was sold, and Sarton moved in October, 1958, to an old house equipped with a barn and thirty-six acres in Nelson, New Hampshire, a small village. *The Small Room*, a novel dealing with women training women as intellectual disciples in the atmosphere of a small women's college, was written there. It also introduced a lesbian love affair between Carryl Cope, a brilliant but flinty scholar, and Olive Hunt, a benefactor of the college. *Mrs. Stevens Hears the Mermaids Singing*, which was written at a time of gloom because of worries over her financial situation, was at first refused publication because it depicted a lesbian affair, and the publishers required excisions before the book was accepted.

Kinds of Love, As We Are Now, Crucial Conversations, and *A Reckoning* explore various marital or amatory dilemmas along with the problem of being feminine and an artist. During this period, Sarton settled briefly in Ogunquit, Maine, and then in York, Maine, in an old house on the coast, writing further volumes of poetry, autobiographical sketches, and journals. Her abiding love for animals is reflected in *The Fur Person*, a story about a gentleman cat's adventures.

Sarton's career reflects her conviction that "art must become the primary motivation for love is never going to fulfill in the usual sense." Increasingly, she has taken her stand as feminist: "We [women] have to be ourselves." Her own sexual orientation seems to have grown partly out of her isolation as a woman and a writer and her sense that marriage and family would detract from her creativity. Despite her age, she continues to be an active and indeed prolific writer.

Analysis

Based upon Sarton's student years in Belgium and memories of her own family, *The Bridge of Years* centers on a Belgian family, Paul and Melanie Duchesnes, and their three daughters, during four segments of their lives. These periods, besides accounting for personal growth in the major characters, also demarcate the stages of political change after World War I: optimism in the immediate postwar period; the decline of public morale and search for political solutions to the Depression of the 1930's; the fear of renewed European conflict attendant upon the rise of Hitler; and the outbreak of that conflict as liberal, humanitarian values come under attack with World War II. The novel is, perhaps, Sarton's most complex work, partly because the prototypes of the main characters were close to Sarton's own experience and the themes were motivated by intellectual friendships established in Europe prior to World War II.

Melanie Duchesne, a designer of furniture, a stickler for fine craftsmanship, a courageous and optimistic woman whose country home is a model of stability, is based upon Sarton's mother and her long-time friend, Céline Limbosch. Paul, the temperamental philosopher who cannot express his thoughts, is partly based on Raymond Limbosch and partly on George Sarton, May's father, especially in his need for an ordered existence and exact routine. Paul's breakthrough into true philosophical statement under the pressure of the war is, as much as anything, Sarton's own search for authentic expression. Her father's leftist socialism and critical intelligence are reflected in Pierre Poiret, the university-student son of close friends of the Duchesnes'. The immemorial Bo Bo, the stiff but protective Teutonic nursemaid, is a portrait of Sarton's childhood governess.

Of the daughters, Colette, the youngest, is the poet, a romanticist living in a fairy world, Sarton's view of herself as a child. Solange, who becomes a veterinarian, has the patient skill with animals that Sarton herself possesses. The eldest daughter, Françoise, with her long affection for Jacques Croll, a fatigued soldier from World War I, believes that art is everything, turning herself inward when Jacques, maneuvered by Melanie, marries a local girl.

Françoise feels compromised when Jacques tips her a wink as he walks down the church aisle with his bride. Her resulting emotional breakdown, and the awareness that art cannot be everything when "life [is] lived near the point of conflict," reflect Sarton's own emotional turmoil in the 1930's as she sought to become an artist.

Paul Duchesne's skepticism about the perfectibility of the human spirit is tempered by his German friend, the intellectual Gerhard Schmidt, who sees the need for individual effort to resist tyranny. After escaping from his homeland during Hitler's purge of intellectuals, he goes to fight with the Loyalists in Spain while his son, Hans, hypnotized by the Nazis, becomes a stormtrooper. This opposition of father and son is repeated in the case of Emile Poiret, a pious Catholic floral illustrator with a sense of cosmic presence in things, and his antireligious son, Pierre. The novel presents facets of the European response to the breakdown of democratic civilization in the 1920's and 1930's and, at a more personal level, reflects the idea that some persons must extend themselves in love if civilization is to continue.

The question of who one is, especially in the context of generations and of change, is a continuing concern of Sarton. It is presented through the dramatic, carefully staged scenes of *The Birth of a Grandfather*, in which the omniscient author moves among the characters, heightening the effect by the questions which they ask themselves. The interior speculation is in the style of Henry James, though the consciousness attributed to a given character does not always seem consistent with his personality or inner life. This novel begins at the Maine island retreat of the wealthy and established Wyeth family. Tom Dorgan, a Boston Irish Catholic, is romantically involved with Betsy Wyeth, Frances and Sprig Wyeth's daughter. In contrast to these young lovers, Lucy, Frances' sister, is undergoing a divorce. It is Frances, the major character, and her husband, Sprig, from the middle-aged generation, whose painful readjustment to marriage and to age form the basis of the plot.

The older generation includes Uncle Joe, an urbane retired diplomat, Aunt Jane, a wise old woman capable of immersing herself in others, and Gran-Quan, Sprig's father, a man consumed by dramatic self-pity over the death of his wife and constantly supported by his sister, Jane. The Wyeths' son, Caleb, is reluctantly in the heart of family matters, biding his time until he gains independence from them. Appropriately enough, a major scene is the family's Fourth of July celebration on a nearby island. The fireworks are, for Frances, like moments of purity amid darkness, but they also herald the sudden death of Aunt Jane and the breaking up of Gran-Quan's private world and descent into insanity. Betsy and Caleb see their parents in new ways: Frances represents human frailty, and Sprig is seen as one sheltered from the pains of life.

The second part of the novel, "Ice Age," set in Cambridge, Massachusetts, shows the threat that tension and obligation bring to family unity. Tom and

Betsy have married, and a child is on the way. This potentially joyful event threatens Sprig, who cannot accept the loss of direction in his life, which has settled into traditional philanthropy and conservation of the family wealth. By contrast, his friend Bill Waterford, who treats life with saving grace, calmly announces his impending death from cancer. Bill's life has had a sense of purpose. Two dinner scenes set forth two perspectives: in one, Hester, Sprig's sister, sees Sprig and Frances trying vainly to avert the emotional threat of Caleb's demand to be allowed to go alone to Greece for a year. In another, Tom Dorgan, innocently holding forth on the coming prospect of family life, exacerbates the conflict of generations, but he also sees that the Wyeths can admit to being wrong and remain loyal to each other. Caleb puts aside his immediate demand for independence, recognizing his father's own imprisonment in his reticence and sense of responsibility.

Coming to terms with Caleb leaves Sprig uncertain about his love for his wife, and a visit to Bill provokes the question of what real life is. Bill's wife, Nora, warns him that one may fail to exercise one's talents out of fear of freedom and power, a question which Sarton has explored in various ways in probing the nature of the artist. Caleb's destination, Greece, awakens other echoes in Sprig, reminding him of the Greek scholarship for which he had once wished; Sprig then realizes his potential for continued growth.

In part three, the grandfather is reborn, both in the sheer physical sense of the new grandchild and in meeting the meaning of his own life. Sprig must surrender his friendship with Bill, and he must test his own talent, no longer relying on Bill's support. Frances wonders whether she has not turned self-detachment into a prison; the answer comes with the realization that birth and death, the march of ongoing generations, has significance. This insight strikes her when, while visiting Bill, she encounters his nearly exhausted wife, Nora; a seemingly unsuitable marriage has worked because Bill was able to give of himself. Upon the departure of Caleb, to whom Sprig has given financial independence so that Caleb may try what he has wanted, Sprig himself turns to translating Greek plays as a self-imposed test. He acknowledges also that he has loved himself rather than Caleb in their relationship. With new honesty and willingness to assume self-defined responsibility, Sprig reconnects to the exuberance of his youth. He and Frances reaffirm their faithfulness, and love wins out as absolute value.

Sarton uses imagistic motifs such as the current in the Charles River or the isles of Greece to suggest important ideas in the novel. The shifting omniscient viewpoint highlights dramatic intensities, but it is used at times without strong motivation or without a careful build-up of character. It also can turn into undisguised narrative commentary. Moral implications do come through in catchwords such as "escape" and "freedom," which reverberate through the novel. Occasionally, moral judgements become banal. The novel has shown Sprig's life as empty of personal demands upon himself and his resistance to his children as a fearful reaction to his own aging, but the moral tends to blunt the focus.

Coming roughly at the middle of Sarton's career, *Mrs. Stevens Hears the Mermaids Singing* is the author's most intense study of the feminine artist. Here, too, the style received mixed reviews, one critic praising the music of the prose, another objecting to the fussiness and humorlessness of the writing. What one critic found to be a well-done presentation of the mystery of the creative impulse, a second found to be "an embarrassing probing of art" and "acute self-consciousness," and a third found the novel's characters "muse-chasers who believe themselves to be delicate vessels of talent." Carolyn Heilbrun, in noting that the novel deals with the poet Hilary Stevens' escape from the passivity of a feminine destiny, sees Sarton as aware that "the real artist is not the fantasy creature imagined by women trapped in domesticity." Art comes, as Hilary insists, at the expense of every human being, the self and the self's ties with other people.

The plot interweaves Hilary's initiation of Mar Hemmer, a potential poet recovering from an intense relationship with a man, with her reveries as she is being interviewed about her own poetic development. Mar, despite his lack of emotional proportion, helps her to see her own life in perspective. Married to an unstable war veteran in England, Hilary began to write poetry after his sudden death. An intellectual friend, Willa MacPherson, encourages her to continue writing poetry and provides one night of passionate sexual exploration. Another friend, however, creates self-doubt, which Hilary identifies with the masculine force in herself. She knows that she can preserve her artistry only by caring about life, which does not necessarily mean sparing others from pain. As Hilary later points out to Mar, poetry and feeling are connected only if the poet understands that "true feeling justifies whatever it may cost." One cannot anesthetize the pain of life.

Philippa Munn, Hilary's proper girlhood governess with whom she is infatuated, plays the role which Sarton's own teachers did in her youth. Poetry diffuses sensuality, Hilary learns; it creates a moment of revelation, not simply of indulgence. As Hilary's wise physician tells her as she lies in the hospital recovering from a breakdown over her husband's death, she must write poems about objects and about a person to whom she can fasten herself deeply, but she should not confuse love for someone with poetry. Poetry can become "passionate decorum" in which love is presented as a mystique; what gives strength to poems is form.

Mrs. Stevens Hears the Mermaids Singing mixes the Platonic tradition of poet as maker whose creations surpass his own conscious understanding with an Aristotelian stress on the formal artifact which has its own laws of being and is autonomous. The notion of the poet as rapt by emotional experience lies also within the Platonic tradition of poetry as ecstasy. The events making up the life of Hilary Stevens have parallels with Sarton's own life, and the novel is a justification of that life. The presentation of the poet as a solitary individual misunderstood by the world also reflects Sarton's Romanticism.

As the heroine of *A Reckoning*, Laura Spelman, resident of an upper-middle-class Boston suburb, faces terminal cancer, she interprets her growing "death-wish" as a return to the Jungian "house of gathering." It is a world of timeless personages; Sarton had been reading Jung before writing the book. She had also become more concerned with feminism and more open about lesbianism. As Laura is alienated from her own body, she works to resolve her unexamined passions by assessing her life. She comes, according to one critic, to an "understanding of life as an amalgam of human relationships, culture, and the natural world."

The novel also shows Harriet Moors, a budding novelist and lesbian, trying to put her life into art, an issue complicated by the opposition of her lover to any fiction that might hint at the truth of their liaison. It seems that not only marriage but also a binding lesbian attachment is fatal to art: Harriet Moors will have to suffer the loss of her lover as the price of continuing with her art.

Laura has to sort out her feelings for her mother, Sybille, a woman of dazzling power whose beauty and charm have oppressed her daughters. Jo, Laura's sister, after her mother had interrupted Jo's passion for a woman, had fled into the sterile intellectuality of academic life. Daphne, Laura's other sister, has become insecure and emotionally dependent. Laura has found escape in marriage. The destructive Sybille is a less flattering version of Céline Limbosch, of whom Sarton has said that she forced friends into decisions they did not wish to make and attacked their authentic being. Even in her senility in a nursing home, Sybille is someone about whom her daughter treads warily. Earlier in her life, Laura had had an intense friendship with Ella; the reader may strain, in fact, to realize it was a lesbian affair. Harriet Moors's visits for advice on her novel rekindles in Laura her memories of Ella. She comes to realize that if love is painful, then art is mutilating. Yet in dying, Laura finds positive answers in music and in poetry. The final reckoning is instigated by Laura's warm and helpful Aunt Minna, whose reading aloud to Laura forces her to consider that "journey into being a woman" and what women are meant to be. Women are locked away from one another in a man's world, she decides. Marriage may be normal destiny, but for those living intensely, a mystical friendship is the hope—of women for women, of men for men. Sybille, according to Ella, feared "the tenderness of communion."

Laura's loss of lonely autonomy is convincingly presented, but the master image, that of weaving a pattern, is imposed rather than dramatized. Ella's appearance at the end does not really complete the final weaving of the pattern by mystical friendship; the scene reminds the reader of sentimental fiction often found in women's magazines. Clearly, too many issues have come within the compass of the heroine's last months. Death may force its victims to focus their lives and aspirations, but the last days of Laura Spelman are not deeply and plausibley linked to her life as a married woman and parent or even to her efforts to approach art. As in *Mrs. Stevens Hears the Mermaids Singing*, reminiscence plays a key role. Whole scenes are recalled in dramatic form, but the very selectivity of memory and its often self-serving quality may raise questions about the honesty and sheer structural relationship between what Laura recalls and what she really was—a Boston upper-middle-class housewife with delusions of creativity, the kind of thing against which Sarton herself has warned. Finally, the linkage of femininty and artistic creation is side-tracked by the lesbian issue. *A Reckoning* lacks the strengths of Sarton's best work: thematic depth, balanced characters, organic use of imagery, adequate plot development, and motivated action. The final reckoning with May Sarton must be deferred.

Major publications other than long fiction
PLAY: *Underground River*, 1947.

POETRY: *Encounter in April*, 1937; *Inner Landscape*, 1939; *The Lion and the Rose*, 1948; *The Land of Silence and Other Poems*, 1953; *In Time Like Air*, 1957; *Cloud, Stone, Sun, Vine: Poems, Seleted and New*, 1961; *A Private Mythology*, 1966; *As Does New Hampshire and Other Poems*, 1967; *A Grain of Mustard Seed: New Poems*, 1971; *A Durable Fire: New Poems*, 1972; *Collected Poems, 1930-1973*, 1974.

NONFICTION: *I Knew a Phoenix: Sketches for an Autobiography*, 1959; *Plant Dreaming Deep*, 1968; *Journal of a Solitude*, 1973; *A World of Light: Portraits and Celebrations*, 1976; *The House by the Sea*, 1977; *Recovering: A Journal*, 1980.

MISCELLANEOUS: *The Fur Person: The Story of a Cat*, 1957.

Bibliography
Anderson, Dawn H. "May Sarton's Women," in *Images of Women in Fiction*, 1972.

Bakerman, Jane S. "'Kinds of Love': Love and Friendship in the Novels of May Sarton," in *Critique: Studies in Modern Fiction*. XX, no. 2 (1978), pp. 83-91.

Elder, Doris L. "Women Writers: May Sarton's *Mrs. Stevens Hears the Mermaids Singing*," in *International Journal of Women's Studies*. I, no. 2 (1978), pp. 150-158.

Shelley, Dolores. "A Conversation with May Sarton," in *Women and Literature*. VII (Spring, 1979), pp. 33-41.

Sibley, Agnes. *May Sarton*, 1972.

Roger E. Wiehe

DOROTHY L. SAYERS

Born: Oxford, England; June 13, 1893
Died: Witham, England; December 17, 1957

Principal long fiction

Whose Body? 1923; *Clouds of Witness*, 1926; *Unnatural Death* 1927; *The Unpleasantness at the Bellona Club*, 1928; *Tristan in Brittany*, 1929 (translation); *The Documents in the Case*, 1930 (with Robert Eustace); *Strong Poison*, 1930; *The Five Red Herrings*, 1931 (also known as *Suspicious Characters*); *Have His Carcase*, 1932; *The Dorothy L. Sayers Omnibus*, 1933, 1934, 1956; *Murder Must Advertise*, 1933; *The Nine Tailors*, 1934; *Gaudy Night*, 1935; *Busman's Honeymoon*, 1937; *The Comedy of Dante, Cantica I*, 1949 (translation); *Cantica II*, 1955 (translation); *The Song of Roland*, 1957 (translation); *Cantica III*, 1962 (translation, with Barbara Reynolds).

Other literary forms

In addition to the twelve detective novels that brought her fame, Dorothy L. Sayers wrote short stories, poetry, essays, and plays, and distinguished herself as a translator and scholar of medieval French and Italian literature. Although she began her career as a poet, with Basil Blackwell bringing out collections of her verse in 1916 and 1918, Sayers primarily wrote fiction from 1920 until the late 1930's, after which she focused on radio and stage plays and a verse translation of Dante. She also edited a landmark anthology of detective fiction, *The Dorothy L. Sayers Omnibus* (1933, 1934, 1956).

Outside of her fiction, the essence of Sayers' mind and art can be found in *The Mind of the Maker* (1941), a treatise on aesthetics that is one of the most illuminating inquiries into the creative process ever written; in her essays on Dante; and in two religious dramas, *The Zeal of Thy House* (1937), a verse play written for the Canterbury Festival that dramatizes Sayers' attitude toward work, and *The Man Born to Be King*, a monumental series of radio plays first broadcast amidst controversy in 1941-1942, which takes up what Sayers regarded as the most exciting of mysteries: the drama of Christ's life and death, the drama in which God is both victim and hero. Of her many essays, the 1946 collection *Unpopular Opinions* and the 1947 *Creed or Chaos?* provide a good sampling of the acumen, wit, and originality with which Sayers attacked a variety of subjects, including religion, feminism, and learning.

In 1972, James Sandoe edited *Lord Peter*, a collection of all the Wimsey stories. Two other collections, both published during Sayers' lifetime (*Hangman's Holiday*, 1933, and *In the Teeth of the Evidence*, 1939), include non-Wimsey stories. At her death, Sayers left unfinished her translation of Dante's *Cantica III: Paradise*, which was completed by her friend and colleague Barbara Reynolds and published posthumously in 1962 as the final volume in the

Penguin Classics edition of Dante that Sayers had begun in 1944. An unpublished fragment of an additional novel, called *Thrones, Dominations* and apparently abandoned by Sayers in the 1940's, was also left unfinished, as was her projected critical/biographical study of Wilkie Collins. This last fragment was published in 1977. From 1973-1977, the British Broadcasting Corporation (BBC) produced excellent adaptations of five of the Wimsey novels for television, thus creating a new audience for Sayers' work.

Achievements

One of the chief pleasures for readers of Dorothy Sayers is the companionship of one of fiction's great creations, Lord Peter Wimsey, that extraordinarily English gentleman, cosmopolite, detective/scholar. Although the Wimsey novels were created primarily to make money, his characterization demonstrates that his creator was a serious, skillful writer. As the novels follow Wimsey elegantly through murder, mayhem, and madness, he grows from an enchanting caricature into a fully realized human being. The solver of mysteries thus becomes increasingly enigmatic himself. Wimsey's growth parallels Sayers' artistic development, which is appropriate, since she announced that her books were to be more like mainstream novels than the cardboard world of ordinary detective fiction.

Lord Peter is something of a descendant of P. G. Wodehouse's Bertie Wooster, and at times he emulates Conan Doyle's Sherlock Holmes, but in Wimsey, Sayers essentially created an original. Sayers' novels integrate elements of earlier detective fiction—especially the grasp of psychological torment typified by Joseph Sheridan Le Ianu and the fine delineation of manners exemplified in Wilkie Collins—with subjects one would expect from a medieval scholar: virtue, corruption, justice, punishment, suffering, redemption, time, and death. The hallmarks of her art—erudition, wit, precision, and moral passion—provoke admiration in some readers and dislike in others.

Sayers' novels are filled with wordplay that irritates those who cannot decipher it and delights those who can. Her names are wonderful puns (Wimsey, Vane, Freke, de Vine, Snoot, Venables), her dialogue is embedded with literary allusions and double entendres in English, French, and Latin, and her plots are spun from biblical texts and English poetry. Reading a Sayers novel, then, is both a formidable challenge and an endless reward. Hers are among the few detective novels that not only bear rereading, but actually demand it, and Sayers enjoys a readership spanning several generations. To know Sayers' novels is to know her time and place as well as this brilliant, eccentric, and ebullient artist could make them known. Because of her exquisite language, her skill at delineating character, and her fundamentally serious mind, Sayers' detective fiction also largely transcends the limits of its time and genre. Certainly this is true of novels such as *Strong Poison, The Nine Tailors, Gaudy Night,* and *Busman's Honeymoon,* books which did much toward making the detective novel part of serious English fiction.

Biography

Dorothy Leigh Sayers was born on June 13, 1893, in the Choir House of Christ Church College, Oxford, where her father, the Reverend Henry Sayers, was Headmaster. Mr. Sayers' family came from County Tipperary, Ireland; his wife, the former Helen Mary Leigh, was a member of the old landed English family that also produced Percival Leigh, a noted contributor to the humor magazine, *Punch*. Sayers' biographer, James Brabazon, postulates that her preference for the Leigh side of the family caused her to insist upon including her middle initial in her name; whatever the reason, the writer wished to be known as Dorothy L. Sayers.

When Sayers was four, her father left Oxford to accept the living of Bluntisham-cum-Earith in Huntingdonshire, on the southern edge of the Fens, those bleak expanses of drained marshland in eastern England. The contrast between Oxford and the rectory at Bluntisham was great, especially as the new home isolated the family and its only child. Sayers' fine education in Latin, English, French, history, and mathematics was conducted at the rectory until she was almost sixteen, when she was sent to study at the Godolphin School, Salisbury, where she seems to have been quite unhappy. Several of her happiest years followed this experience, however, when she won the Gilchrist Scholarship in Modern Languages and went up to Somerville College, Oxford, in 1912. At Somerville, Sayers enjoyed the congenial company of other extraordinary women and men and made some lasting friends, including Muriel St. Clare Byrne. Although women were not granted Oxford degrees during Sayers' time at Somerville, the University's statutes were changed in 1920, and Sayers was among the first group of women to receive Oxford degrees in that year (she had taken first honors in her examination in 1915).

Following her undergraduate days, Sayers did various kinds of work for several years: first, as poetry editor for Blackwell's in Oxford from 1916 to 1918, then as a schoolmistress in France in 1919, and finally in London, where she worked as a free-lance editor and as an advertising copywriter for Benson's, England's largest advertising agency. At Benson's, Sayers helped create "The Mustard Club," a phenomenally successful campaign for Colman's mustard. Around 1920, when Sayers' mind was focused not only upon finding suitable employment but also upon surviving economically, the character of Lord Peter Wimsey was miraculously born, and Sayers' first novel, *Whose Body?*, introduced him to the world in 1923.

These early years in London were scarred by two bitterly disappointing love affairs, one of which left Sayers with a child, born in 1924. The novelist married Oswald Atherton Fleming, a Scottish journalist, in 1926, and shortly thereafter assumed financial responsibility for him as he became ill and ceased working several years after their marriage. Perhaps these pressures encouraged Sayers to keep turning out the increasingly successful Wimsey novels.

By the end of the 1930's, however, Sayers was in a position to "finish Lord Peter off" by marrying him to Harriet Vane, the detective novelist who first appeared in *Strong Poison* and who, like Wimsey, reflected part of Sayers' personality. After the Wimsey novels, Sayers was free to do the kind of writing she had always wanted to do: manifestly serious work such as religious dramas and a translation of Dante that would occupy most of her time from 1944 to 1957. While working on these demanding projects and writing incisive essays on a wide range of issues, Sayers also became something of a public figure, playing the role of social critic and Christian apologist with great brilliance and panache.

On December 17, 1957, Sayers died of an apparent stroke while alone in the house that she had shared with Fleming from 1928 until his death in 1950. Although she left an unpublished autobiographical fragment, "My Edwardian Childhood," much of Sayers' life is reflected in her novels, which depict the Oxford of her college days (*Gaudy Night*), the Fen wastes of her girlhood (*The Nine Tailors*), and the excitement and confusion of the London she knew as a young writer (*Murder Must Advertise*). Excellent though much of her other work is, Sayers will probably be remembered primarily for her novels.

Analysis

If one should wish to know England as it was between the two world wars—how it was in its customs, among its different classes and in its different regions, how it regarded itself and the world, what weaknesses festered, what strengths endured—there is no better place to learn its soul or to revel in its singular delights and peccadilloes than in the novels of Dorothy L. Sayers. When Harriet Vane marries Peter Wimsey in *Busman's Honeymoon*, she happily realizes that she has "married England," revealing that Sayers herself recognized the symbolic import of her hero. As a survivor of World War I, a war that decimated a generation of young Englishmen and left their society reeling, Wimsey represents England's fragile link with a glorious past and its tenuous hold on the difficult present. His bouts of "nerves" and persistent nightmares dramatize the lasting effects of this "War to End All Wars," while his noble attempts at making a meaningful life represent the difficult task of re-creating life from the rubble.

Sayers' England encompasses tiny villages unchanged for centuries (*Busman's Honeymoon*), the golden-spired colleges of Oxford (*Gaudy Night*), the "gloom and gleam" of London (*Murder Must Advertise*), the deceptive calm of the southern seacoast (*Have His Carcase*), the brooding Fens (*The Nine Tailors*), and the primitive north counties (*Clouds of Witness*). The novelist ranges throughout this varied landscape with some constants: accompanied by his indefatigable "man," Bunter (who is Jeeves transformed), Lord Peter reasons his way through all but one mystery (he is absent from *The Documents in the Case*). Through Wimsey's well-wrought consciousness, Sayers maintains a certain *Weltanschauung* that seems a peculiar blend of mathematical rigor and lush, witty, insightful language.

Carolyn Heilbrun's praise for Sayers' special blend of "murder and manners" points out to an understanding of both the novelist's appeal and her place in English fiction: Sayers is an inheritor not only of the more literary branch of detective fiction, but also of the older comedy-of-manners tradition. She can reveal a character, time, or place in a bit of dialogue or one remark. From a brief sentence, for example, the reader knows the Duchess of Denver: "She was a long-necked, long-backed woman, who disciplined herself and her children." A short speech summarizes all *The Unpleasantness at the Bellona Club*, revealing not only a character but also the values and condition of his world:

> Look at all the disturbance there has been lately. Police and reporters—and then Penberthy blowing his brains out in the library. And the coal's all slate. . . . These things never happened before the War—and great heavens! William! Look at this wine! . . . Corked? Yes, I should think it *was* corked! My God! I don't know what's come to this club!

The character upon whom Sayers lavishes most of her considerable talent is Lord Peter. Although it is possible, as some of her critics have said, that Sayers created Wimsey, the perfect mate for an intellectual woman, because actual men had disappointed her, the psychobiographical approach can explain only part of her novels' motivation or meaning. In Wimsey, Sayers dramatizes some significant human problems, including the predicament of the "Lost Generation," the necessity of every person's having a "proper job," and the imperative synthesis of forces that are often perceived as opposites, but which are really complementary: intellect and emotion, good and evil, male and female. When viewed in these terms, Sayers' fictional world fits naturally into the entire cosmos of her creation, because it deals with some of the very subjects she addressed in other, more patently serious forms.

It is appropriate to speak of all Sayers' work as one, for, as she concludes in *The Mind of the Maker*, "the sum of all the work is related to the mind [of the artist] itself, which made it, controls it, and relates it to its own creative personality." From beginning to end, Sayers' work investigates the possibility of creative action; for her the creative act consists of establishing equilibrium among competing powers, of drawing together disparate, even warring elements. Of course, since she writes detective novels, Sayers focuses upon the opposite of creative action in the crimes of her villains, crimes that destroy life, property, sanity, peace. Wimsey, who solves the mysteries and thereby makes a life from destruction, is the creative actor.

The Mind of the Maker argues that there is a discoverable moral law, higher than any other, that governs the universe. In a way, Sayers' novels attempt to discover or reveal this universal moral law, which in its most superficial form is reflected in civil codes. This process of moral discovery, however, becomes increasingly complex and ambiguous; if Sayers' subjects are constant, her understanding of them deepens as her art matures. Since Sayers' artistic maturation parallels her hero's development, a comparison of how Wimsey functions in the early and late novels will elucidate both the consistency and the change that mark Sayers' fiction.

The most striking quality of *Whose Body?* as a first novel is the deftness with which it presents Sayers' hero and his world. In its opening pages, the reader gets to know Lord Peter Wimsey, the dashing man-about-town and collector of rare books (which, amazingly, he seems to read). Keen of mind and quick of tongue, like an exotic bird chirping in a formal English garden that, perhaps, conceals a jolly corpse or two, he is a remarkable personage at birth. Wimsey is also quite marvelously a wealthy man who knows how to spend both his time and his money; his elegant apartment's only acknowledged lack is a harpsichord for his accomplished renditions of Domenico Scarlatti. The product of an older England marked by civility, restraint, and order, Wimsey is accompanied in his first tale by two challengers to his wits and position: his valet, Bunter, and the middle-class Inspector Parker of Scotland Yard, who will make sure that Wimsey never nods during fourteen years of fictional sleuthing. Even his mother, the delightfully balmy Duchess of Denver, is introduced here, and the reader quickly guesses from their relationship that Sayers is interested in how men and women coexist in this world. The Dowager Duchess and her son are as different in appearance as they are similar in character, the narrator remarks, thus signaling that the superficial differences between men and women often conceal more important similarities. Wimsey and his entourage enter the world nearly complete, and their creator has a firm grasp of character, dialogue, and the mystery plot from the beginning of her career.

The theme of *Whose Body?* plants the seeds of one of Sayers' ever-flourishing ideas. Her first and perhaps most horrid villain, Sir Julian Freke, suffers from one of the great problems facing modern man: the disassociation from mind and heart that often renders "civilized" people incapable of moral behavior. The great surgeon Freke, who is aptly named because he is a freakish half-human, denies the importance of intangibles such as the conscience, which he considers akin to the vermiform appendix. With this perfectly criminal attitude, Freke coolly kills and dissects an old competitor, ironically from one of the oldest, least rational of motives, jealousy and revenge. Freke therefore demonstrates Sayers' point: that man, as a creature of both intellect and passion, must struggle to understand and balance both if moral action is to be possible. Freke, the dissector of life, destroys; the destruction he causes awaits the truly healing powers of a creative mind.

The somewhat surprising link between moral action and detective work is suggested by Wimsey, who observes that anyone can get away with murder by keeping people from "associatin' their ideas," adding that people usually do not connect the parts of their experience. The good detective, however, must study the fragments of human life and synthesize the relevant data. This synthesis, the product of imagination and feeling as well as reason, reveals not only "who did it," but how, and why. Thus, according to Sayers' own definitions, her detective pursues moral action in his very sleuthing, not only in its final effects of punishment for the criminal and retribution for society. Wimsey's detective method typifies this creative synthesis by incorporating different aspects of a rich experience: poetry, science, history, psychology, haberdashery, weather reports. When Wimsey finally realizes that Freke is the murderer, he remembers "not one thing, nor another thing, nor a logical succession of things, but everything—the whole thing, perfect and complete . . . as if he stood outside the world and saw it suspended in infinitely dimensional space." In this moment, Wimsey is not merely a successful detective, he is a creator, his mind flashing with godlike insight into human life. The story has moved, therefore, from destruction to creation because disparate aspects of life have been drawn together.

Freke's failure as a human being is exemplified in his failure as a physician, just as Wimsey's successful life is instanced in the skillful performance of his "job," his compulsive "hobby of sleuthing." More than a hobby, detection is actually Wimsey's "proper job." In a crucial discussion with Inspector Parker, Wimsey admits to feeling guilty about doing detective work for fun, but the perceptive Parker warns him that, as a basically responsible person for whom life is really more than a game, he will eventually have to come to terms with the seriousness of his actions. What is clear to the reader at this point is that Wimsey, an English aristocrat displaced by social change and scarred by World War I, is at least carving out a life that is socially useful while it is personally gratifying. He is not simply feeding the Duke of Denver's peacocks.

If Wimsey seems almost too perfect in the early novels, Sayers redeems him from that state by slowly revealing the finite, flawed, and very human man within the sparkling exterior. To make this revelation, she has to create a woman capable of challenging him, which she does in the character of Harriet Vane. By the time he appears in *The Nine Tailors*, Wimsey is less of a god and more of a human being. After all, the great lover has been humiliatingly unsuccessful in wooing Harriet Vane, whom he saved from the hangman four years earlier in *Strong Poison*. The beginning of *The Nine Tailors* finds Wimsey, the super-sleuth, wandering about the Fens, that bleak terrain of Sayers' childhood, muttering about the misery of having one's car break down on a wintery evening and dreaming of hot muffins. When offered shelter at the rectory of Fenchurch St. Paul, the great connoisseur of haute cuisine is delighted with tea and oxtail stew. The greatest change in Wimsey's character and in Sayers' fiction, however, is evidenced in the novel's richer, more subtle structure, and in its newly complex view of crime and punishment, of good and evil.

Indicative of Sayers' increasing subtlety, *The Nine Tailors* is as much a metaphysical meditation on time and change as it is a murder mystery; there is not even a corpse until Part II. In place of Lord Peter's jolly but rather macabre singing of "We insist upon a [dead] body in a bath" (in *Whose Body?*), *The Nine Tailors* resonates with the sound of church bells and an explication of campanology (bell or change-ringing). The bells at Fenchurch St. Paul, which are rung for both weddings and funerals, seem ambiguously to stand for both life and death, good and evil. The whole question of good versus evil is quite complicted here, for unlike the wholly innocent victim of the cold-blooded murder in *Whose Body?*, the man killed here is probably the worst person in the book, and he is accidentally killed by the ringing of holy bells. Locked in the church's bell chamber as a precaution by someone who knows of his criminal past, Geoffrey Deacon is killed by the intense sound of the bells, and ultimately by the hands of every man who unwittingly pulls a bell rope that New Year's Eve. This group includes Wimsey, who just happens to be there because of several coincidences.

Although Deacon perhaps deserves to die, not only for his jewel robbery but also because of a generally dishonorable life, his death forces Wimsey to reexamine himself and his motives. In ringing the changes, Wimsey thought he was simply following a set of mathematical permutations to a neat conclusion; in reality, he was taking a man's life. This greatly sobers the old puzzle-solver, who has always had some qualms about attacking life as a game. Indeed, Wimsey's role in Deacon's death is but an exaggerated version of the detective's role in any mystery: he causes the villain or criminal to come to justice, which usually means death. Wimsey cannot ignore the consequences of his actions in *The Nine Tailors*, because they are direct, obvious, and significant in human terms. He voices his concern about the morality of all his "meddling" to the rector, who assures him that everyone must "follow the truth," on the assumption that this path will lead invariably if somewhat indirectly to God, who has "all the facts" in the great case of life. Thus, it is impossible to be too curious, to probe too far, to ask too many questions, even though some answers or consequences may be painful.

In this great novel, Wimsey actually experiences the central Christian paradox, that of good coming from evil or of the two being inextricably linked. The mystery is over when he realizes, in a grisly pun, that Deacon's killers are already hanged, since they are the very bells in the church's tower. As one of the inscriptions on this ancient church says, the nine tailors, or the nine peals, "make a man," suggesting that the bells not only signify a man when they toll his passing, but also stand as timeless, disinterested judges of human behavior. The dead man, Deacon, mocked honorable work in his thievery, and thus began the cycle of destruction that ends in his own death, a death which ironically leads to Wimsey's discovery or creative act. From evil thus confronted and comprehended, good may grow. Mr. Venables, the rector, wittily pricks Wimsey with the irony that "there's always something that lies behind a mystery . . . a solution of some kind." For Wimsey, as for Sayers, even the solution to a mystery leads to further mysteries; the answer to the mystery of Deacon's death leads to a more subtle inquiry into one of the essential mysteries of life: how to determine responsibility or meaning for human action. In this paradoxical world, victims may be villians and right action is often based in error, chance, or even transgression.

Wimsey leaves this complex novel with greater insight into himself and the ambiguous nature of life; he is, therefore, finally ready to come to terms with the greatest mystery of his life, Harriet Vane, who is also about ready to accept his inquiry. In *Gaudy Night*, Wimsey reaches his fulfillment, a fulfillment that is expressed in terms of resolving the conflict between man and woman, between intellect and emotion, and between good and evil. In fact, Wimsey's fulfillment represents the culmination of Sayers' search for a resolution of these forces. The novel's subject is also one of Sayers' oldest: the moral imperative for every person to do good work that is well done, and the terrible consequences of not doing so. All of these ideas come into play in this subtle novel, which is on one level the mystery of the "Shrewsbury Poison Pen" and on another, more important one, an unusual and profound love story. Reflecting the subtlety and delicacy with which Sayers spins her tale, there is not even a death in this book; the psychological violence caused by the Poison Pen is alarming, but here evil is banal, and all the more powerful for being so.

Gaudy Night takes place at Oxford, which held happy memories for Sayers as the place of her birth and formal education, and the entire novel is a paean to that golden-spired city. Harriet Vane goes to Oxford to attend the Shrewsbury Gaudy, an annual spring homecoming celebration, where she has the opportunity to judge her old classmates and teachers in terms of how well they, as women, have been able to live meaningful lives. Shrewsbury is obviously a fictional version of Somerville, Sayers' college, and just as clearly Vane, a famous detective novelist who is wrestling with the question of "woman's work" and with the problem of rendering reality in fiction, is to some extent Sayers, the self-conscious artist. Having been pursued by Wimsey for five frustrating years, Vane finally accepts him at the end of *Gaudy Night*. She accepts him because the experiences in this book teach her three interrelated things: that Wimsey, as an extraordinary man, will not prevent her from doing her "proper job," a consequence she feared from any relationship with a man; that men and women can live together and not destroy each other, but create a good life; and therefore, that there can be an alliance between the "intellect and the flesh." Vane's discoveries in this novel thus signal the solution of problems that had preoccupied Sayers throughout her career.

Vane learns all of these things through Wimsey's unraveling of the mystery of the Poisen Pen, who is a woman frightfully flawed because she has never been able to strike a balance between the intellect and the flesh, and therefore has never done her proper job. Annie Wilson, the Poison Pen who creates so much confusion and instills so much fear in the intellectual women of Shrewsbury, is the victim of sentimentality and a radically disassociated sensibility; she hates all learning because her dead husband was punished long ago for academic dishonesty. Ironically, Harriet Vane suffers from the same problem, but in its other manifestation; she begins the novel capable of trusting only the intellect, and fears any bonds of the flesh or heart. When she finally sees that neither the sentimentality of Annie nor the hyperintellectualism of Shrewsbury can solve the "problem of life," Harriet realizes that it is only through balancing intellect and passion that creative or truly human action is possible.

Wimsey, who solves the mystery because he is able to bring these forces into equilibrium and to acknowledge the potency of both, is rendered acceptable to Vane because of this ability. Her new willingness to admit her feelings reveals to her what Sayers' readers had known for a long time: she loves Wimsey. The man she loves has changed, too. He is no longer an unattainable paragon who sees good and evil as discrete and life as a game, but a middle-aged man who fears rejection and death, who is idiotically vain about his hands, and who, to Harriet's surprise, looks as vulnerable as anyone else when he falls asleep: the man behind the monocle. All of this does not argue that Wimsey is less extraordinary than he was; in fact, perhaps what is most extraordinary about him now is that he seems a real person—flawed, finite, vulnerable—who is yet capable of that rare thing, creative action. Indeed, his very life seems a work of art.

Wimsey and Vane finally embark upon marriage, that most mundane and mysterious of journeys, in *Busman's Honeymoon*, the final novel that Sayers aptly called a "love story with detective interruptions": the detective novelist had moved that far from the formula. In the closing scene of this last novel, Wimsey admits that his new wife is "his corner," the place where he can hide from a hostile, confusing world and shed tears for the murderer whose execution he caused. This is not the Wimsey who blithely dashed about in the early novels, treating criminals as fair game in an intellectual hunting expedition, but it is the man he could have become after fourteen years of living, suffering, and reflecting. Indeed, it was a masterful stroke for Sayers to create Harriet Vane, a woman who could match Wimsey's wits and passions, because through her and through his loving her, the reader can learn the most intimate facts of this once-distant hero. If a man is to cry in front of anyone, that witness should most likely be his wife, especially if she is an extraordinary person who understands his tears. The early Wimsey may have been the kind of man that an intellectual woman would imagine for a mate, but the mature Wimsey is one with whom she could actually live. The fragment of a later novel called *Thrones, Dominations* indicates that the Wimsey-Vane marriage was just this workable.

Finally, the marriage of Wimsey and Vane symbolizes the paradoxical and joyful truth of good coming out of evil, for if Harriet had not been falsely accused of murder, they would never have met. She quiets Wimsey in one of his familiar periods of painful self-scrutiny about his "meddling" by reminding him that, if he had never meddled, she would probably be dead. The point seems clear: that human action has consequences, many of which are unforeseen and some painful, but all necessary for life. It is not difficult to imagine a novelist with this vision moving on shortly to the drama of Christ's crucifixion and resurrection, nor even the next step, her study and translation of that great narrative of good and evil, desire and fulfillment, mortality and eternity, Dante's *The Divine Comedy* (c. 1320). Indeed, all of Sayers' work is of a piece, creating that massive unity in diversity by which she defined true art.

Major publications other than long fiction

SHORT FICTION: *Hangman's Holiday*, 1933; *In the Teeth of the Evidence*, 1940; *Lord Peter*, 1972 (James Sandoe, editor).

PLAYS: *Busman's Honeymoon*, 1937 (with Muriel St. Clare Byrne); *The Zeal of Thy House*, 1937; *The Devil to Pay*, 1939; *The Man Born to Be King*, 1941-1942.

POETRY: *Op I*, 1916; *Catholic Tales and Christian Songs*, 1918.

NONFICTION: *The Mind of the Maker*, 1941; *Unpopular Opinions*, 1947; *Creed or Chaos?*, 1947; *Introductory Papers on Dante*, 1954; *Further Papers on Dante*, 1957; *Wilkie Collins*, 1977 (fragment).

Bibliography

Brabazon, James. *Dorothy L. Sayers: A Biography*, 1981.

Dale, Alzina Stone. *Maker and Craftsman*, 1978.

Durkin, Mary Brian. O. P. *Dorothy L. Sayers*, 1980.

Gaillard, Dawson. *Dorothy L. Sayers*, 1981.

Gilbert, Colleen B. *A Bibliography of the Works of Dorothy L. Sayers*, 1978.

Hannay, Maragaret P., ed. *As Her Whimsey Took Her*, 1979.

Heilbrun, Carolyn G. "Sayers, Lord Peter, and God," in *American Scholar*. Spring, 1968, pp. 324-330.

Hone, Ralph E. *Dorothy L. Sayers, A Literary Biography*, 1979.

Kenney, Catherine. "Dorothy L. Sayers: The Integrity of the Work," in *Listening*. Fall, 1980, pp. 230-240.

Catherine Kenney

SIR WALTER SCOTT

Born: Edinburgh, Scotland; August 15, 1771
Died: Abbotsford, Scotland; September 21, 1832

Principal long fiction

Waverley: Or, 'Tis Sixty Years Since, 1814; *Guy Mannering*, 1815; *The Antiquary*, 1816; *The Black Dwarf*, 1816; *Old Mortality*, 1816; *Rob Roy*, 1818; *The Heart of Midlothian*, 1818; *The Bride of Lammermoor*, 1819; *A Legend of Montrose*, 1819; *Ivanhoe*, 1820; *The Monastery*, 1820; *The Abbot*, 1820; *Kenilworth*, 1821; *The Pirate*, 1822; *The Fortunes of Nigel*, 1822; *Peveril of the Peak*, 1823; *Quentin Durward*, 1823; *St. Ronan's Well*, 1824; *Redgauntlet*, 1824; *The Betrothed*, 1825; *The Talisman*, 1825; *Woodstock*, 1826; *The Fair Maid of Perth*, 1828; *Anne of Geierstein*, 1829; *Count Robert of Paris*, 1831; *Castle Dangerous*, 1831.

Other literary forms

Sir Walter Scott's first published work was a translation of two ballads by Gottfried August Bürger, which appeared anonymously in 1796. In 1799, he published a translation of Johann Wolfgang von Goethe's drama *Goetz von Berlichingen*. In 1802, the first two volumes of *The Minstrelsy of the Scottish Border* appeared, followed by the third volume in 1803. This was a collection of popular ballads, annotated and often emended and "improved" with a freedom no modern editor would allow himself. A fascination with his country's past, formed in his early years and lasting all his life, led him to preserve these ballads, the products of a folk culture that was disappearing. In 1805 came *The Lay of the Last Minstrel*, the first of the series of long narrative poems that made Scott the most widely read poet of the day. It was followed by *Marmion: A Tale of Flodden Field* (1808). *The Lady of the Lake* (1810) brought him to the height of his popularity as a poet. The later poems were less successful and he was gradually eclipsed by Lord Byron. In 1813, he completed the manuscript of a novel he had laid aside in 1805. This was *Waverley*, which appeared anonymously in 1814. (Scott did not publicly admit authorship of his novels until 1827.) It created a sensation and launched him on the series that remained his chief occupation until the end of his life. Other important works were his editions of Dryden (1808) and of Swift (1814), a series of lives of the English novelists completed in 1824, and *The Life of Napoleon Buonaparte*, begun in 1825 and published in nine volumes in 1827. *Chronicles of the Canongate* (1827) is composed of three short stories: "The Highland Widow," "The Two Drovers," and "The Surgeon's Daughter."

Achievements

The central achievement of Scott's busy career is the series of novels that is conventionally designated by the title of the first of them. The sheer bulk of the Waverley novels is in itself impressive, as is the range of the settings they present. For example, *Ivanhoe* is set in twelfth century England, *The Talisman* in the Holy Land of the Third Crusade, *Quentin Durward* in fifteenth century France, *The Abbot* in the Scotland of Queen Mary, *Kenilworth* in the reign of Elizabeth, and *The Fortunes of Nigel* in that of James I. In spite of his wide reading, tenacious memory, and active imagination, Scott was not able to deal convincingly with so many different periods. Moreover, he worked rapidly and sometimes carelessly, under the pressures of financial necessity and, in later years, failing health. Some of the novels are tedious and wooden, mechanical in their plots and stilted in their dialogue. Scott himself was aware of their flaws and he sometimes spoke and wrote slightingly of them.

Yet most readers find that even the weaker novels have good things in them, and the best of them have a narrative sweep and a dramatic vividness that render their flaws unimportant. The best of them, by common consent, are those set in Scotland as far back as the latter part of the reign of Charles II. When he attempted to go further back, he was less successful, but in such novels as the four discussed below—*Waverley, Old Mortality, Rob Roy,* and *The Heart of the Midlothian*—Scott's sense of history is strong. They are among the most impressive treatments of his great theme, the conflict between the old and the new, between Jacobite and Hanoverian, between the heroic, traditional, feudal values of the Tory Highlands and the progressive commercial interests of the Whig Lowlands, between stability and change. Though some of the other novels offer historical conflict of a comparable kind (*Ivanhoe* and *Quentin Durward*, for example), the Scottish novels present the conflict with particular insight and force and convey a strong sense of the good on both sides of it. Scott values the dying heroic tradition even as he recognizes the benefits that change brings. Earlier writers had mined the past to satisfy a market for the exotic, the strange, or the merely quaint. Scott saw the past in significant relation to the present and created characters clearly shaped by the social, economic, religious, and political forces of their time, thus providing his readers with the first fictions that can properly be called historical novels.

Biography

An important factor in the vividness of the Scottish novels was the strong oral tradition to which Sir Walter Scott had access from his early childhood. After a bout with polio in his second year, he was sent away from Edinburgh to his paternal grandfather's house at Sandyknowe in the Border country, in the hope that the climate would improve his health. It did, and though he remained lame for the rest of his life, his boyhood was an active one. In this region from which his ancestors had sprung, he heard stories of Border raids, Jacobite risings, and religious struggles from people for whom the past survived in a living tradition. Throughout his life he added to his fund of anecdotes, and his notes to the novels show how very often incidents in them are founded on actual events which he had learned about from the participants themselves or from their more immediate descendants.

Scott's father was a lawyer, and in 1786, having attended Edinburgh High School and Edinburgh University, Scott became an apprentice in his father's office. In 1792, he was admitted to the bar, and all his life he combined legal and literary activities. After losing his first love, Williamina Belsches, to a banker, he married Charlotte Carpenter in 1798. In 1805, he entered into a secret partnership with the printer James Ballantyne, and four years later they formed a publishing firm. This firm ran into financial difficulties, and in 1813, Scott escaped ruin only through the intervention of another publisher, Archibald Constable. Scott continued to overextend himself. In 1811, he had bought a farm on the Tweed at a place he named Abbotsford, and in the years that followed he wrote furiously to provide funds for building a splendid house and buying additional land. His ambition was to live the life of a laird. In 1826, the financial collapse of Constable and Ballantyne ruined Scott. In his last years, he worked tirelessly to pay his creditors. The effort told on his health, and he died in 1832, at the age of sixty-one. The debts were finally cleared after his death by the sale of his copyrights.

Analysis

Waverley displays, at the start of Sir Walter Scott's career as a novelist, many of the features that were to prove typical of his best work. In the Jacobite rebellion of 1745, he saw an instance of the conflict between the older feudal and chivalric order, strongly colored with heroic and "romantic" elements, and the newer order of more practical and realistic concerns which had already begun to supplant it. His focus is not on the great public figures whose fates are at stake, and this too is typical. The Pretender, Prince Charles Edward, is not introduced until the novel is more than half over, and most of the major events of this phase of his career are only alluded to, not presented directly. He is shown almost exclusively in his dealings with the fictional character for whom the novel is named, and largely through his eyes.

Edward Waverley, like so many of Scott's heroes, is a predominantly passive character who finds himself caught between opposing forces and "wavering" between his loyalty to the House of Hanover, and the attractions of the Stuart cause. Though his father occupies a post in the Whig ministry, he has been reared by his uncle Sir Everard, a Tory who had supported the earlier Jacobite rebellion of 1715, though not so actively as to incur reprisals when it was put down. His father's connections procure Edward a commission in King George's army, and he is posted to Scotland. Shortly after arriving, he makes an extended visit to his uncle's Jacobite friend, the Baron of Bradwardine, and his daughter Rose. When a Highland raider, Donald Bean Lean, steals several of the Baron's cows, Waverley goes into the Highlands in the company of a follower of Fergus MacIvor, a chieftain who has the influence to secure the return of the cows. Waverley is impressed by Fergus and infatuated with his sister Flora. They are both confirmed Jacobites preparing to declare for the Pretender upon his arrival in Scotland.

As a result of Waverley's protracted absence and of a mutiny among the small band of men from his family estate who had followed him into the army, Waverley is declared absent without leave and superseded in his office. By coincidence, his father also loses his government position. Waverley's resentment at this twofold insult to his family by the Hanoverian government is heightened when, on a journey to Edinburgh to clear himself, he is arrested. Rescued by Donald Bean Lean, he is later brought to Edinburgh (now in the hands of the Jacobites), meets the Pretender, and is won over to his cause. He takes part in the Jacobite victory at Preston, but is separated from Fergus' troop in a skirmish at Clifton, in which Fergus is captured. After a period in hiding, Waverley is pardoned, through the good offices of Colonel Talbot, whom he had saved from death and taken prisoner at Preston. Fergus is executed for treason.

Objections to *Waverley* usually center on the character of the hero, whom Scott himself called "a sneaking piece of imbecility." Certainly it is possible to be impatient with his lack of self-awareness, and the frequency with which he is acted upon rather than acting puts him often in a less than heroic light. Waverley, however, is not intended to be a romantic hero, and his susceptibility to external influence is necessary to enable Scott to show within a single character the conflict between the two forces that compose the novel's theme. For most of the book, Scott's view of the hero is ironic, emphasizing his failings. There is, for example, his vanity. One of the things that reconciles his Jacobite Aunt Rachel to his serving in the Hanoverian army is the fact that he is becoming infatuated with a local girl. Scott mocks Waverley's feelings, first by giving their object the inelegant name of Cecilia Stubbs, and then by telling the reader that on Waverley's last Sunday at the parish church he is too preoccupied with his own dashing appearance in his new uniform to notice the care with which Miss Stubbs has arrayed herself. The complement of this detail occurs later in the novel when Waverley, having joined the Jacobites, puts on Highland dress for the first time, and one of Fergus' followers remarks that he is "majoring yonder afore the muckle pier-glass." More seriously, the memory of "the inferior figure which he had made among the officers of his regiment," resulting from his inability to keep his mind on detail and routine, contributes to his decision to change sides.

In addition to exposing his vanity, Scott often undercuts Waverley's romantic view of experience. On finding himself for the first time in the Highlands, he muses over "the full romance of his situation." It occurs to him that "the only circumstance which assorted ill with the rest, was the cause of his journey—the Baron's milk cows! this degrading incident he kept in the background." If, instead of deploring Waverley's inadequacy as a romantic hero, one attends to the irony with which Scott undercuts his fascination with romance and heroism, one will be better prepared for the author's reluctant dismissal of heroic virtues at the end of the novel. Waverley's character is perfectly appropriate to one who will survive into the new age, an age in which the dashing but destructive energies of Fergus have no place.

The real problem with the character is not his passivity or his ordinariness, but Scott's occasional failure to dramatize certain features of his personality, as opposed to merely making assertions about them. On two occasions he is credited with remarkable conversational powers, but no sample of them is given. During Waverley's period in hiding, Scott declares, "he acquired a more complete mastery of a spirit tamed by adversity, than his former experience had given him," but there is no demonstration of this "mastery." These flaws, however, hardly justify dismissing the characterization as a failure. The eagerness of Waverley's response to the new scenes and experiences he encounters, the growth of his resentment against the established government and his conversion to Jacobitism, his delayed recognition of his love for Rose, the cooling of his regard for Fergus as he comes to see the chieftain's selfishness and then the reawakening of that regard when Fergus is in danger—all these phases of his development are convincingly presented. Moreover, there are a few scenes where he shows real firmness (for example, his confrontation with Fergus when he has been shot at by one of Fergus' men), and several where he displays active generosity.

This said, one may concede that Waverley remains a rather slender figure to carry the weight of a novel of this length. He does not have to, however, for Scott surrounds him with a number of vivid characters from a wide range of classes and backgrounds. It is chiefly through their speech that he makes his characters live. The dialogue is not consistently successful: the bright small talk between Fergus and Flora can be downright dreadful, and some of the language of the other upper-class characters is stiff. The speech of most of the secondary characters, however, is convincing, and the dialect writing is particularly effective. Scott's most important contribution here is the achievement of a wide variety of tones in dialect speech. Before Scott, dialect was almost exclusively a comic device, but he was able to write dialect in different keys all the way up to the tragic. The best evidence of this is the scene in which Fergus and his follower Evan Dhu Maccombich are condemned to death. When Evan Dhu offers his life and the lives of five others in exchange for his chieftain's freedom, volunteering to go and fetch the five others himself, laughter breaks out in the courtroom. In a speech that loses nothing in dignity by being couched in dialect, Evan Dhu rebukes the audience and then proudly rejects the judge's invitation to plead for grace, preferring to share his chieftain's fate.

Fergus is perhaps the most interesting of the major characters. He possesses throughout the capacity to surprise the reader. Scott prepares the reader carefully for his first appearance. Waverley first hears of him in Chapter 15 as an extorter of blackmail or protection money and is surprised to learn that he is nevertheless considered a gentleman. When he is introduced several chapters later, the reader discovers that this feudal leader of a troop of half-savage Highlandmen is a polished and literate individual with a very good French education. He is clearly fond of his sister, and yet quite prepared to exploit her as bait to draw Waverley into the Jacobite ranks. In the early part of the novel, the emphasis is on his courage, his hospitality, and his ability to inspire loyalty, and he is for the most part an attractive figure.

Gradually, however, both Waverley and the reader come to view him more critically. It grows increasingly clear that his commitment to the Jacobite cause is founded on self-interest. On learning that Prince Charles Edward is encouraging Bradwardine to leave his estate to Rose instead of to a distant male relative, he attempts to make the Prince promote his marriage to Rose. When the Prince refuses, he is furious, later saying that he could at that moment have sold himself to the devil or King George, "whichever offered the dearest revenge" (chap. 53). Yet as the Jacobite fortunes ebb, his generosity returns, and for the first time he attempts to use his influence over Waverley for the latter's good, telling him there is no dishonor in his extricating himself from the now certain wreck of their cause and urging him to marry Rose: "She loves you, and I believe you love her, though, perhaps, you have not found it out, for you are not celebrated for knowing your own mind very pointedly." He refuses to allow Waverley to witness his execution, and, by a generous deception regarding the hour at which it is to take place, he spares his sister the pain of a final interview. As he strides out of his cell, it is he who is supporting Waverley.

Throughout the novel, the portrait of Fergus is sharpened by a number of contrasts, explicit and implicit, between him and other characters. The contrast with Waverley is obviously central. There is also a contrast between him and his sister. While Fergus' Jacobitism is tinged with self-interest and he sometimes resorts to duplicity to advance the cause, Flora's devotion to the Stuarts is absolutely pure. She cannot reconcile herself to her brother's dealing with a thief of Donald Bean Lean's stripe even in the interest of the cause, and she resists his wish that she encourage Waverley's infatuation with her in order to win him to their side. Fergus' preoccupation with the more practical aspects of the campaign is set against Bradwardine's comically pedantic concern with form and ceremony in the question of whether and how to exercise his hereditary privilege of drawing off the king's boots. Yet Bradwardine's old-fashioned loyalty lacks all taint of self-interest, and, though he has been largely a comic figure, he behaves after the failure of the rebellion with a gallant fortitude comparable to that of Fergus. In the latter part of the novel, a new character enters to serve as Fergus' complete antithesis. Colonel Talbot, who supplants him in guiding Waverley's fate, differs from Fergus on practically every count—political affiliation, disinterested generosity, attitude toward women, and even age.

Several other characters are paired in contrast. Flora's strength of character, heroic bent, intellectual accomplishments, and striking beauty are repeatedly contrasted with the less remarkable gifts of the placid and domestic Rose. Sir Everard Waverley and his brother Richard are opposite numbers in all respects. When Waverley is arrested on his way to Edinburgh, Melville and Morton, the magistrate and the clergyman who hear his defense, take differing views of his case. One of Fergus' henchmen, Callum Beg, commits a crime for his master when he attempts to shoot Waverley, while Humphry Houghton, one of Waverley's followers, involves himself in a conspiracy and mutiny. Both are carrying out what they mistakenly believe to be their masters' wishes, and they receive differing treatment for their actions.

This network of contrasts contributes much to the unity of a novel that is sometimes criticized as loosely structured. Scott's General Preface to the 1829 edition of the whole series lends credence to this charge: "The tale of Waverley was put together with so little care, that I cannot boast of having sketched any distinct plan of the work. The whole adventures of Waverley, in his movements up and down the country with the Highland cateran Bean Lean, are managed without much skill." Whatever Scott meant by this, it cannot really be said that the book is loosely plotted. A glance at the retrospective explanations contained in Chapters 31 and 65 will remind any reader of the great number of details that at first looked unimportant but that turn out to be essential to the mechanics of the plot. Such after-the-fact explanations may be technically awkward, and they may lay Scott open to the charge of unnecessary mystification in the episodes leading up to them, but they certainly evidence some careful planning.

It is rather for excessive reliance on coincidence that the plot can be criticized. The retrospective explanations just mentioned make some of these appear less unreasonable and incredible, but there are still a great many of them, and this is true of all Scott's novels. Also, the pace of the narrative is at times uncertain. Although the opening chapters describing Waverley's education are important to an understanding of the character, they make an undeniably slow beginning, and some of the set pieces retard the narrative flow.

In spite of its flaws, however, the novel is sustained by its central theme of the process of historical change and by Scott's ability to do justice to both sides in the conflict. Part of him responded strongly to the gallant romance of the Jacobite and to the love of tradition behind it. At the same time, he realized that the world had passed all that by. As Waverley himself points out, there have been four monarchs since James II was deposed, and the divine right absolutism for which the Stuarts stood would have sorted ill with the political and economic realities of the mid-eighteenth century. So Fergus is executed, his head is stuck up over the Scotch gate, and the Edinburgh youth whom Waverley has engaged as a valet comments, "It's a great pity of Evan Dhu, who was a very weel-meaning, good-natured man, to be a Hielandman; and indeed so was [Fergus MacIvor] too, for that matter, when he wasna in ane o' his tirrivies [tantrums]." In a snatch of dialogue, the heroic perspective is replaced by one more down-to-earth and commonplace. The threat to the prevailing order that the rebellion represented is already diminishing in importance in the popular view. To the common man secure in the established order, the energies that burned in Fergus amount to no more than "tirrivies."

Old Mortality deals with an earlier rebellion, one in which the issue is religious. Charles II had won the support of the Scottish Presbyterians by subscribing to the Solemn League and Covenant, which provided for the establishment of Presbyterianism as the state religion in Scotland and in England and Ireland as well. After the Restoration, however, Charles sought to impose episcopacy on Scotland, and the Covenanters were persecuted for their resistance to the bishops. In 1679, the assassination of the Archbishop of St. Andrews by a small party of Covenanters led by John Balfour of Burley sparked a gathering of insurgents who managed at Drumclog to defeat the Cavalier forces under John Graham of Claverhouse that were sent against them. A few weeks later, however, the Covenanters, divided by moderate and extremist factions, were routed at Bothwell Bridge by an army commanded by the Duke of Monmouth. The novel's title is the nickname of an old man who travels through Scotland refurbishing the markers on the graves of the martyred Covenanters.

Out of these events, Scott built one of his starkest and swiftest plots. Once again he portrays a hero caught between conflicting forces. Just after the Archbishop's murder, Henry Morton gives shelter to Burley because Burley and his father had been comrades-in-arms and Burley had saved the elder Morton's life. Henry Morton's moderate principles lead him to condemn the murder, but he also deplores the oppression that provoked it, and Burley hopes that he will eventually take up arms with the Covenanters. Morton is, however, drawn to the Cavalier side by his love for Edith Bellenden (one of Scott's more pallid heroines) and by his friendship for her granduncle.

Morton receives some firsthand experience of the oppressive measures of the Cavaliers when he is arrested for harboring the fugitive Burley and is brought before Claverhouse. This figure is Burley's opposite number, rather as Talbot is Fergus MacIvor's in *Waverley*, except that Talbot is wholly admirable while Claverhouse is a more complex character. Like Burley, Claverhouse sees in Morton qualities of courage and leadership that could be valuable to the rebels. He is about to have him executed when one of his subordinates, Lord Evandale, intervenes. Evandale is a suitor of Edith, and at her request he generously asks Claverhouse to spare his rival's life. Morton is carried along as a prisoner with Claverhouse's troops, and when they are defeated by the Covenanters at Drumclog, he is set free. Under Burley's auspices, he is given a high post in the rebel army.

In this phase of the novel, Morton shows himself a much more active hero than Waverley. He quickly repays his debt to Evandale by saving his life in the rout of the loyalist forces, and he does so again in a later chapter, when Evandale has become Burley's prisoner. He plays a prominent part in the Covenanters' attempts to take Glasgow. He draws up a statement of the rebels' grievances and presents it to Monmouth just before the battle of Bothwell Bridge, and even though the Covenanters obstinately refuse the terms he secures, he does not defect but instead fights heroically in the battle that ensues.

In spite of the vigor with which Morton fulfills his commitment to the Presbyterians, they distrust him, and Scott sharply dramatizes their ignorance, factiousness, bigotry, and cruelty. He also exposes the unscrupulous streak in Burley's enthusiasm. This zealot is convinced that the most barbaric cruelties and the rankest deceptions are justified by his cause. He is surrounded by a gallery of fanatics, of whom the most horrifying is the insane preacher Habbakuk Mucklewrath. In flight after the defeat at Bothwell Bridge, Morton and his servant Cuddie stumble upon a group of Covenanting leaders in an isolated farmhouse at Drumshinnel. They have been praying for guidance, and the arrival of Morton, whom they irrationally regard as the cause of their defeat, convinces them that God has sent him to them as a sacrifice. They conduct a kind of trial, though the verdict of death is never in doubt. It is the Sabbath, however, and they are unwilling to execute him before midnight. Eventually, Mucklewrath jumps up to put the clock ahead, crying, "As the sun went back on the dial ten degrees for intimating the recovery of holy Hezekiah, so shall it now go forward, that the wicked may be taken away from among the people, and the Covenant established in its purity."

This display of the Covenanters' fanaticism is the complement of the earlier trial before Claverhouse, in which Morton was threatened with the arbitrary cruelty of the Cavalier side. Ironically, it is Claverhouse who now arrives to save Morton. (He has been led to the farmhouse by Cuddie, who had been allowed to escape.) Most of the Covenanters are slaughtered. Riding back to Edinburgh in the custody of his rescuers, Morton is divided between horror at Claverhouse's habitual cold indifference to bloodshed and admiration for his urbanity and his valor. Claverhouse admits that he is as much a fanatic as Burley but adds, "There is a difference, I trust, between the blood of learned and reverend prelates and scholars, of gallant soldiers and noble gentlemen, and the red puddle that stagnates in the veins of psalm-singing mechanics, crack-brained demagogues, and sullen boors." Scott counters this assessment in the very next chapter by showing the fortitude of one of the Covenanting leaders, Ephraim MacBriar, as he is brutally tortured and then condemned to death. The reader may also recall that it was prolonged imprisonment by the Cavaliers that drove Mucklewrath insane. As in *Waverley*, Scott sees both sides objectively.

Morton is sentenced to exile, and there is a gap of ten years in the narrative. In 1689, when the Glorious Revolution has put William and Mary on the throne, Morton is free to return to Scotland. Edith is on the point, finally, of accepting marriage to Evandale. Claverhouse, loyal to the Stuarts, is now ironically a rebel in his turn. He is killed in the battle of Killecrankie, but his army is victorious. He had once said to Morton, "When I think of death . . . as a thing worth thinking of, it is in the hope of pressing one day some well-fought and hard-won field of battle, and dying with the shout of victory in my ear—*that* would be worth dying for, and more, it would be worth having lived for!" The rather too crowded closing pages describe the deaths of Burley and Lord Evandale.

The novel displays Scott's dramatic gifts at their best. Though the language of Morton, Edith, and Evandale is sometimes stiff, the dialogue of the rest of the characters is vigorous and precisely adjusted to their various stations and backgrounds, and the language of the Covenanters, loaded with scriptural allusions, idioms, and rhythms, constitutes a particularly remarkable achievement. In addition to the characters already discussed, three others stand out. One is Sergeant Bothwell, who is descended from an illegitimate son of James VI and resents his failure to attain preferment. He is one of the novel's chief embodiments of the bullying oppression and extortion to which the Covenanters are subjected, but he is also capable of the courtesy and bravery that he regards as incumbent on one of his blood. Another is Mause Headrigg, whose compulsive declarations of her extreme Presbyterian principles are always ill-timed, to the chagrin of her pragmatic son Cuddie, who has no ambition to become a martyred Covenanter. The third is Jenny Dennison, Edith's maid. Like her mistress, Jenny has a suitor on each side of the conflict, and Scott thus creates a comic parallel to the Morton-Edith-Evandale triangle. She chooses Morton's servant Cuddie over her other suitor, a soldier in the Cavalier army, and this match foreshadows the eventual union of Edith and Morton. Jenny, however, has more vitality, resourcefulness, and charm than her mistress. She has been criticized for trying to promote Edith's marriage to the wealthy Evandale with a view to securing the future of herself, her husband, and their children. One can admit this fault and go on to point out that it is related to the success of the characterization. The most convincing characters in *Old Mortality* are those in whom Scott reveals a mixture of motivations or a blending of admirable with deplorable traits.

Rob Roy is probably the least successful of the four novels considered here. It resembles *Waverley* in that it takes a young Englishman into the Highlands during a Jacobite rising, this time that of 1715. Like Edward Waverley, Frank Osbaldistone has a romantic and poetical turn and responds eagerly to the unfamiliar world of the Highlands. Like Waverley, he has a touch of vanity and of obstinacy in his temper. Like Waverley, he is slow to understand his feelings for the heroine. That he is not as slow as Waverley was to realize that he loved Rose may be attributed to two factors: There is only one possible object for Frank's affections, not two; and that object, Diana Vernon, bears a much closer similarity to Flora, who captivated Waverley immediately, than to Rose.

Frank Osbaldistone, however, is a less interesting hero than Waverley, largely because he does not experience any serious internal conflict. In spite of his love for Diana, a committed Jacobite, he never considers supporting the Pretender. His conflicts are all external. Having angered his father by refusing to follow him into trade, Frank is sent to stay with his uncle's family in Northumberland, to be replaced in the firm by one of his cousins. Though it is understandable that his father should turn to a nephew when his son has disappointed him, it is not clear what point he has in sending Frank to Osbaldistone Hall. Frank's uncle and five of his cousins are boors with no interests beyond hunting and drinking. The sixth son, Rashleigh, is clever, villainous, ugly, and lame. He is the one chosen to take Frank's place in the firm. He had been tutor to Diana, who is his cousin on his mother's side, but had attempted to seduce her, and she has since kept him at a distance. Nevertheless, their common Jacobite sympathies remain a bond between them. Rashleigh, resenting Diana's obvious liking for Frank and smarting under an insult from him, forms a plan that will ruin the Osbaldistone firm and at the same time hasten the rising of the clans in support of the Pretender. The financial details of this scheme are not clear, and it therefore lacks credibility. This flaw in the plot is fairly serious because in *Rob Roy* commercial activity has considerable thematic importance.

Once in London, Rashleigh wins his uncle's confidence and then absconds with certain crucial documents. Frank's task is to follow him to Glasgow and then into the Highlands to recover them. It is in fact not Frank but Diana Vernon's father (whose identity is a mystery to Frank and the reader until the end of the book) who gets the documents back, and this in spite of the fact that he is also a Jacobite and might thus be expected to further rather than thwart Rashleigh's plot. Punishment comes to Rashleigh not from Frank but from the Highland chieftain Rob Roy. Rashleigh turns traitor to the Jacobites, and, after the failure of the rebellion, he arranges the arrest of Diana and her father. In the process of rescuing them, Rob Roy kills Rashleigh.

Thus, though Frank is a party to his fair share of adventures, he is too often merely a party rather than the chief actor, even though he is clearly meant to be the hero. Although Rob Roy appears at practically every crisis of the story, those appearances are intermittent, and the crises mark stages in the experience of Frank. Everything, down to the use of Frank as first-person narrator, points to him as the central character. (Everything, that is, except the title, but a writer with Scott's sense of what sells would hardly call a book *Osbaldistone*.) At too many crucial points, however, Rob Roy displaces Frank as the focus of the reader's interest. Though their relationship may appear to resemble that of Waverley and Fergus or of Morton and Burley, Morton and even Waverley are more active characters than Frank and thus are never eclipsed by Burley and Fergus to the extent that Frank is by Rob Roy. This seems to be largely a result of the bonds that unite Fergus with Waverley and Morton with Burley in a common enterprise for much of their respective stories. The cause shared by each pair of characters makes it possible for each pair to share the spotlight, so to speak, against a common background without compromising the novel's unity. Rob Roy and Frank, by contrast, do not act together in a public cause, since Frank is not a Jacobite. Furthermore, the distance between them is emphasized in the early part of the novel by the fact that, though he takes action several times in Frank's behalf, Rob Roy's identity is unknown to Frank until the novel is half over. In short, the plot keeps these characters separate as Waverley is not kept separate from Fergus nor Morton from Burley, and as a result the novel seems marred by a divided focus.

There is also a failure to unify the public and the private themes as convincingly as in the other two novels. The vagueness of the link between the ruin of the Osbaldistone firm and the rising of the clans has already been noted. A related problem is the absence of specificity about Diana Vernon's Jacobite activities. A wary reader will recognize Scott's irony in having Frank respond to an early warning about Diana with the words, "Pshaw, a Jacobite?—is that all?" There is, however, a lack of concrete detail about her role in the conspiracy. This is perhaps inevitable, given the first-person point of view and the fact that Diana keeps Frank out of the secret of the conspiracy, but it weakens the characterization of the heroine. In contrast, Flora Mac-Ivor's political obsession is fully convincing. Diana is perhaps not meant to seem as much a fanatic as Flora, yet she too has sacrificed all personal inclination to the cause—or to her father's will. At the end of the novel, the reader learns that her father has been a central figure in the conspiracy and has often stayed at Osbaldistone Hall in the disguise of a priest, and that Rashleigh's hold over Diana resulted from his having penetrated her father's disguise. This is a fairly dramatic situation, but the reader is, so to speak, asked to do the dramatizing for himself in retrospect. The specifics about Diana's part in the conspiracy are too little too late.

Since Sir Frederick Vernon has for the reader no identity until the closing pages, he can never be more than a minor figure. Yet to him, Scott assigns the account of the actual rebellion. In the penultimate chapter, the rebellion and its collapse are perfunctorily described by Sir Frederick in less than two pages. This is a signal failure to unify the personal and historical dimensions. Instead of the climax that it should have been, the 1715 rising seems almost an afterthought.

There is, however, a good deal of effective characterization in the novel. Diana Vernon is probably the most attractive and interesting of Scott's heroines. She is well educated, strong-minded, outspoken, aggressive, and witty. She may not quite hold her own in the company to which critical opinion sometimes promotes her, the company of William Shakespeare's Beatrice and Jane Austen's Elizabeth Bennett, but the dialogue Scott gives her does indeed amply express intelligence and vitality. If there is one false note, it is Scott's allowing her finally to marry Frank, but one's reservations may be qualified by the consideration that Frank seems politically almost neutral. If he does not support the Stuarts, he is not in the debt of Hanover either. It is not quite as if Flora MacIvor had married Edward Waverley.

Diana first appears before Frank on horseback wearing "what was then somewhat unusual, a coat, vest, and hat, resembling those of a man, which fashion has since called a riding-habit." Scott several times underlines her firm and forthright behavior by comparing it to a man's. There is a much stronger masculine streak in the only other important female character in this book which has just four speaking roles for women. Rob Roy's wife Helen is a virago capable of ambushing a British troop with only a small band and of cold-bloodedly ordering the drowning of a hostage. She should have been a powerful figure, but the language she speaks is impossibly bookish and rhetorical, an objection which is not sufficiently answered by Scott's later remarking that her "wild, elevated, and poetical" style is caused by the fact that she is translating from Gaelic into English, "which she had acquired as we do learned tongues."

The characterization of Rob Roy himself is on the whole successful, despite a certain lack of impact in his first few appearances, during which a reader who has skipped Scott's unusually cumbersome prefatory material may not even realize that this is the titular character. He gains added weight by being the chief embodiment of one side of the novel's main thematic conflict. The focus of the novel is not on the Jacobite-Hanoverian struggle but on the related but distinguishable conflict between the half-barbaric feudal life of the Highland clans and the modern commercial world of trade. Rob Roy is an outlaw relying on blackmail to support himself and his followers, who acknowledge no leader but him. Their way of life breeds narrow loyalties (a point emphasized also by the judge in the trial of Fergus MacIvor). Helen MacGregor cannot "bide the sight o' a kindly Scot, if he come frae the Lowlands, far less of an Inglisher." The clansmen are a threat to peace and order because rebellion and disorder are conditions far more likely to improve their lot. As Rob Roy says of the expected uprising, "Let it come . . . and if the world is turned upside down, why, honest men have the better chance to cut bread out of it."

Rob Roy is contrasted with the Glasgow weaver and magistrate Bailie Nichol Jarvie. A business associate of the Osbaldistone firm, he accompanies Frank in his pursuit of Rashleigh. Scott makes Rob Roy and Jarvie kinsmen in order to point out the contrasts between them more sharply. These contrasts are most clearly drawn in two fine scenes, one in the Glasgow jail midway through the novel and the other near the end. In the latter scene, when Bailie Nichol Jarvie deplores the ignorance of Rob Roy's sons, the Highlander boasts, "Hamish can bring down a black-cock when he's on the wing wi' a single bullet, and Rob can drive a dirk through a twa-inch board." Jarvie retorts, "Sae muckle the waur for them baith! . . . An they ken naething better than that, they had better no ken that neither." Rob Roy scorns his kinsman's offer to take his sons as apprentices: "My sons weavers! . . . I wad see every loom in Glasgow, beam, traddles, and shuttles, burnt in hell-fire sooner!" Shortly afterward, however, he admits to Frank that he is troubled at the thought of his sons "living their father's life." That kind of life in fact remained possible for only about three more decades, for after the rising of 1745, the rule of law was extended into the Highlands and the power of the clans was permanently broken.

That defeat in effect completed the Union of England and Scotland that had been established in 1707. In Chapter 27, when Andrew Fairservice, Frank's servant, speaks disparagingly of the Union, Jarvie sternly rebukes him:

> Whisht, sir—whisht! it's ill-scraped tongues like yours, that make mischief atween neighbourhoods and nations. . . . I say, Let Glasgow flourish! . . . judiciously and elegantly putten round the town's arms, by way of by-word—Now, since St. Mungo catched herrings in the Clyde, what was ever like to gar [make] us flourish like the sugar and tobacco trade? Will ony body tell me that, and grumble at the treaty that opened us a road west-awa' yonder?

Jarvie expresses Scott's own sense of the benefits that the growing commercial activity of the eighteenth century had brought to Scotland. Emotionally, he admired the romantic and adventurous character of Rob Roy's way of life, but his reason put him finally on the Bailie's side. Jarvie states the theme in terms of honor versus credit: "I maun hear naething about honour—we ken naething here but about credit. Honour is a homicide and a bloodspiller, that gangs about making frays in the street; but Credit is a decent honest man, that sits at hame and makes the pat play [pot boil]" (chap. 26).

The Heart of Midlothian is regarded by many as Scott's best work. In additon to the familiar virtues of a fully realized specific historical milieu and a large cast of characters from a variety of social levels who create themselves through the dialogue, the novel has for its heroine one of the common people, with whom Scott's powers of characterization were at their surest, and it has a truly serious ethical theme in the heroine's refusal to lie to save the life of her younger sister. Jeanie Dean's dilemma enables Scott to examine the relation of the law to justice and to mercy.

The novel opens with an extended presentation of an actual historical event, the Porteous riots in Edinburgh in 1736. Immediately after the execution of a smuggler named Wilson, John Porteous, Captain of the City Guard, reacts to a minor disturbance among the spectators by needlessly ordering his troop to fire upon the crowd. Several people are killed and Porteous is sentenced to be hanged. On the very day set for his execution, he is reprieved by Queen Caroline. That night a mob storms the prison, the Tolbooth (to which the novel's title is a reference). Porteous is dragged out and hanged.

In Scott's version, the mob is led by George Robertson, an accomplice of Wilson, who would have died along with him had Wilson not generously made possible his escape. Robertson has another reason besides revenge on Porteous for breaking into the Tolbooth. In the prison is Effie Deans, who has been seduced by him and has borne his child. She is to stand trial under a statute which stipulates that if a woman conceals her pregnancy and then can neither produce the infant nor prove that it died a natural death, she shall be presumed to have murdered it and shall suffer the death penalty. Once inside the prison, Robertson seeks her out and urges her to make her escape in the confusion, but she refuses. (One wonders why he did not remove her forcibly, but evidently he has his hands full directing Porteous' fate.) The next night, Robertson summons Effie's sister Jeanie to a remote spot and tells her that the case can be removed from under the statute if Effie is found to have communicated her condition to anyone. Jeanie refuses to lie about her sister's having done this, and she repeats her refusal in an affecting interview with Effie just before the trial. When Effie is condemned to death, Jeanie travels on foot all the way from Edinburgh to London, wins the support of the Duke of Argyle, and persuades Queen Caroline to pardon her sister. A few days after Effie is released, she elopes with Robertson.

At this point the novel is in effect finished, or nearly so, but Scott added a fourth volume to stretch the book to the length for which he had contracted. In it, the Duke of Argyle arranges for Jeanie, her new husband Reuben Butler (a clergyman), and her father to remove to a remote part of Scotland under his protection. This pastoral coda contrasts too strongly with the tone of the rest of the novel, and there is an unfortunate emphasis on the material blessings showered on Jeanie that rather qualifies one's sense of the disinterested heroism of her achievement. The closing chapters are, to be sure, tied to the main plot by the reappearance of Effie and her husband and by the discovery of their son, now a member of a small gang of bandits. Robertson is killed in an encounter with this gang, probably by his own son. There is an interesting variation on the novel's central situation, for the son, probably actually guilty of unnatural murder as his mother Effie was not, escapes when Jeanie goes to the room where he is confined and in her compassion loosens his painfully tight bonds. If this repetition of the novel's central event, Jeanie's saving a prisoner from execution, is aesthetically interesting, it is nevertheless ethically problematic, for the youth is a lawless individual who shows no compunction at what he has done and who does not hesitate, once Jeanie has loosened his bonds, to endanger her life by setting a fire in order to effect his escape. Jeanie's mercy seems in this case ill-judged.

It is the first three volumes that contain the most effective probing of the relation of the law to justice and to mercy. Scott contrasts a number of characters, each of whom stands in a different relation to the law. Wilson is a criminal justly condemned for smuggling, but his last offense is the generous one of saving a life by enabling his young accomplice to escape, and it wins him the sympathy of the populace and sets him in sharp contrast to the enforcer of the law, the Captain of the City Guard. Porteous' excessive zeal in the performance of his office leads to the loss of life and earns him the hatred of the populace when he gives the order to fire upon the crowd. His callousness is also shown by his earlier refusal to loosen Wilson's painfully tight handcuffs on the way to the execution, pointing out that all his pain will soon be at an end.

Among the mob that punishes Porteous, Robertson is concerned to preserve order because he wishes to stress the justice of their action, yet in his own person he has much to fear from justice. He is, moreover, clearly moved more by a desire for revenge than by a true concern for justice, and also, as has already been noted, he has in Effie Deans an ulterior motive for storming the Tolbooth.

Of all the prisoners the novel describes, Effie is in the worst plight, since she is entirely innocent of the crime she is charged with and since the statute does not even require that a crime be proved to have occurred. Moreover, she is in a sense to suffer for the guilt of others, for the government wishes to make an example of her because of the increasing frequency of child murder. Also, the Queen's anger at the response to the pardon of Porteous makes a royal pardon for Effie unlikely. Her situation is rendered more hopeless by these two factors that in strict justice have no bearing on her case.

Effie is linked with Wilson in that he and she have both sacrificed themselves for Robertson. Effie staunchly refuses to reveal her seducer's identity, even when she is "offered a commutation and alleviation of her punishment, and even a free pardon, if she would confess what she knew of her lover." In her desire to protect Robertson, she goes so far as to withhold all information concerning Meg Murdockson, the woman to whom Robertson had sent her when her child was due.

Robertson clearly does not deserve her generosity (nor Wilson's, for that matter). He is completely selfish. Effie is not the first girl he has abused. Meg Murdockson had long been a servant in his family, and he had seduced her daughter Madge. When her mother put Madge's infant out of the way so it would not pose an obstacle to Madge's finding a husband, Madge lost her wits. She is one of a number of pathetic simpletons who wander through Scott's novels, a company that includes David Gellatley in *Waverley* and Goose Gibbie in *Old Mortality*. Robertson's guilt in Madge's case has far-reaching consequences, for it is anger at the prospect of Effie's taking her daughter's place that moves Meg Murdockson to spirit away Effie's infant and later to attempt to waylay Jeanie on her journey to London.

Robertson's real name is Staunton. He has been among other things an actor, and this is appropriate, for, besides being selfish, he is the rankest hypocrite. In the scene where he confronts Jeanie to explain how she can save her sister, he heaps blame on himself liberally, but it is all empty gesture and rhetoric. He expects someone else to solve the problem. Jeanie is to save Effie by telling a lie when he could do it by surrendering himself and telling the truth. When Effie has finally been sentenced, then indeed he leaps on his horse with the intention of securing her reprieve by giving himself up as the leader of the Porteous mob, but he horse loses its footing and Staunton is thrown and severly injured. Jeanie learns of this on her journey to London when, by a remarkable coincidence, she meets him in his father's house, where he is recuperating. He authorizes her to trade his life for that of her sister, but only if her own unsupported plea is refused.

When Effie is reprieved and Staunton marries her, he becomes an actor in good earnest, and so does she. Sir George and Lady Staunton live for years in fear that their past will be discovered, and his unhappiness is much aggravated by the fact that they are childless. A series of coincidences reveals that their son is not dead, but is part of a small gang of bandits in the very vicinity where Jeanie and her family now live. When Staunton arrives in search of him and is killed, Jeanie prepares the body for burial. She discovers "from the crucifix, the beads, and the shirt of hair which he wore next his person, that his sense of guilt had induced him to receive the dogmata of a religion, which pretends, by the maceration of the body, to expiate the crimes of the soul" (chap. 52). The verb *pretends* conveys Scott's view of the appropriateness of Staunton's conversion to Roman Catholicism.

Jeanie Deans, in contrast, is firmly anchored in her father's rigid Presbyterianism and has a horror of every kind of pretense or falsehood. Her principles prevent her from lying to save Effie, but her generosity enables her to accomplish what all of Staunton's empty heroics are powerless to achieve. It is interesting to consider a misunderstanding that arises between Jeanie and her father, David Deans, regarding her testifying at Effie's trial. Deans is a Cameronian, the strictest kind of Scottish Presbyterian, and his memory goes back to the battle of Bothwell Bridge and the persecutions that followed it.

He is doubtful of the propriety of even appearing in court, since doing so might seem to constitute an acknowledgement of a government that has abandoned the Solemn League and Covenant and that exercises what he regards as undue influence over the Kirk. Though Deans has never before hesitated to tell anyone what to do, in the present case he says to himself, "My daughter Jean may have a light in this subject that is hid frae my auld een—it is laid on her conscience, and not on mine—If she hath freedom to gang before this judicatory, and hold up her hand for this poor cast-away, surely I will not say she steppeth over her bounds" (chap. 18). The inconsistency is too touching and too clearly rooted in his love for Effie to be called hypocrisy. It is another instance of the conflict between principles of conduct and emotional claims, and it enriches the character and underlines his relation to the central theme.

When he attempts to convey to Jeanie his resolution of his scruples, she, who has no thought of refusing to appear in court, takes it that he is encouraging her to give false testimony. The misunderstanding increases her sense of isolation and lack of support and thus makes her behavior all the more heroic.

The heroic impact of the journey itself is marred somewhat by the melodramatic events with which Scott seeks to enliven it. The lurid coloring is overdone in the scene of Jeanie's captivity at the hands of Meg, Madge, and two underworld cronies of theirs (to whom the old woman is known as Mother Blood). Scott is more successful when he modulates into comedy in the scene in which the demented Madge, in the absence of Meg and the others, leads Jeanie to a nearby village and then into church, where Madge's fantastic behavior causes her captive considerable embarrassment. The tension between the comic elements here and the very real danger of Jeanie's situation makes a strong effect. Shortly afterward, however, the tone shifts back to melodrama with the coincidental meeting with the convalescent Staunton, and the dramatic temperature drops during one of those retrospective narratives which Scott's complex plotting often forced on him.

The climactic confrontation with the Queen is very well done. Oddly enough, although Scott often had trouble finding a convincingly natural mode of utterance for his invented characters of the upper class, for actual historical figures he often succeeded in writing dialogue that is elevated without being stilted, polished without being wooden. Such is the language of Prince Charles Edward in *Waverley*, of Claverhouse in *Old Mortality*, and of Queen Caroline here.

The psychology of the Queen as well as her language is noteworthy. Jeanie's simple plea is effective, but it is not, or not only, emotional considerations that cause the Queen to grant the pardon. Even her response to Jeanie's main speech—"This is eloquence"—suggests objective evaluation of the speech more than emotional assent, and Scott keeps the scene well clear of sentimentality by a persistent emphasis on the political factors in the Queen's decision. She is divided between resentment of the Scots for their response to her pardoning of Porteous and her inclination to remain on good terms with Jeanie's sponsor, the Duke of Argyle. Even though he is at present out of favor, her policy is based on the principle that political allies may become opponents and opponents may again become allies. Another element in the scene is her complex attitude toward Lady Suffolk, also present at the interview. The Queen has so arranged matters that Suffolk is both her chief confidante and the King's mistress. After inadvertently making a remark that the Queen construes as a reflection on herself, Jeanie rights herself with a chance reference to "the stool of repentance," the punishment in Scotland "for light life and conversation, and for breaking the seventh command." The Queen is amused at the obvious embarrassment of "her good Suffolk."

The novel as a whole indicates that although the law is an absolute necessity, it can never do more than approximate justice because it is made and administered by human beings. It is ironically the generous instincts of Effie (in protecting Staunton) and the uncompromising honesty of Jeanie that make Effie the victim of a law which, it is repeatedly suggested, is a bad law because it exacts punishment in cases where there may have been no crime. It seems unjust too that the strict enforcement in the present instance is caused by factors external to Effie's case, the rise in child murder and the royal anger over the Porteous affair. Moreover, the author tends to place the human agents who enforce the law in an unflattering light. Porteous abuses the authority vested in him. The Doomster, or executioner, is a kind of untouchable who inspires horror in everyone when he makes his ritual appearance at Effie's sentencing. Ratcliffe, a thief four times condemned to the gallows, is the only prisoner besides Effie who rejects the opportunity to escape when the mob breaks into the Tolbooth. His reason is that he wants the post of underturnkey. The authorities actually grant this audacious request after considering how valuable his knowledge of the underworld is likely to prove. Scott provides a striking emblem of the amount of practical compromise involved in the enforcing of the law when he shows Ratcliffe and Sharpitlaw, the superintendent of police, at the start of the interview in which they bargain over Ratcliffe's request: "They sate for five minutes silent, on opposite sides of a small table, and looked fixedly at each other, with a sharp, knowing, and alert cast of countenance, not unmingled with an inclination to laugh."

The scene with the Queen indicates that the prerogative of mercy that is intended to mitigate the sternness of the law or correct miscarriages of justice is likewise governed by considerations of policy and expediency. The outcome of that scene, however, shows that the gap between ideal justice on the one hand, and policy or expediency on the other, can be bridged by the selfless exertions of someone motivated simply by love.

Although the four novels discussed here are likely to appear on anyone's list of the best of Scott, they are by no means the only ones worthy of a modern reader's attention. *The Antiquary*, *The Bride of Lammermoor*, *A Legend of Montrose*, and *Woodstock* have all found advocates among modern critics. There is also a very successful third panel in what might be called the Jacobite triptych that includes *Waverley* and *Rob Roy*; *Redgauntlet*, set in the 1760's, describes the last throes of the Jacobite movement. In addition to a plot full of intrigue, it is noteworthy for its combination of letters and journals with third-person narration and for autobiographical elements in the main characters of Alan Fairford and Darsie Latimer. Obviously Scott will never again have the huge audience he enjoyed throughout the nineteenth century, but he is more than merely a chapter in literary history. In addition to establishing the genre of the historical novel and influencing nineteenth century historiography, he wrote several novels that can be judged major achievements by any but the most narrow and rigid criteria.

Major publications other than long fiction

SHORT FICTION: *Chronicles of the Canongate*, 1827.

PLAYS: *Goetz von Berlichingen* 1799 (translation); *Halidon Hill*, 1822; *Macduff's Cross*, 1823; *The Doom of Devorgoil*, 1839; *Auchindrane: Or, The Ayrshire Tragedy*, 1830.

POETRY: *The Chase, and William and Helen: Two Ballads from the German of Gottfried Augustus Bürger*, 1796 (translation); *The Eve of Saint John: A Border Ballad*, 1800; *The Lay of the Last Minstrel*, 1805; *Ballads and Lyrical Pieces*, 1806; *Marmion: A Tale of Flodden Field*, 1808; *The Lady of the Lake*, 1810; *The Vision of Don Roderick*, 1811; *Rokeby*, 1813; *The Bridal of Triermain: Or, The Vale of St. John, in Three Cantos*, 1813; *The Lord of the Isles*, 1815; *The Field of Waterloo*, 1815; *The Ettrick Garland. Being Two Excellent New Songs*, 1815; (with James Hogg); *Harold the Dauntless*, 1817.

NONFICTION: *Minstrelsy of the Scottish Border*, 1802 (2 volumes); *The Life and Works of John Dryden*, 1808; *A Collection of Scarce and Valuable Tracts*, 1809-1815 (13 volumes); *The Life and Works of Jonathan Swift*, 1814; *Lives of the Novelists*, 1821-1824; *Chronological Notes of Scottish Affairs from the Diary of Lord Fountainhall*, 1822; *Lays of the Lindsays*, 1824; *The Life of Napoleon Buonaparte: Emperor of the French, with a Preliminary View of the French Revolution*, 1827.

Bibliography

Cockshut, A. O. J. *The Achievement of Walter Scott*, 1969.
Daiches, David. *Literary Essays*, 1957.
Devlin, D. D. *The Author of Waverley: A Critical Study of Walter Scott*, 1971.
Lockhart, J. G. *Memoirs of the Life of Sir Walter Scott*, 1837-1838.
Lukács, Georg. *The Historical Novel*, 1962.
Johnson, Edgar. *Sir Walter Scott: The Great Unknown*, 1970.

Lauber, John. *Sir Walter Scott*, 1966.
Welsh, Alexander. *The Hero of the Waverley Novels*, 1963.

John Michael Walsh

MARY WOLLSTONECRAFT SHELLEY

Born: London, England; August 30, 1797
Died: London, England; February 1, 1851

Principal long fiction

Frankenstein, 1818; *Valperga: Or, The Life of Castruccio, Prince of Lucca*, 1823; *The Last Man*, 1826; *The Fortunes of Perkin Warbeck*, 1830; *Lodore*, 1835; *Falkner*, 1837.

Other literary forms

Mary Shelley was a prolific writer, forced into copiousness by economic necessity. Punished by Sir Timothy Shelley, her husband Percy Bysshe Shelley's father, for her violation of his moral codes with his son, Mary Shelley was denied access to the Shelley estate for a long time after her husband's death. Her own father, William Godwin, was eternally in debt himself and spared her none of his troubles. Far from helping her, Godwin threw his own financial woes in her lap. It fell to Mary to support her son by writing, in addition to her novels, a plethora of short stories and some scholarly materials. The stories were mainly available to the public in a popular annual publication called the *Keepsake*, a book intended for gift-giving. Her stories were firmly entrenched in the popular Gothic tradition, bearing such titles as "A Tale of Passion," "Ferdinand Eboli," "The Evil Eye," and "The Bride of Modern Italy." Her scholarly work included contributions to *The Lives of the Most Eminent Literary and Scientific Men* in *Lardner's Cabinet Encyclopedia*. She attempted to write about the lives of both her father and her husband, although her efforts were never completed. She wrote magazine articles of literary criticism and reviews of operas, an art form that filled her with delight. She wrote two travel books, *History of A Six Weeks' Tour Through a Part of France, Switzerland, Germany, and Holland* (1817) and *Rambles in Germany and Italy* (1844). Shelley edited two posthumous editions of her husband's poetry (1824 and 1839) and she wrote several poetic dramas: *Manfred*, now lost, *Proserpine*, and *Midas*. She wrote a handful of poems, most of which were published in *Keepsake*. Her two novellas are *Mathilda*, unfinished and unpublished, and *The Heir of Mondolfo*, published posthumously in 1877.

Achievements

Shelley's literary reputation rests solely on her first novel, *Frankenstein*. Her six other novels, which are of uneven quality, are very difficult indeed to find, even in the largest libraries. Nevertheless, Mary Shelley lays claim to a dazzling array of accomplishments. First, she is credited with the creation of modern science fiction. All subsequent tales of the brilliant but doomed scientist, the sympathetic but horrible monster, both in high and mass culture, owe their lives to her. Even Hollywood's dream factory owes her an imaginative and economic debt it can never repay.

Second, the English tradition is indebted to her for a reconsideration of the Romantic movement by one of its central participants. In her brilliant *Frankenstein* fantasy, Mary Shelley questions many of the basic tenets of the Romantic rebellion: the Romantic faith in man's blissful relationship to nature, the belief that evil resides only in the dead hand of social tradition, and the romantic delight in death as a lover and restorer.

Finally, she has created one of the great literary fictions of the dialogue with the self. The troubled relationship between Dr. Frankenstein and his monster is one of the foundations of the literary tradition of "the double," doubtless the mother of all the doubles in Charles Dickens, Robert Louis Stevenson, and even in Arthur Conan Doyle and Joseph Conrad.

Biography

Mary Shelley, born Mary Wollstonecraft Godwin, lived the life of a great romantic heroine at the heart of the Romantic movement. She was the daughter of the brilliant feminist Mary Wollstonecraft and the equally distinguished man of letters, William Godwin. Born of two parents who vociferously opposed marriage, she was the occasion of their nuptials. Her mother died ten days after she was born, and her father had to marry for the second time in four years to provide a mother for his infant daughter. He chose a rather conventional widow, Mary Jane Clairmont, who had two children of her own, Jane and Charles.

In her childhood, Mary Shelley suffered the torments of being reared by a somewhat unsympathetic stepmother; later, she led the daughter of this extremely middle-class woman into a life of notoriety. The separation traumas in her early years indelibly marked Mary Shelley's imagination: almost all of her protagonists are either orphaned or abandoned by their parents.

Mary Shelley's stormy early years led, in 1812 and until 1814, to her removal to sympathetic "foster parents," the Baxters of Dundee. There, on May 5, 1814, when she was seventeen years old, she met Percy Bysshe Shelley, who was then married to his first wife, Harriet. By March 6, 1815, Mary had eloped with Shelley, given birth to a daughter by him, and suffered the death of the baby. By December 29, 1816, the couple had been to Switzerland and back, had another child, William, and had been married, Harriet having committed suicide. Mary Shelley was then nineteen years old.

By the next year, Mary's stepsister, Jane Clairmont, who called herself Claire Clarmont, had had a baby daughter by Lord Byron, while Mary was working on *Frankenstein*, and Mary herself had given birth to another child, Clara.

The network of intimates among the Shelley circle rapidly increased to include many literati and artists. These included, among others, Leigh and

Marrianne Hunt, Thomas Love Peacock, Thomas Jefferson Hogg, and John Polidori. The letters and diaries of the Shelleys from this period offer a view of life speeded up and intensified, life at the nerve's edge.

While the Shelleys were touring Switzerland and Italy, they sent frantic communications to their friends, asking for financial help. Mary issued frequent requests for purchases of clothing and household items such as thread. There were also legal matters to be taken care of concerning publishing, Shelley's estate, and the custody of his children from his previous marriage.

The leaves of the letters and diaries are filled with urgent fears for the safety of the Shelley children and the difficulties of what was in effect an exile necessitated by the Shelleys' unorthodox style of life. In 1818, Clara Shelley died, barely a year old, and in 1819, William Shelley died at the age of three. Five months later, a son, Percy Florence, was born, the only child of the Shelleys to grow to maturity.

In 1822, Mary Shelley's flamboyant life reached its point of desolation. Percy Shelley, while sailing with his close friend Edward Williams, in his boat, *Ariel*, drowned in the Gulf of Spezia. Mary's letters and diaries of the time clearly reveal her anguish, her exhaustion, and her despair. Her speeding merry-go-round suddenly and violently stopped.

Literary historians find themselves in debate over this point in Mary Shelley's life. Her letters and diaries record unambiguous desolation, and yet many scholars have found indications that Percy Shelley was about to leave her for Jane Williams, the wife of the friend with whom he drowned. There is also some suspicion that Mary's stepsister had recently given birth to a baby by Percy Shelley, a rumor that Mary Shelley denied. Because of Percy Shelley's mercurial nature, such speculations are at least conceivable. Against them stands Mary's diary, a purely private diary, which suggests that she would have no reason to whitewash her marriage among its confidential pages.

Mary's tragedy did not prompt warmth and help from her estranged father-in-law. He refused to support his grandson, Percy Florence, unless Mary gave the child to a guardian to be chosen by him. This she would not do, and she was rewarded for her persistence. Her son became heir to the Shelley estate when Harriet Shelley's son died in 1826. After the death, Mary's son became Lord Shelley. Just as important, however, was the warm relationship that he maintained with Mary until her death. Mary Shelley's life ended in the tranquil sunshine of family affection. Her son married happily and had healthy children. Mary seems to have befriended her daughter-in-law, and, at the last, believed herself to be a truly fortunate woman.

Analysis

Mary Shelley's six novels are written in the Gothic tradition. They deal with extreme emotions, exalted speech, the hideous plight of virgins, the awful abuses of charismatic villains, and picturesque ruins. The sins of the past weigh heavily on their plot structures, and often include previously unsuspected relationships.

Shelley does not find much use for the anti-Catholicism of much Gothic fiction. Her nuns and priests, while sometimes troublesome, are not evil, and tend to appear in the short stories rather than in the novels. She avoids references to the supernatural so common in the genre and tends instead toward a modern kind of psychological Gothic and futuristic fantasy. Like many Gothic writers, she dwells on morbid imagery, particularly in *Frankenstein* and *The Last Man*. Graphic descriptions of the plague in the latter novel revolted the reading public which had avidly digested the grotesqueries of Matthew Gregory Lewis' *The Monk* (1796) and Mr. Singer's *Wanderer of the Alps* (1796).

With the exception of *Frankenstein*, Shelley's novels were written and published after the death of her husband; with the exception of *Frankenstein*, they appear to be attempting to work out the sense of desolation and abandonment that she felt after his death. In most of her novels, Shelley creates men and particularly women who resign themselves to the pain and anguish of deep loss through the eternal hope of love in its widest and most encompassing sense. Reconciliation became Shelley's preponderant literary theme.

Frankenstein is Shelley's greatest literary achievement in every way. In it, she not only calls into the world one of the most powerful literary images in the English tradition, the idealistic scientist Victor Frankenstein and his ironically abominable creation, but also, for the one and only time, she employs a narrative structure of daring complexity and originality.

The structure of *Frankenstein* is similar to a set of Chinese boxes, of narratives within narratives. The narrative frame is composed of the letters of an arctic explorer, Robert Walton, to his sister, Mrs. Saville, in England. Within the letters is the narrative of Victor Frankenstein, and within his narrative, at first, and then at the end within Walton's narrative, is the first-hand account of the monster himself. Walton communicates to England third- and then secondhand accounts of the monster's thoroughly unbelievable existence. Here, it would seem, is the seminal point of Joseph Conrad's much later fiction, *Heart of Darkness* (1902): the communication to England of the denied undercurrents of reality and England's ambiguous reception of that intelligence. In *Frankenstein* as in *Heart of Darkness*, the suggestion is rather strong that England cannot or will not absorb this stunning new perception of reality. Just as Kurtz's fiancée almost a century later cannot imagine Kurtz's "horror," so Mrs. Saville's silence, the absence of her replies, suggests that Walton's stunning discovery has fallen on deaf ears.

The novel begins with Walton, isolated from his society at the North Pole, attempting to achieve glory. He prowls the frozen north "to accomplish some great purpose"; instead, he finds an almost dead Victor Frankenstein, who tells him a story which, in this setting, becomes a parable for Walton. Frankenstein, too, has isolated himself from society to fulfill his great expectations, and he has reaped the whirlwind.

Frankenstein tells Walton of his perfect early family life, one of complete kindness and solicitude. It is a scene across which never a shadow falls. Out of this perfection, Victor rises to find a way of conquering death and ridding himself and mankind of the ultimate shadow, the only shadow in his perfect middle-class life. Like a man possessed, Frankenstein forges ahead, fabricating a full, male, human body from the choicest corpse parts he can gather. He animates the creature and suddenly is overwhelmed by the wrongness of what he has done. In his success, he finds utter defeat. The reanimated corpse evokes only disgust in him. He abandons it in its vulnerable, newborn state and refuses to take any responsibility for it.

From that day, his life is dogged by tragedy. One by one, all his loved ones are destroyed by the monster, who at last explains that he wanted only to love his creator but that his adoration turned to murderous hate in his creator's rejection of him. Ultimately, Frankenstein feels that he must destroy the monster or, at the very least, die trying. He succeeds at both. After Frankenstein's death in the presence of Walton—the only man other than Frankenstein to witness the monster and live—the monster mourns the greatness that could have been and leaves Walton with the intention of hurling himself onto Frankenstein's funeral pyre.

The critical task regarding this fascinating work has been to identify what it is that Frankenstein has done that has merited the punishment which followed. Is the monster a kind of retribution for man's arrogant attempt to possess the secrets of life and death, as in the expulsion from Eden? Is it the wrath of the gods visited on man for stealing the celestial fire, as in the Prometheus legend, a favorite fiction of Percy Shelley? Or is this a rather modern vision of the self-destructiveness involved in the idealistic denial of the dark side of human reality? Is this a criticism of Romantic optimism, of the denial of the reality of evil except as the utterly disposable dead hand of tradition? The mystery endures because critics have suggested all these possibilities; critics have even suggested a biographical reading of the work. Some have suggested that Victor Frankenstein is Shelley's shrewd insight into her husband's self-deceived, uncritical belief in the power of his own intelligence and in his destined greatness.

Valperga, Shelley's second novel, has a fairy-tale aura of witches, princes, maidens in distress, castles, and prophecies. The author uses all these fantasy apparatuses, but actually deflates it as being part of the fantasy lives of the characters which they impose on a fully logical and pragmatic reality. The novel pits Castruccio, the Prince of Lucca, a worldly, Napoleonic conquerer, against the lost love of his youth, the beautiful and spiritual Euthanasia. Castruccio's one goal is power and military dominion, and since he is enormously capable and charismatic, not to mention lucky, he is successful. Nevertheless, that he gains the world at the price of his soul is clearly the central point of the novel.

To gain worldly sway, he must destroy Valperga, the ancestral home of his love, Euthanasia. He must also turn Italy into an armed camp which teems with death and in which the soft virtues of love and family cannot endure. His lust for power raises to predominance the most deceitful and treacherous human beings because it is they who function best in the context of raw, morally unjustified power.

In the midst of all this, Castruccio, unwilling to recognize his limits, endeavors to control all. He wants to continue his aggrandizing ways and have the love of Euthanasia. Indeed, he wants to marry her. She reveals her undying love for him, but will only yield to it if he yields his worldly goals, which he will not do. As his actions become more threatening to her concept of a moral universe, Euthanasia finds that she must join the conspirators against him. She and her cohorts are betrayed, and all are put to death, with the exception of Euthanasia. Instead, Castruccio exiles her to Sicily. En route, her ship sinks, and she perishes with all aboard. Castruccio dies some years later, fighting one of his endless wars for power. The vision of the novel is that only pain and suffering can come from a world obsessed with power.

Surely the name Euthanasia is a remarkable choice for the novel's heroine. Its meaning in Shelley's time was "an easy death"; it did not refer to the policy of purposefully terminating suffering as it does today. Euthanasia's death is the best one in the story because she dies with a pure heart, never having soiled herself with hurtful actions for the purpose of self-gain. Possibly, the import of Shelley's choice is that all that one can hope for in the flawed, Hobbesian world of *Valperga* is the best death possible, as no good life can be imagined. It is probable that this bleak vision is at least obliquely connected with the comparatively recent trauma of Percy Shelley's death and Mary Shelley's grief and desolation.

The degenerating spiral of human history is the central vision of *The Last Man*. Set in the radically distant future of the twenty-first century, this novel begins with a flourishing civilization and ends with the entire population of the world, save one man, decimated by the plague. Lionel Verney, the last man of the title, has nothing to anticipate except an endless journey from one desolate city to another. All the treasures of man are his and his alone; all the great libraries and coffers open only to him. All that is denied to him— forever, it seems—is human companionship.

The novel begins before Lionel Verney's birth. It is a flashback narrated by Lionel himself, the only first-person narrator possible in this novel. Lionel describes his father as his father had been described to him, as a man of imagination and charm but lacking in judgment. He was a favorite of the king, but was forced out of the king's life by the king's new wife, a Marie Antoinette figure. The new queen, depicted as an arrogant snob, disapproves of Verney's father and effects his estrangement from the king by working on her husband's gullible nature.

Verney's father, in ostracized shame, seeks refuge in the country, where he marries a simple, innocent cottage girl and thus begets Lionel and his sister Perdita. Verney's father can never, however, reconcile himself to his loss of status and dies a broken man. His wife soon follows, and Lionel and Perdita live like wild creatures until chance brings the king's son, Adrian, into their path. Their friendship succeeds where the aborted friendship of their fathers failed, despite the continued disapproval of the queen.

What is remarkable to the modern reader is that Shelley, having set her story two hundred years in the future, does not project a technologically changed environment. She projects instead the same rural, agrarian, hand- and animal-driven society in which she lived. What does change, however, is the political system. The political system of *The Last Man* is a republican monarchy. Kings are elected, but not at regular intervals. The bulk of the novel concerns the power plays by which various factions intend to capture the throne by election rather than by war.

Adrian and Lionel are endlessly involved with a dashing, Byronic figure named Lord Raymond, who cannot decide whether he wants life in a cottage with Perdita, or life at the top. Ultimately, Raymond, like the protagonist of *Valperga*, wants to have both. He marries Perdita and gives up all pretensions to power, but then returns with her to rule the land. Power does not make him nor his wife happy.

Despite the sublimation of the power process into an electoral system, the rage for power remains destructive, degenerating finally into war. The plague which appears and irrevocably destroys mankind is merely an extension of the plague of man's will to power. Not only Raymond and Perdita, but also their innocent children, Lionel's wife, Iris, and Adrian's sister, who stayed home to eschew worldly aspirations, are destroyed. No one is immune.

Lionel's survival carries with it a suggestion of his responsibility in the tragedy of mankind. His final exile in a sea of books and pictures suggests that those who commit themselves solely to knowledge and art have failed to deal with the central issues of life. In simply abdicating the marketplace to such as Lord Raymond, the cultivators of the mind have abandoned human-ity. Through Lionel, they reap a bitter reward, but perhaps the implication is that it is a just reward for their failure to connect with their fellow human beings.

A number of critics consider *The Last Man* to be Mary Shelley's best work after *Frankenstein*. Like *Frankenstein*, this novel rather grimly deals with the relationship between knowledge and evil. Its greatest drawback for modern audiences, however, is its unfortunate tendency to inflated dialogue. Every sentence uttered is a florid and theatrical speech. The bloated characteriza-tions obscure the line of Shelley's inventive satire of man's lemminglike rush to the sea of power.

The Fortunes of Perkin Warbeck attempts to chronicle the last, futile struggles of the House of York in the Wars of the Roses. Perkin Warbeck was a historical character who claimed to be Richard, the son of Edward IV of England. Most scholars believe that Richard died in the tower with his brother Edward; Perkin Warbeck claimed to be that child. Warbeck said that he had survived the tower, assumed another identity, and intended to reclaim the usurped throne held by Henry VII.

Shelley's novel assumes that Perkin was indeed Richard and documents his cheerless history from his childhood to his execution in manhood by Henry VII. The novel attempts to explore once more man's fruitless quest for power and glory. Richard is an intelligent, virtuous young man who finds true companionship even in his outcast state, and the love of a number of women, each different, utterly committed, and true. He is unable, however, to forsake the dream of conquest and live simply. As he presses onward to claim the throne, he suffers a series of crushing losses, not one of which will he yield to as a revelation of the wrongheadedness of his quest. His rush toward the throne achieves only the death of innocent persons. When he is executed at the end of the novel, his wife Katherine is given the last words. She needs to find a way of continuing to live without him. She is urged by his adherents to forsake the world, and for his sake to live a reclusive life. Although Katherine appears only briefly in the interminable scenes of war and the grandiose verbiage through which the reader must trudge, her appearance at the end of the novel and her refusal to forsake the world in her grief are the most impressive moments in the work.

In refusing to retreat from the world, Katherine commits herself to the only true value in the novel, love, a value which all the senseless suffering of Richard's quest could not destroy. Katherine, as the widow of the gentle but misguided warrior, becomes a metaphor for the endurance of love in a world which has its heart set on everything but love. Her final, gracious words are a relaxing change from the glory-seeking bombast of the action, "Permit this to be, unblamed—permit a heart whose sufferings have been and are, so many and so bitter, to reap what joy it can from the strong necessity it feels to be sympathized with—to love." Once again, Shelley's basic idea is an enthralling one, but her execution of her plan includes a grandiose superfluity of expression and incident.

Lodore and Shelley's last novel, *Falkner*, form a kind of reconciliation couplet to end her exploration of loss and desolation. Reward for persistence in loving through the trials of death and social obliquy is her final vision. In *Lodore*, an extremely long parade of fatal misunderstandings, the central image is the recovery of a lost mother. The novel begins veiled in mystery. Lord Lodore has exiled himself and his fairylike, delicate daughter, Ethel, to the forests of Illinois in far-off America. Lord Lodore is without his wife, who has done something unnamed and perhaps unnameable to provoke this unusual separation. Reunion with her is the central action of the plot.

Lord Lodore is a perfect gentleman amid the cloddish but honest American settlers. His one goal is to produce the perfect maiden in his daughter, Ethel. Father and daughter are entirely devoted to each other. A series of flashback chapters reveal that Lady Lodore, very much the junior of Lord Lodore, had been overly influenced by her mother, who had insinuated herself between husband and wife and alienated her daughter's affections from Lord Lodore. Lord and Lady Lodore lived what life they had together always on the brink of rapprochement, but utterly confounded by the wiles of the mother-in-law, who managed to distort communicated sentiments to turn husband and wife away from each other, finally effecting a radical separation that neither Lord nor Lady Lodore wanted.

The American idyll ends for Ethel and her father when Ethel is about fifteen years old. The unwanted attentions of a suitor threaten Ethel's perfect life, and her father moves his household once more. Lodore thinks of reestablishing the bond with his estranged wife but is killed in a duel hours before departing for England. His last thoughts of reconciliation are buried with him, because the only extant will is one recorded years ago when he vindictively made Lady Lodore's inheritance dependent on her never seeing Ethel again. Ethel returns to England shaken and abandoned, but not to her mother. Instead, she lives with Lodore's maiden sister.

Ethel is wooed and won by a gentleman, Edward Villiers, coincidentally one of the few witnesses to her father's death and many years older than herself. The marriage of this truly loving couple is threatened because Edward, reared in luxury, is in reduced financial circumstances owing to the irresponsibility of his father, one of the few truly despicable characters in the novel.

Much suffering ensues, during which Edward and Ethel endeavor to straighten out priorities: Which is more important, love or money? Should they part to give Ethel a chance at a more comfortable life, or should they endure poverty for love? They choose love, but Edward is taken to debtor's prison, Ethel standing by for the conjugal visits that the prison system permits.

Through a series of chance encounters, Lady Lodore, now a seemingly shallow woman of fashion, becomes aware of Ethel's needs and of her need to be a mother to the young woman. Telling no one but her lawyer what she intends, she impoverishes herself to release Edward from prison and to set the couple up appropriately. She then removes herself to a humble country existence, anticipating the blessings of martyrdom. She is, however, discovered, the mother and daughter are reunited, and Lady Lodore is even offered an advantageous marriage to a rich former suitor who originally was kept from her by the machinations of his sisters.

Lodore includes many particulars that are close to the biographical details of the author's life: the penury and social trials of her marriage to Shelley, the financial irresponsibility of her father, and the loss of her mother. Shelley's familiarity with her material appears to have dissolved the grandiose pretensions of the previous novels, which may have sprung from her distance from their exotic settings and situations. *Lodore* has the force of life despite its melodramatic plot. If it were more widely available, it would be a rich source of interest for historians and literary scholars. It contains an interesting image of America as envisioned by the early nineteenth century European. It also contains a wealth of interest for students of women's literature.

If *Lodore* offers a happy ending with the return of a long-lost mother, then *Falkner* finds contentment in the restoration of an estranged father. Here, the father is not the biological parent, but a father figure, Rupert Falkner. The plot is a characteristic tangle of Gothic convolutions involving old secrets and sins, obdurate Catholic families, and the pure love of a young girl.

The delightful Elizabeth Raby is orphaned at the age of six under severe circumstances. Because her fragile, lovely parents were complete strangers to the little town in Cornwall to which they had come, their death left Elizabeth at the mercy of their landlady. The landlady is poor, and Elizabeth is a financial burden. The landlady keeps her only because she suspects that the now decimated, strange little family has noble connections. Thus begins a typical Shelley fiction—with abandonment, innocence, and loss of love.

The plot is set in motion by a mysterious stranger who identifies himself as "John Falkner." Falkner undertakes the guardianship of Elizabeth, not only because of her charm, but also because of an unfinished letter found in the family cottage. This letter connects Elizabeth's mother to one "Alithea." The reader comes to learn that Falkner was Alithea's lover, that he carries the guilt of her ruin and death since Alithea was a married woman, and that her husband continues to bear his wife's seducer a vindictive grudge. Happily, for the moment, Alithea's husband believes that the seducer was surnamed Rupert. Alithea's husband was and is an unsuitable mate for a sensitive woman, and the marriage was one from which any woman would have wanted to flee. Alithea's infraction was only against the letter of the marriage bond, not its spirit.

The vindictive husband has conceived a hatred for Alithea's son, Gerard, on account of Alithea's connection with "Rupert." Elizabeth, Falkner's ward, coincidentally meets and forms an attachment to Gerard. Falkner repeatedly attempts to separate them because of *his* guilty feelings. Their attachment blooms into a love which cannot be denied, and Falkner is forced to confess all to Gerard after the boy saves Falkner's life. He is the infamous Rupert, Rupert Falkner.

With the revelation comes the separation of Elizabeth and Gerard, she to stand loyally with Falkner, he to defend his father's honor. For the first time in his life, Gerard finds himself on his father's side, but familiarity breeds contempt. Gerard wants to fight a manly duel for honor, while his father wants to crush Falkner for economic gain in the legal system. Gerard finds this an inexcusable pettiness on his father's part. He then joins Elizabeth to defend Falkner in court. To do this, they will need to go to America to bring back a crucial witness, but the witness arrives and saves them the voyage: Falkner is acquitted. The legal acquittal is also metaphorical: in comparison with the ugly sins of greed, the sins of passion are pardonable.

Elizabeth, the reader knows, is also the product of an elopement in defiance of family, a sin of passion. The proud Catholic family which once spurned her decides to acknowledge Elizabeth. Gerard and Elizabeth, both wealthy and in their proper social position, marry. Falkner will have a home with them in perpetuity.

Once again, Shelley's fictional involvement in the domestic sphere tones down her customary floridity and affords the reader fascinating insights into the thinking of the daughter of an early feminist, who was indeed an independent woman herself. It can only clarify history to know that such a woman as Mary Shelley can write in her final novel that her heroine's studies included not only the "masculine" pursuits of abstract knowledge, but also needlework and "the careful inculcation of habits and order . . . without which every woman must be unhappy—and, to a certain degree, unsexed."

Major publications other than long fiction
SHORT FICTION: *Mary Shelley: Collected Tales and Stories*, 1976.
PLAYS: *Proserpine*, 1922; *Midas*, 1922.
NONFICTION: *History of a Six Weeks' Tour Through a Part of France, Switzerland, Germany, and Holland*, 1817; *Lardner's Cabinet Cyclopaedia*, 1838 (Numbers 63, 71, 96); *Rambles in Germany and Italy*, 1844; *The Letters of Mary Shelley*, 1980 (Betty T. Bennett, editor, 2 volumes).

Bibliography
Levine, George, and V. C. Knoepflmacher, eds. *The Endurance of Frankenstein*, 1979.
Nitchie, Elizabeth. *Mary Shelley*, 1952.
Spark, Muriel. *Child of Light: A Reassessment of Mary Wollstonecraft Shelley*, 1951.
Walling, William A. *Mary Shelley*, 1972.

Martha Nochimson

ALAN SILLITOE

Born: Nottingham, England; March 4, 1928

Principal long fiction

Saturday Night and Sunday Morning, 1958; *The General*, 1960; *Key to the Door*, 1961; *The Death of William Posters*, 1965; *A Tree on Fire*, 1967; *A Start in Life*, 1970; *Travels in Nihilon*, 1971; *Raw Material*, 1972; *The Flame of Life*, 1974; *The Widower's Son*, 1976; *The Storyteller*, 1979; *Her Victory*, 1982.

Other literary forms

Alan Sillitoe, in addition to his novels, has been quite prolific in other genres. He is as well-known for his short stories as he is for his long fiction, especially for *The Loneliness of the Long Distance Runner* (1959), the title story of which was made into a successful motion picture with Sillitoe's screenplay. Some of his other collections of short stories are entitled *The Ragman's Daughter* (1963), *Guzman Go Home* (1968), *A Sillitoe Selection* (1970), and *Men, Women, and Children* (1973). He is also a prolific poet, publishing a number of books, including *Without Beer or Bread* (1957), *The Rats and Other Poems* (1960), *A Falling Out of Love and Other Poems* (1964), *Shaman and Other Poems* (1968), *Love in the Environs of Voronezh and Other Poems* (1968), *Barbarians and Other Poems* (1974), *Storm* (1974), and *Snow on the North Side of Lucifer* (1979). With his wife, the American poet Ruth Esther Fainlight, he adapted a play by Lope de Vega into *All Citizens Are Soldiers* (1969, produced at Stratford-upon-Avon in 1967), and wrote *This Foreign Field* (produced in London in 1970). Three of his plays were collected in book form in 1978. *The City Adventures of Marmalade Jim* (1967) was written for juveniles, and a travel book, *The Road to Volgograd* (1964), recounted his favorable impressions of the Soviet Union and its people. His essays were anthologized in *Mountains and Caverns* (1975).

Achievements

Sillitoe's primary importance as a novelist derives from his authentic representations of the monotony, shallowness, and oppressiveness of British working-class life. The breakdown of the English class system is a journalistic cliché of the twentieth century, and Sillitoe is at least partly responsible for the general acceptance of this truism. *Saturday Night and Sunday Morning* not only gave a frankly honest and authentic portrayal of life among the working classes but also was one of a succession of British literary works that permanently destroyed the delusion that a class of loyal, plucky factory workers were satisfied with their status in British society. Sillitoe's characters often talk wishfully of apocalyptic struggle and of the opportunity to line up factory owners and people with "soft hands" against a firing-squad wall. As a result, Sillitoe has been classified, perhaps erroneously, as one of the "Angry Young Men." Sillitoe at his best, however, differs considerably from the writers with whom he has been commonly compared, for his ability to authentically portray his subjects is generally agreed to be his greatest achievement. At his best, his portrayal of the textures of working-class life is vivid without his exploiting the characters for the sake of a revolutionary or naturalistic philosophy. He allows them to be human beings who are affected individually by social forces. When he has yielded to the temptation to subordinate characterization to message, the results have usually been considered disappointing, except by critics (particularly in Eastern Europe) who favor the more blatantly revolutionary novels and see Sillitoe as having finally faced up to the political responsibilities of his work.

Biography

Alan Sillitoe was born in Nottingham, England, on March 4, 1928, to Christopher and Sylvina (Burton) Sillitoe. His father was a tannery laborer, his grandfather an upholsterer, and his maternal grandfather a blacksmith, putting young Sillitoe in the sociological milieu that would constitute most of his literary subject matter. During most of his childhood, his father was unable to get work, and he later wrote, "My parents constantly fought. I think they would have fought if they had been rich, but fighting among parents when they are poor is somehow much worse." As World War II began, his father more readily found work and the home situation improved. As the second eldest child, Sillitoe often took the responsibility of taking care of his brothers and sisters by telling them stories or putting them to bed. He attended various Nottingham schools; as a student, he did fairly well but later admitted that not much was expected of lower-class children. At eleven, he entered a scholarship examination, which he failed; as a result, he left school at fourteen to work in a Raleigh bicycle company only a few hundred yards from his home. Later, he took jobs in a plywood mill and as a capstan-lathe operator. He gave no thought to becoming a writer and might well have spent his life at factory work were it not for his service in the Royal Air Force.

In 1946, at age eighteen, Sillitoe trained as a radio operator in the air force and was assigned to Malaya. He stayed for nearly two years and, because his radio hut was relatively isolated from the main camp, read works of which he had been only scarcely aware in his teens, when he had read comic books and other juvenile works. Inspired by such works as Leo Tolstoy's *Sevastopol Sketches* (1854-1855) and *The Kreutzer Sonata* (1889), Sillitoe began keeping a journal and, as he later commented, "wrote what I thought were poems." As the war between Communist guerrillas and the colonial government developed, Sillitoe found himself sympathetic to the enemy's cause and hoped only to survive to return to England. When he returned home, he was given a physical examination before his discharge and was discovered to have tuberculosis. He was kept in the RAF for another two years for treatment, spending most of his time in hospital beds. With nothing else to do, he began to write seriously, producing several hundred poems, a few short stories, and a first draft of a novel of 100,000 words. He destroyed the latter, produced in just seventeen days when he was only twenty-one, along with the poems and short stories.

After his discharge, he received a pension that gave him plenty of free time to hone his writing skills. From 1952 to 1958, he traveled in France, Italy, and Spain. He first spent a year in southeast France in a cottage near Menton, then settled on Majorca for five years, where he taught English and did translations. During this time, he met and was encouraged by Robert Graves, also on the island. After ten years of teaching himself to write, Sillitoe's first novel, *Saturday Night and Sunday Morning*, was published in 1958, and critics perceived his portrayal of British working-class life to be a revolutionary force in British literature, winning for him the Author's Club prize. In 1959, after the publication of *The Loneliness of the Long Distance Runner*, he was awarded the Hawthornden Prize for Literature.

On November 19, 1959, he married the American-born poet Ruth Fainlight, who worked with him on the play *All Citizens Are Soldiers* in the early 1960's. They have two children. Since 1970, he has served as literary adviser to W. H. Allen and Company, the publisher of most of Sillitoe's novels, short-story collections, and poetry. Although he considers himself a poet primarily, critics do not agree, seeing his fiction, especially the short stories, as being the best manifestation of his talent.

Analysis

Like D. H. Lawrence, whose father was a miner, Alan Sillitoe is among the few British novelists to have come from the working class. Lawrence, also born and reared in Nottinghamshire, shocked "proper" society with his frank treatment of sexual themes; it is worth noting, however, that the famous trial of *Lady Chatterley's Lover* (1928) did not occur until 1959, the year after the publication of Sillitoe's *Saturday Night and Sunday Morning*, and the same year as the publication of *The Loneliness of the Long Distance Runner*, a fact which has led some critics to remark that the shocking quality of Lawrence's novel lies more in its representation of the illicit relations between a woman of high station and her gardener, an ex-soldier, rather than the sexual content itself. For similar reasons, Sillitoe's first novel was considered shocking in its revelation of the true nature of factory-workers' lives. Drunken Arthur Seaton, the central character, begins the novel by tumbling down a flight of stairs. Seaton is a busy womanizer who becomes responsible for such things as an illegal abortion. Any illusions that British readers may have clung to regarding the nobility of the working class or the redemptive qualities of work were shattered. Furthermore, the illusion that British workers were loyal to their society was destroyed by most of the characters' disrespect for traditional values. The fact that Sillitoe made no attempt to punish his characters for their behavior was an important element in making the book "shocking." Seaton, as it turns out, is rather successfully operating within the factory system he despises. The traditional values are meaningless to him, but his lack of them does not destroy him.

On account of the outrageous behavior and bitter undertone of *Saturday Night and Sunday Morning* and *The Loneliness of the Long Distance Runner*, the themes of Sillitoe's fiction were likened to the rebellious themes of John Osborne, William Cooper, Kingsley Amis, John Wain, Colin MacInnes, and John Braine (the "Angry Young Men"), whose novels, in various ways, underscore the rule of privilege and injustice in the British welfare state. As later critics have pointed out, however, the association is not entirely justified. Amis, Wain, and Osborne were university trained, and their "anger" was directed at the moral and aesthetic cost of rising to the top. They exhibit much class consciousness and are neither proletarian writers nor even socialist writers. The "Angry Young Men" were primarily a group of bourgeois writers who were irritated by the traditional restrictions which kept them from rising even higher in an economic and social sense. Braine was of a working-class background, but his characters exhibit distaste for the lower classes, as if Braine were delighted to have escaped his origins—much the same attitude is present in Lawrence, and is not similar to Sillitoe's attitudes at all.

Sillitoe is more properly associated with antibourgeois writers such as David Storey, Stan Barstow, Keith Waterhouse, Raymond Williams, and John Arden, who violently attacked a society that could easily satiate the physical hungers of its workers while destroying their spirit. Sillitoe's strength in his working-class novels comes from his writing from the point of view of lower-class characters so that the reader comes to understand them from the inside rather than the outside. Sillitoe establishes the basic humanity of the working class, and whatever mindlessness or vulgarity his characters possess is the result of their being in the grip of forces beyond their control. Furthermore, Sillitoe manages to avoid the mistake of many naturalistic and proletarian writers whose characters are mere puppets to their urges and desires. Walter Greenwood's *Love on the Dole* (1933), for example, is an admitted influence upon Sillitoe, but the essential pessimism of this and other proletarian novels is not present in his work. Sillitoe is more complex. His characters have a huge potential beneath their drab exteriors. They are resourceful. They are proudly working class. They maintain their personal integrity and their individual freedom by rejecting the values of a society which has rejected them. The most obvious examples of such characters are Colin Smith, the long distance runner who throws the All-England race in the famous short story, and, of course, Arthur Seaton.

Sillitoe's career, judging from his incredible output, is far from over, and has suffered from the extraordinary expectations created by his earliest published works. Having established so vividly the problems of working-class life in postwar Britain, Sillitoe was expected to come forth with a vision that would transcend the brutish lives of class. Unfortunately, though he has reached out for a solution, he has come up with little more than awkward parables and vague, anarchical ideas. He has not, so far, conveyed the conviction or prophecy of a Lawrence, and his reputation continues to rest on his accurate representations of lower-class life.

Saturday Night and Sunday Morning, Sillitoe's first published novel, has generally been called his best and most important work so far. Critic Anthony West went so far as to assert that with this work alone, Sillitoe had "assured himself a place in the history of the English novel." Negative reaction focused on the nature of the central character himself, Arthur Seaton, who was considered a cad unworthy of attention by some critics, and inadequate as a working-class hero, a view particularly prevalent in Eastern Europe. These reactions can be seen as further confirmation of exactly what most critics praised, the realism of the novel.

Arthur Seaton, the hero, is a rogue who has a meaningless job. Except for the two years of his military service, he has been working in the factory since he was fifteen. As the novel opens, he is twenty-one and living from weekend to weekend, when he gets drunk, fornicates, and, on Sunday morning, fishes. His job consists of drilling steel cylinders, and inevitably, as the day wears on, the numbing boredom causes Seaton to retreat into a world of fantasy. Through his fantasies and his weekend debauchery, Seaton manages to maintain his individuality while so many of his fellow workers gradually become zombies indistinguishable from their machines, ending as his father does— mindlessly sitting in front of a television screen.

Throughout the first chapters of the book, Arthur is a devil-may-care prankster who is sleeping with two sisters, Winnie and Brenda, cutting up with his brother Fred, and enjoying what he calls the "good life." He is defiant, making many gestures, such as refusing free company tea, to maintain his independence. He regards the factory management as "bastards," and his most important concern is not letting them "wear him down." Politically unaffiliated, he trusts neither management nor labor and says "Me, I couldn't care less if the world did blow up tomorrow, as long as I'm blown up with it." Later, however, Arthur undergoes a metamorphosis. He begins to think that adultery is not an adequate substitute for living with the same woman all the time, and faces the problem of reconciling his freedom with his desire for close human relationships. Brenda becomes pregnant, and Arthur is badly beaten by two soldiers. Hence, Arthur yields gradually to the inevitable responsibilities of maturity.

Hugh B. Staples has drawn many parallels between Robert Graves's *The White Goddess* (1947) and Seaton's development, pointing out that Graves, who encouraged Sillitoe's early career, has provided the mythic blueprint for Seaton's growth. In the first chapter, Seaton is pictured curled up like a fetus after tumbling drunk down a flight of stairs at the White Horse Club. Plainly infantile, Seaton follows Graves's symbolic pattern of the death and rebirth of the hero-king. His becoming the hero upon whom the continuity of human life and civilization depends takes place within a year and requires his acceptance of a mature relationship with a woman. Among other details which seem to support Staples' theory are Brenda's hot bath to induce abortion, which can be seen as a parody of Graves's cauldron scene; Seaton's near-acceptance of the cosmic forces that control him during a thunder storm; his symbolic death at the hands of two soldiers; his rebirth during Aunt Ada's Christmas party; and his final engagement to Doreen, which symbolizes his submission to the role of hero-king.

Even with such an intricate network of symbolism, *Saturday Night and Sunday Morning*'s greatest strength remains its vivid realism. The world of the working class is re-created with all its joys and sorrows, and, as Seaton probes the inner recesses of his mind, the reader is allowed to discover Seaton as he discovers himself.

The success of *The Loneliness of the Long Distance Runner* was followed by critical dismay at *The General*, a fable originally written in 1953 and published as a novel after revisions in 1960. Attacked for lack of verisimilitude, the book was plainly misunderstood, though it was obviously intended to be philosophical rather than realistic. It was later adapted into the motion picture *Counterpoint*, with Charlton Heston and Maximilian Schell.

In 1961, *Key to the Door* was published. Consisting of a compilation of works written earlier in his life, it is the most frankly autobiographical of Sillitoe's novels and was praised for the depictions of life during the Depression in the first half of the novel; the second half, however, disappointed many critics because of the Communist tendencies of the hero, Brian Seaton (Arthur Seaton's brother), and because of the insufficient development of his character. Sillitoe's sympathy for Malayan rebels was transferred to Seaton, who refuses to fire upon them, but his sudden committment to their cause was believed to be too abrupt.

The Death of William Posters, *A Tree on Fire*, and *The Flame of Life* compose a trilogy dealing with the character Frank Dawley, who can be considered an older Brian Seaton. As *Key to the Door* ended, Seaton was twenty-one; *The Death of William Posters* begins with a twenty-seven-year-old Dawley fed up with his factory work and on the road in search of his freedom. All his life seems empty, and he abandons his wife and job, finding a lover, living in Spain, and becoming involved in the Algerian revolution. In *A Tree on Fire*, Dawley continues his fighting in Algeria, while his lover

Myra returns to England with their son and is met by Albert Handley, a successful painter. Through Handley, Sillitoe portrays a restive middle class which, rather like the "Angry Young Men," fantasizes a British civil war, while Dawley continues his search for identity. In *The Flame of Life*, Dawley returns to England and becomes involved in a mystical, revolutionary group. The anarchical, violent vision of life presented in the trilogy was received coolly by critics, who accused Sillitoe of subordinating characterization to political propaganda, contrary to his stated aesthetic: "I try to see every person as in individual and not an idea."

The Widower's Son was praised for being Sillitoe's best novel since *Saturday Night and Sunday Morning*, and further clarified his conception of life as a battle and of the world as a jungle in which an individual is surrounded by hostile forces. By rising in society, William Scorton becomes as isolated as many of Sillitoe's earlier characters. He finds little satisfaction in becoming a Colonel, while his relationship with his wife deteriorates. The price of Scorton's rise is seen to be as severe as that of failure, the consequence his father, a retired sergeant-major, most feared for the man. Scorton, feeling out of touch with his roots, lives out a cycle of violence that no one, in Sillitoe's view, is able to escape. As Scorton himself observes, "We're all locked up one way or another, because that's what civilization is: hemmed in by family and hooked by a job." The novel's tone is naturalistic; its sometimes strident didacticism is mitigated by convincing portrayals of Scorton and his father.

The Storyteller received scant praise. In tackling the tale of a professional storyteller, Sillitoe ran into the usual dangers of the novelist writing about writing and was considered to have failed in what is usually his greatest strength, characterization. The elements of allegory on the role of the artist as creator were perceived as being labored, although many scenes within the novel were considered vivid and exciting.

Her Victory, Sillitoe's most recent novel, was better received. In it he tackled the controversial topic of women in society. His central character, Pam, is a forty-year-old Nottingham woman in an unhappy twenty-year marriage. Some reviewers likened it to the many feminist novels published in the late 1970's and early 1980's. Abused by her husband, Pam attempts suicide, but is rescued by a merchant seaman with whom she falls in love. Though generally thought more interesting than many of his previous novels, *Her Victory* was criticized for having neo-Victorian qualities with allusions to Charles Dickens, Joseph Conrad's *Victory* (1915), and George Eliot's *Daniel Deronda* (1876).

Major publications other than long fiction

SHORT FICTION: *The Loneliness of the Long Distance Runner*, 1959; *The Ragman's Daughter*, 1963; *Guzman Go Home*, 1968; *A Sillitoe Selection*, 1970;

Men, Women, and Children, 1973; *The Second Chance*, 1981.

PLAYS: *All Citizens Are Soldiers*, 1969 (adaptation with Ruth Fainlight); *Three Plays*, 1978.

POETRY: *Without Beer or Bread*, 1957; *The Rats and Other Poems*, 1960; *A Falling Out of Love and Other Poems*, 1964; *Shaman and Other Poems*, 1968; *Love in the Environs of Voronezh and Other Poems*, 1968; *Poems*, 1971 (with Ted Hughes and Ruth Fainlight); *Barbarians and Other Poems*, 1974; *Storm*, 1974; *Snow on the North Side of Lucifer*, 1979.

NONFICTION: *The Road to Volgograd*, 1964; *Mountains and Caverns*, 1975.

CHILDREN'S LITERATURE: *The City Adventures of Marmalade Jim*, 1967.

Bibliography

Hurrell, John Dennis. "Alan Sillitoe and the Serious Novel," in *Critique*. IV (Fall/Winter, 1960-1961), pp. 3-16.

Lee, James W. "Myths of Identity: Alan Sillitoe's *The Death of William Posters*; *A Tree on Fire*," in *Old Lines, New Forces*, 1976. Edited by Robert K. Morris.

Penner, Allen Richard. *Alan Sillitoe*, 1972.

Roskies, D. M. "Alan Sillitoe's Anti-Pastoral," in *Journal of Narrative Technique*. X (1980), pp. 170-185.

Staples, Hugh B. "*Saturday Night and Sunday Morning:* Alan Sillitoe and the White Goddess," in *Modern Fiction Studies*. X (Summer, 1964), pp. 171-181.

J. Madison Davis

WILLIAM GILMORE SIMMS

Born: Charleston, South Carolina; April 17, 1806
Died: Charleston, South Carolina; June 11, 1870

Principal long fiction

Martin Faber: The Story of a Criminal, 1833; *Guy Rivers: A Tale of Georgia*, 1834; *The Yemassee: A Romance of Carolina*, 1835; *The Partisan: A Tale of the Revolution*, 1835; *Mellichampe: A Legend of the Santee*, 1836; *Richard Hurdis: Or, The Avenger of Blood, a Tale of Alabama*, 1838; *Pelayo: A Story of the Goth*, 1838; *The Damsel of Darien*, 1839; *Border Beagles: A Tale of Mississippi*, 1840; *The Kinsmen: Or, The Black Riders of the Congaree*, 1841 (revised as *The Scout*, 1854); *Confession: Or, The Blind Heart*, 1841; *Beauchampe: Or, The Kentucky Tragedy, a Tale of Passion*, 1842; *Helen Halsey: Or, The Swamp State of Conelachita, a Tale of the Borders*, 1845; *Count Julian: Or, The Last Days of the Goth, a Historical Romance*, 1845; *Katharine Walton: Or, The Rebel of Dorchester*, 1851; *The Sword and the Distaff: Or, "Fair, Fat and Forty,"* 1852 (revised as *Woodcraft*, 1854); *Vasconselos: A Romance of the New World*, 1853; *The Forayers: Or, The Raid of the Dog-Days*, 1855; *Eutaw: A Sequel to the Forayers*, 1856; *Charlemont: Or, The Pride of the Village*, 1856; *The Cassique of Kiawah: A Colonial Romance*, 1859.

Other literary forms

William Gilmore Simms wrote extensively in all major literary genres. He began as a poet and achieved his first widespread fame in the northern United States with his long poetic work *Atalantis: A Story of the Sea* (1832). Although he continued to write and publish his verse throughout his lifetime, and, indeed, felt himself to be a good poet, his reputation has never rested on his poetic abilities. Still, his poetry is not without interest, for Simms often reveals a sharp eye for natural detail in his descriptions, especially of the Southern landscape. His accomplishments as a writer of short fiction have only recently begun to be appreciated. His emphasis on realism can be seen in such works as "The Hireling and the Slave," and his wonderful command of folk humor can be found in such literary "tall tales" as "Bald-Head Bill Bauldy" and "How Sharp Snaffles Got His Capital and Wife." Longer stories such as *As Good as a Comedy: Or, The Tenesseean's Story* (1852) and "Paddy McGann" contain further elements of the tall tale and folklore. Simms was not a good dramatist; he wrote a number of aborted plays and, in the case of *Pelayo*, adapted a failed drama into novel form. His best play is considered to be *Michael Bonham: A Tale of Texas* (1852), which deals with the Texas war for independence.

In his nonfiction works, Simms often turned to the history of the South.

Of his four major biographies, two—*The Life of Francis Marion* (1844) and *The Life of Nathanael Greene* (1849)—grew out of his abiding interest in the Revolutionary War in the South; both men also appeared as characters in his novels. His historical writings include *The History of South Carolina* (1840), a general history of the state, beginning with its settlement; *South-Carolina in the Revolutionary War* (1853), which concentrated on that part of the state's history which he so often used in his fiction; and his contemporary account of the Civil War, *Sack and Destruction of the City of Columbia, S.C.* (1865), an inspired example of reporting. Although Simms was not always accurate or unbiased, he was a surprisingly good historian. He collected sources throughout his life, made use of private recollections and memoirs, and today his work provides a storehouse of information often overlooked by more standard historical works. Simms's combination of the factual and the imaginative in his historical romances is one of his strongest and most appealing traits.

Achievements

Although during his lifetime William Gilmore Simms's popularity as a novelist ranked second only to that of James Fenimore Cooper, his reputation steadily diminished after his death, so that by the turn of the century he was little more than a footnote in literary histories. With the University of South Carolina Press publications of *The Letters of William Gilmore Simms* (1952-1956, 5 volumes, Mary C. Simms Oliphant, editor) and the first volumes of *The Centennial Edition of the Writings of William Gilmore Simms* (1969-1975, 16 volumes, John C. Guilds and James B. Meriwether, editors), however, there has been a growing interest in his work. Still, the fact remains that Simms's contributions to the development of American literature in the first half of the nineteenth century have been much underrated. Put simply, Simms was the most important antebellum Southern man of letters. He created a body of work that is awesome in size and scope. More than eighty separate volumes were published during his life, and ongoing research is uncovering more of his writings hidden in forgotten periodicals or under various pseudonyms.

When, in 1832, Simms first traveled to New York City, he was determined to establish himself as a writer of national importance. He made the necessary publishing connections and paid homage to the leading Northern literary figures. The publication of his poetic work *Atalantis* in that year was enthusiastically received, but it and his short novel *Martin Faber*, published the following year, were still apprenticeship pieces which followed patterns set down by others. With *Guy Rivers*, *The Yemassee*, and *The Partisan*, Simms not only staked out his own literary territory but also publicly placed himself in competition on a national level. Simms was an ardent supporter of the idea that America must produce its own unique brand of writing, inspired by its own land and people and experiences. Simms's own interest lay in the South, but, as he explained in the Preface to *The Wigwam and the Cabin* (1845), by mastering sectional material, the writer could still be of national importance, since no single writer could adequately depict the country as a whole.

It was in his commitment to the South that Simms achieved his greatness. He saw the South as a land of exciting potential. He loved its rawness as well as its manners, its violence as well as its vitality. Its heritage was rich, he felt, but largely unknown to people both inside and outside the region. Thus, Simms, with his passion for history and folklore, set out to reveal this past to Southerners and Northerners alike, to correct the historical picture he found so lacking. In his romances, he helped to define the popular image of the South from precolonial times up to the American Civil War. The Northerner, Simms maintained, had no right to feel superior to his Southern brethren, but the Southerner had all too often been remiss in preserving and appreciating his own heritage.

As the political disputes between North and South intensified, Simms became a protector of a way of life he felt was being threatened. In this time of trouble, he maintained that the past held lessons for the present: the courageous spirit of the pioneer and the partisan soldier could still inspire, the inherent nobility of the manor-born ladies and gentlemen could still instruct. Thus, Simms's tales of an earlier era, marked by characters of indomitable strength, could be seen as examples for his own time.

The sheer quantity of Simms's work remains staggering and his overall achievement approaches the heroic. Although he sometimes bemoaned the lack of appreciation and support he received in the South, most of his contemporaries, despite occasional carping, freely awarded him the laurels of leadership. A less courageous and confident man would never have faced the challenges that Simms invited. Before the war, he sought, through his own example, to impart a sense of dignity to the Southern artist. For the five years he lived after the war, he struggled to rekindle the pride of a defeated people, in the midst of his own great personal tragedy. As a critic and an editor, as a poet and a writer of fiction, he worked at first with energy and enthusiasm, later out of a kind of desperation against the inevitable, but he never stinted in his devotion to art and to a world which came to lie in ruins around him.

Biography

William Gilmore Simms was born in Charleston, South Carolina, on April 17, 1806, the second son and only surviving child of William Gilmore and Harriet Ann Augusta Singleton Simms. Simms's father came from Ireland after the American Revolution and established a successful mercantile business in Charleston. His mother's family, the Singletons, had lived in the port city for generations. Her grandfather, Thomas Singleton, was one of the Charleston citizens arrested by the British authorities during their occupation and, despite his advanced age, sent in exile to St. Augustine; her father, John Singleton, had fought as a soldier on the side of the patriots. Simms's mother died in 1808, and shortly thereafter, his father, grief-stricken at the loss of his wife, left Charleston to journey westward, placing his only child in the care of his late wife's mother, Mrs. Jacob Gates (she had remarried in 1800 after the death of John Singleton in 1799). The elder Simms went on to lead what must have seemed an incredibly exciting life to his impressionable son; the boy heard tales of his father's fighting under Andrew Jackson in the Indian Wars in Florida and later at the Battle of New Orleans in the War of 1812 before settling in Mississippi, then the edge of the frontier. Thus, Simms the boy grew up surrounded by legends and dreams of almost mythical characters—the Revolutionary War heroes on the Singleton side of the family, and the pioneer-soldier he saw in his own father. Both romantic threads would run throughout Simms's writings. In addition, growing up in historic Charleston allowed him to visit sites of Revolutionary incidents in and near the city. His unflagging interest in history (especially that of South Carolina but also of foreign lands) provided a foundation for his wilder imagination, and his writings would always contain a solid understructure of fact.

Although tradition has held that Simms grew up in genteel poverty in Charleston, feeling ostracized by that aristocratic city's more prominent citizens, his father had, in fact, left him substantial property holdings, and Simms was recognized early for his achievements. Still, it is equally clear that Simms was sensitive to slight—at least partly because of boyhood loneliness after the loss of his immediate family—and his enormous artistic energy no doubt fed on this partial uncertainty.

In 1812, at the age of six, Simms began school in Charleston. He entered the College of Charleston when he was ten, and at twelve he began work in a local apothecary shop. He was already writing poetry and drama. By the age of sixteen, he had published verse in a Charleston newspaper; at seventeen he was editing a juvenile periodical, the first of many editorships he would undertake in his lifetime. The next year, 1824 to 1825, Simms spent with his father in Mississippi. Together they ranged into the wilderness, where Simms met and carefully observed the types of frontiersmen (rascals and rogues among them) and Indians which would people his romances.

When Simms returned to Charleston in 1825, he set about establishing himself as a writer. His first volume of verse, *Monody on the Death of Gen. Charles Cotesworth Pinckney* (1825), made him a prominent local talent. In 1826, he married Anna Malcolm Giles. The next year Simms was admitted to the bar and published his second and third volumes of poetry. In 1828, he bacame editor of the *Southern Literary Gazette*; in 1829, his fourth volume of verse appeared, and his fifth followed in 1830. Also in 1830, he became copartner in the Charleston *City Gazette*; in this role he figured as a leading opponent to the Nullification Movement which was dividing South Carolina into two very fractious parties. Simms's opposition brought him into serious disfavor with many important citizens, and it was an experience which he would remember with a mixture of anger and regret.

The year 1832 was a decisive one for Simms. His wife, Anna, died in February. Overtaxed by emotional and professional demands, Simms gave up his legal practice (never a foremost interest), sold the *City Gazette*, and journeyed to New York City, determined to make his way in earnest as a literary man. In New York, he formed what was to be a lifelong friendship with James Lawson. Simms would use Lawson's home as his northern base until the Civil War finally intervened; Lawson would be among the first to help Simms in the dark days after the war as well. With Lawson's encouragement and advice, Simms published his sixth volume of poetry, *Atalantis*, in 1832. When it proved extremely popular with the Northern audience, Simms followed it with his first novel, *Martin Faber*, and his first collection of short fiction, *The Book of My Lady*, both in 1833. With the publication of *Guy Rivers* in 1834 and of *The Partisan* and *The Yemassee* in 1835, Simms had announced his literary directions, as these three books were the first of his Border, Revolutionary, and Colonial romances, respectively.

The next twenty or so years were generally good ones for Simms. In 1836, he married Chevillette Eliza Roach, the daughter of a prominent land owner in South Carolina. As part of his marriage inheritance, Simms obtained "Woodlands" plantation, which became his most prized retreat, an emblem of all he saw best in the Southern way of life. The demands of his life-style made it necessary that Simms publish as much and as often as possible, but because of the laxity of copyright laws he often received far less than he was due for what he did write. Simms would travel to New York about once a year to confer with his publishers (for a time new works by Simms came out annually) and to visit old friends. He enjoyed his growing reputation as spokesman for the South. Although he was always interested in politics and acted as an informal adviser to a number of political leaders in South Carolina, he served only one term in government, as a member of the South Carolina House of Representatives from 1844 to 1846. His most notable literary position during this time was as editor of *The Southern Quarterly Review* from 1849 to 1854.

Beginning in the 1850's, Simms became a leading and increasingly strident voice in the call for Southern secession from the Union and in the defense of slavery. Unfortunately, he is too often remembered for the attitudes struck in these pronouncements, so at odds with modern understanding, at the expense of his more important creative works. As a public figure, Simms attracted the opprobrium aimed at the South as war became inevitable. His 1856 lecture tour of the North on the role of the South in the American Revolution had to be cut short when Simms enraged his audiences with his vigorous and even pugnacious arguments against the Union stand. He welcomed the final break and was confident of Southern victory, but as the war progressed, he came to see the specter of defeat.

The last years of Simms's life were tragic. In 1862, "Woodlands" was partially burned but was rebuilt through the subscriptions of appreciative South Carolinians. In 1863, his second wife died, a devastating blow to Simms, who had also lost nine of his children. In 1865, "Woodlands" was again set ablaze, this time by stragglers from General Sherman's army. Simms lost in this conflagration his private library of ten thousand volumes, considered to be the finest in the South at the time. During the five years remaining to him after the war, Simms worked as never before, as editor of two newspapers—the Columbia *Phoenix* and the *Daily South Carolinian*—and as the author of still more poems, addresses, short fiction, and serialized novels. Despite his own almost inconceivable losses, Simms did what he could to bring about the resurrection of his land and people. When he died on June 11, 1870, a world and a way of life had clearly passed with him.

Analysis

As early as 1835, in the Preface to *The Yemassee*, William Gilmore Simms attempted to define his goals as a writer. He distinguished his full-length fiction as "romances" rather than novels. Following definitions already in vogue, Simms described the novel as picturing ordinary people in everyday situations, both domestic and common. These works he traced to Samuel Richardson and Henry Fielding. The "romance," on the other hand, he saw as the modern-day equivalent to the ancient epic, drawing its inspiration and power from both drama and poetry. The romance (as practiced by writers such as Sir Walter Scott, Edward Bulwer-Lytton, and James Fenimore Cooper) was of "loftier origins" than the novel. Its characters were individuals caught up in extraordinary, uncertain, even improbable events. As Simms saw it, the writer of a romance was not as bound by strict logic as was the novelist; indeed, the romancer's ingenuity in plotting was often a strong point in the work. As critics have pointed out, a number of Simms's supposed literary sins—stock characters, absurd resolutions, inflated dialogue—resulted from the romantic tradition in which he worked rather than from a lack of art or skill.

To categorize Simms simply as a writer of romances is, however, somewhat misleading, and more recent studies have emphasized the strong sense of realism that is found in his work. During his lifetime, Simms was regularly accused of exceeding the bounds of propriety. He answered these objections on numerous occasions. In his "Advertisement" to *Mellichampe*, for example, he insisted that his purpose was to "adhere as closely as possible, to the features and the attributes of real life." Thus, although he endeavored to invest his stories with noble characters involved in stirring adventures, he wished to write neither "a fairy tale, [n]or a tale in which none but the colors of the rose and rainbow shall predominate."

This sense of realism, which must have seemed uncouth in Simms's own time, has come to be recognized as one of his strongest traits. He was clearly influenced by the "realism" of the legends and frontier tales of his youth and in the writings of the Southern and Southwestern humorists. Augustus Baldwin Longstreet's *Georgia Scenes* was published in 1835, the same year as *The Yemassee* and *The Partisan*. (Simms would himself write several brilliant "tall tales" such as "Bald-Head Bill Bauldy" and "How Sharp Snaffles Got His Capital and Wife.") Simms's sense of realism did not apply only to "low" characters and their exploits, however, as has often been implied. Simms would modify the nobility, the wisdom, even the courage of his "model characters," his aristocrats, if the story warranted it. His heroes could learn, could fail, could grow; and his villains were often surprisingly complex, capable of unexpected decency and courageous deeds.

Underlying all of Simms's romances was a strong awareness of history, of what had actually happened at the time and place about which he wrote. Simms felt free to bend fact to the demands of art, but not to misrepresent the essential truth of the situation. The *facts* of history, he said, standing by themselves, carried little weight, but the artist—the creative writer—by giving *shape* to the facts, could give them life and meaning. Thus, it is the writer who is the true historian, and it was as an "artist-historian" that Simms wrote most of his romances.

As all commentators on Simms like to point out (and as Simms himself was aware), he usually wrote too rapidly and carelessly. He simply produced too much for the good of his own reputation. His faults are often glaring, but they are usually the result of haste and little or no revision. Simms could write with clarity and precision, but he could also sacrifice both for blood and thunder. Simms was a storyteller, and his books, for all their length, keep a steady pace. When he turned his hand to psychological interpretations of characters, when he tried to "analyze the heart," he often did so with the concomitant loss of energy and drive. In his best works, however, he was able to combine complexity of character with a compelling story.

Simms wrote eight romances dealing with the Revolutionary War in the South, and as a group they represent his best work. The novels cover the period from 1775, when the first open warfare began, to 1783, when the British abandoned Charleston and the soldiers returned home to a new and difficult way of life. The internal chronology of the novels does not correspond to the sequence of their composition. "Joscelyn: A Tale of the Revolution," which was meant to be the "opening scene" in Simms's "grand drama" of the South's seven-year war of Revolution, was one of the very last works he wrote, and the only one of the eight never to appear in book form during his lifetime. It appears as volume sixteen of *The Centennial Edition of the Writings of William Gilmore Simms*. "Joscelyn" is set around the Georgia-South Carolina border and describes the early conflicts between those who joined in the growing freedom movement and those who remained loyal to the crown. It also shows that men on both sides of the issue could be motivated by cruelty as well as courage, by selfishness as well as honor.

The next three novels—*The Partisan, Mellichampe,* and *Katherine Walton*— were conceived of by Simms as a trilogy, with developing characters and overlapping plots, although each was also meant to stand as an independent work. These books cover the events of 1780, following the fall of Charleston to the British. *The Partisan* is a big, sprawling book which Simms later described as a "ground-plan," a setting of the stage for the works to come. It introduces numerous characters, both historical—Francis Marion, Lord Cornwallis, Banastre Tarleton, Horatio Gates, Baron DeKalb—and fictional—Major Robert Singleton, Colonel Richard Walton, his daughter Katharine, Lieutenant Porgy—who return in later works in the series. *The Partisan*'s story lines include the development of Marion's guerrilla forces in the swamps of South Carolina, the growth of love between Singleton and Katharine Walton, and the agony of Colonel Walton's decision to align himself with the rebel cause. The novel closes with a detailed description and analysis of the Battle of Camden (in August, 1780), wherein Gates and the Southern Continental Army were soundly defeated by Cornwallis. *Mellichampe* is set in the fall of 1780. It put less emphasis on the large historical picture and was more clearly intended as a work of fiction, although here again the "facts" of the war are not forgotten. In *Mellichampe*, Simms expands his description of Marion's role in the war, develops several minor characters found in *The Partisan*, and illustrates the "excesses of patriotism" and the necessity of honor in times of conflict. The third book of this trilogy, *Katharine Walton*, again takes up the story of Colonel Walton, his daughter, and Robert Singleton. It is set largely in Charleston during the last months of 1780 and describes the social life and attempts at rebellion in the captured city at this very trying time.

The next in the series is *The Scout*, which moves into the central region of South Carolina. It is, in some ways, the most "romantic" and melodramatic of the novels. Its plot of feuding brothers and mysterious outriders is heavy with conventions, but in its description of the marauding outlaw bands which terrorized the back country and in its discussion of Nathanael Greene's siege of the British fort at Ninety-Six (upstate South Carolina) in the summer of 1781, *The Scout* is an impressive and absorbing story. *The Forayers* and *Eutaw*, which were first conceived as one book, follow the retreat of the British from Ninety-Six to Charleston and present the events leading to the climactic battle at Eutaw Springs, South Carolina, in September, 1781, which effectively ended British rule in the state, although the battle itself was a draw.

The last of the Revolutionary War novels is *Woodcraft*, which begins in December, 1782, after the British evacuation. Its theme is the readjustment of soldiers to domestic life, and its main character is Lieutenant Porgy, the wastrel aristocrat soldier whom many feel to be Simms's most successful character. Porgy appears in five of the eight novels, but his most important role is in *Woodcraft*. Basically a comic character (Porgy is often compared to William Shakespeare's Falstaff, although such comparisons rarely go beyond surface descriptions), this fat soldier confronts the challenges of peace after the adventures of war. Born of the landed gentry, Porgy is known to have wasted his inheritance as a young man, and despite his courage and wit, he is not one of Simms's noble heroes. He is, however, among the most likable and (with reservations) the most admirable of Simms's characters, and it is his mood of reconciliation (after one final battle) and acceptance that presides over this last book. Some critics hold *Woodcraft* to be Simms's best work (although *The Forayers* and *Eutaw* might be better choices), and it certainly shows Simms at his most relaxed and amiable.

Commonly listed under the category of Simms's Border Romances are *Guy Rivers*, *Richard Hurdis*, *Border Beagles*, *Beauchampe*, *Helen Halsey*, *Charlemont*, "Voltmeier: Or, The Mountain Men," and "The Cub of the Panther." These works lack the specific historical overview of the Revolutionary War novels—they are closer to Simms's own time and are not as likely to be built around identifiable events—but they do give excellent descriptions of the frontier of the Old South—the customs, speech patterns, and life-styles of settlers, outlaws, and adventurers. The first of these, *Guy Rivers*, was Simms's first full-length novel as well. Set in the mountainous region of Georgia, where gold was being mined in the early 1800's, the story centers on the conflict between Guy Rivers, a notorious outlaw (though once a respected lawyer) and Ralph Colleton, a young South Carolinian whose own frustrations with love and family have led him to the frontier. There he meets Mark Forrester, a native of the region who helps Ralph in his "natural" education. Colleton foreshadows such later Simms's heroes as Robert Singleton, Ernest Mellichampe, and Willie Sinclair (in *The Forayers* and *Eutaw*), while Forrester anticipates Thumbscrew Witherspoon in *Mellichampe* and Supple Jack Bannister in *The Scout*, woodsmen who teach the young aristocrats the need for clear thinking and honorable actions. Rivers is the melodramatic villain of the type that would chew the scenery and threaten feminine virtue in a number of Simms's works: Barsfield in *Mellichampe*, Edward Conway in *The Scout*, Captain Inglehardt in *The Forayers* and *Eutaw*.

Richard Hurdis, the second of the Border novels, is perhaps the best of them. Set in Alabama, the story is loosely based on the outrages of John Murrell and his outlaw gang which roamed throughout Alabama and Mississippi. Simms apparently had met witnesses to or even participants in some of this gang's doings while visiting his father in Mississippi as a boy. The plot is somewhat similar to that of *The Scout*: in each novel, two brothers— one virtuous and one criminally inclined—find themselves at odds; both books are concerned with the attempts to bring outlaw bands to justice. In a sense, *Border Beagles* is a continuation of *Richard Hurdis*; a tale of bandits on the Mississippi frontier, it is generally considered a less effective story than its predecessor.

Beauchampe was Simms's retelling of the notorious Beauchampe-Sharpe "Kentucky tragedy," a murder case in which Beauchampe killed Warham Sharpe, the seducer of Margaret Cooper, whom Beauchampe had married. In 1856, Simms returned to this story in *Charlemont*, which detailed the events leading up to the "tragedy" in *Beauchampe*. Thus, *Beauchampe*, although published first, was, in Simms's words, the "sequel" to *Charlemont*. Simms's last two Border romances were both published in magazines in 1869, at the very end of his life. "Voltmeier" was published again in 1969 as volume one of *The Centennial Edition of the Writings of William Gilmore Simms*. "Voltmeier" and "The Cub of the Panther" were drawn from Simms's personal observations and experiences during trips into the mountainous regions of North Carolina, and they contain some of his best writing.

Simms dealt with the settling of South Carolina in the early eighteenth century in two important works, *The Yemassee* and *The Cassique of Kiawah*. *The Yemassee* was Simms's most popular novel, and, because of its Indian theme, was immediately compared to the works of Cooper. The novel described the 1715 Yemassee Indian War against the colonists. Simms's tale concentrates on two main characters: Governor Charles Craven (a historical figure), who takes the disguise of Gabriel Harrison for much of the book, and Sanutee, the chief of the Yemassee. Simms illustrates Sanutee's problem with sympathy and understanding—the Indian had originally welcomed the settlers and then found himself and his tribe threatened by them—but the novel finally argues in favor of the white men and the advanced civilization they bring with them. Despite *The Yemassee*'s popularity—it is still the work for which Simms is best remembered—the novel is not as impressive as *The Cassique of Kiawah*, a much later and more mature work, which deals with similar material but has received little critical attention. It has been argued that Simms's picture of the Indian was more realistic than Cooper's. He avoided the idea of the "noble savage," but often imbued his Indians with traits of courage and dignity. In addition to these two novels, Simms used colonial and Indian material in several of his shorter works found in *Carl Werner*, *The Wigwam and the Cabin*, and *The Lily and the Totem: Or, The Huguenots in Florida*.

Simms's interest in European history, especially in Spanish history, dated back to his childhood and formed the basis for four foreign romances. *Pelayo* had been conceived when Simms was seventeen as a drama on the conquest of Spain by the Moors. The play was never performed, and the material later grew into a novel. *Count Julian* was the sequel to *Pelayo*, but its publication was delayed for a number of years because its manuscript was lost for a time.

The Damsel of Darien was inspired by the adventures of Vasco Balboa, while *Vasconselos* concerned itself with Hernando DeSoto's explorations in the New World. Most critics and readers would agree that these works are among Simms's weakest.

Simms's first novel was *Martin Faber: The Story of a Criminal*. It recounts the first-person confessions of the title character, who has seduced and murdered one girl and married another, whom he then begins to suspect of adultery. Faber tells his story in prison, just before his execution. The book is a short and emotional work, and was quickly linked to William Godwin's *The Adventures of Caleb Williams: Or, Things as They Are* (1794), although its antecedents could also be found in numerous Gothic romances. Simms returned to this type of story in *Confession: Or, The Blind Heart*, which, in his introduction, Simms linked to Godwin. *Confession* was the reworking of an idea Simms had played with as a younger writer. He explained that he had forgotten the work before he found the manuscript by accident years later. As he reread it, he was "led away" by the psychological aspects of the tale. *Confession* tells of Edward Clifford, a young lawyer who is consumed by jealousy of his wife. Convinced of the worst, Clifford kills the entirely virtuous woman; when he later discovers the truth, he condemns himself to a life of wandering and self-recrimination. The similarities to Shakespeare's *Othello* (1604) are obvious, although Simms maintained that the materials were "gathered from fact."

The same interests in crime, guilt, and retribution are found throughout his other works—he was always intrigued by the psychological complexities of sinners and criminals—and it could be argued that *Beauchampe* and *Charlemont* might better be placed in this group than among the Border tales. These psychological novels, however, are not the works for which Simms is remembered. Although his constantly inquiring imagination was stirred by these situations, he was the master of scope and action rather than the kind of close analysis these topics demanded. The twists and entanglements of plot which could be overridden in his more sweeping works became all too obvious when related at a slower, more concentrated pace.

In his lasting works, Simms's long undervalued contribution to America's literary heritage is clearly evident. His was the voice of the South—the maker of its romances, the singer of its legends, the keeper of its history, and the defender of its traditions. More than any other writer, he embodied his time and place: its grandeur, its courage, and its wrongheadedness.

Major publications other than long fiction
PLAY: *Michael Bonham: A Tale of Texas*, 1852.
POETRY: *Monody on the Death of Gen. Charles Cotesworth Pinckney*, 1825; *Early Lays*, 1827; *Lyrical and Other Poems*, 1927; *The Vision of Cortes*, 1829; *The Tri-Color*, 1830; *Atalantis: A Story of the Sea*, 1832; *Areytos: Or, Songs*

of the South, 1846; *Poems Descriptive, Dramatic, Legendary and Contemplative*, 1853.

SHORT FICTION: *The Book of My Lady*, 1833; *Carl Werner*, 1838; *The Wigwam and the Cabin*, 1845; *Southward Ho!*, 1854.

NONFICTION: *The History of South Carolina*, 1840; *The Geography of South Carolina*, 1843; *The Life of Francis Marion*, 1844; *Views and Reviews in American Literature, History and Fiction*, 1845; *The Life of Captain John Smith*, 1846; *The Life of the Chevalier Bayard*, 1847; *The Life of Nathanael Greene*, 1849; *The Lily and the Totem: Or, The Huguenots in Florida*, 1850; *South-Carolina in the Revolutionary War*, 1853; *Sack and Destruction of the City of Columbia, S.C.*, 1865.

MISCELLANEOUS: *The Letters of William Gilmore Simms*, 1952-1956 (Mary C. Simms Oliphant, editor, 5 volumes); *The Centennial Edition of the Writings of William Gilmore Simms*, 1969-1975 (John C. Guilds and James B. Meriwether, editors, 16 volumes).

Bibliography

Hubbell, Jay B. "William Gilmore Simms," in *The South in American Literature 1607-1900*, 1954.

Kibler, James Everett, Jr. *The Poetry of William Gilmore Simms: An Introduction and Bibliography*, 1979.

_____ . *Pseudonymous Publications of William Gilmore Simms*, 1976.

Parks, Edd Winfield. *William Gilmore Simms as Literary Critic*, 1961.

Ridgely, J. V. *William Gilmore Simms*, 1962.

Trent, William P. *William Gilmore Simms*, 1968.

Wakelyn, Jon L. *The Politics of a Literary Man: William Gilmore Simms*, 1973.

Edwin T. Arnold III

UPTON SINCLAIR

Born: Baltimore, Maryland; September 20, 1878
Died: Englewood, New Jersey; November 25, 1968

Principal long fiction

Springtime and Harvest, 1901; *Prince Hagen*, 1903; *The Journal of Arthur Stirling*, 1903; *Manassas*, 1904; *The Jungle*, 1906; *A Captain of Industry*, 1906; *The Overman*, 1907; *The Metropolis*, 1908; *The Moneychangers*, 1908; *Samuel the Seeker*, 1910; *Love's Pilgrimage*, 1911; *Sylvia*, 1913; *Sylvia's Marriage*, 1914; *King Coal*, 1917; *Jimmie Higgins*, 1919; *100%*, 1920; *They Call Me Carpenter*, 1922; *Oil! A Novel*, 1927; *Boston*, 1928; *Mountain City*, 1930; *Roman Holiday*, 1931; *The Wet Parade*, 1931; *Co-op*, 1936; *The Flivver King*, 1937; *No Pasaran!*, 1937; *Little Steel*, 1938; *Our Lady*, 1938; *World's End*, 1940; *Between Two Worlds*, 1941; *Dragon's Teeth*, 1942; *Wide Is the Gate*, 1943; *Presidential Agent*, 1944; *Dragon Harvest*, 1945; *A World to Win*, 1946; *Presidential Mission*, 1947; *One Clear Call*, 1948; *O Shepherd, Speak!*, 1949; *Another Pamela: Or, Virtue Still Rewarded*, 1950; *The Return of Lanny Budd*, 1953; *What Didymus Did*, 1954; *It Happened to Didymus*, 1958; *Theirs Be the Guilt*, 1959; *Affectionately Eve*, 1961.

Other literary forms

Between 1901 and 1961, Upton Sinclair wrote or rewrote more than forty novels, but in addition to his longer fiction, Sinclair also wrote and published a massive amount of nonfiction, including pamphlets, analyses of diverse subjects, memoirs, twelve plays, and letters by the thousands. The bibliography of his works is testimony to his amazing fluency, but no one who is so prolific can escape being uneven, and this is indeed the case with Sinclair. His career, which spanned more than six decades, was unified in one respect, however, for both his fiction and his nonfiction were devoted to a single aim—the achievement of social justice. Everything that he wrote was written primarily as a means to attain the end he sought, bettering the conditions of life for his fellowman. Thus, much of what Sinclair produced is not belletristic in any full sense, but propaganda to spread his ideas about politics and economics. In books such as the *The Industrial Republic* (1907), he tries to explain how socialism will be arrived at by a natural process in America; the theory is based on the premise that social revolutions are bound to be benevolent. During the period following World War I to the onset of the Depression, most of Sinclair's writing was nonfiction. In a number of books, which he called his Dead Hand series, an ironic allusion to Adam Smith's "Invisible Hand" of *laissez-faire* economics, Sinclair deals with the destructive influence of capitalism on numerous American institutions: *The Profits of Religion* (1918) treats the abuses of institutional religions, showing how the established church supports the ruling classes in exchange for economic advantages; *The Brass Check: A Study in American Journalism* (1919) details the operation of class bias in American journalism; *The Goose-Step: A Study of American Education* (1923) reveals higher education's lackeylike relationship to capitalism, fostered by grants and endowments made to the universities by wealthy families and industry. In *The Goslings: A Study of the American Schools* (1924), the same kind of servile relationship with the capitalist status quo is exposed as existing in elementary and high schools, and in *Mammonart* (1925), Sinclair shows how artists and writers down through history have been duped into serving oppressive economic and political power structures. Not even William Shakespeare, Fyodor Dostoevski, or Joseph Conrad were their own men according to Sinclair's ideological criticism. Although the Dead Hand series is flawed by an excess of socialist polemics, Sinclair did an extensive amount of research to produce each book, and though the case is overstated, there is a grain of truth in his analysis of the all-pervasive influence of the economic and political structure of America on those areas that should be most independent of such pressure—the Church, the press, the educational system, the arts.

Of more interest to the general reader are Sinclair's autobiographical works *American Outpost: A Book of Reminiscences* (1932) and *The Autobiography of Upton Sinclair* (1962), which updates his life for the thirty years intervening between the two books. In his accounts of his life, Sinclair reveals himself to be an honest but self-centered idealist. He chronicles his victories and defeats through childhood, youth, and marriage as the educational experiences of a genius; he offers in generally positive and optimistic terms his lifelong belief in progress and his hatred of social inequality and social exploitation.

Achievements

Sinclair's literary remains weighed in at eight tons when being collected for donation to Indiana University Library. Of modern American writers, he is among the most widely translated, his works having been translated into forty-seven languages in thirty-nine countries, yet his literary reputation has been on a steady decline since the 1940's, despite the fact that *The Jungle* is still widely read in high school and college classrooms. Moreover, Sinclair himself has historical importance for the role he played in the American radical movement.

Sinclair's recurring theme as a novelist was class-conflict, the exploitation of the poor by the rich, of labor by management, of the have-nots by the haves. With few exceptions, the rich are depicted as useless, extravagant, and unprincipled, while the poor are essentially noble characters who are the victims of capitalistic society. Sinclair's literary method, which came to be called "muckraking," was intended to expose the evils of such a society. Apart from *The Jungle*, which is the best-known example of this genre, there is the

Lanny Budd series—ten historical novels that trace the history of the world from 1913 to 1946. *Dragon's Teeth*, the third in the series, won the Pulitzer Prize for Fiction in 1942 by virtue of its vivid portrayal of conditions in Nazi-dominated Europe. In addition to these, the most widely read of Sinclair's novels, he produced novels on almost every topic of then-current social history, including coal strikes in Colorado in *King Coal*, exploitation by the oil industry in California in *The Wet Parade*, and the legal injustices of the Sacco-Vanzetti case in *Boston*. All of Sinclair's fiction was aimed at the middle-class liberal, whom he hoped to convert to his idealistic vision of a brotherhood of labor. Sinclair was thus a spokesman for the progressive era of American history; a chronic protestor and iconoclast, he tried to stir the conscience of his nation and to cause change. In only one case, *The Jungle*, was he successful in prompting the desired changes through legislation. As a propagandist writing in the spirit of Thomas Paine and in the idiom of Karl Marx, Sinclair made a permanent impact by what he said, if not by how he wrote, and to this day, he still serves as one of the chief interpreters of American society to other nations.

Biography

Upton Beall Sinclair was born in Baltimore, Maryland, but reared in New York. Finishing high school at the age of twelve, he was too young for college and had to wait until he was fourteen before he could enter the City College of New York. While an undergraduate, he helped support himself by writing stories and jokes for pulp magazines. In one span of a few weeks, he turned out fifty-six thousand words, an incredible feat even for a prolific prodigy such as Sinclair. In 1898, after taking his B.A. from CCNY, Sinclair enrolled as a special student in the Graduate School of Columbia University, but withdrew after a professor told him "you don't know anything about writing." In 1900, Sinclair married Meta Fuller and began work on his first novel, *Springtime and Harvest*, which was written in Canada. Shortly afterward, in 1902, he joined the Socialist party. The reception of his early fiction gave him little critical encouragement and no cash of which to speak. His first four novels brought him less than one thousand dollars, and the threat of poverty put a strain on his marriage. In 1905, Sinclair, with Jack London, formed the Intercollegiate Socialist Society, an indication of his growing political radicalism.

Sinclair's first fame came with his fifth novel, *The Jungle*; he was even invited to the White House by President Theodore Roosevelt to discuss the book. With the thirty thousand dollars that *The Jungle* earned for him, Sinclair founded a Utopian community, Helicon Colony, in New Jersey. In 1907, an arsonist burned down the Colony and Sinclair's fortune with it. This was the first actual persecution that Sinclair had experienced for professing unpopular views. In private life, he faced further difficulties; his wife divorced him in

1911; he remarried in 1913 and moved West with his new wife, Mary Kimbrough, in 1915. Continuing to write at a furious pace, Sinclair became a publisher during World War I with the *Upton Sinclair Magazine*. He also issued a series of tracts on the effects of capitalism, objecting to its effects on education, art, journalism, and literature.

Not all of Sinclair's energies went into writing. He was instrumental in creating The League for Industrial Democracy and the American Civil Liberties Union. Three times he ran for the California state legislature and three times for governor, usually on the Socialist party ticket but also as a Democrat. In *I, Governor of California and How I Ended Poverty* (1933), he set forth his platform, "End Poverty in California" or "E.P.I.C.," which explained the Depression as a result of private ownership and the economic insanity of limited production. His ideas found a large degree of public acceptance in the early days of the New Deal and he came close to being elected despite the mudslinging of his opponent. Some critics believe that the chief reason for Sinclair's decline as a novelist was his involvement in electoral politics in the 1930's. His novels of that decade are about specific political situations. *The Flivver King* attacks Ford Motor Company and makes a case for labor unions. "Little Steel" is a story about the organization of steel-mill owners against unions. "Pasaram!" is another short story from the 1930's about the brave fight in the Spanish Civil War against right-wing dictators.

During World War II, Sinclair began the historical record of his times in the Lanny Budd series. The novels in this ten-book series show the metamorphosis of the hero, Lanny, from an espouser of socialist causes to an anti-Communist, a change that reflected Sinclair's own changed sympathies.

By the decade of the 1950's, Sinclair had entered semiretirement, during which he nevertheless managed to expand his autobiography and finish six books, including a clever parody of Samuel Richardson's epistolary novel *Pamela* (1740-1741), entitled *Another Pamela*, and a biography of Jesus. In these years, Sinclair finally settled his quarrel with the status quo. In his old age, he came to approve of the American establishment's foot-dragging on civil rights and supported American intervention in Vietnam. The old radical had, like so many before him, softened his position.

Analysis

Upton Sinclair was a prodigy as a writer and wrote with great fluency and consequent unevenness. For him, the essential purpose of literature was to expose social evils and promote change; his end as a writer was the improvement of mankind's condition. Thus, his literary reputation is not really germane to what he was trying to do as a writer. His fiction has more relevance when it is regarded in a political and historical light rather than as literature per se. As the social and economic issues of his time recede into history, so does interest in those books which were simply propaganda.

Although Sinclair was regarded as a literary rebel for his iconoclastic attacks on America's economic, intellectual, and political institutions, he was not in any way an avant-garde writer in terms of style and structure. His subject was society rather than the individual human consciousness. It is necessary in any analysis of Sinclair's fiction to admit at once the defects in his writing. Most of it is journalistic in quality rather than belletristic. In fact, he deliberately wrote against the genteel tradition in American letters. Sinclair employed his rhetoric for practical results rather than to achieve poetic effects. His polemics were couched in fictional form because he believed the novel was a particularly effective medium for his idealistic radicalism.

Sinclair's first four novels were produced between 1900 and 1904. These early works were awkward but full of passionate idealism. In *Prince Hagen* and *The Overman*, which were written before Sinclair discovered socialism, there is already a conflict between the pure-minded and the corrupt oppressors, but no solutions for the problems are proposed. The ideology of socialism provided him with solutions, although Sinclair was not a traditional Socialist: to him, socialism was the purest expression of the American dream. He did not see himself as an overthrower of American values, but as a writer who was helping his countrymen return to a vision of human brotherhood.

Prior to *Manassas*, Sinclair's fiction had been based on personal experience. In this novel about the Civil War, a young Southerner, Alan Montague, the son of a Mississippi plantation owner, becomes a supporter of Abolition. The protagonist is present at many historic moments—the raid at Harper's Ferry, the bombardment of Fort Sumter—and encounters many historical figures, such as Abraham Lincoln, Jefferson Davis, Frederick Douglass, and John Brown. *Manassas* differed from Sinclair's early books in that it was more realistic and objective. As a work of art, however, *Manassas* is not remarkable. The plot is often an inert review of historical facts, the characterizations are shallow, and the story is too filled with coincidence to be plausible. Despite its flaws, *Manassas* marked a turning point in Sinclair's career. In this novel, he revealed attitudes that pointed toward his development as a writer of exposés.

In 1904, Sinclair was asked by the editor of *The Appeal*, a radical paper, to write a novel about wage-slavery and the oppressive conditions of industrial workers which would show that their plight was analogous to that of the black in the Old South. Responding to this offer, Sinclair spent two months in the meat-packing houses of Chicago talking to the workers; he visited the plants also as an official tourist, and in disguise as a worker. The impressions and information Sinclair gathered from this experience were extremely distressing to him. His personal reaction to the corruption he saw was outrage; it is his identification with the exploited workers and his naturalistic descriptions of the oppressive industrial conditions that make his next novel, *The Jungle*, so gripping.

As Sinclair explains in his autobiography, *American Outpost*, he returned to his farm in New Jersey after he had collected his data on the meat-packing industry in Chicago and started writing the novel on Christmas Day, completing it in the summer of 1905 after less than six months' work. Although it was published in serial form as it was being written, Sinclair had trouble finding a publisher for the book; it was refused by five houses before Doubleday & Company took it after their lawyers made a careful investigation to avoid any possible libel suits. When *The Jungle* was published in February, 1906, the public was horrified, not by the novel's account of the conditions of the workers as Sinclair and his socialist friends expected, but by the naturalistic descriptions of the slaughterhouses and the evidence of criminal negligence in meat inspection. *The Jungle*, like most of Sinclair's fiction, straddles genres; it is partly a novel and partly exposé journalism. Sinclair's purpose in writing the book was to protest the exploitation of the workers and to recommend socialism as a corrective ideology to capitalism; the revelations of unsanitary packing-plant procedures were only a means to those ends. Hardly a dozen pages of this long novel are explicitly concerned with the repugnant details of the slaughterhouse, yet what remains in the reader's mind long after the plot line and thematic intentions fade are the scenes of grinding up poisoned rats, children's fingers, and carcasses of steers condemned as tubercular for canning meats; and the rendering of hogs dead of cholera for a fine grade of lard. Most dramatic of all, however, was Sinclair's report that the men who served in the cooking room occasionally fell into the boiling vats and were returned to the world transubstantiated into Durham's Pure Leaf Lard. The vividness of the author's descriptions had two effects: the first was an immediate drop in meat sales across America and Europe; the second was a summons to the White House to detail the abuses in the meat industry to President Theodore Roosevelt. The outraged public brought pressure to bear on politicians, and Congress enacted the Federal Pure Food and Drug Act of 1906.

The sensational revelations of *The Jungle* have drawn attention from the book's literary qualities. *The Jungle* has been compared to the polemical late works of Leo Tolstoy and to the naturalistic fiction of Émile Zola because of its pessimistic determinism. The setting is the grim slums of Chicago and the gory stockyards. The novel tells the story of a group of recent Lithuanian immigrants who have been lured to American from their old-world villages with promises of high wages.

Jurgis Rudkus, the novel's principal character, comes to the stockyard district, along with several of his friends and relatives, expecting to realize the American dream, little aware that they have entered a jungle. Unable to speak English, the immigrants are exploited by almost everyone in power—the politicians, the police, the landlords, and the "Beef Trust" bosses. Jurgis has to pay his foreman part of his low salary to keep his job. He is cheated by a crooked real-estate agent, who sells him a house with a hidden clause which allows the mortgage company to foreclose on Jurgis. After losing his house, Jurgis and his family are afflicted with misery. His job is taken away after he is blacklisted; he serves a jail term for slugging his wife's lascivious boss, who has compromised her honor. In turn, his father dies of disease, his wife and infant son die in childbirth, and finally, he loses his last son in a drowning accident. Jurgis is left without anything; alone and in ill-health, he is a broken man. He becomes a hobo, a petty criminal, and a strike-breaking scab—the lowest form of degradation for him.

In his extremity, Jurgis for the first time reflects upon how unjustly he has been treated by society, which he begins to regard as his enemy, but his views are inchoate. One day, by chance he hears a Socialist speak. The lecture transforms his conception of the world; socialism is like a revelation, for now there is a way by which the workers of the world can win respect. With Jurgis' conversion, the novel as a narrative ends for all practical purposes. The last chapters are devoted to socialist propaganda and socioeconomic analysis. The optimistic conclusion of the novel contrasts sharply with the pessimistic naturalism of the first chapters. Ironically, and to Sinclair's disappointment, the appeal to socialism and the protest against wage-slavery did not win the hearts and minds of his audience, but his realistic portrayal of conditions in the meatpacking industry (as he once remarked) surely turned the stomach of the nation.

The Jungle will never be placed in the first rank of American fiction because of its mixture of fictional and journalistic elements, its unresolved contradictions in theme, and its melodramatic plot and bifurcated structure. Sinclair tried to do too many things at once, and was only partially successful. Most readers think that the true significance of Sinclair's achievement in *The Jungle* lies in the uncensored presentation of the conditions of working-class life. Only Stephen Crane in *Maggie: A Girl of the Streets* (1893) had dealt with slum subjects with such integrity, and Sinclair had no models to follow in depicting this strata of society. In his firsthand observations and deep compassion for the oppressed, he was breaking new ground for literary treatment, which Theodore Dreiser would follow to different purposes.

Following the success of *The Jungle* was difficult for Sinclair. He spent the next eight years trying to repeat what he had done with his first and best "muckraking" book. He produced a number of novels focused on specific problems, but at the other end of the social scale. *The Metropolis* is an exposé of conspicuous consumption among upper-class New York socialites. It is a poor book by Sinclair's own admission and is remarkable only for the absence of socialistic sermons by the author. Sinclair, like F. Scott Fitzgerald, apparently believed that money sets the very wealthy quite apart from the rest of society, but, rather than seeking rapport with his wealthy characters, as Fitzgerald did, Sinclair hoped to reform them. Another novel of this period, *The*

Money Changers, is a story of the machinations of a high financier, obviously patterned on J. P. Morgan; the story tells of the exploits of Dan Waterman, the elderly head of the Steel Trust, who creates a panic on Wall Street purely for personal revenge against a rival steel magnate. Although *The Money Changers* is not very good fiction, it does have an interesting premise, suggesting a connection between sexual desire and the drive for financial power.

Another novel of this period that deserves mention for its subject is *Love's Pilgrimage*; neofeminist in theme, this work examines the pressures on Sinclair's own marriage because of his male insensitivity to his wife's personal, sexual, and intellectual needs. The novel is also interesting for the insight it offers into Sinclair's personality, for he candidly implies that the divorce his first wife sought was deserved because he prudishly withheld from sexual relations on the theory that it would decrease his creative energy.

In 1914, Sinclair was remarried and living in California. The transition in his life resulted in a change in his writing. In the West, Sinclair was drawn back to the problems of the proletariat by labor strife in the Colorado coal mines. As a result of the attempt by the United Mine Workers to organize the miners, the govenor of Colorado had called up the state militia to break up strikes. In 1914, in the town of Ludlow, National Guard troops fired into a camp of strikers and their families, killing eleven women and two children. This shocking event outraged Sinclair as nothing had since he had witnessed the brutal conditions of the stockyards.

Following the methods he had used to collect background material for *The Jungle*, he went to Colorado, visited the miners and their families, and talked with the mining officials and labor leaders. His direct contact with the working-class people stirred his emotions and gave him a more realistic point of departure for his next novel, *King Coal*, than any he had employed since *The Jungle*. In fact, *King Coal* was an attempt to repeat the same sort of muckraking performance that had succeeded so well in the former case. Unfortunately for Sinclair, *King Coal* did not create the response aroused by *The Jungle*, a fact largely resulting from the lag time in the publication of the novel. When *King Coal* appeared in 1917, the events in Ludlow were three years old and yesterday's news. America had just entered World War I, and the nation's mind was on "doughboys" rather than on coal miners.

The poor reception of *King Coal* was a great disappointment to Sinclair, because he knew he had produced the kind of novel he wrote best. *King Coal*, while not as powerful as *The Jungle*, has the rhetorical strength and the factual validity of the earlier book. Sinclair tells the story of a rich young man named Hal Warner, who impersonates a coal miner in order to investigate working conditions in the western coal camps. He becomes a union sympathizer and labor agitator after he becomes convinced that the mine owners are denying the miners their legal rights and are cheating them out of their wages by rigged scales. After witnessing the futility of getting justice for working men inside the legal system, the miners go on a wildcat strike. Hal convinces his coworkers to join the union, and the novel ends with the lines drawn between labor and management while Hal returns to college, vowing to continue his fight for the working people of America.

Although *King Coal* is not as powerful in its naturalistic details as *The Jungle* and lacks the pessimistic determinism of that novel, it is in the opinion of most critics Sinclair's second-best effort at muckraking. If very few Americans responded to Sinclair's account of the dangers of cave-ins, coal dust, and explosions, this result may be because they were never exposed to such perils, whereas all were subject to health hazards as a result of unsanitary food processing. For this reason, the exposé of negligence in Chicago meat-packing plants had a much more profound and practical effect than the exposé of the inhuman conditions in the coal camps of Colorado.

Between World War I and the start of the Depression, Sinclair wrote two remarkable novels based on topical social or political situations. *Oil!* delves into the Tea Pot Dome and other oil scandals of the Harding Administration, and thus has considerable historical significance as well as being one of Sinclair's most readable books. *Boston*, on the other hand, represents Sinclair's best use of a contemporary event for fictional purposes. This novel enfolds the drama of the Sacco-Vanzetti case, but it also encompasses the whole of Boston's society, suggesting that the city itself was responsible for what happened in this tragic case. The central character is again from the upper classes, an elderly Back Bay aristocrat, Cornelia Thornwell, wife to a governor. Full of vitality and intelligence, she thinks that she has spent her life as an artificial adornment to a great family. She determines late in life to emancipate herself from mores and manners of the mansion, and moves out to board with the Brini family, who are honest Italian mill hands, and starts to earn her own living in a factory.

At this point, Vanzetti enters the story. During a strike in the mill, he plays an important role in keeping up the workers' spirits. He also prevents them from organizing, because as an anarchist, Vanzetti did not support unions. Afterward, Vanzetti and his friend Sacco are marked as "anarchist wops" by the police. They are picked up as suspects in a payroll robbery, and in the midst of the deportation mania of the postwar period, the city's reason and sense of justice are beclouded. The courts, judge, jury, and prosecutor seem determined to make the foreigners pay—if not for the crime, then for their politics. The climax of the novel comes when the cogs of justice bring the proletarian saints, Vanzetti and Sacco, to the electric chair with many doubts about their guilt still lingering.

Through a blending of fact and fiction, Sinclair is able to record a complex and tragic story of social injustice, although the story of the runaway grand-mother does get lost in the final pages as the historical facts dominate the plot. As a novel, the two-volume *Boston* is too long except for readers with some special interest in the Sacco-Vanzetti case. As usual, Sinclair was writing for a mass audience, and the novel employs many stock characters and a melodramatic plot; furthermore, a statement of socialist doctrine forms a coda to the novel. Sinclair does, however, create a convincing portrait of Vanzetti. It is in Sinclair's account of the death of this man of dignity and intelligence that the novel gains its greatest power.

The major literary effort of Sinclair's career was launched just before the outbreak of World War II: a ten-novel series offering a fictionalized history of the Western world in the first half of the twentieth century. The series is unified by its central character, Lanny Budd, and is known collectively by his name. One of the Lanny Budd novels, *Dragon's Teeth*, won for Sinclair a Pulitzer Prize in 1943. A chronicle of Germany's slide into Nazism, *Dragon's Teeth* is a scrupulous study of the fateful years between 1930 and 1934, and reflects an extensive research effort on Sinclair's part. In fact, several critics claimed that if the book were stripped of its fictional ingredient, it might well serve as a history text.

Sinclair creates an air of impending doom as he shows how quickly Europe was led to the abyss. His protagonist, Lanny Budd, is a neutral observer traveling the Continent with his millionaire wife, Irma, who is especially obtuse about economics, politics, and national traits. She is a foil to the sensitive and intelligent Lanny, who is aware of the coming crisis. Irma and her upper-class female friends refuse to believe that their smug routine of bridge and dinner parties will be disrupted. The reader in 1942 received these opinions with a great deal of dramatic irony. Meanwhile, Lanny grows increasingly concerned about the absence of morality in the political climate of Germany. Lanny has rather improbable meetings with the big-wigs of the Nazi regime. He goes hunting with Hermann Göring, has cocktails with Joseph Goebbels, and a discussion with Adolf Hitler about the Jewish question. His interest in this topic is not merely academic, since his sister is married to one of Germany's most prominent Jews. The Jews in Germany, however, are like Irma's circle; they refuse to face the realities of Nazism. The novel ends with Lanny's contriving to help his brother-in-law escape the dragon's teeth of the Nazi menace, closing the story on an exciting climax, somewhat like that of a cliffhanger film of the 1940's.

Sinclair continued the adventures of Lanny Budd, interweaving fiction with fact as he related the sequence of world events in *World's End* which covers the years 1913 to 1919; *Between Two Worlds* deals with the events between the Versailles Treaty and the stock market crash of 1929; the author then covers the Nazi "Blood Purge" of 1934 to the Spanish Civil War in *Wide Is the Gate*; the annexation of Austria, the invasion of Czechoslovakia, and the Munich pact in *The Presidential Agent*; the fall of France in *Dragon Harvest*; and America's entry into the war in *A World to Win*. The years of Allied setbacks, 1941-1943, are covered in *Presidential Mission*; *One Clear Call* and

O Shepherd, Speak! deal with the Normandy Invasion and the defeat of the German military machine; and in the sequel to the series, *The Return of Lanny Budd*, Sinclair brings events up to 1949 and the onset of the Cold War between the United States and the Soviet Union.

As a whole, this group of novels is interesting, in part simply because the series surveys a dramatic period of history in considerable detail. Throughout the series, Sinclair's careful research is evident, but the popularity of these novels was also a result of their appeal to patriotism. America's role as the savior of civilization is increasingly emphasized in the later novels in the series. During this period, Sinclair's confidence that progress was represented by socialism and Communism was shaken by the example of the Soviet Union. Like so many early twentieth century political radicals, he became an anti-Communist in the 1950's.

Sinclair was a propagandist first and a novelist second, if propaganda is defined as an "effort directed systematically toward the gaining of support for an opinion or course of action." He wrote millions of words trying to change, improve, or expose oppressive conditions. Because Sinclair so obviously used literature for ulterior purposes and because he was so prolific, serious critics have unduly neglected him; on the other hand, he has been overrated by those foreign critics who delight in finding indictments of America by an American writer. As time puts Sinclair's contribution to American literature into perspective, it seems certain that he will never be regarded as a great novelist, but he will fairly be judged an honest, courageous, and original writer.

Major publications other than long fiction

PLAYS: *Plays of Protest*, 1912; *Hell: A Verse Drama and Photo-Play*, 1923; *The Millennium*, 1924; *The Pot Boiler*, 1924; *Singing Jailbirds*, 1924; *Bill Porter*, 1925; *Oil!*, 1925; *Depression Island*, 1935; *Wally for Queen!*, 1936; *Marie Antoinette*, 1939; *A Giant's Strength*, 1948; *The Enemy Had It Too*, 1950.

NONFICTION: *Our Bourgeois Literature*, 1905; *The Industrial Republic*, 1907; *The Fasting Cure*, 1911; *The Profits of Religion*, 1918; *The Brass Check: A Study in American Journalism*, 1919; *The Book of Life, Mind and Body*, 1921; *The Goose-Step: A Study of American Education*, 1923; *The Goslings: A Study of the American Schools*, 1924; *Mammonart*, 1925; *Letters to Judd*, 1925; *Money Writes!*, 1927; *Mental Radio*, 1930; *American Outpost: A Book of Reminiscences*, 1932; *I, Governor of California and How I Ended Poverty*, 1933; *The Way Out—What Lies Ahead for America?*, 1933; *The EPIC Plan for California*, 1934; *What God Means to Me*, 1936; *Terror in Russia: Two Views*, 1938; *Expect No Peace!*, 1939; *A Personal Jesus*, 1952; *The Cup of Fury*, 1956; *My Lifetime in Letters*, 1960; *The Autobiography of Upton Sinclair*, 1962.

CHILDREN'S LITERATURE: *The Gnomobile: A Gnice Gnew Gnarrative with Gnonsense, but Gnothing Gnaughty*, 1936.

Bibliography
Bloodworth, William. *Upton Sinclair*, 1977.
Harris, Leon. *Upton Sinclair: American Rebel*, 1951.
Kazin, Alfred. *On Native Grounds*, 1942.
Rideout, Walter. *The Radical Novel in the United States*, 1956.
Yoder, Lon. *Upton Sinclair*, 1975.

Hallman B. Bryant

ISAAC BASHEVIS SINGER

Born: Leoncin, Poland; November 21, 1904

Principal long fiction

Shoten an Goray, 1935 (published in the United States as *Satan in Goray*, 1955); *Messiah the Sinner*, 1936 (serialized); *Di Familie Mushkat*, (published in the United States as *The Family Moskat*); *Shadows on the Hudson*, 1957 (serialized); *A Ship to America*, 1958 (serialized); *Der Kuntsnmakher fun Lubin*, 1959 (serialized; published in the United States as *The Magician of Lublin*, 1960); *Der Knekht*, 1961 (serialized; published in the United States as *The Slave*, 1962); *The Manor*, 1967 (serialized in Yiddish in 1953-1955); *The Estate*, 1969; *Sonim de Geshichte fun a Liebe*, 1966 (serialized; published in the United States as *Enemies: A Love Story*, 1972); *The Penitent*, 1974; *Yarme and Kayle*, 1977; *Shosha*, 1978. All of Singer's novels have appeared initially in Yiddish serialized form; there are considerable time gaps of a novel's Yiddish serialization date, and/or its Yiddish book publication date, and/or its translation date.

Other literary forms

The first work that Isaac Bashevis Singer published when he came to the United States was the novel *Messiah the Singer*. It was serialized in three Yiddish daily papers: the *Vorwärts* (*Jewish Daily Forward*, in New York), the *Warshanahaint* (in Warsaw), and the *Pariser Haint* (in Paris). Singer himself considered this work a "complete failure" and never attempted to translate it. Four other Singer novels have been serialized in the *Jewish Daily Forward* but have not been translated to date: *Shadows on the Hudson*, *A Ship to America*, *The Penitent*, and *Yarme and Kayle*. In addition to his novels, Singer has written memoirs, *Mayn Tatn's Bes-din Shtub* (1956, *In My Father's Court*), *A Little Boy in Search of God* (1976), *A Young Man in Search of Love* (1978), and *Lost in America* (1980); more than one hundred stories; numerous books for children; two works on Hasidism, one in collaboration with the artist Ira Moskowitz, entitled *Hasidism* (1973), and the other, *Reaches of Heaven: A Story of the Life of the Baal Shem* (1981). He has also translated, into Yiddish, Stefan Zweig's *Romain Rolland* (1927), Knut Hamsum's *Die Vogler* (1928), *Victoria* (1929), and *Pan* (1931), Erich Maria Remarque's *All Quiet on the Western Front* (1930) and *The Way Back* (1931), Thomas Mann's *The Magic Mountain* (1932), and Leon Glaser's *From Moscow to Jerusalem* (1938); and has written many literary essays and reviews.

Achievements

Singer, acclaimed by some critics as a "genius," referred to by others as "one of the greatest writers of the modern world," is unequivocally the premier fictional historian and chronicler of the Eastern European Jewish community. In the aftermath of the Holocaust, which resulted in the obliteration of Central and Eastern European Jewry, the works of Isaac Bashevis Singer stand as monuments to a vibrant and vital world. Singer does not idolize this community: he depicts it in its totality, in its full humanity. His people are saints and sinners, believers and heretics, fools and scholars, avaricious merchants and ineffectual rabbis, wives and termagants. His imaginative world includes demons, elves, dybbuks, and magicians.

Singer's works are first written in the language of the shtetl, Yiddish. For Singer, Yiddish is more than the vernacular of the people of the Central and Eastern European Jewish community. It is, as he states in his Nobel Prize lecture, "the wise and humble language of us all, the idiom of a frightened and hopeful humanity." His works are difficult to translate because his Yiddish reflects the influence of three languages, Yiddish, Hebrew, and Aramaic, with frequent allusions to rabbinic and Talmudic lore. The richness of his prose, its texture, pace, and rhythm are qualities not easy to capture in translation. Singer works with his translators and participates in the editing. All of his works have first appeared in serial form in the Yiddish paper the *Jewish Daily Forward* (originally a daily, now a weekly) prior to their translation and rendition into book form, except for his first novel, *Satan in Goray*, which was serialized in the magazine *Globus* in Warsaw in 1934.

One of the outstanding characteristics of Singer's tales is his use of demoniac imagery. For Singer, this does not represent a love of the bizarre, the occult, or the Gothic, although he is interested in these. His demons figuratively portray the evil side of human nature, but he believes that supernatural powers—both good and evil—do exist, and he has affirmed his ultimate faith in Providence.

Singer's vision is optimistic when it concerns cosmic matters but pessimistic in dealing with humanity. He differs from his Yiddish literary contemporaries or predecessors in that most were secularists who had relinquished the past in favor of the Enlightenment. Most Yiddish writers after the 1940's portrayed an idealized and sentimental view of that shtetl. Singer could not accept this tradition. He maintains that the greatest gift of God is freedom of choice. Where there is no evil, there is also no freedom. He is aware that good, however, does not always triumph. His Jews are no different from other people: they are not all good. His characters share the traits and illusions of mankind.

Singer is a supreme storyteller. For him, the suspense, the adventure, the age-old pleasures of narrative are paramount: "The story is the very essence of literature." He leaves explanations and interpretations to his readers and critics. Singer has achieved a popular success unusual for a writer of his distinction; his works have become best-sellers and have been translated into fifty-eight languages. He has won the National Book Award twice and was awarded the Nobel Prize in Literature in 1978. A number of his works have been dramatized and performed in theaters all over the country; some have also been made into motion pictures. He is a popular figure on the campuses of colleges and universities, a favorite of interviewers, and has served as writer-in-residence at Oberlin, at the University of California, and at Bard College. He is also a member of the National Institute of Arts and Letters, with the distinction of being the only American writer to write in a language other than English.

Biography

Isaac Bashevis Singer was born in Leoncin, Poland, on November 21, 1904. He was the third child in a family of four siblings, which included an older sister, Hinde Esther, an older brother, Israel Joshua, and a younger brother, Moshe. His parents were Pinchas Mendel Singer, a Hasidic rabbi from Tomoszov, and Bathsheba Zylberman, the daughter of the *Mitnagid*—the opposing sect—rabbi of Bilogray. The couple seemed to be mismatched. Pinchas Mendel, a gentle, pious, spiritual man, was an ardent follower of Hasidism. Bathsheba, a learned, strong-minded woman, was a rationalist and a pragmatist. Israel Joshua, eleven years Singer's senior, inherited his mother's rationalism; Moshe, two years Singer's junior, inherited his father's piety. The confluence of parental legacies, the mysticism of his father and the rationalism of his mother, was Singer's inheritance, reflected in the tensions of his fictive characters: conflicts of the heart and the head, the sacred and the profane, the spiritual and the secular.

Four years after Singer's birth, the family moved to Warsaw, to an apartment on Krochmalna Street. Rabbi Pinchas Mendel became the rabbi of Krochmalna Street, and the Singer home served as its rabbinic court, *bet din*. Singer's memoirs *In My Father's Court* and *A Day of Pleasure: Stories of a Boy Growing Up in Warsaw* (1969) and the novels *Shosha* and *Yarme and Kayle* re-create the intricate life that existed on this cobblestoned shtetl street, a "literary goldmine" to which Singer regularly returns.

In 1917, at the age of thirteen, Singer accompanied his mother on a trip to Bilgoray. They stayed for four years. The visit was crucial in his development as a writer. Bilgoray, far removed from the bustle of cosmopolitan Warsaw, appeared to be untouched by modernity. It was a village wherein young Singer witnessed old world spirituality unblemished by the encroaching Enlightenment. This experience remained with him as an eternal reminder of his rootedness, indeed man's rootedness, in the past, in history, in that which transcends man. Bilgoray plays an important role in many of his tales; Singer says that he could never have written *Satan in Goray* without having been there.

In 1921, Singer entered a rabbinical seminary in Warsaw. He remained a year and then went back to Bilgoray and supported himself by teaching Hebrew. Shortly afterward, he joined his parents in Dzikow, a shtetl close to Bilgoray, where his father had accepted a position as a rabbi. He found this village stifling and depressing, and he was delighted when his brother offered him a job as proofreader for the journal *Literary Pages*, which he coedited. In 1923, Singer moved back to Warsaw to take up this new position. There, he supplemented his income by translating modern European fiction into Yiddish, including works by Hamsun, Zweig, Mann, and Remarque. His family was settled in Galicia, and he never saw his mother and younger brother again.

Singer fell in love with Runya, the mother of his only child, Israel, born the year of Singer's father's death in 1929. Runya was an avid Communist and wanted to live in Russia. She and Singer quarreled heatedly and frequently about political issues. Runya finally took their child and left for Russia in 1934. She was expelled shortly thereafter and went to join her mother in Palestine. Once settled there, she sent their son to Kibbutz Bet Alpha, where he still resides. He has changed his name to Israel Zamir—the Hebrew equivalent for Singer. Singer did not see his son for the next twenty years. In 1955, Zamir decided to visit his father; this episode is described in the short story "The Son" in the collection *A Friend of Kafka and Other Stories* (1970).

Singer's brother, Israel Joshua, was also a writer and served as his mentor. He was the person who exerted the greatest influence on the young Singer, encouraging him when he began to write and instructing him in the rules of good storytelling. The older brother, however, was a realist, while the younger brother was given to mysticism. His brother became part of the Jewish Enlightenment, the *Haskala*, that was overtaking the shtetl at the turn of the century. This caused friction in the Singer home, especially with their father, who was a traditionalist. Joshua—no one called him by his first name—moved out of the house, becoming an artist and then a writer. Singer would often visit his brother and discovered, in his studio, a whole new world. He describes the experience of going from his father's house to his brother's studio in *In My Father's Court*, saying: "it is just one step from the study house to sexuality and back again. Both phases of human existence have continued to interest me." Through his brother, he was introduced to secular literature. Singer lived, for the most part, in his brother's literary shadow. He used pseudonyms for his early writings; some stories were signed "Isaac Bashevis," from his mother's first name, to distinguish his works from those of this brother, while some were signed "Isaac Warshawsky" ("man of Warsaw").

Joshua emigrated to the United States with his family in 1933 and found a job on the Yiddish daily, the *Jewish Daily Forward*. He urged his brother to do likewise. With the shadow of Hitler extending over most of Europe, Singer did not need much coaxing. In 1935, he followed his brother. He has never returned to Poland and claims he never will.

Singer's acclimation to America was difficult. English was a strange language to him, and Yiddish, his mother tongue and his literary language, did not seem to have a future in America. One of his most recent works, *Lost in America*, records this transitional period. He reviewed plays for the *Jewish Daily Forward* but could not resume his writing. At the urgings of his Warsaw friend, Aaron Zeitlin, he completed a novel begun in Warsaw, *Messiah the Sinner*. It was not a success and has never been translated.

The "greatest misfortune" of his life, according to Singer, was the death of his brother, Joshua, in 1944. In the dedication to the English version of *The Family Moskat*, he extols his brother as his "spiritual father and master." Singer's family sagas, *The Family Moskat*, *The Manor*, and *The Estate*, are an effort to emulate his brother, but critics agree that they do not represent the best of Isaac Bashevis Singer, nor are they typical of his work. These novels do present a historical overview of Jewish life in Poland, beginning with the Polish uprising of 1863, in *The Manor*, and culminating in the catastrophe of the Holocaust in World War II, in *The Family Moskat*. The death of his brother seems to have brought Singer out of his literary impotence, leaving him free to be his own man. He has since become a prolific writer and continues to write novels and short stories.

At the suggestion of a friend, Elizabeth Shub, Singer started writing children's books; the first, *Zlateh the Goat and Other Stories* appeared in 1966, and he has gone on to publish more than fifteen books for children. Singer's books for children are not written with the left hand; indeed, the format is particularly congenial to certain aspects of his genius. His children's books have won numerous prizes and have been extremely popular; they have been translated into a dozen languages in addition to English, French, Spanish, Japanese, and Hebrew. Singer has worked with a variety of translators, including his nephew, Joseph. He and his wife, Alma, reside both in New York and in Miami.

Analysis

The oft-quoted line from Isaac Bashevis Singer's story "Gimpel the Fool" epitomizes his theory of fiction and his world view: "No doubt the world is entirely an imaginary world, but it is only once removed from the real world." His approach to his material is both imaginative—demoniac—and historical. Sometimes, these strains run concurrently; at other times, one is subdued by the other. Through his use of the supernatural, he presents a historically accurate picture of the Jewish community from the seventeenth century to the present.

Singer's concern is not only with Jewish history or destiny but also with the individual. He believes that man's soul is a battleground for good and evil impulses. His use of the fantastic suggests the tenuous line between reality and fiction; it also provides an explanation for man's behavior, in what he terms a "spiritual stenography." He suggests that the perversions in which men engage are otherworldly, that man is not always in control of his actions. Although men have freedom of choice, this freedom may be illusory because the forces of evil, if allowed to prevail, can be stronger than the forces of good. Ultimately, however, man's desire for good can triumph if he exerts all his efforts to that end. Singer's solution to man's problems is a return to his ancestral heritage. The struggle between good and evil, between the spiritual and sensual, supplies the tension in his works. Singer contends that man cannot be separated from his passions; they are one and the same. His early novels, especially *Satan in Goray* and *The Magician of Lublin*, illustrate the problem of passions ruling the individual.

Singer's first novel, *Satan in Goray*, written while he was still in Poland, is a Gothic tale, commingling the historical with the phantasmagoric, the mysticism of Hasidism with the influences of Fyodor Dostoevski and Edgar Allan Poe, the sacred with the profane. The work is historical, contemporary, and prophetic. Its vision is dark, its tone is harsh, and it deals with eternal conflicts: between good and evil, between predestination and freedom of choice.

Two historical events constitute the background of this novel: The first is the Cossack rebellion (1648-1649) led by Bogdam Chmielnicki against the Polish landowners, which resulted in the destruction of 100,000 Jews. This was a period of Jewish history remembered for its tremendous loss of life and for its acts of absolute barbarism, surpassed only by the Holocaust of World War II. The second is the messianic movement known as Shabbeteanism, after its originator Shabbetai Zvi (1626-1676). Historically, these movements converged when Shabbetai Zvi, in Smyrna, Turkey, proclaimed himself Messiah in the year 1648, the time of the Chmielnicki massacres.

For Singer, however, historical events are only important in their effects upon individuals. His interest, at all times, lies with the passions that govern man and engage him in a continuous struggle during his lifetime. In this early work, he presents the shtetl of Goray in the aftermath of the Chmielnicki pogrom and indicates how the spiritual decline of the community is related to its physical destruction. The action of the novel takes place in the year 1666 as the survivors of the massacre move back to Goray and attempt to resume their lives. The village, however, cannot be resuscitated. Its people are maimed; its leaders are ineffectual; all are vulnerable. Singer focuses on what happens to man during his time of utmost vulnerability. He presents a good but misguided community, easily led astray by promises of redemption and the cessation of their earthly travails. It is a community which has suffered much, and its prospects for the future are bleak. Its roads and its earth are drenched with the blood of recently murdered people. Life appears meaningless. The inhabitants of the village move about sluggishly. It would seem that the guardian of Israel slumbers while her adversaries are on the alert.

The work is divided into two parts. Part 1 deals with the struggle between good and evil as represented by the opposing factions within the community. Rabbi Benish Ashkenazi, the spiritual leader of this enervated community, one of its last survivors to return, represents the forces of good within the shtetl. He is the voice of traditionalism. He was a strong leader before the events of 1648. He did not allow the study of Cabala with its promise of messianic redemption and with the asceticism of its adherents. At present, he can resume certain rabbinical functions within the community, he can deal with legal matters, but he cannot handle the spiritual and social problems of the villagers. He cannot control the dissension within his family; likewise, he cannot control the growing dissensions in Goray. In both situations, he retreats into his own chambers and ultimately is concerned only with his own salvation. Meanwhile, rumors of the new Messiah have filtered into the secluded village, injecting into it a vitality heretofore absent, resurrecting the shtetl as only messianism can. It is, however, a destructive messianism, one which must be preceded by absolute evil, an abrogation of societal restraints, an immersion into sexual perversity and religious heresy. Part 1 ends with the rabbi's leaving town, after being wounded in a battle with Satan, because he does not want to be buried in Goray. He fears that the evil which has overtaken Goray will contaminate even the dead.

Part 2 concerns the spiritual decline of the community through lack of leadership and perversions of the Law in the name of Shabbeteanism. The battle has been lost. Once the rabbi leaves, total chaos ensues. Part 2 begins with Rechele's marriage to an impotent ascetic—also a believer in Shabbeteanism—and ends with her death, after being impregnated by Satan, who now resides in her body in the form of a dybbuk. In the interim, the community gets a new leader, Reb Gedaliya, an emissary who proclaims the news of the crowning of the Messiah. He is a ritual slaughterer by trade, a charlatan by profession. One of Singer's many perverted religious functionaries, his lust for blood is exceeded only by his lust for Rechele, who is the innocent victim of life's misfortunes. Gedaliya persuades the community that its redemption can take place only upon the abandonment of traditional Jewish life. Singer vividly portrays the manner in which the community loses sight of the relationship between traditional Judaism and redemption and the depths of moral turpitude into which it has plunged. Ultimately, evil—the dybbuk—is exorcised, together with the remaining Shabbeteans, and good returns to Goray. The novel ends in the spirit of a morality tale with these words: "Let none attempt to force the Lord . . . The Messiah will come in God's own time."

Satan in Goray is a bleak tale in which the forces of good and evil fight for the soul of man; man, maimed, vulnerable, and misguided, easily succumbs to the passions of lust and perversity. Critics have seen this work as adumbrating events soon to take place in Europe. The strength of this early novel lies in its use of demonology and the supernatural, which has since become the distinctive quality of Singer's fiction.

Written in 1958, serialized in 1959, and published in English in 1960, *The Magician of Lublin* also deals with the passions of man, yet it is not overcast with the gloom of past events. It reflects an expansiveness often missing in Singer's works. Its focus, unlike that of Singer's earlier novels, *Satan in Goray* and the chronicle, *The Family Moskat*, is not on the Jewish community itself, but on the individual in a timeless context. Its concern is not historical; nevertheless, in tracing the odyssey of a prodigal son, and attempting to reconcile eternal issues, Jewish destiny is suggested. In this work, Singer tempers his use of the supernatural and deals with man as magician.

Singer's magician-protagonist is well-cast. On a literal level, he is representative of the artist. On a symbolic level, every man is, in a sense, a magician, living his life, like Yasha Mazur, the protagonist of *The Magician of Lublin*, "as if walking the tightrope merely inches from disaster." The variegated personality of the hero, "religious and heretical, good and evil, false and sincere," and the lack of dates in the work, would confirm a more symbolic interpretation. In this novel more than in any other, Singer focuses on the single individual and the choices he or she makes. In *Satan in Goray*, historical events negate options. In *The Magician of Lublin*, Singer removes the encumbrances of history and allows his hero to make conscious decisions which determine the progress of his life.

Yasha Mazur is Singer's most interesting protagonist. He is a complex person, vital, exuberant, intense—above all, a man with a personal destiny. Unlike Jacob, the protagonist of *The Slave*, for example, who is a good person, motivated to do right no matter what the circumstances are, Yasha's personality is intricate, and it engages him constantly in a struggle of opposing forces. In *Satan in Goray*, the opposing forces are presented as two distinct elements within the community. The triumph of one necessitates the removal of the other. When evil was victorious, Rabbi Benish Ashkenazi had to leave Goray. In *The Magician of Lublin*, however, these forces are within the individual, enduring aspects of man's nature. Yasha Mazur's entire life is a battle. He can never conquer the adversary. He can only negotiate, appease, or in some other way deal with it, so that it remains dormant. He never knows, however, when it will awaken to begin another round.

Yasha Mazur was reared in a pious Jewish home, studied the Talmud until his father died—his mother died when he was seven—and then joined the circus. He now maintains a home in Lublin with his wife, Esther, but roams the Polish countryside as a "circus performer and hypnotist." As an artist or magician, he moves in various worlds, assumes various guises or personalities, and has a different mistress in each world. He aspires to higher things: he is a successful artist and would like to perform in Warsaw, in the summer theater of the prestigious Saxony Gardens. He is barred from doing so because he is Jewish. The closest he comes to this is the apartment of the middle-class gentile Emilia, located on a street opposite the Saxony Gardens. Yasha's relationship with Emilia focuses the tensions of the work. He thinks he is in love with her, but she refuses the role of mistress. She wants to be his wife. To marry her, Yasha would have to divorce Esther, convert to Christianity, and procure great wealth to maintain the facade he has established in his courting of Emilia. These are formidable decisions that will determine his future.

Singer establishes the dichotomy of predestination and free will early in the work in the contrasting attitudes toward life represented by Yasha and his wife. Esther is a religious woman, married twenty years to Yasha; they have no children. Her entire life consists of making a home for a husband who returns to it only on holidays. She loves him but regrets, at times, not having married someone more stable. The thought of changing her life, however, never crosses her mind. She is a strong believer in Providence and accepts her fate as a lonely woman.

Yasha, although he says that "everything is fate," realizes that he shapes his own destiny in all his choices. He is a magician who consorts with thieves, but he refuses to use his powers for evil purposes. He will not become a thief. When he finally attempts it, out of a desperate need to support Emilia, he fails and injures himself. The man who is so agile that he can walk a tightrope to the awe of his audience, becomes a shlemiel and bungles a simple act of burglary. Although he is Jewish by birth, he is a nonbeliever—or says he is— by choice. He does not pray because God does not answer the prayers of His supplicants: His "gifts" are "plagues, famines, poverty, and pogroms." Nevertheless, to become a Christian for Emilia is a difficult choice for him. He is a libertine, yet considers the institution of marriage sacred and cannot easily make the decision to break up his home for his new infatuation. He is faced with the dilemma of choosing "between his religion and the cross, between Esther and Emilia, between honesty and crime." These choices will "seal his destiny." He finally opts to remain with his own religion and decides also that traditionalism is more meaningful than assimilationism.

Yasha is aware that life is the most powerful seductress. He returns to his home and builds himself a doorless brick prison which frees him from temptation and allows him to meditate on his past actions, yet he discovers that as long as he is alive, he cannot shut out the world. As an artist or a magician, he went out into the world, succumbing to carnal pleasures, drinking, eating, loving unrestrainedly. Having come to the realization that "there must be discipline," he undergoes the transformation from sinner to saint. As an ascetic, in the confines of his self-imposed banishment, considered by all a "holy man," the world comes to him. Even his past love writes him a letter. Yasha's imprisonment has been only partially successful. He has turned his intense feelings in another direction, moving from the sensual to the spiritual. In this work, Singer suggests that man cannot escape his essence: he and his passions are one. The *Magician of Lublin* presents a positive outlook even though it concludes, as does his more recent work, *Shosha*, in a dark cell or room.

Singer's novels *Enemies* and *Shosha* directly address the most tragic time of Jewish history, the Holocaust. *Enemies*, ironically subtitled *A Love Story*, is Singer's only novel set in America; it deals specifically with survivors of the Holocaust. In *Shosha*, Singer returns for another nostalgic look at the destroyed world in which he grew up and attempts to capture the spirit of his people as the perimeters of death close in on them.

Like *The Magician of Lublin*, *Enemies* is a novel written on two levels. Primarily, it fills a gap in Singer's canon. Up until this work, Singer's literary aim was to re-create the destroyed world of Eastern European Jewry, to present the pulsating life that existed specifically in his native Poland. *Enemies* acknowledges the destruction of his fictive world and deals with problems confronting those who survived. In a note that precedes the work, Singer asserts that although he has lived with survivors for years, his work is in no way typical of the Holocaust experience. His novel presents the "exceptional case," unique to the individual who is a victim both of his own personality and his persecutors. Certainly, this can be said of all victims, and Singer's work, despite his abjuration, is a moving depiction of the varied problems many survivors have encountered, as well as a forceful portrayal of what has been termed in literature as *l'univers concentrationnaire*. Singer's note does caution the reader against a rigorous historical interpretation. The Holocaust is a framework within which Singer presents his perennial concern: man battling his adversary in the dark of night, in the fashion of Jacob and the angel. In the biblical narrative, man is not overcome; he walks away, at daybreak, limping but unvanquished. Singer's hero also walks away, but not as a victor.

This novel bears a similarity to *Satan in Goray*, both in its focus on an individual who lives a tormented life, burdened with the knowledge of the tragic destruction of all that is meaningful to him, and in its use of the supernatural. The spiritual powers in this work, representing the forces of good and evil, also reflect a movement away from traditionalism. In addition, they indicate the extent to which the characters, through their previous experiences, have lost touch with reality. *Enemies* also has affinities with *The Magician of Lublin*: the multiple personalities of the protagonist are reflected in his relationships with three strikingly different women.

Enemies is a ghostly story. Herman Broder, the protagonist, is defined through his actions in the Holocaust. He spent those years hiding in a hayloft and has acquired a negative identity in its aftermath. Presently, as a survivor, he is psychologically warped and socially maimed. He lacks the courage to commit suicide, hides behind schizophrenia to "deaden" his consciousness, and assumes the guise of a demon. In New York, Broder becomes a ghost-writer for a rabbi. He shuns contact with others to preserve his anonymity and lives a life of haunting duplicity with his wife (the servant of his family in Poland) and his mistress. The tensions in his spiritual juggling act are intensified by the appearance of his wife from the Old World, assumed to be dead. Ultimately, he disappears, vanishing like a ghost.

The work is divided into three parts. Part 1 establishes the diverse personalities of Herman Broder, "a fraud, a transgressor—a hypocrite," as he sees himself, and the complications they create. Broder's present life in New York is eclipsed by the terrifying experiences of his past. He lives in Brooklyn with his wife, Yadwiga, the Polish woman who worked for his family before the war and who hid him in a hayloft during the Nazi occupation. He married her in gratitude for saving his life, but his relationship with her is deceitful. She does not know about his professional life nor about his mentally disturbed mistress, Masha, who shares with him her experience of the Holocaust. He spends as much time with Masha as he does with Yadwiga, always telling Yadwiga that he is a book salesman and must go out of town to sell books.

The tangled web of Broder's relationships is further complicated when his first wife, Tamara, who has survived being shot twice—one bullet is still lodged within her—comes to New York and seeks him out. Part 1 ends with an additional complication when Masha claims to be pregnant and Broder promises to marry her.

Part 2 attempts a resolution of the problems. Through Broder's conversations with Masha and Tamara, much of the Holocaust experience is recreated. Like Elie Wiesel and other writers of the Holocaust, Singer points out that the full enormity of the events will never be expressed, because words are inadequate to the task. That which is related, however, is extremely powerful. Singer deals with the theological, social, and philosophical problems, both individual and universal, which confront man in coming to terms with the Holocaust and in trying to define himself through the Holocaust— or in spite of it. While presenting the myriad issues with which survivors have been faced—equivocal attitudes toward faith, a missing spouse who turns up after the other has remarried, disorientation in a new environment, reestablishing an identity that had been nonexistent for a time, relating to people as human beings within a society rather than as individuals competing for survival—Singer indicates that the individual is also his own victim, governed by passions he cannot or will not control. Broder would not have married Yadwiga if he had thought that Tamara were alive. Now, however, he wants to hold on to all three women. They satisfy different needs: Yadwiga cares for him and worships him with a childlike simplicity; Masha fulfills his sexual desires and fires his imagination with her night-long storytelling; Tamara is his wife to whom he feels committed. When the intricacies of his life seem overwhelming, he resorts to traditionalism as a life-sustaining measure, yet he cannot maintain his resolve to be a good Jew. He is a weak person by nature, and the impact of the Holocaust has left him without a will, without the power to make meaningful choices and decisions. He is, as he tells Tamara, a "corpse." His only alternative is to vanish. Herman Broder joins Singer's other eternal wanderers, the most famous of whom is Gimpel the Fool. The epilogue, in an almost Darwinian statement, attests the insignificance of the individual in the larger scheme of things by confirming Herman Broder's disappearance and suggesting that life continues nevertheless for those who can battle their enemies successfully.

Shosha is Singer's only novel published in English which is narrated in the first person. Originally appearing in the *Jewish Daily Forward* under the title of *Neshome Ekspeditsyes—Soul Expeditions—*in 1974, it is considered a fictionalized and expanded version of the memoir *A Young Man in Search of Love* which appeared almost simultaneously in 1978. A beautifully wrought work, it is the most poignant of all of Singer's novels to date. Set in Poland in the 1930's, the novel portrays the plight of the Jewish community, overcast with the gloom of the Nazi invasion, yet it brims with the lives, loves, and hopes of its characters. It combines realism with humor and pathos. It is another nostalgic glance at a decimated world, but it is not a gloomy work. It is, as the Yiddish title indicates, the journey of the author's soul, in an affectionate tribute to the vitality of the shtetl, and stands in defiance of his statement at the end of the work: "time is a book whose pages you can turn forward, not back." *Shosha* presents a marvelous picture of Warsaw before the war, focusing on its Yiddish cultural and intellectual life, its writers, artists, philosophers, actors, critics, and dilettantes, as well as its simple people. Within this historical framework, Singer presents his protagonist's life in Poland at the time of greatest stress, a time when Jewish life and culture were disintegrating.

In *Shosha*, the conflict between good and evil which animates all of Singer's works takes the form of the relationship between victim and persecutor. All of the characters are concerned with their immediate gratification. They arouse the reader's sympathy because they become victims of their own blindness and naïveté. In their determination to live normally, they love, argue, philosophize, celebrate holidays. They write plays about dybbuks and talk about dybbuks within themselves. They do not recognize the external evil, the phantom which surrounds them or pursues them.

The first part of the novel charts the circular movement of the protagonist as he attempts to reestablish a sense of belonging, taking the reader to the halcyon days of the narrator's childhood and moving forward to the period preceding the destruction of the shtetl by Hitler. The ancestors of the protagonist, Aaron Greidinger, have lived in Poland for seven hundred years. Krochmalna Street, already familiar to Singer's public through his memoir *In My Father's Court*, is not only a place housing his father's judiciary, but it is also the scene of the narrator's first love, for Shosha, his neighbor, his playmate, his first audience, who believes and trusts him implicitly and unconditionally.

The work delineates the maturation of the narrator, as the serenity of his youthful universe is quickly replaced by the turmoil of world events with their disquieting effect upon the Jews of Poland. The first twenty years of his life pass rapidly as he moves from Krochmalna Street and attempts to define himself as a writer. In Warsaw, the Writers' Club becomes the focal point for the intellectuals, much as the synagogue was the focal point of the traditional Jewish community. It is through the people whom he meets at the Writers' Club that Aaron Greidinger works out his role as writer and lover.

Greidinger's destiny and identity are intimately bound to his youth on Krochmalna Street, and after twenty years, he returns to the area and visits Shosha and her mother. He is amazed that Shosha has changed only slightly during the years: she and Greidinger are the same age, but she looks like a child. Greidinger falls in love with her immediately. He explains to Betty Slonim, the Yiddish actress from America for whom he is writing a play, that he sees himself in Shosha. Shosha represents the naïveté and gentleness of his childhood, a phase of his life that he wants to recapture and repossess. She is Krochmalna Street. She is the shtetl. She is the traditionalism that refuses to keep in step with modernity, but is beautiful nevertheless. She also represents the sources of his creativity, the childlike wonder which Singer the writer still possesses in old age. Part 1 ends with Greidinger's movement back in time, his failure as a playwright, his proposal to Shosha, and his spending most of his time in the small apartment on Krochmalna Street as the political situation worsens for the Jews in Poland.

Part 2 develops the protagonist's affirmation of his unity with his people. It is Yom Kippur, a day of judgment and reckoning for all Jews. The war is getting closer, Poles are more outspoken in their anti-Semitism, and Greidinger spends the day with Shosha, fasting. He marries Shosha two months later during the festival of Hanukkah. By doing so, he forgoes the opportunity to leave Warsaw before the Germans enter. He will not forsake Shosha, knowing that she could not survive by herself during these times. His writing career has improved; he is writing novels that have been accepted by his publisher. Part 2 concludes with the war imminent, but with everyone presenting reasons for not leaving Warsaw prior to the German invasion. The epilogue ties the loose ends together. It takes place thirteen years later, during Greidinger's trip to Israel, where he meets his Warsaw friend, Haiml. While seated in the dark, each tells the story of what happened to his family, his friends, and how he escaped. Shosha died, as expected, because in her fragility, she could not keep ahead of the march of malevolence pursuing her and overtaking Europe.

Although much of the work is strongly autobiographical and historically accurate, it is nevertheless presented as fiction. Aaron Greidinger shares some of the author's background, characteristics, and experiences, but not all.

Shosha was Singer's neighbor and playmate, but he never married her. In fact, Singer did not marry until he came to the United States. Greidinger's family is very much like Singer's and the same fate befalls them, but missing are Singer's sister and his older brother, Israel Joshua, who exerted such a profound influence on him. Unlike Singer, who left Poland in 1935, Greidinger chooses to stay and participate in the fate of the three million other Polish Jews. Greidinger's friends and lovers are fictional but their concerns reflect the concerns of the times, the need to live life at its fullest. They also reflect Singer's interest in the emotions and passions that govern man, that are man's essence.

It is easy to see why Singer occupies a unique place in the literary world. His works transcend the barriers of age, education, and culture, and appeal to all peoples. Chronicler, historian, spiritualist, and moralist, his writings are informed by a deep compassion for men and women who are, after all, only human. Singer may admit to a pessimistic view of man, but it is a sympathetic rather than a cynical pessimism. Throughout the darkness of his presentation, there flickers a spark of faith in the basic goodness of man, the promise of a universal and eternal light.

Major publications other than long fiction

SHORT FICTION: *Shoten an Goray un Anderer Dertailungen*, 1943 (published in the United States as *Satan in Goray and Other Stories*, 1945); *Gimpl Tam un Anderer Dertailungen*, 1957 (published in the United States as *Gimpel the Fool and Other Stories*, 1963); *The Spinoza of Market Street*, 1961; *Short Friday and Other Stories*, 1964; *The Séance and Other Stories*, 1968; *A Friend of Kafka and Other Stories*, 1970; *A Crown of Feathers and Other Stories*, 1973; *Der Shpigl un Andere Derseylungen*, 1975 (published in the United States as *The Mirror and Other Stories*); *Passions and Other Stories*, 1975; *Old Love*, 1979; *The Collected Stories of Isaac Bashevis Singer*, 1982.

NONFICTION: *Mayn Tatn's Bes-din Shtub*, 1956 (published in the United States as *In My Father's Court*, 1966); *A Day of Pleasure: Stories of a Boy Growing Up in Warsaw*, 1969; *Hasidim*, 1973 (with Ira Moskowitz); *A Little Boy in Search of God*, 1976; *A Young Man in Search of Love*, 1978; *Lost in America*, 1980; *Reaches of Heaven: A Story of the Life of the Baal Shem*, 1981.

CHILDREN'S LITERATURE: *Zlateh the Goat and Other Stories*, 1966; *The Fearsome Inn*, 1967; *Mazel and Shlimazel: Or, The Milk of a Lioness*, 1967; *When Schlemiel Went to Warsaw and Other Stories*, 1968; *Elijah the Slave*, 1970; *Joseph and Koza*, 1970; *Alone in the Wild Forest*, 1971; *The Topsy-Turvy Emperor of China*, 1971; *The Wicked City*, 1972; *The Fools of Shelm and Their History*, 1973; *Why Noah Chose the Dove*, 1974; *A Tale of Three Wishes*, 1975; *Naftali the Storyteller and His Horse, Sus, and Other Stories*, 1976; *The Power of Light: Eight Stories*, 1980; *The Golem*, 1982.

MISCELLANEOUS: *Romain Rolland* 1927 (translation); *Die Volger*, 1928 (translation); *Victoria*, 1929 (translation); *Pan*, 1931 (translation); *All Quiet on the Western Front*, 1930 (translation); *The Way Back*, 1931 (translation); *The Magic Mountain*, 1932 (translation); *From Moscow to Jerusalem*, 1938 (translation).

Bibliography

Alexander, Edward. *Isaac Bashevis Singer*, 1980.
Allentuck, Marcia, ed. *The Achievement of Isaac Bashevis Singer*, 1967.
Buchen, Irving. *Isaac Bashevis Singer and the Eternal Past*, 1968.
Kresch, Paul. *Isaac Bashevis Singer: The Magician of West 86th Street*, 1979.
Malin, Irving, ed. *Critical Views of Isaac Bashevis Singer*, 1969.

L. H. Goldman

TOBIAS SMOLLETT

Born: Dalquhurn, Scotland; baptized March 19, 1721
Died: Antignano, Italy; September 17, 1771

Principal long fiction

The Adventures of Roderick Random, 1748; *The Adventures of Gil Blas*, 1749 (translation); *The Adventures of Peregrine Pickle*, 1751; *The Adventures of Ferdinand, Count Fathom*, 1753; *Don Quixote*, 1755 (translation); *The Adventures of Sir Launcelot Greaves*, 1760-1762; *The Expedition of Humphry Clinker*, 1771; *The Adventures of Telemachus, the Son of Ulysses*, 1776 (translation, 2 volumes).

Other literary forms

Tobias Smollett combined his medical practice with an active and varied career as a man of letters. His earliest, though unsuccessful, effort was as a playwright with *The Regicide: Or, James the First of Scotland, a Tragedy* (1749), published by subscription a full ten years after fruitless attempts at having it staged in London. Two other disappointments followed with his inability to secure a production for *Alceste* (1748-1749), a combination of opera, tragedy, and masque, and with the rejection of his first comedy, *The Absent Man* (1751), which was never produced or published. Both of these works have now been lost. His only success on the stage came finally with *The Reprisal: Or, The Tars of Old England* (1757), a comedy; this farce was produced by David Garrick at the Theatre Royal, Drury Lane.

Smollett's deep moral energy surfaced in two early verse satires, "Advice: A Satire" (1746) and its sequel, "Reproof: A Satire" (1747); these rather weak poems were printed together in 1748. Smollett's poetry includes a number of odes and lyrics, but his best poem remains "The Tears of Scotland." Written in 1746, it celebrates the unwavering independence of the Scots, who had been crushed by English troops at the Battle of Culloden.

As Smollett's literary career grew, his hackwork for publishers increased with translations. His most popular work among these projects was *A Complete History of England* (1757-1758) and its sequel, *A Continuation of the Complete History of England* (1760-1765). He took great pride in his achievements as a historian and as a historical editor, *A Compendium of Authentic and Entertaining Voyages* (1756). A diversity of interests from medicine to politics prompted the writing of numerous pamphlets and essays. *An Essay on the External Use of Water* (1752) was a farsighted proposal for the improvement of public hygiene at Bath that caused a furor among the resort's staff and patrons.

Though his health was rapidly deteriorating from overwork, Smollett completed a thirty-five volume edition of *The Works of Voltaire* (1761-1769). In the hope that a warm climate would improve his health, he traveled to France and Italy, and on returning to England published *Travels in France and Italy* (1766). His didactic observations instructed his readers to accept England, for all its faults, as the best nation for securing happiness on earth. His last nonfiction works were *The Present State of All Nations* (1768-1769) and the political satire, *The History and Adventures of an Atom* (1769). Lewis M. Knapp offers the best modern edition of the *Letters of Tobias Smollett* (1970).

Achievements

Smollett cannot be said to have added dignity to the art of the novel in the manner of Henry Fielding's imitation of the epic, nor can it be argued that he gave form to the genre as did Samuel Richardson, yet the eighteenth century novel cannot be discussed without giving full attention to Smollett's stylistic virtuosity and satiric intent.

Smollett successfully challenged Richardson's and Fielding's substantial popular reputation by providing "familiar scenes in an uncommon and amusing point of view." In *The Adventures of Roderick Random* (commonly known as *Roderick Random*), his first novel, he displayed a thorough understanding of the distinction between the novel and the romance, of which Samuel Johnson would speak in *The Rambler* essays (1750-1752). Borrowing from Latin comedy and Elizabethan drama, Smollett created caricatures of human beings with the dexterity of William Hogarth and Thomas Rowlandson. Though his characters lack the psychological depth of Richardson's, they possess breathtaking energy and evocative power.

Only in the past twenty years has Smollett's role in the development of the English novel been fully appreciated. Recent criticism has emphasized the wrongheadedness of viewing Smollett's satiric energy as a deviation from Fielding's epic ambitions for the novel. Instead, Smollett is seen at the beginning of another tradition. Sir Walter Scott and Charles Dickens both valued Smollett's work; Dickens acknowledged his debt to Smollett's picaresque realism and comic characterization in *Pickwick Papers* (1836-1837). Among modern novelists, the savage comedy of writers as various as Evelyn Waugh and Joseph Heller is in Smollett's tradition rather than that of Fielding or Richardson.

Smollett's works continue to provoke critical inquiry. Eight books and numerous dissertations have appeared in the last two decades, as well as many articles. The Oxford English Novels series has published all five of his novels, and the University of Delaware has begun to publish its *Bicentennial Edition of the Works of Tobias Smollett*, under the editorship of O. M. Brack, with *The Expedition of Humphry Clinker* (commonly known as *Humphry Clinker*) appearing in 1979.

Biography

Tobias George Smollett was born at Dalquhurn, Dumbartonshire, in western Scotland, and baptized on March 19, 1721. He was the son of Archibald Smollett, a lawyer, who suffered from ill health, and Barbara Cunningham Smollett, a woman of taste and elegance but no fortune. Smollett's grandfather, of whom the boy was especially proud, had been knighted by King William in 1698, and had become an influential member of the landed gentry as a local Whig statesman. When Smollett's father died only two years after his son's birth, the family suffered from lack of money.

Smollett's education, for all of his family's financial deterioration, was of superior quality though erratic. He entered Dumbarton Grammar School in 1728, remaining for five years, and received the traditional grounding in the classics. His matriculation to Glasgow University (though officially unrecorded) was interrupted when he became a Glasgow surgeon's apprentice while still attending university medical lectures. In the fall of 1739, Smollett was released from his apprenticeship to go to London; now eighteen, he had some reputation as a writer of earthy satires and doggerel. While traveling to London, Smollett carried the manuscript of a tragedy, *The Regicide*, which, he soon realized, would provide no entrée for him with the London theater managers. He is described at this time as "attractive, entertaining as a *raconteur*, and blessed with self-assurance." His future as a London man of letters uncertain, Smollett received advice from a number of Scottish physicians suggesting he continue practicing medicine. On March 10, 1740, he received a medical warrant from the Navy Board and embarked on the *H.M.S. Chichester* as a surgeon's second mate.

The author's naval experience, material used later for *Roderick Random*, began during the outbreak of war with Spain and continued through the bloody Carthagena, West Indies, expedition of 1741. Smollett returned to England in 1742, but was drawn back to Jamaica, where he resided until 1744. While living on the island, he met the daughter of an established family of planters, the Lassells; he married Anne Lassells in 1743. She is described as an affectionate and beautiful woman, in her early twenties, of considerable fortune.

Smollett, on the advice of her family, returned to London alone, where he set up a practice as a surgeon on Downing Street in May, 1744. Having never lost hope of a literary career, he worked on improving his fluency in Spanish and then began translating *Don Quixote*. The years from 1747 to 1750 were marked by considerable literary activity, numerous changes in residence, various trips abroad, a widening circle of acquaintants, and the birth of his only child, Elizabeth, in 1747.

In January, 1748, *Roderick Random* was published; this was followed by the impressive translations of Alain Le Sage and Miguel de Cervantes, and in 1749, *The Regicide* was printed. The success of *Roderick Random* was instantaneous and prolonged, with 6,500 copies sold in twenty-two months; it was to rival the popularity of Fielding's *Joseph Andrews* (1742). The success of *Roderick Random*, which was written in less than six months, became a kind of revenge on the theater managers of London. During this period, Smollett made plans to produce *Alceste*, his opera (George Frederick Handel was contracted for the music), but this effort was to fail; only a lyric from this work survives. His comedy *The Absent Man* was submitted to David Garrick but not accepted; Smollett's failure at drama was a continuing source of frustration throughout his career.

In June, 1750, Smollett purchased his medical degree from Marischal College, Aberdeen, and in the same month moved his family to Chelsea, a fashionable London suburb. It became an ideal home for him, where both his medical practice and his writing flourished; he remained there for thirteen years until forced abroad by his health in 1763. It was in Chelsea that he wrote *The Adventures of Peregrine Pickle* (commonly known as *Peregrine Pickle*), a work of nearly 330,000 words composed at top speed in anticipation of a trip to Paris. On February 25, 1751, his second novel was published to laudatory reviews and wide popularity.

Smollett's involvement with various periodicals began during the 1750's, first as a book reviewer for the *Monthly Review* and later as editor and proprietor of the *Critical Review*. Smollett joined Oliver Goldsmith in launching the *British Magazine* (the *Monthly Repository* beginning in 1760), remaining as coeditor until 1763. With a final venture, Smollett gained public notoriety and untold enemies by agreeing to write the *Briton*, a political effort in support of Lord Bute's ministry. Of Smollett's various journalistic efforts, only the work in the *Critical Review* is exceptional; as a literary periodical, it remains one of the most significant of the last half of the eighteenth century.

In the early 1750's, Smollett was driving himself in order to escape debt. Publishing a medical paper, *An Essay on the External Use of Water*, brought him little money, and in February, 1753, his third novel, *The Adventures of Ferdinand, Count Fathom* (commonly known as *Ferdinand, Count Fathom*), was published with poor financial results. The book attracted few readers, and Smollett was forced to borrow money and to supplement his medical fees with further hackwork. The years of hack writing began in earnest with *A Complete History of England*, a translation of Voltaire's writings, a geographical reference work, and several digests of travel. The period from 1756 to 1763 destroyed Smollett's health, but his reputation as a critic and a successful writer became unquestioned. Unfortunately, this frantic production hardly kept him from debtor's prison. Returning to the novel in the *British Magazine*, Smollett published "the first considerable English novel ever to be published serially"—*The Adventures of Sir Launcelot Greaves* (commonly known as *Sir Launcelot Greaves*). In monthly installments from January, 1760, to December, 1761, the novel gave the six-penny periodical substantial popularity.

In the midst of this literary hard labor, Smollett was imprisoned for three months, having been convicted of libeling an Admiral Knowles in an article in the *Critical Review*. On his release in early 1761, Smollett continued fulfilling his contracts with certain booksellers but also traveled extensively, possibly to Dublin, even though troubled by asthma and tuberculosis. In addition to these difficulties, his spirit was nearly broken by the illness and death of his daughter in April, 1763. This final shock caused him to cut all his London ties and move his family to the Continent, hoping to calm his wife and cure his ailments in the mild climate of the south of France and Italy. He spent two years abroad, returning to England in July, 1765; the literary result of his tour was *Travels in France and Italy*. Though ill-health plagued him he sought for the third time a consulship but was rejected; in 1768 he left England for the last time.

Arriving in Pisa, Italy, Smollett visited with friends at the University, finally settling at his country villa in Antignano, near Leghorn, in the spring of 1770, where he completed his masterpiece, *Humphry Clinker*. Immediately following its publication, he received the rave notices of friends and critics concerning the novel, but he had little time to enjoy the praise. On September 17, 1771, he died from an acute intestinal infection and was buried at the English cemetery at Leghorn.

Analysis

Tobias Smollett is not only a great comic novelist; he is also a morally exhilarating one—a serious satirist of the brutality, squalor, and hideous corruption of mankind. His definite moral purposes are firmly grounded in the archetypal topic of all novelists—man's unceasing battle for survival in the war between the forces of good and evil. Smollett insists that man defy "the selfishness, envy, malice, and base indifference of mankind"; in such a struggle, the hero will ultimately prevail and will be rewarded for his fortitude.

The principal theme of Smollett's first novel, *Roderick Random*, is the arbitrariness of success and failure in a world dominated by injustice and dishonesty. Smollett's decision to use realistic detail as a guise for his satire produces a lively and inventive work; moreover, the hero, Roderick, is not a mere picaro nor a passive fool but an intent satiric observer "who recognizes, reacts, and rebukes." The novel is organized in a three-part structure. The initial stage reveals Roderick's numerous trials as a young man; he loses his innocence during the years of poverty in Scotland, of failure in London, and of brutal experience in the Navy. The middle of the narrative embodies "the lessons of adversity" as the hero declines into near collapse. In a final brief section, Roderick recovers his physical and moral equilibrium and promotes the simple human values of friendship, love, and trust as the only viable bases for a satisfying existence.

Roderick's problem is both to gain knowledge of the world and to assimilate that knowledge. M. A. Goldberg, in *Smollett and the Scottish School* (1959), finds that "at first his responses are dictated by his indignation, by passions . . .

eventually, he learns . . . to govern the emotions with reason." The struggle between these two forces is central to an understanding of eighteenth century England and its literature. In Smollett's first novel, good sense seems a sufficient defense against the sordid viciousness of the world. Good sense, however, can only be achieved, or learned, when the hero can control his pride and passionate nature, which are inextricably linked. Equilibrium, an orderly existence, arises paradoxically from the ashes of his random adventures. This understanding develops as the hero pursues the happiness he thinks he deserves but can never fully attain; as a good empiricist, Roderick gathers knowledge from each reversal, finally achieving a "tranquility of love" with the prudent Narcissa.

In *Roderick Random*, the hero's search for happiness differs significantly from the quest of the traditional picaro. While gaining an education and suffering the rebukes of other men, Roderick remains good and effectual, unlike Don Quixote, who is powerless against cruelty. Roderick's youthful ferocity contributes to the practicality of the satire. Smollett's approach to correcting the ills of society is to allow no attack or insult to go unavenged. A thorough whipping of a bully or the verbal punishment of a pedant lifts the book beyond the picaresque and advances it past the formal verse satire. The center of the satiric discussion implicates the surroundings and not the hero, thus permitting Smollett to offer a long list of evil, self-centered figures who provide an excellent contrast to the goodness and charity of the ill-served protagonist. Only his faithful servant, Strap; his uncle, Tom Bowling; and the maid, Narcissa, join him in opposing his neglectful grandfather, the scoundrel Vicar Shuffle, the tyrannical Captain Oakum, the dandiacal Captain Whiffle, and the rapacious Lord Strutwell.

The last section of the novel provides the hero with the riches of his long quest: family, wealth, and love. The moral of the adventures follows as Roderick's recently discovered father "blesses God for the adversity I had undergone," affirming that his son's intellectual, moral, and physical abilities had been improved "for all the duties and and enjoyments of life, much better than any education which affluence could bestow." The felicity of this final chapter provides a conventional ending, but the crucial point is that Roderick, having completed a rigorous education in the distinctions between appearance and reality, is now deserving of these rewards.

The protagonist of Smollett's long second novel, *Peregrine Pickle*, reminds one of Roderick in every aspect, except that Peregrine is an Englishman, not a Scot. The supporting players are improved; among the novel's outstanding comic creations are Commodore Hawser Trunnion and the spinster, Grizzle Pickle. Often described as the best picaresque novel in English, *Peregrine Pickle* satirizes the upper classes of mid-eighteenth century England. Rufus Putney argues, in "The Plan of *Peregrine Pickle*" (1945), that Smollett "meant to write a satire on the affectations and meannesses, the follies and vices that flourished among the upper classes in order that his readers might learn with Peregrine the emptiness of titles, the sordidness of avarice, the triviality of wealth and honors, and the folly of misguided ambition."

The novel begins by sketching Peregrine's social and emotional background and introducing other principal characters. Following this introductory section, Smollett's protagonist describes his adolescence and education at Winchester and Oxford, where he becomes addicted to coarse practical jokes and to satisfying his overbearing pride. Here the hero meets Emilia, a beautiful orphan with whom he falls in love; because of his capricious nature, however, he cannot remain long with her. Having become alienated from his parents, Peregrine departs on the Grand Tour with the best wishes of his guardian, Trunnion.

Peregrine returns from France an unprincipled, arrogant rogue whose every action supports his vanity. After numerous incidents including the death of Trunnion and his replacement with the eccentric Cadwallader Crabtree as Peregrine's mentor, the hero tests the virtue of Emilia and is rebuffed. The remainder of the novel observes the long distress, the eventual imprisonment, and the final rehabilitation of the protagonist, who by now is convinced of the fraud and folly of the world. As Putney mentions, only after matriculating to the "school of adversity," which reduces his pride and vanity, can Peregrine hope to achieve wealth, marry his true love, triumph over his enemies, and retire to the country. Adversity teaches him to distinguish between the complex vices of the urban sophisticates and the simpler but more substantial pleasures of generosity and love in a rural retreat. Despite its picaresque vigor and satisfactory resolution, the novel suffers from a confusion of purposes: Peregrine's arrogance undermines the credibility of his role as a satirist of high society. Thus, Smollett's satiric intentions are blunted by his aspirations to a novel of character.

Ferdinand, Count Fathom is remembered today for its dedication, in which Smollett gives his famous definition of the novel, and for its place as the first important eighteenth century work to propose terror as a subject for a novel. In *The Novels of Tobias Smollett* (1971), Paul-Gabriel Boucé finds that the major defect of the novel is the author's "mixture of genres, without any transition brought about by unfolding of the story or the evolution of the characters." Fathom's dark cynicism informs the majority of the work, with the last ten chapters unraveling into a weak melodrama; nevertheless, Smollett's satire remains effective as a bitter denunciation of the hypocrisy and violence of elegant society. As an early contribution to the literature of terror, the novel probes the emotions of a young, virtuous girl who undergoes isolation, deprivation, and sadistic brutality at the hands of a rapacious creature. The figure of Fathom is used to undercut sentimental conventions and show their uselessness when civilized norms are forgotten.

Sir Launcelot Greaves completed serialization in December, 1761, and was published as a book in March, 1762. Because of its serial publication, the novel's structure suffers from the frequent contrivance of artificial suspense. Recent criticism, however, has pointed to an underlying thematic unity based upon a series of variations on the theme of madness, with minute investigation into the physical, psychological, and moral aspects of the disorder. Greaves, the quixotic hero, launches a noble crusade for reform. His hopeless demand that a corrupted world listen to reason embraces Smollett's social idealism. If moral intention were the only measure of a novel's worth, then the didactic power of *Sir Launcelot Greaves* would guarantee its success; unfortunately, the delicate balance of the genre remains disordered by the force of an over-obvious moral preoccupation.

Smollett's last novel, *Humphry Clinker*, appeared in the bookstalls on June 15, 1771; Smollett had written the three volumes over a five-year period. It is his masterpiece, and it remains among the great English novels. The work was inspired by the epistles of Christopher Anstey's witty and popular *New Bath Guide* (1766). Using the epistolary method instead of the travel narrative of the early novels, Smollett characterizes his correspondents by means of their wonderfully individual letter-writing styles. Old Matthew Bramble of Brambleton Hall, Wales, travels with his household through Gloucester, Bath, London, Scarborough, Edinburgh, Cameron (Smollett country), Glasgow, Manchester, and home again. Squire Bramble suffers various physical complaints, and his ill-health makes him sensitive to the social ills surrounding him on his journey. Bramble searches for a recovery but finds himself becoming worse, not better, yet his compassionate nature remains undiminished. The journey was begun so that Bramble might distract his young niece, Lydia Melford, from a strolling actor named Wilson. The party also includes Tabitha, his aging, narrow-minded, old-maid sister; her malapropic maid, Winifred Jenkins, the classic example of the illiterate servant; and the modishly cynical nephew, Jery. En route, they adopt, much to Tabitha's delight, a Scottish veteran of Indian warfare, Obadiah Lismahago. Soon, they add Humphry Clinker to the party as a new footman; he turns out to be the natural son of Matthew.

There are three major plots to develop, and numerous minor episodes, all of which hinge upon the charcteristic picaresque device of the journey; Smollett exchanged the rogue hero for a group of picaros—Bramble and nephew Jery—who analyze and observe society. Through careful stages in letter after letter, Matthew's character is revealed to the reader, who learns to trust him as a reliable observer of society's foibles; in this respect *Humphry Clinker* is much stronger than *Peregrine Pickle*, where the satire was blunted by the protagonist's unreliability.

Smollett's satire strikes not individuals but categories of people and assorted social institutions; in particular *Humphry Clinker* is an *exposé* of the false attitudes and disordered life of the eighteenth century *nouveaux riches*. His conservative political views are displayed in Bramble's rages against an unrestricted press, politically biased juries, and the ignorance of the mob, and, as in *Peregrine Pickle*, he contrasts the folly and depravity of urban life with idealized pictures of the country.

Smollett's achievement in *Humphry Clinker* depends on his skillful use of the picaresque and epistolary traditions.His last novel is also distinguished by a warmth and tolerance not found to such a degree in his earlier works. Bramble's cynicism never becomes obnoxious to the reader; the brutality of Roderick is muted here. Smollett allows his hero to accept human society, despite "the racket and dissipation." Finally, for all his burlesque of Samuel Richardson's epistolary method, Smollett's characterization of Lydia has a depth and intensity that raises her above mere romantic convention.

In contrast to many critical reports, *Humphry Clinker* ends on a buoyant note of pure happiness, a happiness which fulfills the eighteenth century dictum of conformity to the universal order. Smollett's novels embrace moral and virtuous methods for pursuing one's goals. Passions and reason must remain in balance, and within this harmony, nature and art can moderate the demands of vice and folly.

Major publications other than long fiction

PLAYS: *The Regicide: Or, James the First of Scotland, a Tragedy*, 1749; *The Reprisal: Or, The Tars of Old England*, 1757.

NONFICTION: *An Essay on the External Use of Water*, 1752; *A Compendium of Authentic and Entertaining Voyages*, 1756; *A Complete History of England*, 1757-1758; *The Modern Part of an Universal History*, 1759-1766; *A Continuation of the Complete History of England*, 1760-1765; *Travels in France and Italy*, 1766; *The Present State of All Nations*, 1768-1769; *The History and Adventures of an Atom*, 1769; *Letters of Tobias Smollett*, 1970 (Lewis M. Knapp, editor).

MISCELLANEOUS: *The Works of Voltaire*, 1761-1769 (translation).

Bibliography

Bold, Alan, ed. *Smollett: Author of the First Distinction*, 1982.
Boucé, Paul-Gabriel. *The Novels of Tobias Smollett*, 1971.
Goldberg, M. A. *Smollett and the Scottish School*, 1959.
Grant, Damian. *Tobias Smollett: A Study in Style*, 1977.
Karl, Frederick R. *The Adversary Literature*, 1974.
Knapp, Lewis M. *Tobias Smollett: Doctor of Men and Manners*, 1949.
Rousseau, G. S., and Paul-Gabriel Boucé, eds. *Tobias Smollett*, 1971.
Spector, Robert D. *Tobias George Smollett*, 1968.
_____ . *Tobias Smollett: A Reference Guide*, 1980.

Paul J. deGategno

C. P. SNOW

Born: Leicester, England; October 15, 1905
Died: London, England; July 1, 1980

Principal long fiction

Death Under Sail, 1932, 1959; *New Lives for Old*, 1933; *The Search*, 1934, 1958; *Strangers and Brothers* series (includes *Strangers and Brothers*, 1940, reissued as *George Passant*, 1972; *The Light and the Dark*, 1947; *Time of Hope*, 1949; *The Masters*, 1951; *The New Men*, 1954; *Homecomings*, 1956, published in the United States as *Homecoming*; *The Conscience of the Rich*, 1958; *The Affair*, 1960; *Corridors of Power*, 1964; *The Sleep of Reason*, 1968; *Last Things*, 1970); *The Malcontents*, 1972; *In Their Wisdom*, 1974; *A Coat of Varnish*, 1979.

Other literary forms

Reflecting his various careers and interests, C. P. Snow published, in addition to his novels, a number of books, including the literary biographies, *Trollope: His Life and Art* (1975) and *The Realists* (1978), as well as many reviews and articles. He had some interest in the drama, encouraging the staging of his novels *The Affair*, *The New Men*, and *The Masters*, writing a full-length play, *The View Over the Park*, produced in London in 1950, and collaborating with his wife, Pamela Hansford Johnson, on six one-act plays published in 1951: *Spare the Rod*, *The Penguin with the Silver Foot*, *Her Best Foot Forward*, *The Supper Dance*, *To Murder Mrs. Mortimer*, and *Family Party*.

Achievements

As a man, Snow's accomplishments were many and varied; as a novelist his achievement was more limited, and yet *(ars longa*, public life frequently *breva)* probably more long-lasting. Snow the scientist and Snow the public figure cannot, however, be divorced from Snow the writer. Just as his novels drew upon his experiences in his nonliterary careers, so were his sociopolitical ideas presented in his novels. Yet, there are less of the details of "doing" science, less of the specificity of the public life than one might have expected from Snow's background had he been more of a "naturalistic" novelist, and there is less ideological content than might have been anticipated from one with Snow's strong views, had he been more of a propagandist.

Snow was rather, a realistic novelist, using his particular knowledge, background, and political ideology not primarily for their own sake, but in the service of his art. This art was conventional, relatively old-fashioned. Snow had limited patience with James Joyce and the literary avant-garde. As a *roman-fleuve*, *Strangers and Brothers* has a few interesting features, but it certainly lacks the subtlety that Snow admired in Marcel Proust. Snow did little to advance novelistic techniques; his own craftsmanship shows scant development over the course of a long writing career. His style has frequently been described as dull or pedestrian; Edmund Wilson found his novels "unreadable."

Snow implicitly defended his own style in discussing Anthony Trollope's, praising his predecessor for using language that was often intentionally made flat in order to be clear. Snow's style is certainly more serviceable than inspired. His imagery is limited and repetitious. Unity and impact are achieved through the recurrence of a limited number of images, such as those of lighted windows and rivers, but the impact is gained at the expense of a degree of monotony.

If Snow's style and imagery are little more than adequate, his plot construction is only somewhat more skillful. Unlike Trollope, whom Snow admired and to whom he has frequently been compared, Snow uses plots that are usually suspenseful; one reads his books partly to see how they will come out. This element of suspense, going back to his first published novel, a "whodunit," no doubt helps explain his having attracted a fairly wide and loyal audience, many of whom were not regular readers of novels. Snow's plots, however, are seldom particularly ingenious or original; essentially, they are a means to the revelation of character.

It is in characterization that Snow's prime virtue as a novelist lies; yet his characterizations excel only within certain limits. These limits arise from his subject matter. As has been frequently noted, Snow is particularly effective in dealing with "man in committee." This focus, related to the election, by thirteen Fellows, of a new head of their college, is central to Snow's most highly praised novel, *The Masters*. A similar focus is present in a number of his other novels, most strongly in *The Affair*. The men operate in committees because of the nature of their work—they are professionals involved in their careers, as academics, businessmen, scientists, civil servants. This *work*—not the physical labor described in a "proletarian novel" but the work of "The New Men," the professional, bureaucratic, technological, managerial, classes—is presented with knowledgeable detail to be found in hardly any other novelist. Snow's work, in effect, filled a vacuum.

Snow filled another vacuum in his treatment of love and sex. While these topics have hardly been ignored by novelists, Snow's consideration of the social dimensions of a love affair or a marriage—the effect, for example, of a particular passion upon a man's career, such as Jago's protective love, in *The Masters*, for his wife—is rare, if not unique, among modern novelists, especially as, in Snow, the passion per se, however important, is never (not even in *Time of Hope*) the central concern.

This concern is character; the conditions of work, the politicking in committee, the impact of love—all these are used to reveal character in action.

Thus, Snow is fundamentally a very traditional novelist, even though his distinctive reputation rests upon his having been a kind of contemporary social psychologist, carefully observing particular segments of modern society. While he is likely to continue to be read for some time for the picture of parts of society that his special experience allowed him to present, he may well still be read when this picture, encrusted by time, is of only historical interest. If, as seems likely, his novels do so survive, it will be because, while dealing with the time-bound particulars of their age, they were able to rise to an understanding of fundamental human motivation, and thus to enjoy the longevity of true art.

Biography

Charles Percy Snow was born on October 15, 1905, in the Midland city of Leicester, the second of four sons. His background was similar to that of his fictional persona, Lewis Eliot. Snow's family had risen to the lower levels of the middle class; his father worked as a clerk in a shoe factory. Like Eliot's father, who led a choir, Snow's father played the organ in church; when he was no longer able to do so he died soon after, at the age of eighty-four.

In school, Snow specialized in science; after graduation he worked as a laboratory assistant while he prepared for the examination which won him a scholarship, in 1925, at the University College of Leicester. He was graduated, in 1927, with First Class Honors in chemistry, and received a grant that allowed him to proceed to a Master of Science degree in physics in 1928. Subsequently, he gained a scholarship to Cambridge, where he entered Christ's College as a research student in physics, published a paper on the infrared investigation of molecular structure, and, in 1930, received a Ph.D. and was elected a Fellow of Christ's College, a post he held until 1950, serving as Tutor from 1935 until 1945.

Like the fictional Lewis Eliot, whose law career hinged upon doing well in examinations and receiving scholarships, Snow must have worked hard (as did the hero of *The Search*) and must have been driven by ambition. His lifelong friend William Cooper (H. S. Hoff) has written novels about the life of the young people in Leicester in which the young Snow appears in fictional form; this work helps confirm the autobiographical quality of Snow's *Time of Hope*. Snow himself suggests the autobiographical aspect of *The Conscience of the Rich*, writing that when he was "very poor and very young," he "was taken up by one of the rich patrician Anglo-Jewish families."

Just as Lewis Eliot changes careers, and as the narrator of *The Search* turns from science to writing, Snow also did not rest in the comfort of being a rising young scientific don. He later wrote that since eighteen or so he knew that he wanted to be a writer, and while an undergraduate he wrote a novel, never published, called *Youth Searching*. He had gone into science because it offered a practical possibility for a poor boy. Although he did good scientific work at Cambridge and published some significant papers, according to William Cooper in *C. P. Snow* (1959), when some of Snow's scientific research went wrong through oversight, he abandoned scientific experimentation and turned more to his writing.

Snow had already published his first novel, *Death Under Sail*, a detective story, in 1932; he looked on it as practice for his later, more serious fiction. The next year he published *New Lives for Old*, combining his interest in science and politics in a work of science fiction. Worried that it would hurt his scientific career, he published this novel anonymously; it has never been reprinted. The first of his "serious" novels, *The Search*, appeared in 1934; like the Lewis Eliot series, it had a significant autobiographical element.

Snow did not move away from science to a complete commitment to literature at this time; rather, he became involved in administration, starting at his college. In 1939, he was appointed to a committee of the Royal Society that was organizing scientists for the war effort. This position led to a career in civil service; during World War II, he worked with the Ministry of Labour, being responsible for scientific personnel; after the war, he recruited scientists for government service. Beginning in 1944, he was associated with the English Electric Company, becoming a member of its Board of Directors in 1947. He was a Civil Service Commissioner from 1945 until 1960.

Snow's public life led to public honors; in 1943 he was made a Commander of the British Empire; in 1957 he was knighted. In 1964, when the Labour party resumed power, Snow, making a decision different from Lewis Eliot's, was made a life peer, Baron Snow, of the City of Leicester, and served for two years as parliamentary secretary of the Ministry of Technology.

During these years of public service, Snow was, of course, also living a personal life. He married the novelist Pamela Hansford Johnson in 1950. Like Margaret Davidson in the *Strangers and Brothers* series, she had been previously married, and like Lewis Eliot, Snow became a stepfather before having a son of his own, Philip Hansford Snow, born in 1952. Lady Snow has written autobiographically; her accounts are especially interesting in suggesting the similarities and differences between her children and the fictional children presented, especially in *Last Things*, by Snow.

Both the public and the personal sides of Snow's life were reflected in the *Strangers and Brothers* series, the idea for which occurred to him, he wrote, on January 1, 1935, while he was in France. It is difficult to determine the degree to which the whole series was worked out in advance. It would seem that Snow developed early certain controlling themes, such as "possessive love" and the idea of the "resonance" of experience upon the narrator, Lewis Eliot, while remaining flexible regarding the number and nature of the volumes that would make up the series. The first volume, *Strangers and Brothers*, which was to give the title to the whole series, appeared in 1940. It was followed in 1947 by *The Light and the Dark*. The subsequent nine volumes of the series appeared at roughly two-year intervals. They continued to draw directly upon his own life, including his eye operations, his cardiac arrest, his interest in the Moors murder case, and his experience in parliament.

The course of Snow's simultaneous literary and public careers brought him increased recognition and honors, including numerous honorary degrees, and apointment as rector of the University of St. Andrews, Scotland. (Like Lewis Eliot, he postponed the first of his eye operations in order to attend this academic installation.) They also involved him in notable controversy, the most famous resulting from his Cambridge lectures in 1959, later published as *The Two Cultures and the Scientific Revolution*. Snow's position, which included a criticism of intellectuals' general lack of understanding of modern science, provoked much discussion and a strong attack, renewed in 1961 by the noted Cambridge literary critic, F. R. Leavis. In 1960, Snow, while on one of his trips to the United States, stirred up another controversy by his lectures at Harvard. In those lectures, he criticized some of the military-scientific decisions made by Winston Churchill's government during World War II.

In his later years, Snow continued to speak out on public policies. He remained a controversial figure, but he gradually acquired the image of an elderly, liberal sage, even if his sagacity was frequently questioned by both the political Left and Right. Following the completion of the *Strangers and Brothers* series, he revised it for an "Omnibus Edition" and continued his writing, publishing *The Malcontents*, *In Their Wisdom*, and ending his career, as he began it, with a detective story (of sorts), *A Coat of Varnish*. His remarkably full life ended on July 1, 1980.

Analysis

Characterization is the foundation of Snow's fiction. While theme and idea, as one might expect from a writer as political and engagé as was C. P. Snow, are important to his work, and while plot is nearly always a major source of interest, character is fundamental. It was his special approach to characterization, at once limited and complex, that allowed him to employ theme and plot, as well as style and imagery, in its service, and which made certain subject matter particularly appropriate. Consequently, his works have their own distinctive and satisfying unity.

In his study of Anthony Trollope, a writer whom he valued highly and with whom he identified in a number of ways, Snow speaks interestingly of characterization. He defines character as persona, distinguishes it from inherent, individual nature, and considers personality to be a fusion of nature and character. These distinctions are certainly relevant to Snow's own work. His starting interest is in "characters," that is, an individual's personal qualities that are conditioned by, and expressed in, social experience. Yet, recognizing that this "character" interacts with "nature," Snow, in attempting to represent a rounded picture of "personality," must demonstrate the interaction. His fiction, then, is simultaneously concerned with showing people their "character" in social situations, indicating their "nature" or personal psychology, and presenting the interplay of the two, the social character and the private nature. All men have, in differing proportions, both a private and a social side to their personalities; all are both strangers and brothers.

Given this approach, it is not difficult to understand why Snow dealt frequently with "man in committee," or why he balanced this social material with presentation of individual passions, such as Lewis Eliot's for Sheila. Work and careers, seen in relation to individual "nature" and love and sex, were the two poles to which his subject matter flowed. As the social side of personality is developed, Snow was able to suggest its changing formation. One observes, for example, Walter Luke's evolution from a brash young scientist to Lord Luke of Salcombe; his persona, but not his basic nature, changes with the years. Because an individual's "nature" is inherent (like his physiology), it is taken as a *donnée*, and its effects are dealt with. It is, for example, a given fact that Roy Calvert is a kind of "manic-depressive"; the reader discovers what the results of this nature will be, both for Calvert himself and for those with whom he interacts.

It was convenient for Snow that this approach to character was quite appropriate to the type of plotting that he apparently preferred. Most of his novels pose a question: "What will Martin decide?" "Who will be elected master?" "Will Roger Quaife succeed?" The reader, in attempting to anticipate the answer, and Snow, in providing and justifying it, must consider the personalities involved. This consideration requires some understanding of the characters' public personae, their social interactions, and their private passions. Plot, a strong element in its own right, is based on character.

Imagery also consistently reinforces Snow's binocular view of personality. The light of brotherhood wages a never-ending Manichaean conflict with the dark of private estrangement. Windows may be lit, inviting people to "come home" to social involvement, but they often walk the dark streets, locked out in their lonely individuality.

Much of Snow's style also reflects his view of personality. E. A. Levenston, in a careful study of Snow's sentence structure (*ES*, 1974), has noticed the prevalence of qualifying "interrupters." Many of these are a result of Snow's comparing the particular to the general, one man's qualities to many men's. Expressions such as "very few men, George least of all," or "Roy was not a snob, no man was less so," run throughout his work.

Thus, Snow was consistent in his craft. If this consistency imposed some limitations on his achievements, it also provided a valuable unity to his whole literary corpus.

For reasons that he later described as "obscure," Snow "signalled" that he intended to abandon his scientific career by writing "a stylised, artificial detective story very much in the manner of the day." *Death Under Sail* is a competent example of this form; it remains quite readable and in some ways foreshadows his more significant work. Told in the first person (curiously, for a book by a twenty-six-year-old, the narrator is sixty-three), it employs light and dark and also water imagery; it includes a political discussion regarding class society being justified through the ranks of the elite being open to talent; and it is concerned with friendship and the "genertion gap." More important, the plot hinges on character. While the novel's characterization is relatively superficial, it involves both social character, as seen in the interaction of a small group (the narrator, the detective, and the suspects), and the individual psychology of concealed motives. It is thus typical of Snow's novels, most of which have the element of a suspense story based on the two sides, public and private, of personality.

Snow's second published novel, *New Lives for Old*, is the weakest of his whole canon, but it is not without its virtues. The story involves the discovery of a rejuvenating process and the subsequent questions of whether the process will be suppressed, its effects on the love-lives of some of the characters, and the political implications of the discovery. These three questions are not well unified; instead of integrating the love interest and the politics, in this one instance Snow treats them as essentially separate stories, at the expense of both. The love story in the middle section becomes tedious; in the last section of the book Snow, atypically, lets a political interest stifle the story. The first part of the book, however, is fairly successful. Here, the plot is related to character, social interactions, private motivations, and moral decisions. Snow is doing what he does best. The falling-off of the work after its relatively effective beginning, however, justifies his decision not to have it reprinted; it is now a difficult book to obtain.

His third published novel, *The Search*, was slightly revised and reprinted twenty-four years after its first appearance. It is generally superior to the first two novels, and more easily related to the *Strangers and Brothers* series, especially *Time of Hope* and *Homecoming*. Although Snow warns the reader, in his Preface to the 1958 edition, that the book's narrator and protagonist, Arthur Miles, is "not much like" Snow himself, clearly there is an autobiographical element in the story of a poor boy's using his talent, determination, and scholarships to make a career in science, later to abandon it to turn to writing. The book was praised for its accurate picture of what it is like to be a scientist; in fact, very little scientific activity per se is present. Rather, professional concerns, ambitions, the relation between love and career, and the decisions made by men in committees constitute the basic material of the book. The protagonist might as easily be a barrister as a scientist. Indeed, *The Search*, while a worthwhile book in its own right, can be seen as a trying out of the material that Snow was to go on to develop in his series. The defects of *The Search* result primarily from attempting to try out too much at once; the book's construction becomes somewhat confused. The virtues arise from Snow's basing his work on personal experience; he employed, more thoroughly than in his first two published novels his skill in showing the interconnections of the personal and public aspects of personality.

The favorable reception given to *The Search* certainly encouraged Snow to continue his career as a novelist; within a year of its publication, he conceived of the series on which his reputation rests. He must have made various plans for the series as a whole; the first volume, however, did not appear until 1940, six years after *The Search*. Writing a *roman-fleuve*, as opposed to a series of individual novels, presents an author with certain problems and various opportunities. While Snow avoided some of the pitfalls, such as narrative inconsistency, he failed to take advantage of some of the potentialities of the form. The overall pattern of this series is more blurred than it need have been. This is indicated by the order in which the books were published; it is not the essentially chronological order of the "Omnibus Edition," published after the series was concluded. While this authorial rearrangement must be accepted, the fact that Snow did not originally insist on it suggests a certain random quality to the series' organization as first conceived of and executed. Furthermore, proposed systems of classification of the books within the series—as, for example, novels of "observed experience" and of "direct experience," or a novels dealing with individuals, groups, or a mixture of both—while useful, fail to make clear a compelling pattern.

Indeed, the individual volumes of the series, with the possible exception of the final *Last Things*, stand on their own and easily can be enjoyed separately. That is not to say that nothing is gained by reading them all in the order that they appear in the "Omnibus Edition." As compared, however, to a work such as Anthony Powell's *roman-fleuve*, *A Dance to the Music of Time*, *Strangers and Brothers* fails to develop the potential cumulative effect of a series.

The series form does allow the overlapping of incident and the "resonance" between events as seen and felt by the narrator, Lewis Eliot. Snow has an interesting concept here but he does too little with it. The reader does not, as in some of the novels of Joyce Cary, see the same events through different eyes; rather, one is given different accounts by a relatively consistent Eliot. The result is that events described for the second time sometimes bore the reader, at other times the reader feels cheated by the inadequacy of the first account. Only occasionally does the technique work well, as, for example, the two accounts, in *The Light and the Dark* and *The Masters*, of Roy Calvert's giving of a self-damning paper to Winslow. The first account omits material in order to focus on Calvert; subsequently, as one learns of the larger implications of the act, it takes on new meaning.

More obvious benefits of a series novel are present in *Strangers and Brothers*; the reader observes more characters, over a longer period of time, than would normally be possible in a single volume. Snow, however, possibly in the interest of verisimilitude, does relatively little with his opportunity. Roy Calvert is killed off, George Passant's change is not traced; one does see more of Martin Eliot and Francis Getliffe, but their developments, such as they are, have little drama. There is little in Snow corresponding to the surprises that Powell gives the reader when, for example, his villain, Widmerpool, makes one of his sudden appearances. Only quite rarely does Snow make effective use of surprise, as when the elderly Hector Rose is found to have acquired a younger, sexy wife.

The time-span of the series does, however, allow Snow to present the succession of generations, and he does a fine job of suggesting how childhood experiences affect parents as they react to their own children and their friend's children. The parents' point of view is an important part of human experience, infrequently treated in fiction; here again, in presenting parental love, Snow effectively filled a vacuum.

A more fundamental aspect of the *roman-fleuve* is of the development of the narrator. Lewis Eliot does change, both in his attitudes and in his style, becoming more ironic in the later volumes. Looking back on earlier events, such as his support of Jago in *The Masters*, he recognizes his errors. While Eliot's development adds interest to the whole series, it would be difficult to maintain that this interest is central.

There are two final aspects of a series novel that make *Strangers and Brothers* something other than eleven separate books—repetition and thematic development. The former is a two-edged device. Any reader of the whole series will be struck by the frequent repetition of certain phrases, sententious remarks, images, and tricks of style, and can readily assemble a list. Are the values of the repetition—interesting variations on a theme and a sense of continuity greater than the drawback—monotony? In Snow's case, it is something of a toss-up. On balance, although many readers may be inclined to say "Oh no! Not another lighted window," the recurring images of light and darkness do form a pattern that unifies the series and reinforces its themes.

Finally, there is theme. Snow himself, in a note preceding *The Conscience of the Rich*, indicated the importance of recurring themes, including "possessive love" and love of, and renunciation of, power. The list could be easily expanded; as has been indicated, the title of the series itself points to a fundamental thematic concern. By seeing these various themes dramatized through different characters in differing circumstances, and learning Lewis Eliot's reactions, the reader certainly gains a perspective that would be impossible in a single volume. Thematic perspective, then, provides the most convincing justification for Snow's series. It is a sufficient justification; the whole is greater than the sum of the parts. That Snow's strength lay more in characterization than thematic presentation may account for the occasional failures of the series, qua series.

A brief discussion of three of the eleven novels of the series may serve to suggest aspects of the volumes considered as individual works. *Time of Hope* is both an early novel and one that focuses upon Lewis Eliot; *The Masters*, generally the most highly regarded of the series, is from the middle period and has a "collective hero"; *Corridors of Power*, a later novel, centers on a protagonist other than Eliot.

Time of Hope was the third volume in the series; in terms of internal chronology, however, it comes first, dealing with the years 1914 to 1933, during which Lewis Eliot matures from a boy of nine to an established barrister, involved in an "impossible" marriage. Strongly unified by its plot, it is perhaps the most emotionally moving volume of the whole series, and one of the more successful.

Indicative of Snow's central concern for the interconnections of the public and private aspects of character, the title refers to both the hope for a better society that Lewis Eliot shares with George Passant's group, and the hero's private ambitions. Asked what he wants from life, Eliot, in a phrase he returns to much later in the series, replies that he wants to see a better world, spend his life not unknown, and gain love.

The suspense in the novel is based on the question of whether Eliot will succeed, whether he will at least be started on the road to realizing these hopes. The conflict and tension behind this question provide the *Angst* that contrasts to the hope. The book begins with a "homecoming," dreaded by the young Eliot. (In a clear parallel with Marcel Proust, Snow picks this up at the start of the very last volume of the series.) Just as he had reason to fear this first homecoming, Eliot later dreads subsequent returns to the woman he manages to marry. Eliot's success is mingled with failure. Through a combination of his "nature," which gives him the drive to struggle, and his social "character," which wins him the help of George Passant, Eliot's "personality" wins through on the public level: he succeeds in becoming a barrister. On the personal level, however, while he "succeeds" in marrying Sheila, his possessive love evokes no response; his marriage is personally disastrous, and a handicap to his career.

Snow in *Time of Hope* thus successfully utilizes his approach to character and his recurring themes in a self-contained story, but one which also prepares for subsequent volumes. His techniques in this volume are typical of the series: The imagery of light and darkness prevails; secondary characters, such as Herbert Getliffe, the barrister under whom Eliot trains, are well drawn; the "nature" of a major character is presented as a *donneé*. Not being shown what makes her the strange person she is, one must take Sheila's problems as given. Fortunately for the story, it is easier to do so than to accept Roy Calvert's inherent depression in *The Light and the Dark*. As a *Bildungsroman*, *Time of Hope* is more conventional than the majority of the volumes in the series. Consequently, it is both one of the more satisfactory of Snow's novels, and one of the less distinctively interesting.

While *Time of Hope* has a clear protagonist, *The Masters*, the first volume
in the revised series, has no one hero. Snow is particularly good at dealing
with interreactions within a group and *The Masters* has been the most highly
regarded of his novels. The title refers to two "masters" or heads of a college;
after the first one dies, a new one must be elected. It is on this election,
involving the votes of thirteen Fellows of the college, that the plot centers.
The election comes down to two candidates, Jago and Crawford. While Lewis
Eliot, now one of the Fellows, supports Jago, and while the reader's sympathies are involved on this side, Snow is careful to avoid making the choice
one between good and evil. There are very few outright villains in Snow's
novels, and Crawford is certainly not one. Politically of the Left, but personally not so well suited for the mastership, he is contrasted to Jago, whom
Eliot finds less appealing politically but much more appealing as a man. Thus,
the issue is essentially between personal "nature" and public "character." The
different Fellows line up on this basis, thereby reflecting their own natures
and characters; their ultimate votes demonstrate the balance of these two
aspects of "personality."

Interestingly, given Snow's famous dispute, following the publication of the
The Masters, over "the two cultures," the literary and the scientific, one might
see Jago, a scholar of English literature, as the humanists' candidate, and
Crawford, a member of the Royal Society, as the scientists'. Snow, opposed
to the split between the "cultures," does not have the Fellows vote on the
basis of this split. Walter Luke, a scientist, judges by nature and sticks with
Jago. Francis Getliffe, also a scientist, although recognizing Jago's virtues, is
motivated by "public" principle, and supports Crawford. Eustace Pilbrow, a
literary scholar, agrees with Getliffe. Nightingale, another scientist, jealous
of Crawford's professional success, initially supports Jago. Paradoxically,
Despard-Smith, because he identifies with Jago, supports Crawford.

Having established the initial lineup of votes, Snow skillfully shows the
interactions of motives that cause some of them to shift. One particularly
important consideration is the question of Jago's wife; her character, thought
to be unsuitble for that of a Master's spouse, becomes an issue in the election.
The personal issue here involves another form of "possessive love," and sets
up a "resonance" for Eliot, who is ambivalently trapped in his marriage to
Sheila. Snow handles the development of the plot and the suspense leading
to the election quite effectively. In ringing so many insightful changes on the
interactions of the personalities within a small group, Snow wrote what may
be his own masterpiece.

In the later volumes of the series, Eliot moves from college to national and
international political maneuvers; the implications are that there is not that
much difference. Nevertheless, the "Tolstoyan" view of history—that individuals are secondary to the larger forces of history which is explicitly men-

tioned more than once in the series—is more pronounced in the later volumes. Snow suggests that with other men, probably the same policies would be carried out, the same forces would operate. Thus, the *mechanisms* of politics are of primary interest, but to understand them, one must understand the men who work and are worked by them. As Snow once said, one must understand how the world "ticks" if one is to change it for the better.

Corridors of Power, the ninth volume in the series, gives the reader a picture of how the high-level decision making that he also described in *The New Men* and questioned in *Science and Government* (1961), does operate. However deterministic its underlying historical philosophy, the novel supports the statement of one of its characters that what is important is how something is done, who it is done by, and when it is done.

The story centers on Roger Quaife, a politician committed to an "enlightened" view of the use of atomic weapons. Once again, one sees both the public and private side of a protagonist, the "nature" and "character" that interact to form Quaife's "personality"; again, however, the nature is essentially a *donneé*—Quaife is to be taken as found. Ostensibly happy in his marriage, Quaife has a mistress; she is a factor, although not a decisive one, in his political career. Snow is quite good at showing the interactions of career considerations and more personal feelings within the triangle composed of Quaife, his wife Caro, and his mistress Ellen. Sex is seen as a *relationship*, social as well as emotional and physical. In order to present this relationship, however, verisimilitude must be stretched a bit, because Lewis Eliot, the narrator, has to be in places and hear confidences from which one would expect him to be barred. Not only does Eliot learn much about private lives, but also he is rather surprisingly ubiquitous at political councils. Here, in describing some of the behind-the-scenes maneuvers, Snow is quite effective, as he is with the presentation of secondary characters, such as the member of Parliament "Sammikins," and, expecially, the important civil servant, Hector Rose.

After the completion and revision of the *Strangers and Brothers* series, Snow not only worked on biographical studies (*Trollope, The Realists, The Physicists*) but also continued his novel-writing. Although the final volume in the series, *Last Things*, was diffuse in plotting, he returned, in his final novels, to the use of a strong plot line. Both *The Malcontents* and *A Coat of Varnish* are forms of the "whodunit," and *In Their Wisdom*, like *The Sleep of Reason*, maintains the reader's interest in the outcome of a law case.

The Malcontents received generally poor reviews. It does have obvious weaknesses; the dialogue, usually one of Snow's stronger points, is somewhat unconvincing. Well attuned to the talk of his cohorts, Snow's ear for the speech of contemporary youth was less acute. A more serious defect is related to the mystery-story requirement of providing a goodly number of suspects. Too many characters are introduced at the beginning; the reader has an initial problem in differentiating them, and the book gets off to a slow start. Once the story is underway, however, the narrative interest is strong. It involves the interaction of a group of seven young people, planning to take action against the Establishment. One of them is known to be an informer. Typically for a Snow novel, to appreciate fully the narrative one must consider the formative aspects of each individual's personality. Class background, family relations, ideological positions, and love interests all enter in. Diffused through seven characters, however, Snow's analysis of these factors is somewhat superficial, with the exception of Stephen Freer, whose relationship to the older generation is presented with sensitivity. An underlying sympathy for the ends, if not the means, of the young radicals informs much of the book. This sympathy, while somewhat Olympian, avoids being patronizing and becomes one of the novel's virtues.

In Their Wisdom is a more successful work. Again, to develop narrative interest, a problem is posed. In this instance, it involves an argument over a will and the results of a trial over the disputed legacy. Just as the reader's sympathy is involved, in *The Masters*, on Jago's side, here there is no question of whom to support in the contest. Julian, a selfish and opportunistic young man, is Snow's closest approach to a clear villian. By simplifying some of the characters, Snow is able to devote more attention to the others. Jenny is particularly interesting, different from characters in Snow's earlier books. In showing her life of genteel poverty and the effect upon her of the trial and its outcome, Snow once again effectively intertwines the personal and the public. Although it devotes an excessive amount of space to the House of Lords, *In Their Wisdom* is one of Snow's more successful novels.

His last novel, *A Coat of Varnish*, was a return to the detective-story genre of his first book. A less pure example of this genre than *Death Under Sail*, however, it is somewhat unsatisfactory considered simply as a mystery. The title refers to a line within the book, to the effect that civilization is a thin coat of varnish over barbarism, a notion relevant also to *The Sleep of Reason*. A fairly interesting cast of characters is introduced, but none of them is treated with the depth of analysis of which Snow was capable. Here, character is secondary to plot, and plot itself is used to comment on society. To try to work out who is guilty, one must understand motives: Money, sex, and power. In understanding these motives, one gains, Snow expects, an understanding of society. Although this is one of Snow's weaker novels, certainly not ending his career triumphantly, it does manage a degree of fulfillment of the Horatian formula, to delight and to instruct.

Perhaps one should ask for no more. Throughout his career as a novelist, Snow, although with varying degrees of success, never failed to provide a number of intelligent readers with these twin satisfactions. This may not put him in the ranks of a Leo Tolstoy or a Proust; it is, nevertheless, no small accomplishment.

Major publications other than long fiction

PLAYS: *The Supper Dance*, 1951 (with Pamela Hansford Johnson); *Family Party*, 1951 (with Pamela Hansford Johnson); *Spare the Rod*, 1951 (with Pamela Hansford Johnson); *To Murder Mrs. Mortimer*, 1951 (with Pamela Hansford Johnson); *The Pigeon with the Silver Foot*, 1951 (with Pamela Hansford Johnson); *Her Best Foot Forward*, 1951 (with Pamela Hansford Johnson); *The Public Prosecutor*, 1969 (adaptation with Pamela Hansford Johnson).

NONFICTION: *Richard Aldington: An Appreciation*, 1938; *Writers and Readers of the Soviet Union*, 1943; *The Two Cultures and the Scientific Revolution*, 1959 (revised as *Two Cultures and a Second Look*, 1964); *Science and Government*, 1961; *A Postscript to Science and Government*, 1962; *Magnanimity*, 1962; *C. P. Snow: A Spectrum, Science, Criticism, Fiction*, 1963; *Variety of Men*, 1967; *The State of Siege*, 1969; *Public Affairs*, 1971; *Trollope: His Life and Art*, 1975; *The Realists*, 1978; *The Physicists*, 1981.

Bibliography

Boytinck, Paul. *C. P. Snow: A Reference Guide*, 1980.

Cooper, William. *C. P. Snow*, 1959.

Davis, Robert Gorham. *C. P. Snow*, 1965.

Johnson, Pamela Hansford. *Important to Me: Personalia*, 1974.

Karl, Frederick R. *C. P. Snow: The Politics of Conscience*, 1963.

Morris, Robert K. *Continuance and Change: The Contemporary British Novel Sequence*, 1972.

Shusterman, David. *C. P. Snow*, 1975.

Thale, Jerome. *C. P. Snow*, 1965.

William B. Stone

TERRY SOUTHERN

Born: Alvarado, Texas; May 1, 1924

Principal long fiction

Flash and Filigree, 1958; *Candy*, 1958 (as Maxwell Kenton, with Mason Hoffenberg); *The Magic Christian*, 1959; *Blue Movie*, 1970.

Other literary forms

In addition to *Red-Dirt Marijuana and Other Tastes* (1967), a mixed and uneven collection of short stories and essays originally published in the *Paris Review* and other journals, Terry Southern has been primarily involved in writing screenplays, for which he has won greater recognition than as a novelist. His first screenplay, written in collaboration with David Burnett, was *Candy Kisses* (1955); he received instant acclaim with his second, *Dr. Strangelove: Or, How I Learned to Stop Worrying and Love the Bomb* (1964), written in collaboration with Stanley Kubrick and Peter George and based on George's novel *Red Alert* (1958). Most of his screenplays, in fact, have been written in collaboration with others; among them, *The Loved One* (1965), based on Evelyn Waugh's novel, was written with Christopher Isherwood; *The Cincinnati Kid* (1966) with Ring Lardner, Jr.; *Barbarella* (1967) with Roger Vadim and others; *Easy Rider* (1968) with Peter Fonda and Dennis Hopper; *The End of the Road* (1969), based on John Barth's novel, with Aram Avakian; and *The Magic Christian* (1971), based on his own novel, with Peter Sellers and Joseph McGrath. Southern's account of the filming of *The Loved One* appears in a "production log" published in 1965, and *Blue Movie* is dedicated to "the great Stanley K.," further indications of Southern's recent involvement with the cinema. The screenplay for *Easy Rider* was published in 1969.

Achievements

Southern's novels have received extensive attention though little extended analysis or evaluation. His film work, however, has been rewarded by the British Screen Writers' Award in 1964 and by two Academy Award nominations, in 1963 for *Dr. Strangelove* and in 1968 for *Easy Rider*. In both his novels and his screenplays, Southern's work is characterized by a highly irreverent, often salacious variety of satire often labeled "black humor." Most of Southern's film work has been done in collaboration with directors, authors, or actors; in each case, however, Southern's distinctively wild talent is evident through satiric exaggeration far in excess of conventional satire. The result is a consistently macabre examination of sex, often in combination with death, that manages to make telling points regarding bourgeois values while maintaining some of the most wildly comic situations to be found in all of modern fiction. Southern has not always been able to observe the fine line between utter tastelessness and relevant satire, but his books, when compared to more recent fictional black humor, now seem relatively tame and lacking in much of the shock value they had when they were published.

Biography

Terry Southern was born in Alvarado, Texas, on May 1, 1924, the only son of T. M. (a pharmacist) and Helen Simonds Southern (a dress designer). Between the ages of eleven and fifteen, according to the book jacket for *Flash and Filigree*, he filled sixty-seven notebooks with adventure tales based on Edgar Allan Poe's stories, and from sixteen to eighteen he rewrote, as exercises, all of Nathaniel Hawthorne's stories and half of Poe's. His early ambition was to become a physician like his grandfather, an ambition maintained throughout high school in Dallas and during premedical studies at Southern Methodist University. These plans were cut short by induction into the United States Army, and, following two years service in Europe (from 1943 to 1945), he continued his college studies, first at the University of Chicago, then at Northwestern University, where he received his B.A. in 1948. Aided by the GI Bill, he then studied in Paris at the Sorbonne until 1950, continuing to live in Paris after these funds were depleted, and began writing stories and essays, mostly for the *Paris Review* but also for *Esquire* and *Harper's Bazaar*. In 1952, he returned to the United States, and settled in Greenwich Village. He met Carol Kauffman, a nursery-school teacher, in the same year, and he married her in 1956; they have one son, Nile.

After a time working at various jobs, Southern turned increasingly to freelance writing and journalism. The following years were spent partly in Geneva (where Carol Southern taught at the United Nations' nursery school) and partly in the United States, where the Southerns eventually settled in East Canaan, Connecticut.

After destroying three early novels, Southern discovered the work of the late British writer Henry Green (1905-1973), realizing that he had been gradually developing a similar style and subject. Green helped Southern to get his first novel, *Flash and Filigree*, published in England, after which it appeared in the United States. With the publication of *The Magic Christian*, Southern's growing word-of-mouth reputation attracted the attention of the director Stanley Kubrick; following collaboration with Kubrick on the screenplay for *Dr. Strangelove*, Southern wrote increasingly for the screen.

While in Paris in the late 1950's, Southern and Mason Hoffenberg (using the joint pseudonym "Maxwell Kenton") collaborated on *Candy* for Maurice Girodias, whose Olympia Press published many erotic and literary works, especially by English-speaking writers unable to secure publication of such books in their own countries. After being banned by the de Gaulle government and reissued under another title, *Lollipop*, the book was published in the United States; because of legal uncertainty about authorship and copyright, it was published both in an authorized edition under Southern and Hoffenberg's names and in unauthorized editions by various pornographic and other publishers under the authors' joint pseudonym and without royalties. The consequent uproar, coming at the same time as the release of *Dr. Strangelove*, helped Southern's critical reputation and enabled him to purchase a farm in the Connecticut Berkshires, where he has since lived when not in Hollywood working on screenplays.

Southern's subsequent novels have not had as sensational a reception as his earliest ones, though *Blue Movie* again raised the question of whether he was writing pornography or satire about pornography. At the present time, only *Blue Movie* is in print; Southern's other books now appear somewhat dated.

Analysis

Flash and Filigree (1958), like Southern's other novels, is short on plot but long on comic incidents. There are, in fact, two distinct plots related only through the central characters' common place of employment. In one, Dr. Frederick Eichner, a sports-car fanatic and world's greatest dermatologist— the "Flash" of the title—works at a clinic and is reluctantly involved in a grotesque trial on account of a speeding accident. Medical personnel—as a result of Southern's early career plans—are present for more than their share of satire in his novels, and Eichner is merely the first of a parade of such characters. Eichner's increasingly complicated life includes the hiring of an alcoholic detective, a bizarre courtroom scene, and a truly memorable foil, the cause of much of Eichner's distress, Felix Treevly. Treevly's encounters with Eichner include a wild account of self-inflicted infection, jury-tampering, and transvestism, and Eichner's method of solving his problem with Treevly is both ingenious and effective.

The other plot involves a young nurse at the clinic, Babs Mintner, the first in Southern's series of beautiful, ingenuous young women who reluctantly lose their innocence, a series culminating in Candy Christian. In Mintner's case—and she is clearly the "filigree," or decorative ornamentation, for the clinic—the loss is a sexual one, a long, drawn-out, utterly clichéd contest of wills with her boyfriend in the backseat of a convertible at a drive-in movie that ends with her "defeat" and the inevitable "Do you love me?" Other satiric touches include a closet lesbian head-nurse who enjoys watching Babs change clothes, a lecherous dwarf (another of Southern's favorite satiric touches), ineffectual comic policemen, medical routine and dialogue, and, most frequent of all, the trite, revealing language of everyday discourse.

Indeed, Southern's chief talent may be his ability to capture perfectly the language of ordinary people involved in out-of-the-ordinary circumstances;

it is certainly situation and language far more than plot that is notable in this novel, as well as in his later ones. Ultimately, though, *Flash and Filigree* seems like a slight effort, and despite the hyperbolic praise given it by early reviewers, it now seems as dated as an old situation comedy.

Candy is a remarkably funny novel, clearly derived from Voltaire's *Candide* (1759) both in title and in substance. Indeed, the kind of character suggested by Babs Mintner in *Flash and Filigree* became a virtually new type in *Candy*, a type often encountered in fiction since the publication of *Candy*. Candy Christian is both lovely and innocent—but with a kind of innocence that permits her to have sexual relations with almost anyone who "needs" her, while she remains chaste in her mind. Much of the novel is a picaresque plot in which Candy attempts to find her lost father, but this traditional theme is handled with wicked glee by Southern, as he introduces a series of utterly outrageous and wildly funny scenes: Candy's aunt ordering "a bit of giant Male Organ—piping hot!" in a fine restaurant, a physician's masturbation-therapy sessions, a gynecologist's examining Candy in a New York bar, an erotic variety of Zen, and, ultimately, an incestuous encounter with her father in a Tibetan temple. Southern plays with time and space freely in the novel; rapid, inexplicable changes in setting are simply accepted by the reader as he relishes Candy's tortuous path to "spiritual advancement" through the help of Grindle, a "monk" who repeatedly seduces Candy while convincing her that such fleshly encounters are merely controlled expressions of mystical, transcendant truth.

Southern's chief satiric subject in *Candy* is clearly innocence, especially sexual innocence, and the question of whether he is satirizing and parodying pornography or actually writing pornography has often been raised, though without any clear answer. Certainly his frequent inclusion of explicit sexual scenes and the familiar jargon of pornography suggest one view, while his heightened, self-aware handling of sex as related to larger satiric targets suggests something quite different. Candy's sexual encounters never become a matter of rational consideration of her motives, other than the alleged "need" on the part of her seducers; in a word, Candy is simply everyman's ideal combination of virgin and whore, endlessly available, never questioning. Candy's naïveté enables her to absorb all experiences—and all lovers—with the same equanimity, openness, lack of distinction and lack of sophistication. The book, therefore, is far from conventional pornography, though it still appears in editions (and shops) catering to readers of such works. The book seems in retrospect a particularly explicit form of black humor, one in which some of America's most cherished values and beliefs are simply turned upside down, but with an implicit sense that Southern is actually defending these values and beliefs, much as satire—traditionally a conservative (in its literal sense) variety of humor—has always done.

Southern's next novel, *The Magic Christian*, is another episodic work composed of two distinct but related plots. The central character, Guy Grand, is the connecting link between the two plots; Grand, a billionaire with unlimited imagination as well as wealth, spends his life arranging grotesque practical jokes. These practical jokes have a point, however, as the reader soon discovers: Each is intended to expose the greed, arrogance, perverted values, and vanity of the victims. Among the dozen or more pranks described in detail in the novel are the entering of a black panther in a dog-show (the panther promptly eats its competition); inserting sexual or murder scenes in such films as *The Best Years of Our Lives* and *Mrs. Miniver*; manufacturing automobiles (intended to appeal to the *nouveau riche*) that are so long they cannot turn corners; promoting cosmetics whose use results in the exact opposite of their presumed effect; having a large vat set up in downtown Chicago with ten thousand one-hundred-dollar bills floating in a heated mixture of manure, urine, and blood from the stockyards and then watching the well-dressed commuters wade in the muck for the money; using a 75mm. howitzer to hunt game in Kenya; and, finally, the ultimate appeal to snobbery, the floating of an ultraexclusive ship, the *Magic Christian*, in which utter anarchy occurs before the pasengers discover that their journey was a prank, that they are back in New York harbor, and that their ship simply plows into the pier upon return as an abrupt conclusion to their expensive outing.

In all of these cases, Grand finds that money can indeed buy whatever he wants, even though putting on these potentially damaging situations costs him a small portion of his immense fortune. Grand is insatiable in his efforts to ridicule people's desire to possess more; but even he realizes that using his wealth for such jokes is ultimately boring. Hence, his attempt to top each successive prank by another, more outrageous one, culminates in the sea-voyage; after that, all he can do is "keep in touch," as he phrases it, by reverting to lesser practical jokes that would help to keep his reputation alive, such as opening a grocery store and selling everything in two hours at absurdly low prices, then simply closing the store when the word spreads.

Grand's practical jokes constitute the chief plot in the novel, memorable simply because it is so outrageous. The other, lesser plot deals with Grand's conversations with his two genteel aunts. Each chapter begins with such a conversation, with the balance of the chapter containing Grand's reminiscing about some of his past escapades. Hence the two plots alternate between the present (the teas with his aunts) and the past (in which most of the pranks are set), suggesting more than a simple contrast in time. Grand is seen not as a malicious man but simply as a bored one, as a man who will do anything and go to any expense to be amused. While this amusement seems to be at the expense of others, the victims benefit financially from the episodes.

The questions which had been raised about alleged "pornographic" elements in some of Southern's earlier novels were raised even more vehemently in regard to *Blue Movie*, his latest work. Briefly, *Blue Movie* is the story of

Boris, a distinguished Hollywood director who believes that he can make an explicit sex-film that will be professionally and artistically effective, made by professionals and with name talents, and that will be accepted by the general moviegoing public. Far less avaricious and vulgar than his associates, Boris believes that *The Facts of Love* (a film with a number of segments, each illustrating a different sexual activity) will succeed if he can simply get the best in the business to work with him. Much of the book is thus a comic examination of grotesque producers, agents, financiers, actors and actresses and their obsessions and insecurities, and, of course, the ever-vigilant watchdogs of cinema, notably the Roman Catholic Church. Virtually every type likely to be encountered in the making of an erotic film is encountered in the pages of the novel: a sexy actress á la Marilyn Monroe or Jayne Mansfield, who is shy and simple by nature and who wants to be remembered for her art, not her body; a French lesbian actress; an utterly gross, sex-driven producer; well-developed black male extras from Morocco; and so on. These types are redeemed from cliché by Southern's judicious touches in characterizaton; each is seen as somewhat more believable and vulnerable than one would expect, and at times the reader feels genuine sympathy and compassion for their frenetic seeking after Dionysian thrills and their desire to be accepted.

Boris is the one person in the novel who seems consistently human and admirable; he has to persuade, even cajole, people who respect his art to work with him; in some cases, he cannot even tell his actors exactly what they will be doing in the film until the cameras are rolling. Boris' ambition to make an artistically satisfying sexual omnibus is not novel, yet one cannot help but admire his goal and intent; his ability to work around his more vulgar hangers-on is itself a matter of some admiration.

Southern's explicit sexual detail and array of sexual situations even now lead some readers to find the novel offensive and tedious. The catalog of sexual activities he presents is a wide one, including, besides the usual heterosexual activities, incest, gang rape, homosexuality, necrophilia, and others, generally presented as routine activities without much guilt. Southern uses sex in the novel for its own sake, to reflect on the obsessive nature of human sexuality, and as a vehicle of satire against Hollywood and the film industry. The cynical approach taken by Boris' subordinates in this matter is made even clearer—and more grotesque—following the death of his sex-goddess, when even this tragic incident is perceived as material to be exploited.

Southern's own possible cynicism is seen less in the portion of the novel concerned with sex—admittedly the larger portion—than in his treatment of the role of the Vatican. At the novel's end, the master copies of the film, including the negative, are stolen by a cardinal and a gang of "Vatican toughs," never to be seen again, whether in private or in public. At least that is the impression one gets—until the final page, on which a *New York Times* typographic parody reports unusual private occurrences in a dark court at the

Vatican, the participants in these events walking slowly away, contemplatively and with eyes glittering, a clear indication that the film will forever be available only for the delectation of the Vatican hierarchy.

Southern is an uneven writer, and much of his work has been done in collaboration with others. Still, he clearly has manic gifts for situation and character, though little talent for careful plotting. Even when the satire is overdone, its effectiveness cannot be denied. He once observed that the importance of writing is "to astonish," not to shock, and this he clearly does with flair and imaginative zest. His desire to "blast" smugness when it is encountered is a worthy goal, even if he sometimes seems to use a cannon to kill a mosquito. One can only regret the fact that he has not published any additional novels, for "smug"targets are as much in need of annihilation now as in Southern's prime.

Major publications other than long fiction

SHORT FICTION; *Red-Dirt Marijuana and Other Tastes*, 1967.

NONFICTION: *Writers in Revolt*, 1963 (edited with Richard Seaver and Alexander Trocchi); *The Journal of "The Loved One": The Production Log of a Motion Picture*, 1965.

Bibliography

Algren, Nelson. "The Donkeyman by Twilight," in *The Nation*. May 18, 1964, pp. 509-512.

Galloway, David D. "Clown and Saint: The Hero in Current American Fiction," in *Critique*. VII (1965), pp. 46-65.

Hill, Hamlin. "Black Humor and the Mass Audience," in *American Humor: Essays Presented to John C. Gerber*. 1977, pp. 1-11.

McLaughlin, John J. "Satirical Comical Pornographical *Candy*," in *Kansas Quarterly*. I (1969), pp. 98-103.

Maland, Charles. "*Dr. Strangelove* (1964): Nightmare Comedy and the Idelogy of Liberal Consensus," in *American Quarterly*. XXXI (1979), pp. 697-717.

Murray, D. M. "Candy Christian as a Pop-Art Daisy Miller," in *Journal of Popular Culture*. V (1971), pp. 340-347.

Scholes, Robert. "Black Humor in Hawkes and Southern," in *Fabulation and Metafiction*. 1979, pp. 163-168.

Silva, Edward T. "From *Candide* to *Candy*: Love's Labor Lost," in *Journal of Popular Culture*. VIII (1974), pp. 783-791.

Wakeman, John, ed. "Terry Southern," in *World Authors 1950-1970*, 1975.

Walling, William. "*Candy* in Context," in *New York Literary Forum*. I (1978), pp. 229-240.

Paul Schlueter

MURIEL SPARK

Born: Edinburgh, Scotland; February 1, 1918

Principal long fiction

The Comforters, 1957; *Robinson*, 1958; *Memento Mori*, 1959; *The Ballad of Peckham Rye*, 1960; *The Bachelors*, 1960; *The Prime of Miss Jean Brodie*, 1961; *The Girls of Slender Means*, 1963; *The Mandelbaum Gate*, 1965; *The Public Image*, 1968; *The Driver's Seat*, 1970; *Not to Disturb*, 1971; *The Hothouse by the East River*, 1973; *The Abbess of Crewe: A Modern Morality Tale*, 1974; *The Takeover*, 1976; *Territorial Rights*, 1979; *Loitering with Intent*, 1981.

Other literary forms

In addition to her novels, Muriel Spark has produced a sizable amount of work in the areas of poetry, the short story, drama, biography, and criticism. Her volumes of poetry include *The Fanfarlo and Other Verse* (1952) and *Collected Poems I* (1967). Her first collection of short stories, entitled *The Go-Away Bird and Other Stories* appeared in 1958, follwed by *Collected Stories I* in 1967. *Voices at Play*, a collection of short stories and radio plays, appeared in 1961, and a play, *Doctors of Philosophy*, was first performed in London in 1962 and published in 1963. Spark's literary partnership with Derek Stanford resulted in their editing *Tribute to Wordsworth* (1950), a collection of essays on the centenary of the poet's death, and *My Best Mary: The Selected Letters of Mary Shelley* (1953). Spark and Stanford also edited *Letters of John Henry Newman* (1957) and coauthored a critical and biographical study of Emily Brontë entitled *Emily Brontë: Her Life and Work* (1953), with Spark contributing the biographical essay. She has produced a study of Mary Shelley, *Child of Light: A Reassessment of Mary Wollstonecraft Shelley* (1951), and *John Masefield* (1953). Spark also edited *Selected Poems of Emily Brontë* (1952) and *The Brontë Letters* (1954).

Achievements

Critical opinion about Spark's status as a novelist is sharply divided. In general, she has been less highly valued by American critics; Frederick Karl, for example, has dismissed her work as being "light to the point of froth" and says that it has "virtually no content." English critics such as Frank Kermode, Malcolm Bradbury, and David Lodge, on the other hand, consider Spark a major contemporary novelist. Kermode compliments her on being "obsessed" with novelistic form, calls *The Mandelbaum Gate* a work of "profound virtuosity," and considers her to be a "difficult and important artist." Bradbury, who has regarded Spark as an "interesting, and a very amusing, novelist" from the beginning of her career, now thinks that she is also a "very high stylist" whose work in the novella shows a precision and economy of form and style. In a reassessment of *The Prime of Miss Jean Brodie*, Lodge comments on the complex structure of the novel and Spark's successful experimentation with authorial omniscience.

Throughout her career, Spark has been able to combine popular success with critical acclaim. In 1951, she received her first literary award, the *Observer* Story Prize for the Christmas story "The Seraph and the Zambesi." A radio drama based on *The Ballad of Peckham Rye* won the Italia Prize in 1962, and in the same year she was named Fellow of the Royal Society of Literature. In 1965, Spark received the prestigious James Tait Black Memorial Prize for Fiction for the *The Mandelbaum Gate*. To date, she has produced sixteen novels and has consistently maintained a high level of artistic development and achievement.

Biography

Muriel Sarah Spark was born in Edinburgh, Scotland, on February 1, 1918, of a Jewish father, Bernard Camberg, and an English mother, Sarah Uezzell Camberg. She attended James Gillespie's School for Girls in Edinburgh, an experience that later formed the background for *The Prime of Miss Jean Brodie*. She lived in Edinburgh until 1937, when she married S. O. Spark and moved to Africa. She was divorced from Spark a year later and, in 1944, returned to England, after having lived in South Africa and Rhodesia. From 1944 to 1946, she worked in the Political Intelligence Department of the British Foreign Office, an experience she later drew upon when writing *The Hothouse by the East River*. Her interest in poetry led to her serving as General Secretary of the Poetry Society in London from 1947 to 1949 and as editor of the *Poetry Review*; in 1949, she introduced a short-lived journal entitled *Forum Stories and Poems*. In the 1950's, she began a successful career as a critic and editor which included books on William Wordsworth, Mary Shelley, Emily Brontë, John Masefield, and John Henry Newman, publishing several of these works with her literary partner and friend Derek Stanford.

The major turning point in Spark's career as a writer occurred in 1954, when she converted to Roman Catholicism. Brought up in the Presbyterian religion, she says that she had "no clear beliefs at all" until 1952, when she became "an Anglican intellectually speaking," although she did not formally join the Anglican Church until late in 1953. The Church of England was, however, a halfway house for Spark, who was an Anglo-Catholic for only nine months before her conversion to Roman Catholicism. She believes that the writings of John Henry Newman were an important factor in her move to the Catholic Church. Her conversion initially caused her a great deal of emotional suffering, and she says that her mind was, for a period of time, "far too crowded with ideas, all teeming in disorder." This feeling of mental chaos gave way later to what she has called "a complete reorganization" of her mind that enabled her to begin writing fiction. Several persons encouraged her to produce a novel, among them Graham Greene and Macmillan and Company, which was looking for new writers at the time; the result was *The Comforters*.

In 1961, Spark traveled to Jerusalem to research the background for *The Mandelbaum Gate*, and, in 1964, moved from her home in London to New York. She lived for less than a year in an apartment close to the United Nations Building, a location which later became the setting for *The Hothouse by the East River*. In 1967, she was awarded the Order of the British Empire and left England to settle permanently in Rome, a move which is reflected in the European settings of most of her novels written after *The Mandelbaum Gate*.

Analysis

Muriel Spark frequently uses the word "minor" to describe her achievement as a novelist, a term which, in her vocabulary, is not as derogatory as it may at first appear. She believes that the artist is by definition a "minor public servant" and claims that she chooses to write "minor novels deliberately." This characterization of the artist and of her own intentions as a writer reflects her concerns about the novel as a form and the creative process in general, issues which are present throughout her work. She has admitted that while writing her first novel, *The Comforters*, she had difficulty resigning herself to the fact that she was writing a novel, a genre which, in her opinion, was a "lazy way of writing poetry." For Spark at that time, poetry was the only true literature, while the novel was an "inferior way of writing" whose "aesthetic validity" was very much in doubt. Although she has apparently revised her earlier low estimation of the novel, she says that she still thinks of herself as a poet rather than a novelist and believes that her novels are "the novels of a poet."

Spark's distrust of the novel form also results from her suspicions about fiction's relationship to truth; she has said that she is interested in "absolute truth" and that fiction is a "kind of parable" from which a "kind of truth" emerges which should not be confused with fact. The truth which the novel can embody is similar to her definition of "legend" in *Emily Brontë: Her Life and Work*. Speaking of the literary legends which surround a writer such as Emily Brontë, she says that these stories, though not literally true, are "the repository of a vital aspect of truth" which should be accorded respect in their own right. It is imperative, however, for writers and readers to discriminate among types of truth and between life and art, a discrimination that Charmian Colston, the aged novelist in *Memento Mori*, is capable of making. She tells another character that "the art of fiction is very like the practice of deception," and, when asked if the practice of deception in life is also an art, replies, "In life . . . everything is different. Everything is in the Providence of God." Spark, who is careful to maintain this distinction in her statements about her work, has described her own novels as a "pack of lies."

Caroline Rose in *The Comforters*, who shares this distrust of fiction, struggles against being a character in a novel because she resents being manipulated by the novelist. At one point, she describes the author of the fiction as an "unknown, possibly sinister being." The writer's "sinister" nature results from his ability to create fictions which are imaginative versions and extensions of the truth rather than the truth itself; and, perhaps more important, the novelist deprives his characters of their free will and independence. As Patricia Stubbs has observed, Spark perceives a parallel between God and the novelist, and the act of creating fiction is, in a sense, "dabbling in the devil's work."

As a result, Spark's novels are filled with would-be artists and artist-figures, people who attempt to create fictions in real life and consequently bring about discord and mischief. In *The Prime of Miss Jean Brodie*, Miss Brodie begins to view the people around her as characters in a story she is creating and attempts to bring about sexual pairings and heroic deeds in her self-made "plot" with disastrous results. Both Alec Warner in *Memento Mori* and Dougal Douglas in *The Ballad of Peckham Rye* are involved in "research" into the lives of the people around them; Douglas carries his curiosity about others a step further, fictionalizing an autobiography for an actress and later becoming the author of "a lot of cock-eyed books." In two later novels, *The Public Image* and *Territorial Rights*, fictions are devised even more consciously— and are potentially more dangerous. In *The Public Image*, film actress Annabel Christopher is, for the most part, merely the product of a clever publicity campaign with its accompanying lies, distortions, and omissions. After her husband's suicide, she becomes the victim of his well-planned attempt to destroy her career, for he has left behind a group of letters which would impugn her sexual morality and destroy her carefully devised "public image." In *Territorial Rights*, Robert Leaver stages his own kidnaping and sends threatening letters filled with truth and lies to his family and friends. In addition, he leaves fragments of a "novel" he is supposedly writing which contain a sensational mixture of fact and fiction which could hurt many of the people around him. Just as these characters are guilty of trying to manipulate reality by inserting carefully constructed "fictions" into the lives of real people, Sir Quentin Oliver in *Loitering with Intent* overtly plagiarizes a fictional model to accomplish his ends. After reading Fleur Talbot's novel *Warrender Chase*, he begins to orchestrate the lives of the members of the Autobiographical Association according to its plot, an action which causes Fleur to complain that "He's trying to live out my story."

The ubiquitous "listening devices" and spying present in Spark's fiction are another aspect of her fascination with the process of creating fictions. Dougal Douglas, the artist-to-be, sells tape recorders to African witch doctors; the

Abbey in *The Abbess of Crewe* is bugged; and Curran in *Territorial Rights* has a sudden moment of paranoia in a restaurant when he wonders if his fellow diners are all spies armed with "eavesdropping devices." As the servants in *Not to Disturb* realize, recording and preserving experience allows the person doing the recording to alter, and, in a sense, to create reality. Armed with tape recorders and cameras, they are busy creating their own version of the events of an evening which culminates in the deaths of the Baron and Baroness Klopstock and their secretary; the servants are artist-figures, manipulating the plot of the story which they will soon sell to the public media. Spark sees the novelist, like the "typing ghost" who plagues Caroline Rose in *The Comforters*, as an eavesdropper who spies upon his characters and then manipulates their actions in order to create a fiction; and she peoples her novels with characters who are also engaged in this process.

Because Spark is so intent upon acknowledging her fiction as fiction, most of her novels are consciously artificial in both form and content. She has no desire to be a realistic novelist or to write the "long novel"; she said she grew bored writing her only lengthy novel, *The Mandelbaum Gate*, because of its length. Rather, she claims to speak in a "kind of shorthand" in which the narrative voice is curiously impersonal. Not surprisingly, in several novels, among them *Not to Disturb* and *The Driver's Seat*, she has experimented with her own version of the *nouveau roman*. In Spark's fiction, however, unlike that of many of the antinovelists, all details, no matter how arbitrary they at first appear, are ultimately significant. In fact, a word that appears throughout her statements about fiction and in her novels is "economy." In *The Takeover*, the narrator mentions the "intuitive artistic sense of economy" that characterizes the creative person, and Spark has emphasized her belief that the artist should carefully select only the most appropriate details in order to create meaning.

At the same time, because she believes that it is "bad manners to inflict emotional involvement on the reader," she writes novels in which the narrator's witty detachment from the subject matter signifies her goal of creating art which remains distanced from the human suffering it presents. Literature, she believes, should not continue to sympathize with the victims of violence and tyranny; art should instead abandon sentimental depictions of the human condition so that it can "ruthlessly mock" the forces which cause the individual to suffer. She believes that art needs "less emotion and more intelligence" and should aspire to become an art of satire and ridicule. The world, for Spark, is essentially absurd, and "the rhetoric of our time should persuade us to contemplate the ridiculous nature of the reality before us, and teach us to mock it."

Spark's first novel, *The Comforters*, reflects the two pivotal experiences of her life: her conversion to Roman Catholicism and her change as a writer from poet to novelist. Spark has said that in order to overcome her aesthetic skepticism about the novel form, it was necessary for her "to write a novel about somebody writing a novel." In addition, she believes that *The Comforters* is a result of the "complete reorganization" of her mind that followed her conversion and that its theme is "a convert and a kind of psychic upheaval." Caroline Rose, the novel's central character, is in the process of coming to terms with both these issues. A recent convert to Catholicism who dislikes many of her fellow Catholics, Caroline is writing a book called *Form in the Modern Novel* and trying to understand why she has begun to overhear a disembodied "novelist," complete with typewriter, who is writing a novel about her and her friends.

The Comforters is about the battle between the author and her characters, a battle in which Caroline struggles to preserve her free will in the face of the novelist's desire to control the events of the story. Caroline finds the experience of being "written into" someone else's narrative painful, just as her friend Laurence Manders protests that "I dislike being a character in your novel" when he discovers that Caroline is writing fiction which includes the story of their relationship. Caroline believes that it is her "duty" to "hold up the action" of the novel, to "spoil" it, and she asserts her right to make her own decisions, finding, however, that this is usually impossible; the predetermined "plot" of the novelist prevails.

Caroline remains unaware, however, that she in turn is capable of affecting the novel as it is being written. The narrator admits that Caroline's "remarks" continue to interfere with the book and that she does not realize her "constant influence" on the story's development. From Caroline's perspective, she has only partial knowledge of the plot, and she complains that the voices she overhears only give her "small crazy fragments" of a novel in which there may be other characters whom she does not know. In this sense, Caroline is a surrogate for Spark the novelist, a character who "discovers" the plot, as does its creator, while it is being written. As a result, *The Comforters* concludes with Caroline leaving London to write a novel which apparently will be *The Comforters*.

Spark would appear to be working out both the technique and the morality of writing fiction in her first novel. Caroline's fascination with "form in the modern novel" is also Spark's fascination, and Spark writes a story about the problems involved in writing a story: *The Comforters* is about the struggle between the novelist's will to impose form and the continued growth and development of the characters, who begin to become independent entities in the narrative, insisting upon the right to break free of the restraints of plot and situation. One of the reasons Caroline Rose gives for opposing the novelist is that Caroline "happens to be a Christian"; Spark, as a Catholic, is uneasy with the idea of the novelist "playing God" and depriving her characters of choice.

The Comforters is also about Catholicism and the recent convert's attempts to find an identity as a Catholic. Georgina Hogg, the Catholic in the novel whom Caroline particularly despises, symbolizes Caroline's (and Spark's) reservations about individual Catholics. These reservations are not, it should be emphasized, about Catholicism as a religion. Rather, Mrs. Hogg represents a Catholicism which, in the hands of a certain type of individual, becomes simply dogma. Mrs. Hogg, who lacks insight or any true feeling about her religion, uses her sense of self-righteousness to impinge upon the people around her. In the novel, she is called a "sneak," a "subtle tyrant," and a "moral blackmailer," and she is indeed guilty of all these accusations. At one point in the story, Caroline decides that Mrs. Hogg is "not a real-life character . . . merely a gargoyle"; she is so lacking in identity that she literally "disappears" when there are no other people around to perceive her existence. As several characters observe, Georgina Hogg "has no private life," a phrase which ironically underscores her lack of substance as a character and a Catholic.

Mrs. Hogg's lack of identity is a major theme of the novel, and a problem which several other characters share. Helena Manders, when she has a sudden sense of how "exhilarating" it is to be herself, actually perceives her personality as belonging to someone else. Eleanor Hogarth, as Caroline realizes, has completely lost contact with her true personality because she has for so long been satisfied with mimicking others, adopting other roles to play. Caroline's auditory hallucinations are another aspect of this problem, for she feels that her free will as an individual is being taken from her: Is she Caroline Rose, or simply a character in someone else's novel? At the same time, she is obsessed with the identity of what she calls the "typing ghost," at one point making a list entitled "*Possible identity*" which speculates about who the typist-novelist may be—Satan, a woman, a hermaphrodite, or a Holy Soul in Purgatory.

The characters' lack of identity is related to their isolation and inability to communicate with one another. "Is the world," asks Caroline, "a lunatic asylum then? Are we all courteous maniacs discreetly making allowances for everyone else's derangement?" Although she rejects this idea, *The Comforters* certainly depicts a world in which individuals search for an identity while remaining locked into a very subjective set of preconceptions about everything external to them. The way out of this trap, at least for Caroline, is to write a novel, the novel which Spark has actually written. *The Comforters* represents Spark's successful confrontation with and resolution of the issues of Catholicism, creativity, and the novel as a genre. Her interest in the novel as a form and the process of creating fictions has continued throughout her career as a novelist.

In an interview, Spark has said that the eponymous protagonist of *The Prime of Miss Jean Brodie* represents "completely unrealised potentialities," a descriptive phrase which reflects the same ambiguity with which she is treated in the novel. The story of an Edinburgh schoolmistress and her effects on the lives of six of her pupils, *The Prime of Miss Jean Brodie* concentrates on the relationship between Jean Brodie and Sandy Stranger, the student who eventually "betrays" her. Like many other characters in Spark's fiction, Miss Brodie begins to confuse fact and fiction, and it is when Sandy perceives that her teacher has decided that Rose Stanley must begin an affair with art teacher Teddy Lloyd that Sandy realizes that Jean Brodie is no longer playing a game or advancing a theory: "Miss Brodie meant it." As David Lodge notes in his article on the novel in *The Novelist at the Crossroads* (1971), Sandy and Jenny intuitively understand when their fiction, a made-up correspondence between Miss Brodie and music teacher Gordon Lowther, should be buried and forgotten; unlike her students, Jean Brodie does not know when fantasies should be discarded.

In addition to seeing herself as an artist-figure who can manipulate the lives of her students and lovers, Jean Brodie is also guilty, in Sandy's eyes, of serious religious and political errors. Although she has not turned to religion at the time, a very young Sandy is frightened by her vision of all the "Brodie set" in a line headed by their teacher "in unified compliance to the destiny of Miss Brodie, as if God had willed them to birth for that purpose." Later, Sandy is horrified to discover that her former teacher "thinks she is Providence" and that she can see the beginning and the end of all "stories." Jean Brodie's lack of guilt over any of her actions results from her assurance that "God was on her side"; she elects herself to grace with an "exotic suicidal enchantment" which drives her to the excesses that eventually result in her forced retirement. Jean Brodie's view of herself as "above the common moral code," a phrase she applies to Rose, her chosen surrogate for an affair with Teddy Lloyd, is related to her political views as well. An early admirer of Benito Mussolini and Adolf Hitler whom Sandy later characterizes as a "born fascist," she sees herself as duty-bound to shape the personalities and the destinies of the young girls around her. "You are mine," she says to her "set," whom she has chosen to receive what she calls the "fruits of her prime," which will remain with the girls "always," a prophecy which is partially true.

The complexity of *The Prime of Miss Jean Brodie* lies in the fact that Jean Brodie is not simply a villainous character who oversteps her bounds as a teacher and begins to exert a potentially corruptive force on the young people entrusted to her. Although she flirts with Fascism (after the war she calls Hitler "rather naughty"), she at the same time encourages a fierce individualism in her chosen students, who, as the headmistress of the Marcia Blaine School for Girls sadly learns, are totally lacking in "team spirit." She makes good her promise to "put old heads on young shoulders" and creates the "capacity for enthusiasm" for knowledge that remains with several of her students for life. The lecture to her girls on her theory of education—"It means a leading out. To me education is a leading out of what is already there in the pupil's soul. . . . Never let it be said that I put ideas into your heads"—is, like the portrait of Jean Brodie that Spark presents in the novel, open to several interpretations. Although in the later years of her prime, Miss Brodie *does* attempt to put "ideas" into the girls' heads, at the same time she bequeaths to her students a knowledge of and sensitivity to art, culture, and ideas that would have been impossible in a more conventional educational situation.

Just as *The Prime of Miss Jean Brodie* is about "unrealised potentialities," Miss Brodie also communicates to her students a knowledge of the unlimited potential inherent in all experience. In her late thirties, Jenny Gray has an experience that reawakens a memory of her "sense of the hidden possibility in all things" that she felt as an eleven-year-old student under the tutelage of Jean Brodie. More important, however, is the teacher's influence on Sandy Stranger. In his book on Spark, Derek Stanford says that "Truth, for Muriel Spark, implies rejection," and Sandy laments in the novel that she has had nothing, particularly in the religious realm, to react against or reject. Jean Brodie finally provides this catalyst, and Sandy's decision to "put a stop" to her results from a variety of reasons: her moral indignation over Miss Brodie's "plans" for Rose and Joyce Emily, sexual jealousy of Teddy Lloyd's continued infatuation with her teacher, and her awakening sense of Christian morals.

As an adult, however, Sandy acknowledges that Jean Brodie was her most important formative influence and in a sense responsible for the course her life has taken. Her conversion to Catholicism and taking of the veil are the result of her affair with Teddy Lloyd, an affair she instigates in order to subvert Jean Brodie's plans. Although Spark does not indicate the exact subject of the psychological treatise that has made Sandy famous, other than the fact that it concerns the nature of "moral perception," its title, "The Transfiguration of the Commonplace," reveals that it in some way deals with the mind's ability to alter everyday reality. Clearly, this topic owes a debt to Jean Brodie's communication to her students of the endless "possibilities" which surrounded them and is a reflection of Jean Brodie's constantly changing nature in the novel. The narrator observes that, unlike her colleagues, Miss Brodie is in a "state of fluctuating development"; like her students, her "nature was growing under their eyes, as the girls themselves were under formation." One element of Jean Brodie's "prime" is her nonstatic personality, and the problem, of course, is the direction in which the changes take place. As the narrator notes, "the principles governing the end of her prime would have astonished herself at the beginning of it."

In *The Prime of Miss Jean Brodie*, Spark is at the height of her powers as a novelist, and nowhere else in her fiction is she more in control of her subject. The "flash-forwards" which occur throughout the novel cause the reader to concentrate on the characters' motivations and interrelationships rather than on any intricacies of the plot, and Spark makes use of the principle of "economy" which she so values on almost every page, providing only the most telling details of the story while refraining, for the most part, from any authorial interpretation. In fact, the idea of economy is an important thematic element in the book. Sandy is first fascinated by the economy of Jean Brodie's fusing her tales of her dead lover, Hugh, with her current associations with Gordon Lowther and Teddy Lloyd, and later she is angered and intrigued by the economy of the art teacher's paintings, which make Jean Brodie's students resemble their teacher. When Sandy betrays Miss Brodie to the headmistress, she uses this principle after concluding that "where there was a choice of various courses the most economical was the best." Both in form and style, *The Prime of Miss Jean Brodie* shows Spark utilizing her own "intuitive artistic sense of economy."

In *The Driver's Seat*, Spark writes her revisionist version of the *nouveau roman*. She has said that she disagrees with the philosophical tenets of the antinovel, and she adopts many of its techniques to prove the invalidity of its philosophy. Although *The Driver's Seat* initially appears to be filled with randomly chosen, objectively described phenomena, ultimately the novel denies the entire concept of contingency. As Frank Kermode states in *The Sense of an Ending* (1966), Spark's fiction is not about any kind of "brutal chaos" but rather presents a "radically non-contingent reality to be dealt with in purely novelistic terms." Every event, every description becomes, in the light of the ending of *The Driver's Seat*, significant.

The novel concerns a young woman named Lise who leaves her home in northern Europe to travel south. Spark carefully fails to specify which cities are involved in order to create the same impersonal, anonymous air in the novel that characterizes Lise's world in general. The purpose of her journey is to find a man to murder her, and in this story Spark inverts the typical thriller: the "victim" relentlessly stalks her murderer and finally "forces" him to act. Lise, who has abandoned the sterile loneliness of her former existence symbolized by her apartment, which "looks as if it were uninhabited," takes control of her life for the first time and decides to take the most dramatic final step possible. In the opening scene, she shouts at a salesgirl who attempts to sell her a dress made of nonstaining fabric because, having already decided that she is to be stabbed to death, she wishes for clothing which will provide the more lurid touch of bloodstains. At the conclusion of the scene, Lise again shouts at the salesgirl "with a look of satisfaction at her own dominance over the situation," and the remainder of the novel is about Lise's carefully planned murder and the trail of information and clues she leaves for Interpol all across Europe.

Unlike Caroline Rose in *The Comforters*, whose response to being a character in a novel is to write a novel about characters in a novel, Lise actually wrests control of the plot from the narrator, who is forced to admit ignorance of her thoughts and intentions. "Who knows her thoughts? Who can tell?"

asks the narrator, who is even unsure as to whether or not Lise tints her hair or the reason she attracts so much attention. As a result, the narrator is forced to give only external information, but this information is, as the reader begins to realize, all pertinent to the outcome of the novel. Only at the conclusion, after Lise's death, does the narrator seem privy to the interior knowledge accessible to the omniscient author.

One of the most important themes in *The Driver's Seat* is, as in many other Spark novels, the inability of people to communicate with one another. In the majority of the conversations, no logical connections are made between the participants, who remain isolated in their own worlds of obsessional concerns. It would even appear that the more sane the individual, the less likely it is that any communication can take place. Instead, it is the more psychotic characters who are capable of nonverbal, intuitive understanding. Lise realizes immediately, as does Richard, that he is the man who is capable of murdering her, and he initially avoids any conversation with her. The three men who do converse with her, Bill, Carlos, and the sickly looking man on the plane, are not, as she phrases it, "her type"; this is because they attempt to communicate verbally with her. As Lise says of the salesman in the department store, "Not my man at all. He tried to get familiar with me. . . . The one I'm looking for will recognize me right away for the woman I am, have no fear of that." The verb "sense," which is used several times in the novel, signifies the subterranean, psychotic apprehension of other people which is the only perception taking place in *The Driver's Seat.*

Although most of Mrs. Friedke's conversations with Lise have the same illogical, uncommunicative structure that characterizes the other dialogues, she does momentarily enter Lise's realm of supernatural perception. She buys a paper knife for her nephew Richard similar to the one Lise decides against purchasing at the beginning of her journey, and this gift becomes the weapon Richard uses to murder Lise. She also prophetically insists that "you and my nephew are meant for each other . . . my dear, you are the person for my nephew." It is at this point that Lise reveals how she will recognize the man for whom she is searching.

In a phrase that tells a great deal about her past life, she says that she will know him not as a feeling of "presence" but as a "lack of absence." Malcolm Bradbury, in his essay on Spark in *Possibilities: Essays on the State of the Novel* (1973), says that Spark's fiction "conveys significant absences, a feeling of omission, and so has considerable resemblances to a good deal of contemporary art, including the *nouveau roman.*" Lise's search for a "lack of absence" is a statement about the emptiness and lack of meaning in her own existence and the type of novel Spark has chosen to write about her: the form of the antinovel is used to comment both on the psychosis of the main character and the failure of the *nouveau roman* to deal with the ultimate significance of phenomena. In the *nouveau roman,* the present tense frequently signifies the meaninglessness and ephemerality of events; in *The Driver's Seat*, the present tense is used to create a world of terrifying inevitability in which the smallest details become integral elements in Lise's carefully plotted death.

Spark calls *The Driver's Seat* "a study, in a way, of self-destruction," but also admits that the novel is impossible for her to describe. She says that she became so frightened while writing the story that she was forced to enter a hospital in order to complete it. The fear the novel inspired in her—and many readers—cannot be explained simply by Lise's self-destructiveness; Lise's decision to assert herself, to play god with her life independent of any control by the novelist or a higher power, also contributes to the frightening dimension of the novel. Spark, who has said that she believes that "events are providentially ordered," creates a character who decides to *become* providence and the author of her own story; unlike Jean Brodie, who mistakenly thinks she can see the "beginning and the end" of all stories, Lise successfully orchestrates the novel's conclusion.

In *Loitering with Intent*, Spark's heroine, novelist Fleur Talbot, frequently quotes from Benvenuto Cellini's *The Autobiography of Benvenuto Cellini* (c. 1558-1560): "All men . . . who have done anything of merit, or which verily has a semblance of merit . . . should write the tale of their life with their own hand." *Loitering with Intent* is the fictional autobiography of its "author," Fleur Talbot, and a meditation by Spark on her own career as a novelist; it is, in addition, a meditation on the creative process and the relationship between fiction and autobiography. Spark shows that she has come a long way from her early distrust of the novel: *Loitering with Intent* is a paean to the artistic, fiction-making sensibility. Although the habitual tension between life and art and the danger of confusing the two are still present in this novel, Spark firmly comes down on the side of art, defending it against individuals who would seek to "steal" its myth and pervert its truth.

Fleur Talbot frequently comments on "how wonderful it is to be an artist and a woman in the twentieth century." At the conclusion, she admits that she has been "loitering with intent"; that is, she has used her observations about the people and events around her as fictional material, taking joy both in the comic and tragic occurrences in the lives of the individuals who become characters in her own "autobiography." "I rejoiced in seeing people as they were," she says, and the word "rejoice" occurs many times in the novel as Fleur repeatedly uses Cellini's phrase, saying that she "went on her way rejoicing." In her later life she is accused by her friend Dottie of "wriggling out of real life," but Fleur makes no apologies for the way in which she handles the relationship between her life and her creativity; instead, *Loitering with Intent* calls into question the use "real" people make of the fictions of others.

Fleur becomes the secretary of Sir Quentin Oliver, head of the spurious Autobiographical Association he has formed in order to bring people together to compose their memoirs. Like the character of Warrender Chase in the novel Fleur is in the process of completing, Sir Quentin begins to exert a devastating influence on the Association's members, psychologically manipulating them not for blackmailing purposes but for the enjoyment of pure power. Instead of encouraging them to fictionalize their autobiographies, as Fleur attempts to do, Sir Quentin begins to fictionalize their lives with tragic results. Fleur says that

> I was sure . . . that Sir Quentin was pumping something artificial into their real lives instead of on paper. Presented fictionally, one could have done something authentic with that poor material. But the inducing them to express themselves in life resulted in falsity.

Fiction, when acknowledged as fiction, can help the individual to comprehend reality more clearly, as Fleur notes when she tells a friend that she will have to write several more chapters of *Warrender Chase* before she will be able to understand the events of the Autobiographical Association. In the same way, she says that one can better know one's friends if they are imaginatively pictured in various situations. Sir Quentin, however, inserts "fictions," frequently stories and events taken from Fleur's novel, into the lives of the Association's members.

The relationship between Sir Quentin and Fleur symbolizes the battle between life and art that is waged in *Loitering with Intent*, for Fleur accuses him of "using, stealing" her myth, "appropriating the spirit" of her legend, and trying to "live out the story" she creates in *Warrender Chase*. Although she believes that it is wrong for Sir Quentin to take her "creation" from her, she in turn believes that he may well be a creation of hers, particularly when he begins to resemble her character Warrender Chase as the story progresses. She takes pride in saying that she could almost "have invented" Sir Quentin and that at times she feels as if she *has* invented him; in fact, this feeling so persists that she begins to wonder if it is Warrender Chase who is the "real man" on whom she has partly based the fictional character of Sir Quentin. From Fleur's point of view, this kind of inversion of life and art is necessary and productive for the artistic process and is not dangerous because it results in a bona fide fiction that acknowledges itself as fiction; Sir Quentin's appropriation of her "myth," however, is dangerous because he refuses to acknowledge the fictiveness of his creation. One irony of this situation is editor Revisson Doe's refusal to publish *Warrender Chase* because it too closely resembles the activities of the Autobiographical Association: Sir Quentin's literal and figurative theft of Fleur's novel almost results in its never becoming a work of art available to the public.

The relationship between life and art has another dimension in *Loitering with Intent*. In this novel, Spark is also concerned with the psychic potential of the artist, the ability of the creative imagination to foresee the future in the process of creating fictions. Just as Fleur remarks that writing a novel or imagining her friends in ficitional situations helps her to understand them better, so does the artist often predict the future while constructing a work of art. At the end of the novel, Dottie admits that Fleur had "foreseen it all" in *Warrender Chase*, and the events of *Loitering with Intent* do bear an eerie resemblance to the plot of Fleur's first novel. In her book on Emily Brontë, Spark said that "Poetic experience is . . . such that it may be prophetic." In *Loitering with Intent*, Fleur uses reality as raw material for her novel, while Sir Quentin attempts to use art to tamper with the lives of real people; at another level, however, Fleur's poetic imagination perceives and creates future events.

Loitering with Intent also permits Spark to look back on her life as a novelist and defend many of her fictional techniques. Fleur's philosophy of art is, to a great degree, Spark's philosophy, and Fleur's descriptions and explanations of her craft could easily be addressed by Spark directly to her readers. Like Spark, Fleur is a believer in economy in art, observing "how little one needs . . . to convey the lot, and how a lot of words . . . can convey so little." Fleur does not believe in authorial statements about the motives of her characters, or in being "completely frank" with the reader; in fact, "complete frankness is not a quality that favours art." She defends herself against the charge of writing novels that are called "exaggerated" by critics and states that her fiction presents "aspects of realism." The novel, she believes, is not a documentary transcription of reality but should always seek to transform its subject. "I'm an artist, not a reporter," she informs her readers.

Fleur also answers the critics who in the past have accused Spark of treating her material in a flippantly detached manner. She says that she treats the story of Warrender Chase with a "light and heartless hand" which is her method when giving a "perfectly serious account of things" because to act differently would be hypocritical: "It seems to me a sort of hypocrisy for a writer to pretend to be undergoing tragic experiences when obviously one is sitting in relative comfort with a pen and paper or before a typewriter." At one point in the novel, Spark even challenges the "quality" of her readers, having her narrator remark that she hopes the readers of her novels are of "good quality" because "I wouldn't like to think of anyone cheap reading my books." The most significant theme of *Loitering with Intent*, however, is joy: the joy the artist takes in the everyday reality that contributes to the imaginative act, and the euphoria the artist feels in the act of creation. Spark has indeed traveled a great distance from her early suspicions of the fictive-making process and of the novel as form.

Major publications other than long fiction
SHORT FICTION: *The Go-Away Bird and Other Stories*, 1958; *Voices at Play*, 1961 (with radio plays); *Collected Stories I*, 1967.

PLAY: *Doctors of Philosophy*, 1963.

POETRY: *The Fanfarlo and Other Verse*, 1952; *Selected Poems of Emily Brontë*, 1952 (edited); *Collected Poems I*, 1967.

NONFICTION: *Tribute to Wordsworth*, 1950 (edited with Derek Stanford); *Child of Light: A Reassessment of Mary Wollstonecraft Shelley*, 1951; *Emily Brontë: Her Life and Work*, 1953 (with Derek Stanford); *John Masefield*, 1953; *My Best Mary: The Selected Letters of Mary Shelley*, 1953 (edited with Derek Stanford); *The Brontë Letters*, 1954 (edited); *Letters of John Henry Newman*, 1957 (with Derek Stanford).

CHILDREN'S LITERATURE: *The Very Fine Clock*, 1958.

Bibliography

Bradbury, Malcolm. "Muriel Spark's Fingernails," in *Possibilities: Essays on the State of the Novel*, 1973.

Kemp, Peter. *Muriel Spark*, 1974.

Kermode, Frank. *The Sense of an Ending*, 1966.

Lodge, David. "The Uses and Abuses of Omniscience," in *The Novelist at the Crossroads*, 1971.

Malkoff, Karl. *Muriel Spark*, 1968.

Stanford, Derek. *Muriel Spark*, 1963.

Stubbs, Patricia. *Muriel Spark*, 1973.

Whittaker, Ruth. "Angels Dining at the Ritz: The Faith and Fiction of Muriel Spark," in *The Contemporary English Novel*, 1979.

Angela Hague

CHRISTINA STEAD

Born: Rockdale, Australia; July 17, 1902
Died: Sydney Australia; March 31, 1983

Principal long fiction

Seven Poor Men of Sydney, 1934; *The Beauties and Furies*, 1936; *House of All Nations*, 1938; *The Man Who Loved Children*, 1940, 1965; *For Love Alone*, 1944; *Letty Fox: Her Luck*, 1946; *A Little Tea, A Little Chat*, 1948; *The People with the Dogs*, 1952; *Dark Places of the Heart*, 1966; *The Little Hotel*, 1974; *Miss Herbert: The Suburban Wife*, 1976.

Other literary forms

Christina Stead began her career with a volume of short stories, *The Salzburg Tales* (1934), and she has contributed short stories to both literary and popular magazines. Her volume *The Puzzleheaded Girl* (1967) is a collection of four novellas. Her other literary output includes reviews and translations of several novels from the French. She also edited two anthologies of short stories, one with her husband William Blake. The *Christina Stead Anthology*, edited by Jean B. Read, was published in 1979.

Achievements

Stead is considered to be in the first rank of Australian novelists; in 1974, she received Australia's Patrick White Award. One of Stead's novels, *The Man Who Loved Children*, received special critical acclaim. Stead resisted critic's attempts to represent her as a feminist writer, but she did received attention from feminist critics for her depiction of women constricted by their social roles.

Biography

Christina Ellen Stead's parents were David George Stead, a naturalist and fisheries economist, and Ellen Butters Stead, who died of a perforated appendix when Christina was two years old. David Stead then married Ada Gibbons, a society woman, and they had six children to whom Stead became big sister. Stead trained at the Sydney Teachers College, where she became a demonstrator in experimental psychology. As a public school teacher, she taught abnormal children and administered psychological tests in the schools. Stead suffered voice strain, however, and she later saw it as a symptom of her being unfit for the work. Like Teresa Hawkins in *For Love Alone*, Stead studied typing and shorthand to embark on a business career. In 1928, she left Sydney, sailing on the *Oronsay* for England. In London and Paris, she worked as a grain clerk and a bank clerk, experiences that became background for her novel about finance, *House of All Nations*. By that time, Stead had met the economist and writer, William Blake (born William Blech), whom she married in 1952. Stead settled in the United States from 1937 to 1946, publishing several novels and working for a time as a writer with M-G-M in Hollywood. At the end of World War II, Stead returned to Europe with Blake, living in various places on the Continent and returning to England when she feared that she was losing her feel for the English language. In 1968, Stead's husband died, and a few years later, in 1974, she returned to live with one of her brothers in Australia. She died in Sydney on March 31, 1983, at the age of eighty.

Analysis

Christina Stead was preeminently a novelist of character. She identified herself as a psychological writer, involved with the drama of the person. Her stories develop out of the dynamics of characters asserting their human energy and vigor and developing their wills. Stead established personality and communicated its energy and vitality through her creation of a distinctive language for each character. This individuating language is explored in the characters' dialogues with one another (Sam Pollit talking his fantastic baby talk to his children), in their interior monologues (Teresa Hawkins, walking miles to and from work, meditating on her need to find a life beyond the surface social conventions), and in letters (the letter to Letty Fox from her former lover, who wants his money back after she has had an abortion). The language establishes the sense of an individual person with obsessions and characteristic blindnesses. One gets to know the quality of the mind through the texture of the language. Christopher Ricks expressed Stead's accomplishment by saying that she re-creates the way people talk to themselves "in the privacy of [their] skulls." His phrase gives the sense of how intimately and deeply the language belongs to the person: it is in the skull and the bone.

In her novel *Letty Fox*, Stead has Letty sum up her adventures to date by saying, "*On s'engage et puis on voit.*" The statement (roughly translated as "one gets involved and then one sees") is an existentialist one that reconciles what critics see as two forces in Stead's fiction: a preoccupation with character that links her to nineteenth century novelists, and an analysis of social, psychological, and economic structures behind individual lives that links Stead to her contemporaries.

The phrase "*On s'engage et puis on voit*" sums up Stead's method. First, she immerses the reader in the particular atmosphere of the character's mind and world; only then does she lead the reader to see a significance behind the individual passion. The phrase implies that one cannot see clearly by being disengaged, looking down on the human spectacle with the detachment of an objective physical scientist. Instead, one must become part of that experience, seeing it as a participant, in order to understand its reality. Some of the constant preoccupations of Stead's characters include family, love, marriage, money, and individual power.

Stead's masterpiece, as critics agree, is the larger-than-life depiction of a family, *The Man Who Loved Children*. Out of print for twenty-five years, the book has enjoyed a second life because of a partly laudatory review by the poet Randall Jarrell that was included as an introduction when the novel was reissued. *The Man Who Loved Children* immerses its readers in the life of the Pollit family, in its swarming, buzzing intimacy. The father, Sam Pollit, is a garrulous idealist who advocates eugenics for the unfit but who fantasizes for himself babies of every race and a harem of wives who would serve his domestic comfort. On the surface, Sam's passions are his humanitarian ideals and his love for his children, but his underlying passion is what Geoffrey Chaucer said women's was—his own way or his own will. Sam is an egotistical child himself; he sees only what he wants to see. His characteristic talk is his overblown, high-sounding rhetoric expressing schemes to right the world and the fanciful, punning baby talk, whining and wheedling, that he uses with the children.

Henny, wife to Sam and stepmother to Louisa, is Sam's compulsive antagonist, worn down with childbearing and the struggle to manage the overextended household. Henny's passion is to survive, to fight dirt and debt and the intermittent sexuality that involves her in continual childbearing. Henny's characteristic talk is insult and denunciation, castigating with graphic details and metaphors the revolting sights, sounds, smells, tastes, and touches that assault her. Stead emphasizes Henny's eyes in descriptions of the fierce eyeballs in her sockets and her mouth in descriptions of her incessantly drinking tea and mouthing insults.

Stead's way of explaining the unbridgeable gap between the minds and sensibilities of the marriage partners is to say that they have no words in common. Sam's abstraction can never communicate with Henny's particularity. They have no words that they understand mutually, and so for most of the book the two characters communicate with each other only through messages relayed by the children or by terse notes concerning household necessities. In spite of that essential gap, a sixth child is conceived and born to the couple during the novel, and the resources of the household are further strained, finally to the breaking point.

What brings the family to destruction is a complex of causes, many of which are fundamentally economic. The death of David Collyer, Henny's once rich father, is a blow to the family's fortunes. The family loses its home, and Henny's creditors no longer expect that her father will pay her debts. Collyer's death also leaves Sam without a political base in his government job, and Sam's enemies move to oust him. The money crisis is intensified by Sam's refusal to fight for his job. Instead, he retires to their new ramshackle home to do repairs and to play with the children. Sam grandly waits to be exonerated, while Henny struggles to keep the family fed and clothed.

Another cause of the breakup of the family is the birth of Sam and Henny's newest baby. Part of the trouble is economic: the new child means more expenses when Henny had promised her money-conscious eldest son Ernie that there would be no more children. The birth also brings an anonymous letter charging falsely that the child is not Sam's because Sam has been away in Malaya for several months. The letter, filled with spite, probably has been sent by one of Henny's disappointed creditors, but it exacerbates the mutual resentment of the couple and drives them closer and closer to serious violence against each other. (The pregnancy has not only invaded Henny's body and multiplied her worries, but it has also cost her her lover, who deserts her when he hears of the pregnancy. Henny is more than ever in Sam's power.)

A pivotal character in the fierce struggle between the parents is Louisa, oldest daughter of Sam and stepdaughter of Henny. Louisa's emergence from childhood upsets the hierarchy of the household. The man who "loved children" does not love them when they question his authority and threaten his position as "Sam the Bold," leader of the band of merry children. In retaliation, Sam calls Louisa names from "Loogoobrious" to "Bluebeak." In disputing Sam's ability to make it rain (his cosmic power), Louisa and Ernie—who is quick to jump in with what he has learned in school about evaporation—introduce norms from the world outside the family.

By the end of the novel, the family tears itself apart. Sam is unconsciously comparing himself to Christ and seeing Nature as his bride, while he says that women are "cussed" and need to be "run" and that he will send Henny away and keep the children. When Louisa asks for freedom to be sent to her dead mother's relatives in Harper's Ferry, Sam says that he will never let her leave, that she must not get married but must stay and help him with the children and his work. The quarreling between the parents increases until Louisa thinks that they will kill each other. The quarrels become physical battles, and Henny screams to the children to save her from their father. In despair, Ernie makes a dummy out of his clothes and hangs himself in effigy. Sam teases and humiliates the children, insisting that they stay up all night and help him boil down a marlin, an image that is reminiscent of Henny with its staring eye, deep in its socket, and its wound in its vitals.

Louisa sees the two parents as passionate and selfish, inexorably destroying each other and the children, completely absorbed in their "eternal married hate." To save the children, Louisa considers poisoning both parents. Sam provides both the rationale, that the unfit should make room for the fit, and the means, cyanide that he ghoulishly describes as the bringer of death. Louisa succeeds in getting the grains of cyanide into only one large cup of tea when Henny notices what she has done and drinks it, exonerating Louisa and saying "damn you all." Even with Henny dead and Louisa's confession of her plan and its outcome, Sam refuses to believe her and refuses to let her go. Louisa's only escape is to run away, thus seizing her freedom.

The power of the novel derives partly from the archetypal nature of the conflicts—between parents and children for independence; between man and woman, each for his own truth and identity; between parents for their children, their objects of greatest value. The power also results from the particularity of the characterization, the metaphors that Stead employs to communicate the nature of each family member, and the astounding sense of individual language mirroring opposed sensibilities.

The epigraph to another Stead novel *Letty Fox: Her Luck*, says that one can get experience only through foolishness and blunders. The method which Letty follows in her adventures puts her in the stream of picaresque heroes; the novel's subtitle, "her luck," makes more sense with reference to the notion of a submission to experience, to one's fate, than it does with reference to the common meaning of "luck" as "good fortune." Letty's "luck" is that she survives and learns something about the ways of the world.

Stead once said that in *For Love Alone*, the novel which preceded *Letty Fox*, she wrote about a young girl of no social background, who tries to learn about love, and that readers did not understand the story. Thus, in *Letty Fox*, she gave American readers a story which they could understand: the story of a modern American girl searching for love and trying to obtain status through marriage.

In both novels, the social structure tells young women that they have no valid identity except through the men they marry. In *For Love Alone*, Teresa Hawkins, like her friends, fears becoming an old maid. Even though Letty Fox has had a series of lovers and a series of responsible, interesting jobs, she does not feel validated without the security of marriage.

This firmly held conventional belief is belied by Letty's own family situation. Her beloved father Solander has a mistress, Persia, with whom he has lived faithfully for many years. The family women wonder how Persia can hold Solander without a paper and without a child. On the other hand, Mathilde, Letty's mother, has the marriage title but little else. She has three daughters—Letty, Jacky, and the much younger Andrea, conceived in a late reconciliation attempt—but Persia has Solander.

Like the picaresque hero, on her own, Letty learns the ways of the world. She truly loves Luke Adams, who tantalizes her with pretended concern for her youth and innocence and fans her fascination with him. She lives for a summer with a married man and has an abortion for which she must repay him. Originally confused by Lucy Headlong's interest in her, Letty refuses a Lesbian affair with her. Letty sees a range of choices in the lives of the women around her: from her serious sister Jacky, in love with an elderly scientist, to her younger sister Andrea, sharing the early maternal experience of her girlhood friend.

Letty wants the security of marriage, but the men she knows do not want to make serious commitments. In *For Love Alone*, Teresa remarks the short season for the husband hunt, with no time for work or extended study. In the marriage market for the comparatively long season of seven years, Letty does not catch a husband, even when her vicious cousin Edwige does.

Except in the matter of marriage, Letty trusts her own responses and takes credit for her own integrity. When her lover Cornelius is about to leave her for his mistress in Europe and his wife, Letty faces him with the truth of relationships from a woman's point of view. She tells Cornelius that she has got ambition and looks. She works for men, and she is their friend. She suffers without crying for help and takes responsibility for her life. Yet she sees men run after worthless, shiftless women and honor the formality of marriage when there is no substance to their relationships with them. All of these facts might be just part of the injustice of the world, but Cornelius and many other men Letty knows also expect that she should be their lover and yet admit that there is no love involved but only a relationship of mutual convenience. Like the British poet William Blake, Letty sees prostitution as an invention of men who have tried to depersonalize the most intimate relationship between people. Letty affirms the reality of the sexual experience in its intimacy and its bonding.

With all her clear sight and all her independence, however, Letty does not feel safe and validated until she is married to her longtime friend Bill Van Week. Ironically, Letty marries Bill when he has been disinherited by his millionaire father, so the security Letty attains is not financial. In summing up her life to date, Letty does not claim total honesty, but—like a typical picaresque hero—she does claim grit. She says that with her marriage, her journey has begun. Here Stead limits the awareness of her character. At the end of the novel, Letty says that marriage gives her not social position but self-respect. In this retreat, Letty joins the social mainstream but denies her individual past experience. Self-respect is not an award; it is not issued like a diploma or a license. Letty, who may stand up very well to the practical problems of real life with Bill, is by no means liberated, and her awareness is finally limited.

Published in Britain as *Cotter's England*, *Dark Places of the Heart* is an exploration of the influence of Nellie Cotter Cook on the people around her— her family, friends, and acquaintances. A central concern is the relationship between Nellie and her brother Tom, a jealous relationship with which Nellie seems obsessed. Like Michael and Catherine Baguenault, the brother-sister pair in *Seven Poor Men of Sydney*, Nellie and Tom seem too close to each other, too intimately attuned to each other's sensibilities. In their battles, Nellie calls Tom a man out of a mirror, who weaves women into his life and then eats their hearts away. Tom calls Nellie a spider, who tries to suspend a whole human being on a spindly thread of sympathy. Tom also criticizes Nellie's bent for soul-saving, saying that it gets people into trouble.

The motif of hunger and starvation runs through the novel. When Tom brings a chicken to the family home in Bridgehead, no one in the family knows how to cook it. When George goes away to Italy, he writes that Nellie should buy cookery books, a suggestion that she scorns. Seemingly exhibiting a strange kind of hunger, Nellie craves for followers who will make her destiny.

Nellie's and Tom's battles often center on Tom's relationships with women, which precipitate a tug-of-war between Nellie and Tom for the love of the woman in question. Many allusions and incidents in the novel suggest that Nellie's interest is Lesbian. Nellie begins her luring of these women by demanding their friendship and, ultimately, by forcing them to prove their loyalty through death. Such demands literalize the existentialist definition of love, that the lover puts the beloved beyond the value of the world and his life, making that beloved his standard of value, his absolute. The demand is messianic, and in this novel the cost is the suicide of Caroline Wooler, after her witnessing what seems to be a Lesbian orgy. Caroline climbs a building under construction and jumps to her death.

Nellie views Caroline's death as a personal triumph. At the end of the novel, with her husband dead, Nellie goes with the window-washer Walter to a temple, a "Nabob villa," where she explores "problems of the unknowable." Like Sam Pollit, who at his worst compared himself to Christ, Nellie Cook is drawn finally to outright mysticism, an interest that combines, in Nellie's case at least, a fascination with death, a craving for a high destiny, and an uncontrollable urge to manipulate other people. It seems that for Stead, the "dark places of the heart" make people dissatisfied with their humanity.

Major publications other than long fiction

SHORT FICTION: *The Salzburg Tales*, 1934; *The Puzzleheaded Girl*, 1967.

ANTHOLOGIES: *Modern Women in Love*, 1945 (with William Blake); *Great Stories of the South Sea Islands*, 1956.

MISCELLANEOUS: *Colour of Asia*, 1955 (translated); *The Candid Killer*, 1956 (translated); *In Balloon and Bathyscaphe*, 1956 (translated).

Bibliography

Beston, John B. "An Interview with Christina Stead," in *World Literature Written in English*. XV (1976), pp. 87-95.

Geering, R. G. *Christina Stead*, 1969.

Lidoff, Joan. "Christina Stead: An Interview," in *Aphra*. VI (1976), pp. 39-64.

_____ . "Domestic Gothic: The Imagery of Anger, Christina Stead's *The Man Who Loved Children*," in *Studies in the Novel*. II (1979), pp. 201-215.

Ricks, Christopher. "Domestic Manners," in *The New York Review of Books*. IV (June 17, 1965), pp. 14-15.

Smith, Graeme Kinross. "Christina Stead—A Profile," in *Westerly*. I (March, 1976), pp. 67-75.

Sturm, Terry. "Christina Stead's New Realism," in *Cunning Exiles: Studies of Modern Prose Writers*, 1974. Edited by Don Anderson and Stephen Knight.

Yglesias, Jose. "Marx as Muse," in *The Nation*. April 5, 1965, pp. 368-370.

Kate Begnal

WALLACE STEGNER

Born: Lake Mills, Iowa; February 18, 1909

Principal long fiction

Remembering Laughter, 1937; *The Potter's House*, 1938; *On a Darkling Plain*, 1940; *Fire and Ice*, 1941; *The Big Rock Candy Mountain*, 1943; *Second Growth*, 1947; *The Preacher and the Slave*, 1950; *A Shooting Star*, 1961; *All the Little Live Things*, 1967; *Angle of Repose*, 1971; *The Spectator Bird*, 1976; *Recapitulation*, 1979; *Joe Hill*, 1980.

Other literary forms

Wallace Stegner has also published two collections of short fiction, *The Women on the Wall* (1950) and *The City of the Living* (1956); two biographies, *Beyond the Hundredth Meridian: John Wesley Powell and the Second Opening of the West* (1954) and *The Uneasy Chair: A Biography of Bernard DeVoto* (1974); a collection of critical essays, *The Writer in America* (1951); a historical monograph, *The Gathering of Zion: The Story of the Mormon Trail* (1964); and two volumes of personal essays on the Western experience. *Wolf Willow: A History, a Story, and a Memory of the Last Plains Frontier* (1962) and *The Sound of Mountain Water* (1969). Stegner has also published a number of edited works, both nonfiction and fiction.

Achievements

Stegner has had three distinct audiences since the start of his career: the popular magazine audience; readers interested in modern American literature; and a regional audience interested in the culture and history of the American West. Since the 1930's, he has published seventy-two short stories, with fifty of them appearing in such magazines as *Harper's*, *Mademoiselle*, *Colliers*, *Cosmopolitan*, *Esquire*, *Redbook*, *The Atlantic*, *The Inter-Mountain Review*, and the *Virginia Quarterly*. Bernard DeVoto, Van Wyck Brooks, and Sinclair Lewis recognized his talent early, and DeVoto was instrumental in encouraging Stegner to continue writing. Stegner has enjoyed a solid critical reputation as a regional American writer concerned largely with the problems and themes of the Western American experience.

He has also won numerous honors throughout his career. He was elected to the American Academy of Arts and Sciences and the National Academy of Arts and Letters, and he was awarded fellowships by Phi Beta Kappa, the Huntington Library, The Center for Advanced Studies in the Behavioral Sciences, and by the Guggenheim, Rockefeller, and Wintergreen Foundations. In 1937, he won the Little Brown Novelette Prize for *Remembering Laughter*. He also won the O. Henry Memorial Award for short stories in

1942, 1948, and 1950, and in 1971 he won the Pulitzer Prize for Fiction for his *Angle of Repose*. Other awards for his work include the Houghton Mifflin Life-in-America Award in 1945 and the Commonwealth Club Gold Medal in 1968. In 1981, he became the first recipient of the Robert Kirsch Award for Life Achievement in the *Los Angeles Times* Book Awards.

As a master of narrative technique and a respected literary craftsman, Stegner has had the opportunity to influence many young writers associated with the Stanford University Creative Writing Program, where he taught from 1945 to 1971, including Eugene Burdick, one of the authors of *The Ugly American* (1958), Ken Kesey, and Thomas McGuane. His own theory of literature is rather traditional and appears in his only extended piece of criticism, *The Writer in America*. The creative process, he believes, is basically the imposition of form upon personal experience. The committed writer must discipline himself to the difficult work of creation, choosing significant images from the insignificant and selecting significant actions for his characters. The writer must change the disorderliness of memory into symmetry without violating his readers' sense of what is true to life.

Biography

Wallace Earle Stegner was born on February 18, 1909, in Lake Mills, Iowa, the second son of George and Hilda Paulson Stegner. He was descended from Norwegian farmers on his mother's side and unknown ancestors on his father's side. His father was a drifter and a resourceful gambler—a searcher for the main chance, the big bonanza. In Stegner's early years, the family moved often, following his father's dream of striking it rich, from Grand Forks, North Dakota, to Bellingham, Washington, to Redmond, Oregon, to East End Saskatchewan, where they lived from 1914 to 1921. East End left him with memories of people and landscapes that played an important role in *The Big Rock Candy Mountain*. The family moved in 1921 to Salt Lake City, Utah, where Stegner attended high school and began college. Here, Stegner went through the pains of adolescence and, although not himself a Mormon, he developed a strong attachment to the land and a sympathy for Mormon culture and values which are reflected in his later books such as *Mormon Country* (1942), *The Gathering of Zion*, and *Recapitulation*.

From 1925 to 1930, Stegner attended the University of Utah, where he balanced his interest in girls and his studies with a job selling rugs and linoleum in the family business of a close friend. By a fortunate chance, he studied freshman English with Vardis Fisher, then a budding novelist, and Fisher helped stimulate Stegner's growing interest in creative writing. In 1930, he entered the graduate program at the University of Iowa, completing his M.A. in 1932 and completing his Ph.D. in 1935 with a dissertation on the Utah naturalist Clarence Dutton, entitled "Clarence Edward Dutton: Geologist and Man of Letters," later revised and published as *Clarence Edward Dutton:*

An Appraisal by the University of Utah in 1936. This work fed his interest in the history of the American West and the life of the explorer John Wesley Powell, the subject of his *Beyond the Hundredth Meridian.* Teaching English and creative writing occupied him for several years, beginning with a one-year stint at tiny Augustana College in Illinois in 1934. Next, he went to the University of Utah until 1937, moving from there to teach freshman English at the University of Wisconsin for two years. He also taught at the Bread Loaf School of English in Vermont for several summers and enjoyed the friendship of Robert Frost, Bernard DeVoto, and Theodore Morrison. In 1940, he accepted a part-time position at Harvard University in the English writing program. There, during the Depression, he was involved in literary debates between the literary left led by F. O. Matthiessen, and the conservative DeVoto.

In 1945, Stegner accepted a professorship in creative writing at Stanford University, where he remained for twenty-six years until his retirement in 1971. The Stanford years were his most productive; he produced a total of thirteen books in this period. In 1950, he made an around-the-world lecture tour, researched his family's past in Saskatchewan and Norway, and spent much of the year as writer-in-residence at the American Academy in Rome. He was also an active environmentalist long before ecology became fashionable. During the Kennedy Administration, he served as Assistant to the Secretary of the Interior (1961) and as a member of the National Parks Advisory Board (1962).

Analysis

Wallace Stegner is a regional writer in the best sense. His settings, his characters, and his plots derive from the Western experience, but his primary concern is with the meaning of that experience. Geographically, Stegner's region runs from Minnesota and Grand Forks, North Dakota, through Utah and Northern Colorado. It is the country where Stegner lived and experienced his youth. Scenes from this region appear frequently in his novels. East End, Saskatchewan, the place of his early boyhood, appears as Whitemud, Saskatchewan, in *The Big Rock Candy Mountain,* along with Grand Forks and Lake Mills, Iowa, his birthplace. Salt Lake City figures prominently in *Recapitulation* and *The Preacher and the Slave,* the story of Joe Hill, a union martyr. *Wolf Willow,* furthermore, is historical fiction, a kind of history of East End, Saskatchewan, where he spent his early boyhood, and *On a Darkling Plain* is the story of a much decorated and seriously wounded veteran of World War I who withdraws from society in an isolated shack on the plains outside of East End.

In a much larger sense, Stegner is concerned with the spiritual West—the West as an idea or a consciousness—and with the significance of the Western values and traditions. He is also concerned with the basic American cultural conflict between East and West and with the importance of frontier values in American history. Bo Mason, modeled after Stegner's father, the abusive head of the Mason family in *The Big Rock Candy Mountain*, is an atavism, a character who may have been at home in the early frontier, who searches for the elusive pot of gold—the main chance of the Western myth. Never content with domestic life or with stability, Bo Mason, like George Stegner, moves his family from town to town always looking for an easy fortune. As a man of mixed qualities—fierce pride, resourcefulness, self-reliance, and a short, violent temper—he is ill at ease in the post-frontier West, always chafing at the stability of community and family ties. He continually pursues the old Western myth of isolated individualism that preceded twentieth century domestication of the region. He might have made a good mountain man. Stegner stresses his impact on his family and community and shows the reader the basic tragedy of this frontier type trapped in a patterned world without easy bonanzas.

In *Angle of Repose*, Stegner explores the conflict between the values of self-reliance, impermanence, and Western optimism and the Eastern sense of culture, stability, and tradition. In a way, this is the basic conflict between Ralph Waldo Emerson's party of hope (the West) and the party of the past (the East). He also explores the idea of community as a concept alien to the Western myth. Indeed, community as the close-knit cooperation between individuals is shown in Stegner's work as the thing that ended the frontier. In *The Big Rock Candy Mountain* and in *Recapitulation*, there is a longing for community and a pervasive feeling that the Mason family is always outside the culture in which it exists, particularly in Utah, where Mormon culture is portrayed as innocent, solid, stable, and as a result attractive. Mormon life is characterized by the absence of frontier individualism and by a belief in permanence and group experience, an anomaly in the Western experience.

A third major concern throughout Stegner's work is his own identity and the meaning of Western identity. Bruce Mason in *The Big Rock Candy Mountain* is much concerned with his relationship as an adolescent to the Utah culture and its sense of community.

Stegner's fifth novel, *The Big Rock Candy Mountain*, is an obviously autobiographical account of his childhood and adolescence. A family saga, the novel follows the history of the rootless Mason family as it follows the dreams of Bo Mason, a thinly disguised version of Stegner's father, as he leads them to Grand Forks, North Dakota, to the lumber camps of Washington, then back to Iowa and up to Whitemud, Saskatchewan, and finally to Salt Lake City and Reno. Family identity problems are played out against the backdrop of an increasingly civilized and domesticated West against which the self-reliant and short-tempered character of Bo Mason stands out in stark relief. His qualities, which might have had virtues in the early settlement of the West, create family tensions and trauma that cause Bruce Mason (Stegner) to develop a hatred for his father only partially tempered by a grudging respect. Bo Mason relentlessly pursues the American dream and the Western myth of easy success rooted in the early frontier: he endlessly pursues the Big Rock Candy Mountain.

Throughout this odyssey, the family longs for stability and community, for a place to develop roots. Even in Salt Lake City, where Bruce spends his adolescence, Bo keeps the family changing houses to hide his bootlegging business during the Prohibition period. His activities in the midst of puritanical Mormon culture only highlight the contrast between the Masons and the dominant community. Even in his later years, Bo pursues his dream in Reno by operating a gambling house.

Stegner vividly illustrates how this rootless wandering affects family members. Else, Bo's wife, representing the feminine, domesticating impulse, is a saintly character—long-suffering, gentle, and protective of her two sons. She longs for a home with permanence but never finds it. Her initial good nature and mild optimism eventually give way to pessimism as resettlements continue. Three of the family members die: Else is destroyed by cancer; Chet, the other son, who is defeated by both marriage and career, dies young of pneumonia; and Bo, with all his dreams shattered and involved with a cheap whore after Else's death, shoots himself. Only Bruce is left to make sense of his family's experiences, and he attempts to understand his place in the family saga as he strives to generalize his family's history. In the final philosophical and meditative chapters, Stegner tries to link Bruce (and therefore himself) to history, to some sense of continuity and tradition. His family history, with its crudeness and tensions, is made to represent the history of the frontier West with its similar tensions and rough edges. Bruce, who long sought solace and identity in books, excels in school and finally follows the civilized but ironic path of going to law school at the University of Minnesota. He has, finally, reached a higher level of culture than his family ever attained. *The Big Rock Candy Mountain* has achieved a reputation as a classic of American regionalism, while it also deals with broader national themes and myths.

Angle of Repose, published in 1971 and awarded the Pulitzer Prize for Fiction, is regarded by many critics as Stegner's most finely crafted novel. The metaphoric title is a mining and geological term designating the slope at which rocks cease to fall, the angle of rest. Stegner uses it to apply to the last thirty years of the marriage of Susan Burling and Oliver Ward, two opposite personalities, after their often chaotic early married years. This ambitious work, covering four generations, is a fictionalized biography of the turn-of-the-century writer and illustrator Mary Hallock Foote (1847-1930) and her marriage to Arthur De Wint Foote, an idealistic pioneer and self-educated mining engineer.

Lyman Ward, the narrator, was reared by his grandparents Susan Burling Ward and Oliver Ward, fictionalized versions of the Footes, and is a retired history professor from Berkeley who was crippled in middle age by a progressively arthritic condition. He has been transformed by the disease into a grotesque creature who loses first his leg and then his wife Ellen, who runs off with the surgeon who amputated Lyman's leg. Bitter and disillusioned by his wife's behavior and his son Rodman's radical idealism and contempt for the past, he retires to Grass Valley, California, to write his grandparents' biography. Here, he is assisted by Shelly Hawkes, a Berkeley dropout who shares Rodman's attitude toward history.

As he reads through his grandparents' correspondence, he simultaneously recounts the development of their marriage and discovers the dynamics of their personalities. Susan Ward, cultured, educated in the East, and artistically talented, marries Oliver Ward, an idealistic mining engineer, her second choice for a husband. Without having resolved her disappointment at his lack of culture and appreciation for the arts, she marries him and begins two decades of following him through the West as he looks for professional and financial success in the unstable mining industry. The years in New Almeden, California, Leadville, Colorado, Michoacán, Mexico, and southern Idaho increasingly wear Susan down, despite brief interludes of stability and the frequent company of other Eastern scientists and engineers during her Western exile.

In Boise Canyon, Idaho, as Oliver's grand irrigation project falls apart, Susan falls into infidelity with Frank Sargent, Oliver's colorful assistant, and steals away to the countryside under the pretext of taking five-year-old Agnes Ward for a walk. Soon, Agnes' body is found floating in a nearby canal, and the day after her funeral, Frank Sargent commits suicide. Suspecting the worst, Oliver leaves his wife for two years until persuaded to return. For the remaining fifty years of their marriage, Oliver treats her with a kind silence and lack of physical affection, never truly forgiving her infidelity. Lyman learns that his grandparents' angle of repose was not the real thing, not a time of harmony, but a cold truce full of human weakness. His naïve image of his grandparents based on childhood memories is undercut as he comes to understand them in a more sophisticated way. He learns to respect their strength and complexity.

Lyman's discoveries are all the more poignant because of the similarities between his grandparents' experience and his own relationship with an unfaithful wife who has broken trust, and who, it is implied, will seek a reconciliation. As in *The Big Rock Candy Mountain*, the two main characters symbolize two conflicting impulses in the settlement of the West—Oliver, the dreamer and idealist, pursuing his vision of success in a world with few amenities, and Susan, the finely cultured Easterner, yearning for stability and society. Lyman discovers links between his family's past and present and encounters universals of history such as suffering and infidelity which are more poignant to him because he discovers them in his own family history.

Finally, the novel suggests that frontier values and the civilizing impulses need their own angle of repose. In essence, American experience has not yet reached its angle of rest; frontier and domestic values lie instead in a kind of uneasy truce.

A continuation of the family saga played out in *The Big Rock Candy Mountain, Recapitulation*, published in 1979, is the moving drama of Bruce Mason's return to Salt Lake City to face his past. Toward the end of a successful career as a diplomat in the United States Foreign Service, Mason returns to the scene of his turbulent adolescence and the death of his family to attend his maiden aunt's funeral. Upon his arrival at the funeral home, the attendant presents him with a message to call Joe Mulder, his best friend in high school and in college at the University of Utah. Bruce was virtually a member of Joe's family for three years during the time when his father's bootlegging business threatened to jeopardize his social life.

Bruce remembers the 1920's and his adolescence before the stock market crash. Trying to find himself, he slowly remembers the time when he was an outsider in Mormon country, a time when he found many of the values that sustained him after the death of his family. Well-liked in high school by his teachers, Bruce was also picked on by the bigger boys and the less able students and acutely embarrassed by the family's house, which doubled as a speakeasy. His first major romance with Nola, a Mormon country girl who was half Indian, led to his first sexual encounter. Bruce was infatuated with her but knew her intellectual limits—that ideas put her to sleep and art bored her. Throughout the narrative, he recounts the disintegration of his family during his adolescence.

Stegner stresses Bruce's close relationship with Joe Mulder, but Bruce is emotionally incapable of meeting Joe because he hates being treated as "The Ambassador," a visiting dignitary—a title that would only exaggerate the changes and losses of the past forty-five years. In a sense, he finds that he cannot go home again. He would have nothing in common with Joe except memories of adolescent love affairs, and youthful myths. Their past could never be altered or renewed.

A second major theme in *Recapitulation* is the need to belong to some larger community. The Mormon sense of community, whatever its intellectual failings, is viewed nostalgically. Bruce envies the close-knit families of his friends. Nola's family, for example, seems like a tribe, a culture unto itself full of unspoken values and understandings. His decision to attend law school in Minnesota irrevocably removes him from Nola, Utah, his adolescence, and ultimately from his chance to belong. When he returns to Utah, he is in the later stages of a successful but lonely adult life. His first job out of law school was in Saudi Arabia—a place without available women. He finally becomes a Middle Eastern specialist and a permanent bachelor.

Stegner ends the novel with Bruce, lonely, nostalgic, and emotionally incomplete, unable to make contact with Joe Mulder and with his past in a satisfying way. Even though the act of thinking through his past has served him therapeutically, he will continue as a diplomat, making formal contacts with people, living in the surface world of protocol, unable to connect emotionally with people. As the last of his family, he is a solitary figure, a man of deep feelings which he is unable to express. He is, finally, a man who has partially tamed the frontier restlessness and anger of his father and risen above his family's self-destructive tendencies. Still, Bruce carries on the family's feeling of rootlessness, in a more formal, acceptable way. In the Foreign Service, he never develops roots and is shifted from one diplomatic post to another. In a more formal sense than his father, Bruce is still a drifter. Stegner ends the novel fittingly with Bruce Mason being called back to the diplomatic service as United States Representative to an important OPEC meeting in Caracas, Venezuela, reluctantly pulled away from his efforts to understand his past.

Major publications other than long fiction

SHORT FICTION: *The Writer's Art: A Collection of Short Stories*, 1950 (edited with Richard Scowcroft and Boris Ilyin); *The Women on the Wall*, 1950; *The City of the Living and Other Stories*, 1956.

NONFICTION: *An Exposition Workshop*, 1939 (edited); *Readings for Citizens at War*, 1941 (edited); *Mormon Country*, 1942; *One Nation*, 1945 (with the editors of *Look*); *Look at America: The Central Northwest*, 1947; *The Writer in America*, 1951; *Beyond the Hundredth Meridian: John Wesley Powell and the Second Opening of the West*, 1954; *This Is Dinosaur: The Echo Park and Its Magic Rivers*, 1955 (edited); *The Exploration of the Colorado River of the West*, 1957 (edited); *Report on the Lands of the Arid Region of the United States*, 1962 (edited); *Wolf Willow: A History, a Story, and a Memory of the Last Plains Frontier*, 1962; *The Gathering of Zion: The Story of the Mormon Trail*, 1964; *Modern Composition*, 1964 (edited, 4 volumes); *The American Novel: From Cooper to Faulkner*, 1965 (edited); *The Sound of Mountain Water*, 1969; *The Uneasy Chair: A Biography of Bernard DeVoto*, 1974; *Ansel Adams: Images 1923-1974*, 1974; *The Letters of Bernard DeVoto*, 1975 (edited); *One Way to Spell Man*, 1982.

ANTHOLOGIES: *Stanford Short Stories*, 1946, 1947 (with Richard Scowcroft); *Great American Short Stories*, 1957 (with Mary Stegner); *Selected American Prose: The Realistic Movement*, 1958; *Twenty Years of Stanford Short Stories*, 1966.

Bibliography
Canzoneri, Robert. "Wallace Stegner: Trial by Existence," in *Southern Review*. IX (Fall, 1973), pp. 796-827.
Hudson, Lois Phillips. "*The Big Rock Candy Mountain*: No Roots and No

Frontier," in *South Dakota Review*. IX (Spring, 1971), pp. 3-13.

Lewis, Merrill, and Lorene Lewis. *Wallace Stegner*, 1972.

Milton, John. "Conversations with Wallace Stegner," in *South Dakota Review*. IX (Spring, 1971), pp. 45-57.

Peterson, Audrey C. "Narrative Voice in Stegner's Angle of Repose," in *Western American Literature*. X (Summer, 1975), pp. 125-133.

Robinson, Forrest, and Margaret Robinson. *Wallace Stegner*, 1977.

Richard H. Dillman

GERTRUDE STEIN

Born: Allegheny, Pennsylvania; February 3, 1874
Died: Neuilly-sur-Seine, France; July 27, 1946

Principal long fiction

Three Lives, 1909; *The Making of Americans*, 1925; *Lucy Church Amiably*, 1930; *A Long Gay Book*, 1932; *The World Is Round*, 1939; *Ida, A Novel*, 1941; *Brewsie and Willie*, 1946; *Quod Erat Demonstrandum*, 1950.

Other literary forms

Any attempt to separate Gertrude Stein's novels from her other kinds of writing must be highly arbitrary. Stein thought the novel to be a failed literary form in the twentieth century, claiming that no real novels had been written after Marcel Proust and even including her own novelistic efforts in this assessment. For this and other reasons, it might be claimed that few, if any, of Stein's works are novels in any traditional sense. In fact, very few of Stein's more than six hundred titles in more than forty books can be adequately classified into any traditional literary forms. Her philosophy of composition was so idiosyncratic, her prose style so seemingly nonrational, that her writing bears little resemblance to whatever genre it purports to represent. Depending on one's definition of the novel, Stein wrote anywhere between six and twelve novels, ranging in length from less than one hundred to 925 pages. The problem is that none of Stein's "novels" has a plot in any conventional sense, that few have conventionally developed and sustained characters, and that several seem almost exclusively autobiographical, more diaries and daybooks than anything else. It is not any easier to categorize her other pieces of writing, most of which are radically *sui generis*. If references to literary forms are made very loosely, Stein's work can be divided into novels, autobiographies, portraits, poems, lectures, operas, plays, and explanations. Other than her novels, her best-known works are *The Autobiography of Alice B. Toklas* (1933); *Tender Buttons* (1914); *Four Saints in Three Acts* (1934); *Lectures in America* (1935); *Everybody's Autobiography* (1937); and *Portraits and Prayers*, 1934.

Achievements

Whether towering or crouching, Stein is ubiquitous in contemporary literature. A child of the nineteenth century who staunchly adhered to many of its values halfway through the twentieth, she nevertheless dedicated her creative life to the destruction of nineteenth century concepts of artistic order and purpose. In her own words, she set out to do nothing less than to kill a century, to lay the old ways of literary convention to rest. She later boasted that "the most serious thinking about the nature of literature in the twentieth century has been done by a woman," and her claim has great merit. During the course of her career, Stein finally managed to convince almost everyone that there was indeed some point, if not profundity, in her aggressively enigmatic style. The ridicule and parody that frustrated so much of her early work had turned to grudging tolerance or outright lionizing by 1934, when Stein made her triumphant American lecture tour; for the last fifteen or so years of her life, she was published even if her editor had not the vaguest idea of what she was doing (as Bennett Cerf later admitted he had not). On the most concrete level, Stein's distinctive prose style is remarkably significant even when its philosophical dimensions are ignored. William Gass has observed, Stein "did more with sentences, and understood them better, than any writer ever has."

More important was Stein's influence on other leaders in the development of modernism. As a student of William James, a friend of Alfred North Whitehead and Pablo Picasso, Stein lived at the center of the philosophical and artistic revolutions of the twentieth century. She was the natural emblem for modernism, and in her person, career, and legend, many of its salient issues converged. In the light of more recent developments in the novel and in literary theory, it has also been argued that Stein was the first postmodernist, the first writer to claim openly that the instance of language is itself as important as the reality to which it refers. Among major writers, Ernest Hemingway was most obviously influenced by his association with her, but her genius was freely acknowledged by F. Scott Fitzgerald, Sherwood Anderson, and Thornton Wilder. William Saroyan explained her influence most directly when he asserted that no American writer could keep from coming under it, a sentiment reluctantly echoed by Edmund Wilson in *Axel's Castle* (1931), even before Stein's great popular success in the mid-1930's.

Biography

Gertrude Stein was born on February 3, 1874, in Allegheny, Pennsylvania, but she was seven before her family settled into permanent residence in Oakland, California, the city she was later to describe as having "no there there." Her birth itself was contingent on the deaths of two of her five brothers and sisters: her parents had decided to have only five children, and only after two children had died in infancy were Gertrude and her older brother, Leo, conceived. Identity was to become one of the central preoccupations of her writing career, and the tenuous nature of her own birth greatly influenced that concern.

Stein's early years were comfortably bourgeois and uneventful. Her father, a vice-president of the Union Street Municipal Railway System in San Francisco, was authoritarian, moody, aggressive, but vacillating, and he may have helped foster her sense of independence, but he undoubtedly left her annoyed by him in particular and by fatherhood in general. Her mother barely figured in her life at all: a pale, withdrawn, ineffectual woman, she left most of the rearing of her children to governesses. By the time Stein was seventeen, both parents had died and she had grown even closer to her immediate older brother, Leo. In 1893, she entered Harvard Annex (renamed Radcliffe College the following year), thus rejoining Leo, who was a student at Harvard. There, Stein studied with William James and Hugo Munsterberg and became involved in research in psychology. Together with the great influence exerted on her thinking by William James, this early work in psychology was to provide her with both a subject and a style that would continue in many forms throughout her career. She was awarded her A.B. by Harvard in 1898, almost a year after she had entered medical school at The Johns Hopkins University. Her interest in medicine rapidly waned, and she left Johns Hopkins in 1901, failing four courses in her final semester.

After leaving medical school, Stein spent two years moving back and forth between Europe and America. During that time, she was involved in an agonizing love affair with another young woman student at Johns Hopkins, May Bookstaver. The affair was painfully complicated, first by Stein's naïveté, then by the presence of a more sophisticated rival for May's love, Mabel Haynes. The resulting lover's triangle led Stein, in an effort to understand May, to begin formulating the theories of personality that dominated her early writing. The frustration and eventual despair of this Lesbian relationship profoundly influenced Stein's view of the psychology of personality and of love. Most directly, Stein's troubled affair with May Bookstaver provided her with many, if not most, of the concerns of three of her books, *Q.E.D.*, *The Making of Americans*, and *Three Lives*, the first two of which she began while living in New York in the winter of 1903.

After a brief stay in New York, she lived with Leo, first in Bloomsbury in London, and then, beginning in 1903, in Paris at 27 rue de Fleurus, the address she was to make so well-known to the world. In Paris, Gertrude and Leo became more and more interested in painting, buying works by new artists such as Henri Matisse and Picasso. Leo's preference was for works by Matisse, while Gertrude favored the more experimental works of Picasso, marking the beginning of a distancing process that would lead to Leo's complete separation from his sister in 1913. Leo was bright, opinionated, and fancied himself by far the greater creative talent of the two, but his brilliance and energy never produced any creative or significant critical work, and he grew to resent both his sister's independent thinking and her emerging ability to write. Later in his life, he would dismiss Gertrude as "dumb," her writing as "nonsense."

In 1907, Stein met another young American woman in Paris, Alice Toklas, and Alice began to displace Leo as the most important personal influence in Gertrude's life. Alice learned to type so she could transcribe Stein's handwritten manuscripts, beginning with portions of *The Making of Americans* in

1908. In 1909, Alice moved in with Gertrude and Leo at 27 rue de Fleurus, and by 1913, Alice had replaced Leo as Gertrude's companion and as the manager of her household. Stein later referred to her relationship with Alice as a "marriage," and few, if any, personal relationships have ever influenced a literary career so profoundly. Apart from providing Stein with the persona for her best-known work, *The Autobiography of Alice B. Toklas*, Alice typed, criticized, and valiantly worked to publish all of Stein's work for the rest of her career and for the twenty years that Alice lived after Stein's death. While it is doubtful that Alice was directly responsible for any of Stein's writing, her influence on its composition and on Stein's life was tremendous.

Gertrude and Alice spent the first months of World War I in England as houseguests of Alfred North Whitehead, returning to Paris briefly in 1914, then spending more than a year in Spain. They joined the war effort in 1917 when Stein ordered a Ford motor van from America for use as a supply truck for the American Fund for French Wounded, an acquisition which began Stein's lifelong fascination with automobiles, particularly with Fords. She and Alice drove this van, named "Auntie," until the war ended, work for which she was later awarded the Medaille de la Reconnaissance Française.

Modernism had burst on the American consciousness when the Armory Show opened in New York in 1913, and this show, which had confronted Americans with the first cubist paintings, also led to the association in the public mind of Stein's writing with this shockingly new art, particularly since Stein's first periodical publications had been "Matisse" and "Picasso" in *Camera Work*, the year before. Stein's mammoth, 925-page novel, *The Making of Americans*, was published in 1925, and in 1926, she lectured at Oxford and Cambridge, attempting to explain her idiosyncratic writing style. Her "landscape" novel, *Lucy Church Amiably*, appeared in 1930, but it was in 1933, with the publication of the best-selling *The Autobiography of Alice B. Toklas*, that Stein first captured the public's interest. She became front page news the following year when her opera *Four Saints in Three Acts* was first performed and when she embarked on a nationwide lecture tour, later described in *Everybody's Autobiography* and *Lectures in America*.

Stein and Toklas spent World War II in Bilignin and then in Culoz, France. While Stein and Toklas were both Jewish, they were never persecuted by occupying forces, owing in part to the influence of Bernard Fay, an early admirer of Stein's work who directed the Bibliotheque Nationale for the Vichy regime. When, after the war, Fay was sentenced to life imprisonment for his Vichy activities, Stein was one of his few defenders. That her art collection survived Nazi occupation virtually intact can only have been through Fay's intercession. During the war, Stein finished another novel, *Mrs. Reynolds* (unpublished), and *Wars I Have Seen* (1945), an autobiographical work. Her novel *Brewsie and Willie*, a series of conversations among American GIs, was published in 1945.

Stein died following an operation for cancer in the American Hospital in Neuilly-sur-Seine, France, on July 27, 1946. While Alice Toklas' account of Stein's last words may be apocryphal, it certainly is in keeping with the spirit of her life. As Alice later reconstructed their last conversation, Stein had asked her "What is the answer?" Then, when Alice remained silent, Stein added, "In that case, what is the question?"

Analysis

While Gertrude Stein's persistence finally earned her access to readers, it could never guarantee her readers who would or could take her strange writing seriously. As a result, more confusing and contradictory information surrounds her career than that of any other twentieth century writer of comparable reputation. Usually responding in any of four basic ways, readers and critics alike seemed to view her as (1) a literary charlatan of the P. T. Barnum ilk, interested in publicity or money rather than in art; (2) something of a naïve child-woman incapable of comprehending the world around her; (3) a fiery-eyed literary revolutionary, den mother of the avant-garde; or (4) an ageless repository of wisdom and genius. Ultimately, the reader's acceptance or rejection of these various categories will greatly determine his or her response to Stein's writing, which forces the reader to make as many cognitive choices as does that of any major writer.

Stein's many explanations of her writing further complicate its interpretation: even her "explanations" frustrate as much as they reveal, explicitly setting her up in cognitive competition with her reader, a competition suggested by her favorite cryptogram, which works out to read: "I understand you undertake to overthrow my undertaking." Stein proposes a rhetoric not of misunderstanding, but of antiunderstanding; that is, her "explanations" usually argue precisely against the desirability of explaining.

As Stein bluntly put the matter, "understanding is a very dull occupation." "Understanding" has a special denotation for Stein, sometimes meaning as little as paying attention to or reading. "To understand a thing means to be in contact with that thing," she proclaimed. Central to her mistrust of explanations and interpretations was Stein's often anguished belief that her thoughts could never really be matched to anyone else's. She was deeply troubled by this doubt as she wrote *The Making of Americans*, referring in that work to "the complete realization that no one can believe as you do about anything" as "complete disillusionment in living." Starting from this assumption that no one can ever really understand what someone else says or writes because of the inherent ambiguity of language, Stein not only decided to force her readers to confront that ambiguity, but also claimed it as a primary virtue of her writing. She announced triumphantly that "if you have vitality enough of knowing enough of what you mean, somebody and sometimes a great many will have to realize that you know what you mean and so they will agree that you mean what you know, which is as near as anybody can come to understanding any one." Stein's focus here is on relationships or process rather than on product—on the act of trying to become one with, rather than focusing on the ultimate result of that act.

Stein's thinking about understanding manifests itself in a number of distinctive ways in her writing, as do her theories of perception and of human psychology. Moreover, during the nearly fifty years of her writing career, her style developed in many related but perceptibly different stages, such as her "cubist" or her "cinema" phases. As a result, no single analysis can do more than describe the primary concerns and features of one of her stylistic periods. There are, however, three central concerns that underlie and at least partially account for all of the stages in the development of her style. These concerns are with the value of individual words, with repetition as the basic rhythm of existence, and with the related concept of "movement" in writing. Her articulations of these central concerns all run counter to her reader's expectations about the purpose and function of language and of literature. Her writing surprised her readers in much the same way that her penchant for playing only the black keys on a piano surprised and frustrated all but the most patient of her listeners.

One of Stein's goals was to return full meaning, value, and particularity to the words she used. "I took individual words and thought about them until I got their weight and volume complete and put them next to another word," she explained of seemingly nonsense phrases such as "toasted Susie is my ice cream," or "mouse and mountain and a quiver, a quaint statue and pain in an exterior and silence more silence louder shows salmon a mischief intender." This sort of paratactic juxtaposition of seemingly unrelated words rarely occurs in Stein's novels, but represents a problem for her reader in many other ways in her writing. She frequently chose to stress or focus on a part or aspect of the object of her description that the reader normally does not consider. The "things" Stein saw and wrote of were not the "things" with which readers are familiar: where another observer might see a coin balanced on its edge, Stein might choose either of the descriptive extremes of seeing it literally as a thin rectangle, or figuratively as the essence of money. Characteristically, her most opaque parataxis refers to essences or processes rather than to objects or static concepts.

A related quirk in Stein's style results from her intellectual or emotional attachment to particular words and phrases at certain stages of her career. As she admitted in *The Making of Americans*,

> To be using a new word in my writing is to me a very difficult thing. . . . Using a word I have not yet been using in my writing is to me a very difficult and a peculiar feeling. Sometimes I am using a new one, sometimes I feel a new meaning in an old one, sometimes I like one I am very fond of that one that has many meanings many ways of being used to make different meanings to everyone.

Stein said she had learned from Paul Cézanne that everything in a painting was related to everything else and that each part of the painting was of equal importance—a blade of grass as important to the composition of the painting as a tree. She attempted to apply these two principles to the composition of her sentences, taking special delight in using normally "overlooked" words, arguing that articles, prepositions, and conjunctions—the transitive elements in grammar—are just as important and more interesting than substantives such as nouns and verbs. Her reassessment both of the value of words and of the conventions of description resulted in what Michael J. Hoffman in *The Development of Abstractionism in the Writings of Gertrude Stein* (1965) has described as Stein's "abstractionism." It also resulted in her including in her writing totally unexpected information in perplexingly paratactic word-strings.

A second constant in Stein's style is the pronounced repetition of words, phrases, and sentences, with no change or with only incremental progressions of sounds or associations. Works such as *The Making of Americans* and *Three Lives* contain long passages in which each sentence is a light variation on some core phrase, with great repetition of words even within a single sentence. Stein termed this phenomenon "insistence" rather than repetition, citing her former teacher, William James, as her philosophical authority. James's argument in his *The Principles of Psychology* (1890) that one must think of the identical recurrence of a fact in a fresh manner remarkably resembles Stein's contention that "in expressing anything there can be no repetition because the essence of that expression is insistence, and if you insist you must each time use emphasis and if you use emphasis it is not possible while anybody is alive that they should use exactly the same emphasis." Repetition or insistence is perhaps the central aspect of what has been called Stein's "cinema style," based on her claim that in writing *The Making of Americans* she was "doing what the cinema was doing." She added that her writing in that book was "like a cinema picture made up of succession and each moment having its own emphasis that is its own difference and so there was the moving and the existence of each moment as it was in me."

Stein's discussion of "what the cinema was doing" appears in her *Lectures in America* and also suggests the third basic concern of her writing: movement. By "movement," she referred not to the movement of a message to its conclusion or the movement of a plot or narrative, but to "the essence of its going" of her prose, a timeless continuous present in the never-ending motion of consciousness. Stein also credits Cézanne with discovering this concern, "a feeling of movement inside the painting not a painting of a thing moving but the thing painted having inside it the existence of moving." She seemed to understand Cézanne's achievement in terms of William James's model of consciousness as an ever-flowing stream of thought. Accordingly, she used her writing not to record a scene or object or idea (products of thought), but to try to capture the sense of the process of perceiving such things. Stein's subject is almost always really two things at once: whatever attracted her attention—caught her eye, entered her ear, or crossed her mind—and the mobile nature of reality, particularly as it is perceived by human consciousness. In fact, Stein was usually more concerned with the nature of her own perception and with that of her reader than she was with its objects. She wanted to escape the conventions of linguistic representation, arbitrary arrangements similar to the "rules" for perspective in painting, and to present "something moving as moving is not as moving should be." As confusing as her resulting efforts sometimes are, her concern with motion makes sense as an attempt to mimic or evoke the nature of consciousness as she understood it.

From James at Harvard and possibly from Henri Bergson in Paris, Stein had learned that the best model for human consciousness was one that stressed the processual, ever-flowing nature of experience. She added to this belief her assumption that the essence of any subject could only be perceived and should only be represented through its motion, echoing Bergson's claim that "reality is mobility." Unfortunately, this belief led her writing into one of its many paradoxes: she could only attempt to represent the continuous stream of experience through the segmented, inherently sequential nature of language. Streams flow; words do not. Instead, they proceed one by one, like the cars pulled by a train engine. While James would certainly have objected to Stein's sequential cinema model as an approximation of the stream of consciousness, her motion-obsessed writing probably suggests the flow of consciousness as well as does any literary style.

Written in 1903, but put out of her mind until 1932, and not published until 1950, Stein's *Quod Erat Demonstrandum* (first published as *Things as They Are*) is her most conventional novel. Its sentences employ no unexpected syntax or diction, its central concerns are clear, its time scheme is linear, and its characters are conventionally drawn. If anything, Stein's style in this first novel is markedly old-fashioned, including highly formal sentences that frequently sport balanced serial constructions. "Adele vehemently and with much picturesque vividness explained her views and theories of manners, people and things, in all of which she was steadily opposed by Helen who differed fundamentally in all her convictions, aspirations and illusions." While its conventional style (crudely reminiscent of that of Henry James) is completely unlike that of any other Stein novel, *Q.E.D.* is a very significant work for the consideration of Stein's career. Apart from convincingly refuting the suspicion of some of her detractors that Stein was incapable of rational writing, this book establishes her preoccupation with psychological typecasting and vaguely hints at the importance of repetition in her thinking and writing.

Q.E.D. charts the growth, turbulence, and eventual dissolution of the relationships among three young women: Adele, the book's central consciousness, an obviously autobiographical figure; Helen Thomas, the object of Adele's love; and Mable Neathe, Adele's calculating rival for Helen's affection. These three characters closely parallel Stein, May Bookstaver, and Mabel Haynes, and the story of their relationship is the story of Stein's first, agonizing love affair. While the novel follows these three young women for three years, not much happens. Most of the book relates conversations and correspondence between Adele and Helen, showing Adele's torment first from her not yet understood desire for Helen, then from her growing realization that she is losing Helen to Mabel. Of principal interest to the reader is Stein's self-characterization in her portrayal of Adele.

Three Lives is easily Stein's best-known and most respected piece of fiction. Technically three novellas, this work is unified by its three subjects, by its central concern with the nature of consciousness, and by its attempt to blend colloquial idioms with Stein's emerging style, here based largely on her understanding of Cézanne's principles of composition, particularly that "one thing was as important as another thing." "The Good Anna," "Melanctha," and "The Gentle Lena" are the three sections of this work. Anna and Lena are poor German immigrants who patiently work as servants in Bridgepoint, Baltimore; Melanctha is a young black woman who discovers sexuality and love, then turns from a frustrating relationship with a sincere young black doctor to a dissipative affair with a gambler. Since all three women are essentially victimized by their surroundings and die at the end of their stories, this work is deterministic in the naturalist tradition, but *Three Lives* marks the transition from naturalism to modernism as Stein departs from nineteenth century literary conventions. She abandons conventional syntax to try to follow the movement of a consciousness rather than of events, and she develops a new narrative style only partially tied to linear chronology. The result is an interior narrative of consciousness in which Stein's prose style serves as the primary carrier of knowledge. Through the rhythms of her characters' speech and the rhythms of her narration, Stein gives her reader a sense of the basic rhythms of consciousness for these three women—what Stein would elsewhere refer to as their "bottom natures."

Possibly Stein's most widely celebrated piece of writing, "Melanctha" recasts the anguishing love triangle of *Q.E.D.* into the conflict between Melanctha and Jeff Campbell, whose inherently conflicting "bottom natures" or personality types parallel the conflict between Helen and Adele in the earlier work. "Melanctha" has been praised by Richard Wright, among others, as one of the first realistic and sympathetic renderings of black life by a white American author, but Melanctha's race is actually incidental to Stein's central concerns with finding a style to express the rhythms of personality and the frustrating cycles of love.

While it was not published until 1925, Stein's *The Making of Americans* occupied her as early as 1903 and was in fact begun before *Q.E.D.* and *Three Lives*. This mammoth novel began as a description of the creation of Americans from a representative immigrant family: "The old people in a new world, the new people made out of the old, that is the story that I mean to tell, for that is what really is and what I really know." Stein's projected family chronicle soon lost its original focus, becoming first a history of everyone, then a study of character types rather than of characters. Leon Katz, who has worked with this book more than has anyone else, calls it "a massive description of the psychological landscape of human being in its totality." Although the book ostensibly continues to follow events in the lives of two central families, the Herslands and the Dehnings, its real concern is almost always both larger and smaller, ranging from Stein's questions about her own life and identity to questions about the various personality types of all of humanity. As Richard Bridgman suggests, this is "an improvised work of no identifiable genre in which the creator learned by doing," one "full of momentary wonders and botched long-range schemes, lyrical outbursts and anguished confessions." Accordingly, Bridgman concludes that *The Making of Americans* is best thought of "not as a fictional narrative nor a philosophic tract, but as a drama of self-education." In a way, the book chronicles the "making" of Gertrude Stein, presenting a phenomenology of her mind as it works its way through personal problems toward the distinctive "cinema style."

Underlying a great part of the writing in this book is Stein's belief that human personality consists of variations on a few basic "bottom natures" or kinds of identity which can be perceived through a character's repeated actions. "There are then many things every one has in them that come out of them in the repeating everything living have always in them, repeating with a little changing just enough to make of each one an individual being, to make of each repeating an individual thing that gives to such a one a feeling of themselves inside them." There are two basic personality types, "dependent independent" and "independent dependent," polarities identified in part by the way the person fights: the first kind by resisting, the second by attacking. Concerns with character-typing dominate the book's first two sections, "The Dehnings and the Herslands" and "Martha Hersland," (the character most closely modeled on Stein's own life), while the third section, "Alfred and Julia Hersland," contains mostly digressions about contemporary matters in Stein's life. The fourth section, "David Hersland," becomes a meditation on the nature of aging and death ("He was dead when he was at the beginning of being in middle living."), and the final section, "History of a Family's Progress," is—even for Stein—an incredibly abstract and repetitive series of reflections on the concerns that had given rise to the novel. This final section contains no names, referring only to "some," "any," "every," or "very many."

Stein later described her efforts in this book as an attempt "to do what the cinema was doing"; that is, to give a sense of motion and life through a series of highly repetitive statements, each statement only an incremental change from the preceding one, like frames in a strip of film. One of the main effects of this technique is to freeze all action into a "continuous present." Not only do Stein's sentences exist in overlapping clusters, depending more for their meaning on their relationships to one another than on individual semantic content, but also her verbs in *The Making of Americans* are almost exclusively present participles, suspending all action in the present progressive tense. "The business of Art," Stein later explained, "is to live in the actual present, that is the complete actual present, and to express that complete actual present." As a result, while *The Making of Americans* does ostensibly present a history of four generations of the Hersland family, there exists in it little or no sense of the passage of time. Instead, the book presents a sense of "existence suspended in time," a self-contained world existing quite independently of the "real world," a basic modernist goal that has also become one of the hallmarks of postmodernism.

A 416-page version, abridged by Stein, was published in 1934, but has not been accepted by Stein scholars as adequately representative of the longer work. For all its difficulty, *The Making of Americans* is one of modernism's seminal works and an invaluable key to Stein's literary career.

Described by its author as "a novel of Romantic beauty and nature and which Looks Like an Engraving," *Lucy Church Amiably* shares many characteristics with Stein's best-known opera, *Four Saints in Three Acts*, and with the several works she called "geographies." The book was Stein's response to the area around Belley, France, where she and Alice spent many summers. Stein's title plays on the existence of the church in a nearby village, Lucey. As Richard Bridgman has observed, Lucy Church refers throughout the book to both that church and to a woman who resembles a relaxed Gertrude Stein. As Bridgman also notes, "the book is essentially a long, lyric diary," with Stein including in it information about the geography, residents, and flora of the surrounding area. This information appears, however, in Stein's distinctive paratactic style:

> In this story there is to be not only white black tea colour and vestiges of their bankruptcy but also well wishing and outlined and melodious and with a will and much of it to be sure with their only arrangement certainly for this for the time of which when by the way what is the difference between fixed.

This novel can perhaps best be thought of as a pastoral and elegiac meditation on the nature of place.

In 1939, Stein's novel for children, *The World Is Round*, was published, with illustrations by Clement Hurd. The book focuses on a series of events in the lives of a nine-year-old girl, Rose, and her cousin, Willie. These events are more enigmatic than dramatic, but seem to move both children through several kinds of initiations. Identity worries both Rose and Willie ("Would she have been Rose if her name had not been Rose and would she have been

Rose if she had been a twin"), as does the contrast between the uncertainties of their lives and the advertised verities of existence, emblemized by the "roundness" of the world. Comprising both the children's meditations and their songs, the book is, for Stein, relatively conventional. Although its sentences are highly repetitive and rhythmic, they present a compelling view of a child's consciousness, and Stein scholars agree on the importance and success of this little-known work.

Originally intended as "a novel about publicity," *Ida, A Novel* expands many of the concerns of *The World Is Round*, extending them from Ida's birth well into her adult life. As is true of all of Stein's novels, there is not anything resembling a plot, and many of the things that happen in Ida's life are surrealistically dreamlike. "Funny things" keep happening to the young Ida, and while the nature of these things is never explained, most of them seem to involve men. Frequently, these men have nothing at all to do with her, or they only glance at her, but Ida sees them as vaguely threatening, and insofar as her novel can be said to have a central concern, it is with certain problems of sexuality. Although Stein later described Ida as having been based on the Duchess of Windsor, this connection is only superficial, and Ida is better seen as another in the long line of Stein's autobiographical characters.

Stein's novel, *Brewsie and Willie*, redirected her revolutionary spirit from literary to social and economic problems. In this series of conversations among American GIs and nurses awaiting redeployment from France to the United States after World War II, Stein pessimistically considered the future of her native land. Stein had long held that the United States was "the oldest country in the world" because it had been the first to enter the twentieth century. By 1945, she felt that America had grown "old like a man of fifty," and that its tired, middle-aged economic system had become stale and repressive. In *Brewsie and Willie*, she describes that economic system as "industrialism," portraying a stultifying cycle of depleting raw materials for overproduction and installment buying. This cycle also locked the worker into "job thinking," making of him a kind of automaton, tied to his job, locked into debt, and, worst of all, robbed of freedom of thought. Through conversations involving Brewsie (Stein's spokesman), Willie, and several other GIs and nurses, Stein portrays an apprehensive generation of young Americans who see the potential dangers of postwar America but who fear they do not "have the guts to make a noise" about them. These conversations cover a wide range of subjects, from a comparison of French and American baby carriages to the tentative suggestion that the American system must be torn down before "pioneering" will again be possible.

Stein makes little or no effort in this book to differentiate the voices of her speakers, but she does rather amazingly blend her own voice with those of the GI's. The result is a style that is characteristically Stein's but that also has the rhythm and the randomness of overheard conversation. Often overlooked,

Brewsie and Willie is one of the most remarkable documents in Stein's writing career.

However idiosyncratic Stein's writing may seem, it must be remembered that a very strong case can be made for its substantial philosophical underpinnings. To her way of thinking, language could refuse few things to Stein, and the limitations of language were exactly what she refused to accept. She bent the language to the very uses that process philosophers such as James and Bergson and Whitehead feared it could not be put. Her stubborn emphasis on the individual word—particularly on transitive elements—her insistent use of repetition, and her ever-present preoccupation with the essential motion of words were all part of Stein's monumental struggle with a language she felt was not accurately used to reflect the way people perceive reality or the motion of reality itself. In a narrow but profound sense, she is the most serious realist in literary history. Stein was not a philosopher—her magpie eclecticism, associational flights, and thundering *ex cathedra* pronouncements ill-suited her for systematic explanation—but in her writing a wealth of philosophy appears.

Major publications other than long fiction

PLAY: *Four Saints in Three Acts*, 1934.

POETRY: *Tender Buttons*, 1914.

NONFICTION: *The Autobiography of Alice B. Toklas*, 1933; *Portraits and Prayers*, 1934; *Lectures in America*, 1935; *The Geographical History of America*, 1936; *Everybody's Autobiography*, 1937; *Wars I Have Seen*, 1945.

Bibliography

Bridgman, Richard. *Gertrude Stein in Pieces*, 1970.

Hoffman, Frederick J. *Gertrude Stein*, 1961.

Hoffman, Michael J. *The Development of Abstractionism in the Writings of Gertrude Stein*, 1965.

Haas, Robert Bartlett. *A Primer for the Gradual Understanding of Gertrude Stein*, 1971.

Mellow, James R. *Charmed Circle: Gertrude Stein and Company*, 1974.

Sutherland, Donald. *Gertrude Stein: A Biography of Her Work*, 1951.

Brooks Landon

JOHN STEINBECK

Born: Salinas, California; February 27, 1902
Died: New York, New York; December 20, 1968

Principal long fiction

Cup of Gold, 1929; *The Pastures of Heaven*, 1932; *To a God Unknown*, 1933; *Tortilla Flat*, 1935; *In Dubious Battle*, 1936; *The Red Pony*, 1937, 1945; *Of Mice and Men*, 1937; *The Grapes of Wrath*, 1939; *The Moon Is Down*, 1942; *Cannery Row*, 1945; *The Wayward Bus*, 1947; *The Pearl*, 1947; *Burning Bright*, 1950; *East of Eden*, 1952; *Sweet Thursday*, 1954; *The Short Reign of Pippen IV*, 1957; *The Winter of Our Discontent*, 1961.

Other literary forms

In addition to his seventeen novels, John Steinbeck published a story collection, *The Long Valley* (1938), and a few other uncollected or separately printed stories. His modern English translations of Sir Thomas Malory's Arthurian tales were published posthumously in 1976. Three plays he adapted from his novels were published as well as performed on Broadway: *Of Mice and Men* (1938), *The Moon Is Down* (1943), and *Burning Bright* (1951). Three of the six film treatments or screenplays he wrote—*The Forgotten Village* (1941), *A Medal for Benny* (1945), and *Viva Zapata!* (1952, 1975)—have been published; the other three also were produced as films—*Lifeboat* (1944), *The Pearl* (1945), and *The Red Pony* (1949), the latter two adapted from his own novels. His nonfiction was voluminous, and much of it remains uncollected. The more important nonfiction books include: *Sea of Cortez* (1941, 1951), *Bombs Away* (1942), *A Russian Journal* (1948), *Once There Was a War* (1958), *Travels With Charley* (1962), *America and Americans* (1966), *Journal of a Novel* (1969), and *Steinbeck: A Life in Letters* (1975).

Achievements

From the publication of his first bestseller, *Tortilla Flat*, in 1935, Steinbeck was a popular and widely respected American writer. His three earlier novels were virtually ignored, but the five books of fiction published between 1935 and 1939 made him the most important literary spokesman for the Depression decade. *In Dubious Battle*, *The Red Pony*, and *Of Mice and Men* established him as a serious writer, and his master work, *The Grapes of Wrath*, confirmed him as a major talent. During these years, his popular and critical success rivaled that of any of his contemporaries.

Although his immense popularity, public recognition, and the impressive sales of his works persisted throughout his career, Steinbeck's critical success waned after *The Grapes of Wrath*, reaching a nadir at his death in 1968, despite his Nobel Prize for Literature in 1962. During World War II, his development as a novelist faltered for many reasons, and Steinbeck never recovered his artistic momentum. Even *East of Eden*, the work he thought his masterpiece, proved an artistic and critical failure though a popular success. Since his death, Steinbeck remains widely read, both in America and abroad, while his critical reputation has enjoyed a modest revival. Undoubtedly the appreciation of his considerable talents will continue to develop, as few writers have better celebrated the American dream or traced the dark lineaments of the American nightmare.

Biography

John Ernst Steinbeck was born on February 27, 1902, in Salinas, California. The time and place of his birth are important because Steinbeck matured as an artist in his early thirties during the darkest days of the Depression, and his most important fictions are set in his beloved Salinas Valley. In one sense, Steinbeck's location in time and place may have made him a particularly American artist. Born just after the closing of the frontier, Steinbeck grew up with a frustrated modern America and witnessed the most notable failure of the American dream in the Depression. He was a writer who inherited the great tradition of the American Renaissance of the nineteenth century and who was forced to reshape it in terms of the historical and literary imperatives of twentieth century modernism. Steinbeck's family background evidenced this strongly American identity. His paternal grandfather, John Adolph Steinbeck, emigrated from Germany, settling in California after serving in the Civil War. His mother's father, Samuel Hamilton, sailed around Cape Horn from northern Ireland, finally immigrating to the Salinas Valley. John Ernst Steinbeck and Olive Hamilton were the first-generation descendants of sturdy, successful, and Americanized immigrant farm families. They met and married in 1890, settling in Salinas, where the father was prominent in local business and government, and the mother stayed home to rear their four children—three daughters and a son, the third child named for his father. The Steinbecks were refined, intelligent, and ambitious people who lived a quiet middle-class life in the small agricultural service town of Salinas.

Steinbeck seems to have enjoyed a happy childhood, and in fact he often asserted that he did. His father made enough money to indulge him in a small way, even to buy him a red pony. His mother encouraged him to read and to write, providing him with the classics of English and American literature. At school, he proved a popular and successful student and was elected president of his senior class.

After graduation from Salinas High School in 1919, Steinbeck enrolled at Stanford University. His subsequent history belies the picture of the happy, normal young man. He was soon in academic difficulties and dropped out of college several times to work on ranches in the Salinas Valley and observe "real life." His interests were varied, but he settled on novel-writing as his ambition, despite his family's insistence that he prepare for a more prosaic career. This traumatic rejection of middle-class values would prove a major force in shaping Steinbeck's fiction, both his social protest novels and his lighter entertainments such as *Cannery Row*.

Leaving Stanford without a degree in 1925, Steinbeck sojourned in New York for several months, where he worked as a laborer, a newspaper reporter, and a free-lance writer. Disillusioned in all his abortive pursuits, Steinbeck returned to California, where a job as winter caretaker of a lodge at Lake Tahoe provided the time to finish his first novel, *Cup of Gold*. The novel, a romance concerned with the Caribbean pirate Henry Morgan, was published by a small press directly before the crash of 1929, and it earned the young writer little recognition and even less money. In 1930, he married Carol Henning and moved with her to Los Angeles and later to Pacific Grove, a seaside resort near Monterey, where he lived in his parents' summer house. Still supported by his family and his wife, the ambitious young writer churned out the manuscripts of several novels.

A friend, Edward F. (Ed) Ricketts, a marine biologist trained at the University of Chicago, encouraged Steinbeck to treat his material more objectively. Under Rickett's influence, Steinbeck modified his earlier commitment to satire, allegory, and romanticism and turned to modern accounts of the Salinas Valley. Steinbeck's next two novels, *Pastures of Heaven* and *To a God Unknown*, are both set in the Valley, but both still were marked by excessive sentimentality and symbolism. Both were virtually ignored by the public and the critics. Steinbeck's short fiction, however, began to receive recognition; for example, his story "The Murder" was selected as an O. Henry Prize story in 1934.

Tortilla Flat, a droll tale of Monterey's Mexican quarter, established Steinbeck as a popular and critical success in 1935. (Unfortunately, his parents died just before he achieved his first real success.) The novel's sales provided money to pay his debts, to travel to Mexico, and to continue writing seriously. His next novel, *In Dubious Battle*, established him as a serious literary artist and began the period of his greatest success, both critical and popular. This harshly realistic strike novel followed directions established in stories such as "The Raid," influenced by the realistic impulse of American literature in the 1930's. Succeeding publications quickly confirmed this development in his fiction. His short novels *The Red Pony* and *Of Mice and Men* followed in 1937, his story collection, *The Long Valley*, in 1938, and his epic of the Okie migration to California, *The Grapes of Wrath*, in 1939. His own play version of *Of Mice and Men* won the Drama Critics Circle Award in 1938, and *The Grapes of Wrath* received the Pulitzer Prize in 1940. Steinbeck had become one of the most popular and respected writers in the country, a spokesman for an entire culture.

In 1941, Pearl Harbor changed the direction of American culture and of

John Steinbeck's literary development. During the war years, he seemed in a holding pattern, trying to adjust to his phenomenal success while absorbing the cataclysmic events around him. Steinbeck's career stalled for many reasons. He left the California subjects and realistic style of his finest novels, and he was unable to come to terms with a world at war, though he served for a few months as a front-line correspondent. Personal developments paralleled these literary ones. Steinbeck divorced his first wife and married Gwen Conger, a young Hollywood starlet; no doubt she influenced his decision to move from California to New York. Steinbeck began to write with an eye on Broadway and Hollywood.

Steinbeck was forty-three when World War II ended in 1945; he died in 1968 at the age of sixty-six. Over those twenty-three years, Steinbeck was extremely productive, winning considerable acclaim—most notably, the Nobel Prize in Literature in 1962. Yet the most important part of his career was finished. The war had changed the direction of his artistic development, and Steinbeck seemed powerless to reverse his decline.

Again, his personal life mirrored his literary difficulties. Although Gwen Conger presented him with his only children—Tom, born in 1944, and John, born in 1946—they were divorced in 1948. Like his first divorce, this one was bitter and expensive. In the same year, his mentor Ricketts was killed in a car accident. Steinbeck traveled extensively, devoting himself to film and nonfiction projects. In 1950, he married Elaine Scott, establishing a supportive relationship which allowed him to finish his epic Salinas Valley novel *East of Eden*.

Steinbeck tried again and again to write his way back to the artistic success of his earlier years, notably in *The Wayward Bus*, but his commercial success kept getting in the way. *East of Eden*, Steinbeck's major postwar novel, attempted another California epic to match the grandeur of *The Grapes of Wrath*. Although the book was a blockbuster best-seller, it was an artistic and critical failure. Steinbeck himself seemed to recognize his own decline, and in his last years he virtually abandoned fiction for journalism.

Of his last novels, only *The Winter of Our Discontent* transcends mere entertainment, and it does not have the literary structures to match its serious themes. Despite the popularity of nonfiction such as *Travels with Charley*, despite awards such as the Nobel Prize and the United States Medal of Freedom, despite his personal friendship with President Lyndon Johnson as a supporter of Vietnam, Steinbeck was only the shell of the great writer of the 1930's. He died in New York City on December 20, 1968.

Analysis

John Steinbeck remains a writer of the 1930's, perhaps *the* American writer of the 1930's. Although his first novel, *Cup of Gold*, was published in 1929, its derivative "Lost Generation" posturing gives little indication of the masterpiece he would publish at the end of the next decade, *The Grapes of Wrath*. Steinbeck developed from a romantic, imitative, often sentimental apprentice to a realistic, objective, and accomplished novelist in only a decade. The reasons for this change can be found in the interplay between a sensitive writer and his cultural background.

A writer of great talent, sensitivity, and imagination, John Steinbeck entered into the mood of the country in the late 1930's with an extraordinary responsiveness. The Depression had elicited a reevaluation of American culture, a reassessment of the American dream: a harsh realism of observation balanced by a warm emphasis on human dignity. Literature and the other arts joined social, economic, and political thought in contrasting traditional American ideals with the bleak reality of breadlines and shantytowns. Perhaps the major symbol of dislocation was the Dust Bowl; the American garden became a wasteland from which its dispossessed farmers fled. The arts in the 1930's focused on these harsh images and tried to find in them the human dimensions which promised a new beginning.

The proletarian novel, documentary photography, and the documentary film stemmed from similar impulses; the radical novel put more emphasis on the inhuman conditions of the dislocated, while the films made more of the promising possibilities for a new day. Painting, music, and theater all responded to a new humanistic and realistic thrust. The best balance was struck by documentary photographers and filmmakers: Dorothea Lange, Walker Evans (James Agee's associate), and Arthur Rothstein in photography; Pare Lorentz, Willard Van Dyke, and Herbert Kline in film. As a novelist, Steinbeck shared this documentary impulse, and it refined his art.

In Dubious Battle tells the harsh story of a violent agricultural strike in the "Torgas Valley" from the viewpoint of two Communist agitators. Careful and objective in his handling of the material, the mature Steinbeck provided almost a factual case study of a strike. In a letter, he indicated that this was his conscious intention:

> I had an idea that I was going to write the autobiography of a Communist. Then Miss McIntosh [his agent] suggested I reduce it to fiction. There lay the trouble. I had planned to write a journalistic account of a strike. But as I thought of it as fiction the thing got bigger and bigger . . . I have used a small strike in an orchard valley as the symbol of man's eternal, bitter warfare with himself.

For the first time, Steinbeck was able to combine his ambition to write great moral literature with his desire to chronicle his time and place.

Significantly, the novel takes its title from John Milton's *Paradise Lost* (1667) in which the phrase is used to describe the struggle between God and Satan, but it takes its subject from the newspapers and newsreels of the 1930's. The underlying structure demonstrates the universal struggle of good and evil, of human greed and selfishness versus human generosity and idealism.

Jim, the protagonist killed at the conclusion, is obviously a Christ figure, an individual who has sacrificed himself for the group. Here, Steinbeck needs no overblown symbolic actions to support his theme. He lets his contemporary story tell itself realistically and in documentary fashion. In a letter, he describes his method in the novel: "I wanted to be merely a recording consciousness, judging nothing, simply putting down the thing." This objective, dispassionate, almost documentary realism separates *In Dubious Battle* from his earlier fiction and announces the beginning of Steinbeck's major period.

Of Mice and Men was written in 1935 and 1936 and first published as a novel in 1937 at the height of the Depression. Steinbeck constructed the book around dramatic scenes so that he could easily rewrite it for the stage, which he did with the help of George S. Kaufmann. The play opened late in 1937, with Wallace Ford as George and Broderick Crawford as Lennie. A movie version, directed by Lewis Milestone (*All Quiet on the Western Front*, 1931; *Rain*, 1932; and so on), with Burgess Meredith and Lon Chaney, Jr. in the central roles, appeared in 1939. The success of the play and film spurred sales of the novel and created a wide audience for Steinbeck's next book, *The Grapes of Wrath*.

Like his classic story of the "Okie" migration from the Dust Bowl to the promised land of California, *Of Mice and Men* is a dramatic presentation of the persistence of the American dream and the tragedy of its failure. His characters are the little people, the uncommon "common people," disoriented and dispossessed by modern life yet still yearning for a little piece of land, that little particle of the Jeffersonian ideal. Lennie is the symbol of this visceral, inarticulate land-hunger, while George becomes the poet of this romantic vision. How their dream blossoms and then dies is Steinbeck's dramatic subject; how their fate represents that of America in the 1930's and after becomes his theme. His title, an allusion to the Scottish poet Robert Burns, suggests that the best laid plans "of mice and men often gang a-gley"; so the American vision had gone astray in the Depression decade Steinbeck documented so movingly and realistically.

The Red Pony involves the maturation of Jody Tiflin, a boy of about ten when the action opens. The time is about 1910 and the setting is the Tiflin ranch in the Salinas Valley, where Jody lives with his father, Carl, his mother, Ruth, and the hired hand, a middle-aged cowboy named Billy Buck. From time to time, they are visited by Jody's grandfather, a venerable old man who led one of the first wagon trains to California. "The Gift," the first section of the novel, concerns Jody's red pony, which he names Gabilan, after the nearby mountain range. The pony soon becomes a symbol of the boy's growing maturity and his developing knowledge of the natural world. Later, he carelessly leaves the pony out in the rain, and it takes cold and dies, despite Billy Buck's efforts to save it. Thus Jody learns of nature's cruel indifference to human wishes.

In the second part, "The Great Mountains," the Tiflin ranch is visited by a former resident, Gitano, an aged Chicano laborer reared in the now vanished hacienda. Old Gitano has come home to die. In a debate which recalls Robert Frost's poem "The Death of the Hired Man," Carl persuades Ruth that they cannot take Old Gitano in, but—as in Frost's poem—their dialogue proves pointless. Stealing a broken-down nag significantly named Easter, the old man rides off into the mountains to die in dignity. Again, Jody is faced with the complex, harsh reality of adult life.

In "The Promise," the third section, Jody learns more of nature's ambiguous promises when his father has one of the mares put to stud to give the boy another colt. The birth is complicated, however, and Billy Buck must kill the mare to save the colt, demonstrating that life and death are inextricably intertwined. The final section, "The Leader of the People," ends the sequence with another vision of death and change. Jody's grandfather comes to visit, retelling his time-worn stories of the great wagon crossing. Carl Tiflin cruelly hurts the old man by revealing that none of them except Jody is really interested in these repetitive tales. The grandfather realizes that Carl is right, but later he tells Jody that the adventurous stories were not the point, but that his message was "Westering" itself. For the grandfather, "Westering" was the source of American identity. With the close of the frontier, "Westering" has ended, and the rugged Westerners have been replaced by petty landholders such as Carl Tiflin and aging cowboys such as Billy Buck. In his grandfather's ramblings, Jody discovers a sense of mature purpose, and by the conclusion of the sequence, he too can hope to be a leader of the people.

The Red Pony traces Jody's initiation into adult life with both realism and sensitivity, a balance which Steinbeck did not always achieve. The vision of the characters caught up in the harsh world of nature is balanced by their deep human concerns and commitments. The evocation of the ranch setting in its vital beauty is matched only in the author's finest works, such as *Of Mice and Men*. Steinbeck's symbols grow naturally out of this setting, and nothing in the story-sequence seems forced into a symbolic pattern, as in his later works. In its depiction of an American variation on a universal experience, *The Red Pony* deserves comparison with the finest of modern American fiction, especially with initiation tales such as William Faulkner's *The Bear* (1942) and Ernest Hemingway's Nick Adams stories.

Responding to a variety of social and artistic influences, Steinbeck's writing had evolved toward documentary realism throughout the 1930's. In fiction, this development is especially clear in *In Dubious Battle*, *Of Mice and Men*, and *The Long Valley*. Even more obvious was the movement of his nonfiction toward a committed documentation of the social ills plaguing America during the Depression decade. Steinbeck's newspaper and magazine writing offered detailed accounts of social problems, particularly the plight of migrant agricultural workers in California's fertile valleys. The culmination of this development was *Their Blood Is Strong* (1938), a compilation of reports originally written for the *San Francisco News* and published with additional text by Steinbeck and photographs by Dorothea Lange originally made for the Farm Security Administration.

It is significant that Steinbeck first conceived of *The Grapes of Wrath* as just such a documentary book. In March, 1938, Steinbeck went into the California valleys with a *Life* magazine photographer to make a record of the harsh conditions in the migrant camps. The reality he encountered seemed too significant for nonfiction, however, and Steinbeck began to reshape this material as a novel, an epic novel.

Although his first tentative attempts at fictionalizing the situation in the agricultural valleys were heavily satiric, as indicated by the early title *L'Affaire Lettuceberg*, Steinbeck soon realized that the Okie migration was the stuff of an American epic. Reworking his material, adding to it by research in government agency files and by more journeys into the camps and along the migrant routes, Steinbeck evolved his vision. A grand design emerged; he would follow one family from the Oklahoma Dust Bowl to California. Perhaps this methodology was suggested by the sociological case histories of the day, perhaps by the haunted faces of individual families which stared back at him as he researched in Farm Security Administration files.

In discussing his plans for his later documentary film, *The Forgotten Village* (1941), Steinbeck remarked that most documentaries concerned large groups of people but that audiences could identify better with individuals. In *The Grapes of Wrath*, he made one family representative of general conditions. The larger groups and problems he treated in short interchapters which generalized the issues particularized in the Joad family. Perhaps the grand themes of change and movement were suggested by the documentary films of Pare Lorentz (later a personal friend), *The Plow That Broke the Plains* (1936) and *The River* (1938), with their panoramic geographical and historical visions. Drawing an archetypal theme from Sir Thomas Malory, John Bunyan, John Milton, and the Bible—the ultimate source of his pervasive religious symbolism—Steinbeck made the journey of the Joads into an allegorical pilgrimage as well as a desperate race along Route 66. During this journey, the Joad family disintegrates, but the larger human family emerges. Tom Joad makes a pilgrim's progress from a narrow, pessimistic view to a transcendental vision of American possibilities. The novel ends on a note of hope for a new American dream.

The Grapes of Wrath was a sensational best-seller from the beginning. Published to generally favorable reviews in March, 1939, it was selling at the rate of more than twenty-five hundred copies a day two months later. Controversy helped spur sales. As a semidocumentary, its factual basis was subject to close scrutiny, and many critics challenged Steinbeck's material. Oklahomans resented the presentation of the Joads as typical of the state (many still do), while Californians disapproved of the depiction of their state's leading industry. The book was attacked, banned, burned—but everywhere it was read. Even in the migrant camps, it was considered an accurate picture of the conditions experienced there. Some 430,000 copies were sold in a year, and in 1940, the novel received the Pulitzer Prize and the Award of the American Booksellers Association (later the National Book Award). Naturally, all the excitement attracted the attention of Hollywood, in spite of the fact that the controversy over the novel seemed to preclude a film version, or at least a faithful film version. Nevertheless, Darryl F. Zanuck produced and John Ford directed a faithful adaptation starring Henry Fonda in 1940; the film, like the novel, has become a classic, and it gave Steinbeck's vision of America in the 1930's even wider currency.

Indeed, Steinbeck's best work was filmic in the best sense of that word—visual, realistic, objective. These qualities nicely balanced the allegorical and romantic strains inherent in his earlier fiction. During World War II, however, his work, much to its detriment, began to cater to the film industry. In fact, much of his postwar writing seems to have found its inspiration in Hollywood versions of his work. His own screen adaptation of an earlier story, *The Red Pony* (1949), proves a sentimentalized reproduction of the original. Still, he was occasionally capable of recapturing his earlier vision, particularly in his works about Mexico—*The Pearl* and *Viva Zapata!*

Mexico always had been an important symbolic place for Steinbeck. As a native Californian, he had been aware of his state's Mexican heritage. Even as a boy, he sought out Chicano companions, fascinated by their unconcern for the pieties of WASP culture; he also befriended Mexican fieldhands at the ranches where he worked during his college summers. Later, his first literary success, *Tortilla Flat*, grew from his involvement with the *paisanos* of Monterey, people who would today be called Chicanos.

For Steinbeck, Mexico was everything modern America was not; it possessed a primitive vitality, a harsh simplicity, and a romantic beauty—all of which are found in *The Pearl*. Mexico exhibits the same qualities in the works of other modern writers such as Malcolm Lowry, Aldous Huxley, Graham Greene, Hart Crane, and Katherine Anne Porter. All of them lived and worked there for some time, contrasting the traditional culture they discovered in Mexico with the emptiness of the modern world. Steinbeck also was fascinated by a Mexico still alive with social concern. The continued extension of the Revolution into the countryside had been his subject in *The Forgotten Village*, and it would be developed further in *Viva Zapata!* For Steinbeck, Mexico represented the purity of artistic and social purposes that he had lost after World War II.

This sense of the writer's personal involvement energizes *The Pearl*, making it Steinbeck's best work of fiction in the years following the success of *The Grapes of Wrath*. At the beginning of the novella, the storyteller states: "If this story is a parable, perhaps everyone takes his own meaning from it and reads his own life into it." The critics have read Steinbeck's short novel in a number of ways, but strangely enough, they have not considered it as a parable of the author's own career in the postwar period. Much like Ernest Hemingway's *The Old Man and The Sea* (1952), *The Pearl* uses the life of a simple fisherman to investigate symbolically an aging artist's difficult maturation.

Steinbeck was presented with the tale during his Sea of Cortez expedition in 1940. In his log, he recounts "an event which happened at La Paz in recent years." The story matches the basic outline of *The Pearl*, though Steinbeck made several major changes, changes significant in an autobiographical sense. In the original, the Mexican fisherman was a devil-may-care bachelor; in *The Pearl*, he becomes the sober young husband and father, Kino. Steinbeck himself had just become a father for the first time when he wrote the novella, and this change provides a clue to the autobiographical nature of the parable. The original bachelor thought the pearl a key to easy living; Kino sees it creating a better way of life for the people through an education for his baby son, Coyotito. If the child could read and write, then he could set his family and his people free from the social and economic bondage in which they toil. Kino is ignorant of the dangers of wealth, and *The Pearl* is the tale of how he matures by coming to understand them. Steinbeck, too, matured from his youthful innocence as he felt the pressures of success.

As in his best fiction of the 1930's Steinbeck fuses his universal allegory with documentary realism. Perhaps planning ahead for a screenplay, Steinbeck's prose in the novel often takes a cinematic point of view. Scenes are presented in terms of establishing shots, medium views, and close-ups. In particular, Steinbeck carefully examines the natural setting, often visually contrasting human behavior with natural phenomena. As in his best fiction, his naturalistic vision is inherent in the movement of his story; there is no extraneous philosophizing.

Steinbeck's characters in *The Pearl* are real people in a real world, but they are also universal types. Kino, the fisherman named for an early Jesuit explorer, Juana, his wife, and Coyotito, their baby, are almost an archetypal family, like the Holy Family in a medieval morality play. Kino's aspirations are the same universal drives to better himself and his family that took the Okies to the California valleys. Like the Joads, this symbolic family must struggle at once against an indifferent natural order and a corrupt social order. Unfortunately, aside from the screenplay of *Viva Zapata!*, Steinbeck would never again achieve the fusion of parable and realism which energizes *The Pearl*.

In his Nobel Prize speech of 1962, Steinbeck indicated what he tried to accomplish in his work:

> The ancient commission of the writer has not changed. He is charged with exposing our

many grievous faults and failures, with dredging up to the light our dark and dangerous dreams, for the purpose of improvement.

No writer has better exposed the dark underside of the American dream, but few writers have so successfully celebrated the great hope symbolized in that dream—the hope of human development. Steinbeck's best fictions picture a paradise lost but also posit a future paradise to be regained. In spite of his faults and failures, John Steinbeck's best literary works demonstrate a greatness of heart and mind found only rarely in modern American literature.

Major publications other than long fiction
SHORT FICTION: *Saint Katy the Virgin*, 1936; *The Long Valley*, 1938.
PLAY: *Burning Bright*, 1951.
NONFICTION: *Their Blood Is Strong*, 1938; *The Forgotten Village*, 1941; *Sea of Cortez*, 1941; *Bombs Away*, 1942; *A Russian Journal*, 1948; *Once There Was a War*, 1958; *Travels with Charley*, 1962; *Letters to Alicia*, 1965; *America and Americans*, 1966; *Journal of a Novel*, 1969; *Steinbeck: A Life in Letters*, 1975 (Elaine Steinbeck and Robert Wallsten, editors).

Bibliography
Astro, Richard. *John Steinbeck and Edward Ricketts: The Shaping of a Novelist*, 1973.
French, Warren. *John Steinbeck*, 1975.
Hayashi, Tetsumaro, ed. *A Study Guide To Steinbeck: A Handbook to His Major Works*, 1974, 1979.
Kiernan, Thomas. *The Intricate Music: A Biography of John Steinbeck*, 1979.
Levant, Howard. *The Novels of John Steinbeck: A Critical Study*, 1974.
Lisca, Peter. *The Wide World of John Steinbeck*, 1957.
McCarthy, Paul. *John Steinbeck*, 1980.
Moore, Harry T. *The Novels of John Steinbeck*, 1939.

Joseph R. Millichap

LAURENCE STERNE

Born: Clonmel, Ireland; November 24, 1713
Died: London, England; March 18, 1768

Principal long fiction
The Life and Opinions of Tristram Shandy, Gent., 1759-1767; *A Sentimental Journey Through France and Italy*, 1768.

Other literary forms
Laurence Sterne began his literary career with political pieces in the *York-Courant* in 1741. Two years later, he published a poem, "The Unknown World," in *The Gentleman's Magazine* (July, 1743). His song, "How Imperfect the Joys of the Soul," written for Kitty Fourmantel, appeared in Joseph Baildon's *Collection of New Songs Sung at Ranelagh* (1765), and a four-line epigram, "On a Lady's Sporting a Somerset," was attributed to Sterne in *Muse's Mirror* (1778). His sermons were published in three installments: two volumes in 1760, another two in 1766, and a final three volumes in 1769. A political satire entitled *A Political Romance* was published in 1759 but quickly suppressed. After Sterne's death, *Letters from Yorick to Eliza* appeared in 1773, and his daughter arranged for the publication of *Letters of the Late Rev. Mr. Sterne to His Most Intimate Friends* (1775, 3 volumes). These volumes include an autobiographical *Memoir* and the *Fragment in the Manner of Rabelais*. In 1935, Oxford University Press published the definitive edition of Sterne's letters, edited by Lewis Perry Curtis. The *Journal to Eliza*, composed in 1767, was not published until 1904.

Achievements
When Sterne went to London in March, 1760, he was an obscure provincial parson. He rode as a guest in Stephen Croft's cart, and he brought with him little more than his "best breeches." Two months later, he returned to York in his own carriage. Robert Dodsley, who the year before had refused the copyright of *The Life and Opinions of Tristram Shandy, Gent.* (commonly called *Tristram Shandy*) for 50 pounds, now gladly offered Sterne 250 pounds for the first two volumes, 380 pounds for the next two, as yet unwritten, and another 200 pounds for two volumes of sermons. The famous artist William Hogarth agreed to provide a frontispiece to the second edition of Volume I and another for Volume III; Joshua Reynolds painted Sterne's portrait. Like Lord Byron, Sterne could have said that he awoke to find himself famous. As Sterne did say, in a letter to Catherine Fourmantel, "I assure you my Kitty, that Tristram is the Fashion." Despite the carpings of a few—Horace Walpole thought *Tristram Shandy* "a very insipid and tedious performance," and Samuel Richardson thought it immoral—the novel was the rage of Lon-

don, inspiring so many continuations and imitations that Sterne had to sign the later volumes to guarantee their authenticity.

After the novel's initial popularity, sales did drop off. In Book VIII, Tristram complains that he has "ten cart-loads" of Volumes V and VI "still unsold." Dodsley abandoned publication of the work after Volume IV, and Sterne's new publisher, Thomas Becket, complained in April, 1763, that he had 991 copies of Volumes V and VI unsold (from a printing of four thousand). Samuel Johnson's famous comment, though ultimately incorrect, probably reflected the opinion of the day: "Nothing odd will do long. *Tristram Shandy* did not last." Even Sterne may have tired of the work; the volumes grew slimmer, and Volume IX appeared without its mate, Volume X having, in Sterne's apt words for an obstetrical novel, "miscarried."

Yet *Tristram Shandy* has lasted. It retains its readership, even if it has continued to justify Sterne's complaint of being "more read than understood." Twentieth century readers have made great, perhaps exaggerated, claims for the novel, seeing it as the harbinger of the works of Marcel Proust, James Joyce, and Albert Camus, who, it is said, derived from Sterne the concept of relative time, the stream of consciousness, and a sense of the absurd. Even if one discounts such assertions, there can be no question of the work's importance in the development of the novel or of *Tristram Shandy*'s place in the first rank of eighteenth century fiction.

Less has been claimed for *A Sentimental Journey Through France and Italy* (commonly called *A Sentimental Journey*), yet this work, apparently so different and so much simpler than *Tristram Shandy*, greatly influenced Continental, especially German, literature of the Romantic period. Though critics debate the sincerity of the emotions in the work, eighteenth century readers generally did not question Yorick's sentimentality, which contributed to the rise of the cult of sensibility exemplified by such works as Henry Mackenzie's *The Man of Feeling* (1771) and Sarah Morton's *The Power of Sympathy* (1789). Because of its brevity, its benevolence, and its accessibility, *A Sentimental Journey* has enjoyed continued popularity since its first appearance. Though lacking the stature of *Tristram Shandy*, it remains a classic.

Biography

Laurence Sterne was born in Clonmel, Tipperary, Ireland, on November 24, 1713. On his father's side, he could claim some distinction. His great-grandfather, Richard Sterne, had been Archbishop of York, and his grandfather, Simon Sterne, was a rich Yorkshire country squire. Roger Sterne, Laurence's father, was less distinguished. Sterne describes his father as "a little smart man—active to the last degree, in all exercises—most patient of fatigue and disappointments, of which it pleased God to give him full measure." Sterne added that his father was "of a kindly, sweet disposition, void of all design." Many have seen Roger Sterne as the model for Uncle Toby

Shandy. At the age of sixteen, Roger joined the Cumberland Regiment of Foot, and on September 25, 1711, he married Agnes Nuttall. Agnes, according to her son, was the daughter of "a noted sutler in Flanders, in Queen Ann's wars," whom Roger married because he was in debt to her father. Actually, she may have been the daughter of a poor but respectable family in Lancashire.

From his birth to the age of ten, Sterne led a nomadic life, wandering from barracks to barracks across Great Britain. During these years, he may have acquired some of the military knowledge that appears throughout *Tristram Shandy*, or at least that fondness for the military which marks the work.

When Sterne was ten, his uncle Richard sent him to school near Halifax, in Yorkshire, and in 1733, Sterne's cousin sent him to Jesus College, Cambridge, where his great-grandfather had been a master and where both his uncle Jaques and his cousin had gone. At Cambridge, Sterne met John Hall, who later renamed himself John Hall-Stevenson. Hall-Stevenson was to be one of Sterne's closest friends throughout his life; his library at "Crazy Castle" would furnish much of the abstruse learning in *Tristram Shandy*, and he would himself appear in both that novel and *A Sentimental Journey* as "Eugenius," the sober adviser. While at Cambridge, Sterne suffered his first tubercular hemorrhage.

After receiving his bachelor's degree in January, 1737, Sterne had to choose a profession. Since his great-grandfather and uncle had both gone into the Church, Sterne followed their path. After Sterne served briefly in St. Ives and Catton, his uncle Jaques, by then Archdeacon of Cleveland and Canon and Precentor of the York Cathedral, secured for him the living of Sutton on the Forest, a few miles north of York. A second post soon followed; Sterne received the prebend of Givendale, making him part of the York Cathedral chapter and so allowing him to preach his turn there.

At York, Sterne met Elizabeth Lumley, a woman with a comfortable fortune. Their courtship had a strong sentimental tinge to it. Indeed, if Sterne actually wrote to Elizabeth the letters that his daughter published after his death, his is the first recorded use of the word *sentimental*, and the emotions expressed in these letters foreshadow both *A Sentimental Journey* and the *Journal to Eliza*. Even if these letters are spurious, Sterne's description of his courtship in the *Memoirs* is sufficiently lachrymose to rival the death of Le Fever in *Tristram Shandy*. Unfortunately for Sterne, he, unlike Tristram, did go on; on March 30, 1741, he married Elizabeth. The unfavorable portrait of Mrs. Shandy owes much to Sterne's less than sentimental feelings toward his wife, whom he called in March, 1760, the "one Obstacle to my Happiness."

The year 1741 was also important for Sterne because it marked his first appearance in print. His uncle Jaques was a strong Whig, and he recruited his nephew to write in support of the Whig candidate for York in that year's election. Sterne wrote, the Whig won, and Sterne received the prebend of

North Newbold as a reward. The Whig success was, however, short-lived. When the Walpole government fell in 1742, Sterne wrote a recantation and apology for his part in "the late contested Election," and thereby earned the enmity of his uncle, an enmity which ended only with Jaques's death in 1759.

For the next eighteen years, Sterne lived as a typical provincial clergyman, attending to the needs of his parishioners and publishing two sermons. One of these, "For We Trust We Have a Good Conscience," Sterne reprints in its entirety in the second volume of *Tristram Shandy*. In 1751, he received the commissaryship of Pickering and Pocklington, despite his uncle's efforts to secure this position for Dr. Francis Topham. Sterne and Topham collided again in 1758, when Topham attended to include his son in a patent and thus secure for him a post after his own death. When the dean of York Cathedral blocked the inclusion, a pamphlet war ensued. Sterne fired the final shot; his *A Political Romance* so squashed Topham that he agreed to abandon the fray if Sterne would withdraw his pamphlet. Sterne did withdraw *A Political Romance*, but he was not finished with Topham, who was to appear in *Tristram Shandy* as Phutatorius and Didius.

A Political Romance is little more than a satirical squib, but it shows that Sterne was familiar with the works of Jonathan Swift. In its use of clothes symbolism as well as in its severity it recalls *A Tale of a Tub* (1704), and it shows that Swift's work was running in Sterne's head between 1758 and 1759. He was making other use of Swift, too. On May 23, 1759, Sterne wrote to Robert Dodsley, "With this You will receive the Life & Opinions of *Tristram Shandy*, which I choose to offer to You first." By this time, the first volume of the novel was finished. Although Dodsley refused the copyright for the 50 pounds Sterne requested, Sterne continued to write, completing a second volume and revising the first to remove "all locality" and make "the whole . . . more saleable," as he wrote to Dodsley several months later.

Salable it was. The York edition sold two hundred copies in two days when it appeared in December, 1759, and when Sterne went up to London, he was told that the book was not "to be had in London either for Love or money." Dodsley, who had been unwilling to risk 50 pounds on the copyright, now purchased it for 250 pounds, gave another 380 pounds to publish the still unwritten Volumes III and IV, and yet another 200 pounds for two volumes of Sterne's sermons. Sterne was honored by the great. Thomas Gray wrote to Thomas Wharton, "Tristram Shandy is still a greater object of admiration, the Man as well as the Book. One is invited to dinner, where he dines, a fortnight beforehand."

In March, 1760, Sterne also succeeded to the curacy of Coxwold, a better position than his earlier one at Sutton. In May, 1760, he therefore settled at Coxwold, renting Shandy Hall from Earl Fauconberg. Here he worked on the next two volumes of *Tristram Shandy*, which he brought to London at the end of the year. In 1761, he repeated this pattern, but he did not return to Yorkshire after delivering the manuscript of Volumes V and VI. Having suffered a tubercular hemorrhage, he set off for the warmer, milder air of France.

There he repeated his earlier triumph in London, and he incidentally acquired materials for Book VII of *Tristram Shandy* and *A Sentimental Journey*. Sterne remained in France for almost two years; when he returned to England, he hastily wrote the next two volumes of *Tristram Shandy*, which appeared in January, 1765. In October of that year, he brought twelve sermons to London rather than more of his novel. After leaving the manuscript with his publisher, he again set off for the Continent; he would combine the adventures of this trip with those of his earlier one in writing *A Sentimental Journey*.

In June, 1766, Sterne was back in Coxwold, where he wrote what proved to be the last installment of *Tristram Shandy*. This he brought with him to London in late December; shortly after his arrival, he met Eliza Draper, the wife of an East India Company clerk twenty years her senior. Though initially unimpressed with her, Sterne was soon madly in love. When Sterne met her, she had already been in England some two years, and she was to return to India less than three months later, yet she was to color Sterne's last year of life. Before she sailed on the *Earl of Chatham* on April 3, 1767, Sterne visited her daily, wrote letters to her, drove with her, exchanged pictures with her. After their separation, Sterne continued his letters; those he wrote between April 13 and the beginning of August, 1767, comprise the *Journal to Eliza*. When he broke off this journal with the words "I am thine—& thine only, & for ever" to begin *A Sentimental Journey*, her spirit haunted that work, too, as the Eliza upon whom Yorick calls.

By December, Sterne had finished the first half of *A Sentimental Journey* and again set off for London and his publisher. On February 27, 1768, *A Sentimental Journey*, Volumes I and II, appeared. Less than a month later, on March 18, Sterne died. He was buried in London on March 22; on June 8, 1769, he was reinterred in the Coxwold churchyard in Yorkshire.

Analysis

Readers may be tempted to see Laurence Sterne's works either as *sui generis* or as eighteenth century sports that had no mate until Marcel Proust and James Joyce. In fact, Sterne was very much a product of his age. His humor owes much to such earlier writers as François Rabelais, Miguel de Cervantes, Michel de Montaigne, Sir Thomas Browne, and Jonathan Swift, all of whom influenced his experimentation with the form of the newly emerged novel. Even this experimentation is typical of the age. Thomas Amory's *The Life and Opinions of John Buncle Esquire* (1756-1766) may have suggested to Sterne his complete title *The Life and Opinions of Tristram Shandy, Gent.* Like *Tristram Shandy*, Amory's book is full of digressions, and its narrator is conceited.

Sterne's experimentation did go beyond the traditional; one need look no farther than the typography, the varying length of the chapters in *Tristram Shandy*—from four lines to sixty pages—or the unusual location of certain conventional elements—for example, the placing of *Tristram Shandy's* Preface after the twentieth chapter of Book III or Yorick's writing the Preface to *A Sentimental Journey* after Chapter Six. At the same time, Sterne relied on the conventions of the novel. He is meticulous in his descriptions of clothing, furniture, and gesture. His characters are fully developed: they walk, sometimes with a limp, they cough, they bleed, they dance. From Swift, Daniel Defoe, and Samuel Richardson, Sterne took the first-person narrator. From Richardson, he adopted the technique of writing to the moment; from Henry Fielding, he got the idea of the novel as a comic epic in prose. From numerous sources—Rabelais, Cervantes, and Swift, to name but three—he learned of the satiric potential of the genre.

A Political Romance reveals Sterne's powerful satiric abilities, but this work has little in common with the novels. True, the personal satire of the pamphlet does persist. Sterne lampoons Dr. Burton (Dr. Slop), Dr. Richard Meade (Dr. Kunastrokius), and Francis Topham (Phutatorius, Didius) in *Tristram Shandy*; Tobias Smollett (Smeldungus) and Samuel Sharp (Mundungus) in *A Sentimental Journey*. For the most part, though, Sterne is after bigger game. As he wrote to Robert Dodsley, the satire is general; and, as he wrote to Robert Foley some years later, it is "a laughing good tempered Satyr," another distinction between the novels and the pamphlet.

The objects of this general satire are several: system-makers of all types, pedants, lawyers, doctors, conceited authors, prudes, self-deceivers. A common thread uniting all these satiric butts is folly, the folly of believing that life should conform to some preconceived notion, of trying to force facts to fit theories rather than the other way around.

Sterne's insistence on common sense and reason is consistent with the Augustan tradition, which itself is rooted in Anglican beliefs that Sterne emphasized in his sermons as well as in his fiction. Although Sterne's satire is good-tempered, it attacks man's tendency to evil, a tendency noted in Article IX of the Thirty-nine Articles of the Anglican Church. Like his fellow Augustans, Sterne saw this tendency to evil in many spheres. Like them, therefore, he attacked these deviations from the norm as established by religion and reason (which for Sterne are the same), by nature, by tradition, and by authority. The characters in *Tristram Shandy* and Yorick in *A Sentimental Journey* (who is the only sustained character in that work) are laughable because they deviate from the norm and because they refuse to accept their limitations.

Sterne repeatedly reminds the reader of man's finiteness. Thus, death haunts the novels: in *Tristram Shandy*, Toby, Walter, Mrs. Shandy, Yorick,

Trim, and Bobby are all dead, and Tristram is dying. In *A Sentimental Journey*, a resurrected Yorick sees death all around him—a dead monk, dead children, a dead ass, dead lovers. Another, less dramatic symbol of the characters' limitation is their inability to complete what they begin. *Tristram Shandy* and *A Sentimental Journey* remain fragments. Trim never finishes his tale of the King of Bohemia and his seven castles. Walter never finishes the *Tristrapaedia*. Obadiah never goes for yeast. Yorick never finishes the story of the notary. Nor can characters communicate effectively with one another: Walter's wife never appreciates his theories; Toby's hobbyhorse causes him to understand all words in a military sense; Dr. Slop falls asleep in the middle of Trim's reading; Yorick in *A Sentimental Journey* never pauses long enough to develop a lasting friendship.

Death, the prison of the self, the petty and great disappointments of life—these are the stuff of tragedy. Yet, in Sterne's novels they form the basis of comedy, for the emphasis in these novels is not on the tragic event itself but rather on the cause or the reaction. Bobby's death, for example, is nothing to the reader, not only because one never meets Bobby alive but also because one quickly becomes involved in Walter's oration and Trim's hat. In *A Sentimental Journey*, Sterne focuses on Yorick's reaction to Maria rather than on her poignant tale: consequently, one laughs at Yorick instead of crying with Maria. The prison of words that traps the characters is not the result of man's inherent isolation but rather of a comic perversity in refusing to accept the plain meaning of a statement. The tragic is further mitigated by its remoteness. Though Tristram writes to the moment, that moment is long past; Tristram's account is being composed some fifty years after the events he describes, and Yorick, too, is recollecting emotions in tranquility. The curious order of *Tristram Shandy* and the rapid pace of *A Sentimental Journey* further dilute the tragic. Yorick dies in Book I but cracks the last joke in Book IX. Yorick has barely begun a sentimental attachment with a *fille de chambre* in Paris when he must set off for Versailles to seek a passport. Though the disappointments, interruptions, failures, and deaths recur, individually they quickly vanish from view. What remains are the characters, who are comic because they refuse to learn from their failures.

Sterne's world is therefore not tragic; neither is it absurd. In the world of the absurd, helpless characters confront a meaningless and chaotic world. For Sterne, the world is reasonable; he shares the Augustan world view expressed so well by Alexander Pope: "All Nature is but Art, unknown to thee,/ All Chance Direction which thou canst not see." The reasonableness of the world is not, however, to be found in the systematizing of Walter Shandy or the sentimentalism of Yorick. People can live in harmony with the world, Sterne says, only if they use common sense. The comedy of these novels derives in large part from people's failure or laziness to be sensible.

In *Aspects of the Novel* (1927), E. M. Forster writes: "Obviously a god is hidden in *Tristram Shandy* and his name is Muddle." There is no question that the muddle is present in the novel. Chapters Eighteen and Nineteen of Book IX appear as part of Chapter Twenty-five. The Preface does not appear until the third volume. There are black, marbled, and white pages. In Book IV, a chapter is torn out and ten pages dropped. Uncle Toby begins knocking the ashes out of his pipe in Book I, Chapter Twenty-one, and finishes this simple action in Book II, Chapter Six. The novel begins in 1718 and ends, if it may be said to end, in 1713. Although called *The Life and Opinions of Tristram Shandy, Gent.*, the novel recounts the life of Uncle Toby and the opinions of Walter Shandy.

One must distinguish, though, between the muddle that the narrator, Tristram, creates, and the ordered universe which Sterne offers. Theodore Baird has demonstrated that one can construct an orderly sequence of events from the information in *Tristram Shandy*, beginning with the reign of Henry VIII (III,xxxiii) through the wounding of Trim in 1693 (VIII,xix; II,v), the siege of Namur at which Toby is wounded in 1695 (I,xxv), the conception and birth of Tristram Shandy in 1718 (I-III), the death of Bobby (1719; IV,xxxii and v,ii), the episode of Toby and the fly (1728; II,xii), the death of Yorick (1748; I,xii), and the composition of the novel (1759-1766). Tristram does attempt to impose some order upon these events; the first five and a half books trace his life from his conception to his accident with the window sash and his being put into breeches. He then breaks off to recount the amours of Uncle Toby, which again appear essentially in sequence, with the major exception of Book VII, Tristram's flight into France.

Although Tristram attempts to order these events, he fails. He fails not because life is inherently random or absurd, but because he is a bad artist. He pointedly rejects the advice of Horace, whose *Ars Poetica* (13-8 B.C., *The Art of Poetry*) was highly respected among eighteenth century writers. He will not pause to check facts and even refuses to look back in his own book to see whether he has already mentioned something; this is writing to the moment with a vengeance. He refuses to impose any order at all upon his material, allowing his pen to govern him instead of acting the part of the good writer who governs his pen.

In governing his pen, the good writer carefully selects his material. Many a man has told a plain, unvarnished tale in less space than Tristram, but Tristram cannot decide what is important. Must one know what Mrs. Shandy said to Walter on the night of Tristram's begetting, which, incidentally, may not be the night of Tristram's begetting at all, since the night described is only eight months before Tristram's birth rather than nine—does Tristram realize this fact? Does one need so vivid an account of how Walter falls across the bed upon learning of Tristram's crushed nose? Is it true that one cannot understand Toby's statement, "I think it would not be amiss brother, if we rung the bell," without being dragged halfway across Europe and twenty-three years back in time? Such details serve the purpose of Tristram's creator by highlighting the follies of a bad writer, but they hardly help Tristram proceed with his story.

Tristram's failure to select his material derives in part from laziness. "I have a strong propensity in me to begin this chapter very nonsensically, and I will not balk my fancy," he writes (I,xxiii), for it requires intellectual effort to balk a fancy. In part, too, this failure to select reflects Tristram's belief that everything concerning himself is important. His is a solipsistic rendering of the humanist's credo, "*Homo sum, humani nihil a me alienum puto*"—I am a man, and nothing that relates to man can be foreign to me. He is confident that the more the reader associates with him, the fonder he (the reader) will become. Hence, the reader will want to know about his failure with Jenny, about his aunt Dinah's affair with the coachman, about his attire as he writes, about his casting a fair instead of a foul copy of his manuscript into the fire. Tristram sets out to write a traditional biography, beginning with a genealogy and proceeding to birth, education, youthful deeds that foreshadow later achievements, marriage, children, accomplishments, death, and burial. He becomes so bogged down in details, however, that he cannot get beyond his fifth year. The episode of Toby and the fly must substitute for a volume on education, and the setting up of his top replaces an account of his youthful deeds.

Although Tristram refuses to impose any system on his writing, he is a true son of Walter Shandy in his willingness to impose systems on other aspects of his world. He devises a scale for measuring pleasure and pain, so that if the death of Bobby rates a five and Walter's pleasure at delivering an oration on the occasion rates a ten, Walter proves the gainer by this catastrophe. Tristram has another scale for measuring his own writing; he awards himself a nineteen out of twenty for the design of the novel. Tristram attaches much significance to the way he is conceived, believing that one's conception determines his entire life. His declared method of describing character is similarly reductive, focusing strictly on the individual's hobbyhorse. He has a theory on knots, on window-sashes, and on the effect of diet on writing. Tristram thus serves as a satire on systematizers as well as on bad writers.

The more obvious butt of Sterne's satire on system-makers is Walter Shandy. The Augustan Age has also been called the Age of Reason, and Sterne recognizes the importance of reason. At the same time, the Augustans recognized that a person's reason alone is often an insufficient guide because it can be corrupted by a ruling passion, as Yorick's sermon in *Tristram Shandy* reveals. Tristram fails as an author because he trusts exclusively to his own logic instead of following conventional guidelines. Walter Shandy is another example of one who becomes foolish because of his reliance on his own reason. Like Pope's dunces, Walter is well read, and like Pope's dunces, he fails to benefit from his learning because he does not use common sense. He will look in the Institutes of Justinian instead of the more obvious, and more reliable, catechism—part of Sterne's joke here is that the source Walter cites does not contain what he wants. Walter will consult Rubenius rather than a tailor to determine of what cloth Tristram's breeches should be made. From his reading and reasoning he develops a host of theories: that Caesarian birth is the best way of bringing a child into the world, that Christian names determine one's life, that auxiliary verbs provide a key to knowledge. Each of these theories rests on a certain logic. Walter is correct that no one would name his child Judas. From this true observation, though, he erects a most absurd theory, proving Tristram's statement that "when a man gives himself up to the government of a ruling passion,—or, in other words, when his Hobby-Horse grows headstrong,—farewell cool reason and fair discretion" (II,v). Neither Walter nor his son will rein in his hobbyhorse, and, as a result, they become ridiculous.

They may also become dangerous. While Walter is busily engaged in composing his *Tristrapaedia* that will codify his theories of child rearing, Tristram grows up without any guidance at all. Walter is willing, indeed eager, to have his wife undergo a Caesarian operation because he believes that such an operation will be less harmful to the infant than natural childbirth. That such an operation will cause the death of Mrs. Shandy is a fact that apparently escapes him.

Even the benign and lovable Uncle Toby makes himself ridiculous by yielding to his hobbyhorse. Not only does this hobbyhorse lead him into excessive expense and so deprive him of money he might put to better use, but also it keeps his mind from more worthwhile occupations. Repeatedly, Sterne, through Tristram, likens Toby's garden battlefield to a mistress with whom Toby dallies; the Elizabethan sense of hobbyhorse is precisely this—a woman of easy virtue. As Tristram notes early in the novel, when "one . . . whose principles and conduct are as generous and noble as his blood" is carried off by his hobbyhorse, it is better that "the Hobby-Horse, with all his fraternity, (were) at the Devil" (I,viii). Deluding himself that he is somehow contributing to the defense of England, Toby blinds himself to the real horrors of war. Wrapped up in his military jargon, he isolates himself verbally from those around him; a bridge or a train has only one meaning for him. No less than Tristram, he is betrayed by words, but in his case as in Tristram's the fault lies not with the words but with the individual betrayed.

Nor is Toby's hobbyhorse dangerous to himself alone. It keeps him away from the Widow Wadman and so prevents his fulfilling his legitimate social responsibilities of marrying and begetting children; his hobbyhorse renders him sterile even if his wound has not. This hobbyhorse also comes close to rendering Tristram sterile, for Trim removes the weights from the window sash to make cannon for Toby's campaigns.

Each of the major characters is trapped in a cell of his own making. Tristram can never finish his book because his theory of composition raises insurmountable obstacles. The more he writes, the more he has to write. Walter's and Toby's hobbyhorses blind them to reality and prevent their communicating with each other or anyone else. The Shandy family is well named; "shandy" in Yorkshire means crackbrained. Significantly, the novel begins with an interrupted act of procreation and ends with sterility. As in Pope's *The Dunciad* (1728-1743), the uncreating word triumphs because of human folly.

Sterne's vision is not quite as dark as Pope's, though; the novel ends not with universal darkness but with a joke. Yorick, the voice of reason and moderation, remains to pull the reader back to reality. Yorick is a jester, and the role of the jester is to remind his audience of the just proportion of things as well as to make them laugh. Yorick does not put a fancy saddle on a horse that does not deserve one. He will destroy a sermon because it is too bad (unlike Tristram, who destroys a chapter because it is too good). He makes only modest claims for his sermons and is embarrassed even by these (unlike Tristram, who repeatedly proclaims himeslf a genius). Yorick thus offers in word and deed an example of living reasonably and happily.

Sterne offers a second consolation as well. Even though characters isolate themselves with their hobbyhorses, even though they cannot or will not understand one another's words, they can and do appreciate one another's feelings. These emotional unions are short-lived, but they are intense and sincere. Walter will continue to make fun of Toby even after promising not to, but at the moment the promise is made, the two are united spiritually and physically. Tristram and Jenny quarrel, but they also have their tender moments. Trim looks for a carriage in a book by shaking the leaves, and he mistakes fiction for reality in a sermon, but he allows his parents three halfpence a day out of his pay when they grow old. The benevolence that Sterne urged in his sermons is capable of bridging self-imposed isolation. Though one laughs at the characters in *Tristram Shandy*, one therefore sympathizes with them as well; one sees their weaknesses but also their underlying virtue. Though they have corrupted that virtue by yielding to a natural tendency to evil, they redeem themselves through their equally natural tendency to kindness.

Tristram Shandy offended many contemporary readers because of its bawdy tales; reviewers much preferred such seemingly sentimental episodes as the death of Le Fever and urged Sterne to refine his humor. *A Sentimental Journey* superficially appears to have been written to satisfy these demands. It is full of touching scenes, of tears, of charity, of little acts of kindness. Moreover, in a letter to Mrs. William James in November, 1767, Sterne describes the novel as dealing with "the gentle passions and affections" and says his intention is "to teach us to love the world and our fellow creatures better than we do." Sterne's letters, and especially his *Journal to Eliza*, reveal him as a man of feeling, and *Tristram Shandy* satirizes all aspects of human life except for benevolence. Sterne's sermons reinforce his image as a believer in the importance of charity. As a Latitudinarian, he believed that the Golden Rule constitutes the essence of religion, that ritual and church doctrine, while important, are less significant than kindness. Since Yorick in *Tristram Shandy* is Sterne's spokesman, it is tempting to see Yorick in *A Sentimental Journey* as having the same normative function. Though the narrator of *Tristram Shandy* is a dunce and a satiric butt, can one not still trust the narrator of *A Sentimental Journey*?

No. In a famous letter to Dr. John Eustace, Sterne thanks Eustace for the gift of a curious walking stick: "Your walking stick is in no sense more shandaic than in that of its having *more handles than one.*" Readers could regard *Tristram Shandy* as total nonsense, as a collection of bawdy stories, as a realistic novel, as a satire on the realistic novel, or as a satire on the follies of mankind. Sterne's second novel, too, is "shandaic." The reader can see it as a tribute to the popular spirit of sentimentality, or he can view it as a satire of that spirit. Yet a careful reading of the book will demonstrate why Sterne wrote to the mysterious "Hannah" that this novel "shall make you cry as much as ever it made me laugh." In other words, Sterne is sporting with rather than adopting the sentimental mode.

The object of Sterne's laughter is Yorick. The Yorick who recounts his travels is not the same normative parson as appears in *Tristram Shandy*. He is by now twice dead—dead in William Shakespeare's *Hamlet* (1600-1601) and dead again in *Tristram Shandy* some fifteen years prior to the events of *A Sentimental Journey*. This second resurrection may itself be a joke on the reader, who should recall Yorick's death in Book I of the earlier novel.

This revived Yorick bears a great similarity to Tristram. He is, for one thing, a systematizer. He establishes three degrees of curses; he discovers "three epochas in the empire of a French woman" ("Paris"); he is able to create dialogues out of silence; he derives national character not from "important matters of state" but rather from "nonsensical minutiae" ("The Wig— Paris"). Like Tristram, too, Yorick is vain. He gives a sou to a beggar who calls him "My Lord *Anglois*" and another sou for "*Mon cher et très charitable Monsieur.*" He does not worry about being unkind to a monk but is concerned that as a result a pretty woman will think ill of him.

Even his style, though less difficult to follow than Tristram's, bears some similarities to that of Sterne's earlier narrator. In the midst of the account of his adventures in Versailles, Yorick introduces the irrelevant anecdote of Bevoriskius and the mating sparrows, thus combining Tristram's habit of digressing with Walter's love of abstruse learning. Yorick later interpolates an account of the Marquis d'E****, and while telling about Paris he presents a "Fragment" that does nothing to advance the story. Like Tristram, too, Yorick cannot finish his account, breaking off in mid-sentence. Apparently, he is more governed by his pen than governing.

Yorick also reminds the reader of the narrator in Swift's *A Tale of a Tub*, who believes that happiness is the state of being well deceived. Yorick is disappointed to learn that his small present to Le Fleur has been sufficient only to allow his servant to buy used clothes: "I would rather have imposed upon my fancy with thinking I had bought them new for the fellow, than that they had come out of the *Rue de friperie*" (Le Dimanche—Paris"). Instead of inquiring about the history of the lady at Calais, he invents a pleasant account of her until he gets "ground enough for the situation which pleased me" ("In the Street—Calais"). He deceives himself into believing that he is accompanying a pretty *fille de chambre* as far as possible to protect her when actually he wants her company. Even his benevolence is self-deception. He conjures up images to weep over—a swain with a dying lamb, a man in the Bastille, an imaginary recipient of charity. When in this last instance he confronts the reality, his behavior is hardly benevolent, though.

Sterne is not satirizing benevolence as such. In his sermons "The Vindication of Human Nature" and "Philanthropy Recommended" he rejects the notion that man is inherently selfish and stresses his belief in man's natural benevolence. Yet he had to look no farther than his own nose to discover that benevolence can become a hobbyhorse that can carry a person away from the path of reason. Yorick's hobbyhorse of benevolence is no less dangerous than Uncle Toby's or Walter Shandy's. Yorick will weep over a carriage, over a dead ass, over a caged starling. He admits that he does not even need an object for his sympathy: "Was I in a desert, I would find out wherewith in it to call forth my affection" ("In the Street—Calais"). Real human misery, however, he cannot understand. He can weep over his imagined prisoner in the Bastille, but he cannot imagine the real suffering there. He can be callous to the poor, but never to a pretty young woman.

Yorick's benevolence is thus a compound of self-deception and lust. He will give no money to the poor monk until he wants to impress a pretty woman. He gives a sou to a beggar with a dislocated hip, but he gives an unsolicited crown to a pretty *fille de chambre*, and he gives three *louis d'or* to a pretty grisette. He imagines that in offering to share his chaise with another pretty young lady, he is fighting off "every dirty passion" such as avarice, pride, meanness, and hypocrisy. Actually, he is yielding to desire.

True benevolence is guided by reason, and it is not a thing of the moment only, as Sterne points out in his sermon on the Good Samaritan. Yorick's benevolence is impulsive and short-lived. The cry of a caged starling moves him greatly: "I never had my affections more tenderly awakened," he says ("The Passport—The Hotel at Paris"). The hyperbole of the language is itself a warning of Yorick's inability to temper emotion with reason. After such a reaction, his attitude changes abruptly; Yorick buys the starling but never frees it. After tiring of it, he gives it away to another as callous as himself. At Namport, he mourns for a dead ass and praises its owner for his kindness, adding, "Shame on the world! . . . Did we love each other, as this poor soul but loved his ass—'twould be something" ("Namport—The Dead Ass"). By the next page, Yorick is sending his postillion to the devil. Yorick goes out of his way to find the mad Maria, whom Sterne had introduced in Book VII of *Tristram Shandy*. He weeps with Maria at Moulines; she makes such an impression on him that her image follows him almost to Lyon—an entire chapter!

Yorick is humorous because, like Tristram, Walter, and Toby, he is the victim of his hobbyhorse. He gallops away from reason, failing to examine his motivation or to temper his sudden fanciful flights. In "Temporal Advantages of Religion," Sterne provides a picture of the ideal Christian traveler. "We may surely be allowed to amuse ourselves with the natural or artificial beauties of the country we are passing through," Sterne notes, but he warns against being drawn aside, as Yorick is, "by the variety of prospects, edifices, and ruins which solicit us." More important, Yorick forgets the chief end of man's earthly sojourn: "Various as our excursions are—that we have still set our faces towards Jerusalem . . . and that the way to get there is not so much to please our hearts, as to improve them in virtue." Yorick has come to France for knowledge, but he learns nothing. His benevolence is much closer to wantonness than to virtue; it is fitting that he ends his account in the dark, grasping the *fille de chambre*'s end of Volume II.

In *A Sentimental Journey*, as in *Tristram Shandy*, Sterne mocks excess. He shows the folly that results from the abdication of reason. Though he introduces norms such as Yorick in *Tristram Shandy* or the old soldier in *A Sentimental Journey*, the ideal emerges most clearly from a depiction of its opposite—perverted learning, bad writing, unexamined motives. When Sterne came to London in 1760, Lord Bathurst embraced him as the heir to the Augustan satirists; Lord Bathurst was right.

Major publications other than long fiction
NONFICTION: *A Political Romance*, 1759; *Letters from Yorick to Eliza*, 1773; *Sterne's Letters to His Friends on Various Occasions*, 1775; *Letters of the Late Rev. Mr. Sterne to His Most Intimate Friends*, 1775 (3 volumes); *In Elegant Epistles*, 1790; *Journal to Eliza*, 1904.

RELIGIOUS WRITINGS: *The Sermons of Mr. Yorick*, 1760, 1766 (Vols. I-IV); *Sermons by the Late Rev. Mr. Sterne*, 1769 (Vols. V-VII).

Bibliography
Cash, Arthur Hill. *Sterne's Comedy of Moral Sentiments: The Ethical Dimension of the Journey*, 1965.
Cross, Wilbur Lucius. *The Life and Times of Laurence Sterne*, 1929.
Dilworth, Ernest Nevin. *The Unsentimental Journey of Laurence Sterne*, 1948.
Farrell, William J. "Nature Versus Art as a Comic Pattern in *Tristram*

Shandy," in *English Literary History*. XXX (1963), pp. 16-35.

Hartley, Lodwick. *Laurence Sterne in the Twentieth Century: An Essay and a Bibliography of Sternean Studies, 1900-1965*, 1966.

_____ . *This Is Lorence*, 1943.

New, Melvin. *Laurence Sterne as Satirist: A Reading of Tristram Shandy*, 1970.

Putney, Rufus D. "The Evolution of *A Sentimental Journey*," in *Philological Quarterly*. XIX (1940), pp. 349-369.

_____ . "Laurence Sterne: Apostle of Laughter," in *The Age of Johnson: Essays Presented to Chauncey Brewster Tinker*, 1949. Edited by Frederick W. Hilles.

Joseph Rosenblum

ROBERT LOUIS STEVENSON

Born: Edinburgh, Scotland; November 13, 1850
Died: Apia, Samoa; December 3, 1894

Principal long fiction

Treasure Island, 1883; *Prince Otto*, 1885; *The Strange Case of Dr. Jekyll and Mr. Hyde*, 1886; *Kidnapped*, 1886; *The Black Arrow*, 1888; *The Master of Ballantrae*, 1888; *The Wrong Box*, 1889; *The Wrecker*, 1892 (with Lloyd Osbourne); *Catriona*, 1893; *The Ebb-Tide*, 1894 (with Lloyd Osbourne); *Weir of Hermiston*, 1896 (unfinished); *St. Ives*, 1897 (completed by Arthur Quiller-Couch).

Other literary forms

In addition to his novels, Robert Louis Stevenson published a large number of essays, poems, and short stories, most of which have been collected under various titles. The best edition of Stevenson's works is the South Seas Edition (32 volumes) published by Scribner's in 1925.

Achievements

A man thoroughly devoted to his art, Stevenson was highly regarded during his lifetime as a writer of romantic fiction. Indeed, few, if any, have surpassed him in that genre. Combining a strong intellect and a wide-ranging imagination with his ability to tell a story, he produced novels that transport the reader to the realms of adventure and intrigue. After his death, his literary reputation diminished considerably, until he was regarded primarily as a writer of juvenile fiction, unworthy of serious critical attention. With the growth of scholarly interest in popular literature, however, Stevenson is sure to enjoy a revaluation. Certainly his narrative skill speaks for itself, and it is on that base that his literary reputation should ultimately rest. Anyone who has vicariously sailed with Jim Hawkins in quest of buried treasure or sipped a potion that reduces intellect to instinct with Henry Jekyll can vouch for the success of Stevenson as a writer and agree with what he wrote in "A Gossip of Romance" (1882): "In anything fit to be called reading, the process itself should be absorbing and voluptuous; we should gloat over a book, be rapt clean out of ourselves, and rise from the perusal, our mind filled with the busiest kaleidoscopic dance of images, incapable of sleep or of continuous thought."

Biography

The only child of Thomas and Margaret (Balfour) Stevenson, Robert Louis Stevenson was born on November 13, 1850, in Edinburgh, Scotland. He was in poor health even as a child, and he suffered throughout his life from a tubercular condition. Thomas, a civil engineer and lighthouse keeper, had hopes that Stevenson would eventually follow in his footsteps, and the young-ster was sent to Anstruther and then to Edinburgh University. His fragile health, however, precluded a career in engineering, and he shifted his efforts to the study of law, passing the bar in Edinburgh in 1875.

Even during his preparation for law, Stevenson was more interested in literature, and, reading widely in the essays of Michel de Montaigne, Charles Lamb, and William Hazlitt, he began imitating their styles. Their influence can be seen in the style that Stevenson ultimately developed—a personal, conversational style, marked by an easy familiarity.

Between 1875 and 1879, Stevenson wandered through France, Germany, and Scotland in search of a healthier climate. In 1876, at Fontainebleau, France, he met Fanny Osbourne, an American with whom he fell in love. She returned to California in 1878, and in that same year became seriously ill. Stevenson set out immediately to follow her. Traveling by steerage, he underwent considerable hardships on his journey, hardships that proved det-rimental to his already poor health. In 1880, he married Fanny and settled for a few months in a desolate mining camp in California. After a return to Scotland, the couple journeyed to Davos, Switzerland, for the winter.

Again returning to Scotland in the spring, Stevenson worked on his novel, *Treasure Island*. Moving back and forth between Scotland and Switzerland was not conducive to improved health, and Stevenson decided to stay per-manently in the south of France. Another attack of illness, however, sent him to Bournemouth, England, a health resort, until 1887, during which time he worked assiduously on his writing. In August of that year he sailed for Amer-ica, settling at Saranac Lake in New York's Adirondacks. There he wrote *The Master of Ballantrae* in 1889. He finally settled in the islands of Samoa in the South Seas, a setting that he used for *The Wrecker* and *The Ebb-Tide*. He died there on December 3, 1894, ending a short but productive life.

Analysis

By the time that Robert Louis Stevenson published his first novel, *Treasure Island*, the golden age of Victorianism in England was over. The empire was far-flung and great, but the masses of England had more immediate concerns. The glory of the Union Jack gave small comfort to a working class barely able to keep its head above water. If earlier novelists wrote for the middle-class reader, those of the last twenty years of the century revolted against the cultural domination of that class. Turning to realism, they dealt with the repression caused by a crushing environment. Stevenson, however, disdained moral and intellectual topics, preferring the thin, brisk, sunny atmosphere of romance. Consequently, he stands apart from such figures as Thomas Hardy, Arnold Bennett and George Gissing.

In "A Humble Remonstrance," Stevenson spoke of the function of a writer of romance as being "bound to be occupied, not so much in making stories true as in making them typical; not so much in capturing the lineament of each fact, as in marshalling all of them to a common end." Perhaps, then, Stevenson should be seen not simply as an antirealistic writer of romance, but as a writer whose conception of realism was different from that of his contemporaries.

In his study of Stevenson, Edwin Eigner points out that the novelist's heroes are drawn from real life and are usually failures. Moreover, says Eigner, "very few of the characters, whether good *or* evil, manage even to fail greatly." Stevenson himself wrote in his essay "Reflection and Remarks on Human Life" that "our business in this world is not to succeed, but to continue to fail, in good spirits." His own ill-health may have caused him to see life in terms of conflict, and in his case a conflict that he could not win. This element of failure adds a somber dimension to Stevenson's romances—a note of reality, as it were, to what otherwise might have been simply adventure fiction. It is the element of adventure superimposed on reality that gives Stevenson's writing its peculiar character. A writer's stories, he remarked, "may be nourished with the realities of life, but their true mark is to satisfy the nameless longings of the reader, and to obey the ideal laws of the daydream." In doing this, the writer's greatest challenge, according to Stevenson, is to give "body and blood" to his stories. Setting, circumstance, and character must all fall into place to give a story the power to make an impression on the mind of the reader—"to put the last mark of truth upon a story and fill up at one blow our capacity for sympathetic pleasure." In this way a story becomes more than merely literature; it becomes art.

Stevenson regarded the tales of the *Arabian Nights* as perfect examples of the storyteller's art: tales that could captivate the reader in his childhood and delight him in his old age. Such was the goal that he sought in his own works: to bring the reader to the story as an involved spectator, who does not shy away from the unpleasantries or the villainy, but finds in witnessing them the same pleasure he does in witnessing the more optimistic and uplifting aspects of the piece. Perhaps this is Stevenson's greatest achievement: he illustrates with his stories a sometimes forgotten truth—"Fiction is to the grown man what play is to the child."

"If this don't fetch the kids, why, they have gone rotten since my day," Stevenson wrote in a letter to Sidney Colvin on August 25, 1881. He was speaking of *Treasure Island*, the novel on which he was then at work. He need not have worried, for since its publication it has been a favorite of children everywhere—and, indeed, of many adults. Stevenson wrote the book, according to his own account, in two bursts of creative activity of about fifteen days each. "My quickest piece of work," he said. The novel was begun as an amusement for his stepson Lloyd Osbourne, then twelve years old. Upon its completion in November of 1881, the novel was serialized in the magazine *Young Folks*; since it did not raise circulation to any degree, it was not considered particularly successful. The book was an altogether different story.

As a tale of adventure, *Treasure Island* stands as one of the best. Buried treasure has always had an aura of mystery and intrigue about it, and this case is no exception. Young Jim Hawkins is the hero of the novel; the adventure starts when Bill Bones, an old seaman, comes to Jim's father's inn, the Admiral Benbow, to wait for a one-legged seaman, who does not arrive. Bones does have two other visitors: a seaman named Black Dog, whom he chases away after a fight, and a deformed blind man named Pew, who gives him the black spot, the pirates' death notice. Bones is so frightened that he dies of a stroke. In the meantime, Jim's father has also died, leaving Jim and his mother alone. Opening Bones's locker, they find an oilskin packet that Jim gives to Squire Trelawney and Dr. Livesey.

Finding in the packet a treasure map, Trelawney and Livesey decide to outfit a ship and seek the treasure. Jim is invited to come along as cabin boy. Just before they sight the island where the treasure is supposed to be, Jim overhears the ship's cook, the one-legged Long John Silver, and some of the crew plotting a mutiny. When Silver and a party are sent ashore, Jim smuggles himself along to spy on them.

When Trelawny and Livesey learn of Silver's duplicity, they decide to take the loyal crew members and occupy a stockade they have discovered on the island, leaving the ship to the pirates. Unable to take the stockade, Silver offers a safe passage home to its defenders in return for the treasure map. The offer is refused, and, after another attack, the party in the stockade is reduced to Trelawney, Livesey, Captain Smollett, and Jim. Jim rows to the ship, shoots the only pirate on board and then beaches the ship. Returning to the stockade, he finds his friends gone and Silver and the pirates in control. Silver saves Jim's life from the other pirates and reveals the treasure map, which Dr. Livesey had given him secretly when the former had come to treat some of the wounded pirates. What Silver does not know is that Ben Gunn, the lone resident of the island, has already found the treasure and moved it to his own quarters. When the pirates find no treasure, they turn on Jim and Silver, but Gunn and Jim's friends arrive in time to rescue them. The ship is floated by the tide, and Jim, his friends, and Silver leave the island. Silver jumps ship with only a bag of coins for his efforts, but the rest of the group divide the treasure. "Drink and the devil had done for the rest."

Though Jim may be the hero of the novel, it is Long John Silver who dominates the book. He is an ambiguous character, capable of murder, greed, and double-dealing on the one hand and magnanimity on the other. He was Stevenson's favorite character—and the one who ultimately raises the book from a pedestrian adventure story to a timeless, mythically resonant tale which has absorbed generations of readers. The unifying theme of *Treasure Island* is man's desire for wealth. Trelawney and Livesey may be more moral in society's eyes than Silver, but their motivation is certainly no higher. As for Jim, he cannot, like Silver, give a belly laugh in the face of such a world and go off seeking another adventure. One such adventure is enough for Jim, and that one he would rather forget.

Serialized in *Young Folks* in 1883, *The Black Arrow* was labeled by Stevenson as "tushery," a term he and William Henley used for romantic adventures written for the market. In a letter to Henley in May, 1883, he said, "Ay, friend, a whole tale of tushery. And every tusher tushes me so free, that may I be tushed if the whole thing is worth a tush." Stevenson had hopes, however, that *The Black Arrow* would strike a more receptive note in *Young Folks* than did *Treasure Island*, and in this respect, his hopes were realized.

Though it lacks the depth of *Treasure Island*, *The Black Arrow* was enormously popular in its time and does not deserve its critical neglect. Set in the fifteenth century against the background of a minor battle of the Wars of the Roses and the appearance of the infamous Richard, Duke of Gloucester, the story recounts the adventures of Dick Shelton as he attempts to outwit his scheming guardian, Sir Daniel Brackley. An unscrupulous man, Sir Daniel has fought first on one side of the war and then on the other, adding to his own lands by securing the wardships of children orphaned by the war.

Planning to marry Dick to Joanna Sedley, an orphaned heiress, Sir Daniel has ridden away to take charge of the girl. In his absence, Moat House, his estate, is attacked by a group of outlaws led by a man with the mysterious name of John Amend-All, who pins a message to the church door of Moat House swearing vengeance on Sir Daniel and others for killing Dick's father, Henry Shelton.

Dick, deciding to remain quiet until he can learn more of the matter, sets out to inform Sir Daniel of the attack. In the meantime, Joanna, dressed as a boy, has eluded Sir Daniel. On his way back to Moat House, Dick meets Joanna in the guise of "John Matcham." Unaware that Sir Daniel has planned the marriage and unaware that John is Joanna, Dick offers to help his companion reach the abbey at Holywood. They eventually arrive at Moat House, where Dick learns that John is really Joanna and that his own life is in danger. He escapes and, after a lengthy series of intrigues and adventures, saves the life of Richard of York, Duke of Gloucester, and rescues Joanna from Sir Daniel, who is killed by Ellis Duckworth (John Amend-All). Dick then marries Joanna and settles at Moat House.

As an adventure story, *The Black Arrow* is thoroughly sucessful. The movement from episode to episode is swift, and the reader has little opportunity to lose interest. The love story between Dick and Joanna is deftly handled, with Joanna herself a delightfully drawn character. Still, the novel does not venture beyond the realm of pure adventure. Like many adventure stories, it is often contrived and trivial, but this fact does not detract from its readability.

Stories and theories abound regarding the writing of *The Strange Case of Dr. Jekyll and Mr. Hyde*. In "A Chapter of Dreams" (1888), Stevenson himself gave an account of the composition of the novel, explaining that "for two days I went about racking my brain for a plot of any sort; and on the second night I dreamed the scene at the window; and a scene afterwards split in two, in which Hyde, pursued for some crime, took the powder and underwent the change in the presence of his pursuers. All the rest was made awake, and consciously." The whole, according to Stevenson, was written and revised within a ten-week period.

The novel is based on the idea of the double personality in every man, an idea with which Stevenson had long been concerned. Referring to Jekyll, he said to Will H. Low, a painter, that "I believe you will find he is quite willing to answer to the name of Low or Stevenson." Not the first to use the idea in literature, Stevenson does give it a different twist. Hyde is not the double of the sinner, a conscience as it were; but, as one reviewer put it, Hyde is a personality of "hideous caprices, and appalling vitality, a terrible power of growth and increase."

As the story opens, Richard Enfield and Mr. Utterson, a lawyer, are discussing the activities of a Mr. Hyde, who has recently trampled down a small child. Both friends of Dr. Henry Jekyll, they are perturbed that the latter has named Hyde as heir in his will. A year later, Hyde is wanted for a murder, but he escapes. Soon after, Dr. Jekyll's servant Poole tells Utterson of strange goings on in his employer's laboratory. He is concerned that possibly Jekyll has been slain. Poole and Utterson break into the laboratory and find a man dead from poison. The man is Edward Hyde. A note in the laboratory contains Jekyll's confession of his double identity.

Early in life, he had begun leading a double existence: a public life of convention and gentility and a private life of unrestrained vice. Finally, he discovered a potion that transformed him physically into Edward Hyde, his evil self. Though Jekyll wanted desperately to be rid of Hyde, he was not strong enough to overcome his evil side. He finally closed himself in his laboratory, seeking a drug that would eliminate Hyde. Failing in his search, he committed suicide.

As an exploration into the darkest recesses of the human mind, *The Strange Case of Dr. Jekyll and Mr. Hyde* is skillfully constructed. Not only are Jekyll and Hyde presented in a haunting fashion, but Utterson also is a character brought clearly to life. The plot, sensational though it is, does not rely on the standard Gothic claptrap to hold the reader. On the contrary, the story is subtly undertold, and the reader is drawn into the horror of it by Stevenson's penetrating imagination and his easy mastery of language and style. The reader, said one reviewer, "feels that the same material might have been spun out to cover double the space and still have struck him as condensed and close knit workmanship. It is one of those rare fictions which make[s] one understand the value of temperance in art."

Stevenson completed *Kidnapped* in the spring of 1886, intending it originally as a potboiler, and it surely has all the ingredients of high adventure: a stolen inheritance, a kidnaping, a battle at sea, and several murders. Having gained an interest in Scottish history from his travels through the Highlands, Stevenson used as his principal source of historical information *Trial of James Stewart* (1753), a factual account of the 1752 Appin murder trial.

Kidnapped is the story of David Balfour, whose only inheritance from his father is a letter to Ebenezer Balfour of Shaws, David's uncle. On the way to see Mr. Rankeillor, the family lawyer, to get the true story of the inheritance, David is tricked and sent off on a ship for slavery in the American colonies. He meets Alan Breck, an enemy of the monarch because of his part in a rebellion against King George, and, though David is loyal to the King, the two become fast and true friends. Escaping from the ship, they have numerous adventures, finally returning to Scotland, where David learns the truth of the inheritance. His father and uncle had both loved the same woman; when David's father married the woman (David's mother), he generously gave up his inheritance to his brother Ebenezer. Ebenezer knew that such an arrangement would not hold up legally, and thus he tried to kill David. David accepts Ebenezer's offer of two-thirds of the income from the inheritance, and, with the money, he helps Alan reach safety from the king's soldiers who are pursuing him.

Kidnapped is rich in its depiction of the Scottish Highlands, and the novel's dialogue is particularly effective. The contrast between David, a Lowlander, and a Whig, and Alan, a Highlander and a Jacobite, for example, is well drawn. Ignoring their differences, the two, like Huck and Jim in Mark Twain's *The Adventures of Huckleberry Finn* (1884), prove that their friendship is more important than geographical and political differences.

Whatever Stevenson thought of *Kidnapped*, his friend Edmund Gosse thought it the "best piece of fiction that you have done." Many would argue with Gosse's statement. While it perhaps has more human interest than does *Treasure Island*, it lacks the sharpness and force of Stevenson's masterpiece.

Although not as well known as *Treasure Island* and *Kidnapped*, *The Master of Ballantrae* is considered by many to be Stevenson's best novel. Stevenson himself saw it as a "most seizing tale," a "human tragedy." Despite his preoccupation with character delineation in the story, he still regales the reader with a plethora of adventurous incidents. Set in eighteenth century Scotland, *The Master of Ballantrae* recounts the story of two brothers as they compete for title and love. When Stuart the Pretender returns to Scotland in 1745 to claim the English throne, Lord Durrisdeer decides to send one son to fight with Stuart and to keep one at home, hoping that way to make his estate secure regardless of the outcome of the struggle. James, Master of Ballantrae and his father's heir, joins Stuart, and Henry remains behind. When news of

Stuart's defeat and James's death comes, Henry becomes Master of Ballantrae. He marries Alison Graeme, who had been betrothed to James.

James, however, is not dead, and, after adventures in America and France, returns to Scotland. Goading Henry and pressing his attentions on Alison, James soon angers his brother to the point of a midnight duel. Henry thinks that he has killed James, but again the latter escapes death—this time going to India. He surprises Henry once more by showing up alive at Durrisdeer. Taking his family, Henry secretly leaves for America, but James, with his Indian servant Secundra Dass, follows. Searching for treasure that he buried on his previous trip to America, James falls sick and dies, but Henry, thinking his brother able to return at will from death, goes to the grave one night and sees Secundra Dass performing strange ministrations over James' exhumed body. Although the servant is unable to revive James, Henry believes that he sees his brother's eyes flutter and dies from heart failure. Thus, both Masters of Ballantrae are united in death.

The Master of Ballantrae, perhaps more than any other of Stevenson's novels, goes beyond the bounds of a mere adventure story. Adventure is a key element in the book, but the characters of James and Henry Durie are drawn with such subtlety and insight that the novel takes on dimensions not usually found in Stevenson's works. Like Long John Silver in *Treasure Island*, James Durie is not an ordinary villain. Henry, who moves from a kind of pathetic passivity in the first part of the novel to a villainy of his own, is unable to assume the true role of Master of Ballantrae. Overmatched and possessed by James, he lacks the dash and charm and strength of personality that makes the latter the real Master of Ballantrae. "In James Durie," wrote one reviewer, "Mr. Stevenson has invented a new villain, and has drawn him with a distinction of touch and tone worthy of Vandyke." With all the attributes of a hateful fiend, James nevertheless has a wit and a courage that are captivating.

Perhaps the novel does, as Stevenson himself feared, leave the reader with an impression of unreality. Still, whatever its shortcomings, *The Master of Ballantrae* has all the trademarks of Stevenson's fiction: an intricately and imaginatively designed plot, power of style, clear evocation of scene, and lifelike characters. G. K. Chesterton felt that Stevenson was the "first writer to treat seriously and poetically the aesthetic instincts of the boy." In his own way, Stevenson contributed a fair number of readable and memorable works to the English literary heritage, and that heritage is the richer for it.

Major publications other than long fiction
SHORT FICTION: *The New Arabian Nights*, 1882; *More New Arabian Nights*, 1885; *The Merry Men and Other Tales and Fables*, 1887; *Island Nights' Entertainments*, 1893.
PLAYS: *Deacon Brodie*, 1880; *Macaire*, 1885 (with William Ernest Henley);

The Hanging Judge, 1914 (with Fanny Van de Grift Stevenson).

POETRY: *Moral Emblems*, 1882; *A Child's Garden of Verses*, 1885; *Underwoods*, 1887; *Ballads*, 1890; *Songs of Travel*, 1895.

NONFICTION: *An Inland Voyage*, 1878; *Picturesque Notes on Edinburgh*, 1878; *Travels with a Donkey in the Cevennes*, 1879; *Virginibus Puerisque*, 1881; *Familiar Studies of Men and Books*, 1882; *The Silverado Squatters: Sketches* 1883; *Memories and Portraits*, 1887; *The South Seas: A Record of Three Cruises*, 1890; *Across the Plains*, 1892; *A Footnote to History*, 1892; *Amateur Emigrant*, 1895; *In the South Seas*, 1896.

Bibliography

Balfour, Graham. *The Life of Robert Louis Stevenson*, 1915.
Eigner, Edwin. *Robert Louis Stevenson and Romantic Tradition*, 1966.
Saposnik, Irving. *Robert Louis Stevenson*, 1974.

Wilton Eckley

HARRIET BEECHER STOWE

Born: Litchfield, Connecticut; June 14, 1811
Died: Hartford, Connecticut; July 1, 1896

Principal long fiction

Uncle Tom's Cabin: Or, Life Among the Lowly, 1852; *Dred: A Tale of the Great Dismal Swamp*, 1856; *The Minister's Wooing*, 1859; *Agnes of Sorrento*, 1862; *The Pearl of Orr's Island*, 1862; *Oldtown Folks*, 1869; *Pink and White Tyranny*, 1871; *My Wife and I*, 1871; *We and Our Neighbors*, 1875; *Poganuc People*, 1878.

Other literary forms

In 1843, Harriet Beecher Stowe gathered a number of her sketches and stories into a volume called *The Mayflower: Or, Sketches of Scenes and Characters of the Descendants of the Pilgrims* (1843). For forty years thereafter, she published short fiction and miscellaneous essays in magazines. In *A Key to Uncle Tom's Cabin* (1853), she assembled a mass of sources and analogues for the characters and incidents of her most famous novel. Her 1869 *The Atlantic* article "The True Story of Lady Byron's Life," and a subsequent elaboration, *Lady Byron Vindicated* (1870), caused a sensation at the time. She also published a geography for children (1833, her earliest publication, issued under her sister Catharine's name), poems, travel books, collections of biographical sketches, and a number of other children's books.

Stowe's stories and sketches remain readable. Her best collection, *Sam Lawson's Oldtown Fireside Stories* (1872), differs from the novel *Oldtown Folks* mainly in degree of plotlessness. Selections from Stowe's frequently long and chatty letters can be found in the *Life of Harriet Beecher Stowe* (1889), written by her son Charles Edward Stowe, and in more recent biographies, but hundreds of her letters remain unpublished and scattered in various archives.

Achievements

Known primarily today for her antislavery novel *Uncle Tom's Cabin*, Stowe also interpreted the life of her native New England in a series of novels, stories, and sketches. Along with Ralph Waldo Emerson and Oliver Wendell Holmes, she contributed to the first issue of the *The Atlantic* (November, 1857) and for many years thereafter contributed frequently to that Boston-based magazine. As an alert and intelligent member of a famous family of Protestant ministers, she understood the Puritan conscience and outlook as well as anyone in her time, and as a shrewd observer of the commonplace, she deftly registered Yankee habits of mind and speech. All of her novels feature authentic New England characters; after *Uncle Tom's Cabin* and *Dred*, she turned to settings which included all six New England states. Despite a contradictory idealizing tendency, she pioneered in realism.

One of the first American writers to apply a talent for dialect and local color to the purposes of serious narrative, she exerted a strong influence on Sarah Orne Jewett, Mary Wilkins Freeman, and other regionalists of the later nineteenth century. Without a doubt, however, her greatest achievement was the novel which, beginning as an intended short serial in a Washington antislavery weekly, the *National Era*, forced the American reading public to realize for the first time that slaves were not only a national problem but also people with hopes and aspirations as legitimate as their own. Critics as diverse as Henry Wadsworth Longfellow, Heinrich Heine, William Dean Howells, and Leo Tolstoy in the nineteenth century, and Edmund Wilson and Anthony Burgess in the twentieth, have used superlatives to praise *Uncle Tom's Cabin*.

Biography

When Harriet Elizabeth Beecher was born on June 14, 1811, the seventh child of Lyman and Roxana Beecher, her father's fame as a preacher had spread well beyond the Congregational Church of Litchfield, Connecticut. All seven Beecher sons who lived to maturity became ministers, one becoming more famous than his father. Harriet, after attending Litchfield Academy, a well-regarded school, was sent to the Hartford Female Seminary, which was founded by her sister Catharine—in some respects the substitute mother whom Harriet needed after Roxana died in 1816 but did not discover in the second Mrs. Beecher. In later years, Harriet would consistently idealize motherhood. When Catherine's fiancé, a brilliant young man but one who had not experienced any perceptible religious conversion, died in 1822, the eleven-year-old Harriet felt the tragedy. In 1827, the shy, melancholy girl became a teacher in her sister's school.

In 1832, Lyman Beecher accepted the presidency of Lane Seminary in Cincinnati, Ohio, and soon Catharine and Harriet had established another school there. Four years later, Harriet married a widower named Calvin Stowe, a Lane professor. In the years that followed, she bore seven children. She also became familiar with slavery, as practiced just across the Ohio River in Kentucky; with the abolitionist movement, which boasted several notable champions in Cincinnati, including the future Chief Justice of the United States Supreme Court, Salmon P. Chase; and with the Underground Railroad. As a way of supplementing her husband's small income, she also contributed to local and religious periodicals.

Not until the Stowes moved to Brunswick, Maine, in 1850, however, did she think of writing about slavery. Then, urged by her brother Henry, by then a prominent minister in Brooklyn, New York, and by other family members in the wake of Congress's enactment of the Fugitive Slave Act, and spurred by a vision she experienced at a church service, she began to construct

Uncle Tom's Cabin. Even as a weekly serial in the *National Era*, it attracted much attention, and its publication in 1852 as a book made Stowe an instant celebrity. After that year, from her new base in Andover, Massachusetts, where her husband taught, she twice visited Europe, met Harriet Martineau, John Ruskin, the Brownings, and Lady Byron, among others, and the scope of her fame increased even further.

Stowe wrote another slavery novel, *Dred*, and then turned her literary attention to New England. The drowning of her son Henry, a Dartmouth student, in the summer of 1857, marred for her the successes of these years. In the fall of 1862, infuriated by the lack of British support for the North in the Civil War and skeptical that President Lincoln would fulfill his promise to issue a proclamation of emancipation, Stowe visited Lincoln, who is reported to have greeted her with the words, "So this is the little lady who made this big war." She left Washington satisfied that the president would keep his word.

Following Calvin Stowe's retirement from Andover, the family moved to Hartford, the winters usually being spent in northern Florida. Two of the most sensational scandals of the post-Civil War era involved Stowe, the first arising when she published an imprudent and detailed account of Lord Byron's sins as revealed to her some years earlier by the now deceased widow of the poet, the second being an adultery suit brought against her brother Henry in which Stowe characteristically defended him to the hilt. The Byron affair in particular turned many people against her, although her books continued to be commercial successes throughout the 1870's. The most severe personal abuse ever directed at a respectable nineteenth century woman bothered Stowe far less than another personal tragedy: the alcoholism and eventual disappearance of her son Fred in San Francisco, California, in 1870.

In the last twenty-three years of her life, Stowe became the central attraction of the Hartford neighborhood known as Nook Farm, also the home of Charles Dudley Warner and Mark Twain, the latter moving there in part because of its Beecher connections. Her circle of friends included Annie Fields, wife of *The Atlantic* publisher; George Eliot, with whom she corresponded; and Holmes, always a staunch supporter. In her final years, her mind wandered at times, but she was still writing lucid letters two years before her death on July 1, 1896, at the age of eighty-five.

Analysis

In 1869, after finishing her sixth novel, *Oldtown Folks*, Harriet Beecher Stowe began a correspondence with George Eliot by sending her a copy. Although an international celebrity, Stowe wanted the approval of this younger and less famous woman who had contributed notably to a movement just beginning to be critically recognized: literary realism. Like Stowe, Eliot came from a deeply religious background and had formed a union with an unromantic, bookish, but supportive man. Unlike the American novelist, Eliot had rejected religion for rationalism and romanticism for realism. Had Calvin Stowe's first wife not died, it would have been unthinkable for Harriet Beecher to live with him as Eliot did with George Henry Lewes. In life, the former Miss Beecher cheerfully married the unexciting scholar; in *The Minister's Wooing*, she would not permit her heroine Mary Scudder to marry her scholarly suitor (as Eliot's Dorothea Brooke in *Middlemarch* was permitted to marry hers, Dr. Casaubon).

Stowe's hope, in a measure fulfilled, that Eliot would like *Oldtown Folks* may be taken as signifying her desire to be recognized as a realist, even though her own realism was strongly tinged with the romanticism Eliot had come to despise. The young Harriet Beecher had probably learned something from John Bunyan's *The Pilgrim's Progress* (1678, 1684), but most of her other reading—*The Arabian Nights*, Cotton Mather's *Magnalia Christi Americana* (1702), and the works of Sir Walter Scott and Lord Byron—had little to teach an incipient realist. Nor did American literature in the 1830's, when she began to write, furnish any likely models. As a result, the reader finds in her works a mingling of realistic and romantic elements.

Stowe's settings, particularly the New England ones, ring true. She understood her cultural roots, and she proved able to recollect childhood impressions almost photographically. She possessed a keen ear for dialect and a sharp eye for the idiosyncrasies of people she scarcely seemed to have noticed until they turned up in her writing. She used the novel to probe urgent social issues such as slavery and women's rights. Although she liked nature and worked hard at describing it accurately, she disdained her native region's characteristic transcendental interpretations of it. She displayed the realist's aversion to mystery, mysticism, and the legendizing of history.

On the other hand, the romantic tendencies of Stowe's fiction stand out against its realistic background. Her heroines are invariably saintly, as are certain of her black males such as Uncle Tom and, in *Dred*, Uncle Tiff. Her recalcitrant heroes often undergo rather unconvincing conversions. Occasionally, she introduces a mythic, larger-than-life character such as Dred. In common with most of the generation of American realists who followed her, she never renounced the heroic but sought to demonstrate its presence among humble and common people. Her heroes differ from those of Twain, William Dean Howells, and Henry James, however, in drawing their strength from a firm Christian commitment: Stowe's piety has been something of an impediment to her modern readers.

The looseness of plotting about which Stowe's critics have complained so much derives in large measure from her inability to develop convincing central characters in most of her novels. Four of her last five novels have plural nouns—words such as *neighbors* and *folks* and *people*—in their titles, but even *Uncle Tom's Cabin* is not about Uncle Tom in the sense that Charles

Dickens' *David Copperfield* (1849-1850) or Gustave Flaubert's *Madame Bovary* (1857) is about its title character. In fact, Stowe changed the title of *Dred* for a time to *Nina Gordon*, a more central character but one who dies many chapters from the end. *My Wife and I* and *Oldtown Folks* are narrated by relatively colorless central characters.

One of Stowe's most persistent and indeed remarkable narrative traits also works against her realism on occasions. As she confides at the beginning of Chapter fourty-four of *Dred*, "There's no study in human nature more interesting than the aspects of the same subject in the points of view of different characters." That she periodically allowed this interest to distract her from the task at hand is clear. Although she experimented with different points of view—omniscient, first-person, dramatic, and circulating (the last primarily through the use of the epistolary method)—she worked before the time when novelists such as Joseph Conrad, James Joyce, and William Faulkner developed techniques capable of sustaining this kind of interest. It should be pointed out that Stowe uses the expression "points of view" in the sense of "opinions," and she is more likely to present the conflict of opinions through conversations than through living, breathing embodiments of motivating ideas.

It is as a realist before her time that Stowe is most profitably considered. Even where her realism does not serve a socially critical purpose, as it does in *Uncle Tom's Cabin* and *My Wife and I*, she makes her readers aware of the texture, the complexity, of social life—particularly the conflicts, tensions, and joys of New England community life. Understanding how people grow from their geographic, social, religious, and intellectual roots, she is able to convey the reality of isolated Maine coastal villages and the jaunty postwar Manhattan of aspiring journalists. In her best work, she depicts evil not as the product of Mephistophelean schemers or motiveless brutes but of highminded people incapacitated by a crucial weakness, such as the irresolute Augustine St. Clare of *Uncle Tom's Cabin*, the temporizing Judge Clayton of *Dred*, and the imperceptive Dr. Hopkins of *The Minister's Wooing*.

Uncle Tom's Cabin: Or, Life Among the Lowly, remains one of the most controversial of novels. Extravagantly admired and bitterly detested in the 1850s, it still arouses extreme reactions more than a century later. An early barrage of challenges to its authenticity led Stowe to work furiously at the assembling of *A Key to Uncle Tom's Cabin* the next year. In 262 closely printed, double-columned pages, she impressively documented horrors that verified "the truth of the work." This book unfortunately encouraged the development of an essentially nonliterary mass of criticism, with the result that the novel early gained the reputation of a brilliant piece of propaganda—even President Lincoln supposedly accepting the Civil War as its legacy—but unworthy of serious consideration on artistic grounds.

It did not help the novel's cause that the inevitable later reaction against this enormously popular story coincided with the effort, spearheaded by Henry James, to establish the novel as a form of art rather than as a mere popular entertainment. A writer who strove too singlemindedly for mere verifiability did not merit consideration as an artist. In the same year that *Uncle Tom's Cabin* began appearing serially, Nathaniel Hawthorne—James's chief example of the American artist—prefaced his *The House of the Seven Gables* (1851) with a firm declaration of its imaginary basis which contrasted sharply with his attempt to provide a "historical" one for *The Scarlet Letter* one year earlier. Hawthorne's star as a writer of fiction gradually rose; Stowe's sank. Like "Old Ironsides," the vigorous youthful poem of Stowe's staunch friend of later years, *Uncle Tom's Cabin* was relegated to the status of a work that made things happen—important historically but damned by that very fact to the region of the second-rate.

In *A Key to Uncle Tom's Cabin*, Stowe herself called *Uncle Tom's Cabin* "a very inadequate representation of slavery," but her excuse is significant: "Slavery, in some of its workings, is too dreadful for the purposes of art." She was acknowledging a problem that would continue to bedevil realists for most of the rest of the century. The most prominent spokesman for realism, Howells, agreed with her, and until the 1890's, realists would generally exclude things considered "too dreadful." As late as 1891, Thomas Hardy induced mass revulsion by allowing his heroine to be raped in *Tess of the D'Urbervilles* (1891) while referring to her in his subtitle as "a pure woman."

Stowe sandwiched the story of Uncle Tom, the meek Christian capable of turning the other cheek even to the sadistic Simon Legree, between the resolute George and Eliza Harris' escape from slavery and the Harris family's fortuitous reunion at the end of the novel. If the plot is untidy and contrived, a number of the individual characters and episodes have remained among the most memorable in fiction. The famous scene in which Eliza crosses the Ohio River ice in early spring is "true" not because the feat had been accomplished (although Stowe knew it had) but because she makes the reader feel Eliza's desperation, the absolute necessity of the attempt, and the likelihood that a person who grew up in her hard school would develop the resources to succeed.

The meeting between Miss Ophelia and Topsy illustrates Stowe's talent for dramatizing the confrontation of stubborn viewpoints. Sold down the river by his first owner, Tom has rescued the angelic daughter of Augustine St. Clare and has been installed to the St. Clare household. Miss Ophelia, a Vermont cousin of St. Clare, has been brought south to take care of Eva, whose mother is languidly incompetent. St. Clare despises slavery but feels powerless to resist it; Ophelia's intransigent New England conscience will not permit her to acquiese in it. After listening to a considerable amount of her antislavery rhetoric, St. Clare gives his cousin a little black girl rescued from alcoholic parents. Ophelia is revolted by Topsy, so utterly different from the golden, cherubic Eva. Topsy, shrewd and skeptical beyond her years, embodies the insidiousness of slavery itself. Neither was premeditated but simply "grow'd" and now must somehow be dealt with as found. Ophelia must find room in her heart for the little "black spider" or lose face with her cousin. Her struggle with Topsy—and with her own physical aversion—is fierce and richly comical, and its successful outcome believable.

For the modern reader, the death scenes in the novel are more of a problem. Little Eva's protracted illness and beatific death exactly pleased the taste of Stowe's time. Today, her father's senseless and sudden death as a result of his attempt to mediate a tavern brawl seems more like real life—or would if Stowe had not permitted St. Clare to linger long enough to undergo a deathbed religious conversion. Modern reaction to Stowe's climactic scene is complicated by the hostility of writers such as James Baldwin to the character of Uncle Tom, who, in dying at the hands of Legree's henchmen, wins their souls in the process. Whether or not the conversion of Sambo and Quimbo convinces today's reader, Tom's character has been firmly established, and he dies in precisely the spirit the reader expects.

Far less satisfactory is the subsequent escape of two of Legree's slaves from his clutches. Stowe did nothing beforehand to induce belief in a brutal master who could melt into helpless impassivity at the sight of a lock of his dead mother's hair. Finding it expedient to make Legree superstitious, she established this side of his character belatedly and ineptly, and she failed to understand that her conception of the power of motherhood was not universally shared.

In short, the reader's admiration is interrupted by idealistic and sentimental material that does not support Stowe's goal of depicting life as it was. Nor is this inconsistency surprising. No American had ever written such a novel: realistic in impulse and directed at a current social problem of the greatest magnitude. She had no models and could not, like Twain after her, draw upon experiences as Missourian, journalist, western traveler, and—before he wrote his greatest books—neighbor of Stowe and reader of her work.

Like Twain and Howells after her, Stowe did not banish Romanticism from her novels, but her commitment to realism is clear. Thirty years before Twain boasted of his accomplishments with dialect in *The Adventures of Huckleberry Finn* (1884), and nearly two decades before Bret Harte popularized the concept of local color, Stowe used dialects—not with perfect consistency but not for the conventional purpose of humor either. For the first time in major American fiction, dialect served the purpose of generating a credible environment for a serious narrative. In the process, she changed the perceptions of hundreds of thousands of readers forever.

Within a year, the book had made Stowe internationally known. When, after several years of minor literary activity, she returned to the subject of slavery, events were unfolding that led inexorably to war. Her brother Henry was outraging North and South alike by holding his own mock slave auction in his Brooklyn church. John Brown was launching his personal Civil War in Kansas. In the chamber of the United States Senate, abolitionist Charles Sumner was nearly beaten to death by a Southern colleague. Stowe herself had been busy with antislavery petitions and appeals.

From this context emerged *Dred*, a more somber novel. As it opens, Nina Gordon has returned to her North Carolina plantation from New York upon the death of her father. She has dallied with several suitors but has sense enough to prefer Edward Clayton, an idealistic young lawyer from another part of her native state. After successfully prosecuting a white man who had hired and then physically abused Nina's domestic slave Milly, Clayton's ambition to counteract such abuses legally is checked when an appeals judge—a man of undoubted probity and, ironically, Claytons' own father—reverses the earlier decision on the grounds that no slave has any rights under state law. Meanwhile, Nina's attempt at benign management of her plantation is set back by the appearance of her wastrel brother Tom, who especially enjoys tormenting her able quadroon steward Harry. Although bearing a strong resemblance to George Harris of *Uncle Tom's Cabin*, Harry is different in two important ways. First, Stowe develops the frustration of this educated and sensitive man much more thoroughly. Second, Harry is, unknown to Nina, the Gordon children's half-brother.

When Nina dies in a cholera epidemic, Tom asserts control over the plantation, and Clayton returns home with the resolve to press for changes in a legal code that permits a man to own and mistreat his own brother. Harry is driven to rebel and flee into the nearby swamp, where he falls under the influence of Dred, whom the author styles after the son of the famous black rebel Denmark Vesey, but who resembles even more closely that other noted rebel, Nat Turner.

What happens next exemplifies Stowe's familiarity with the clergy and her talent for controversy. Invited by his uncle to a Presbyterian ministers' conference, Clayton seeks there the moral support for legal reform. Even though he finds one minister passionately committed to rights for slaves, the majority of the brethren turn out to be complacent trimmers, and Clayton learns that he can expect no help in that quarter. Stowe strategically places the conference between two scenes of desperation, both of which illustrate the social system's assault on the family. In the former, Uncle Tiff, the black guardian of two white children whose father is a shiftless squatter on the Gordon plantation, vows to preserve them from the corrupting influence of their slatternly step-mother and takes them to Dred's hidden fastness in the swamp. In the latter, another quadroon Gordon offshoot, Cora, confesses in court to the murder of her own two children to "save" them, as she puts it, from being sold away.

In the swamp, Tiff and the children are succored by Dred, who is one of Stowe's most bizarre creations: half Robin Hood, half self-appointed executioner for the Lord. Too mythic a hero for a realistic novel, Dred unfortunately develops quickly into a very tedious one too, ranting interminably in his guise of Old Testament prophet. Even he is no match, however, for the committed Christian Milly, although she can accomplish no more than the postponement of his planned revenge against the hated whites. When Tom Gordon organizes a party to ransack the swamp for Dred and Harry, the former is killed, and Harry and his wife, along with Tiff and his young charges, escape to the North. In an obviously Pyrrhic victory, Clayton, baffled by his neighbors in his attempt to educate the slaves on his own estate, takes them off to Canada, where they continue to work for him in their freedom.

Tiff is another saintly domestic slave, but he has no power to reclaim any Sambo or Quimbo from degradation. There are no spectacular personal conversions in *Dred* and no hope of any social one. Milly, who has had to endure the loss by death or sale of all her numerous children, seems to win a legal victory over a cruel master and a moral one over the vindictive fugitive Dred, but both turn out to be illusory. Not only the fugitive blacks but also Clayton the hero must leave the country. If *Uncle Tom's Cabin* stands as a warning to a divided society, *Dred* is a prophecy of disintegration.

Stowe's next two novels have much in common. Both *The Minister's Wooing* and *The Pearl of Orr's Island* are anchored in New England coastal communities, and both put Yankee manners and speech on display. Each novel boasts a saintly heroine who effects the conversion of a dashing young man with a strong affinity for the sea. Although the former novel paints Newport, Rhode Island, less colorfully than the latter does coastal Maine, *The Minister's Wooing* is a more carefully constructed novel which analyzes New England character more profoundly.

More than any other Stowe novel, *The Minister's Wooing* focuses on its principals: Samuel Hopkins, Congregationalist minister of Newport, and Mary Scudder, daughter of Hopkins' widowed landlady. In several respects, the minister is the historical Dr. Hopkins, learned protégé of the great Jonathan Edwards, eminent theologian in his own right, and vigorous opponent of slavery in a town consecrated to the slave trade. In the 1780's, when the novel is set, however, the real Hopkins was in his sixties and possessed a wife and eight children; Stowe makes him middle-aged and a bachelor. Another celebrity of the time plays a significant role: Aaron Burr in the years before he became senator, vice-president, and killer of Alexander Hamilton in a duel. Burr is depicted as a charming, unscrupulous seducer of women—a distortion of the historical Burr, no doubt, but one based on the man's reputation.

Stowe's motive for involving these men in her story of pious young Mary Scudder is utterly serious. As friend and student of Edwards, Hopkins represents the stern, uncompromising Puritan past. As Edwards' worldly and skeptical grandson, Burr stands for the repudiation of the past. Mary's choice is not—what would be easy for her—between Hopkins and Burr but between Hopkins and her young lover James Marvyn, who resembles Burr only in his impatience with the hard and incomprehensible doctrines of his forebears. James has grown up with Mary but has gravitated to the sea, and is not quite engaged to her when he is reported lost in a shipwreck. Mrs. Scudder thereafter nudges Mary toward a union with the unexciting minister, himself an admirer of the young lady's ardent—if for his taste too sunny—Christianity.

Stowe neatly balances the claims of Hopkins's exacting Old Testament theology and Mary's simpler faith in the loving kindness of Jesus. In comforting the lost James's mother, long appalled by the minister's remorseless logic and now driven to near-psychosis by her son's supposed death, Mary's cheerful faith receives its first test. She also befriends an aristocratic young Frenchwoman—Burr's intended victim—and learns of the world of adulterous intrigue. As in her previous novels, Stowe introduces a black servant who has looked on life long and maintained a practical Christianity that is proof against all temptation to despair. Having been freed by her master, Mr. Marvyn, under the minister's influence, Candace works freely for the Marvyns and venerates Dr. Hopkins, not failing, however, to draw Mrs. Marvyn gently from "the fathomless mystery of sin and sorrow" to the "deeper mystery of God's love." Meanwhile, Mary's faith deepens, Stowe probably raising more than a few Protestant eyebrows by likening her explicitly to the Virgin Mary, who "kept all things and pondered them in her heart."

In real life, Catharine Beecher's beloved did not survive his shipwreck, and Stowe's elder sister agonized long over the possibility of his having died unregenerate. In life, Henry Stowe did not miraculously escape drowning. James Marvyn, on the other hand, after a considerable interval in which he inexplicably fails to notify either Mary or his family of his survival, returns a week before Mary's scheduled wedding with the minister. After having promised herself to Hopkins, Mary will not of course renege, so it falls to Miss Prissy, her dressmaker and friend, to approach the formidable theologian with the fact—which he is incapable of divining—that James is Mary's true love. Miss Prissy is one of Stowe's well-conceived realistic characters; an incurable gossip and a hypocrite in her professed admiration for the minister's sermons, she is nevertheless willing to assume the unpleasant initiative on behalf of her friend. Apprised of the true situation, the minister releases Mary and promptly marries her to Marvyn.

As she had in her first *The Atlantic* short story, Stowe depicts in this novel the psychology of bereavement; what she refuses to present is not death itself but the possibility of a good-hearted lad's dying unregenerate. She demonstrates how the rigorous faith of a Hopkins can be a barrier, even a poison, to the unstable, but of the efficacy of Christianity to restore lost lambs, she can conceive no doubt. Even the heterodox Burr nearly succumbs to Mary's entreaties to reform. Stowe's less saintly believers, such as Miss Prissy, and her magnanimous skeptics, like Augustine St. Clare of *Uncle Tom's Cabin*, are more credible. As for Hopkins, willing to jeopardize his church financially and socially by his insistence that the most influential of his parishoners renounce his connections with the slave trade, his final renunciation of Mary is quite consistent with his previous rock-ribbed selflessness.

Oldtown Folks, at which Stowe worked in the postwar years and published whole in 1869—for she refused to serialize it in the usual way—repeats many of the concerns of *The Minister's Wooing* and even reintroduces Jonathan Edwards' grandson, here known as Ellery Davenport. Longer, more varied, and much more rambling, this novel contains a considerable amount of Stowe's best writing. In the Preface, her narrator, Horace Holyoke, vows to "interpret to the world the New England life and character of the early republic." Today, no one would choose a loose, leisurely narrative to achieve such an ambition, and perhaps no one but Stowe would have attempted it in the 1860's. It is no coincidence that *Oldtown Folks* attracted the attention of Perry Miller, the distinguished twentieth century interpreter of the New England tradition.

The Minister's Wooing had been a theological novel in which no one had very much fun. As if to redress the deficiency, Stowe widens her focus, invests this work with more of the engaging minor characters of *The Pearl of Orr's Island*, and shows her villagers enjoying themselves. Her twenty-seventh chapter, "How We Kept Thanksgiving at Oldtown," which has become an anthology piece in recent years, argues that Oldtown (based on her husband's hometown of Natick, Massachusetts) has fun precisely because the inhabitants take human life seriously enough "to believe they can do much with it." Sam Lawson—Stowe's most famous character outside *Uncle Tom's Cabin*—far from exemplifying the protestant work ethic, is the town idler, universally valued for his skill at "lubricating" with his humorous andecdotes and relaxed manner the "incessant streampower in Yankee life." By contrast, the character most devoted to work, Miss Asphyxia Smith, is easily the most hateful character in the book.

Sam also serves the tenuous plot interest by coming upon two of its three principals (Narrator Horace Holyoke is the other) in an abandoned house to which they had fled from Miss Asphyxia's clutches, for, like Uncle Tiff's young charges in *Dred*, Harry and Tina Percival have been successively deserted by their scalawag father and subjected to the slow death of their mother. Tina, who is adopted by Mehitabel Rossiter, a woman of no physical beauty but much strength of character and intellect, grows into a beautiful, kindhearted, but willful woman—exactly the type favored by the unprincipled Davenport. Harry grows up as Horace's companion in the nearby Holyoke household.

Tina, not knowing that Davenport numbers among his previous victims Ellen Rossiter, Mehitabel's younger sister, marries him, and it appears that Stowe will not permit her protagonist the usual eleventh-hour rescue. Tina endures ten years with the erratic Davenport, generously adopting his daughter by Ellen Rossiter, but then, in a switch on the Aaron Burr story, Davenport is killed in a duel. Two years (but only three paragraphs) later, Tina and Horace marry and settle in Boston. At the end of the novel, the Horace Holyokes are discoverd back in Oldtown visiting its most durable inhabitant, Sam Lawson.

Any synopsis leaves untouched the merits of *Oldtown Folks*: the interplay of its varied and vital minor characters and the development of its seduction theme. Of the former, Miss Asphyxia, "a great threshing-machine of a woman"; Horace's peppery grandmother, "a valiant old soul, who fearlessly took any bull in life by the horns, and was ready to shake him into decorum"; and Lawson, half nuisance, half good neighbor, are only three of the most memorable. As seducer, Davenport takes advantage of several factors: the intransigence of Calvinism in its death throes, embodied in brilliant but outdated theorizers such as this novel's version of Hopkins, Dr. Stern; the Calvinist legacy of neurosis, skepticism, and rebellion (Miss Rossiter, Tina, and Davenport himself); and the ineffectuality of well-intentioned observers such as Horace and Harry. Thwarted by orthodoxy, which has become a cruel instrument in the hands of its conservative defenders, and averse to the rationalism that played such a large part in the creation of the new republic, the Oldtowners are easily taken in by Davenport, who has turned the passion and intellectual energy inherited from Edwards and the rest of his Puritan forebears to the service of selfish and worldly ends.

In *My Wife and I* and its sequel, *We and Our Neighbors*, Stowe turns to contemporary Manhattan life, a frivolous and even more worldly existence dotted nevertheless by young men and women of impulses Stowe characterizes as Christian but which may strike today's reader as more generally humanitarian. The full spectrum of views on women's rights is on display, including a conviction, expressed by a young woman struggling for the opportunity to study medicine, that "marriage ought never to be entered on as a means of support." The main business of the two novels, however, is to educate Harry Henderson for marriage and thus to provide a base of operations for his wife, who dedicates herself to neighborliness and charitable offices. Stowe retains her observant eye and spicy descriptive powers, but her narrator cannot "interpret" the Gilded Age as Horace Holyoke in *Oldtown Folks* could interpret post-Revolutionary New England.

Pink and White Tyranny, the story of a man who married and must endure a selfish and demanding woman, must rank, along with the earlier *Agnes of Sorrento*, among Stowe's weakest books. Finally, in *Poganuc People*, she returns to the milieu of *The Minister's Wooing*, *The Pearl of Orr's Island*, and her Oldtown books. Poganuc is the Litchfield of her childhood and Dolly Cushing her closet approximation to an autobiographical heroine. The principal conflict is not between the old religion and the new worldliness but between entrenched Congregationalism and upstart Episcopalianism. The novel begins and ends at Christmas when the liturgical and social differences between the two denominations stand out most sharply. Like Maggie Tulliver in Eliot's *The Mill on the Floss* (1860) Dolly is precocious, sensitive, and consequently often uncomfortable, but instead of developing the crises of her heroine's maturation, as does Eliot, Stowe whisks her off to a fashionable Boston marriage with a successful merchant, after which the author makes a final survey of the Poganuc people going about their business under the immemorial elms of the village.

Stowe seldom brought her psychological insights to bear on the development of her main characters, with the result that the less important ones invariably seem more convincing. Whether because her most productive years antedated the time of the realistic novel and particularly the psychological novel, or because she felt too strongly the nineteenth century prohibition against a woman exploring the conflicts and repressions of her own life, Stowe left unwritten what might have constituted her richest vein of realism. She never wrote a novel expressing what it felt like to be a vocationless Harriet Beecher approaching womanhood or the second Mrs. Calvin Stowe struggling with sickness, poverty, and the multitudinous demands of husband and children. The woman who wrote of domesticity in her time avoided calling attention to its tensions, exactions, and restrictions. Whatever else family life meant to Stowe, it helped prepare her to do what no American novelist had done before: write powerfully and feelingly about slavery.

Major publications other than long fiction

SHORT FICTION: *The Mayflower: Or, Sketches of Scenes and Characters of the Descendants of the Pilgrims*, 1843; *Sam Lawson's Oldtown Fireside Stories*, 1872.

POETRY: *Religious Poems*, 1867.

NONFICTION: *Sunny Memories of Foreign Lands*, 1854; *Lady Byron Vindicated*, 1870; *Palmetto Leaves*, 1873.

CHILDREN'S LITERATURE: *First Geography for Children*, 1833 (published under sister Catharine's name).

MISCELLANEOUS: *A Key to Uncle Tom's Cabin*, 1853.

Bibliography

Adams, John R. *Harriet Beecher Stowe*, 1963.

Crozier, Alice C. *The Novels of Harriet Beecher Stowe*, 1969.

Foster, Charles H. *The Rungless Ladder: Harriet Beecher Stowe and New England Puritanism*, 1954.

Moers, Ellen. *Harriet Beecher Stowe and American Literature*, 1978.

Rugoff, Milton. *The Beechers: An American Family in the Nineteenth Century*, 1980.

Stowe, Charles E. *Life of Harriet Beecher Stowe*, 1889.
Wilson, Forrest. *Crusader in Crinoline: The Life of Harriet Beecher Stowe*, 1941.

Robert P. Ellis

JESSE STUART

Born: Riverton, Kentucky; August 8, 1907

Principal long fiction

Trees of Heaven, 1940, *Taps for Private Tussie*, 1943; *Foretaste of Glory*, 1946; *Hie to the Hunters*, 1950; *The Good Spirit of Laurel Ridge*, 1953; *Daughter of the Legend*, 1965; *Mr. Gallion's School*, 1967.

Other literary forms

Jesse Stuart initially gained prominence as a poet. His first collection, *Harvest of Youth* (1930), contained eighty-one poems, which are considered largely juvenilia. His second collection, *Man with a Bull-Tongue Plow* (1934), was composed of 703 poems written in sonnetlike forms (Stuart does not always hold strictly to the sonnet structure). The book was a popular and critical success and brought Stuart his first recognition. His next volume of poetry, *Album of Destiny* (1944), was less well-received, although Stuart considered it his best. Since then, he has published two other books of verse: *Kentucky Is My Land* (1952) and *Hold April* (1962). Altogether, Stuart has published more than two thousand poems.

Stuart has also been a prolific short-story writer. From his more than three hundred published short stories, Stuart has gathered several collections, including: *Head o' W-Hollow* (1936), *Men of the Mountains* (1941), *Tales from the Plum Grove Hills* (1946), *Clearing in the Sky and Other Stories* (1950), *Plowshare in Heaven: Tales True and Tall from the Kentucky Hills*, (1958), *Save Every Lamb* (1964), and *My Land Has a Voice* (1966). *Huey, the Engineer*, a story first published in *Esquire* (August, 1937), was later printed in an anthology, *The Best Short Stories of 1938*. It is generally agreed that Stuart's best work has been in the short story.

Stuart's biographical and autobiographical writings, which are among his most important, include *Beyond Dark Hills* (1938), *The Thread That Runs So True* (1949), *The Year of My Rebirth* (1956), and *God's Oddling* (1960). In addition, he has written five books for children: *The Beatinest Boy* (1953), *A Penny's Worth of Character* (1954), *Red Mule* (1955), *The Rightful Owner* (1960), and *Andy Finds a Way* (1961).

Achievements

As a writer, Stuart has been both a spokesman for and a popularizer of Appalachia, a region and people that have long bewildered and fascinated the rest of the nation. In some ways, Stuart is responsible for, if not creating, then strengthening and prolonging a number of the myths and stereotypes which have beleaguered this area, although Stuart has insisted that he has rarely exaggerated the truth. Stuart himself seems larger than life, and since so much of his fiction is heavily dependent on his own life, it is difficult to determine where the actual leaves off and the imaginative begins. There is Stuart as the mountain boy from a large, poor family, who works his way through school fired by a need for knowledge; then, as an educator who returns to his region and almost single-handedly (and sometimes two-fistedly) brings learning into a backward land; and finally as an extremely successful writer who scribbles poems by the bushel while plowing fields, who produces novels in a few weeks' time, and who gains a reputation as a true primitive, a writer who creates as a force of nature. Still, there is no denying the impressive scope of Stuart's achievements. A man of boundless energy and enthusiasm, he has established himself as perhaps the foremost American regionalist writer of the twentieth century.

Stuart was labeled as an original from the time of his first important work, *Man with a Bull-Tongue Plow*, in 1934. He claims to have written these poems primarily for his own pleasure, as reflections and observations on the world of nature in which he lived; but when they were published, their vitality, apparent artlessness, and obvious sincerity captivated a large section of the literary establishment and the reading public. Stuart, the writing mountain man, was called "a modern Robert Burns," the kind of easy pigeonholing which reveals a misunderstanding of both men. When Stuart followed the poems with a collection of stories (*Head o' W-Hollow*), a book of autobiography (*Beyond Dark Hills*), and an impressive novel (*Trees of Heaven*), he had declared himself a writer to be reckoned with. The recognition and awards came quickly. In 1934, he received the Jeannette Sewal Davis poetry prize of one hundred dollars for *Man with a Bull-Tongue Plow* (beating out such other contenders as Ezra Pound and William Carlos Williams). In 1937, he was awarded the John Simon Guggenheim Literary Award for his poetry and short stories. In 1941, he was given the Academy of Arts and Sciences Award for *Men of the Mountains*, his second short-story collection. In 1943, his second novel, *Taps for Private Tussie*, was chosen for the Thomas Jefferson Southern Award of $2500 as the best Southern novel of the year. *The Thread That Runs So True*, which detailed Stuart's experiences as a young teacher in a one-room Kentucky schoolhouse, was selected by the National Educational Association as the "most important book of 1949" written on the subject of education (indeed, the president of the NEA, Dr. Jay Elmer Morgan, called it "the best book on education written in the last fifty years"). In 1954, Stuart was named poet laureate of Kentucky; in 1955, he was given the Centennial Award for Literature by Berea College. The recognition which has meant the most to Stuart came in 1961, when the 1960 Fellowship of the Academy of American Poets was bestowed on him for "distinguished service to American poetry."

Biography

Hilton Jesse Stuart was born on August 8, 1907, in W-Hollow in Greenup County, a very mountainous and, at the time, relatively isolated section of Kentucky which Stuart would use as the locale for most of his writings. He was the first child of Mitchell and Martha Hilton Stuart; six other children followed, but two died in infancy from pneumonia. Stuart's father's family had lived in Kentucky for generations. They were a clannish people—"Tall Figures of the Earth," in Stuart's own words. His grandfather, Mitchell Stuart, had fought in the Civil War, and Stuart honored this individualistic and often cantankerous old man in one of his first poems, "Elegy for Mitch Stuart," published by H. L. Mencken in *The American Mercury* in 1934. Stuart's father was a quieter man than "Mitch" Stuart; he worked as a coal miner, railroad man, and farmer, and his influence on his son was immense. Stuart used him as the prototype for some of his most impressive charcters, and described his relationship with his father in his autobiographical *Beyond Dark Hills* and in *God's Oddling*, a biography of his father. His mother's family came to Kentucky from North Carolina and were apparently more "cultured"; it was she who encouraged her son to read and first supported him in his continuing quest for education.

The Stuarts moved from farm to farm throughout W-Hollow when Jesse was a boy, a way of life which gave him a sympathy for the plight of the landless. When he was seventeen, Stuart's enthusiasm for learning earned him the positon of teacher in a one-room school, two years before he was graduated from Greenup High School. Following graduation in 1926, Stuart left the mountains, working for a short time in a carnival; then undergoing military training at Camp Knox, Kentucky; and finally spending an unhappy period in the Ashland, Kentucky, steel mills. Later in 1926, he was accepted at Lincoln Memorial University (Harrogate, Tennessee), where he studied under Professor Harry Harrison Kroll, a published writer and one of Stuart's greatest influences. While at Lincoln Memorial, with Kroll's encouragement, Stuart began writing poems, some of which were published in the school newspaper. After being graduated in 1929, Stuart returned to the mountains and served a year as principal and teacher of Warnock High School. In 1930, his first book, *Harvest of Youth*, was privately published; Stuart dedicated it to Harry Harrison Kroll.

In September of 1931, Stuart entered Vanderbilt University to undertake a master's degree in English. There he met such beginning writers as Robert Penn Warren and John Crowe Ransom, and he studied under his most important mentor, Donald Davidson. Stuart's year at Vanderbilt was a time of trial. He was working part-time to support his studies, he was homesick for the mountains, and he was uncertain of his future. When he was assigned by Professor Edwin Mims to write an autobiographical paper, Stuart complied with a work of more than three hundred pages, which, when revised several years later, became *Beyond Dark Hills*. Mims was impressed by Stuart's talents, rough though they were, and further encouraged him to continue his writing. Still, the year was largely one of frustration, capped by a dormitory fire which destroyed most of Stuart's possessions and his nearly finished thesis on the writings of John Fox, Jr. Thus, Stuart left Vanderbilt without a degree, but with experience, inspiration, connections, and material which he would use in his later work.

In September of 1932, Stuart became superintendent of Greenup County schools, but after a year spent embroiled in political turmoil, resigned to become principal of McKell High School, where he incorporated many of his then-radical educational theories. While serving as principal of McKell, from 1933 to 1937, he published *Man with a Bull-Tongue Plow* and *Head o' W-Hollow*. He also began to lecture throughout the country on matters of education and literature. In 1937, Stuart received a Guggenheim Fellowship and traveled to Scotland after obtaining a year's leave of absence from McKell, but when he returned in April of 1938, he found that a new administration had reneged on the agreement. Following another year's teaching in Ohio (just across the state line), while continuing his fight with the Kentucky school authorities (during which time his life was threatened and he was once actually beaten by an assailant), Stuart quit teaching in disgust and returned to farming. On October 14, 1939, he married Naomi Deane Norris; their only child, Jessica Jane, was born in 1942.

Stuart wrote about many of these experiences in two of his major books, *Beyond Dark Hills* and *The Thread That Runs So True*. After his retirement from teaching, he devoted a greater part of his time to his career as a writer and lecturer. His first novel, *Trees of Heaven*, appeared in 1940; his second, *Taps for Private Tussie*, in 1943, proved his greatest success, financially and critically, and was a main selection of the Book-of-the-Month Club. From 1944 to 1945, Stuart served in the United States Naval Reserves, but continued to write. In 1954, he suffered a near-fatal heart attack after one of his many lectures and was left practically helpless for a year. Stuart described the experience in his "journal," *The Year of My Rebirth*. In 1956, he again returned to the field of education, serving as principal once more at McKell High School for the year, a time he later discussed in his last novel, *Mr. Gallion's School*. In 1960-1961, he taught at the American University in Cairo, Egypt, in part because of his desire to challenge the spread of communism in this section of the world. In 1962-1963, he undertook a seven-month lecture tour overseas for the State Department for the same reasons. In 1966, Stuart became writer-in-residence at Eastern Kentucky University. Stuart has spent the last few years living in W-Hollow, the world he has made his own.

Analysis

Jesse Stuart's works are a part of the rich literary heritage drawn from the people and traditions of the Appalachian mountains. He is grouped with such writers as George Washington Harris, Mary Noailles Murfree, John Fox, Jr., Elizabeth Madox Roberts, James Still, Wilma Dykeman, and Harriette Arnow as creators (and sometimes debunkers) of one of America's most lasting stereotypes, the Southern mountaineer or "hillbilly." Of these writers, Stuart surely stands at the head, for he has captured the imagination and sympathy of the reading public as has none of the rest.

There are several reasons for Stuart's abiding popularity. His writings are, for the most part, easily accessible. His main interest is in telling a story or relating an emotion, and he does so with simplicity of style and directness of approach. Indeed, Stuart's works are rarely overtly analytical; his characters are not introspective, which has led to charges of an anti-intellectual strain in his writings. Certainly, Stuart does tend to answer complex problems with easy solutions: if a man is determined, brave, and honest, Stuart suggests, the greatest challenge will be overcome. His autobiographical works especially emphasize this idea, and, in truth, such solutions seem to have been borne out in Stuart's own life.

Stuart also has proven popular because of the uniqueness and inherent romance of his material. As Stuart presents them, his characters are a primitive people, in some ways unspoiled by the corruptions of the outside society, but often in need of the civilizing influences that such a society can offer through education. Thus, some of these people, such as Theopolis Akers in *The Good Spirit of Laurel Ridge*, glory in their separation from the rest of the world, while others, like so many of the Tussie clan, are desperately in need of some edifying influence. Because these characters are drawn in broad strokes and are easily labeled as "good" or "bad" (perhaps "worthy" or "worthless" would be more appropriate terms), they exist more as character types, clothed in the charm of dialect and locale, than as real, breathing people. Still, Stuart is capable of surprising subtlety in his work, a quality often overlooked by some of his critics. He can force his readers to question their initial judgments of such characters as Anse Bushman in *Trees of Heaven*, Grandpa Tussie in *Taps for Private Tussie*, or even Theopolis Akers in *The Good Spirit of Laurel Ridge*.

The land plays an all-important role in Stuart's works. He attended Vanderbilt University at the time of the Agrarian-Fugitive Movement (*I'll Take My Stand* was published by Twelve Southerners in 1930, the year before Stuart arrived), and he came into contact with a number of its leaders, but Stuart never became a disciple himself. Although he agreed with many of the ideas of the movement, Stuart felt that "Their farming was on paper," whereas he had farmed in order to eat. His writings, however, always reflect the importance of place in a man's life, and *Man with a Bull-Tongue Plow* was essentially a celebration of the land and man's relationship with it. He clearly admires characters such as Theopolis Akers, Deutsia Huntoon in *Daughter of the Legend*, and Tarvin Bushman in *Trees of Heaven*, who live in harmony with nature and draw their strength and their morality from the world-spirit. In Stuart's work, nature can be dangerous to the unwary, but it offers peace and wisdom to those who approach it with respect.

Perhaps Stuart's greatest strength as a writer is his fine sense of the comic. He has been linked to such humorists as A. B. Longstreet, G. W. Harris, Mark Twain, Erskine Caldwell, and William Faulkner, and rightfully so. His most serious books, such as *Mr. Gallion's School*, are among his weakest, while *Taps for Private Tussie*, his comic masterpiece, continues to delight. Stuart's humor is basically good-natured. He laughs at the foibles of man, enjoys his foolishness, and shakes his head at absurdities. He rarely condemns. Even in a satirical work such as *Foretaste of Glory*, in which he recounts the many hypocrisies to which men are given, Stuart deals gently with his characters. His comedy derives from the tall-tale tradition and is at its best when it ventures into that region wherein the absurd and the tragic coexist.

Although Stuart has achieved honor and success in almost every form of literature, he has been most effective in the short story. Despite his early fame as a poet, his verse has never received the attention it warrants. His novels generally are loosely structured; they tend to be episodic and uneven as he moves from one event to the next. His plots also rely heavily on convention or cliché. Still, in his large body of writing, Stuart has created a unique fictional world, peopled with characters recognizably his own. It is a world that is likely to last.

Stuart wrote *Trees of Heaven* in 1939 after returning from Europe. He married Naomi Deane Norris while writing the book, and their romance is reflected in the love story of Tarvin Bushman and Subrinea Tussie. *Trees of Heaven* is a big, rambling book, less a well-constructed novel than a conglomeration of facts, observations, tales, and characterizations built around a very simple plot. Anse Bushman is a prominent landowner and farmer, one who takes great pride in the quality of his work and the number of his possessions. Boliver Tussie is a squatter who lives on the land that Anse owns. The two men are antithetical to each other. Anse works—and drives others to work—to such a degree that labor and ownership have become obsessions to him. Boliver opts for a more relaxed, indeed, indolent approach to life, unburdened by responsibility. The conflict arises when Tarvin Bushman, the only child still living with Anse, falls in love with Subrinea Tussie, Boliver's beautiful daughter. Through Tarvin's intervention, Anse agrees to take on the Tussies as sharecroppers, although he first compels Boliver to sign a contract specifying what he can and cannot do while living on Anse's land. The contract is an attempt to control not only the Tussies' work habits, but their moral and social behavior as well. Although Boliver is offended by some of these demands, he is in no position to argue with Anse; thus, he agrees to stop drinking, to avoid dancing, and to abstain from fathering any more children until the harvest is over. Two such differing life-styles cannot coexist peacefully, and when Anse becomes suspicious of his son's relationship with Subrinea and becomes convinced that the Tussies are taking advantage of his generosity, he evicts the family and takes their crops. After an accident, however—Anse is almost killed by a falling tree limb—he becomes a wiser, more tolerant man. Tarvin and Subrinea (who is already pregnant) marry, and, as the book ends, they are going to bring back the Tussies to work the land once again.

Although Anse Bushman is the central character of this novel and the one for whom the reader has the most sympathy and respect, he is by no means an entirely admirable character. His emphasis on work has driven away his other children, and his wife, Fronnie, has succumbed to premature aging. Indeed, toward the end of the book, she is clearly teetering on the edge of madness, haunted by nightmares of Anse's spiritual damnation and fearful that Tarvin will be caught up by his father's obsessions. Anse is a dictatorial old man who cannot balance his love of family with his greed for land. Still, Stuart does not present him as a villain; the reader can understand Anse and generally sides with him in his struggle against the Tussies. At the same time, the Tussies are more likable than one might expect. Their shiftlessness is a relief from Anse's discipline, but they are quite capable of hard work when the occasion demands and show a true love of the land on which they have lived for generations. In fact, Boliver Tussie is a farmer equal to Anse Bushman, although he is usually careless and negligent. The Tussies are a convincing thorn in Anse's side, but he is wrong in his attempt to impose his lifestyle on them.

It is difficult to label *Trees of Heaven* as either a romantic or realistic novel, for it contains elements of each. The love story between Tarvin and Subrinea is idyllic and is the weakest part of the novel, while Stuart's detailed and factual discussions of farming and sheep raising interfere with the progress of the plot. The description of the Tussies and their kind—families that have become inbred over the years and that are capable of viciousness and violence—is sometimes at odds with their basically comic role in the book. The threat of bloodshed runs throughout the story, but it is generally averted through the author's manipulations.

Trees of Heaven is narrated in the present tense and is structured around the change of the seasons. Both devices give it a sense of timelessness, as if the characters, the place, and the actions were occurring in the present in their own world. The use of present tense sometimes leads to repetition and oversimplification, however, and its effectiveness is not sustained throughout the book. Still, *Trees of Heaven* is an impressive first novel, a work of considerable art and scope.

Stuart's second novel, *Taps for Private Tussie*, is generally considered to be his best. Certainly it is his most successful comic work, although the tale it tells is marked by numerous tragic events. Indeed, Stuart claims that he wrote the story as a "sad thing" and was surprised that others laughed at the antics it described. The book is more carefully constructed than *Trees of Heaven* and is effectively held together through the use of a first-person narrator, a young boy who tells the the story with an appealing mixture of naïveté and native wisdom.

Private Kim Tussie is reported killed in action during World War II, and his family sets about burying the returned body. Like the Tussies in *Trees of Heaven*, this branch of the family is also made up of squatters. At the beginning of the book, they are living in a schoolhouse abandoned for the summer. The immediate family is composed of Kim's parents, Grandpa and Grandma Tussie, his wife, Vittie, his unmarried brother, Mott, and the boy-narrator, Sid. When Vittie collects Kim's ten-thousand-dollar insurance policy, the Tussies are able to fulfill their long-held dreams, First, they move from the schoolhouse (from which they are being evicted) to a "mansion," a fourteen-room house on the outskirts of town. Then they buy furniture for each of the rooms to replace that which has been destroyed on leaving the schoolhouse. Soon, as Grandma has predicted, other Tussies begin to arrive, hoping to benefit from Grandpa's "good fortune." The first of these is Uncle George, Grandpa's brother, who has been married five times. Others follow until finally there are forty-six Tussies living in the house. George and Mott have, by this time, begun vying for the attentions of Aunt Vittie, and as George grows more successful, Mott turns increasingly to drink.

After a period of communal living, the Tussies are again turned out of their home, which they have destroyed through their careless behavior, because Grandpa has lost his relief benefits, upon which they had depended. With the last of the insurance money, Grandpa buys a small piece of land, and the family moves into a run-down shack for the winter. Uncle George marries Vittie; Sid is forced to begin school; and Mott sinks into dissipation. Grandpa learns the pride of ownership and plans to farm the following spring, while Sid discovers the joy of education and begins to consider his future, but these plans are upset when Mott kills two of his cousins while drunk and is himself killed by Uncle George. Grandpa then prepares for his own approaching death and confines himself to bed, awaiting the end. At this point, hope returns with the appearance of Kim himself, who was not killed after all, and who stands ready to take Grandpa's place as the head of the remaining group. Uncle George is tracked down by a posse, Sid learns that Vittie is his mother, and the novel ends with a mixture of death and regeneration.

Taps for Private Tussie is an extremely enjoyable book. Grandpa Tussie is one of Stuart's most successful and memorable characters, a good and loving man despite his weaknesses. Sid Tussie comes from a long line of boy-narrators in American literature, including, most obviously, Huckleberry Finn, but also those boys in the works of Sherwood Anderson, William Faulkner, and

Erskine Caldwell. Once again Stuart displays his sympathies for a basically unsympathetic group of people. Stuart distinguishes Sid from the Tussies through the revelation that he does not have Tussie blood and is therefore "superior" (he is smarter and more ambitious than the average Tussie). The book acts as a satire on the welfare system: Grandpa Tussie has so long depended on his relief check that he has forgotten the satisfaction of self-sufficiency; when he rediscovers it in the land, it is too late. Stuart often shows man at his worst—fawning, lying, killing—but *Taps for Private Tussie* finally offers hope of renewal. The Kim who left for war was, as Sid remembers, a vicious and hateful man; the one who returns has been reborn and shows the boy kindness and understanding. Grandpa must die, but Sid will begin to live with a new sense of self.

Foretaste of Glory was begun while Stuart served in the Navy during World War II and was developed from stories he remembered and told about his home. It was not published until 1946, and it was poorly received by the people in Greenup County, Kentucky, who took the book as an affront. It recounts the events of one night—September 18, 1941—in Blakesburg, Kentucky, when the night sky is set ablaze by the uncommon appearance of the aurora borealis. Most of the townspeople are convinced that the display prefigures the end of the world, the Second Coming. Stuart examines the reactions of selected characters when faced with their apparent Day of Judgment. The book is constructed in an episodic manner, although some characters do appear in more than one episode, and certain ideas are repeated as Stuart mocks social distinctions, political alliances (as in *Taps for Private Tussie*), and basic hypocrisies. Stuart was attempting in this work to capture an overall sense of the community, in much the same manner as Sherwood Anderson did in *Winesburg, Ohio* (1919). The book is a satire, for most of the characters reveal their deceits and admit their sins as they await the arrival of the Lord, but the tone is not malicious. The author is more understanding and amused than cruel or vindictive. Although the book has been highly praised by some readers, its very concept finally limits its effectiveness. The narratives become redundant, the episodes are uneven, and the excitement is simply not sustained.

Although Stuart considers *The Good Spirit of Laurel Ridge* the best novel he has written, it is a flawed work. Its plot and too many of its characters are unconvincing, although many readers have been charmed by its view of natural man in the natural world. The story is insubstantial. Theopolis Akers has lived all of his life on Laurel Ridge. His wife is dead; his daughter, Lucretia, was taken away from him when she was a child because of his drinking; and his simpleminded son, Jack, roams the land and appears only in the spring to see the butterflies. As the book begins, Op has undergone a cataract operation, and Lucretia has come to live with him as he regains his sight. Although the operation is successful, she decides to stay in the mountains with her father. A pretty girl, she is soon being courted by a local mountain swain, Hootbird Hammertight, but she is more interested in a mysterious stranger who is hiding out in the hills, a figure Op declares to be the ghost of Ted Newsome, a young man murdered for love many years ago. Op is convinced that spirits—both good and bad—inhabit this area of the mountains, and in his tales and memories he insists on the otherworldliness of Laurel Ridge.

Op's way of life has been disturbed by Lucretia's arrival, although her father comes to accept her. When, however, in a completely unrealistic plot contrivance, two other relatives—Alfred and Julia Pruitt, Lucretia's city cousins—arrive, Op finds himself pushed to the limits. Alf Pruitt is set up as a foil to Op, his city ways and suburban dread placed in stark contrast to Op's natural acceptance of life. Alf most fears the atom bomb, but modern civilization in general has driven him to distraction. Through Op's influence and in a series of mildly comic adventures, Alf learns the importance of nature, but he remains a nervous, essentially unhappy man. Finally, it is revealed that the ghost "Ted Newsome" is really a soldier Lucretia had known in the city. He is AWOL because he mistakenly believes that he has killed a man in a fight, and both he and Lucretia have come to Laurel Ridge to escape. When the military police track him down, just as he is about to be hanged by a group of angry mountaineers, the officer explains that the soldier has killed no one and that he can make amends with a brief prison sentence. Thus, he and Lucretia return to the city. Alfred and Julia also return, having benefited from their stay in the hills, although ultimately unable to adapt to such a rough way of life. Op is again left alone, a man at peace with himself.

The Good Spirit of Laurel Ridge is filled with the folklore of the hills, and Op Akers is a good storyteller and describer of these tales and customs. The plot, however, is so conventional and the ending such a cliché that the book's potential charm is never fully realized. Stuart's satire on the modern world, exemplified in Alf Pruitt, is much too heavy-handed and obvious to work for long. Despite its popularity, *The Good Spirit of Laurel Ridge* is not one of Stuart's better works.

Generally considered Stuart's weakest novel, *Daughter of the Legend* in fact contains some of his best writing. Again, the plot of the novel is slight. The narrator, Dave Stoneking, a lumberjack, tells of his tragic love for Deutsia Huntoon, a Melungeon living in the mountains of eastern Tennessee. After a courtship in which Deutsia introduces Dave to a finer appreciation of nature than he has so far held, they are married and enjoy an idyllic winter together. In the spring, however, Deutsia dies in childbirth, and Dave leaves the land of the Melungeons a rather bitter man. The book is notable for two reasons. First, in his discussion of the Melungeon people, Stuart calls for racial compassion and understanding. The Melungeons are people of mixed heritage, and when Dave marries into their race, he suffers the discriminations they have long felt. His attempts to rectify these injustices give the book a contemporary social awareness missing from many other works by Stuart. In addition, *Daughter of the Legend* includes one of Stuart's finest comic episodes in the chapter dealing with the death and burial of Sylvania, a six-hundred-pound seller of moonshine. Although Stuart had written this tale as a short story years before, it fits smoothly into the novel and presents an ironic counterpoint to the more sentimental death of Deutsia.

Stuart's last published novel, *Mr. Gallion's School*, is a semifictional account of his experiences as principal of McKell High School, to which he returned in 1956 following his heart attack. George Gallion is a thinly disguised version of Stuart himself. Against great odds, Mr. Gallion attempts to restore order and a sense of worth to the school. He must fight not only the defeatist attitudes of the students and teachers but also a corrupt and ineffectual political system which uses the schools as pawns in its power game. That Mr. Gallion succeeds so completely in his fight illustrates the weaknesses of the book. On a strictly realistic level, Stuart oversimplifies both the problems and the solutions. Indeed, the book often becomes a treatise on the author's theories of education. While *Mr. Gallion's School* holds the reader's attention, it is by no means one of Stuart's best novels.

Although Jesse Stuart has been the subject of numerous studies, he has never been accorded the kind of intensive scholarly study one might expect. This is caused, no doubt, by his reputation as a "popular" writer. His often romantic and sentimental picture of the Appalachian mountains has come under attack in the past few decades, especially by many of the young writers and critics from the area, who see Stuart as having helped to create the misleading and often condescending image of the mountaineer. Stuart's skills as a writer are considerable, however, and among his many publications are works which will continue to be read and admired.

Major publications other than long fiction
SHORT FICTION: *Head o' W-Hollow*, 1936; *Men of the Mountains*, 1941; *Tales from the Plum Grove Hills*, 1946; *Clearing in the Sky and Other Stories*, 1950; *Plowshare in Heaven: Tales True and Tall from the Kentucky Hills*, 1958; *Save Every Lamb*, 1964; *My Land Has a Voice*, 1966; *Come Gentle Spring*, 1969; *Come Back to the Farm*, 1971; *Votes Before Breakfast*, 1974.
POETRY: *Harvest of Youth*, 1930; *Man with a Bull-Tongue Plow*, 1934; *Album of Destiny*, 1944; *Kentucky Is My Land*, 1952; *Hold April*, 1962.
NONFICTION: *Beyond Dark Hills*, 1938; *The Thread That Runs So True*, 1949; *The Year of My Rebirth*, 1956; *God's Oddling*, 1960; *To Teach, To Love*, 1970.
CHILDREN'S LITERATURE: *Mongrel Mettle: The Autobiography of a Dog*, 1944; *The Beatinest Boy*, 1953; *A Penny's Worth of Character*, 1954; *Red Mule*, 1955; *The Rightful Owner*, 1960; *Andy Finds a Way*, 1961.

Bibliography

Blair, Everetta Love. *Jesse Stuart: His Life and Works*, 1967.
Clarke, Mary Washington. *Jesse Stuart's Kentucky*, 1967.
Foster, Ruel E. *Jesse Stuart*, 1968.
Le Master, J. R., and Mary Washington Clarke, eds. *Jesse Stuart: Essays on His Work*, 1977.
Pennington, Lee. *The Dark Hills of Jesse Stuart*, 1967.

Edwin T. Arnold III